AN INTRODUCTION
TO DATA STRUCTURES

An Introduction to Data Structures

Larry R. Nyhoff

Calvin College
Department of Computer Science
Grand Rapids, MI

An Alan R. Apt Book

PRENTICE HALL
Upper Saddle River, New Jersey 07458

Library of Congress Cataloging-in-Publication Data

Nyhoff, Larry R.
    C++: an introduction to data structures / Larry R. Nyhoff.
    p.   cm.
  Includes bibliographical references and index.
  ISBN 0-02-388725-7
  1. C++ (Computer program Language)   2. Data structures (Computer
science) I. Title.
  QA76.73.C153 N868 1998
  005.13'3--dc21

            98-48724
            CIP

Publisher: Alan R. Apt
Aquisitions editor: Laura Steele
Editorial and production supervision: Sharyn Vitrano, Ann Marie Kalajian
Editor-in-chief: Marcia Horton
Director of production and manufacturing: David W. Riccardi
Art director: Heather Scott
Cover Designer: John Christiana
Director of Creative Services: Paula Maylahn
Editorial assistant: Kate Kaibni
Composition: V&M Graphics, Inc.
Interior Design: Elm Street Publishing; Emily Friel

© 1999 by Prentice-Hall, Inc.
Upper Saddle River, NJ 07458

Cover image: A Leaded Glass Window designed by Frank Lloyd Wright for The Avery Coonley Playhouse, Riverside, Illinois, Circa 1912. Chrisites Images, New York. The designs of Frank Lloyd Wright are Copyright © the Frank Lloyd Wright Foundation, Scottsdale, AZ. All rights reserved.

The author and publisher of this book have used their best efforts in preparing this book. These efforts include the development, research, and testing of the theories and programs to determine their effectiveness. The author and publisher make no warranty of any kind, expressed or implied, with regard to these programs or the documentation contained in this book. The author and publisher shall not be liable in any event for incidental or consequential damages in connection with, or arising out of, the furnishing, performance, or use of these programs.

Printed in the United States of America
10 9 8 7 6 5 4 3

ISBN 0-02-388725-7

Prentice-Hall U.K. Limited, *London*
Prentice-Hall of Australia Pty. Limited, *Sydney*
Prentice-Hall Canada, Inc., *Toronto*
Prentice-Hall Hispanoamericano, S.A., *Mexico*
Prentice-Hall of India Private Limited, *New Delhi*
Prentice-Hall of Japan, Inc., *Tokyo*
Simon & Schuster Asia Pte. Ltd., *Singapore*
Editora Prentice-Hall do Brazil, Ltda., *Rio de Janeiro*

Preface

This text is designed for the course CS2 as described in the curriculum recommendations of the ACM (Association of Computing Machinery). It aims to meet the major objectives of this course as spelled out in these recommendations, one of which is:

- To continue developing a disciplined approach to the design, coding, and testing of programs written in a high-level language.

This text continues the Object-Centered-Design paradigm developed in the C++ text of which I am one of the authors—*C++: An Introduction to Computing*—and culminates in true OOP (Object-Oriented Programming), which has become the modus operandi in programming and system development. It also continues the coverage of C++, including more advanced topics not usually covered in a first course and that students need to learn such as recursion, function and class templates, inheritance, and polymorphism. Standard C++ as prescribed in the final November 1997 ANSI/ISO draft is used throughout.

Two other objectives of CS2 are:

- To teach the use of data abstraction using as examples data structures other than those normally provided as basic types in current programming languages; for example, linked lists, stacks, queues, and trees.

- To provide an understanding of the different implementations of these data structures.

This text emphasizes abstract data types (ADTs) throughout. It is a study of data structures in the spirit of OOP. All of the usual data structures are covered as recommended. It also treats the containers and algorithms from the Standard Template Library, which are up-to-date and powerful standard data types and tools in C++. In addition, some of the C-style topics appropriate in a data structures course are included, because many students will get jobs as C programmers; many libraries are written in C; C-style data structures are usually implemented very efficiently; and they are often used to implement some of the more modern standard data types.

Another objective of the CS2 course is:

- To introduce searching and sorting algorithms and their analysis.

Both searching and sorting are covered in detail in the text. It also covers algorithm development, analysis, and introduces algorithm verification, thus providing a first look at important tools for later courses in computer science.

The curriculum recommendations also include the following objective for the CS2 course:

- To provide an introduction to the various areas of computer science and thereby provide a foundation for further studies in computer science.

This text continues the portrayal of the discipline of computer science begun in *C++: An Introduction to Computing* by including examples and exercises from different areas of computer science in an attempt to provide a foundation for further study in theoretical and/or applied computer science. The topics include:

- A description of the software development process.
- Abstract data types
- Object-oriented programming
- Computational complexity of algorithms, illustrated by the analysis of standard searching and sorting algorithms
- An introduction to correctness proofs
- Data encryption schemes (DES and public key)
- Data compression using Huffman codes
- Doubly-linked lists and large integer arithmetic
- Random number generation and simulation
- Lexical analysis and parsing
- Reverse Polish notation and generation of machine code
- Simple systems concepts such as input/output buffers, parameter-passing mechanisms, address translation, and memory management

SUPPLEMENTARY MATERIALS

A number of supplementary materials have been planned for this text:

- A solutions manual containing solutions to all of the exercises and many of the programming problems (available from the publisher to instructors who adopt the text for use in a course)
- A companion website (www.prenhall.com/nyhoff) containing presentation slides, source code, and additional resources.
- A lab manual containing tested lab exercises that coordinate with the text (sold separately)

ACKNOWLEDGMENTS

I express my sincere appreciation to all who helped in any way in the preparation of this text. I especially thank my editor Laura Steele, whose support and encouragement have kept me going and whose friendship over the past several years has made textbook writing for Prentice Hall an enjoyable experience. My gratitude for friendship, perceptive suggestions and directions, and unflagging support and encouragement goes to Alan Apt, a publisher respected throughout the publishing and academic communities. I also appreciate the management of reviews and mega-many other details handled so promptly and with pleasant demeanor by Assistant Editor (extraordinaire) Kate Kaibni. I must also thank Assistant Managing Editor Eileen Clark, Art Director Heather Scott, Production Editors Sharyn Vitrano and Ann Marie Kalajian and all the others who did such a fantastic job of designing this attractive book and actually getting it into print. Their attention to details has compensated for my lack thereof and their cooperation and kind words were much appreciated. I also owe a debt of gratitude to Ralph Ewton (Univ. of Texas—El Paso) whose thorough, painstaking, and perspicacious comments, criticisms, and suggestions have strengthened the presentation immensely. I also appreciate the following reviewers of the manuscript for their many valuable observations and recommendations: Adair Dingle (Seattle Univ.), Jens Gregor (Univ. of Tennessee), Bob Holloway (Univ. of Wisconsin), Robin Rowe (SAIC, Pt. Loma Research Center), Andrew Sung (New Mexico Tech), and Mansour Zand (Univ. of Nebraska). Of course, I must once again pay homage to my wife Shar and our children and grandchildren—Jeff, Dawn, Rebecca, Megan, and Sara; Jim; Greg, Julie, Joshua and Derek; Tom, Joan, and Abigail—for their love and understanding through all the times that their needs and wants were slighted by my busyness. Above all, I give thanks to God for giving me the opportunity, ability, and stamina to prepare this text.

Larry Nyhoff

Contents

3 MORE ABOUT DATA STRUCTURES AND ADTS— C++ TYPES 85

AN INTRODUCTION
TO DATA STRUCTURES

Chapter 1

SOFTWARE DEVELOPMENT

Chapter Contents

Problem solving with a computer requires the use of both hardware and software. The **hardware** of a computing system consists of the actual physical components, such as the central processing unit (CPU), memory, and input/output devices that make up the system. **Software** refers to programs used to control the operation of the hardware in order to solve problems. Software development is a complex process that is both an art and a science. It is an art in that it requires a good deal of imagination, creativity, and ingenuity. But it is also a science in that it uses certain standard techniques and methodologies. The term **software engineering** has come to be applied to the study and use of these techniques.

Although the problems themselves and the techniques used in their solution vary, several phases or steps are common in software development:

- ▶ Problem Analysis and Specification: The problem is analyzed and a specification for the problem is formulated.
- ▶ Design: A plan for solving the problem is designed.
- ▶ Coding: The plan is implemented in some programming language producing a program and, for some problems, one or more libraries.
- ▶ Testing, Execution, and Debugging: The program is tested and errors (*bugs*) are removed.
- ▶ Maintenance: The program is updated and modified, as necessary, to keep it up to date and/or to meet users' needs.

In this chapter we briefly review and illustrate by means of a case study each phase of this **software life cycle**, describing some of the questions and complications

1

that face software developers and some of the software engineering techniques that they use in dealing with them.

1.1   PROBLEM ANALYSIS AND SPECIFICATION

CPSC 185 - Assignment 4

Due : Wednesday, March 11

One method of calculating depreciation is the sum-of-the-years digits method. It is illustrated by the following example. Suppose that $15,000 is to be depreciated over a five-year period. We first calculate the "sum-of-the-years digits," $1 + 2 + 3 + 4 + 5 = 15$. Then 5/15 of $15,000 ($5,000) is depreciated the first year, 4/15 of $15,000 ($4,000) is depreciated the second year, 3/15 the third year, and so on.

Write a program that reads the amount to be depreciated and the number of years over which it is to be depreciated. Then for each year from 1 through the specified number of years, print the year number and the amount of depreciation for that year under appropriate headings. Execute the program with the following data: $15,000 for 3 years; $7,000 for 10 years; $500 for 20 years; $100 for 1 year.

To: Bob Byte, Director of
         Computer Center
From: Chuck Cash, V.P. of Scholar-
         ships and Financial Aid
Date: Wednesday, March 11

Because of new government regulations, we must keep more accurate records of all students currently receiving financial aid and submit regular reports to FFAO (Federal Financial Aid Office). Could we get the computer to do this for us?

CC

The preceding assignment sheet (on the left) is typical of programming problems given in introductory programming courses. The exercises and problems in such courses are usually quite simple and clearly stated. This often makes a description of the behavior of a program to solve such problems quite straightforward:

The program should display on the screen a prompt for an amount to be depreciated and the number of years over which it is to be depreciated. It should then read these two values from the keyboard. Once it has the amount and the number of years, it should compute the sum of the integers from $1, 2, \ldots,$ up to the number of years. It should then display on the screen a table with appropriate headings that shows the year number and the depreciation for that year, for the specified number of years.

Such a description is also called a *specification* for the problem.

For most real-world problems, however, formulating a specification is not so easy and straightforward, as the preceding memo (on the right) illustrates. The initial descriptions of such problems are often vague and imprecise. The person posing the problem often does not understand it well and does not understand how to solve it or what the computer's capabilities and limitations are. Formulating a behavioral description of what is needed to solve the problem may take considerable time and effort: asking questions, gathering information, clarifying ambiguities, and so on.

For example, one of the first steps in formulating a specification is to give a complete and precise description of the problem's *input*—what information is available for solving the problem. Often the problem's statement includes irrelevant items of information, and one must determine which items will be useful in solving the problem. Usually, additional questions must be answered. For example, what information is available for each student? How will this information be accessed? What data will the user enter during program execution?

Analysis of what is needed to solve the problem requires determining what *output* is required, that is, what information must be produced to solve the problem. It may be necessary to answer many questions to determine this. For example, what must be included in the reports to be submitted to FFAO? Must these reports have a special format? Must similar reports be generated for any other government agencies or university departments? Must reports be prepared for mailing to individual students? Must computer files of student records be updated?

Additional information may be also required before the specification of the problem is complete. What hardware and software are available? What are the performance requirements? For example, what response time is necessary? How critical is the application in which the software is being used? If fault-free performance is required, must a proof of correctness accompany the software? How often will the software be used? Will the users be sophisticated or will they be novices, so that the software must be extra user-friendly and robust?

For some problems, decisions must be made regarding the feasibility of a computer solution. Is it possible to design software to carry out the processing required to obtain the desired output from the given input? If so, is it economically feasible? Could the problem better be solved manually? How soon must the software be available? What is its expected lifetime?

If it is determined that a computer-aided solution is possible and is cost-effective, then the problem's specification becomes a blueprint that guides the development of the software, and it serves as the *standard* or *benchmark* to use in validating the final product to determine that it does in fact solve the problem. Consequently, this specification must be complete, consistent, and correct.

When software is being developed under contract for a company or agency, it may be necessary to argue, perhaps in a court of law, that the software does (or does not) perform according to specification. In such cases and others, the specification must be stated very precisely and for this reason, a number of **formal methods** such as Z, VDM (Vienna Development Method), and Larch have been developed for formulating specifications. These methods are usually studied in more advanced software engineering courses, and in this text, problem specifications will be stated somewhat less formally.

1.2   DESIGN

Once the specification of a problem has been given, a plan for developing a program or a system of modules, libraries, and programs that solve the problem must be designed. This design phase is the most challenging phase of software development. Because the computer has no inherent problem-solving capabilities, designing a plan for solving a problem with the aid of the computer requires ingenuity and creativity on the part of the programmer. Various design methodologies have been developed over the years, and here we will describe an approach that has been termed **object-centered design (OCD)**[1] because it is consistent with and leads to **object-oriented programming** (**OOP**), which has become the *modus operandi* in programming and system development.

Object-centered design involves several stages:

1. Identify the *objects* in the problem's specification and their types.
2. Identify the *operations* needed to solve the problem.
3. Arrange the operations in a sequence of steps, called an *algorithm*, which, when applied to the objects, will solve the problem.

In this text we will focus much of our attention on this design phase of the software development process, and so in this section we will look at each of the stages in more detail.

OBJECTS

Once we have formulated a specification that describes what the program or system is to do, we are ready for the next step, which is to identify the **objects** in the problem. One approach is to go through the description and identify all of the *nouns*. The objects that the program will have to define can then be selected from this list. For example, for the depreciation problem we might identify the following objects:

Description	Type	Name
The screen	ostream	cout
A prompt	string	none
Amount to depreciate	double	*amount*
Number of years	int	*numYears*
The keyboard	istream	cin
Sum of 1, 2, . . . , *numYears*	int	*sumOfYears*
Table headings	string	none
A year number	int	*year*
Annual depreciation	double	*depreciation*

---

[1]This is the approach described in Joel Adams, Sanford Leestma, and Larry Nyhoff, *C++: An Introduction to Programming*, 2d ed., Prentice Hall, Inc., Upper Saddle River, NJ, 1997.

Other attributes of the objects could also be listed—for example, whether it is a variable or a constant and whether it is user-defined or is predefined in the language.

The most important attribute of each object is its **type**, which determines what values the object may have, what operations can be performed on it, and what these operations produce. In a first programming course you learn about the **simple data types** provided in the programming language for objects that are single entities. For example, in C++, int (or one of its variations such as unsigned, short int, and long int) is used for a single integer such as 123; double (or float, or long double) for a single real value such as 3.1415926535898; char for individual characters such as 'A'; and bool for a single logical value true or false; enum for a single enumerated value; a *pointer* to store a single memory address.

However, some objects are collections of values, and data types, usually called **structured data types** or **data structures**, are needed to store these collections of values. The most common of these, and one with which you should already be familiar, is the **array**.[2] Nearly every high-level programming language provides arrays and also perhaps other more modern extensions such as valarrays and vectors in C++ (see Secs. 6.8 and 6.4). Arrays are used to organize data items that are all of the same type—for example, a collection of test scores (integers) or a collection of names (strings). They may be **one-dimensional,** in which case, each item in the array is accessed by specifying its location in the array, usually by enclosing it in brackets or parentheses and attaching it as an index to the array name. Arrays may also be **multidimensional**, in which case access to an element requires using more than one index to specify its location. For example, in C++, if score is a one-dimensional array of integers and sales is a two-dimensional array of real numbers defined by

```
const int MAXSCORES  = 100,
          MAXROWS    = 10,
          MAXCOLUMNS  = 10;

int score[MAXSCORES];
double sales[MAXROWS][MAXCOLUMNS];
```

then the fifth score can be accessed with the array reference score[4], and the entry in the first row and third column of sales can be accessed with sales[0][2]. (Recall that arrays in C++ are **zero-based**; that is, the first index is 0 so that, for example, 100 integers can be stored in score[0], score[1], score[2], ..., score[99].)

Most programming languages also provide **structures**, also called **records** or simply **structs**. They differ from arrays in that the objects in the collection need not be of the same type, and therefore are useful for storing nonhomogeneous collections of data items. For example, a student record might consist of an identification number that is a positive integer; a name that is itself a structure consisting of a last name (a string), a first name (a string), and a middle initial (a character); an address that might also be a structure consisting of strings of various lengths; a grade-point average that is a real number; and other items of information of various types.

---

[2] Arrays in C++ are reviewed in Sec. 2.3.

Most languages provide still more data types. For instance, C++ provides unions, classes, strings, istreams, ostreams, iostreams, ifstreams, ofstreams, fstreams, valarrays, vectors, bitsets, lists, maps, multimaps, sets, multisets, stacks, queues, deques, priority queues, and more! However, even though the language in which you do most of your programming is rich in predefined data types (and C++ is such a language), sometimes it will be necessary to define new types to store the data for a particular problem. A large part of this text is devoted to studying in detail several of the data types provided in C++ and how they can be used to implement other important data types.

OPERATIONS

Data is useless if it cannot be processed, and we must, therefore, also identify which operations are needed to process the data and solve the problem. For the depreciation problem we are considering, we have the following operations:

Description	Name
Display `strings` (the prompt and table headings)	<<
Read a `double` (amount to be depreciated)	>>
Read an `int` (number of years)	>>
Calculate `sumOfYears`	??
Display the depreciation table	??

Some of the operations such as input (>>) and output (<<) are provided in C++ but others require some additional work. For example, calculating `sumOfYears` requires calculating

$$\text{sumOfYears} = 1 + 2 + \cdots + \text{numYears}$$

which is not a predefined operation. Similarly, displaying the depreciation table is not an operation defined in the language. We will have to define these operations ourselves.

ALGORITHM

Once we have identified the objects and operations in the problem, we organize them into a sequence of steps, called an **algorithm**, for solving the problem. For example, a first version of an algorithm for solving the depreciation problem might be

1. Display via `cout` a prompt for the amount to be depreciated and the number of years.

2. Read from `cin` a `double` value and store it in `amount`.

3. Read from `cin` an `int` value and store it in `numYears`.

4. Calculate $\text{sum} = 1 + 2 + \cdots + \text{numYears}$.

5. Display via `cout` the depreciation table.

As we have noted, we must define operations for steps 4 and 5 of this algorithm, and we will define functions `YearSum()` and `DisplayTable()` to carry out these operations.

Designing each function is a **subproblem** of the original problem and must be solved using the same problem-solving approach. To save space, we will simply outline the solutions.

DESIGN OF FUNCTION YearSum()

SPECIFICATION. The function YearSum() should accept an integer n. It should then compute and return the value of the sum $1 + 2 + \cdots + n$.

OBJECTS.

The integer n of type int received by the function
An integer *sum* of type int to be returned by the function

OPERATIONS.

  i. Accept an integer value n

  ii. Initialize an integer variable *sum* to 0

  iii. Accumulate a sum by repeatedly adding each integer $1, 2, \ldots, n$ to *sum*

  iv. Return the value of *sum*

ALGORITHM 1

1. Accept an integer for n.

2. Initialize *sum* to 0.

3. For each integer i in the range 1 to n:
      Assign *sum* + i to *sum*.

4. Return the value of *sum*.

Each of these steps can be carried out in C++: Make n an int function parameter; define an int local variable *sum* with initial value 0; write a for loop that uses += to accumulate the value for *sum*; and use a return statement to return the value of sum.

Often there are several different algorithms that can be used to solve a problem. For example, a well-known summation formula from mathematics states that the sum of the first n positive integers is given by [3]

$$1 + 2 + 3 + \cdots + n = \frac{n \times (n + 1)}{2}$$

and so the problem can be solved with the following algorithm:

---

[3] This formula is usually credited to Carl Friedrich Gauss, one of the greatest mathematicians of all time. One day in school the students were asked (perhaps as punishment) to sum the integers from 1 to 100. Gauss produced the correct answer (5050) almost immediately, perhaps by observing that writing the sum forward and then backwards,

$$sum = 1 + 2 + 3 + \cdots + 98 + 99 + 100$$
$$sum = 100 + 99 + 98 + \cdots + 3 + 2 + 1$$

and then adding corresponding terms in these two equations gives

$$2 \times sum = 101 + 101 + 101 + \cdots + 101 + 101 + 101 = 100 \times 101$$

Thus the sum is equal to $sum = \dfrac{100 \times 101}{2} = 5050$. A similar approach gives the general formula.

ALGORITHM 2

1. Accept an integer for n.

2. Return the value of $\dfrac{n \times (n + 1)}{2}$.

This algorithm is better than the first one because it solves the same problem *in less time*. For example, to compute the sum of the integers from 1 through 1000, Algorithm 1 must repeat the loop in step 3 1000 times, which means that it must perform 1000 additions, 1000 assignments, 1000 increments of i, and 1000 comparisons of i with n, for a total of 4000 operations. For an arbitrary value of n, $4n$ operations are required. We say that the number of operations performed by Algorithm 1 *grows linearly* with the value of n and denote this in *big-O notation* by saying the growth rate of Algorithm 1 is $O(n)$. By contrast, Algorithm 2 does 1 addition, 1 multiplication, and 1 division, for a total of 3 operations, regardless of the value of n. Thus the time taken by Algorithm 2 is *constant*, no matter what the value of n. We say that its computing time is $O(1)$, which indicates that it grows at a rate proportional to 1.

This is a first look at an important area of computer science called *analysis of algorithms*, which, along with big-O notation, is considered more carefully in Chap. 7. When there are two or more algorithms for a problem, we analyze the number of operations each requires to determine which of them is better. Algorithm 2 solves the problem in constant time while Algorithm 1 solves the problem in time proportional to n, and consequently, Algorithm 2 is to be preferred.

DESIGN OF FUNCTION `DisplayTable()`

SPECIFICATION. The function `DisplayTable()` should accept an integer *numYears* and two real values *amount* and *yearSum*. It should display appropriate table headings. Then, for each year from 1 to *numYears*, it should calculate the depreciation for that year and display the year number and that depreciation.

OBJECTS.

    An integer *numYears* of type `int` and real values *amount* and *yearSum* of type `double`

    An output stream (`cout`)

    A loop control variable *year* of type `int` to range over the integers $1, 2, \ldots,$ *numYears*

    A real value *depreciation* of type `double`

OPERATIONS.

  i. Accept an integer value (*numYears*) and real values (*amount*, *yearSum*)

  ii. Display table headings via `cout`

 iii. Repeatedly display via `cout` the value of *year*

 iv. Repeatedly calculate and display the value of

$$depreciation = \left(\frac{numYears - year + 1}{yearSum} \right) \times amount$$

ALGORITHM

1. Accept an integer value for *numYears* and real values for *amount and yearSum*.

2. Display table headings.

3. For each value of *year* in the range 1 to *numYears*:

    a. Calculate $depreciation = \left(\dfrac{numYears - year + 1}{yearSum} \right) \times amount$.

    b. Display year and depreciation.

As before, each step in this algorithm can be implemented in C++: Make *numYears* an `int` function parameter and *amount* and *yearSum* `double` parameters; use `<<` to display the function headings; write a for loop that uses `-`, `+`, `/`, `*`, `=`, and `<<` to calculate and display the values of *year* and *depreciation*.

SOME FINAL COMMENTS ABOUT ALGORITHMS

We see that data and the operations on that data are both important and cannot be separated. Stated differently, the way in which the data is organized and the algorithms for operations on the data are inextricably linked; neither can be carried out independently of the other. Quite a few years ago, Niklaus Wirth, the originator of the Pascal language, realized this when he entitled one of his texts

Algorithms + Data Structures = Programs

The word *algorithm* is derived from the name of the Arab mathematician, Abu Ja'far Mohammed ibn Musa al Khowarizmi (c. A.D. 825), who wrote a book describing procedures for calculating with Hindu numerals. In modern parlance, the word has come to mean a "step-by-step procedure for solving a problem or accomplishing some end." In computer science, however, the term algorithm refers to a procedure that can be executed by a computer, and this requirement imposes additional limitations on the instructions that comprise these procedures:

1. They must be *definite* and *unambiguous* so that it is clear what each instruction is meant to accomplish.

2. They must be *simple* enough that they can be carried out by a computer.

3. They must satisfy a *finiteness* property; that is, the algorithm must terminate after a finite number of operations.[4]

In view of the first two requirements, unambiguity and simplicity, algorithms are usually described in a form that resembles a computer program so that it is easy to implement each step of the algorithm as a computer instruction or as a sequence of instructions. Consequently, algorithms are commonly written in **pseudocode**, a pseudo-programming language that is a mixture of natural language and symbols, terms, and other features commonly used in one or more high-level programming languages. Because it has no standard syntax, pseudocode varies from one programmer to another, but it typically includes the following features:

---

[4] This is not always a requirement for programs. For example, an operating system is a program whose execution is not supposed to terminate.

1. The usual computer symbols $+, -, *$, and $/$ are used for the basic arithmetic operations.

2. Symbolic names (identifiers) are used to represent the quantities being processed by the algorithm.

3. Some provision is made for indicating comments, for example, using the C++ convention of enclosing them between a pair of special symbols such as /* and */.

4. Key words that are common in high-level languages are allowed, for example, *read* or *enter* for input operations and *display, print,* or *write* for output operations.

5. Indentation is used to set off blocks of instructions.

The finiteness property requires that an algorithm will eventually halt; that is, it will terminate after a finite number of steps. In particular, this means that the algorithm may not contain any infinite loops. For example, if an algorithm includes a set of statements that are to be executed repeatedly while some boolean expression is true, then these statements must eventually cause that boolean expression to become false so that repetition is terminated. Also, when an algorithm terminates, we obviously expect that it will have produced the required results. Thus, in addition to demonstrating that a given algorithm will terminate, it is also necessary to verify its correctness (see Sec. 7.6).

As a practical matter, simply knowing that an algorithm will terminate may not be sufficient. For example, a scheduling algorithm that requires 2^n operations to schedule n events will eventually terminate for large values of n but will require too much time to be of practical value. Useful algorithms, therefore, must terminate in some reasonable amount of time. Also, as we have seen, we may have to decide between two or more algorithms that perform differently. In Chap. 7 we will consider some techniques that are useful in estimating the computing time of an algorithm and for comparing algorithms.

The analysis and verification of algorithms and of the programs that implement them are much easier if they are well structured, which means that they are designed using three basic control structures:

1. *Sequence*:   Steps are performed in a strictly sequential manner.
2. *Selection*:   One of several alternative actions is selected and executed.
3. *Repetition*:   One or more steps is performed repeatedly.

These three control mechanisms are individually quite simple, but together they are sufficiently powerful that any algorithm can be constructed using them.

Algorithms that are carefully designed using only these control structures are much more readable and understandable and hence can be analyzed and verified much more easily than can unstructured ones. To illustrate, consider the following unstructured algorithm:

ALGORITHM (UNSTRUCTURED VERSION)

/* Algorithm to read and count several triples of distinct numbers
   and print the largest number in each triple.
--*/

1. Initialize *count* to 0.
2. Read a triple *x*, *y*, *z*.
3. If *x* is the end-of-data flag then go to step 14.
4. Increment *count* by 1.
5. If *x* > *y* then go to step 9.
6. If *y* > *z* then go to step 12.
7. Display *z*.
8. Go to step 2.
9. If *x* < *z* then go to step 7.
10. Display *x*.
11. Go to step 2.
12. Display *y*.
13. Go to step 2.
14. Display *count*.

The "spaghetti logic" of this algorithm is vividly displayed in the first diagram in Fig. 1.1.

In contrast, consider the following structured algorithm. The clarity and simple elegance of its logical flow are shown in the second diagram in Fig. 1.1.

ALGORITHM (STRUCTURED VERSION)

/* Algorithm to read and count several triples of distinct numbers
and print the largest number in each triple.
--*/

1. Initialize *count* to 0.
2. Read the first triple of numbers *x*, *y*, *z*.
3. While *x* is not the end-of-data-flag do the following:

    a. Increment *count* by 1.
    b. If *x* > *y* and *x* > *z* then
        Display *x*.
      Else if *y* > *x* and *y* > *z* then
        Display *y*.
      Else
        Display *z*.
    c. Read the next triple *x*, *y*, *z*.

4. Display *count*.

1.3 CODING

Coding is the process of implementing the design plan in some programming language such as C++. If the design phase has been carried out carefully, some parts of this translation process are often nearly automatic.

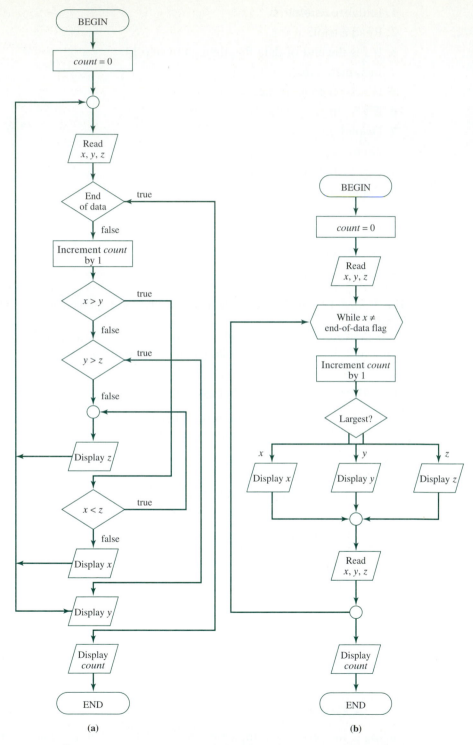

FIGURE 1.1   (a) Unstructured algorithm (b) structured algorithm.

The first decision that must be made is what programming language to use. This obviously depends on the languages available to the programmer and those that he or she is able to use. Also, the problem may have characteristics that make one language more suitable than another. For example, if the problem requires scientific computing with extended precision and/or complex numbers, FORTRAN may be the most suitable language. Problems that involve extensive file manipulation and report generation may perhaps best be done with COBOL. In this text we will use C++. Figure 1.2 shows a C++ program that implements the objects and algorithms for the operations given in the preceding section for solving the depreciation problem.[5]

FIGURE 1.2   CALCULATING DEPRECIATION

```
/* This program calculates and displays depreciation tables.
 *
 * Input:  Amount to be depreciated and the number of years
 * Output: A depreciation table
 ******************************************************************/

#include <iostream>              // <<, >>, cout, cin, fixed, showpoint
#include <cassert>               // assert()
#include <iomanip>               // setprecision(), setw()
using namespace std;

int YearSum(int n);
void DisplayTable(int numYears, double amount, double yearSum);

int main()
{
   int numYears;                 // number of years, and
   double amount;                // amount to depreciate

   cout << "This program computes a depreciation table using\n"
           "the sum-of-the-years'-digits method.\n\n"
           "Enter the number of years over which to depreciate: ";
   cin >> numYears;
   cout << "Enter the amount to be depreciated: ";
   cin >> amount;

   double sum = YearSum(numYears);
   DisplayTable(numYears, amount, sum);
}
```

[5] New names for standard libraries along with *namespaces*, which make it possible to group together things that logically belong together, are recent additions to C++. With older compilers it may be necessary to use the older library names—for example, iostream.h instead of iostream, assert.h instead of cassert, and iomanip.h instead of iomanip—and remove the using namespace std; line, which specifies that we want to use the standard libraries from the namespace named std. Without this line we would have to *qualify* each item such as cout from the libraries with the prefix std::; for example

```
        std::cout << "Enter the amount to be depreciated: ";
```

```
/* YearSum(n) computes the sum of the integers from 1 to n.
 *
 *   Receive:       n, an integer
 *   Precondition: n > 0
 *   Return:        The sum 1 + 2 + ... + n
 *********************************************************/

int YearSum(int n)
{
  assert(n > 0);
  return n * (n + 1) / 2;
}


/* DisplayTable() displays a depreciation table for a given
 * amount over numYears years using the sum-of-the-years'-digits
 * method; yearSum is the sum 1 + 2 + ... + numYears.
 *
 *   Receive: numYears, an integer
 *            amount, a real
 *            yearSum, a real
 *   Output:  A depreciation table
 *   Uses:    setprecision() and setw() from iomanip library
 ***********************************************************************/

void DisplayTable(int numYears, double amount, double yearSum)
{
  cout << "\nYear -  Depreciation"
       << "\n--------------------\n";

  double depreciation;

  cout << showpoint << fixed << setprecision(2);

  for (int year = 1; year <= numYears; year++)
  {
    depreciation = (numYears - year + 1) * amount / yearSum;
    cout << setw(3) << year
         << setw(13) << depreciation << endl;
  }
}
```

SAMPLE RUN:
```
This program computes a depreciation table using
the sum-of-the-years'-digits method.

Enter the number of years over which to depreciate: 5
Enter the amount to be depreciated: 15000
Year -  Depreciation
--------------------
  1        5000.00
  2        4000.00
  3        3000.00
  4        2000.00
  5        1000.00
```

Regardless of the language that is used, *source code should be correct, readable, and understandable.* Of these three properties, correctness is obviously the most important. No matter which of the other qualities a piece of code has—it is well structured, is well documented, looks nice, and so on—it is worthless if it does not produce reliable results. Code testing is therefore an important step in software development and is reviewed in more detail in the next section.

It is often difficult for beginning programmers to appreciate the importance of the other characteristics and of developing good programming habits that lead to code that is readable and understandable. They have difficulty because programs developed in an academic environment are often quite different from those developed in real-world situations, in which programming style and form are critical. Student programs, subprograms,[6] and libraries are usually quite small (usually less than a few hundred lines of code); are executed and modified only a few times (almost never, once they have been handed in); rarely are examined in detail by anyone other than the student and the instructor; and are not developed within the context of budget restraints. Real-world software, on the other hand, may be very large (several hundreds of thousands of lines of code);[7] may be developed by teams of programmers; is commonly used for long periods of time and thus requires maintenance if it is to be kept current and correct; and often is maintained by someone other than the original programmer. As hardware costs continue to decrease and programming costs increase, the importance of reducing these maintenance costs and the corresponding importance of writing code that can be easily read and understood by others, continues to increase.

A number of programming practices contribute to the development of correct, readable, and understandable code. Because good programming habits are essential, we shall review some of these guidelines once again. One principle is that *programs and subprograms should be well structured.* The following guidelines are helpful in this regard:

- ▶ *Use a modular approach for a complex problem.* Rather than write one large subprogram or program, write individual subprograms that solve a part of the problem and that are relatively short and self-contained.

- ▶ *Use the basic control structures when developing each code segment.* Any program unit can be written using only the sequential, selection, and repetition structures. These structures should be combined to form nested blocks of code that are entered only at the top and normally have only one exit.

- ▶ *Use local variables within subprograms.* Variables used only within a subprogram should be declared within that subprogram.

- ▶ *Use parameters to pass information to and from subprograms.* Avoid using **global variables** to share information between subprograms because it destroys their independence. It can be difficult to determine the value of a global variable at some point in the program because it may have been changed by any of the program units.

---

[6] Functions in C++, functions and subroutines in Fortran, functions and procedures in Pascal, and so on.

[7] And this may even exceed one million lines, for example, in some operating systems such as Windows NT.

▶ *To protect arguments that should not be modified by a subprogram, declare the corresponding parameters to be value parameters or constant reference parameters rather than reference parameters.* Otherwise, the subprogram may unexpectedly change the value of an argument in some other program unit.

▶ *Don't use "magic numbers."* For example, the following statement violates what has been termed the "Houdini principle" because it allows numbers to arise suddenly without explanation, almost as if by magic:

```
popChange = (0.1758 - 0.1257) * population;
```

The integer literals 0.1758 and 0.1257 should be replaced by constant identifiers (or variables whose values are read or assigned during execution), as in

```
const double BIRTH_RATE = 0.1758,
             DEATH_RATE = 0.1257;
       .
       .
       .

popChange = (BIRTH_RATE - DEATH_RATE) * population;
```

The second assignment statement is more readable than the first. Also, if these numbers must be changed, one need only change the definitions of BIRTH_RATE and DEATH_RATE rather than conduct an exhaustive search of the program to locate all their occurrences. Similarly, using a constant identifier such as INT_MAX (in the C++ library climits) rather than some machine-dependent constant such as 32767 increases portability.

▶ *Strive for simplicity and clarity.* Clever programming tricks intended only to demonstrate the programmer's ingenuity or to produce code that executes only slightly more efficiently should be avoided.

▶ *Identify any preconditions and postconditions a program or subprogram has, and check them.* **Preconditions** describe the state of processing before the program or subprogram is executed. Typically, these are assumptions made about the program unit, often one or more restrictions on what comprises a valid input or received value. In a similar way, **postconditions** describe the state of processing after the program unit is executed. The assert() mechanism, which evaluates a boolean expression and terminates execution if it is false, can be used to check preconditions and postconditions.

☞   A second principle is that *all source code should be documented.* In particular

▶ *Each program should include opening documentation.* Comments should be included at the beginning of the program to explain what it does, how it works, any special algorithms it implements, and so on, and may also include a summary of the problem's specification, assumptions, and other items of information such as the name of the programmer, the date the program was written, when it was last modified, and references to books and manuals that give additional information about the program.

▶ *Each subprogram should be documented in a manner similar to programs.* In particular, it should include (at least) a brief description of what it does, what (if anything) it receives, what (if anything) it returns, any input or output, and where appropriate, preconditions and postconditions.

▶ *Comments should be used to explain key code segments and/or segments whose purpose or design is not obvious.* However, don't clutter the code with needless comments, as in

```
counter++;    // add 1 to counter
```

▶ *Use meaningful identifiers.* For example,

```
wages = hoursWorked * hourlyRate;
```

is clearer than

```
w = h * r;
```

or

```
z7 = alpha * x;
```

Don't use "skimpy" abbreviations just to save a few keystrokes when entering the source code. Also, follow what has been called the "Shirley Temple principle" and avoid "cute" identifiers, as in

```
bacon_brought_home = hoursWasted * pittance;
```

☞   A third principle has to do with a program's appearance: *Source code should be aesthetic; it should be formatted in a style that enhances its readability.* In particular, the following are some guidelines for good programming style:

▶ *Put each statement of the program on a separate line.*

▶ *Use uppercase and lowercase letters in a way that contributes to program readability;* for example, put identifiers for variables in lowercase, capitalizing the first letter of each word after the first as in `totalHoursWorked`; put identifiers for constants in uppercase, separating words by underscores, as in `TAX_RATE`; put identifiers for types and functions in lowercase, but capitalizing the first letter of each word as in `DisplayInfo()`.

▶ *Put each { and } on separate lines.*

▶ *Align each { and its corresponding }. Indent the statements enclosed by { and }.*

▶ *When a statement is continued from one line to another, indent the continued line(s).*

▶ *Align the identifiers in each constant and variable declaration, placing each on a separate line*; for example

```
const double TAX_RATE = 0.1963,
              INTEREST_RATE = 0.185;

int employeeNumber;

double hours,
       rate,
       wages;
```

▶ *Insert blank lines between declarations and statements and between blocks of statements to make clear the structure of the program.*

▶ *Separate the operators and operands in an expression with spaces to make the expression easy to read.*

▶ *Declare constants at the beginning of a function. Declare variables near their first use.* This makes it easy to find constants when they must be modified. It also reduces the tendency to declare unused variables, since declarations are deferred until they are needed.

▶ *Label all output produced by a program.* For example,

```
cout << "Employee # " << employeeNumber
     << "  Wages = $" << employeeWages;
```

produces more informative output than

```
cout <<  employeeNumber << "   " << employeeWages;
```

1.4 TESTING, EXECUTION, AND DEBUGGING

Errors may occur in any of the phases of the software development life cycle. For example, the specifications may not accurately reflect information given in the problem or the customer's needs and/or desires; the algorithms may contain logic errors; and the program units may not be coded or integrated correctly. The detection and correction of errors is an important part of software development and is sometimes referred to as verification and validation. **Verification** refers to checking that documents, program modules, and the like that are produced are correct and complete and that they are consistent with one another and with those of the preceding phases. **Validation** is concerned with checking that these products match the problem's specification. Verification is sometimes described as answering the question "Are we building the product right?" and validation as answering the question "Are we building the right product?"

Because errors may occur at each phase of the development process, different kinds of tests are required to detect them: **unit tests** in which a subprogram or other code segment is tested individually; **integration tests** that check whether the various program units have been combined correctly; and **system tests** that test to see whether the overall system of programs, subprograms, and libraries performs correctly. In this section we restrict our attention to some of the techniques used in unit testing, probably the most rigorous and time-consuming of the various kinds of testing. It is surely the most fundamental kind of testing, since incorrectness of an individual program unit implies incorrectness of the larger system of which it is a part.

Only in the rarest cases is the first attempt at writing a program unit free of errors. **Syntax errors** (caused by incorrect punctuation, misspelled keywords, etc.) and **run-time errors** such as division by zero and integer overflow that occur during execution are usually quite easy to detect and correct, since system-generated error messages can help locate and explain these errors. **Logic errors**, however, are far more difficult to detect and locate because the program executes but does not produce the correct results. These errors may be due to inaccurate coding of an algorithm or in the design of the algorithm itself.

There are many kinds of tests that can be used to locate errors. One classification of testing techniques is into black-box tests and white-box tests. In a **black-box test** or **functional test** of a function, a code segment, or other program unit, the outputs produced for various inputs are checked for correctness without considering the structure of the program unit itself. That is, the program unit is viewed as a black box that accepts inputs and produces outputs, but the inner workings of the box are not examined. In a **white-box** (glass-box or clear-box) **test** or **structural test**, the performance of the program unit is tested by examining its internal structure. Test data is carefully selected so that the various parts of the program unit are exercised.

To illustrate some of the testing techniques that can be used to detect logic errors, let us consider a function to perform a binary search for some item in an ordered list stored in an array. The specification for this function is

SPECIFICATION FOR BINARY SEARCH

Purpose:	Function is to perform a binary search of an ordered list stored in an array for a specified item, and if found, determine its position in the array
Input:	None
Receive:	An array having *n* elements ordered in ascending order and a value *item* having the same type as the array elements
Output:	None
Pass back:	*found* and *mid* where *found* is true and *mid* is the position of *item* if the search is successful; otherwise *found* is false

It has been estimated that 80 percent of all beginning programmers will not write a binary search algorithm correctly the first time. One common attempt is

BINARY SEARCH ALGORITHM (INCORRECT VERSION)

1. Set *found* = false.

2. Set *first* = 0.

3. Set *last* = $n - 1$.

4. While *first* ≤ *last* and not *found* do the following:
    a. Calculate *mid* = (*first* + *last*) / 2.
    b. If *item* < *a*[*mid*] then
        Set *last* to *mid*.
        Else if *item* > *a*[*mid*]
            Set *first* to *mid*
        Else
            Set *found* to true.

A C++ function that implements this algorithm is

```
/* INCORRECT FUNCTION --------------------------------------
   BinarySearch() performs a binary search of a for item.

   Receive:    item and an array a having n items, arranged
               in ascending order
   Pass back:  found and mid, where found is true and
               mid is the position of item if the search
               is successful; otherwise found is false
------------------------------------------------------------*/

void BinarySearch(NumberArray a, int n,  ElementType item,
                  bool & found, int & mid)
{
   int first = 0,      // first and last positions in sublist
       last = n - 1;   // currently being searched
   found = false;
   while (first <= last && !found)
   {
      mid = (first + last) / 2;
      if item < a[mid]
         last = mid;
      else if item > a[mid]
         first = mid;
      else
         found = true
   }
}
```

This function might be tested using a black-box approach with n = 7 and the following array a of integers:

$$a[0] = 45$$
$$a[1] = 64$$
$$a[2] = 68$$
$$a[3] = 77$$
$$a[4] = 84$$
$$a[5] = 90$$
$$a[6] = 96$$

A search for `item` $= 77$ returns the values `true` for `found` and 3 for `mid`, which is the location of 77 in the array. Testing with `item` $= 90$ and `item` $= 64$ also yields correct results. If the value 76 is used for `item`, `found` is returned as `false`, indicating that the `item` is not in the array. These tests might lead one to conclude that this procedure is correct.

☞   Experienced programmers know, however, that *special cases must always be considered when selecting test data*, since it is often these cases that cause a program unit to malfunction. For example, in processing lists like that in this problem, one special case that must be tested is searching at the ends of the list. For function `BinarySearch()`, therefore, we should test it with values of 45 and 96 for `item` as well as with values less than 45 and values greater than 96. For `item` $= 45$, the function returns `found` $=$ `true` and `mid` $= 0$, as it should. A search for `item` $= 96$ fails, however; the search procedure did not terminate and it was necessary for the programmer to terminate execution using "break" keys (e.g., `Ctrl` + `c`) on the keyboard.

White-box testing would also detect an error because in this approach, we choose data to test the various paths that execution can follow. For example, one set of data should test a path in which the first condition `item < a[mid]` in the `if` statement is true on each iteration so that the first alternative `last = mid` is always selected. Using values less than or equal to 45 will cause execution to follow this path. Similarly, values greater than or equal to 96 will cause execution to follow a path in which the second condition `item > a[mid]` in the `if` statement is true on each iteration so that the second alternative `first = mid` is always selected.

Once an error has been detected, various techniques can be used to locate the error. One approach is to trace the execution of a program segment by inserting temporary output statements to display values of key variables at various stages of program execution. For example, inserting the statements

```
cerr << "DEBUG:  At top of while loop in BinarySearch()\n"
     << "first = " << first << ", last = " << last
     << ", mid = " << mid << endl;
```

after the statement that assigns a value to `mid` at the beginning of the while loop in the preceding procedure `BinarySearch()` results in the following output in a search for 96:

```
DEBUG:  At top of while loop in BinarySearch()
first = 0, last = 6, mid = 3
DEBUG:  At top of while loop in BinarySearch()
first = 3, last = 6, mid = 4
DEBUG:  At top of while loop in BinarySearch()
first = 4, last = 6, mid = 5
DEBUG:  At top of while loop in BinarySearch()
first = 5, last = 6, mid = 5
DEBUG:  At top of while loop in BinarySearch()
first = 5, last = 6, mid = 5
DEBUG:  At top of while loop in BinarySearch()
first = 5, last = 6, mid = 5
         .
         .
         .
```

One must be careful, however, to put such temporary output statements in places that are helpful in locating the source of the error and not use so many of these statements that the volume of output hinders the search for the error.

One can also manually trace an algorithm or program segment by working through it step by step, recording the values of certain key variables in a **trace table.** This technique is known as **desk checking** the algorithm/program segment. For example, tracing the while loop in the binary search algorithm using the preceding array *a* with *item* = 96, recording the values of *first, last,* and *mid,* gives the following trace table:

Step	*first*	*last*	*mid*
Initially	0	6	—
4a	0	6	3
4b	3	6	3
4a	3	6	4
4b	3	6	4
4a	4	6	5
4b	4	6	5
4a	5	6	5
4b	5	6	5
4a	5	6	5
4b	5	6	5
4a	5	6	5
4b	5	6	5
.	.	.	.
.	.	.	.
.	.	.	.

Either manual or automatic tracing of this procedure reveals that when *item* = 96, the last array element, *first* eventually becomes 5, and *last* becomes 6, and *mid* is then always computed as 5, so that *first* and *last* never change. Because the algorithm does locate each of the other array elements, the beginning programmer might "patch" it by treating this special case separately and inserting the statement

```
if (item == a[n - 1])
{
    mid = n;
    found = true:
}
```

before the while loop. The function now correctly locates each of the array elements, but it is still not correct, as searching for any item greater than a[6] will still result in an infinite loop.

☞   *Attempting to fix a program unit with "quick and dirty" patches like this is almost always a bad idea* because it fails to address the real source of the problem and thus makes the program unnecessarily complicated and "messy." The real source of difficulty in the preceding example is not that the last element of the array requires special consideration but that the updating of *first* and *last* within the while loop is not correct. If *item* < a[*mid*], then the part of the array preceding location *mid*, that is, a[*first*], . . . , a[*mid* − 1], should be searched, not a[*first*], . . . , a[*mid*]. Thus, in this case, *last* should be set equal to *mid* − 1, not *mid*. Similarly, if *item* > a[*mid*], then *first* should be set equal to *mid* + 1 rather than *mid*.

Testing of a program unit should be done several times using a variety of inputs, ideally prepared by people other than the programmer, who may be making nonobvious assumptions in the choice of test data. If any combination of inputs produces incorrect output, then the program contains a logic error. Thorough testing of a program will increase one's confidence in its correctness, but it must be realized that it is almost never possible to test a program with every possible set of test data. No matter how much testing has been done, more can always be done. Thus, *testing is never finished; it is only stopped.* No matter how extensively a program unit is tested, there is no guarantee that all the errors have been found. Obscure "bugs" will often remain and will not be detected until some time later, perhaps after the software has been released for public use. As these bugs turn up, the cycle of testing and correction must be repeated and a "fix" or "patch" or a new release sent to the users. There are cases in which apparently correct programs have been in use for more than ten years before a particular combination of inputs produced an incorrect output caused by a logic error. The particular data set that caused the program to execute the erroneous statement(s) had never been input in all that time!

In some applications such as defense systems and spacecraft guidance systems, program errors are more than just a nuisance and cannot be tolerated. In such cases, relying on the results of test runs may not be sufficient because *testing can only show the presence of errors, not their absence.* It may be necessary to give a deductive proof that the program is correct and that it will always produce the correct results (assuming no system malfunction). Correctness proofs are considered in Chap. 7.

1.5   MAINTENANCE

Once a program and possibly a collection of subprograms and libraries developed for solving a problem has been validated and verified, it begins its useful life and will, in many cases, be used for several years. It is likely, however, that it will require some modification. As we noted in the previous section, some software systems, especially large ones developed for complex projects, will often have obscure bugs that were not detected during testing and that will surface after the software is released for public use. One important aspect of system maintenance is fixing such flaws in the software.

It may also be necessary to modify software to improve its performance, to add new features, and so on. Other modifications may be required because of changes in the computer hardware and/or the system software such as the operating system. External factors such as changes in government rules and regulations or changes in the organizational structure of the company may also force software modification. These changes are easier to make in systems that are developed in a modular manner with well-structured program units than in poorly designed ones because the changes can often be made by modifying only a few of the units or by adding new ones.

Software maintenance is a major component of the life cycle of software. Studies have shown that in recent years more than 50 percent of computer center budgets and more than 50 percent of programmer time have been devoted to software maintenance and that worldwide, billions and perhaps trillions of dollars have been spent on software maintenance. A major factor that has contributed to this high cost in money and time is that many programs and systems were originally written with poor structure, documentation, and style. This problem is complicated by the fact that maintenance must often be done by someone not involved in the original design. Thus it is mandatory that programmers do their utmost to design programs and systems of programs that are readable, well documented, and well structured so they are easy to understand and modify and are thus easier to maintain than is much of the software developed in the past.

✔ Quick Quiz 1.5

1. The term _____ refers to the study and use of certain standard techniques and methodologies in developing software.

2. List the five steps of software development.

3. A description of the behavior of a program for solving a problem is called a _____ of the problem.

4. Formulating a specification for most real-world problems is usually quite easy and straightforward. (True or false)

5. The three stages of object-centered design are to: (1) Identify the problem's _____; (2) identify the _____ needed to solve the problem; (3) arrange these in a sequence of steps called a(n) _____ that solves the problem.

6. The most important attribute of an object is its _____.

7. Algorithms are commonly written in _____.

8. What three control structures are used in developing structured algorithms?

9. _____ is the process of implementing a design plan in some programming language.

10. Using global variables to share information between subprograms is a good programming practice. (True or false)

11. _____ describe the state of processing before a program or subprogram is executed and _____ describe the state of processing after it is executed.

12. Distinguish between verification and validation.

13. Name and describe three kinds of programming errors.

14. Distinguish between black-box and white-box testing.

15. Testing can only show the presence of errors in a program, not their absence. (True or false)

✍ EXERCISES 1.5

1. Name and describe the five phases of the software life cycle.
2. What are the three phases of object-centered design?
3. What are some of the ways in which problems in introductory programming courses differ from real-world problems?
4. What are structured data types? Give some examples from C++.
5. Define an algorithm, naming and describing the properties it must possess.
6. What is pseudocode?
7. Name and describe the three control structures used in developing structured algorithms.
8. What are some of the ways in which student programs differ from real-world software?
9. Name three kinds of programming errors and give examples of each. When during program development is each likely to be detected?
10. What are some situations in which maintenance may be required?

☞ PROGRAMMING POINTERS

1. Always formulate a *specification* for the behavior of a program for solving a problem and develop a *design plan* for it before beginning to write code.
2. Identifying a problem's *objects*, the *operations* needed to solve the problem, and developing an *algorithm* for applying these operations to the objects to solve the problem is the essence of object-centered design.
3. Some algorithms for solving a problem may be much more efficient than others.
4. Source code should be *correct, readable,* and *understandable.*
5. Make all programs and subprograms *well structured.* (See Sec. 1.3 for guidelines.)
6. *Document* all source code. (See Sec. 1.3 for guidelines.)
7. Make source code *aesthetic.* (See Sec. 1.3 for guidelines.)
8. Consider *special cases* when selecting test data, because they often cause a program to malfunction.
9. "Quick and dirty" patching of a program unit is almost never a good idea.
10. Testing can only show the presence of errors, not their absence. Testing is never finished; it is only stopped.

ADT TIPS

1. The most important attribute of each object is its *type*, which determines what values the object may have, what operations can be performed on it, and what these operations produce.
2. Simple data types are for objects that are single entities; structured data types are for objects that are collections of objects.

PROGRAMMING PROBLEMS

1. Write the following unstructured program segment in structured form (but different from those given in Problems 2 and 3):

```
        int row = 0,
            col;
   A:  col = 0;
        if (col < n) goto B;
        goto A;
   B:  if (row < n) goto C;
        goto E;
   C:  if (mat[row][col] == item) goto D;
        col++;
        if (col < n) goto B;
        row++;
        goto A;
   D:  cout << "item found\n";
        goto F;
   E:  cout << "item not found\n";
   F:  ;
```

2. Although the following program segment is structured, it is not a correct solution to Exer. 1.

```
/* Search the entries of the n X n matrix mat in
   rowwise order for an entry equal to item */

bool found;
for (int row = 0; row < n; row++)
  for (int col = 0; col < n; col++)
    if (mat[row][col] == item)
      found = true;
    else
      found = false;
if (found)
  cout << "item found\n";
else
  cout << "item not found\n";
```

(a) Write a program that incorporates this program segment and then perform black-box testing of it, beginning with the matrix $\mathtt{mat} = \begin{bmatrix} 45 & 77 & 93 \\ 78 & 79 & 85 \\ 72 & 96 & 77 \end{bmatrix}$ and $\mathtt{item} = 77$ as the first set of test data. Produce enough output to show that your testing has turned up an error.

(b) Use program tracing to determine what is wrong with this program segment.

3. The following program segment is correct, but it is not a good solution to Exer. 1. Why not? (Consider its efficiency.)

```
/* Search the entries of the n X n matrix mat in
   rowwise order for an entry equal to item */

bool found = false;
for (int row = 0; row < n; row++)
   for (int col = 0; col < n; col++)
      if (mat[row][col] == item)
         found = true;
if (found)
   cout << "item found\n";
else
   cout << "item not found\n";
```

4. The following function performs a linear search of a list l of length ll for the item it, returning 0 or 1 depending on whether or not it is found. Many principles of good programming are violated. Describe some of these and rewrite the function in an acceptable format.

```
int LS(int l[], int ll, int it)
/* Search l for it */
{
int i=0,f=0;A:if (l[i]==it)
goto B; if (i==ll) goto
C;/*ADD 1 TO i*/i++;goto A;
B:f=1;C:return f;
}
```

Chapter 2

INTRODUCTION TO DATA STRUCTURES AND ABSTRACT DATA TYPES— C-STYLE TYPES

Chapter Contents

The design phase of the software life cycle described in Chap. 1 included (among other things) deciding how to organize the data involved in a problem and how to design algorithms for the operations on the data. The main purpose of this text is to explore these two topics in detail. The data to be processed must be organized in a way that reflects the relationships among the data items to allow the data to be processed efficiently. As we have already noted, deciding how to store these data items and designing algorithms to perform the operations on the data cannot be separated; they must be done in parallel.

Because these data structures and algorithms must be implemented in some programming language, they must be designed to take advantage of the features of that language. This means that where possible, they should be based on the predefined data types, operations, and other features provided in the language. In this chapter we define and illustrate data structures and their implementations, describe how some of the predefined C++ data types are implemented, and also how they can be used to implement new data types.

29

2.1   DATA STRUCTURES, ABSTRACT DATA TYPES, AND IMPLEMENTATIONS

To illustrate the process of organizing and structuring data in a problem, let us consider the following example. Suppose that Trans-Fryslan Airlines operates a single ten-passenger airplane. TFA would like to modernize its operations and, as a first step, needs a program that will determine for each flight which seats are unoccupied so that they can be assigned.

In this problem, it is clear that the basic object is a collection of ten seats and, for each seat, some indication of whether it is occupied. We must be able to perform the following operations: (1) Examine the collection of seats to determine which of them are unoccupied; (2) reserve a seat, and (3) cancel a seat assignment. To perform these operations, it is convenient to think of the seats as organized in a list.

After organizing the data as a list of ten seats and identifying the basic operations to be performed, we can consider possible ways to implement this structure. A variety of implementations are possible. For example, we might define an enumeration

```
enum SeatStatus (OCCUPIED, UNOCCUPIED);
```

and represent the list of seats by 10 simple variables of type `SeatStatus`:

```
SeatStatus seat1, seat2, ... , seat10;
```

Although this is a simple representation of the list of seats, the algorithms to perform the required operations are somewhat awkward. For example, the algorithm to scan the list of seats and to produce a listing of those seats that are unoccupied might be as follows:

ALGORITHM TO LIST UNOCCUPIED SEATS

1. If `seat1` is UNOCCUPIED
   Display 1.

2. If `seat2` is UNOCCUPIED
   Display 2.

3. If `seat3` is UNOCCUPIED
   Display 3.
   .
   .
   .

10. If `seat10` is UNOCCUPIED
   Display 10.

An algorithm for reserving a seat would be even more awkward and, in fact, is completely unreasonable!

ALGORITHM TO RESERVE A SEAT

1. Set `done` to false.

2. If `seat1` is UNOCCUPIED do the following:

  a. Display "Do you wish to assign Seat #1?".

  b. Get `response` from user.

  c. If `response` is 'y' then do the following:

    i. Set `seat1` to OCCUPIED.

    ii. Set `done` to `true`.

 3. If not `done and seat2` is UNOCCUPIED then do the following:

  a. Display "Do you wish to assign Seat #2?".

  b. Get `response` from user.

  c. If `response` is 'y' then do the following:

    i. Set `seat2` to OCCUPIED.

    ii. Set `done` to `true`.

     ⋮

An algorithm for canceling a seat assignment would be equally ridiculous.

 C++ functions could be written to implement these algorithms, but they would be clumsy. They would be inflexible and difficult to modify and would become even more awkward if TFA replaced its ten-seat airliner with a larger aircraft having more seats.

 These difficulties certainly suggest that it may be appropriate to consider other ways to represent the data of this problem. One alternative is to represent the list of seats as an array (or as a `vector`) whose elements are of type `SeatStatus`:

```
const int MAX_SEATS = 10; // upper limit on the number of seats

enum SeatStatus {OCCUPIED, UNOCCUPIED};
typedef SeatStatus SeatList[MAX_SEATS];

SeatList seat;
```

Because the elements of an array can be easily accessed by using the subscript operator, the algorithms to implement the required operations are much simpler:

ALGORITHM TO LIST UNOCCUPIED SEATS

 1. For `number` ranging from 0 to `MAX_SEATS` −1 do the following:

  If `seat[number]` is UNOCCUPIED

   Display `number`.

ALGORITHM TO RESERVE A SEAT

 1. Read `number` of seat to be reserved.

 2. If `seat[number]` is UNOCCUPIED

  Set `seat[number]` to OCCUPIED.

 Else

  Display a message that the seat having this `number` has already been assigned.

The algorithm for canceling a seat assignment is similar to that for reserving a seat.

Although this is a very simple example, it does illustrate several general concepts. One is that solving a problem involves processing data and an important part of the solution is the careful organization of the data. This requires that we identify

1. The *collection of data items* and

2. Basic *relationships* among them and *operations* that must be performed on them

 Such a collection with operations and relations is called an **abstract data type** (commonly abbreviated as **ADT**). In this example, the collection of data items is a list of seats or some representation of them (for example, a seating chart of the plane), together with the basic operations: (1) Scan the list to determine which seats are occupied, and (2) change a seat's status from unoccupied to occupied or from occupied to unoccupied. The word *abstract* refers to the fact that the data and the basic operations and relations defined on it are being studied independently of how they are implemented. We are thinking of *what* can be done with the data, not *how* it is done.

An **implementation** of an ADT consists of **storage structures** commonly called **data structures** to store the data items and **algorithms** for the basic operations and relations. In the preceding example, two implementations are given. In the first, the storage structure consists of 10 simple variables, and in the second implementation, it is an array. In both cases, algorithms for the basic operations are given, but those in the second implementation are considerably easier than those in the first.

The terms *abstract data type* and *abstract data structure* are often used interchangeably. However, we will use abstract data type when data is studied at a logical or conceptual level, independent of any programming language or machine considerations. An ADT in computer science is analogous to structures such as groups and vector spaces in mathematics. The term data structure is appropriate when data is being organized (structured) in a program unit.

This idea of **data abstraction**, in which the definition of the data type is separated from its implementation, is an important concept in software design. It makes it possible to study and use the structure without being concerned about the details of its implementation. In fact, this is usually the approach used for predefined data types such as `int`, `double`, `char`, `bool`, arrays, and structs. Most of the time programmers use these data types without worrying how they are implemented. Nevertheless, these data types can be used more effectively and efficiently if the programmer has some understanding of the implementation used. For this reason, in the next several sections we review some of the basic data types of C++ and examine their implementations.

C++ provides a very large collection of data types. Some of these are built into the language and others are provided in standard libraries. Some of the most commonly used types are summarized in Fig. 2.1.

2.2   SIMPLE DATA TYPES

As we indicated in the preceding section, problem solving invariably involves manipulating some kind of data. In its most basic form, data values (as well as instructions) are encoded in the memory of a computer as sequences of 0s and 1s. This is because the devices that make up a computer's memory are two-state

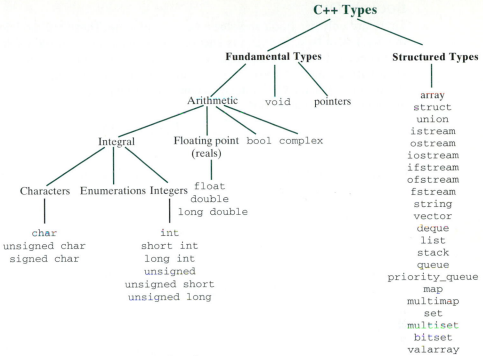

FIGURE 2.1   Some C++ data types.

devices and hence are ideally suited for storing information that is coded using only two symbols. If one of the states is interpreted as 0 and the other as 1, then a natural scheme for representing information is one that uses only the two binary digits, or **bits**, 0 and 1. The two-state devices used in computer memory are organized into groups called **bytes**, each of which consists of eight bits. These bytes are in turn organized into **words**. These memory units—bits, bytes, and words—are the basic storage structures for all simple data types and indeed, for all data stored in a computer. In *byte-addressable* computers,[1] the bytes are numbered, and the number associated with a byte is called its **address**. The contents of each byte or sequence of bytes can be accessed by means of its address.

Basic data types such as int, float, double, char, and bool in C++ are called **simple data types** because a value of one of these types is atomic; that is, it consists of a single entity that cannot be subdivided. Nevertheless, each can be viewed as an abstract data type because it consists of a collection of values and one or more basic operations and relations defined on these values. Their implementations use the basic memory cells as storage structures, and the algorithms for the basic operations and relations are implemented by the hardware and/or software of the computer system. In this section we examine the implementations of these simple data types.

---

[1]As opposed to *word-addressable* computers in which words have addresses.

BOOLEAN DATA

There are only two boolean values: `false` and `true`. These are modeled in C++ by the `bool` data type. If `false` is encoded as 0 and `true` as 1, then a single bit is all that is needed to store a `boolean` value. Usually, however, an entire word or byte is used with all bits set to 0 for `false` and any other bit string representing `true`. Accordingly, when a C++ integer is converted to type `bool`, 0 is converted to `false` and any nonzero value to `true`:

$$\text{bool}(int\_val) = \begin{cases} \text{false if } int\_val \text{ is 0} \\ \text{true if } int\_val \text{ is not 0} \end{cases}$$

Conversely, when a `bool` value in C++ is converted to an integer, `false` is converted to 0 and `true` to 1:

$$\text{int}(bool\_val) = \begin{cases} 0 \text{ if } bool\_val \text{ is false} \\ 1 \text{ if } bool\_val \text{ is true} \end{cases}$$

Three boolean operations are defined in C++: `&&` (and), `||` (or), and `!` (not). Because a boolean expression of the form p `&&` q is true only in the case that p and q both are true, the bit operation that implements `&&` is defined by the following table:

&&	0	1
0	0	0
1	0	1

Similarly, a boolean expression of the form p `||` q is false only in the case that p and q both are false, and so the corresponding bit operation is defined by

||	0	1
0	0	1
1	1	1

The boolean operation `!` is implemented simply by bit complementation—"flip" the bits

x	$!x$
0	1
1	0

CHARACTER DATA

The schemes used for the internal representation of character data are based on the assignment of a numeric code to each of the characters in the character set. Several standard coding schemes have been developed, such as ASCII (American Standard Code for Information Interchange) and EBCDIC (Extended Binary Coded Decimal

Interchange Code) and Unicode.[2] In C++, characters are normally processed using type `char`, and are stored in one 8-bit byte. For example, the ASCII code of `c` is 99 $= 01100011_2$, which can be stored in a single byte:[3]

Unicode is designed for use with most of the written languages of the world and must therefore provide codes for many characters. Whereas a single byte can encode only 256 characters, Unicode provides codes for more than 65,000 characters. To accomplish this it uses 16-bit codes. For example, the code for `c` (99—same as in ASCII) would be stored in two bytes:

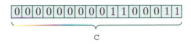

The code for the non-ASCII character π (Greek pi) is $960 = 0000001111000000_2$ and can also be stored in two bytes:

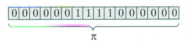

C++ provides the *wide character type* `wchar_t` to store characters in larger character sets like Unicode.

One important operation involving character values is comparison to determine whether two characters are equal or whether one is less than another. This comparison is carried out using the integer codes that represent the characters. Two characters are equal if their codes are equal, and one character is less than the other if the code of the first is less than the code of the second.

In C++, character values can be processed as integer values:

$$\text{int}(char\_value) = \text{the numeric code of } char\_value$$

For values of unsigned `char` type these are usually in the range 0 to 255 and values of `signed char` type are in the range -127 to 127. Which of these is used for plain `char` is implementation dependent.

Sequences of characters can be stored in consecutive bytes, one byte for each character in the string. For example, the character string `code` can be stored in a 32-bit word with the code for `c` in the first byte, the code for `o` in the second byte, and so on:

Character strings can be processed by using `char` arrays in C++ (see Sec. 2.3).

---

[2]See Appendix A for a table of ASCII codes for all characters.
[3]See Appendix B if you are not familiar with other number systems such as binary, octal, and hexadecimal.

INTEGER DATA

UNSIGNED INTEGERS.   The set of *nonnegative integers*, sometimes called *cardinal numbers*, is {0, 1, 2, 3, . . . }. It is modeled in C++ by the data types unsigned short, unsigned, and unsigned long (which are shorthands for unsigned short int, unsigned int, and unsigned long int, respectively). Typically, unsigned short values are stored in 2 bytes and unsigned long values in 4 bytes. Which of these two is used for plain unsigned values is implementation-dependent. Thus the integer 58 can be represented as a 16-bit binary numeral

$$58 = 0000000000111010_2$$

and stored in two bytes:

0	0	0	0	0	0	0	0	0	0	1	1	1	0	1	0

SIGNED INTEGERS.   The set {. . . , −3, −2, −1, 0, 1, 2, 3, . . . } of *integers* is modeled in C++ by the data types, short (or short int), int, and long (or long int). Which of these will be used to represent an integer literal such as 12345 is implementation-dependent. If we wish to specify that it is to be stored as an unsigned value, we can attach the suffix U: 12345U. Attaching the suffix L, 12345L, specifies that it is to be stored as a long value. Attaching both specifies an unsigned long value: 12345LU or 12345UL.

Most schemes for representing integers use one bit to indicate the sign of a number. One simple way to do this is to set the leftmost bit to 1 if the number is negative, 0 if it is not, and use the remaining bits to store the magnitude of the number, using its base-two representation. This representation is called the **sign-magnitude** representation for integers. For example, the 8-bit sign-magnitude representation of 6 is

and the sign-magnitude representation of −6 is

Although this is a very simple scheme for representing integers, the algorithms for the basic arithmetic operations are not as easy as they are in some other representations. In particular, addition of integers with opposite signs is rather difficult.

One scheme commonly used to represent integers for which the algorithms for the basic operations are simpler is called **two's complement** notation. In this scheme, the nonnegative integers are represented as in the sign-magnitude notation. The representation of a negative integer −n is obtained by first finding the base-two representation for n, complementing it (that is, changing each 0 to 1 and each 1 to 0), and then adding 1 to the result.[4] Thus the two's complement representation of -6 using a string of 16 bits is obtained as follows:

1. Represent 6 as a 16-bit base-two number   0000000000000110

2. Complement this bit string   1111111111111001

3. Add 1   1111111111111010

The integer -6 can thus be stored in two bytes as

1	1	1	1	1	1	1	1	1	1	1	1	1	0	1	0

Since 2^n different patterns can be formed with n bits, it follows that there are 2^n different integers that can be represented by a string of n bits. For example, using $n = 16$ bits, we can represent $2^{16} = 65536$ different integers. If the two's complement scheme is used, the integers in the range -32768 through 32767 can be represented as follows:

Two's Complement	Decimal
1000000000000000	-32768
1000000000000001	-32767
1000000000000010	-32766
1000000000000011	-32765
.	.
.	.
.	.
1111111111111101	-3
1111111111111110	-2
1111111111111111	-1
0000000000000000	0
0000000000000001	1
0000000000000010	2
0000000000000011	3
.	.
.	.
.	.
0111111111111101	32765
0111111111111110	32766
0111111111111111	32767

[4] A simpler way to do this third step is: Scan from the right, changing 1s to 0s until a 0 is encountered; change it to 1 and stop.

Note that the leftmost bit of the two's complement representation of each of the negative integers −32768 through −1 is 1, whereas the leftmost bit of the two's complement representation of the nonnegative integers 0 through 32767 is 0. Thus the leftmost bit is the sign bit, with 0 indicating a nonnegative value and 1 indicating a negative value.

The algorithms to implement the usual arithmetic operations on unsigned integers and for signed integers represented using two's complement notation are similar to the familiar algorithms for carrying out these operations on base-ten numbers. The basic addition and multiplication tables are

+	0	1
0	0	1
1	1	10

×	0	1
0	0	0
1	0	1

Thus, for example, the sum $5 + 7$ is calculated by adding, bit by bit, the base-two representations of these numbers, carrying when necessary:

$$111 \leftarrow \text{carry bits}$$
$$0000000000000101$$
$$+ \quad 0000000000000111$$
$$0000000000001100$$

Similarly, the sum $5 + (-6)$ is calculated as

$$0000000000000101$$
$$+ \quad 1111111111111010$$
$$1111111111111111$$

which yields the two's complement representation of −1. Comparison of two integers in two's complement notation is somewhat awkward, however, since the representation of negative integers seems to indicate that these integers are greater than the positive integers.

Another useful scheme for representing integers is **excess** or **biased notation**. In this scheme, the representation of an integer as a string of n bits is formed by adding a *bias*, typically 2^{n-1}, to the integer and representing the result in base-two. Thus, the 8-bit biased representation of −6 using a bias of $2^7 = 128$, is obtained as follows:

1. Add the bias to −6, giving 122

2. Represent the result in base-two notation: 01111010

The integers in the range from −8 through 7 can be represented using four bits and a bias of $2^3 = 8$ as follows:

Biased	Decimal
0000	−8
0001	−7
0010	−6
0011	−5
0100	−4
0101	−3
0110	−2
0111	−1
1000	0
1001	1
1010	2
1011	3
1100	4
1101	5
1110	6
1111	7

Note that the leftmost bit is again a sign bit, with 0 indicating a negative value and 1 a nonnegative value.

Although algorithms for the basic arithmetic operations are more complicated in this scheme than in the two's complement scheme, two integers can be compared more easily. This is one reason that a biased representation is typically used for the exponent in the floating-point representation of real numbers, to be described momentarily.

OVERFLOW.   The details of how integers are represented internally are usually of little concern to the programmer because they are automatically handled by the computer. One aspect that is important, however, is that there is a limit to the range of integers that can be stored. The largest unsigned integer that can be stored in two bytes is $2^{16} - 1 = 65535$, and in four bytes, $2^{32} - 1 = 4294967295$. The largest signed integer that can be stored in two bytes is $2^{15} - 1 = 32767$, and in four bytes, $2^{31} - 1 = 2147483647$. The smallest signed integer that can be stored in two bytes is $-2^{16} = -32768$, and in four bytes, $-2^{32} = -2147483648$. An attempt to store an integer outside the allowed range will result in the loss of some of the bits of its binary representation—a phenomenon known as **overflow**.

We could enlarge the range of integers that can be stored by using more bytes, but this does not resolve the problem of overflow because the range of representable integers is still finite. Thus the integer types in C++ are not perfect representations of the mathematical concept of integer since in mathematics, the set of integers is infinite.

REAL DATA

Real values, also called *floating-point* values, are modeled in C++ by the single-precision type `float`, the double-precision type `double`, and the extended-precision type `long double`. Type `double` is the default type used for processing real data. A suffix F can be attached to a real literal, as in `123.45F`, to specify that it is to be processed as a `float` value; attaching L specifies a `long double` value.

In a decimal numeral representing a real value, the digits to the right of the decimal point are also coefficients of powers of 10. In this case, however, the exponents are negative integers. For example, the numeral 0.317 can be written in expanded form as

$$3 \times 10^{-1} + 1 \times 10^{-2} + 7 \times 10^{-3}$$

The point in a base-two numeral representing a real value is called a **binary point**, and the positions to the right of the binary point represent negative powers of the base 2. For example, the expanded form of 110.101 is

$$(1 \times 2^2) + (1 \times 2^1) + (0 \times 2^0) + (1 \times 2^{-1}) + (0 \times 2^{-2}) + (1 \times 2^{-3})$$

and thus it has the decimal value

$$4 + 2 + 0 + \frac{1}{2} + \frac{0}{4} + \frac{1}{8} = 6.625$$

There is some variation in the schemes used for storing real numbers in computer memory, but one floating-point representation was standardized in 1985 by the Institute for Electrical and Electronic Engineers (IEEE) and has become almost universal. This **IEEE Floating-Point Format** specifies how real numbers can be represented in two formats: *single precision*, which uses 32 bits, and *double precision*, which uses 64 bits. The double precision format is simply a wider version of the single precision format, so we will consider only single precision.

We begin by writing the binary representation of the number in **floating-point form**, which is like scientific notation except that the base is two rather than ten,

$$b_1.b_2b_3 \cdots \times 2^k$$

where each b_i is 0 or 1, and $b_1 = 1$ (unless the number is 0). $b_1.b_2b_3 \ldots$ is called the **mantissa** (or **fractional part** or **significand**) and k is the **exponent** (or **characteristic**). To illustrate it, consider the real number 22.625, which can be represented in binary as

$$10110.101_2$$

Rewriting this in floating-point form,

$$1.0110101_2 \times 2^4$$

is easy since multiplying (dividing) a base-two number by 2 is the same as moving the binary point to the right (left). 1.0110101_2 is the mantissa and 4 is the exponent.

In the IEEE format for single-precision real values,

▶ the leftmost bit stores the sign of the mantissa, 0 for positive, 1 for negative

▶ the next 8 bits store the biased binary representation of the exponent with bias 127

▶ the rightmost 23 bits store the bits to the right of the binary point in the mantissa (the bit to the left need not be stored since it is always 1, unless the number is 0)

For 22.625, the stored exponent would be $4 + 127 = 10000011_2$ and the stored mantissa would be $01101010000000000000000_2$:

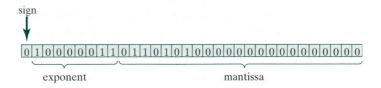

The IEEE representation for double precision uses an 11-bit exponent with a bias of 1023 and 53 bits for the signed mantissa.

Because the binary representation of the exponent may require more than the available number of bits, we see that the **overflow** problem discussed in connection with integers also occurs in storing a real number whose exponent is too large. An 8-bit exponent restricts the range of real values to approximately -10^{38} to 10^{38}, and overflow occurs for values outside this range. A negative exponent that is too small to be stored causes an **underflow**. Real values represented using an 8-bit exponent must be greater than approximately 10^{-38} or less than -10^{-38}, and underflow occurs between these values:

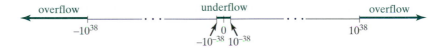

Also, there obviously are some real numbers whose mantissas have more than the allotted number of bits; consequently, some of these bits will be lost when such numbers are stored. In fact, most real numbers do not have finite binary representations and thus cannot be stored exactly in any computer. For example, the binary representation of the real number 0.7 is

$$(0.10110011001100110011001100110\ldots)_2$$

where the block 0110 is repeated indefinitely. Because only a finite number of these bits can be stored, the stored representation of 0.7 will not be exact. For example, if only the first twenty-four bits are stored and all the remaining bits are truncated, the stored representation of 0.7 will be

$$0.101100110011001100110011001$$

which has the decimal value 0.6999999284744263. If the binary representation is rounded to 24 bits, then the stored representation of 0.7 is

$$0.101100110011001100110011010$$

which has the decimal value 0.7000000476837159. In either case, the stored value is not exactly 0.7. This error in the stored representation of a real value, called **round-off error**, can be reduced, but not eliminated, by storing a larger number of bits.

A 24-bit mantissa gives approximately 7 significant decimal digits for real values and a 48-bit mantissa gives approximately 14 significant digits.

This approximation error may be compounded when real numbers are combined in arithmetic expressions. To illustrate, consider adding the three real numbers 0.4104, 1.0, and 0.2204; for simplicity, assume that the computations are done using decimal representation with four-digit precision. The normalized floating-point representations of these values are 0.4104×10^0, 0.100×10^1, and 0.2204×10^0. The first step in the addition of two values is to "align the decimal point" by increasing the smaller of the two exponents and shifting the mantissa. Thus, the sum of the first two values is obtained by adding 0.0410×10^1 and 0.1000×10^1, which gives 0.1410×10^1. Adding the third number again requires adjusting the exponent and shifting the mantissa, 0.0220×10^1, and the final result is 0.1630×10^1, or 1.630. On the other hand, if the two smaller values are added first, giving 0.6308×10^0, and then the larger number is added, the result is 0.1631×10^1, or 1.631 (assuming rounding). In a long chain of such calculations, these small errors can accumulate so that the error in the final result may be very large. This example also illustrates that two real quantities that are algebraically equal, such as $(A + B) + C$ and $(A + C) + B$, may have computed values that are not equal. Consequently, some care must be taken when comparing two real values with the relational operators == and !=.

It should now be clear that, as with integers, only a finite range of real numbers can be stored because of the limited number of bits allotted to the exponent. Unlike integers, however, not all real numbers within this range can be stored because of the limit on the number of bits in the mantissa. In fact, only a finite subset of these real numbers can be stored exactly, and this means that there are infinitely many real numbers that cannot be stored exactly.

SUMMARY

We have seen that each of the basic data types for boolean, character, integer, and real data can be represented by bit strings. It is the *interpretation* of a bit string and the operations that may be applied to it that determine what kind of value is represented by that bit string. A given bit string may represent a boolean, character, integer, or real value, depending on the interpretation used. For example, the bit string

$$0\ 1\ 0\ 0\ 1\ 0\ 0\ 1\ 0\ 1\ 0\ 1\ 0\ 0\ 0\ 1$$

can be interpreted as the integer value

$$2^{14} + 2^{11} + 2^8 + 2^6 + 2^4 + 2^0 = 18769$$

or as a real value (assuming IEEE floating-point representation and that the next 16 bits are 0)

$$\left(\frac{1}{2} + \frac{1}{4} + \frac{1}{16} + \frac{1}{128} \right) \times 2^{19} = 430080.0$$

or (if ASCII code is used) as the pair of characters

$$\mathtt{IQ}$$

or (if boolean values are stored one per 16-bit word) as the single boolean value true

or (if each boolean value is stored in one byte) as a pair of boolean values

true, true

or (if each boolean value is stored in one bit) as a sequence of 16 boolean values

false, true, false, false, true, . . . , true

It might even be interpreted as a machine-language instruction in which the first eight bits represent the opcode $01001001_2 = 73$ of some operation to be applied to the data value stored in the memory location whose address $01010001_2 = 81$ is given by the last eight bits.

✔ Quick Quiz 2.2

1. What is an abstract data type (ADT)?

2. What is an implementation of an ADT?

3. _____ refers to the separation of the definition of a data type from its implementation.

4. A(n) _____ is a binary digit; a(n) _____ is a group of eight binary digits.

5. An attempt to store an integer greater than the maximum allowed will result in _____ .

6   The decimal value of 10111_2 is _____.

7. The decimal value of 101.11_2 is _____.

8. In the floating-point representation 1.011×2^5, 1.011 is called the _____ .

9. In floating-point representation of a real value, a negative exponent that is too small to be stored causes a(n) _____ .

10. If a and b are integers that can be stored exactly, then all integers between a and b can also be stored exactly. (True or false)

11. If a and b are real values that can be stored exactly, then all real values between a and b can also be stored exactly. (True or false)

✍ EXERCISES 2.2

In Exercises 1–6, indicate how each of the bit strings of length 16 can be interpreted as (a) a boolean value; (b) a pair of boolean values; (c) a sequence of 16 boolean values.

1. 0000000001000000
2. 0110111001101111
3. 1011111111111110
4. 1100000000000001
5. 1001100110011001
6. 1010101010101010

7. Interpret the bit string in Exercise 1 as a pair of characters assuming ASCII representation (see Appendix A).

8. Repeat Exercise 7 but for the bit string in Exercise 2.

9–14. Find the integer (base-ten value) represented by the bit strings of length 16 in Exercises 1–6, assuming a sign-magnitude representation.

15–20. Find the integer (base-ten value) represented by the bit strings of length 16 in Exercises 1–6, assuming two's complement representation.

21–26. Find the integer (base-ten value) represented by the bit strings of length 16 in Exercises 1–6, assuming biased notation with bias 2^{15}.

For Exercises 27–32, find the real value represented by the bit string, assuming IEEE single-precision representation.

27. 01000000010000000000000000000000

28. 01000000110000000000000000000000

29. 01000011111111100000000000000000

30. 00111111111000000000000000000000

31. 01010101010101010000000000000000

32. 11000000010110000000000000000000

Find the 16-bit two's complement representation of the integers in Exercises 33–38.

33. 99	**34.** 5280	**35.** 255
36. −255	**37.** 1024	**38.** −1024

Show how each of the real numbers in Exercises 39–44 will be stored using IEEE single-precision representation if extra bits in the mantissa are (a) truncated or (b) rounded.

39. 0.625	**40.** 25.625	**41.** 14.78125
42. 0.015625	**43.** 0.1	**44.** 2.01

Indicate how the character strings in Exercises 45–50 would be stored in two-byte words using ASCII.

45. BE	**46.** be	**47.** ABLE
48. Mr. Doe	**49.** 1234	**50.** 12.34

2.3   ARRAYS

In addition to simple data types, most high-level programming languages also provide **structured data types**. Values of these types are *collections* rather than individual data items. In this section we consider the most common of these data types, the array.

As an abstract data type, an **array** may be defined as follows:

ADT ARRAY

Collection of data elements:

A *fixed-size* sequence (*ordered* set) of elements, all of the same type

Basic operation:

Direct access to each element in the array so that values can be retrieved from or stored in this element.

Thus an array has a specific fixed number of elements and these are ordered so that there is a first element, a second element, and so on. All the array elements must be of the same type; thus we might have an array of integers, an array of characters, or even an array of arrays. An array is therefore an appropriate data structure to consider for organizing *homogeneous* data collections, that is, those in which all the data items are of the same type, and especially those collections whose sizes remain fairly constant and in which there is an order associated with the data items.

Direct or **random access** means that each array element can be accessed simply by specifying its location in the array, so that the time required to access each element in the array is the same for all elements, regardless of their positions in the array. For example, in an array of 100 elements, the time required to access the seventy-fifth element is the same as that for the fifth. This is quite different from a **sequential access** structure in which one can access an element only by first accessing all those that precede it. Clearly, in this case, the time required to access the seventy-fifth element would be considerably greater than that needed for the fifth.

In most high-level languages, an array is denoted by a variable whose value is the collection of values that comprise the array. As described later, the value of an array variable is actually the address in memory where the first element is stored. A particular element of the array is then accessed by attaching to the array name one or more **indices** (also called **subscripts**) that specify the position of that element in the array. If only one index is used, the array is said to be **one-dimensional**; arrays involving more than one index are called **multidimensional** arrays.

ONE-DIMENSIONAL ARRAYS

In this section we consider C-style arrays. For compatibility, C++ retains these arrays, although it has added more powerful array types (`valarrays` and `vectors`) that will be described later (see Chap. 6).

A C++ array declaration must specify two features of the array: the number of elements and the type of the elements.

C++ ARRAY DECLARATION

Forms:

```
element_type array_name[CAPACITY];

element_type array_name[CAPACITY] = {initializer_list};
```

where
   `element_type` is any type;
   `array_name` is the name of the array object being defined;
   `CAPACITY` is the number of values the object can contain; it is optional in the
      second form; and
   `initializer_list` is a list of comma-separated values of type `element_type`.

Purpose

Instructs the compiler to reserve a block of consecutive memory locations[5] to hold *CAPACITY* objects of type *element_type*, and associates the name *array_name* with that storage. The array is **zero-based**; that is, the elements of the array are indexed $0, 1, 2, \ldots, CAPACITY - 1$.

In the second form, the array elements are initialized with the values in *initializer_list*. If there are fewer initial values than the array's capacity, 0 is assumed for the remaining elements. It is an error to list more initial values than the declared capacity.[6]

Note how the properties of a C++ array implement the definition of an array as an ADT:

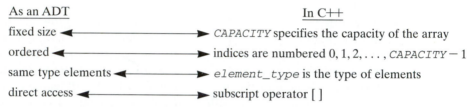

As an ADT	In C++
fixed size	*CAPACITY* specifies the capacity of the array
ordered	indices are numbered $0, 1, 2, \ldots, CAPACITY - 1$
same type elements	*element_type* is the type of elements
direct access	subscript operator [ ]

To illustrate array declarations, consider arrays a, b, c, and d to store collections of 10 integers declared by

```
int a[10],
    b[10] = {0,11,22,33,44,55,66,77,88,99},
    c[10] = {10, 20, 30},
    d[10] = {0};
```

or better, using a named constant to specify the array capacity,

```
const int CAPACITY = 10;

int a[CAPACITY],
    b[CAPACITY] = {0,11,22,33,44,55,66,77,88,99},
    c[CAPACITY] = {10, 20, 30},
    d[CAPACITY] = {0};
```

The elements of the array a are named a[0], a[1],...,a[9] and are initially undefined; they usually contain whatever "garbage" values remain from prior use of the memory block allocated to the array. The elements of the array b are initialized with the specified values, $b[0] = 0, b[1] = 11, b[2] = 22, \ldots, b[9] = 99$:

---

[5]These memory locations are "logically" consecutive; for a very large capacity and/or very large element types, they may not be physically adjacent.
[6]How the compiler is to handle this error is not specified in the C++ standard. In some cases, the array will be filled with values from the list and any remaining values ignored.

	b[0]	b[1]	b[2]	b[3]	b[4]	b[5]	b[6]	b[7]	b[8]	b[9]
b	0	11	22	33	44	55	66	77	88	99

Note that the array capacity can be omitted when an initializer list is used, so the definition of b could also be written

```
int b[] = {0,11,22,33,44,55,66,77,88,99};
```

The first three elements of the array c are initialized with 10, 20, and 30, and the remaining elements with 0:

	c[0]	c[1]	c[2]	c[3]	c[4]	c[5]	c[6]	c[7]	c[8]	c[9]
c	10	20	30	0	0	0	0	0	0	0

All the elements of d will be initialized to 0. Note that this is *an easy way to initialize an array to contain all zeros*:

	d[0]	d[1]	d[2]	d[3]	d[4]	d[5]	d[6]	d[7]	d[8]	d[9]
d	0	0	0	0	0	0	0	0	0	0

If several arrays of 10 integers are needed (especially as parameters of functions), it is better to associate a name with this array type with the `typedef` mechanism,

```
const int CAPACITY = 10;
typedef int IntegerArray[CAPACITY];
```

and then use it to declare the array objects:

```
IntegerArray a,
            b = {0,11,22,33,44,55,66,77,88,99},
            c = {10, 20, 30},
            d = {0};
```

Although arrays may be initialized in their definitions, *the assignment operator = is not defined for arrays*. Copying one array to another must be done elementwise. For example, the statements

```
for (int i = 0; i < CAPACITY; i++)
   b[i] = a[i];
```

can be used to copy the elements of a into the elements of b.

CHARACTER ARRAYS.   Because C has no class mechanism, it has no standard string class for storing character strings. As a result, strings are stored in character arrays. For compatibility, C++ retains this and other features of C for storing character strings.

Character arrays may be initialized in the same manner as numeric arrays, for example,

```
const int NAME_CAPACITY = 10;
char name[NAME_CAPACITY] =
                {'J', 'o', 'h', 'n', ' ', 'D', 'o', 'e'};
```

but they may also be initialized with a character string literal:

```
char name[NAME_CAPACITY] = "John Doe";
```

Both definitions construct name as an array object whose *capacity* is 10 and whose *size* is 8 because there are eight characters in "John Doe".

When fewer values are supplied than the declared capacity of the array, as in these declarations, the zeros used to fill uninitialized elements are interpreted as the **null character** '\0' whose ASCII code is 0, which C uses as an end of string mark.[7]

name | J | o | h | n | | D | o | e | \0 | \0
[0] [1] [2] [3] [4] [5] [6] [7] [8] [9]

String-processing functions can use this null character to find the end of the string. For example, the following statements can be used to output the characters stored in name:

```
for (int i = 0; name[i] != '\0'; i++)
    cout << name[i];
```

 To provide room for the null character, the capacity of a character array must always be at least 1 more than the size of the largest string to be stored in the array. The standard C string-processing functions (in cstring) cannot be expected to perform correctly on character arrays in which there is no terminating null character.

THE SUBSCRIPT OPERATION

An array declaration instructs the compiler to reserve a block of consecutive memory locations that is large enough to store the elements of the array. The address of the first element is called the **base address** of the array and the name of the array is actually a **pointer** to this element; that is, its value is the base address of the array.

The addresses of other array elements are translated into offsets from this base address. This **address translation** is performed by the **subscript operator [ ]**.[8] For

---

[7] \0 is the escape sequence for the null character (just as \101 is the escape sequence for the letter A). Since its octal numeric code is 000, it could also be written as \000. We will use the customary short version \0 in this text.

[8] The subscript operator can be defined for other types by defining a function **operator[]()** whose parameters are these two operands. For example, if x is an object of some type, the statement
```
cout << x[i];
```
could also be written
```
cout << operator[](x, i);
```
The subscript operator computes the address x + i of the element in location i in x and then **dereferences** it to access the contents of the memory location. Thus x[i] is equivalent to *(x + i) where * is the **dereferencing operator** (see Sec. 8.4). For example, the preceding output statement could also be written
```
cout << *(x + i);
```

example, if *b* is the base address of a and ints are stored in four bytes, then the first integer a[0] will be stored in the four bytes beginning at address *b*, the second integer a[1] in the four bytes beginning at address $b + 4$, the next integer a[2] in the four bytes beginning at address $b + 8$, and in general, a[i] in four bytes beginning at address $b + 4i$.

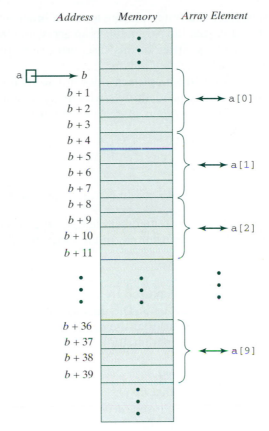

In general, if each element of array a is of type Element_Type and thus requires n = sizeof(Element_Type) bytes for storage, the ith array element a[i] will be stored in the block of n bytes beginning at address $b + n \times i$.

ARRAYS AS PARAMETERS

Functions can be written that accept arrays via parameters and then operate on the arrays by operating on individual array elements. For example, we can output the elements of an int array with the following function:

```
/* Print() displays the values in an array of integers.
 *
 *   Receive:    out, the ostream being written to
 *               theArray, an array of int values
 *               itsSize, the number of values it holds
 *   Output:     Each value in theArray, on a separate line,
 *                  to the ostream out
 *   Pass back:  The modified ostream out
 ****************************************************************/
```

```
void Print(ostream & out, int theArray[], int itsSize)
{
   for (int i = 0; i < itsSize; i++)
      out << theArray[i] << "   " << endl;
}
```

As this example illustrates, placing a pair of brackets ([]) after the name of a parameter indicates that the parameter is an array, and that it is not necessary to specify the capacity of the array. In this case, *there is no restriction on the capacity of the array that is passed to the function.*

☞   As we will see, this approach does not work for multidimensional arrays. It is better to associate type identifiers with arrays (using typedef as described earlier) and *use these type identifiers to declare the types of array parameters*; for example,

```
const int CAPACITY = 100;
typedef int IntArray[CAPACITY];
              .
              .
              .
void Print(ostream & out, IntArray theArray, int itsSize)
```

☞ It is also important to remember that *passing an array into a function is actually passing an address*. For example, in the function call

```
Print(cout, a, 10);
```

the base address of a is passed to theArray so that in the function theArray has the same base address as a. This means that any modification to theArray also modifies a. It also means that the capacity of a is lost to the function and must be passed in as a separate parameter if it is needed.

OUT-OF-RANGE ERRORS

☞ It is important to note that *no checking is done to ensure that indices stay within the range determined by an array's declaration*. Letting an index get out of bounds can produce some puzzling results. For example, consider the following program segment:

```
IntArray a = {0, 1, 2, 3},
         b = {4, 5, 6, 7},
         c = {8, 9, 10, 11};

int below = -3,
    above = 6;

cout << "a = "; Print(cout, a, 4);
cout << "b = "; Print(cout, b, 4);
cout << "c = "; Print(cout, c, 4);

b[below] = -999;
b[above] = 999;

cout << "\na = "; Print(cout, a, 4);
cout << "b = "; Print(cout, b, 4);
cout << "c = "; Print(cout, c, 4);
```

The output produced on one system is[9]

```
a = 0   1   2    3
b = 4   5   6    7
c = 8   9   10   11

a = 0   -999   2    3
b = 4   5      6    7
c = 8   9      999  11
```

Even through there are no assignments of the form a[i] = *value* or c[i] = *value* to change values stored in a and c, the second element of a was changed to -999 and the third element of c was changed to 999. This happened because the address translation carried out by the subscript operator simply counted forward or backward from the base address of the array. The illegal array reference b[-3] was three memory locations before the base address of b, which, on this system, was the same as a[1]. Similarly, b[6] accessed the same memory location as that for c[2]. Thus modifying b[-3] and b[6] changed a[1] and c[2], respectively.

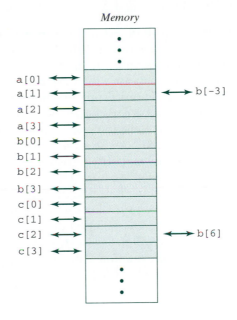

Memory

~~~~~~~~~~~~~~~~

[9]The output on your system may not agree exactly with that shown in the sample run. For example, some systems allocate memory from higher addresses to lower and the output in this case will probably appear as follows:

```
a = 0   1   2    3
b = 4   5   6    7
c = 8   9   10   11

a = 0   1      999  3
b = 4   5      6    7
c = 8   -999   10   11
```

PROBLEMS WITH ARRAYS

There are other difficulties besides the out-of-range errors that can occur with array indices. One of these is

▶ The capacity of an array cannot change during program execution.

This means that an array's capacity must be set large enough to store the largest data set to be processed. This can either result in a considerable waste of memory—for example, storing 25 elements in an array of capacity 5000—or result in array indices getting out of range with unfortunate results like those just described.

C++ does provide a mechanism for allocating arrays at run-time (see Sec. 8.5). It also provides the type `vector`, which uses (and effectively hides) this mechanism. As we will see in Sec. 6.4, when we use `vector` we are in fact (indirectly) using run-time allocation.

A deeper problem with arrays is that:

▶ Arrays are not self-contained objects because an operation on an array
  needs at least two pieces of information: the array and some way to
  identify its size (the number of values stored in it) or a way to find the last
  value stored in it.

One of the principles of object-oriented programming is that *an object should be self-contained*, which means that it should carry within itself all of the information necessary to describe and operate on it. Arrays violate this principle. In particular, they carry neither their size nor their capacity within them.

For this reason, array-processing functions usually require two (and sometimes three) parameters just to characterize the array being processed. This was demonstrated by the `Print()` function given earlier. We must pass to `Print()` not only the array to be displayed but also its size, and this is *not consistent with the aims of object-oriented programming*. If we wish to treat a sequence of values as a single object (which is the reason for storing the values in an array), then it should be necessary to pass only that one object to the function.

The C++ class mechanism allows different data members to be stored within a single object. This provides a solution to the second problem—by storing an array, its capacity and its size within a class structure, a single class object can encapsulate all three pieces of information. This is the approach used by the `vector` and `valarray` types described in Chap. 6.

MULTIDIMENSIONAL ARRAYS

Most high-level languages also support arrays with more than one dimension. Two-dimensional arrays are particularly useful when the data being processed can be arranged in rows and columns. Similarly, a three-dimensional array is appropriate when the data can be arranged in rows, columns, and ranks. When several characteristics are associated with the data, still higher dimensions may be appropriate, with each dimension corresponding to one of these characteristics.

TWO-DIMENSIONAL ARRAYS.   To illustrate the use of two-dimensional arrays, suppose we wish to store and process a table of test scores for several different students on several different tests:

	Test 1	Test 2	Test 3	Test 4	Test 5
Student 1	99.0	93.5	89.0	91.0	97.5
Student 2	66.0	68.0	84.5	82.0	87.0
Student 3	88.5	78.5	70.0	65.0	66.5
⋮	⋮	⋮	⋮	⋮	⋮
Student 30	100.0	99.5	100.0	99.0	98.0

A **two-dimensional array** is an appropriate data structure to store these values. A simple form of a declaration for such an array in C++ is

```
element_type array_name[NUM_ROWS][NUM_COLUMNS];
```

For example, we could declare a two-dimensional array scoresTable to store this table of test scores by:

```
const int NUM_ROWS = 30,
          NUM_COLUMNS = 5;

double scoresTable[NUM_ROWS][NUM_COLUMNS];
```

Alternatively, we could use a typedef to declare an array type TwoDimArray,

```
const int NUM_ROWS = 30,
          NUM_COLUMNS = 5;
typedef double TwoDimArray[NUM_ROWS][NUM_COLUMNS];
```

and then use this type identifier to define the array variable scoresTable:

```
TwoDimArray scoresTable;
```

In either case, the notation

```
scoresTable[2][3]
```

refers to the score 84.5 in row 2 and column 3 of scoresTable. In general, the notation

```
scoresTable[r][c]
```

refers to the entry in row r and column c, that is, to the score for student r on test c. The elements of a two-dimensional array are typically processed using nested loops to vary the two indices, most often in a rowwise manner. For example, the following statements might be used to input the scores for a class of students and store them in scoresTable:

```
int numStudents, numTests;

cout << "# students and # of tests? ";
cin >> numStudents >> numTests;

cout << "Enter " << numTests << " test scores for student\n";
for (int r = 0; r < numStudents; r++)
{
  cout << '#' << r + 1 << ':';
  for (int c = 0; c < numTests; c++)
    cin >> scoresTable[r][c];
}
```

THREE-DIMENSIONAL ARRAYS.   The two-dimensional array scoresTable models one page of a gradebook. To model the entire gradebook, we can use a three-dimensional array:

```
const int NUM_ROWS = 30, NUM_COLUMNS = 5, NUM_RANKS = 10;
typedef double ThreeDimArray[ROWS][COLUMNS][RANKS];

ThreeDimArray gradeBook;
```

The array reference gradeBook[2][3][4] then refers to the score for student 2 (numbered from 0) on test 3 (numbered from 0) on page 4 of the gradebook (numbered from 0).

HIGHER-DIMENSIONAL ARRAYS.   In some problems, arrays with even more dimensions may be useful. For example, to illustrate an array with more than three dimensions, consider an automobile dealership that characterizes the vehicles it sells with five attributes: make, style, color, year, and a model code. We might maintain an inventory of these vehicles using a five-dimensional array inv declared by

```
enum Make {FORD, CHEVROLET, DODGE, NUM_MAKES};
enum Style {SEDAN, CONVERTIBLE, VAN, MINI_VAN,
            SPORT_UTILITY, NUM_STYLES};

enum Color {BLUE, GREEN, BROWN,
            RED, YELLOW, GRAY, NUM_COLORS};

typedef int InventoryArray[NUM_MAKES, NUM_STYLES,
                           NUM_COLORS, int, int];

InventoryArray inv;
```

The statement

```
inv[FORD][MINI_VAN][BLUE][1997][4]--;
```

could then be used to record the sale of one blue 1997 Model-4 Ford minivan.

In general, n-dimensional arrays can be defined and subscript operators can be used to access the array elements. C++ places no limit on the number of dimensions of an array, but the number of values in each dimension must be specified. The general form of an array declaration is

---

GENERAL C++ ARRAY DECLARATION

Form:

```
element_type array_name[DIM₁][DIM₂]...[DIMₙ]
                        = {initializer_list};
```

where

`element_type` is any type;
`array_name` is the name of the array being defined;
each DIM_i must be a nonnegative integer (constant) value; and
the optional `initializer_list` is a list of values of type `element_type`, possibly enclosed with internal braces { and }.

Purpose:

Defines an n-dimensional object whose elements are of type `element_type`, in which $DIM_1, DIM_2, \ldots, DIM_n$ are the number of elements in each dimension. If the `initializer_list` is present, the values are placed in the array in a generalized rowwise order, that is, with the leftmost indices varying most slowly.

ARRAY OF ARRAYS DECLARATIONS.   One way to view a multidimensional array is as an **array of arrays**; that is, an array whose elements are other arrays. For example, consider the table of test scores described earlier:

```
const int NUM_ROWS = 30,
          NUM_COLUMNS = 5;


double scoresTable[NUM_ROWS][NUM_COLUMNS];
```

Since NUM_ROWS is 30, this table can be thought of as a one-dimensional array, whose 30 elements are its rows:

scoresTable:

```
[0] [                              ]
[1] [                              ]
[2] [                              ]
[3] [                              ]
              •
              •
              •
[29][                              ]
```

Of course, each of the rows in `scoresTable` is itself a one-dimensional array of five real values:

scoresTable:

```
        [0]   [1]   [2]   [3]   [4]
[0] [     |     |     |     |     ]
[1] [     |     |     |     |     ]
[2] [     |     |     |     |     ]
[3] [     |     |     |     |     ]
                 •
                 •
                 •
[29][     |     |     |     |     ]
```

A table can thus be viewed as a one-dimensional array whose components are also one-dimensional arrays.

C++ allows array declarations to be given in a form that reflects this perspective. If we first declare the type identifier `ScoreList` as a synonym for an array of test scores,

```
const int NUM_SCORES = 5;
typedef double ScoreList[NUM_SCORES];
```

the objects of type `ScoreList` are one-dimensional arrays of `double` values. We can then use this new type to declare a second type `TwoDimScoreTable` as an array whose elements are `ScoreList` objects:

```
const int NUM_ROWS = 30;
typedef ScoreList TwoDimScoreTable[NUM_ROWS];
```

This declares the name `TwoDimScoreTable` as a new type, whose objects are two-dimensional arrays of `double` values. The resulting type can then be used to define a two-dimensional array `TwoDimScoreTable` object, as before:

```
TwoDimScoreTable scoresTable;
```

Regardless of which approach is used, the notation

```
scoresTable[2]
```

refers to row 2 in the table,

	[0]	[1]	[2]	[3]	[4]
[2]					

and the notation

```
scoresTable[2][4]
```

to the last entry in this row.

This idea can be extended to higher-dimensional arrays. For example, the three-dimensional array gradebook considered earlier can also be thought of as an array of arrays. In particular, since the gradebook is a sequence of pages, the entire three-dimensional array can be viewed as an array of pages of test scores, meaning a one-dimensional array whose components are two-dimensional arrays. If we adopt this point of view, we might declare the three-dimensional array gradeBook by adding the declarations

```
const int NUM_PAGES = 10;
typedef TwoDimScoreTable ThreeDimScoreArray[NUM_PAGES];
ThreeDimScoreArray score;
```

to the preceding declarations. The notation

```
score[2]
```

refers to the entire scores table recorded on the third page (counting from 0), which might be the following two-dimensional array of test scores:

	[0]	[1]	[2]	[3]	[4]
[0]	99.0	93.5	89.0	91.0	97.5
[1]	66.0	68.0	84.5	82.0	87.0
[2]	88.5	78.5	70.0	65.0	66.5
⋮	⋮	⋮	⋮	⋮	⋮
[29]	100.0	99.5	100.0	99.0	98.0

As in the previous example, each row in a scores table can be viewed as a one-dimensional array of test scores, and each table can therefore be viewed as a one-dimensional array of the test-score arrays. The doubly-indexed expression

```
score[2][0]
```

refers to the first row in the table of scores on page 0,

99.0	93.5	89.0	91.0	97.5

and the triply-indexed expression

```
score[2][0][4]
```

accesses the last score in this row:

97.5

The implementation of multidimensional arrays is somewhat more complicated than that for one-dimensional arrays. Memory is organized as a sequence of memory locations and thus is one-dimensional in nature. Consequently, we must determine how to use a one-dimensional structure to store a higher-dimensional one.

To illustrate, suppose that t is a 3 × 4 array of characters declared by

```
char t[3][4];
```

or equivalently,

```
typedef char Row[4];
typedef Row Table[3];

Table t;
```

in which the following table is to be stored:

$$\begin{bmatrix} A & B & C & D \\ E & F & G & H \\ I & J & K & L \end{bmatrix}$$

Since a character can be stored in a single byte, this array declaration instructs the compiler to reserve 12 consecutive bytes to store the array elements. These elements might be stored in **rowwise** order (also called *row major* order), with the first four bytes beginning at the base address of t used to store the elements in the first row of t, the next four bytes for the second row, and so on.

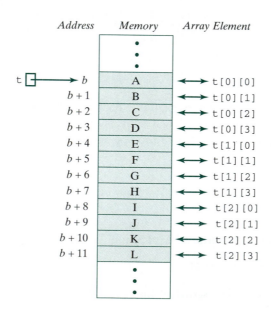

It also is possible to store the elements in **columnwise** (or *column major*) order, with the first three bytes storing the elements in the first column of t, the next three bytes storing the elements in the second column, and so on. In either case, an address translation must be carried out by the subscript operator to determine where in memory a given array element t[i][j]is stored.

The formulas for this address translation can be derived from those given earlier for one-dimensional arrays if a two-dimensional array is viewed as a one-dimensional array whose elements are also one-dimensional arrays.[10] To see this, we will assume rowwise storage and view t as a one-dimensional array having three elements (the rows of t), each of which requires four bytes for storage. Thus, by the address translation formula for one-dimensional arrays, the ith row of t, t[i], is stored in the byte whose address is

$$\text{base}(\texttt{t[i]}) = \text{base}(\texttt{t}) + 4i$$

Since this ith row of t is itself a one-dimensional array with base address base(t[i]), the jth element in this row, t[i][j], is stored in the byte having the address

$$\text{base}(\texttt{t[i]}) + j$$

that is, t[i][j] is stored in the byte whose address is

$$\text{base}(\texttt{t}) + 4i + j$$

Similarly, the address translation formulas for one- and two-dimensional arrays can be used to derive formulas for three-dimensional arrays if they are viewed as one-dimensional arrays whose elements are two-dimensional arrays (or as two-dimensional arrays whose elements are one-dimensional arrays). For example, consider the three-dimensional array b declared by

```
double b[3][4][3];
```

or equivalently

```
typedef double Across[3];
typedef Across Slice[4];
typedef Slice ThreeDimArray[3];

ThreeDimArray b;
```

b can thus be viewed as a one-dimensional array having three elements, b[0], b[1], and b[2], each of which is a two-dimensional array with 4 rows and 3 columns:.

---

[10] See Appendix D for general address formulas.

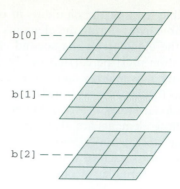

If each double requires 8 bytes of storage, then 96 bytes will be needed to store each of the tables b[0], b[1], and b[2]. Thus, b[i] is stored beginning at the byte with address

$$\text{base}(\texttt{b[i]}) = \text{base}(\texttt{b}) + 96\texttt{i}$$

Since each b[i] is a two-dimensional array, the address translation formulas for two-dimensional arrays give as the beginning address for b[i][j][k]

$$\text{base}(\texttt{b[i]}) + 24\texttt{j} + 8\texttt{k}$$
$$= \text{base}(\texttt{b}) + 96\texttt{i} + 24\texttt{j} + 8\texttt{k}$$

Address translation formulas for arrays having more than three dimensions can be derived similarly, but their complexity increases as the number of dimensions increases.

✔ Quick Quiz 2.3

1. Define array as an ADT.

2. _____ access means that each array element can be accessed simply by specifying its location in the array.

3. An array is an appropriate data structure for organizing homogeneous data collections. (True or false)

4. List the elements (if any) that an array a will contain if it is declared by

        int a[5] = {1};

5. '\0' denotes the _____ character.

6. Elements of an array are accessed with the _____ operator.

7. The address of the first element is called the _____ of the array and the name of the array is actually a(n) _____ to this element.

8. Passing an array into a function is actually passing an address. (True or false)

9. Array indices are checked to ensure they are not out of range. (True or false)

10. What are two problems with arrays?

11. t[3][5] is a value in column 3 of two-dimensional array t. (True or false)

✍ EXERCISES 2.3

Exercises 1–23 assume that `char`s are stored in one byte, `int`s in 4 bytes, `double`s in 8 bytes, values of type `T` in 10 bytes, and values of type `Day` in 4 bytes, where `Day` is the enumeration defined by

```
enum Day {SUN, MON, TUE, WED, THU, FRI, SAT, NUM_DAYS};
```

For Exercises 1–4, find how many bytes are required for an array a of the specified type.

1. `char a[10]`

2. `double a[10]`

3. `T a[7]`

4. `int a[26]`

5. `Day a[NUM_DAYS]`

6. For array a in Exercise 1, find where a`[3]` and a`[9]` are stored.

7. For array a in Exercise 2, find where a`[3]` and a`[9]` are stored.

8. For array a in Exercise 3, find where a`[4]` and a`[6]` are stored.

9. For array a in Exercise 4, find where a`[1]` and a`[2]` are stored.

10. For array a in Exercise 5, find where a`[TUE]` and a`[SAT]` are stored.

11–15. For the arrays in Exercises 1–5, indicate with diagrams like those in the text where each element of a is stored if the base address of a is b. Also, give the general address translation formula for a`[i]`.

In Exercises 16–19, find where the indicated elements of a two-dimensional array `t` of the specified type are stored, if the base address of `t` is 100 and storage is rowwise.

16. `char t[5][5]`; t`[1][3]` and t`[2][2]`

17. `double t[4][10]`; t`[0][8]` and t`[3][2]`

18. `int t[8][7]`; t`[3][2]` and t`[1][6]`

19. `T t[7][6]`; t`[TUE][3]` and t`[FRI][2]`

20–23. Proceed as in Exercises 16–19, but for columnwise storage.

24. Derive a general address translation formula for t`[i][j]`, where `t` is a two-dimensional array whose elements require w bytes of memory for storage. Assume that memory is allocated in a (a) rowwise manner; (b) columnwise manner.

25. Derive a general address translation formula for b`[i][j][k]` for a three-dimensional array `b` whose elements require w bytes of memory for storage, by viewing `b` as a one-dimensional array whose elements are two-dimensional arrays.

26. Derive the address translation formula for f`[i][j][k][l]`, where `f` is a four-dimensional array defined by

```
double f[N1][N2][N3][N4];
```

by viewing `f` as a one-dimensional array with `N1` elements, each of which is a three-dimensional $N2 \times N3 \times N4$ array of `double`s. Assume that three-dimensional arrays are allocated storage as described in the text.

27. Give one possible address translation formula for an element $h[i_1][i_2]...[i_q]$ of a q-dimensional array defined by

```
Element_Type h[N1][N2]...[Nq];
```

assuming that each element requires n = `sizeof(Element_Type)` bytes for storage.

28. A *lower triangular* matrix m is a square matrix in which the only positions that may contain nonzero entries are on and below the main diagonal from the upper-left corner to the lower-right corner; all entries above this diagonal are zero:

$$\begin{matrix} X & 0 & 0 & \cdots & 0 \\ X & X & 0 & \cdots & 0 \\ X & X & X & \cdots & 0 \\ \vdots & \vdots & \vdots & \ddots & \vdots \\ X & X & X & \cdots & X \end{matrix}$$

That is, m is a two-dimensional array in which $m[i][j]$ is 0 if $i < j$. Memory would be utilized more efficiently if instead of storing all the entries of m, only those on and below the diagonal were stored. Derive an address translation formula in this case for $m[i][j]$ where $i \geq j$, assuming that each entry of m can be stored in 8 bytes and row-wise storage is used, beginning at the byte with address b.

29. Proceed as in Exercise 28 but for an *upper triangular* matrix m, in which the only positions that may contain nonzero entries are on and above the diagonal; all entries below this diagonal are zero:

$$\begin{matrix} X & X & X & \cdots & X \\ 0 & X & X & \cdots & X \\ 0 & 0 & X & \cdots & X \\ \vdots & \vdots & \vdots & \ddots & \vdots \\ 0 & 0 & 0 & \cdots & X \end{matrix}$$

30. A *tridiagonal* matrix is a square matrix m in which the only positions where nonzero entries may appear is in the "band" consisting of locations on the diagonal, immediately above the diagonal (on the "superdiagonal") and immediately below it (on the "subdiagonal"); all entries not in this band are zero:

$$\begin{matrix} X & X & 0 & 0 & \cdots & 0 & 0 \\ X & X & X & 0 & \cdots & 0 & 0 \\ 0 & X & X & X & \cdots & 0 & 0 \\ 0 & 0 & X & X & \cdots & 0 & 0 \\ \cdot & \cdot & \cdot & \cdot & \cdots & \cdot & \cdot \\ \cdot & \cdot & \cdot & \cdot & \cdots & \cdot & \cdot \\ \cdot & \cdot & \cdot & \cdot & \cdots & \cdot & \cdot \\ 0 & 0 & 0 & 0 & \cdots & X & X \end{matrix}$$

that is, $m[i][j]$ is 0 if $|i-j|>1$. Devise an efficient storage scheme for such matrices, and derive an address translation formula.

2.4 STRUCTURES

Arrays are essential in programming and are provided in almost every high-level programming language. In this section we consider another important data type called a *structure* or a *record* in some languages (e.g., Pascal).

WHY ARE STRUCTURES NEEDED?

To understand what structures are and why they are needed, consider the following outline of the approach used up to now to design a program (and software in general):

1. Identify the *objects* in the problem.

   1a. . . .

2. Identify the *operations* in the problem.

   2a. If the operation is not predefined, write a *function* to perform it.

   2b. If the function is useful for other problems, store it in a *library*.

3. Organize the objects and operations into an algorithm.

4. Code the algorithm as a program.

5. Test, execute, and debug the program.

6. Maintain the program

Because predefined types in the programming language being used may not be adequate, we add

   1a. *If the predefined types are not adequate to model the object, create a new data type to model it .*

For example, we might create an enumeration type like that in the exercises of Sec. 2.3

```
enum Day {SUN, MON, TUE, WED, THU, FRI, SAT};
```

to better represent the days of the week instead of using integers (1, 2, 3, 4, 5, 6, 7) or strings ("Sunday", "Monday", "Tuesday", . . .).

Now suppose, however, that the object being modeled has *multiple attributes*. For example, a temperature such as 32°F has two attributes: number of *degrees* and a *scale* (Fahrenheit, Celsius, Kelvin). We might thus picture a temperature object as follows:

32.0	F
degrees	*scale*

Similarly, a date object like

December	31	1999
month	*day*	*year*

has three attributes: a *month*, a *day*, and a *year*.

Because such objects cannot be represented easily using simple types, programming languages such as C and C++ provide structures to create new types with multiple attributes. Thus we might add to our design methodology

1. Identify the objects in the problem.

   1a. If the predefined types are not adequate to model the object, create a new type to model it.

   1b. *If the object has multiple attributes, create a structure to represent objects of that type.*

As an abstract data type, we can define a **structure** (or **record**) as follows:

 ADT STRUCTURE (OR RECORD)

Collection of data elements:

A *fixed-size* sequence (*ordered* set) of elements, not necessarily of the same type. The elements are called **members** or **fields**.

Basic Operation:

Direct access to each member of the structure so that values can be retrieved from or stored in this member.

A structure differs from an array, therefore, in that its elements may be of different types.

C-STYLE STRUCTS

In C and in C++, a structure is called a **struct**. Declarations of structs in C and in their simplest form in C++ have the following forms:

C++ STRUCT DECLARATIONS

Declaration of a struct (simplified)

```
struct TypeName
{
    declarations of members   // of any types
};
    . . .
```

Forms of declarations of struct objects

```
TypeName struct_name;

TypeName struct_name = {initializer_list};
```

where
   the members may be of any type; and
   in the second form, the types of the values in `initializer_list` match the types of the corresponding members in the struct declaration.

Purpose:

Instructs the compiler to reserve a block of memory locations to hold objects of the specified types and associates the name *struct_name* with that storage. In the second form, the struct's members are initialized with the values in *initializer_list*.

To illustrate, we might declare a type `Temperature` by

```
struct Temperature
{
   double degrees;    // number of degrees
   char scale;        // temp. scale (F, C, K, ...)
};
```

and then define `Temperature` objects `FREEZING` and `temp` by

```
Temperature temp;
const Temperature FREEZING = {32, 'F'};
```

which define `temp` to be a `Temperature` object with its members undefined and `FREEZING` to be a constant with its `degrees` member initialized to 32 and its `scale` member to F:

```
FREEZING  32.0     F
          degrees scale
```

A type `Date` for processing dates might be declared by

```
struct Date
{
   string month;    // name of month
   int day,         // day number
       year;        // year number
};
```

and a `Date` object `endOfCentury` defined by

```
Date endOfCentury = {"December", 31, 1999};
```

which initializes `endOfCentury`'s `month` member to `December`, its `day` member to 31, and its `year` member to 1999:

```
endOfCentury  December    31  1999
              month       day year
```

As another example, records maintained for users of a computer system might contain a user identification number, a password, a resource limit, and the resources used to date; for example,

unsigned	string	double	double
12345	UR2MUCH	100.00	37.45
idNumber	password	resourceLimit	resourcesUsed

A data type for these records can be declared by

```
struct ComputerUsageInfo
{                               //  user's
   unsigned idNumber;           //   id number
   string password;            //   password
   double resourceLimit,       //   limit on computer resources
          resourcesUsed;       //   resources used to date
};
```

A `ComputerUsageInfo` object `userRecord` can then be defined by

```
ComputerUsageInfo userRecord;
```

The data members of a struct may be of any type. They need not be simple types as in the preceding examples, but they may be structured data types such as arrays or other structures. For example, for a student in a computer science class, we might wish to store the student's name, birthdate, computer-usage information, and a list of four test scores. For this we can use the preceding structured types `Date` and `ComputerUsageInfo` to specify the types of two of the data members of a struct `StudentClassRecord`:

```
const int MAX_SCORES = 4;
struct StudentClassRecord
{                               //  student's
   string name;                //   complete name
   Date birthdate;             //   birthdate
   ComputerUsageInfo usage;    //   user info
   int score[MAX_SCORES];      //   test scores
};
```

The statement

```
StudentClassRecord aStudent;
```

then defines a `StudentClassRecord` object `aStudent` and

```
CONST int COURSE_LIMIT = 50;
StudentClassRecord cpsc186[COURSE_LIMIT];
```

an array of 50 `StudentClassRecord` objects. Each object contains four data members in which the first is a string, the second is a struct with three members (`month`, `day`, `year`), the third is a struct with four members (`idNumber`, `password`, `resourceLimit`, `resourcesUsed`), and the fourth is an array of four `doubles`.

Structs such as `aStudent` that contain other structures are sometimes called **nested structures** to indicate that some structures are "nested" inside other structures. They are also frequently referred to as **hierarchical structures**, as suggested by the following diagram:

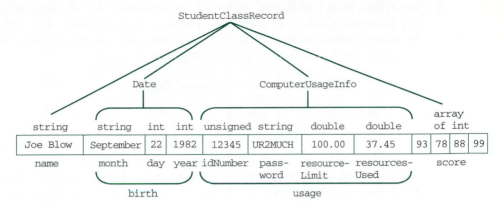

STRUCT OPERATIONS

Just as the subscript operator [] provides direct access to the elements of an array in C and C++, *member access operators* provide direct access to the members of a struct (or class). One of these is the **dot operator (.)** used in expressions of the form

        struct_object.member_name

The following are some examples:

```
// Calculate the Celsius equivalent of temp
Temperature tempCels;
tempCels.degrees = (temp.degrees - 32.0) / 1.8;
tempCels.scale = 'C';

// Input values into the members of currentDate
cin >> currentDate.month >> currentDate.day
    >> currentDate.year;

// Sum the scores in aStudent
int sum = 0;
for (int i = 0; i < 4; i++)
  sum += aStudent.score[i];

// Output the birth month and id number of aStudent
cout << "Birth month: " << aStudent.birth.month << endl
     << "Id Number:   " << aStudent.usage.idNumber << endl;
```

A sequence of similar assignment statements could be used to copy one struct to another by copying one member at a time. However, this can be accomplished more simply with an assignment statement of the form

        struct_variable = struct_object;

where the struct variable and the struct object have the same type.

UNIONS

Some languages provide a data structure called a **union** that is similar to a structure but differs from it in that the members of a structure are allocated different memory locations, whereas the members of a union share memory; that is, they all have the same memory address.[11] In C++, the syntax of a union is the same as that for a struct except that the word `struct` is replaced by `union`:

```
union TypeName        // TypeName is optional
{
   declarations of members
};
```

Unions can be used to build structures that have **fixed parts** and **variant parts**. All objects of such a type have the same members in corresponding fixed parts but there may be different members in the variant parts. Such structures are called **variant records** in some languages such as Pascal and are useful in certain specialized problems. To illustrate, suppose computer-usage records for employees at a computer center have one of three structures:

Support staff	Id number
	Password
	Resource limit
	Resources used to date
	Department code
Research	Id number
	Password
	Account number
	Security clearance (1–10)
	Department code
Administration	Id number
	Password
	Division

All of these structures can be incorporated into a single struct by storing the common information (id number and password) in the fixed part of the struct and the other information in a union whose members are structs containing the varying parts in these structures:

```
struct SupportInfo
{                                 // support-person's
   double resourceLimit,   //   limit on computer resources
          resourcesUsed;   //   resources used to date
   char department;        //   department in which employed
};
```

---

[11]See Appendix D for an example program that demonstrates this.

```
struct ResearchInfo
{                                // researcher's
  int account,                   //   research account
  securityClearance;             //   security clearance: 1-10
  char department;               //   department in which employed
};

struct AdministrationInfo
{                                // administrator's
  char division;                 //   division
};

struct ComputerUsageInfo
{                                // user's
  unsigned idNumber;             //   id number
  string password;               //   password
  char category;                 //   tag: 'S' = support,
                                 //        'R' = research,
                                 //        'A' = administration

  union                          //   varying info
  {
    SupportInfo support;
    ResearchInfo research;
    AdministrationInfo administration;
  };
};
```

Note that a member `category` has also been added as a *tag field* to specify which of the three variants is in effect for a given employee.

In OOP languages, structures like this are not needed because *inheritance* makes it possible to encapsulate the fixed information in a *base class* and from it *derive a class* for each variant. As we show in Chap. 10, the OOP approach would be to define a base class containing the common information (id number, password, and category), and then derive classes that inherit these members (and operations) from the base class and contain new members (and operations) for the attributes peculiar to that class. We might picture this as follows:

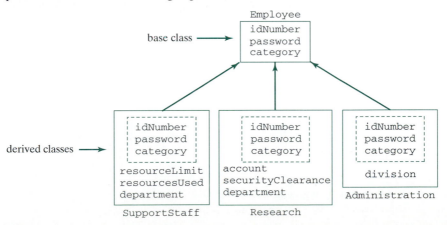

STRUCTS IN MEMORY

We have seen that to store an array, sufficient memory is allocated to store all the array elements, and that each array reference involves two steps: First, an address translation must be performed to locate where that array element is stored, and second, the bit string stored there must be interpreted in the manner prescribed by the type specification for the array elements. Similarly, storing a structure also requires sufficient memory to store all of the members that comprise the structure. Address translation is again required to determine the location in which a particular member is stored, but this address translation is slightly more complex than for arrays because different members usually require a different number of bytes for storage. Also, unlike arrays, different interpretations of the bit strings are usually required for different members, because the members of a structure need not be of the same type.

To illustrate, consider customer records that consist of a customer's account number, name, an account balance, and the type of account,

```
enum AccountType {WHOLESALE, EDUCATIONAL,
                  REGULAR, HIGH_RISK};
struct Customer
{
   int number;
   char name[20];
   double balance;
   AccountType account;
};

Customer c;
```

and suppose that `ints` and `enums` are stored in 4 bytes, `chars` in 1 byte, and `doubles` in 8 bytes. This definition of struct `c` instructs the compiler to reserve a block of 40 bytes to store such a struct, the first of which, as for arrays, is called the *base address*. The four bytes beginning at this base address might then be allocated to `c.number`, the next 20 bytes to `c.name`, the next 8 bytes to `c.balance`, and the next 4 bytes to `c.account` as pictured on the next page. When one of these members is accessed, the bit string stored in the associated bytes is interpreted according to the type specified for that field in the struct declaration.[12]

---

[12]See Appendix D for general address formulas.

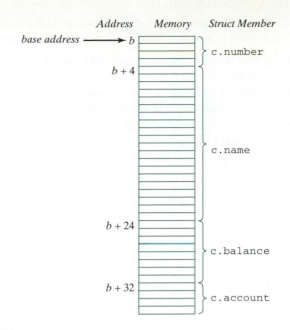

Quick Quiz 2.4

1. Define structure as an ADT.

2. A structure is an appropriate data structure for organizing nonhomogeneous data collections. (True or false)

3. The elements of a structure are called _____ .

4. Elements of a struct in C++ are accessed with the _____ operator.

5. What is the main difference between a struct and a union in C++?

✐ EXERCISES 2.4

For each of Exercises 1–10, design a struct to store the given information, writing appropriate type declarations for the structures.

1. Time in civilian format (hours, minutes, seconds, and an A.M./P.M. indicator).

2. Time in military format ($xxyy$ where $0 \leq xx \leq 23, 0 \leq yy \leq 59$).

3. Length measured in yards, feet, and inches.

4. Angles measured in degrees, minutes, and seconds.

5. Cards in a deck of playing cards.

6. Listings in a telephone directory.

7. Description of an automobile (make, model, style, color, and the like).

8. Description of a book in a library's card catalogue (author, publisher, and the like).

9. Teams in a baseball league (name, won/lost record, and the like).

10. Position of a checker on a checkerboard.

For each of Exercises 11–14, design a struct with a variant part to store the given information, writing appropriate type declarations for the structures.

11. Time in either civilian or military format (see Exercise 1) as specified by a tag field in the struct.

12. Information about a person: name, birthday, age, sex, social security number, height, weight, hair color, eye color, marital status, and if married, number of children.

13. Statistics about a baseball player: name; age; birth date; position (pitcher, catcher, infielder, outfielder); for a pitcher: won/lost record, earned-run average, number of strikeouts, and number of walks; if a starting pitcher, number of complete games; and if a relief pitcher, number of innings pitched and number of saves; for the other positions: batting average; slugging average; bats right, left, or switch hitter; fielding percentage; also, for an infielder, what positions he can play; and for a catcher, whether he can catch a knuckleball.

14. Weather statistics: date; city and state, province, or country; time of day; temperature; barometric pressure; weather conditions (clear skies, partly cloudy, cloudy, stormy); if cloudy conditions prevail, cloud level and type of clouds; for partly cloudy, percentage of cloud cover; for stormy conditions, snow depth if it is snowing, amount of rainfall if it is rainy, size of hail if it is hailing.

For Exercises 15–19, assume that values of type char are stored in one byte, ints in 4 bytes, double values in 8 bytes. Give diagrams like those in the text showing where each field of the following structs would be stored:

15.
```
struct Date
{
   char month[8];
   int day, year;
};
```

16.
```
struct Point
{
   double x, y;
};
```

17.
```
struct ClassRecord
{
   int snumb;
   char name[16];
   char sex;
   int testScore[5];
};
```

18.
```
struct StudentRecord
{
   int snumb;
   char[16] name;
   GradeInfo grades;
   double finalNumScore;
   char letterGrade;
};
```

where the type GradeInfo is declared by

```
struct GradeInfo
{
   double homework, tests, exam;
};
```

19.
```
struct Transaction
{
  char customerName[24];
  int customerNumber;
  NumericDate transDate;
  char transType;          // tag
  union
  {
    double deposit;        // tag = 'D'
    double withdrawal;     // tag = 'W'
    LoanInfo loan;         // tag = 'L'
    TransferInfo transfer; // tag = 'T'
  };
};
```

where types `NumericDate`, `LoanInfo`, and `TransferInfo` are declared by:

```
struct NumericDate
{
  int month, day, year;
};
struct LoanInfo
{
  int number;
  double payment, interest, newbalance;
};
struct TransferInfo
{
  int account;
  double amount;
  char code;
};
```

2.5 PROCEDURAL PROGRAMMING

In the **procedural-programming paradigm** engendered by many *procedural* languages such as C, FORTRAN, Pascal, and Modula-2, programmers concentrate on writing subprograms (procedures/functions/subroutines) to perform various tasks. This is because the basic approach in this problem-solving methodology is as follows:

1. Identify the basic tasks to be performed in solving a problem, which may involve dividing the problem into simpler subproblems and identifying subtasks for these subproblems.

2. Implement the actions required to do these tasks and subtasks as subprograms, passing the data items being processed from one subprogram to another.

3. Group these subprograms together to form a program or perhaps a collection of programs/modules/libraries, which together make up a complete system for solving the problem.

This procedural approach to programming might thus be said to be *action-oriented*— or as someone else has described it, it concentrates on the *verbs* of a problem's specification in designing a solution.

EXAMPLE: A TIME DATA TYPE

To illustrate this procedural approach, we will show how C-style structs can be used to create a data type. In the next chapter we will redo this problem using the OOP approach.

PROBLEM.   To create a type `Time` for processing times in standard hh:mm AM/PM form and in military-time form.

DATA ATTRIBUTES.   `Time` objects will have the following four attributes:

> Hours (an integer in the range 0 through 12)
> Minutes (an integer in the range 0 through 59)
> AM or PM indicator (the character 'A' or 'P')
> Military time (a nonnegative integer)

Each `Time` value will therefore consist of four values corresponding to these four attributes.

SOME OPERATIONS.   Many operations would be necessary to provide a complete model of time. For simplicity, we will consider only the following:

> Set the time
> Display the time
> Advance the time
> Determine if one time is less than another time

IMPLEMENTATION.   We need storage structures for the four values that comprise a `Time` object. Because these are not all of the same type, we will use a struct. We will write functions to perform the operations on `Time` objects. We can then package the declarations together in a header file `Time.h` and the definitions of the functions in an implementation file `Time.cpp`. Fig. 2.2 shows these files. It also shows a test-driver program.

FIGURE 2.2   A TIME DATA TYPE—PROCEDURAL APPROACH

```
/** Time.h -------------------------------------------------------
   This header file defines the data type Time for processing time.
   Basic operations are:
     Set:      To set the time
     Display:  To display the time
     Advance:  To advance the time by a certain amount
     LessThan: To determine if one time is less than another
--------------------------------------------------------------*/

#include <iostream>
using namespace std;

struct Time
{
  unsigned hour,
           minute;
  char AMorPM;         // 'A' or 'P'
  unsigned milTime;    // military time equivalent
};
```

```
/* Set sets the time to a specified value.
 *
 *   Receive:    Time object t
 *               hours, the number of hours in standard time
 *               minutes, the number of minutes in standard time
 *               AMPM ('A' if AM, 'P' if PM)
 *   Pass back: The modified Time t with data members set to
 *                 the specified values
 *********************************************************************/

void Set(Time & t, unsigned hours, unsigned minutes, char AMPM);


/* Display displays time t in standard and military format using
 * output stream out.
 *
 *   Receive:    Time t and ostream out
 *   Output:     The time T to out
 *   Pass back: The modified ostream out
 *********************************************************************/

void Display(const Time & t, ostream & out);


/* Advance increments a time by a specified value.
 *
 *   Receive:    Time object t
 *               hours, the number of hours to add
 *               minutes, the number of minutes to add
 *   Pass back: The modified Time t with data members incremented
 *                 by the specified values
 *********************************************************************/

void Advance(Time & t, unsigned hours, unsigned minutes);


/* < determines if one time is less than another time.
 *
 *   Receive:  Times t1 and t2
 *   Return:   True if t1 < t2, false otherwise.
 *********************************************************************/

bool LessThan(const Time & t1, const Time & t2);


//========= Time.cpp -- implements the functions in Time.h =========

#include "Time.h"

/** Utility functions -- might be added as basic operations later **/

int ToMilitary(unsigned hours, unsigned minutes, char AMPM);

void ToStandard(unsigned military,
                unsigned & hours, unsigned & minutes, char & AMPM);
```

```
void Set(Time & t, unsigned hours, unsigned minutes, char AMPM)
{
  if (hours >= 1 && hours <= 12 &&
      minutes >= 0 && minutes <= 59 &&
      (AMPM == 'A' || AMPM == 'P'))
  {
    t.hour = hours;
    t.minute = minutes;
    t.AMorPM = AMPM;
    t.milTime = ToMilitary(hours, minutes, AMPM);
  }
  else
    cerr << "*** Can't set time with these values ***\n";
    // t remains unchanged
}

void Display(const Time & t, ostream & out)
{
  out << t.hour << ':'
      << (t.minute < 10 ? "0" : "") << t.minute
      << ' ' << t.AMorPM << ".M.  ("
      << t.milTime << " mil. time)";
}

void Advance(Time & t, unsigned hours, unsigned minutes)
{
  // Advance using military time
   t.milTime += 100 * hours + minutes;
   unsigned milHours = t.milTime / 100,
            milMins = t.milTime % 100;

  // Adjust to proper format
   milHours +=  milMins / 60;
   milMins %= 60;
   milHours %= 24;
   t.milTime = 100 * milHours + milMins;

  // Now set standard time
   ToStandard(t.milTime, t.hour, t.minute, t.AMorPM);
}

bool LessThan(const Time & t1, const Time & t2)
{
  return (t1.milTime < t2.milTime);
}

/***** UTILITY FUNCTIONS *****/

/* ToMilitary converts standard time to military time.
 *
 *   Receive: hours, minutes, AMPM
 *   Return:  The military time equivalent
 ****************************************************************/
```

```cpp
int ToMilitary (unsigned hours, unsigned minutes, char AMPM)
{
  if (hours == 12)
    hours = 0,

  return hours * 100 + minutes + (AMPM == 'P' ? 1200 : 0);
}

/* ToStandard converts military time to standard time.
 *
 *  Receive: military, a time in military format
 *  Return:  hours, minutes, AMPM -- equivalent standard time
 ***************************************************************/

void ToStandard(unsigned military,
                unsigned & hours, unsigned & minutes, char & AMPM)
{
   hours = (military / 100) % 12;
   if (hours == 0)
      hours = 12;

   minutes = military % 100;
   AMPM = (military / 100) < 12 ? 'A' : 'P';
}

#include <iostream>

//========= Test driver =========

#include "Time.h"
#include <iostream>
uses namespace std;

int main()
{
  Time mealTime,
       goToWorkTime;

  Set(mealTime, 5, 30, 'P');

  cout << "We'll be eating at ";
  Display(mealTime, cout);
  cout << endl;

  Set(goToWorkTime, 5, 30, 'P');  // Try other values also: 'A' -> 'P'
  cout << "You leave for work at ";
  Display(goToWorkTime, cout);
  cout << endl;
  if (LessThan(MealTime, goToWorkTime))
    cout << "If you hurry, you can eat first.\n";
  else
    cout << "Sorry you can't eat first.\n";
```

```
    Advance(goToWorkTime, 0, 30);    // Try other values also: 0 -> 12)
    cout << "You go into work later at ";
    Display(goToWorkTime, cout);
    cout << endl;
    if (LessThan(MealTime, goToWorkTime))
      cout << "If you hurry, you can eat first.\n";
    else
      cout << "Sorry you can't eat with us.\n";
    cout << endl;


}
```

EXECUTION:

```
We'll be eating at 5:30 P.M.   (1730 mil. time)
You leave for work at 5:30 P.M. (1730 mil. time)
Sorry you can't eat first.
You go into work later at 6:00 P.M. (1800 mil. time)
If you hurry, you can eat first.
```

PP VERSUS OOP

Note how `Time` objects are passed around for processing among the functions `Set()`, `Display()`, `Advance()`, and `LessThan()`. This is characteristic of procedural programming (PP). We store the data in some data structure and ship it around among various functions/procedures/subroutines for processing.

In the **object-oriented-programming paradigm** using *OOP* languages like C++, programmers concentrate on creating types called *classes*, which contain *data members* and *function members* that operate on the data—the functions are actually part of the structure, and we "send a message" to an object telling it to "operate on itself" using one of the functions. The programmer determines what objects are needed for a problem and how they should work together to solve the problem. The focus of OOP is thus on objects rather than on subprograms, on the *nouns* in the specification of the problem rather than on the *verbs*.

If we think of the `Time` data type as modeling a digital watch, then the procedural approach is analogous to wrapping up your digital watch whenever it needs to be set, displayed, advanced, or compared with another one and sending it off to the manufacturer. The manufacturer performs the required task and then returns the watch to you. Although procedural programming is useful in many situations, it is not the best approach to use for this problem.

In the next chapter we will develop a `Time` data type using the OOP approach. To set a digital watch in OOP, we push a button sending a message to the watch to put itself in set mode and accept new values for hours and minutes; to display it, we push a button that sends a message to the watch to turn on its backlight; and so on. This approach obviously models a digital watch more realistically than the procedural approach.

☞ *PROGRAMMING POINTERS*

1. An attempt to store an integer greater than the maximum allowed will result in the loss of some of the bits of its binary representation; a phenomenon known as *overflow*.

2. For a floating-point value, generating a negative exponent that is too small to be stored causes an *underflow*.

3. *Roundoff error*, the error in the stored representation of a real value, may be compounded when real numbers are combined in arithmetic expressions.

4. In C++

   ▶ Arrays are zero-based.

   ▶ Supplying more initial values in an array declaration than the array's capacity is an error. If too few initial values are supplied, 0 is used to initialize the remaining elements.

   ▶ The capacity of `char` arrays should be large enough to store the terminating null character.

   ▶ It is a good practice to associate type identifiers with arrays (using `typedef`) and use these type identifiers to declare the types of array objects.

   ▶ Modifying an array parameter in a function modifies the corresponding array argument.

   ▶ No checking is done to ensure that array indices stay in range.

   ▶ Members of a struct are accessed using the dot operator.

   ▶ Members of a struct are stored in separate memory locations; members of a union share memory locations.

ADT TIPS

1. *Data abstraction*, in which the definition of the data type is separated from its implementation, is an important concept in software design.

2. An array is an appropriate data structure for organizing *homogeneous* data collections.

3. Array weaknesses:

   ▶ Capacity cannot change during execution.

   ▶ They are not self-contained.

PROGRAMMING PROBLEMS

SECTION 2.2

1. Write C++ functions to add and multiply nonnegative integers in base-two. Use these functions in a program that reads two bit strings representing nonnegative integers, calls these functions to find their sum and product, and then displays the corresponding bit strings.

SECTION 2.3

2. Letter grades are sometimes assigned to numeric scores by using the grading scheme commonly known as *grading on the curve*. In this scheme, a letter grade is assigned to a numeric score according to the following table:

x = Numeric Score	Letter Grade
$x < m - \dfrac{3}{2}\sigma$	F
$m - \dfrac{3}{2}\sigma \le x < m - \dfrac{1}{2}\sigma$	D
$m - \dfrac{1}{2}\sigma \le x < m + \dfrac{1}{2}\sigma$	C
$m + \dfrac{1}{2}\sigma \le x < m + \dfrac{3}{2}\sigma$	B
$m + \dfrac{3}{2}\sigma \le x$	A

Here m is the mean score and σ is the standard deviation; for a set of n numbers $x_1, x_2, \ldots, x_n$, these are defined as follows:

$$m = \frac{1}{n}\sum_{i=1}^{n} x_i \qquad \sigma = \sqrt{\frac{1}{n}\sum_{i=1}^{n}(x_i - m)^2}$$

Write a program to read a list of real numbers representing numeric scores, calculate their mean and standard deviation, and then determine and display the letter grade corresponding to each numeric score.

3. Peter the postman became bored one night and to break the monotony of the night shift, he carried out the following experiment with a row of mailboxes in the post office. These mailboxes were numbered 1 through 150, and beginning with mailbox 2, he opened the doors of all the even-numbered mailboxes, leaving the others closed. Next, beginning with mailbox 3, he went to every third mail box, opening its door if it were closed, and closing it if it were open. Then he repeated this procedure with every fourth mailbox, then every fifth mailbox, and so on. When he finished, he was surprised at the distribution of closed mailboxes. Write a program to determine which mailboxes these were.

4. Write a program to add two large integers with up to 300 digits. One approach is to treat each number as a list, each of whose elements is a block of digits of that number. For example, the integer 179,534,672,198 might be stored with $block[0] = 198$, $block[1] = 672$, $block[2] = 534$, $block[3] = 179$. Then add two integers (lists), element by element, carrying from one element to the next when necessary.

5. Proceeding as in Exercise 4, write a program to multiply two large integers with up to 300 digits.

6. A demographic study of the metropolitan area around Dogpatch divided it into three regions—urban, suburban, and exurban—and published the following table showing the annual migration from one region to another (the numbers represent percentages):

	Urban	Suburban	Exurban
Urban	1.1	0.3	0.7
Suburban	0.1	1.2	0.3
Exurban	0.2	0.6	1.3

For example, 0.3 percent of the urbanites (0.003 times the current population) move to the suburbs each year. The diagonal entries represent internal growth rates. Using a two-dimensional array with an enumerated type for the indices to store this table, write a program to determine the population of each region after 10, 20, 30, 40, and 50 years. Assume that the initial populations of the urban, suburban, and exurban regions are 2.1 million, 1.4 million, and 0.9 million, respectively.

7. If A and B are two $m \times n$ matrices, their *sum* is defined as follows: If A_{ij} and B_{ij} are the entries in the ith row and jth column of A and B, respectively, then $A_{ij} + B_{ij}$ is the entry in the ith row and jth column of their sum, which will also be an $m \times n$ matrix. Write a program to read two $m \times n$ matrices, display them, and calculate and display their sum.

8. The *product* of an $m \times n$ matrix A with an $n \times p$ matrix B is the $m \times p$ matrix $C = A * B$ whose entry C_{ij} in the ith row and jth column is given by

$$C_{ij} = \text{the sum of the products of the entries in row } i \text{ of } A$$
$$\text{with the entries in column } j \text{ of } B$$

$$= A_{i1} * B_{1j} + A_{i2} * B_{2j} + \ldots + A_{in} * B_{nj}$$

Write a program that will read two matrices A and B, display them, and calculate and display their product (or a message indicating that it is not defined).

9. A *magic square* is an $n \times n$ matrix in which each of the integers $1, 2, 3, \ldots, n^2$ appears exactly once and all column sums, row sums, and diagonal sums are equal. For example, the following is a 5×5 magic square in which all the rows, columns, and diagonals add up to 65:

17	24	1	8	15
23	5	7	14	16
4	6	13	20	22
10	12	19	21	3
11	18	25	2	9

The following is a procedure for constructing an $n \times n$ magic square for any odd integer n. Place 1 in the middle of the top row. Then after integer k has been placed, move up one row and one column to the right to place the next integer $k + 1$, unless one of the following occurs:

▶ If a move takes you above the top row in the jth column, move to the bottom of the jth column and place $k + 1$ there.

▶ If a move takes you outside to the right of the square in the ith row, place $k + 1$ in the ith row at the left side.

▶ If a move takes you to an already filled square or if you move out of the square at the upper right-hand corner, place $k + 1$ immediately below k.

Write a program to construct an $n \times n$ magic square for any odd value of n.

10. Suppose that each of the four edges of a thin square metal plate is maintained at a constant temperature and that we wish to determine the steady-state temperature at each interior point of the plate. To do this, we divide the plate into squares (the corners of which are called *nodes*) and find the temperature at each interior node by averaging the four neighboring temperatures; that is, if T_{ij} denotes the old temperature at the node in row i and column j, then

$$\frac{T_{i-1,j} + T_{i,j-1} + T_{i,j+1} + T_{i+1,j}}{4}$$

will be the new temperature.

To model the plate, we can use a two-dimensional array, with each array element representing the temperature at one of the nodes. Write a program that first reads the four constant temperatures (possibly different) along the edges of the plate, and some guess of the temperature at the interior points, and uses these values to initialize the elements of the array. Then determine the steady-state temperature at each interior node by repeatedly averaging the temperatures at its four neighbors, as just described. Repeat this procedure until the new temperature at each interior node differs from the old temperature at that node by no more than some specified small amount. Then print the array and the number of iterations used to produce the final result. (It may also be of interest to print the array at each stage of the iteration.)

11. The game of *Life*, invented by the mathematician John H. Conway, is intended to model life in a society of organisms. Consider a rectangular array of cells, each of which may contain an organism. If the array is viewed as extending indefinitely in both directions, then each cell has eight neighbors, the eight cells surrounding it. In each generation, births and deaths occur according to the following rules:

▶ An organism is born in any empty cell having exactly three neighbors.

▶ An organism dies from isolation if it has fewer than two neighbors.

▶ An organism dies from overcrowding if it has more than three neighbors.

▶ All other organisms survive.

To illustrate, the following shows the first five generations of a particular configuration of organisms:

Write a program to play the game of *Life* and investigate the patterns produced by various initial configurations. Some configurations die off rather rapidly; others repeat after a certain number of generations; others change shape and size and may move across the array; and still others may produce "gliders" that detach themselves from the society and sail off into space.

SECTION 2.5

12. Suppose that a file consists of records of computer users, each of which contains a user's id number (integer), name (string of length 30 in the form *last-name, first-name*), password (5-character string), resource limit (integer), and resources used to date (real). (See the website described in the preface for a sample `UserIdFile`.) At the end of each month, a report is produced that shows the status of each user's account. Write a program to read these records and print a report like the following that shows the status of each user's account. The three asterisks indicate users that have already used 90 percent or more of the resources available to them.

```
                    USER ACCOUNTS - 12/31/1998


                                      RESOURCE      RESOURCES
     USER NAME           USER-ID       LIMIT          USED
     =========          =======      ========      =========
     Miltgen, Joseph    100101        $750          $380.81
     Small, Isaac       100102        $650          $598.84***
          .                .             .              .
          .                .             .              .
          .                .             .              .
```

13. Consider a master file containing permanent student records and an update file containing current information for each student. (See the website described in the preface for sample `StudentFile` and `StudentUpdate` files.) Each record in the master file consists of a student's number (integer), last name (15-character string), first name (10-character string), middle initial (character), hometown (25-character string), phone number (7-digit integer), sex (character), class level (1-digit integer), major (4-character string), total credits earned to date (integer), and cumulative GPA (real). Each record in the update file contains a student's number and a list of five course records, each consisting of a course name (string), a letter grade (2-letter string), and the number of course credits (integer). The records in each file are arranged so that the student numbers are in ascending order. Write a program that reads the information for each student from these files, storing it in appropriate structures, and produces an updated grade report of the form

```
              GRADE REPORT - Semester #1
                    12/31/1998

                 Dispatch University

          10103 James L. Johnson


          COURSE             CREDITS         GRADE
          ======             =======         =====
          ENGL176            4                 C
          EDUC268            4                 B
          EDUC330            3                 B+
          P_ED281            3                 C
          ENGR317            4                 D

          Cumulative Credits:   33
          Semester GPA:       2.22
          Cumulative GPA:     2.64
```

(To calculate the semester GPA: Multiply the credits by the numeric grade—A = 4.0, A− = 3.7, B+ = 3.3, B = 3.0, . . . , D− = 0.7, F = 0.0—for each course to find the number of honor points earned for that course; sum these to find the total number of new honor points; then divide the total number of new honor points by the total number of new credits. To update the cumulative GPA, first calculate the number of old honor points = old credits times old cumulative GPA; add the new honor points; and then divide this total by the updated total number of credits.)

14. Write a declaration of a union to represent geometric figures: circle, square, rectangle, and triangle. For a circle, the union should store its radius; for a square, the length of a side; for a rectangle, the length of two adjacent sides; and for a triangle, the lengths of the three sides. Then write a program that reads one of the letters C (circle), S (square), R (rectangle), T (triangle), and the appropriate numeric quantity or quantities for a figure of that type and then calculates its area. For example, the input R 7.2 3.5 represents a rectangle with length 7.2 and width 3.5, and T 3 4 6.1 represents a triangle having sides of lengths 3, 4, and 6.1. (For a triangle, the area can be found with *Hero's formula*

$$area = \sqrt{s(s-a)(s-b)(s-c)}$$

where a, b, and c are the lengths of the sides and s is one-half the perimeter.)

Chapter 3

MORE ABOUT DATA STRUCTURES AND ADTs—C++ TYPES

Chapter Contents

Some data types are implemented directly with the corresponding predefined data types in the programming language being used. For example, in the preceding chapter we considered the structured data types that C++ inherits from C, its parent language: arrays, structs, and unions. For such structures the programmer usually need not be concerned with the details of the storage structures and algorithms used in their implementations because these are handled by the compiler and other system software.

In many applications, however, new data types must be designed and implemented by the programmer. We begin this chapter with a new look at ADTs and show how they are implemented using classes in C++. We will illustrate them with some of the C++ classes that you should already know about. We will also show how the data type `Time` described in the preceding chapter in the context of procedural programming can be redesigned as a class that is consistent with the object-oriented paradigm. And because your study of classes may have focused on *using* classes with very little (if any) practice in *building* classes, we will be much more detailed in our study of classes than we were for the data types in the preceding chapter. If your experience with classes is more extensive, you may choose to skim or skip over some of these extended presentations.

3.1   CLASSES

In the preceding chapter we described *structs* as they are used in the C programming language. C++ retains structs from its parent language, but it also provides *classes*. Structs and classes have similarities:

- ▶ Both can be used to model objects with different attributes (characteristics) represented as *data members*. They can thus be used to organize nonhomogeneous data sets.

- ▶ They have essentially the same syntax.

The basic difference is

- ▶ *Members of a class by default are private* (cannot be accessed by nonmember functions) unless explicitly declared to be public. *Members of a struct by default are public* (can be accessed by nonmember functions via the dot operator). In C++ they can be explicitly declared to be private.

Thus choosing whether to use a struct or a class in C++ is not based on their capabilities. In C++, a struct is simply a class in which all members are public by default. It is common practice, however, to use classes to prevent users of a new data type from accessing the data members. (We can also enforce this with structs, but this is not their default nature.)

DIFFERENCES BETWEEN "TRADITIONAL" (C) STRUCTS AND OOP (C++) STRUCTS AND CLASSES

Structs and classes in C++ are extensions of C's structs. Like C-style structs, they may contain **data members** to represent *attributes* (*characteristics*) of objects being modeled. But the main difference between structs and classes in C++ and structs in C is that they may also contain **function members** (also called **member functions** or **methods**[1]) to represent *operations* (*behaviors*) of those objects. This is an important difference because

- ▶ It provides a way to implement ADTs because the storage for the data items and the functions for the basic operations can be **encapsulated** in a single structure.

- ▶ It leads to a new style of programming—*object-oriented* rather than *procedural*. Objects can now be **self-contained**, carrying their own operations around with them—sometimes called the **I-can-do-it-myself principle**—instead of having to be shipped off to external functions that operate on them and send them back.

CLASS DECLARATIONS

Two common forms of a class declaration are

---

[1]It is common to call the two parts of a class *data members* and *member functions*. ("Data members" and "function members" are really more correct.) We will use the terms *function members* and *member functions* interchangeably.

CLASS DECLARATION

Form 1

```
class ClassName
{
public:
   Declarations of public members
private:
   Declarations of private members
};
```

Form 2

```
class ClassName
{
private:  ◄─────────────────────────────── optional
   Declarations of private members
public:
   Declarations of public members
};
```

Notes

1. By default, members are private; thus, in the second form, the **access specifier** `private:` is optional, but it is commonly included for clarity. In the first form, the access specifier `public:` is needed to specify the public section of the class and `private:` to specify where the public section ends and the private section begins.

2. Although not commonly done, a class may have several private and public sections; the keyword `private:` marks the beginning of each private section and the keyword `public:` marks the beginning of each public section.

3. The data members are normally placed in the private section(s) of a class and the function members in the public section(s).

4. Private members can be accessed only by member functions (and by friend functions described later).

5. Public members can be accessed by both member and nonmember functions.

The order of the public and private sections in a class does not matter. Some programmers prefer to put the public section first and others the private section first. In this text we will use the first form to emphasize the operations that make up the public user interface.

Class declarations are usually placed in a library, which is then called a **class library**. A class library has traditionally consisted of a header file `ClassName.h` and an implementation file `ClassName.cpp`[2] However, the increasing use of class templates as described in Chap. 6 for which the class library must reside in a single file has diminished this distinction between header and implementation files.

A particular instance of a class is called an **object**:

```
ClassName object_name;
```

(This is the "object" in *object-oriented programming*.) An object can access its public members by using the **dot operator**:

```
object_name.member_name
```

EXAMPLE: C++'s STANDARD I/O CLASSES

The standard C++ library contains many different classes and class templates (see Sec. 6.3). Some of the most familiar are the input/output classes `istream`, `ostream`, and `iostream`. They are general-purpose models for input and output that programmers can use without having to concern themselves with the messy details of how data actually gets from the keyboard to the program or from the program to the screen. Another useful standard class is the `string` class described in Sec. 3.4.

An `istream` object can be thought of as a stream of characters flowing from an arbitrary input device to an executing program and an `ostream` object as a stream of characters flowing from an executing program to an arbitrary output device:

The recently added class `iostream` supports both stream input and stream output.[3] These classes are defined in the library `<iostream>` that also defines the following standard stream objects:

cout: standard output stream of `char` (same destination as C's `stdout`)

cerr: standard unbuffered output stream for error messages (same destination as C's `stderr`)

clog: standard buffered output stream for error messages (same destination as C's `stderr`)

cin: standard input stream of `char` (same destination as C's `stdin`)

---

[2]Or with some other compiler-dependent suffix such as `.cp` or `.cc`.

[3]`iostream` is derived from both `istream` and `ostream`, which themselves are really specializations of the class templates `basic_istream` and `basic_ostream` to type `char`. Using `wchar_t` instead of `char` produces wide-character streams `wistream` and `wostream`. `basic_istream` and `basic_ostream` are derived from the `basic_ios` base class that handles the low-level details of formatting, buffers, and so on.

Operation	Description
For istream	
>>	input (extraction) operator
get()	input a single character or a string of characters
getline()	input a line
gcount()	count characters read by last input member function
ignore()	skip over characters
peek()	look at next character to be read
read()	input a character or a specified number of characters
readsome()	input at most a specified number of characters
putback()	put a character back into read buffer
unget()	put back most recent character read
seekg()	set current position
tellg()	get current position
For ostream	
<<	output (insertion) operator
put()	output a single character
write()	output a specified number of characters
flush()	empty the buffer
seekp()	set current position
tellp()	get current position

TABLE 3.1 **istream** AND **ostream** OPERATIONS

Table 3.1 lists some of the most commonly used istream and ostream operations defined as member functions of these classes. Expanded descriptions of these are given in Appendix D.

3.2   EXAMPLE OF A USER-DEFINED TYPE: A Time CLASS

In Sec. 2.4 we developed a Time type using a procedural programming approach. Time objects were structs with four data members—hours, minutes, AMorPM, and milTime—and these objects were processed by passing them around among various functions—Set(), Display(), Advance(), and LessThan(). As we noted there, we might think of the approach as follows: Whenever it is necessary to set the time, display it, advance it, or compare it with another time, we wrap up the watch and send it off to the manufacturer or some service company who will process it and then return it to us, perhaps changing the watch as requested—set or advanced—or sending back some value—the time displayed on the watch or in the case of LessThan(), a value of true or false to indicate the outcome of the comparison.

We will now use an OOP approach that models the watch more realistically. In this approach we can think of sending messages to the watch, perhaps by pushing buttons, and asking it to perform various operations on itself. To emphasize this *I-can-do-it-myself principle*, we will use names of the form *myThis* and *myThat* for the data members as a reminder that a `Time` object is operating on itself.

As noted in the introduction, we will proceed quite slowly and methodically in our study of classes and how they are used to define data types because this may be your first look at how such classes are designed and built. Accordingly, the first version of a class `Time` in Fig. 3.1 is deliberately kept simple by focusing on only two of the operations, set and display.

 FIGURE 3.1   INTERFACE FOR A `Time` DATA TYPE—OOP APPROACH.

```
/** Time.h -------------------------------------------------------
 This header file defines the data type Time for processing time.
 Basic operations are:
   Set:     To set the time
   Display: To display the time
-------------------------------------------------------------*/

#include <iostream>
using namespace std;

class Time
{
/******** Member functions ********/
public:

/* Set sets the data members of a Time object to specified values.
 *
 *  Receive:  hours, the number of hours in standard time
 *            minutes, the number of minutes in standard time
 *            am_pm ('A' if AM, 'P' if PM)
 *  Return:   The Time object containing this function with its
 *            myHours, myMinutes, and myAMorPM members set to hours,
 *            minutes, and am_pm, respectively, and myMilTime to
 *            the equivalent military time
 ****************************************************************/

void Set(unsigned hours, unsigned minutes, char am_pm);

/* Display displays time in standard and military format using
 * output stream out.
 *
 *  Receive:       ostream out
 *  Output:        The time represented by the Time object containing
 *                 this function
 *  Passes back:   The ostream out with time inserted into it
 ****************************************************************/

void Display(ostream & out) const;
```

```
/********** Data Members **********/
private:
   unsigned myHours,
            myMinutes;
   char myAMorPM;          // 'A' or 'P'
   unsigned myMilTime;     // military time equivalent


   }; // end of class declaration
```

Note the keyword `const` at the end of the heading for member function `Display()`. This makes `Display()` a **const function**, which means that it cannot modify any of the data members in the class. Any attempt to do so will produce a compiler error. Whenever a member function does not modify any of the class data members, it is good practice to prototype and define that member function as a `const` function.

WHY NOT MAKE ALL MEMBERS PUBLIC?   *The main reason for making the class data members private is so that only member (and friend) functions can access them.* The reason for restricting access to the data members is that as classes are developed, used, and upgraded, it often becomes clear that they can be improved by using data members different from those used in the initial design. Possible reasons for this include

- The class will better model some real-world object
- Operations can be performed more efficiently
- Operations can be implemented more easily

If data members are public, programmers tend to write programs that access them directly, and these programs then depend directly on those data members. Thus if a class upgrade replaces a data member, programs that use the class must also be modified, which means

- Increased upgrade time
- Increased programmer cost
- Decreased programmer productivity
- Reduced profits due to
  —Software late getting to market with the possible result of losing out to competitors
  —Loss of customer confidence in software reliability

For these reasons, it is good practice to

Always define data members of a class as private.

Keeping the data members "hidden" forces programs to interact with an object through its member functions, which thus provide the **interface** between programs and the class. If this interface does not change, then programs that use an object will not require change.

IMPLEMENTATION OF A CLASS

The definitions of member functions are usually placed in the corresponding implementation file—for example, in `ClassName.cpp`. Because different classes may have members with the same names, the names of the functions must be **qualified** with the name of the class to which they belong. This is done using the **scope operator** `::` to prepend the class name to the function name

```
ReturnType ClassName::FunctionName(param_declaration_list)
{
    . . .
}
```

Figure 3.2 shows an implementation file for the `Time` class.

FIGURE 3.2   IMPLEMENTATION OF A `Time` DATA TYPE—OOP APPROACH

```cpp
/** Time.cpp -- implements the Time member functions **/

#include "Time.h"

/*** Utility Functions -- Prototypes ***/

int ToMilitary(unsigned hours, unsigned minutes, char am_pm);

//----- Function to implement the Set operation -----

void Time::Set(unsigned hours, unsigned minutes, char am_pm)
{
  // Check class invariant
  if (hours >= 1 && hours <= 12 &&
      minutes >= 0 && minutes <= 59 &&
      (am_pm == 'A' || am_pm == 'P'))
  {
    myHours = hours;
    myMinutes = minutes;
    myAMorPM = am_pm;
    myMilTime = ToMilitary(hours, minutes, am_pm);
  }
  else
    cerr << "*** Can't set time with these values ***\n";
    // Object's data members remain unchanged
}

//----- Function to implement the Display operation -----

void Time::Display(ostream & out) const
{
  out << myHours << ':'
      << (myMinutes < 10 ? "0" : "") << myMinutes
      << ' ' << myAMorPM << ".M.   ("
      << myMilTime << " mil. time)";
}
```

```
/*** Utility Functions -- Definitions ***/

/* ToMilitary converts standard time to military time.
 *
 *   Receive: hours, minutes, am_pm
 *   Return:  The military time equivalent
 *************************************************************/

int ToMilitary(unsigned hours, unsigned minutes, char am_pm)
{
  if (hours == 12)
    hours = 0;

  return hours * 100 + minutes + (am_pm == 'P' ? 1200 : 0);
}
```

To test this first version of class `Time`, we might use a test driver program like that in Fig. 3.3.

 FIGURE 3.3   TEST DRIVER FOR Time DATA TYPE

```
// Test driver

#include "Time.h"
#include <iostream>
using namespace std;

int main()
{
  Time mealTime;

  mealTime.Set(5, 30, 'P');

  cout << "We'll be eating at ";

  mealTime.Display(cout);

  cout << endl;
}
```

EXECUTION:

```
We'll be eating at 5:30 P.M.   (1730 mil. time)
```

Again, note the difference from the procedural approach. Rather than ship the object `mealTime` off to various functions for processing, *we send messages to the object to operate on itself.* For example, to set my digital watch to 5:30 P.M., I don't wrap it up and mail it off somewhere to have it set; rather, I push a button. To display the time, I don't wrap up my watch and mail if off somewhere and have them tell me what time it is. I have it display the time to me itself, perhaps pushing a button to turn on the backlight so that I can see it.

SOME OBSERVATIONS

 ▶ Because member functions are members of a class object, they can operate on that object without it being passed to them as a parameter. Another way to view this is

- *A member function receives the class object to be operated on implicitly, rather than explicitly via a parameter.*

 This is not the case for nonmember functions however; thus,

- *If a nonmember function needs to operate on an object, it must receive it via a parameter.*

 ▶ For nontrivial member functions, we usually put their prototypes inside the class declaration and their definitions in the implementation file; in this case, the function names must be qualified with the scope operator (::) in the implementation file.

▶ If a member function is simple, we may want to specify that it be an **inline** function, which suggests to the compiler that it replace a function call with the actual code of the function, thus avoiding the usual overhead of a function call (see Sec. 4.3). This can be done in two ways:

1. *Prototype the function inside the class declaration, but define it below the class declaration in the header file, qualifying its name as usual;* for example:

   In `ClassName`.h:

   ```
   class ClassName
   {
   // Public section -- function members
              . . .
   ReturnType SimpleFunction(param_list);
              . . .
   // Private section -- data members
              . . .
   }; // end of class declaration

   inline ReturnType ClassName::SimpleFunction(param_list)
   {
      // function body
   }
   ```

2. *Simply put the definition of the function inside the class declaration—its name need not be qualified. The compiler will treat it as an inline function;* for example

   In `ClassName`.h:

   ```
   class ClassName
   {
   // Public section -- function members
              . . .
   ```

```
ReturnType ClassName::SimpleFunction(param_list)
{
    // function body
}
        . . .
// Private section — data members
        . . .
}; // end of class declaration
```

☞ ▶ A **class invariant** should be formulated and tested to ensure that the data members always contain valid values. This means that other member functions are guaranteed of each data member's validity and need not check it themselves. Whenever an operation modifies any of the data members, it should always establish that the class invariant still holds. For example, for class Time, the class invariant is

```
myHours >= 1 && myHours <= 12 &&
myMinutes >= 0 && myMinutes <= 59 &&
(myAMorPM == 'A' || myAMorPM == 'P')
```

In Set(), we tested the arguments to ensure that this invariant would be true after the function is executed:

```
if (hours >= 1 && hours <= 12 &&
      minutes >= 0 && minutes <= 59 &&
      (am_pm == 'A' || am_pm == 'P'))
{
   myHours = hours;
   . . .
}
else
   . . .
```

An alternative way to test this is to use the **assert() mechanism** (from cassert)—at least during debugging. It

▶ Accepts a boolean condition
▶ If that condition is true, execution continues as usual
▶ If the condition is false, execution halts and an error message is displayed

For example, we could also have defined Set() as follows:

```
#include <cassert>
. . .

//----- Function to implement the Set operation -----
```

```
void Time::Set(unsigned hours, unsigned minutes, char am_pm)
{
   assert(hours >= 1 && hours <= 12 &&
          minutes >= 0 && minutes <= 59 &&
          (am_pm == 'A' || am_pm == 'P'));
   myHours = hours;
   myMinutes = minutes;
      . . .
}
```

To test it, we might modify `driver.cpp` by having `mealTime` attempt to set itself to an illegal value; for example

```
mealTime.Set(13, 30, 'P');
```

This will cause execution to terminate and a message similar to the following will usually be displayed:

```
Time.cpp: failed assertion
'hours >= 1 && hours <= 12 && minutes >= 0 &&
minutes <= 59 && (am_pm == 'A' || am_pm == 'P')'
IOT trap
```

In our first method of testing the class invariant, we simply display an error message if the invariant fails and return to the calling function. In the second approach, the `assert()` mechanism displays an error message and terminates program execution. A third alternative is to **throw an exception** that the calling function can **catch** and take appropriate action.[4] For example, we might change the definition of `Set()` as follows:

```
//----- Function to implement the Set operation -----

void Time::Set(unsigned hours, unsigned minutes, char am_pm)
{
   // Check class invariant
   if (hours >= 1 && hours <= 12 &&
       minutes >= 0 && minutes <= 59 &&
       (am_pm == 'A' ||am_pm == 'P'))
   {
      . . .
   }
   else
   {
      char error[] =
         "*** Can't set time with these values ***\n";
      throw error;
   }
}
```

---

[4]See Appendix D for more information about exceptions.

To catch this exception, a calling function might contain

```
try
{
  mealTime.Set(13, 30, 'P');
  cout << "This is a valid time\n";
}
catch (char badTime[])
{
  cout << "ERROR: " << badTime << endl;
  exit(-1);
}
cout << "Proceeding. . .\n";
```

When executed, the output produced will be

```
ERROR: *** Can't set time with these values ***
```

If we change the `Set()` message for `mealTime` to

```
mealTime.Set(8, 30, 'P');
```

the output will be

```
This is a valid time
Proceeding. . .
```

☞ ▸ Whenever a member function does not modify any of the class data
members, that function should be prototyped and defined as a const
function. A compiler error will result if the function attempts to modify
any of the data members of the class.

CLASS CONSTRUCTORS

Constructing an object consists of

1. *Allocating memory* for the object, and

2. *Initializing* the object.

In our example, the definition

```
Time mealTime;
```

causes the compiler to allocate memory for the `Time` object `mealTime`, but its data
members are not initialized. If we forgot to use the `Set()` operation to do this,
we may later be processing "garbage" values in the data members of `mealTime`.
It would be better if the programmer knew the values with which every `Time` object
will be initialized. This could be either with

▸ initial values specified in the declaration of `mealTime`

▸ default values if no initial values are specified

This can be accomplished using **constructor functions**, which have the following properties:

1. *Their primary role (for now) is to initialize the data members of all objects (either with default values or with values provided as arguments).*

2. *Their names are always the same as the class name.*

3. *They are always member functions and are (almost always) prototyped or defined in the public section.*

4. *They do not return a value; they have no return type (not even* void*). For this reason, documentation that describes their behavior commonly specifies the following items:*

   ▶ *What values they receive* (if any) via parameters

   ▶ ***Preconditions:*** Conditions that must be true before the function is called

   ▶ ***Postconditions:*** Conditions that must be true when the function terminates

5. *Often they are quite simple and can be inlined in either of the two ways described earlier.*

6. *A constructor gets called whenever an object is declared.*

7. *If no constructor is given in a class, the compiler allocates memory for each data member and initializes it with default values determined by the types of the data members.*

To illustrate, we will add two constructors to our Time class: a **default constructor** that has no arguments and that initializes a Time object to a default value of our choosing (12:00 midnight) and an **explicit-value constructor** that has arguments whose values are used to initialize the data members. Figure 3.4 shows these constructors.

FIGURE 3.4   CLASS CONSTRUCTORS FOR Time DATA TYPE

In **Time.h**

```
.  .  .


class Time
{
/******** Member functions ********/
public:

/***** Class constructors *****/

/* --- Construct a class object (default).
 *  Precondition:  A Time object has been declared.
 *  Postcondition: The Time object is initialized to 12:00 A.M.;
 *                 that is, the myHours, myMinutes, and myAMorPM
 *                 members are initialized to 12, 0, 'A', respectively,
 *                 and myMilTime to 0.
 ***************************************************************************/

Time();
```

```
/* --- Construct a class object (explicit values).
 *   Precondition:    A Time object has been declared.
 *   Receive:         Initial values initHours, initMinutes, and
 *                    initAMPM
 *   Postcondition:   The myHours, myMinutes, and myAMorPM members
 *                    of the Time object are initialized to initHours,
 *                    initMinutes, and initAMPM, respectively, and
 *                    myMilTime to the corresponding military time.
 ***********************************************************************/

Time(unsigned initHours, unsigned initMinutes, char initAMPM);
   . . .
// other member function prototypes
   . . .
/********** Data Members **********/
private:
   . . .
}; // end of class declaration

//----- Definition of default constructor
inline Time::Time()
{
  myHours = 12;
  myMinutes = 0;
  myAMorPM = 'A';
  myMilTime = 0;
}
```

Add to **Time.cpp**

```
#include <cassert>
   . . .

//----- Function to implement the explicit-value  constructor -----

Time::Time(unsigned initHours, unsigned initMinutes, char initAMPM)
{
  // Check class invariant
  assert(initHours >= 1 && initHours <= 12 &&
         initMinutes >= 0 && initMinutes <= 59 &&
         (initAMPM == 'A' || initAMPM == 'P'));

  myHours = initHours;
  myMinutes = initMinutes;
  myAMorPM = initAMPM;
  myMilTime = ToMilitary(initHours, initMinutes, initAMPM);
}
```

Alternatively, we could simply put the definition of the default constructor inside the class declaration:

```
/***** Class constructors *****/

/* --- Construct a class object (default).
   . . .
Time()
{
  myHours = 12;
  myMinutes = 0;
  myAMorPM = 'A';
  myMilTime = 0;
}
```

To test our constructors, we might use the following declarations in a driver program:

```
Time mealTime,
     bedTime(11,30,'P');
```

The first declaration constructs `mealTime` using the default constructor, since there are no arguments passed to the constructor. Memory is allocated for `mealTime` and the data members initialized to 12, 0, 'A', and 0, respectively. The second declaration constructs `bedTime` using the explicit-value constructor. Memory is allocated for `bedTime`, the arguments 11, 30, and 'P' are used to initialize the data members `myHours`, `myMinutes`, `myAMorPM`, and `myMilTime` to 11, 30, 'P', and 2330, respectively.

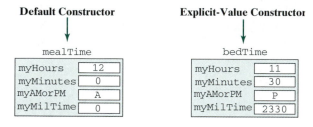

Execution of the statements

```
mealTime.Display(cout);
cout << endl;
bedTime.Display(cout);
cout << endl;
```

will produce

```
12:00 A.M. (0 mil. time)
11:30 P.M. (2330 mil. time)
```

If we change the declarations to

```
Time mealTime,
     bedTime(13,30,'P');
```

failure of the assertion in the explicit-value constructor will cause execution to terminate:

```
Time.cpp: failed assertion
'hours >= 1 && hours <= 12 && minutes >= 0 &&
minutes <= 59 && (am_pm == 'A' || am_pm == 'P')'
IOT trap
```

☞   If we do not provide a constructor for a class, the compiler will generate a default constructor that will initialize the data members with default values determined by their types.[5] *If we provide a constructor for a class, we must also provide a default constructor, because the compiler will not supply one.* And without a default constructor, declarations of the form

```
ClassName object_name;
```

which require a default constructor will not be allowed.

OVERLOADING FUNCTIONS.   Notice that in our class `Time`, there are two functions with the same name `Time()`. This is allowed in C++ provided that the parameter lists of the functions differ in the number and/or types of parameters—that is, *they have different **signatures**.* The compiler will use the arguments in a function call to determine which function to use. This is an example of **function overloading** in C++.

DEFAULT ARGUMENTS.   An alternative to using two different constructors is to replace their prototypes in `Time.h` with a single constructor that uses **default arguments** to supply values for parameters for which there is no corresponding argument. (It is important to remember that *parameters with default arguments must appear after all parameters without default arguments.*)

```
/*--- Construct a class object.
 *   Precondition:  A Time object has been declared.
 *   Receive:       Initial values initHours, initMinutes,
 *                  and initAMPM (defaults 12, 0, 'A')
 *   Postcondition: The myHours, myMinutes, and myAMorPM
 *                  members of the Time object are initialized
 *                  to initHours, initMinutes, and initAMPM,
 *                  respectively, and myMilTime to the
 *                  corresponding military time.
 ***************************************************************/

Time(unsigned initHours = 12, unsigned initMinutes = 0,
     char initAMPM = 'A');
```

The declarations

```
Time t1, t2(5), t3(5, 30), t4(5, 30, 'P');
```

---

[5]It will also provide a *destructor* to destroy objects after their lifetimes are over. We can also supply our own class destructor as described in Sec. 8.5.

will then create four `Time` objects: `t1` is initialized using all three of the default arguments (12, 0, and 'A') to initialize the data members `myHours`, `myMinutes`, and `myHours`; `t2` is initialized using the supplied value (5) for `myHours` and the last two default arguments (0 and 'A') for `myMinutes` and `myAMorPM`; for `t3`, the supplied values (5 and 30) are used for `myHours` and `myMinutes` and the last default argument ('A') is used for `myAMorPM`; and `t4` uses only the supplied arguments (5, 30, and 'P') to initialize `myHours`, `myMinutes`, and `myHours`. The following diagrams summarize:

t1		t2		t3		t4	
myHours	12	myHours	5	myHours	5	myHours	5
myMinutes	0	myMinutes	0	myMinutes	30	myMinutes	30
myAMorPM	A	myAMorPM	A	myAMorPM	A	myAMorPM	P
myMilTime	0	myMilTime	500	myMilTime	530	myMilTime	1730

Note that it is not possible to use supplied values for the first and third data members and a default value for the second because arguments are matched with parameters from left to right. For example, the declaration `Time t(5, 'P');` will produce a compilation error because `'P'` is used as a value for `myMinutes`.

COPY OPERATIONS—INITIALIZATION AND ASSIGNMENT

Two default copy operations are provided for all classes:

1. Copy in initialization
2. Copy in assignment

Each constructs a copy of an object by making (byte-by-byte) copies of the data members of the object. (In cases where this is not appropriate, we can define a *copy constructor* for the first kind of copy and overload the assignment operator for the second kind. Copy constructors are described in more detail in Sec. 8.5.)

To illustrate these copy operations, suppose that `bedTime` and `mealTime` are the `Time` objects considered earlier. Then

```
Time t = bedTime;
```

is a legal definition of `Time` object `t` as is

```
Time t(bedTime);
```

Both allocate memory for `t` and then copy the members of `bedTime` into these memory locations, thus initializing `t` to be a copy of `bedTime`:

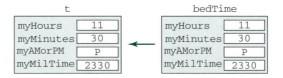

t		bedTime	
myHours	11	myHours	11
myMinutes	30	myMinutes	30
myAMorPM	P	myAMorPM	P
myMilTime	2330	myMilTime	2330

The same initialization results from

```
Time t = Time(11, 30, 'P');
```

which uses the explicit-value constructor to construct a (temporary) Time object and then copies it into t.

Although the preceding copy operations may look like assignments, they are not—a default copy constructor is called to do the initialization. However, C++ does provide a default copy operation for assignment. For example, the assignment statement

```
t = mealTime;
```

will copy the members of mealTime into t, replacing any previous values stored in the members of t:

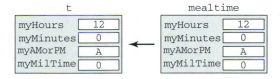

ACCESS FUNCTIONS

Because the data members are private, they can be accessed only by member (and friend) functions. It is often necessary, however, to make the values stored in some or all of these members more widely accessible. For this, **access** functions can be provided in the class.

To illustrate, suppose we wish to add *retrievers* to class Time that will retrieve the value stored in a data member of an object. We will do this only for the myHours member; the others are essentially the same. A specification for this retriever is

Receives: A Time object (perhaps implicitly)
Returns: The value stored in the myHours member of that object

As usual, the specification tells us how to prototype the function:

▶ Because it will be a member function, no parameters (Time or otherwise) will be needed.

▶ The function returns myHours, which is an integer.

In addition, because all this function does is retrieve the value stored in a data member, it is simple enough to inline. And because it does not modify any of the class's data members, it should be a constant function. Figure 3.5 shows how to add this accessor to the class Time.

FIGURE 3.5   ACCESSORS FOR **Time** DATA TYPE

In **Time.h**

```
   . . .


class Time
{

/******** Member functions ********/
public:
   . . .


/***** Data Retrievers *****/

/* Hour Accessor
 *   Receive: The Time object containing this function (implicitly)
 *   Return:  The value stored in the myHours member of the Time
 *            object containing this function
 ***************************************************************/


unsigned Hour() const;

// and similar functions for myMinutes,
// myAMorPM, and myMilTime retrieval
   . . .
/********** Data Members **********/
 private:
   . . .
}; // end of class declaration
   . . .


//----- Definition of Hour()
inline unsigned Time::Hour() const
{ return myHours; }
```

INPUT/OUTPUT—OVERLOADING OPERATORS—FRIEND FUNCTIONS

OUTPUT.   One of the first functions to add to a class is an output function so that it can be used for debugging the class while it is being built. In our first version of class Time, we have used a member function Display() to output Time objects. For example, to output the Time object mealTime to the screen, we sent a message to it instructing it to display itself using cout:

```
   mealTime.Display(cout);
```

It would be more convenient, however, to overload the output operator << for a Time object so that statements like

```
   cout << "We'll be eating at " << mealTime << endl;
```

can be used instead of

```
cout << "We'll be eating at " ;
mealTime.Display(cout);
cout << endl;
```

OVERLOADING OPERATORS.   We have noted that functions in C++ can be overloaded; that is, two functions may have the same name, provided they have different signatures. This also means that operators may be overloaded because they can be implemented as functions:

Operator	Function
Δ	operatorΔ()

Thus, we can overload an arbitrary operator Δ by defining a function with the name operatorΔ() but whose signature is distinct from any existing definition of operatorΔ().[6] If it is defined as a member function of a class C, the compiler will treat an expression of the form

```
a Δ b
```

where a is of type C as a call to this function member with the second operand (b) as its only (explicit) argument:

```
a.operatorΔ(b)
```

This means that in overloading operator<<() for class Time, we cannot make it a member function. To see this, suppose it was a member function. Then an output statement such as

```
cout << mealTime;
```

would be treated by the compiler as cout.operator<<(mealTime). But this would mean that operator<<() must be a member of class ostream, not a member of class Time.

If, however, an operator function of the form operatorΔ() is a nonmember function, then an expression of the form

```
a Δ b
```

will be treated by the compiler as the function call

```
operatorΔ(a, b)
```

This means that if we define operator<<() to have two parameters, the first an ostream and the second of type Time, then

```
cout << mealTime;
```

___

[6]Only the operators ::, ., and .* cannot be overloaded.

will be treated by the compiler as the function call

```
operator<<(cout, mealTime);
```

To overload the output operator `<<` for our `Time` class, therefore, we need to define a function of the form

```
ReturnType  operator<<(ostream_parameter, Time_parameter)
{
}
```

The `ostream` parameter will be a *reference parameter* because output changes the `ostream`. And as is common for class objects, we will use a **const reference parameter** for the second parameter. This avoids the overhead of making a copy of the object and making it a const parameter that protects the corresponding argument. Thus our function becomes

```
ReturnType  operator<<(ostream & out, const Time & t)
{
}
```

The next question we must address is what the function's return type should be and what should be returned. Consider a chained output expression of the form

```
cout << x << y
```

Because `<<` is left-associative, this is equivalent to

```
(cout << x) << y
```

The subexpression `cout << x` is thus evaluated first and, as we have seen, this can be accomplished with a call to function `operator<<()`:

```
(operator<<(cout, x)) << y
```

After this function call is completed, we want the chained output expression to become

```
cout << y
```

This means that the first function call must return an `ostream` and it must be `cout`; that is, it must return the `ostream` (`cout`) that is associated with the first parameter (`out`). We can accomplish this as follows:

- ▶ Make the function's return type `ostream &`[7]
- ▶ Have the function return its first parameter (`out`)

---

[7]If a function's return type is `T` and it returns a value `v` of type `T`, it actually returns a *copy* of `v`. Making the return type `T &` returns a reference to `v`, that is, an alias for `v`, so that both refer to the same `T` value.

An alias for out will be returned and since out is an alias for cout (because it is a reference parameter), the function operator() will actually produce output to cout and will return this modified ostream. The output function for our new type Time thus becomes

```
ostream & operator<<(ostream & out, const Time & t)
{
  // statements that output to ostream out
  // the time corresponding to t

  return out;
}
```

Now we must determine where to put this function. The compiler will evaluate

```
cout << t1;
```

with the function call

```
operator<<(cout, t1);
```

in which t1 is an argument to the function. Consequently, we cannot simply put the prototype of operator<<() inside the class declaration because it would then be treated as a member function, which, as we have seen, will confuse the compiler. There are two ways to proceed.

OUTPUT OPTION 1.   Put the prototype of operator<<() in the header file Time.h but outside the class. Actually, because of its simplicity, we have decided to inline it and so have put its definition in Time.h, as shown in Fig. 3.6.

FIGURE 3.6   OUTPUT OPERATOR FOR Time DATA TYPE—OPTION 1

In **Time.h**

```
   . . .
class Time
{
/******** Member functions ********/
public:
   . . .

void Display(ostream & out);
   . . .

/********** Data Members **********/
private:
   . . .
}; // end of class declaration
   . . .
```

```
/* --- operator<< displays time in standard and military format
 * using ostream out.
 *   Receives:      An ostream out and a Time object t
 *   Output:        The time represented by the Time object t
 *   Passes back:   The ostream out with t inserted into it.
 *   Return value:  out
 ***************************************************************/

inline ostream & operator<<(ostream & out, const Time & t)
{
  t.Display(out);
  return out;
}
```

EXAMPLE OF USE IN A DRIVER PROGRAM:

```
cout << mealTime << endl << bedTime << endl;
```

OUTPUT PRODUCED:

```
5:30 P.M.  (1730 mil. time)
11:30 P.M. (2330 mil. time)
```

This option actually uses a member function (`Display()`) to carry out the output and `operator<<()` simply sends a message to the object to output itself on a specified `ostream`. This method is preferred by many programmers, even though it does require two functions—a member function and a nonmember function to call it.

OUTPUT OPTION 2.   Some programmers prefer to simplify the preceding method by eliminating the member function (`Display()`) and use only `operator<<()`. However, it does not work to simply make this replacement in the class declaration, because this makes `operator<<()` a member function of class `Time` and, as we have seen, this cannot be. If we make this replacement

```
class Time
{

public:
    . . .

  ostream & operator<<(ostream & out, const Time & t);
  // We're not finished with this prototype

}; // end of class declaration
```

and modify the definition of `Display()` in `Time.cpp` appropriately for `operator<<()` (see Fig. 3.7), an error results when we try to compile `Time.cpp`. One compiler generated the following unusual error message:

```
'Time::operator<<(ostream &, const Time &)'
 must take exactly one argument
```

Although it isn't obvious, the error stems from the fact that as a member function of class `Time`, `operator<<()` actually has three parameters:

    out,
    t, and
    the `Time` object containing it (an *implicit parameter*)

However, `operator<<()` normally has just two parameters, and

☞   *C++ does not allow an overloaded operator definition to change the operator's **arity** (the number of operands the operator takes).*

But we cannot simply remove the prototype from the class `Time` because then we start getting error messages stating that the data members are private. We seem to be caught in a Catch-22 situation:

    `operator<<()` cannot be a member function.
    If `operator<<()` is not a member function, then the compiler won't allow it to access the private members of the class.

One way to proceed is to use access functions to retrieve the values stored in the data members. However, it is a nuisance to have to write access functions for every data member and for every class. What is needed is a "compromise" mechanism by which a class can grant a nonmember function permission to access its data members. In C++ this is done by prototyping the nonmember function within the class (like a member) but preceding its prototype (but *not its definition*) with the keyword **friend**.

☞   *A function that a class names as a friend is a nonmember function to which the class has granted permission to access members in its private sections.*

It is important to note that *because a friend function is not a member function*

  ▸ Its definition is not qualified using the class name and the scope operator (::)
  ▸ It receives the class object on which it operates as a parameter (explicitly)
  ▸ It uses the dot operator to access the data members

Figure 3.7 shows how this output option can be used for our class `Time`. The definition of `operator<<()` in `Time.cpp` is an easy modification of that for `Display()`. But note that because the `Time` object `t` being displayed is being passed in as a parameter, we must use the dot operator to access its `myHours`, `myMinutes`, `myAMorPM`, and `myMilTime` members.

FIGURE 3.7   OUTPUT OPERATOR FOR Time DATA TYPE—OPTION 2

In `Time.h`

```
   . . .

class Time
{
/******** Member functions ********/
public:
   . . .

/***** I/O Functions *****/

 * operator<< displays time in standard and military format
 * using ostream out.
 *   Receives:      An ostream out and a Time object t
 *   Output:        The time represented by the Time object containing
 *                  this function
 *   Passes back:   The ostream out with t inserted into it.
 *   Return value:  out
 ********************************************************************/

friend ostream & operator<<(ostream & out, const Time & t);
   . . .
/********** Data Members **********/
   . . .
}; // end of class declaration
   . . .
```

Add to `Time.cpp`

```
//----- Function to implement ostream output -----

ostream & operator<<(ostream & out, const Time & t)
{
  out << t.myHours << ':'
      << (t.myMinutes < 10 ? "0" : "") << t.myMinutes
      << ' ' << t.myAMorPM << ".M.   ("
      << t.myMilTime << " mil. time)";

  return out;
}
```

EXAMPLE OF USE IN A DRIVER PROGRAM:

```
Time mealTime,
     bedTime(11, 30, 'P');
  . . .

mealTime.Set(5, 30, 'P');
cout << "Eat at " << mealTime
     << "\nand sleep at " << bedTime << endl;
```

EXECUTION:
```
Eat at 5:30 P.M.   (1730 mil. time)
and sleep at 11:30 P.M.   (2330 mil. time)
```

INPUT.   To add an input operator to our Time class, we proceed in much the same way as for output and use one of the following options:

1. Add a member function ReadTime() that reads values and stores them in the data members of a Time object; then call it from a nonmember function operator>>()

2. Declare operator>>() to be a friend function so that it can access the data members of a Time object and store input values in them

Figure 3.8 shows the second approach.

FIGURE 3.8   INPUT OPERATOR FOR Time DATA TYPE

In **Time.h**, declare **operator>>()** as a friend function

```
   . . .
class Time
{
/******** Member functions ********/
public:
   . . .

/***** I/O Functions *****/
   . . .

/* --- operator>> inputs a Time value from istream in.
 *
 *   Receives:     An istream in and a Time object t
 *   Input :       Values for the data members of t
 *   Passes back:  The istream in with values removed from it
 *                 t with values stored in its data members
 *   Return value: in
 *   Note:  Times are input in the format hh:mm xM
 ****************************************************************/

friend istream & operator>>(istream & in, Time & t);
   . . .

/********** Data Members **********/
   . . .
}; // end of class declaration
   . . .
```

Add to `Time.cpp`

```
//----- Function to implement istream input -----

istream & operator>>(istream & in, Time & t)
{
   char ch;     // gobble up separators
   in >> t.myHours >> ch >> t.myMinutes >> t.myAMorPM>> ch;

   // Check the class invariant
   assert(t.myHours >= 0 && t.myHours <= 12 &&
          t.myMinutes >= 0 && t.myMinutes <= 59 &&
          (t.MyAMorPM == 'A' || t.myAMorPM == 'P'));
   t.myMilTime = ToMilitary(t.myHours, t.myMinutes, t.myAMorPM);
   return in;
}
```

EXAMPLE OF USE IN A DRIVER PROGRAM:

```
Time mealTime,
     bedTime;
     . . .
cout << "Enter meal time and bedtime (hh:mm xM): ";
cin >> mealTime >> bedTime;

cout << "We'll be eating at " << mealTime << endl;
cout << "We'll hit the hay at " << bedTime << endl;
```

EXECUTIONS:

```
Enter meal time and bedtime (hh:mm xM): 5:30 PM  11:30 PM
We'll be eating at 5:30 P.M.  (1730 mil. time)
We'll hit the hay at 11:30 P.M.  (2330 mil. time)

Enter meal time and bedtime (hh:mm xM): 5:30 PM  1:00 AM
We'll be eating at 5:30 P.M.  (1730 mil. time)
We'll hit the hay at 1:00 A.M.  (100 mil. time)
```

OTHER OPERATIONS: RELATIONAL OPERATORS AND ADVANCE

The original version of this new data type Time in the preceding chapter had two other operations: comparing two Time objects to determine if one is less than another and advancing a Time object by a given number of hours and minutes. We will now consider how these can be added to the class Time.

RELATIONAL OPERATORS.   We will describe how to add only the less-than (<) operator; the other relational operators are similar.

We begin with a specification of less-than:

Receives: Two Time objects (perhaps one implicitly)

Returns: True if the first Time object is less than the second; false otherwise

Now we must decide whether the function `operator<()` for this operation should be a member function. To help with this decision, it is useful to consider the question from two different perspectives:

From an internal perspective: I compare myself with another `Time` object and determine if I am less than that other object

From an external perspective: Two `Time` objects are compared to determine if the first is less than the second

Either point of view is reasonable, but in keeping with the OOP I-can-do-it-myself principle of making objects self-contained, we will opt for using member functions. In this case, we might better rephrase our specification as:

Receives: A `Time` object (and the current object implicitly)

Returns: True if I (the `Time` object containing this function) am less than the time object received; false otherwise

Figure 3.9 incorporates the < operation into class `Time` using this approach. Because of the simplicity of this function we have inlined it.

FIGURE 3.9   LESS-THAN OPERATOR FOR **Time** DATA TYPE

In **Time.h**

```
    . . .
class Time
{
/******** Member functions ********/
public:
    . . .


/***** Relational operators *****/

/* --- operator< determines if the current Time object is less
 *      than another Time object.
 *
 *   Receive: Time t and the Time object containing this
 *              function (implicitly)
 *   Return:  true if the Time object containing this function
 *              is less than t; false otherwise
 *   ***********************************************************/

bool operator<(const Time & t) const;

/********** Data Members **********/
private:
    . . .
}; // end of class declaration
    . . .
```

```
//----- Definition of operator<
inline bool Time::operator<(const Time & t) const
{ return myMilTime < t.MilTime(); }
```

Note that in the `return` statement, we used the member function `MilTime()` to access the `milTime` data member. This is not necessary, however. We could have written

```
    return myMilTime < t.myMilTime;
```

Ordinarily, a nonfriend function would not be allowed to access the private data members of an object, but

    A class's member functions can access private data members of class objects that it receives as parameters.

ADDING `Advance()`.   The last operation we add to our class `Time` is the operation to advance a time by a specified number of hours and minutes. A specification for this operation is

Receives: A `Time` object (perhaps implicitly), hours, minutes

Returns: The `Time` object with data members incremented by these values

Again we must decide whether the function `Advance()` for this operation should be a member function. Should it operate from inside a `Time` object or from outside on `Time` objects? The I-can-do-it-myself principle leads us to select the first option and make it a member function as shown in Fig. 3.10.

FIGURE 3.10   ADVANCE OPERATOR FOR `Time` DATA TYPE

In `Time.h`

```
   . . .
class Time
{
/******** Member functions ********/
public:
   . . .

/***** Increment operator *****/

/* --- Advance() increments a Time by a specified value.
 *
 *   Receive:   hours, the number of hours to add
 *              minutes, the number of minutes to add
 *   Return:    The Time object containing this function with its
 *              data members incremented by these values
 ***************************************************************/

void Advance(unsigned hours, unsigned minutes);
```

```
/********** Data Members **********/
   . . .
}; // end of class declaration
   . . .
```

Add to **Time.cpp**

```
//----- Function to implement Advance() -----

void Time::Advance(unsigned hours, unsigned minutes)
{
   // Increment the myMilTime member
   myMilTime += 100 * hours + minutes;

   // Adjust to proper format
   unsigned  milHours = myMilTime / 100,
             milMins = myMilTime % 100;
   milHours +=  milMins / 60;
   milMins %= 60;
   milHours %= 24;
   myMilTime = 100 * milHours + milMins;

   // Now set the standard time data members
   ToStandard(myMilTime, myHours, myMinutes, myAMorPM);
}

// ToStandard() is the utility function we used in our "procedural"
// implementation of Time in Figure 2.2.  We add its declaration
// and definition to Time.cpp.
```

SUMMARY AND A FEW OTHER ITEMS

When an object needed to solve a problem cannot be conveniently represented using the predefined C++ data types, the class mechanism can be used to create a new data type *NewTypeName* to represent the object, which is then usually stored in a class library with

- ▶ The class declaration stored in the header file (*NewTypeName*.h)
- ▶ The definitions of nontrivial class operations stored in an implementation file (*NewTypeName*.cpp)
- ▶ The implementation file compiled separately

The usual procedure for a program to use this new data type is

- ▶ Insert the class declaration into the program using
  #include "*NewTypeName*.h"
- ▶ Compile the program (and *NewTypeName*.cpp) separately
- ▶ Link the program's object file and the library's object file

GENERAL FORM OF A CLASS DECLARATION.   A common form for a class declaration is

```
class ClassName
{
 public:
   declarations/prototypes of public members
 private:
   declarations of private members
};
```

▶ Class members can be either *data members* or *member functions*.

▶ Public members can be accessed by nonmember functions using the *dot operator*:

```
classObjectName.publicMemberName
```

▶ Private members can be accessed only by member functions and by friends of the class.

▶ A member function has full access to all private members of a class; its full name begins with the name of its class and the *scope operator*:

```
ReturnType NewTypeName::FunctionName(parameter_list)
{ . . . }
```

▶ The name of a *class constructor* function is the name of the class. A constructor is invoked each time execution encounters a class object's declaration, making it an ideal way to initialize a class object's data members.

▶ Every class must have a default constructor (with no arguments). If no constructor is defined for a class, the compiler will provide a default constructor; otherwise, the programmer must provide one.

▶ Any function that a class names as a *friend* is not a member function but still has access to the private members of the class.

THE PROBLEM OF REDUNDANT DECLARATIONS.   A class such as Time might be used in a program, in libraries, in other class libraries, and thus it could easily happen that it gets included several times in the same file; for example,

A program needs the Time class, so it #includes "Time.h"
The program also needs library Lib, so it #includes "Lib.h"
   but Lib.h also #includes "Time.h"

This would cause "redeclaration" errors during compiling.

A common way to prevent the declarations in a library such as Time.h from being included more than once in a file is to use **conditional compilation**. The declarations in Time.h are wrapped inside preprocessor directives like those shown in Fig. 3.11[8] A complete version of class Time can be found at the website given in the preface.

---

[8]The preprocessor scans through a file removing comments, #including files, and processing other directives (which begin with #) before the file is passed to the compiler.

FIGURE 3.11   PREVENTING REDUNDANT DECLARATIONS

```
#ifndef TIME
#define TIME

class Time
{
/******** Member functions ********/
public:
   . . .
/********** Data Members **********/
private:
   . . .
}; // end of class declaration

// Definitions of member and nonmember functions.

#endif
```

The first directive `#ifndef TIME` tests to see whether the identifier TIME has been defined. (It is common practice to use the name of the class in uppercase for this identifier.) If it has not, processing proceeds to the second directive `#define TIME`, which defines TIME (to be 1), and then continues on through what follows and on to the `#endif` and beyond. If it has been defined, the preprocessor removes all code that follows until a `#elif`, `#else`, of `#endif` directive is encountered.

Thus, the first time the preprocessor encounters the declaration of class Time, it defines the name TIME. If it encounters the class declaration again, since TIME has been defined, all code between `#ifndef TIME` and `#endif` is stripped, thus removing the redeclaration.

MORE THAT COULD BE DONE.   This completes our development of the class Time. There obviously are other operations that could (and should) be added or modified. For example, we could add the remaining relational operators. This is straightforward, almost exactly like what we did for <. We could also add the increment operations ++ and += in place of Advance() and perhaps the decrement operations -- and -= as well. And there are other changes and modifications we could make, but we must move on to other topics.

✔ Quick Quiz 3.2

1. What is the basic difference between structs and classes?
2. Unlike C's structs, C++ structs and classes can contain both _____ members and _____ members.
3. What is the I-can-do-it-myself principle?
4. A particular instance of a class is called a(n) _____ .
5. Why should data members of a class be private?
6. Members of a class are qualified with the class name using the _____ operator.

7. Declaring a function to be _____ suggests to the compiler that it replace a function call with the actual code of the function.

8. A(n) _____ should be formulated and tested to ensure that a class's data members always contain valid values.

9. What are two aspects of constructing an object?

10. _____ are conditions that must be true before the function is called; _____ are conditions that must be true when the function terminates.

11. A(n) _____ constructor initializes the data members of an object to default values and a(n) _____ constructor initializes them to specific values supplied as arguments.

12. Functions can be overloaded provided they have different _____ .

13. Two default copy operations provided for all classes are copy in _____ and copy in _____ .

14. An operator Δ can be overloaded by defining a function with the name _____ .

15. Using a const reference parameter avoids making a copy of the corresponding argument but yet protects that argument from being changed. (True or false)

16. A _____ function is a nonmember function that can access a class's data members.

17. _____ compilation can be used to prevent a file from being included more than once.

✍ EXERCISES 3.2

1. The input operator >> was added to the Time class by making operator>>() a friend function. Make the necessary changes so that operator>>() calls an auxiliary member function Read(), in the same way that operator<<() called Display().

2. The less-than operator < was added to the Time class by making operator<() a member function. Make the necessary changes for operator<() being a nonmember function.

3. Using the approach for less-than in the text or that in Exercise 2, add the relational operator == to the class Time.

For Exercises 4–9, define the private portion of a class to model the given item.

4. Date for dates consisting of a month, day, and year

5. PhoneNumber for telephone numbers consisting of area code, local exchange, and number

6. Checker for the position of a checker on a board

7. CartesianPoint for a point (x, y) in a Cartesian coordinate system

8. PolarPoint for a point (r, θ) in a polar coordinate system

9. Card for cards in a deck of playing cards

10–15. Add appropriate operations to the classes in Exercises 4–9 and implement them with functions. To test these classes you should write driver programs as instructed in Programming Problems 6–11 at the end of this chapter.

For Exercises 16–18, develop a class for the given information, selecting operations that are appropriate for an object of that type. To test these classes you should write driver programs as instructed in Programming Problems 12–14 at the end of this chapter.

16. Information about a person: name, birthday, age, gender, social security number, height, weight, hair color, eye color, and marital status

17. Statistics about a baseball player: name, age, birthdate, position (pitcher, catcher, infielder, outfielder)

18. Weather statistics: date; city and state, province, or country; time of day; temperature; barometric pressure; weather conditions (clear skies, partly cloudy, cloudy, stormy)

For Exercises 19–21, write appropriate class declarations to describe the information in the specified file. See Programming Problems 12 and 13 at the end of Chap. 2 and the website described in the preface for descriptions of these files.

19. `StudentFile`

20. `InventoryFile`

21. `UserIdFile`

3.3 STRINGS AS ADTS

The word *compute* usually suggests arithmetic operations performed on numeric data; thus computers are sometimes thought to be mere "number crunchers," devices whose only purpose is to process numeric information. This is not the case, however, for in Chap. 2 we considered coding schemes used to represent characters and we also introduced some of C++'s capabilities for processing characters and strings.

String processing is an important part of many problems. For example, in processing employee information it might be necessary to store the name of each employee along with other information. A program for maintaining an inventory might require processing product names, names of manufacturers, their addresses, and so on. Many problems involve sequences of characters such as words and sentences in text-editing and word-processing, files and messages that must be encrypted for security and/or reliability, searching for words, phrases, and patterns in text files, and so on. As computers have evolved from number crunchers to general-purpose machines, the number of problems in which strings must be input, stored, processed, and output has increased. What is needed is a string data type in which string objects can store character strings and operate on them in various ways.

The operations needed to process strings vary from one problem to the next. However, in most text-editing and word-processing applications they include those listed in the following description of strings as an abstract data type (and usually more).

ADT STRING

Collection of Data Elements

A finite sequence of characters drawn from some given character set

Basic Operations

▸ Input & Output   Read and display strings

▸ Length   Find the number of characters in a string

▸ Compare   Determine if two strings are the same, or if one string precedes another in lexicographic order

▶ Concatenate	Join two strings together
▶ Copy	Copy a string or a substring of a given string to another string
▶ Find	Locate one string or a character within another
▶ Insert	Insert one string into another
▶ Delete	Delete part of a string
▶ Replace	Replace part of a string with another string

To illustrate these basic operations, suppose that *str1* is the string "en", *str2* is "list", and *str3* is "light". The length of *str1* is 2, the length of *str2* is 4, and the length of *str3* is 5. Because 'e' < 'l', *str1* < *str2*. In comparing *str3* with *str2*, we search from the left for the first nonmatching characters and find 's' > 'g', which means that *str2* > *str3*. The concatenation of *str1* with *str2* is

"enlist"

and the concatenation of *str2* with *str1* is

"listen"

and the concatenation of *str1* with *str3* with *str1* gives

"enlighten"

Copying the substring of *str2* of length 2 beginning at the second character gives the string

"is"

and replacing this substring with "aria" gives

"lariat"

C-STYLE IMPLEMENTATION OF STRINGS

The C programming language does not provide a predefined string data type but it does provide some string-processing capabilities, which are thus part of C++. Because a C++ programmer is likely to see some of these features in older programs and perhaps use them in a program where the full-blown C++ standard `string` type isn't needed, we will take a quick look at this C-style implementation of strings.

Recall that implementing a data structure requires (1) choosing appropriate storage structures to store the data items and (2) designing algorithms to carry out the basic operations and relations. Thus we begin by looking first at the storage structure.

STORAGE STRUCTURE.   Because strings are finite sequences of characters, it seems natural to use arrays of characters for storing strings. As we saw in Sec. 2.3, C uses `char` arrays to store strings, but appends a null character \0 at the end of the string. For example, the definitions

```
char animal[10] = "elephant",
     bird[] = "robin";
```

construct the `char` array `animal` with 10 elements initialized with the characters in the string `elephant` followed by two null characters,

animal | e | l | e | p | h | a | n | t | \0 | \0 |
       | [0] | [1] | [2] | [3] | [4] | [5] | [6] | [7] | [8] | [9] |

and the `char` array `bird` with six elements initialized with the characters in the string `robin` followed by a null character:

bird | r | o | b | i | n | \0 |
     | [0] | [1] | [2] | [3 | [4] | [5] |

FUNCTIONS FOR BASIC OPERATIONS.   String-processing functions can use this null character to find the end of the string. For example, the statements

```
for (int i = 0; animal[i] != '\0'; i++)
    cout << animal[i];
```

can be used to output the eight characters stored in `animal` without displaying whatever characters (perhaps blanks or garbage characters) are in the remaining array locations. Implementation of several of the other basic string operations such as find, insert, delete, and replace are similar in their use of the subscript operator `[]` to access individual positions in the array and the null character to detect the end of the string stored in the array. Functions for these operations are left as exercises.

Character arrays can be output in C++ using the output operator. For example, the statement

```
cout << animal;
```

produces the same output as the preceding `for` loop. They can be input using the input operator. For example, the statement

```
cin >> animal;
```

can be used to input a string into `animal`. The input operator first skips leading white space (unless the format manipulator `noskipws` has been used). It then extracts characters from `cin` storing them in the `char` array `animal` until the end of the file is reached or a white-space character is encountered, which will not be removed from the `istream`. After this, it terminates the string with a null character. Thus if we input

```
tom cat
```

the value read for `animal` will be

```
tom
```

If the input statement is encountered again, the space preceding `cat` will be skipped and the string `cat` read and assigned to `animal`.

Because `>>` continues to read characters until the end of the file or white-space is encountered, the array can overflow. Thus reading into a `string` variable is usually preferred. An alternative is to use the `istream` member function `width()` to set the maximum number of characters to be read by the next `>>`. For example, for

```
cin.width(10);
cin >> animal;
```

no more than 9 characters will be read from `cin` for `animal`. (Remember that space is reserved for the terminating null character.)

Other input functions that can be used are the `istream` member functions `get()`, `getline()`, `read()`, and `readsome()`, and the member function `write()` can be used for output. Many other string operations listed earlier in our ADT description of a string are implemented by C-style functions provided in the C++ library `<cstring>`. Other useful string-processing functions are the conversion functions in `<cstdlib>` and the character-processing functions from `<cctype>`. These functions are all described in Appendix C.[9]

A STRING CLASS

To design an OOP string type we could design a class `Strings` that uses a `char` array as one of its data members to store the string's characters and various string-processing member functions to operate internally on these data members:

```
/***** Strings.h *****/

class Strings
{
/*** Prototypes of member and friend
     string-processing functions ***/
public:
   . . .

/*** Data Members ***/
private:
  static const int STRING_LIMIT = . . . ;
  char myStorage[STRING_LIMIT];

};  // end of class declaration
```

---

[9]The C++ standard specifies that a library provided in C with a name of the form `<lib.h>` be renamed in C++ as `<clib>` in which the prefix c is attached and the extension `.h` is dropped. In particular, C's string library `<string.h>` is renamed `<cstring>`. Early versions of C++ libraries also were named with the `.h` extension; for example, `<iostream.h>`, which has the new name `<iostream>`. Many versions of C++ support both names and some programmers still use them. One must be careful, however; including `<string.h>` in a program will include the C string library and *not* the C++ string library.

To implement the length operation we could have a member function `Length()` search `myStorage` for a terminating null character, which we would ensure is placed at the end of each string by all constructors and other operations that modify the string:

```
int i = 0;
for (; myStorage[i] != '\0'; i++);
return i;
```

Or we could simply have `Length()` call the C function `strlen()`,

```
return strlen(myStorage);
```

which would perform a similar search for the null character. For efficiency, we might add a `myLength` data member that gets updated whenever the string gets modified. The `Length()` member function then becomes a simple accessor function.

Like the length operation, there are different algorithms that can be used to implement the other basic string operations. To illustrate, consider a function for the find operation:

```
/*--- Find the position of a substring in a Strings object.
 *
 *   Receive: str, a Strings object, and the Strings object
 *            containing this function (implicitly)
 *   Return:  The index of the first occurrence of str in
 *            this Strings object (-1 if it is not present)
 ************************************************************/
int Find(const Strings & str) const;
```

As an illustration of a "brute force" implementation of this operation, suppose we wish to find the index of `str1` = 'abcabd' in `str2` = 'abcabcabdabba'. The search for `str1` in `str2` begins at the first position of each. The first five characters match but a mismatch occurs when the next characters are compared:

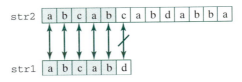

We then backtrack and start the search over again at the second character in `str2`:

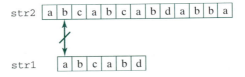

A mismatch occurs immediately, so we must backtrack again and restart the search with the third character in `str2`:

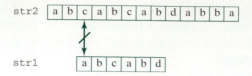

Once again a mismatch occurs, so we must backtrack again and restart at the fourth character in str2:

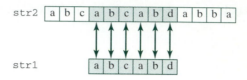

Now the six characters in str1 match the corresponding characters in positions three through eight in str2.

The following function implements this brute force approach. It is not very efficient but a more efficient algorithm is described in Sec. 3.7.

```cpp
/***** Strings.cpp *****/

int Strings::Find(const Strings & str) const
{
   int i = j = index = 0;
   /* index i runs through str.myStorage,
      j through the current object's myStorage,
      index keeps track of starting position of
         str.myStorage in current object's myStorage */

   while (i < str.Length()) && j < Length()
   {
      if (str.myStorage[i] == myStorage[j])
      {                        // continue matching
         j++;
         i++;
      }
      else                     // backtrack and start over
      {                        // at next position of
         index++;              // current object's myStorage
         j = index;
         i = 0;
      }
   }

   if (i == str.Length()) // str found
      return index;
   else
      return -1;              // str not found
}
```

Functions for the other basic string operations can also be written. Some of them, like `Length()`, are easy if we use the C string-processing functions. We leave these functions as exercises.

One problem with this version of a `Strings` class is that the data member `myStorage` used for the actual string characters has a fixed size, which means that we run the risk of array overflow when strings grow and we waste memory when we make `STRING_LIMIT` large enough to handle long strings and then process strings that are small. The usual way to circumvent this weakness is to use *run-time* arrays for which memory is allocated during execution rather than before execution at compile time. This makes it possible to construct `Strings` objects with small `myStorage` members and when necessary, allocate a larger array during program execution, copy the string from `myStorage` into it, delete the array currently allocated for `myStorage`, and then assign the new array to it. The details of run-time arrays are described in Sec. 8.5. Another approach is to use a *linked list* for the storage structure, perhaps only for long strings, which can grow with no upper limit (except available memory) and shrink with no memory waste. Linked lists are considered in Chap. 8.

Developing a complete `Strings` class that provides dynamic storage for strings is somewhat tedious, but not difficult. We shall not build such a class, however, because the recent C++ standard includes a standard `string` class that provides a large collection of string operations, and it doesn't make sense for us to "reinvent the wheel." Of course, someone using an older C++ compiler that does not provide the standard C++ `string` class may find it necessary to construct a string class. But if this standard `string` class is available, we would construct our own string class only in problems where only a few of the string operations are needed and the extended capabilities of the standard `string` class are deemed unnecessary overkill or when different string operations are needed (see Sec. 3.6). At the other end of the spectrum, if a problem needs more operations than the standard `string` class provides, we can derive a new class from it and add the new operations.

The next section describes the standard C++ `string` class in detail. We will use this class in this text for most of the examples that require string processing.

✍ EXERCISES 3.3

Exercises 1–6 ask you to write functions for some of the basic string operations listed in the ADT specification for a string type at the beginning of this section. In these exercises, assume that these will be for the last version of the class `Strings` described in this section. To test these functions you should write driver programs as instructed in Programming Problems 15–20 at the end of this chapter.

1. The compare operation
2. The concatenate operation
3. The copy operation
4. The insert operation
5. The delete operation
6. The replace operation

7. The array-based implementation of strings described in this section wastes space when processing dynamic strings whose lengths vary considerably. An alternative implementation is to establish some "work-space" array `storage` to store the characters of strings to be processed and then represent each string as a struct or class whose fields are indices `start` and `length`, which specify where in `storage` the string is stored. For example, if `s` is a string variable with `s.start = 10` and `s.length = 8`, the string of characters for `s`, "`John  Doe`", can be found in positions 10 through $10 + 8 - 1 = 17$ of `storage`:

storage

Write a class declaration with the data members needed for this work-space storage structure for a strings type. (Member or friend functions for the basic operations are added in the following exercises.)

8. The work space in Exercise 7 must be managed in some appropriate way. Devise a scheme for doing this.

For Exercises 9–18, write functions for the class in Exercises 7 and 8 for the basic string operation. For each, tell where the function's prototype and the function's definition are to placed—inside the class declaration, in the class header file but after the class declaration, in the class's implementation file, and so on. Be sure to document your functions carefully and completely. To test these functions you should write driver programs as instructed in Programming Problems 21–30 at the end of this chapter.

9. The output operation

10. The input operation

11. The length operation

12. The compare operation

13. The concatenate operation

14. The copy operation

15. The find operation

16. The insert operation

17. The delete operation

18. The replace operation

3.4 THE C++ STRING TYPE

In the preceding section we described how strings can be processed using `char` arrays (ala C), and we also described how a self-contained class could be constructed for a string type. But as we noted, there usually is no need to build our own string class because one is provided in the C++ library `<string>`.[10] In this section we will describe the main operations of this `string` class.

[10]The class `string` is really a specialization of the class template `basic_string` to type `char`. Also, see Footnote 8 regarding the name of this class library.

DEFINITIONS AND CONSTRUCTORS

There are several different ways that a string object can be defined. In addition to the default constructor there are constructors that initialize the object with another string object, with a char array or part of it, or with copies of a character.

`string s;`	Constructs s as an empty string
`string s(str_ca);`	Initializes s to contain a copy of `string` or `char` array `str_ca`
`string s(ca, n);`	Initializes s to contain a copy of the first n characters in char array `ca`
`string s(str, pos, n);`	Initializes s to contain a copy of the n characters in `string` str, starting at position pos; if n is too large, characters are copied only to the end of `str`
`string s(n, ch);`	Initializes s to contain n copies of the character `ch`

For example, in the definitions

```
char vowels[] = "aeiou";
string name1,  name2(""), name3 = "",
       s("abcdefghijklmn"),
       s1(vowels, 3),
       s2(s), s3(s, 2), s4(s, 2, 5),
       snore(10, 'z');
```

the first three construct `name1`, `name2`, and `name3` as `string` objects and initialize them with the **empty string**, which contains no characters. A literal for the empty string can be written as two consecutive double quotes (`""`). The last six declarations construct `string` objects s, s1, s2, s3, s4, and `snore` and initialize them to contain the following strings:

```
s:     abcdefghijklmn
s1:    aei
s2:    abcdefghijklmn
s3:    cdefghijklmn
s4:    cdefg
snore: zzzzzzzzzz
```

STORAGE

A `string` object must store the individual characters that make up the string value it represents. Some implementations use `char` arrays for short strings and dynamic storage structures for longer strings that grow and shrink because of frequent insertions and deletions. Exactly what the storage structure for strings is and how it is managed is implementation-dependent. There are, however, `string` member functions that provide some information about it; others are described in Appendix D. In these descriptions, s is of type `string`:

`s.capacity()`	Returns the capacity of the storage allocated in s
`s.size(),s.length()`	Returns the length of s
`s.empty()`	Returns `true` if s contains no characters, `false` otherwise
`s.max_size()`	Returns the maximum length of s

INPUT/OUTPUT

String input and output are quite similar to input and output for other types of objects. The output operator << can be used to display `string` literals and expressions. Input can be accomplished by using the input operator >> or the nonmember function `getline()`. In the descriptions of these operations, `ostr` is an `ostream`, `istr` is an `istream`, and s is a `string`:

`ostr << s`	Inserts characters of s into `ostr`; returns `ostr`
`istr >> s`	Extracts characters from `istr` and stores them in s until `s.max_size()` characters have been extracted, the end of file occurs, or a white-space character is encountered, in which case *the white-space character is not removed* from `istr`; returns `istr`
`getline(istr, s, term)`	Extracts characters from `istr` and stores them in s until `s.max_size()` characters have been extracted, the end of file occurs, or character `term` is encountered, in which case `term` *is extracted from* `istr` *but is not stored in* s. If `term` is omitted, `'\n'` is used.

To illustrate, consider the statements

```
cin >> name1;
cout << "name1: " << name1 << endl;
```

If we input the string `A1-Ley-Cat`, the output produced will be

```
name1: A1-Ley-Cat
```

If we replace the dashes with spaces, however, and input the string `A1 Ley Cat`, the output produced will be

```
name1: A1
```

because the input operator >> stops reading characters when the blank is encountered; the rest of the input (`" Ley Cat"`) is left in the input stream `cin` and will be read in subsequent input statements.

By contrast, if we use the same inputs for the statements

```
getline(cin, name2)
cout << "name2: " << name2 << endl;
```

the output produced in the first case will be

```
name2: Al-Ley-Cat
```

and in the second case,

```
name2: Al Ley Cat
```

because `getline()` reads an entire line of input.

Care must be taken when using both `>>` and `getline()`. For example, consider the statements

```
cin >> name1;
cout << "name1: " << name1 << endl;
getline(cin, name2)
cout << "name2: " << name2 << endl;
getline(cin, name3);
cout << "name3: " << name3 << endl;
```

If we input

```
Al Ley Cat
Road Runner
```

the output produced will be

```
name1: Al
name2: Ley Cat
name3: Road Runner
```

However, if we input

```
Al
Ley Cat
Road Runner
```

the output produced will be

```
name1: Al
name2:
name3: Ley Cat
```

Input stops when `>>` encounters the end-of-line character following `Al`, but it *does not remove it from the input stream* `cin`. Consequently, when `getline()` attempts to read a line for `name2`, it encounters the end of line immediately, and assigns an empty string to `name2`. To remove the end-of-line character (and characters preceding it), we could use `ignore`:

```
cin.ignore(80, '\n');
```

STRING STREAMS

The streams we have considered up to now have been connected to input and output devices or to files. It is also possible to connect a stream to a `string` and to read input from the string or to write output to it. This is made possible by means of **string streams** defined in the `<sstream>` library:[11]

`istringstream`	For input from a string
`ostringstream`	For output to a string
`stringstream`	For input from and output to a string

The member function `str()` can be used to convert a `string` to a string stream and vice versa:

`strstream.str(s);`	Set string stream `strstream` to a copy of `string` `s`
`str(strstream)`	Returns a `string` that is a copy of the string in `strstream`

The short program in Fig. 3.12 is a simple demonstration of string streams. It constructs an `istringstream` from the `string date`, uses the input operator `>>` to read the individual words and integers, and displays these on separate lines. This should indicate that one use for `istringstream`s is to input a string and then parse it. The program then produces some formatted output to the `ostringstream ostr` and then uses `str()` to make a copy of the string in an `ostream` and in an `ofstream`. This illustrates how we can do some rather elaborate formatting one time, outputting it to a string, from where it can be output anywhere we might want.

FIGURE 3.12   STRING STREAMS

```
#include <iostream>
#include <fstream>
#include <iomanip>
#include <cassert>
#include <sstream>
using namespace std;

int main()
{
  string date = "Independence Day:  July 4, 1776";

  istringstream istr(date);

  string word1, word2, month;
  int day, year;
  char comma;
```

---

[11]The corresponding types for wide characters (of type `wchar_t`) are `wistringstream`, `wostringstream`, and `wstringstream`.

```
istr >> word1 >> word2 >> month >> day >> comma >> year;
cout << "Contents of string stream istr, one word per line:\n"
     << word1 << endl << word2 << endl << month << endl
     << day << comma << endl << year << endl << endl;

int one = 1;
ofstream outfile("file3-12.out");
assert(outfile.is_open());

ostringstream ostr;

ostr << "New Year's " << word2 << "  January"
     << setw(2) << one << ", " << year + 224 << endl;
cout << ostr.str();
outfile << ostr.str();
}
```

EXECUTION:

```
Contents of string stream istr, one word per line:
Independence
Day:
July
4,
1776

New Year's Day:   January 1, 2000
```

LISTING OF FILE `file3-12.out`:

```
New Year's Day:   January 1, 2000
```

MODIFIERS

In our description of a string as an ADT, we listed concatenation, insertion, deletion, and replacement as basic string operations that combine or modify strings. The concatenation operation is provided in `string` by the (overloaded) + operator, and the others by member functions, the common forms of which are given here (see Appendix D for others). s, t, and `str` are `strings`, ca is a `char` array, str_ca is a string or a `char` array, ch is a character, and n, n1, n2, pos1, and pos2 are integers.

`s + t,  t + s`	Returns the result of concatenating s and t; t may be a string, a character array, or a character
`s.append(str_ca)`	Appends str_ca at the end of s; returns s
`s.append(ca, n)`	Appends the first n characters in ca at the end of s; returns s
`s.append(n, ch)`	Appends n copies of ch at the end of s; returns s

`s.insert(pos, str)`	Inserts a copy of `str` into `s` at position `pos`; returns `s`
`s.insert(pos1, str, pos2, n)`	Inserts a copy of `n` characters of `str` starting at position `pos2` into `s` at position `pos1`; if `n` is too large, characters are copied only until the end of `str` is reached; returns `s`
`s.insert(pos, ca, n)`	Inserts a copy of the first `n` characters of `ca` into `s` at position `pos`; inserts all of its characters if `n` is omitted; returns `s`
`s.insert(pos, n, ch)`	Inserts `n` copies of the character `ch` into `s` at position `pos`; returns `s`
`s.erase(pos, n)`	Removes `n` characters from `s`, beginning at position `pos` (default value 0); returns `s`
`s.replace(pos1, n1, str)`	Replaces the substring of `s` of length `n1` beginning at position `pos1` with `str`; if `n1` is too large, all characters to the end of `s` are replaced; returns `s`
`s.replace(pos1, n1, ca, n2)`	Replaces a substring of `s` as before but with the first `n2` characters in `ca`; returns `s`
`s.swap(str)`	Swaps the contents of `s` and `str`; return type is `void`
`swap(str1, str2)`	Swaps the contents of `str1` and `str2`; return type is `void`

COPIERS

There are several operations that make copies of a string or a part of a string. Some of these, such as the assignment operator, assign this copy to another `string` object. (See Appendix D for other forms of these operations.) `s`, `ca`, `str_ca`, `pos`, `n`, and `ch` are as before.

`s = val`	Assigns a copy of `val` to `s`; `val` may be a string, a character array, or a character
`s += val`	Appends a copy of `val` to `s`; `val` may be a string, a character array, or a character
`s.assign(str_ca)`	Assigns a copy of `str_ca` to `s`; returns `s`
`s.assign(ca, n)`	Assigns to `s` a string consisting of the first `n` characters in `ca`; returns `s`
`s.assign(n, ch)`	Assigns to `s` a string consisting of `n` copies of `ch`; returns `s`
`s.substr(pos, n)`	Returns a copy of the substring consisting of `n` characters from `s`, beginning at position `pos` (default value 0)

ACCESSING INDIVIDUAL CHARACTERS

The (overloaded) subscript operator `operator[]()` and the member function `at()` can be used to access the character at a specified position in a string (counting from 0).

> `s[i]`   Returns a reference to the character at position `i` in string `s`. No exception is raised if `i` is out of range.
>
> `s.at(i)`   Returns a reference to the character at position `i` in string `s`. An out-of-range exception is raised if `i` is out of range.

The subscript operator does not check for out-of-range indices, but `at()` does. For example, the out-of-range error in the following example will be caught:

```
string s = "ABCDE";
int i = 5;
try
{
    cout << s.at(i) << endl;
}
catch (out_of_range)
{
    cout << "Out-of-range error\n";
}
cout << "Done checking\n";
```

The output produced will be

```
Out-of-range error
Done checking
```

The out-of-range error message will not be displayed, however, if `s.at(i)` is replaced by `s[i]`. If the definition of `i` is changed to

```
int i = 4;
```

the output produced will be

```
E
Done checking
```

SEARCH OPERATIONS

The `string` class provides a plethora of operations for locating strings and individual characters in a string. The following are some of the forms of these search operations; see Appendix D for others; `str_ca_ch` is a `string`, `char` array, or a `char`; `s`, `pos`, `n`, are `ch` are as before.

> `s.find(str_ca_ch, pos)`   Returns the first position ≥ `pos` such that the next `str.size()` characters of `s` match those in `str_ca_ch`; returns `npos` if there is no such position; 0 is the default value for `pos`

s.find_first_of (str_ca_ch, pos)	Returns the first position $\geq$ pos of a character in s that matches any character in str_ca_ch; returns npos if there is no such position; 0 is the default value for pos
s.find_first_not_of (str_ca_ch, pos)	Returns the first position $\geq$ pos of a character in s that does not match any of the characters in str_ca_ch; returns npos if there is no such position; 0 is the default value for pos
s.find_last_of (str_ca_ch, pos)	Returns the highest position $\leq$ pos of a character in s that matches any character in str_ca_ch; returns npos if there is no such position; npos is the default value for pos
s.find_last_not_of (str_ca_ch, pos)	Returns the highest position $\leq$ pos of a character in s that does not match any character in str_ca_ch; returns npos if there is no such position; npos is the default value for pos
s.rfind(str_ca_ch, pos)	Returns the highest position $\leq$ pos such that the next str_ca_ch.size() characters of s match those in str_ca_ch; returns npos if there is no such position; npos is the default value for pos

Here are a few examples that illustrate these functions:

```
s = "abcdeabcdeabcdeABCDE";
cout << "s: " << s << endl;

cout << "s.find(\"cde\"): "
    << s.find("cde") << endl;

cout << "s.rfind(\"cde\"): "
    << s.rfind("cde") << endl;

cout << "s.find_first_of(\"udu\"): "
    << s.find_first_of("udu")
    << "\ns.find_first_of(\"udu\", 5): "
    << s.find_first_of("udu", 5) << endl;

cout << "s.find_last_of(\"udu\"): "
    << s.find_last_of("udu")
    << "\ns.find_last_of(\"udu\", 10): "
    << s.find_last_of("udu", 10) << endl;

cout << "s.find_first_of(\"usurp\"): "
    << s.find_first_of("usurp")
    << "\n*** NOTE:  string::npos = "
    << string::npos << endl;

cout << "s.find_first_not_of(\"udead\"): "
    << s.find_first_not_of("udead") << endl;

cout << "s.find_last_not_of(\"udead\"): "
    << s.find_last_not_of("udead") << endl;
```

They produce the following output:

```
s: abcdeabcdeabcdeABCDE
s.find("cde"): 2
s.rfind("cde"): 12
s.find_first_of("udu"): 3
s.find_first_of("udu", 5): 8
s.find_last_of("udu"): 13
s.find_last_of("udu", 10): 8
s.find_first_of("usrp"): 4294967295
*** NOTE:  string::npos = 4294967295
s.find_first_not_of("udead"): 1
s.find_last_not_of("udead"): 19
```

COMPARISONS

All of the usual relational operators are overloaded in the `string` class; `string`s may be compared with other `string`s or with C-style strings (i.e., `char` arrays.) Also, a `compare()` function is provided that is similar to the C function `strcmp()` but which may also be used to compare parts of strings. Some common forms of these operations are as follows (see Appendix D for others); s, t, and str_ca are as before.

`s < t, t < s`	Returns `true` or `false` as determined by the relational
`s <= t, t <= s`	operator; t may be a string or a character array
`s > t, t > s`	
`s >= t, t >= s`	
`s == t, t == s`	
`s != t, t != s`	
`s.compare(str_ca)`	Returns a negative value, 0, or a positive value according as s is less than, equal to, or greater than str_ca

string AND C-STYLE STRINGS

Some problems require a C-style string instead of a `string` object. For example, the name supplied to the `open()` operation for the file streams `ifstream`, `ofstream`, and `fstream` must be a string literal or a string stored in a `char` array. The C++ `string` class provides three member functions to convert a `string` object s into a C-style string:

`s.c_str()`	Returns a `char` array containing the characters stored in s, terminated by a null character
`s.data()`	Returns a `char` array containing the characters stored in s, but not terminated by a null character
`s.copy(charArray, pos, n)`	Replaces `charArray` with n characters from s, starting at position `pos` or at position 0, if `pos` is omitted; if n is too large, characters are copied only until the end of s is reached; returns the number of characters copied

✔ Quick Quiz 3.4

1. To store strings, C uses a(n) _____ array with a(n) _____ appended at the end.
2. " " is a(n) _____ string.
3. A(n) _____ can be used to connect a stream to a `string` and to read input from the string or to write output to it.

Questions 4–17 assume the declarations
```
string s1,
       s2 = "neu",
       s3 = "roses are red";
```
and that the data entered for input operations is
```
The cat in the hat
```

4. `s1.size()` = _____, `s2.size()` = _____, `s3.size()` = _____

5. `cin >> s1;` will assign _____ to s1

6. `getline(cin, s1);` will assign _____ to s1

7. After `s1 = s2 + s3;` is executed, s1 will have the value _____.

8. `s2[1]` = _____

9. `s2.append("tron")` = _____

10. After `s3.insert("colo", 10)` is executed, s3 will have the value _____.

11. `s3.erase(4, s3.length()-4)` = _____

12. `s3.replace(0, 1, s2.substr(0,1))` = _____

13. `s3.find("re")` = _____.

14. `s3.find_first_of(s2)` = _____

15. `s2 < s3.` (True or false)

16. `s3.compare(s2)` = _____

✍ Exercises 3.4

The following exercises ask you to write functions to do various kinds of string processing. To test these functions you should write driver programs as instructed in Programming Problems 31–41 at the end of this chapter.

1. Write a function to count occurrences of a string in another string.

2. Write a function that accepts the number of a month and returns the name of the month.

3. Write a function that accepts the name of a month and returns the number of the month.

4. Write a function that, given a string of lowercase and uppercase letters, returns a copy of the string in all lowercase letters; and another function that, given a string of lowercase and uppercase letters, returns a copy of the string in all uppercase letters. (*Hint:* Use the functions provided in <cctype>.)

5. Write a function `replace_all()`, such that a call
```
newString = replace_all(str, substring, newSubstring);
```
will return a copy of string *str* with each occurrence of *substring* replaced by *newSubstring*.

6.   Write a function that, given the three components of a name (the first name, middle name or initial, and last name), returns a single string consisting of the last name, followed by a comma, and then the first name and middle initial. For example, given "John", "Quincy", and "Doe", the function should return the string "Doe, John Q.".

7.   Proceed as in Exercise 6, but design the function to accept a single string object consisting of a first name, a middle name or initial, and a last name. As before, the function should return a single string consisting of the last name, followed by a comma, and then the first name and middle initial. For example, given "John Quincy Doe", the function should return the string "Doe, John Q.".

8.   Write a function that reads a string of digits, possibly preceded by + or −, and converts this string to the integer value it represents. Be sure that your function checks that the string is well formed, that is, that it represents a valid integer. (*Hint:* Use the functions provided in `<cctype>` and `<cstdlib>`.)

9.   Proceed as in Exercise 8, but for strings representing real numbers in either decimal or scientific form.

10. A `string` is said to be a palindrome if it does not change when the order of its characters is reversed. For example,

```
madam
463364
ABLE WAS I ERE I SAW ELBA
```

are palindromes. Write a function that, given a string, returns true if that string is a palindrome and returns false otherwise.

11. Write a function that accepts two strings and determines whether one string is an *anagram* of the other, that is, whether one string is a permutation of the characters in the other string. For example, "dear" and "dare" are anagrams of "read."

3.5   AN EXAMPLE: TEXT EDITING

The preparation of textual material such as letters, books, and computer programs often involves the insertion, deletion, and replacement of parts of the text. The software of most computer systems includes an **editor** or **word processor** that makes it easy to carry out these operations. These and other text-editing operations can often be performed by using the basic string operations. The simple command-driven text-editor program in Fig. 3.13 illustrates this.

A C-style `char` array COMMAND_MENU for the menu of editing commands is used rather than a `string` simply because the only operation performed on COMMAND_MENU is output; the C function `toupper()` is used to convert commands to uppercase; and C++'s standard `string` data type is used to process the file names and lines of text.

In the design of this program, the following objects and operations were identified:

OBJECTS

COMMAND_MENU (`char` array):	menu of editing commands (insert, delete, replace, length, position, get a new line of text, quit)
inFileName, outFileName (`string`):	file names

inFile, outFile, cout, cin:	streams to these files, to the screen, from the keyboard
line, str1, str2 (string):	line of text to be edited and strings used in editing
command (char):	editing command
position, numChars (int):	position in a string; how many characters to delete

OPERATIONS

Open streams to files
I/O of strings from/to files, from keyboard, to the screen
String editing operations: insert, delete, replace, length, position

The algorithm for using these objects and operations is straightforward:

ALGORITHM FOR TEXT-EDITING

1. Get inFileName; construct outFileName; and open streams inFile and outFile.

2. Display COMMAND_MENU.

3. Read line from inFile and display it on the screen.

4. Repeat the following:

    a. Terminate repetition if the end of the file has been reached.

    b. Get command, convert it to uppercase, and do the appropriate processing:

        L: Display length of line

        P: Find and display position of str1 in line

        I: Insert str1 in line at position

        D: Delete numChars characters starting at position − 1

        R: Find str1 in line at position; replace it with str2

        N: Output line to outFile and read new line from inFile

        Q: Output line to outFile; repeatedly read new line from inFile and output line to outFile until the end of inFile is reached

        Otherwise, display an error message

    c. If the end of the file has not been reached, display the edited line.

5. Display an "editing complete" message.

FIGURE 3.13   TEXT EDITING

```
/* This program performs several basic text-editing operations
 * on lines of text read from a file; after editing has been
 * completed, each line is written to a new file whose name
 * is that of the input file with the suffix ".out" appended.
 *
 * Input (keyboard): names of files, editing commands
 * Input (file):     lines of text
 * Output (screen):  a menu of editing commands, unedited and edited
 *                   lines of text
 * Output (file):    edited lines of text
 ------------------------------------------------------------------*/
```

```cpp
#include <iostream>
#include <fstream>
#include <string>
using namespace std;

int main()
{
  const char COMMAND_MENU[] =
        "Editing commands are:\n"
        "   L      : Determine the length of current line\n"
        "   P str : Find position (counting from 0) of string str\n"
        "   I str : Insert string str\n"
        "   D p n : Delete n characters beginning at position p\n"
        "   R str : Replace substring str with another string\n"
        "   N      : Get next line of text\n"
        "   Q      : Quit editing\n";

  string inFileName,
         outFileName;
  cout << "Enter the name of the input file: ";
  getline(cin, inFileName);
  outFileName = inFileName;
  outFileName.append(".out");
  ifstream inFile(inFileName.data());
  ofstream outFile(outFileName.data());
  if (!inFile.is_open() || !outFile.is_open())
  {
    cerr << "Error in opening files.";
    exit(-1);
  }
  cout << COMMAND_MENU << endl
       << "Enter an editing command following each prompt >\n";
  char command;              // editing command
  string line,               // line of text to be edited
         str1, str2;          // strings used in editing
  int position,              // position of a string in line
      numChars;              // number of characters to delete

  getline(inFile, line);
  cout << line << endl;
  for (;;)
  {
    if (inFile.eof()) break;

    cout << '>';
    cin >> command;
    switch(toupper(command))
    {
      case 'L' : cout << "Length = " << line.length() << endl;
                 break;
```

```
        case 'P' : cin.ignore(1); getline(cin, str1);
                   position = line.find(str1);
                   if (position != string::npos)
                     cout << "Position is " << 1 + position << endl;
                   else
                     cout << str1 << " not found\n";
                   break;
        case 'I' : cin.ignore(1); getline(cin, str1);
                   cout << "Insert where? ";
                   cin >> position;
                   line.insert(position - 1, str1);
                   break;
        case 'D' : cin >> position >> numChars;
                   line.erase(position, numChars);
                   break;
        case 'R' : cin.ignore(1); getline(cin, str1);
                   position = line.find(str1);
                   if (position == string::npos)
                   {
                     cout << str1 << " not found\n";
                     break;
                   }
                   cout << "With what? ";
                   getline(cin, str2);
                   line.replace(position, str1.length(), str2);
                   break;
        case 'N' : outFile << line << endl;
                   getline(inFile, line);
                   cout << "\nNext line:\n";
                   break;
        case 'Q' : outFile << line << endl;
                   for (;;)
                   {
                     getline(inFile, line);
                     if (inFile.eof()) break;
                     outFile << line << endl;
                   }
                   break;
        default :  cout << "\n*** Illegal command ***\n"
                        << COMMAND_MENU << line << endl;
      }// end of switch
    if (!inFile.eof())
      cout << line << endl;
  }
  cout << "\n*** Editing complete ***\n";
}
```

LISTING OF TEXT FILE USED IN SAMPLE RUN:

```
Foursscore and five years ago, our mothers
brought forth on continent
a new nation conceived in liberty and and dedicated
to the preposition that all men
are created equal.
```

SAMPLE RUN:

```
Enter the name of the input file: file3-13
Editing commands are:
   L     : Determine the length of current line
   P str : Find position (counting from 0) of string str
   I str : Insert string str
   D p n : Delete n characters beginning at position p
   R str : Replace substring str with another string
   N     : Get next line of text
   Q     : Quit editing

Enter an editing command following each prompt >
Foursscore and five years ago, our mothers
>D 4 1
Fourscore and five years ago, our mothers
>R five
With what? seven
Fourscore and seven years ago, our mothers
>r mo
With what? fa
Fourscore and seven years ago, our fathers
>N

Next line:
brought forth on continent
>P con
Position is 18
brought forth on continent
>I this
Insert where? 18
brought forth on this continent
>N

Next line:
a new nation conceived in liberty and and dedicated
>P and
Position is 35
a new nation conceived in liberty and and dedicated
>D 35 4
a new nation conceived in liberty and dedicated
```

```
>N

Next line:
to the preposition that all men
>R pre
With what? pro
to the proposition that all men

>N
Next line:
are created equal.
>N

Next line:

*** Editing complete ***
```

LISTING OF EDITED FILE (`file3-13.out`) PRODUCED:

```
Fourscore and seven years ago, our fathers
brought forth on this continent
a new nation conceived in liberty and dedicated
to the proposition that all men
are created equal.
```

3.6   DATA ENCRYPTION (OPTIONAL)

The basic string operations such as length, position, concatenate, copy, insert, and delete that we considered in the preceding section are the operations most useful in text-editing applications. There are, however, some important kinds of string processing that require other basic operations. In this section we consider one such application, data encryption, and the basic operations of *substitution* and *permutation* that are important in this application.

Encryption refers to the coding of information in order to keep it secret. Encryption is accomplished by transforming the string of characters comprising the information to produce a new string that is a coded form of the information. This is called a **cryptogram** or **ciphertext** and may be safely stored or transmitted. At a later time it can be deciphered by reversing the encrypting process to recover the original information, which is called **plaintext**.

Data encryption has been used to send secret military and political messages from the days of Julius Caesar to the present. Recent applications include the Washington-Moscow hotline, electronic funds transfer, electronic mail, database security, and many other situations in which the transmission of secret data is crucial. Less profound applications have included Captain Midnight secret decoder rings that could be obtained in the 1950s for twenty-five cents and two Ovaltine labels, puzzles appearing in the daily newspaper, and a number of other frivolous applications. In this section we describe some encryption schemes ranging from the Caesar cipher scheme of the first century B.C. to the Data Encryption Standard and the public key encryption schemes of the twentieth century.

The simplest encryption schemes are based on the string operation of **substitution,** in which the plaintext string is traversed and each character is replaced by some other character according to a fixed rule. For example, the **Caesar cipher** scheme consists of replacing each letter by the letter that appears k positions later in the alphabet for some integer k. (The alphabet is thought of as being arranged in a circle, with A following Z.) In the original Caesar cipher, k was 3, so that each occurrence of A in the plaintext was replaced by D, each B by E, . . ., each Y by B, and each Z by C. For example, using the character set

A B C D E F G H I J K L M N O P Q R S T U V W X Y Z

we would encrypt the string "IDESOFMARCH" as follows:

Plaintext: I D E S O F M A R C H
             ↓ ↓ ↓ ↓ ↓ ↓ ↓ ↓ ↓ ↓ ↓
Ciphertext: L G H V R I P D U F K

To decode the message, the receiver uses the same **key** k and recovers the plaintext by applying the inverse transformation, that is, by traversing the ciphertext string and replacing each character by the character k positions earlier in the alphabet. This is obviously not a very secure scheme, since it is possible to "break the code" by simply trying the 26 possible values for the key k.

An improved substitution operation is to use a **keyword** to specify several different displacements of letters rather than the single offset k of the Caesar cipher. In this **Vignère cipher** scheme, the same keyword is added character by character to the plaintext string, where each character is represented by its position in the character set and addition is carried out modulo 26. For example, suppose the character set and positions of characters are given by

Position	0	1	2	3	4	5	6	7	8	9	10	11	12
Character	A	B	C	D	E	F	G	H	I	J	K	L	M

	13	14	15	16	17	18	19	20	21	22	23	24	25
	N	O	P	Q	R	S	T	U	V	W	X	Y	Z

and that the keyword is DAGGER. The plaintext IDESOFMARCH is then encrypted as follows:

Plaintext: I D E S O F M A R C H
                     ↓ ↓ ↓ ↓ ↓ ↓ ↓ ↓ ↓ ↓ ↓
Repeated key word: D A G G E R D A G G E
                     ↓ ↓ ↓ ↓ ↓ ↓ ↓ ↓ ↓ ↓ ↓
Ciphertext: L D K Y S W P A X I L

Again, the receiver must know the key and recovers the plaintext by subtracting the characters in this keyword from those in the ciphertext.

A different substitution operation is to use a *substitution table,* for example:

Original character:	A	B	C	D	E	F	G	H	I	J	K	L	M
Substitute character:	Q	W	E	R	T	Y	U	I	O	P	A	S	D

	N	O	P	Q	R	S	T	U	V	W	X	Y	Z
	F	G	H	J	K	L	Z	X	C	V	B	N	M

The string IDESOFMARCH would then be encoded as follows:

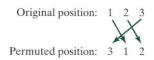

Plaintext: I D E S O F M A R C H

Ciphertext: O R T L G Y D Q K E I

To decode the ciphertext string, the receiver must again know the key, that is, the substitution table.

Since there are 26! (approximately 10^{28}) possible substitution tables, this scheme is considerably more secure than the simple Caesar cipher scheme. Experienced cryptographers can easily break the code, however, by analyzing frequency counts of certain letters and combinations of letters.

Another basic string operation in some encryption schemes is **permutation**, in which the characters in the plaintext or in blocks of the plaintext are rearranged. For example, we might divide the plaintext string into blocks (substrings) of size 3 and permute the characters in each block as follows:

Original position: 1 2 3

Permuted position: 3 1 2

Thus the message IDESOFMARCH is encrypted (after the addition of a randomly selected character X so that the string length is a multiple of the block length)

Plaintext: I D E S O F M A R C H X

Ciphertext: D E I O F S A R M H X C

To decode the ciphertext string, the receiver must know the key permutation and its inverse

Original position: 1 2 3
Permuted position: 2 3 1

DATA ENCRYPTION STANDARD

Most modern encryption schemes use both of these techniques, by combining several substitution and permutation operations. Perhaps the best known is the **Data Encryption Standard (DES)** developed in the early 1970s by the federal government and the IBM corporation. The scheme is described in *Federal Information Processing Standards Publication 46* (FIPS Pub 46)[12] and is outlined in Fig. 3.14, which is a diagram from this government publication.

---

[12]Copies of this publication can be obtained from the National Institute of Standards and Technology of the U.S. Department of Commerce.

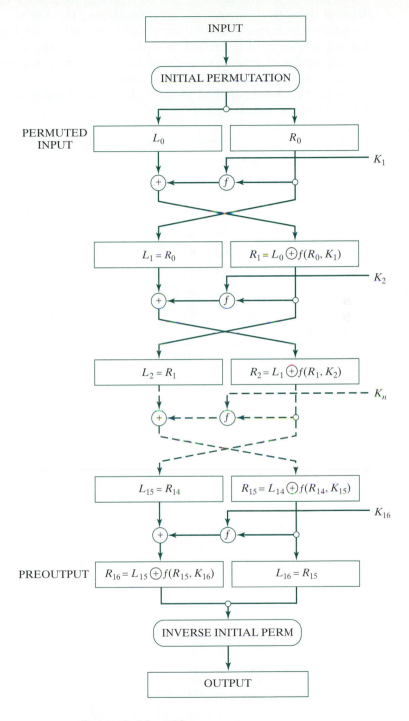

FIGURE 3–14   DES.

The input is a bit string of length 64 representing a block of characters in the plaintext string (for example, the concatenation of the ASCII codes of eight characters), and the output is a 64-bit string that is the ciphertext. The encryption is carried out as a series of permutations and substitutions. The substitution operations used are similar to those in earlier examples: Some are obtained by the addition of keywords and others use a substitution table.

The first operation applied to the 64-bit input string is an initial permutation (*IP*) given by the following table:

IP							
58	50	42	34	26	18	10	2
60	52	44	36	28	20	12	4
62	54	46	38	30	22	14	6
64	56	48	40	32	24	16	8
57	49	41	33	25	17	9	1
59	51	43	35	27	19	11	3
61	53	45	37	29	21	13	5
63	55	47	39	31	23	15	7

For example, the first bit in the permuted result is the fifty-eighth bit in the original string; the second bit is the fiftieth; and so on. This permuted string is then split into two 32-bit substrings: a left substring, denoted by L_0 in the diagram in Fig. 3.14, and a right substring, denoted by R_0. A **cipher function** denoted by f uses substitutions and a key K_1 to transform R_0 into a new 32-bit string denoted by $f(R_0, K_1)$. This string is then added to L_0 using bit-by-bit addition modulo 2 (that is, they are combined using the exclusive or operation $\oplus$) to produce the right substring R_1 at the next stage. The original R_0 becomes the left substring L_1.

This basic sequence of operations is performed 16 times with 16 different key strings $K_1, \ldots, K_{16}$, except that no "crossover" is performed at the last stage. These operations produce a 64-bit string $R_{16} L_{16}$ labeled "PREOUTPUT" in the diagram. The inverse of the initial permutation (IP^{-1}) is then applied to this preoutput string to yield the final ciphertext.

IP^{-1}							
40	8	48	16	56	24	64	32
39	7	47	15	55	23	63	31
38	6	46	14	54	22	62	30
37	5	45	13	53	21	61	29
36	4	44	12	52	20	60	28
35	3	43	11	51	19	59	27
34	2	42	10	50	18	58	26
33	1	41	9	49	17	57	25

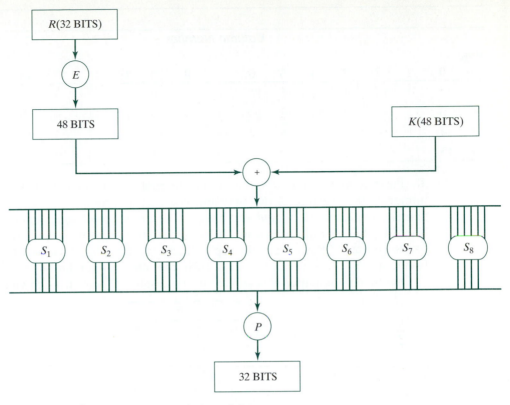

Figure 3–15   **Calculation of *f*(*R, K*).**

The details of the operation f are shown in Fig. 3.15. The right substring denoted by R is first expanded into a 48-bit string using the following bit-selection table E:

		E			
32	1	2	3	4	5
4	5	6	7	8	9
8	9	10	11	12	13
12	13	14	15	16	17
16	17	18	19	20	21
20	21	22	23	24	25
24	25	26	27	28	29
28	29	30	31	32	1

Thus the first 6-bit block consists of bits 32, 1, 2, 3, 4, and 5 of R; the second block consists of bits 4, 5, 6, 7, 8, and 9; and so on. A substitution operation is then applied to this 48-bit string by combining it with a 48-bit key string K using the exclusive or operation. Another substitution using a different table is then applied to each of the 6-bit blocks to produce 4-bit blocks so that the final result is again a 32-bit string. For example, the substitution table for S_1 is

							S_1								
							Column Number								
Row No.	0	1	2	3	4	5	6	7	8	9	10	11	12	13	14	15
0	14	4	13	1	2	15	11	8	3	10	6	12	5	9	0	7
1	0	15	7	4	14	2	13	1	10	6	12	11	9	5	3	8
2	4	1	14	8	13	6	2	11	15	12	9	7	3	10	5	0
3	15	12	8	2	4	9	1	7	5	11	3	14	10	0	6	13

To illustrate how it is used, suppose that the first 6-bit block is 101000. The binary numeral 10 consisting of the first and last bits determines a row in this table, namely, row 2, and the middle four bits 0100 determine a column, namely, column 4. The 4-bit binary representation 1101 of the entry 13 in the second row and the fourth column of this table is the replacement for this 6-bit block. Similar substitution tables $S_2, \ldots, S_8$ are used to transform the other seven 6-bit blocks.

One final permutation P is applied to the resulting 32-bit string to yield $f(R, K)$:

	P		
16	7	20	21
29	12	28	17
1	15	23	26
5	18	31	10
2	8	24	14
32	27	3	9
19	13	30	6
22	11	4	25

The 16 different keys used in DES are extracted in a carefully prescribed way from a single 64-bit key. Thus the user need supply only one key string to be used for encryption and decryption, rather than 16 different keys. The algorithm for decrypting ciphertext is the same as that for encryption, except that the 16 keys are applied in reverse order.

DES has been adopted by the National Institute of Standards and Technology (formerly the National Bureau of Standards) as the standard encryption scheme for sensitive federal documents. It has been the subject of some controversy, however, because of questions about whether the 48-bit keys used in the substitutions are long enough and the substitution keys are sophisticated enough to provide the necessary security.

PUBLIC-KEY ENCRYPTION

Each of the encryption schemes considered thus far requires that both the sender and the receiver know the key or keys used in encrypting the plaintext. This means that although the cryptogram may be transmitted through some public channel such as a telephone line that is not secure, the keys must be transmitted in some secure manner, for example, by a courier. This problem of maintaining secrecy of the key is compounded when it must be shared by several persons.

Recently developed encryption schemes eliminate this problem by using two keys, one for encryption and one for decryption. These schemes are called **public-key encryption schemes** because the encryption key is not kept secret. The keys used in these systems have the following properties:

1. For each encryption key there is exactly one corresponding decryption key, and it is distinct from the encryption key.

2. There are many such pairs of keys, and they are relatively easy to compute.

3. It is almost impossible to determine the decryption key if one knows only the encryption key.

4. The encryption key is made public by the receiver to all those who will transmit messages to him or her, but only the receiver knows the decryption key.

In 1978, Rivest, Shamir, and Adelman proposed one method of implementing a public key encryption scheme.[13] The public key is a pair (e, n) of integers, and one encrypts a message string M by first dividing M into blocks $M_1, M_2, \ldots, M_k$ and converting each block M_i of characters to an integer P_i in the range 0 through $n - 1$ (for example, by concatenating the ASCII codes of the characters). M is then encrypted by raising each block to the power e and reducing modulo n:

$$\text{Plaintext:} \quad M = M_1 M_2 \cdots M_k \rightarrow P_1 P_2 \cdots P_k$$
$$\text{Ciphertext:} \quad C = C_1 C_2 \ldots C_k, \quad C_i = P_i^e \% n$$

(Here % is the mod operator in C++.) The cipher text C is decrypted by raising each block C_i to the power d and reducing modulo n, where d is a secret decryption key. Clearly, to recover the plaintext, we need

$$P_i = C_i^d \% n = (P_i^e)^d \% n = P_i^{e \cdot d} \% n$$

for each block P_i. Thus e and d must be chosen so that

$$x^{e \cdot d} \% n = x$$

for each nonnegative integer x.

The following algorithms summarize this Rivest-Shamir-Adelman (RSA) public key encryption system:

RSA ENCRYPTION ALGORITHM

/*   This algorithm encrypts a plaintext using the RSA scheme with a
     public encryption code (e, n) to produce a ciphertext.
     Receive: Plaintext M.
     Return: Ciphertext C.
---*/

[13]R. L. Rivest, A. Shamir, and L. Adelman, "A method for obtaining digital signatures and public-key cryptosystems," *Communications of the ACM* 21, 2 (February 1978): 120–126.

1. Pad M with some randomly selected character if necessary so that $length(M)$ is a multiple of $blockLength$.

2. Calculate $numberOfBlocks = length(M) / blockLength$.

3. Initialize index j to 1.

4. For $i = 1$ to $numberOfBlocks$:

    a. Extract the substring M_i from M consisting of the $blockLength$ characters beginning at position j.

    b. Convert M_i to numeric form to give P_i.

    c. Calculate $C_i = P_i^e \% n$

    d. Increment j by $blockLength$.

RSA DECRYPTION ALGORITHM

/*   This algorithm decrypts a ciphertext using a secret decryption
     key d to produce a plaintext.
     Receive: Ciphertext C consisting of numeric blocks C_i,
                $i = 1, \ldots, numberOfBlocks$
     Return: Plaintext M.
---*/

1. Initialize M to the empty string.

2. For $i = 1$ to $numberOfBlocks$:

    a. Calculate $P_i = C_i^d \% n$

    b. Convert P_i to a string of characters M_i.

    c. Concatenate M_i onto M.

To illustrate, suppose that $(17, 2773)$ is the public encryption code and that characters are converted to numeric values using the following table:

Character:	A	B	C	D	E	F	G	H	I	J	K	L	M
code:	00	01	02	03	04	05	06	07	08	09	10	11	12

Character:	N	O	P	Q	R	S	T	U	V	W	X	Y	Z
code:	13	14	15	16	17	18	19	20	21	22	23	24	25

To encrypt a string such as $M =$ "IDESOFMARCH" using the RSA algorithm, we divide M into 2-character blocks $M_1, M_2, \ldots, M_6$ (after appending the randomly selected character X) and represent each block M_i as an integer P_i in the range 0 through $2773 - 1 = 2772$ by concatenating the numeric codes of the characters that comprise the block:

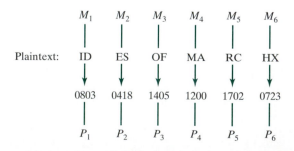

Each of these blocks P_i is then encrypted by calculating $C_i = P_i \ \% \ 2773$:

Ciphertext:	0779	1983	2641	1444	0052	0802
	C_1	C_2	C_3	C_4	C_5	C_6

For this encryption key, the corresponding decrypting key is $d = 157$. Thus, we decrypt the ciphertext by calculating $C_i^{157} \ \% \ 2773$ for each block C_i. For the preceding ciphertext this gives

Decrypted ciphertext: 0803   0418   1405   1200   1702   0723

which is the numeric form of the original message.

Two points in the preceding discussion of the RSA encryption scheme require further explanation: (1) How are n, e, and d chosen? (2) How can the exponentiation be performed efficiently?

The number n is the product of two large "random" primes p and q,

$$n = p \cdot q$$

In the preceding example, we used the small primes 47 and 59 to simplify the computations, but Rivest, Shamir, and Adelman suggest that p and q have at least one hundred digits. The decrypting key d is then selected to be some large random integer that is relatively prime to both $p - 1$ and $q - 1$, that is, one that has no factors in common with either number. In our example, $d = 157$ has this property. The number e is then selected to have the property that

$$e \cdot d \ \% \ [(p - 1) \cdot (q - 1)] \text{ is equal to } 1$$

A result from number theory then guarantees that e and d will have the required property described earlier, namely, that

$$P_i^{e \cdot d} \ \% \ n = P_i$$

for each block P_i.

We can efficiently carry out the exponentiations required in encryption and decryption by repeatedly squaring and multiplying, as follows:

EXPONENTIATION ALGORITHM

```
/*   Algorithm to calculate y = x^k mod n.
     Input:    Integers x, k, and n.
     Return:   y.
-----------------------------------------------------------------*/
```

1. Find the base-2 representation $b_t \cdots b_1 b_0$ of the exponent k.

2. Initialize y to 1.

3. For $i = t$ down to 0:
   a. Set $y = y^2 \ \% \ n$.
   b. If $b_i = 1$ then
          Set $y = (y * x) \ \% \ n$.

Recall that the encrypting key (e, n) is a public key, so that no attempt is made to keep it secret. The decrypting key d is a private key, however, and so must be kept secret. To break this code, one would need to be able to determine the value of d from the values of n and e. Because of the manner in which d and e are selected, this is possible if n can be factored into a product of primes. The security of the RSA encryption scheme is based on the difficulty of determining the prime factors of a large integer. Even with the best factorization algorithms known today, this is a prohibitively time-consuming task. A study of a few years ago gave the following table displaying some estimated times, assuming that each operation required one microsecond.

Number of Digits in Number Being Factored	Time
50	4 hours
75	104 days
100	74 years
200	4 billion years
300	5×10^{15} years
500	4×10^{25} years

Although the research on factorization continues, no efficient algorithms have been found that significantly reduce the times in the preceding table. Improved algorithms and the use of high-speed computers have made factorization possible in less time than the table shows, but not significantly less for large numbers. This public key encryption scheme thus appears (so far) to be quite secure and is being endorsed by a growing number of major computer vendors; and the adoption of a public key encryption standard is being considered by the National Institute of Standards and Technology.

✎ EXERCISES 3.6

1. A pure permutation encryption scheme is very insecure. Explain why by describing how an encryption scheme that merely permutes the bits in an n-bit string can easily be cracked by studying how certain basic bit strings are encrypted. Illustrate for $n = 4$.

2. Consider a simplified DES scheme that encrypts messages using the DES approach pictured in Fig. 3.14 but with only two keys, K_1 and K_2, instead of 16 keys $K_1, \ldots, K_{16}$, and that in the calculation of $f(R, K)$ pictured in Fig. 3.15 uses the same substitution table S_1 for each of the 6-bit blocks instead of eight different tables $S_1, \ldots, S_8$. Encrypt the string "AARDVARK" using this simplified DES scheme with keys $K_1 =$ "ABCDEF" and $K_2 =$ "SECRET" and assuming that strings are converted into bit strings by replacing each character by its binary ASCII codes.

3. Using the character codes $00, 01, \ldots, 25$ given in the text

   a. Find the RSA ciphertext produced by the key $(e, n) = (5, 2881)$ for the plaintext "PUBLIC."

   b. Verify that $d = 1109$ is a decrypting key for the RSA scheme in **(a)**.

4. If the RSA ciphertext produced by key $(e, n) = (13, 2537)$ is 0095 and the character codes $00, 01, \ldots, 25$ given in the text are used, find the plaintext.

5. A public key encryption scheme can be used to provide positive identification of the sender of a message by incorporating a *digital signature* into it. To illustrate, suppose that Al wishes to send a message M to Bob. Al first "signs" M by encrypting it using his secret decrypting key, which we might indicate by

$$S = D_{Al}(M)$$

He then encrypts S using Bob's public encryption key and sends the result to Bob:

$$M' = E_{Bob}(S)$$

Bob first decrypts the ciphertext M' with his secret decrypting key to obtain the signature S

$$D_{Bob}(M') = D_{Bob}(E_{Bob}(S)) = S$$

and then extracts the message M by using Al's public encryption key:

$$E_{Al}(S) = E_{Al}(D_{Al}(M)) = M$$

Bob's pair (M, S) is similar to a paper document that Al signed, since only Al could have created S. For the message $M =$ "HI" and using the character codes $00, 01, \ldots, 25$ given in the text, find M' if Al and Bob have published RSA encryption keys $(3, 1081)$ and $(1243, 1829)$, respectively.

6. Write a function to implement the algorithm given in the text for calculating $y = x^k \% n$ by repeated squaring and multiplication.

3.7   PATTERN MATCHING (OPTIONAL)

In Sec. 3.3 we described several basic string operations and implemented a few of them. In particular we considered a function `Find()` to locate one string in another string. As we noted, the brute force algorithm that it implemented is not the best possible. Because the find operation is a special case of the more general pattern-matching problem that occurs in many applications, such as text editing and text processing, a good deal of work has gone into designing more efficient algorithms. In this section we describe one such algorithm, called the *Knuth-Morris-Pratt algorithm*. Another efficient approach is the *Boyer-Moore* method described in several algorithms texts.

To review the brute force method and to discover how it can be improved, consider again the example of finding the first occurrence of the pattern "abcabd" in the line of text "abcabcabdabba":

text: | a | b | c | a | b | c | a | b | d | a | b | b | a |

pattern: | a | b | c | a | b | d |

We begin matching characters in *pattern* with those in *text* and find that the first five characters match, but the next characters do not:

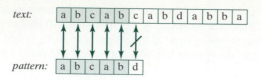

When such a mismatch occurs, we must backtrack to the beginning of *pattern*, shift one position to the right in *text*, and start the search over again:

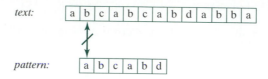

This time a mismatch occurs immediately, and so we backtrack once more to the beginning of *pattern*, shift another position to the right in *text*, and try again:

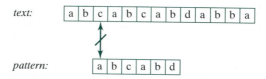

Another mismatch of the first characters occurs, so we backtrack and shift once again:

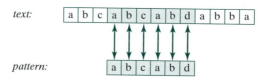

On the next search, all of the characters in *pattern* match the corresponding characters in *text*, and thus the pattern has been located in the line of text.

In this example, only three backtracks were required, and two of these required backing up only one character. The situation may be much worse, however. To illustrate, suppose that the text to be searched consists of one hundred characters, each of which is the same, and the pattern consists of 49 of these same characters followed by a different character, for example,

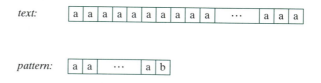

In beginning our search for *pattern* in *text*, we find that the first 49 characters match but that the last character in *pattern* does not match the corresponding character in *text*:

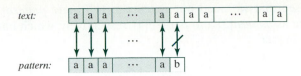

We must therefore backtrack to the beginning of *pattern*, shift one position to the right in *text*, and repeat the search. As before, we make 49 successful comparisons of characters in *pattern* with characters in *text* before a mismatch occurs:

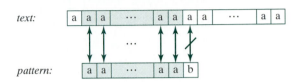

This same thing happens again and again until eventually we reach the end of *text* and are able to determine that *pattern* is not found in *text*. After each unsuccessful scan, we must backtrack from the last character of *pattern* way back to the first character and restart the search one position to the right in *text*.

The source of inefficiency in this algorithm is the backtracking required whenever a mismatch occurs. To illustrate how it can be avoided, consider again the first example in which *pattern* = "abcabd" and *text* = "abcabcabdabba":

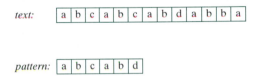

In the first scan, we find that *pattern*[0] = *text*[0], *pattern*[1] = *text*[1], *pattern*[2] = *text*[2], *pattern*[3] = *text*[3], and *pattern*[4] = *text*[4], but *pattern*[5] ≠ *text*[5]:

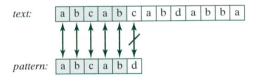

Examining *pattern*, we see that *pattern*[0] ≠ *pattern*[1]; thus *pattern*[0] cannot possibly match *text*[1] because *pattern*[1] did. Similarly, since *pattern*[0] is different from *pattern*[2], which matched *text*[2], neither can *pattern*[0] match *text*[2]. Consequently, we can immediately "slide" *pattern* three positions to the right, eliminating the backtracks to positions 1 and 2 in *text*. Moreover, examining the part of *pattern* that has matched a substring of *text*,

abcab

we see that we need not check *pattern*[0] and *pattern*[1] again since they are the same as *pattern*[3] and *pattern*[4], respectively, which have already matched characters in *text*.

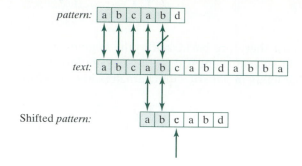

This partial match means that we can continue our search at position 5 in *text* and position 2 in *pattern*; no backtracking to examine characters before that in the position where a mismatch occurred is necessary at all!

Now consider the general problem of finding the index of a pattern $p_0 p_1 \cdots p_m$ in a text $t_0 t_1 \cdots t_n$ and suppose that these strings are stored in the arrays *pattern* and *text* so that $pattern[i] = p_i$ and $text[j] = t_j$. Also suppose that in attempting to locate *pattern* in *text* we have come to a point where the first i characters in *pattern* have matched characters in *text*, but a mismatch occurs when *pattern*[i] is compared with *text*[j].

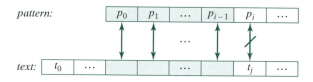

To avoid backtracking, we must shift *pattern* to the right so that the search can continue with *text*[j] and *pattern*[k], for some $k < i$.

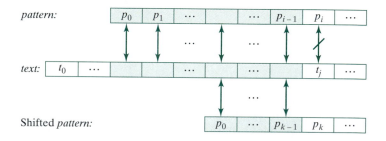

It is clear from this diagram that in order to do this, the first k characters of *pattern* must be identical to the k characters that precede *pattern*[i] and that *pattern*[k] must be different from *pattern*[i] so that *pattern*[k] has a chance of matching *text*[j]:

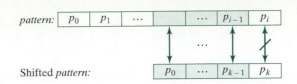

Let us denote this value k by $next[i]$. Thus, as we have just observed, $next[i]$ is the position in *pattern* at which the search can continue by comparing $pattern[next[i]]$ with the character $text[j]$ that did not match $pattern[i]$; that is, we slide *pattern* to the right to align $pattern[next[i]]$ with $text[j]$ and continue searching at this point. If no such k exists, we take $next[i] = -1$ to indicate that the search is to resume with $pattern[0]$ and $text[j + 1]$. (In this case, we can think of sliding *pattern* to the right to align the nonexistent character in position -1 with $text[j]$ and resume the search.)

KNUTH-MORRIS-PRATT PATTERN MATCHING ALGORITHM

/*   Algorithm to find a pattern in a text string. The pattern is stored in positions 0 through m of the array *pattern*, and the text is stored in positions 0 through n of the array *text*.

Input: Strings *text* and *pattern*
Return: Location of *pattern* in *text*, -1 if not found
- -*/

1. Initialize each of *index*, i, and j to 0.

/* *index* is the beginning position of the substring of *text* being compared with *pattern*, and indices i and j run through *pattern* and *text*, respectively. */

2. While $i \leq m$ and $j \leq n$:

If $pattern[i] = text[j]$ then   // match
    Increment each of i and j

Else do the following: // mismatch
    a. /* Slide *pattern* to the right the appropriate distance */
        Add $i - next[i]$ to *index*.
    b. /* Determine where the search is to continue */
        If $next[i] \neq -1$ then
            Set i equal to $next[i]$.
        Else
            Set i equal to 0 and increment j by 1.

3. If $i > m$ then *index* is the index of *pattern* in *text*; otherwise, *pattern* does not appear in *text*.

To illustrate, consider the following pattern

    pattern = abcaababc

and assume that the we are given the following table of *next* values for this pattern:

i	0	1	2	3	4	5	6	7	8
pattern[i]	a	b	c	a	a	b	a	b	c
next[i]	−1	0	0	−1	1	0	2	0	0

Now suppose that we wish to determine the index of *pattern* in

   text = aabcbabcaabcaababcba

Initially, *index, i,* and *j* are 0. Both *text*[0] and *pattern*[0] are 'a', and so both *i* and *j* are incremented to 1. A mismatch now occurs:

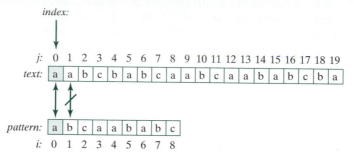

Since *next*[1] = 0, *index* is set to *index* + (1 − *next*[1]) = *index* + (1 − 0) = 1, *i* is set to *next*[1] = 0, *j* retains the value 1, and the search continues by comparing *pattern*[*next*[1]] = *pattern*[0] with *text*[1]. The next mismatch occurs when *i* = 3 and *j* = 4:

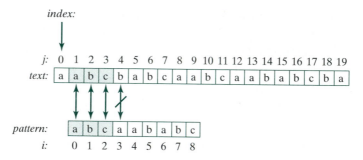

Since *next*[3] = −1, *index* is set to *index* + (3 − (−1)) = 5, *i* is set to 0, and *j* is incremented to 5. The search then resumes by comparing *pattern*[0] with *text*[5], and continues until the next mismatch, when *j* = 11 and *i* = 6:

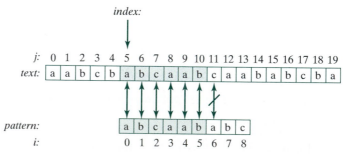

Now, *next*[6] = 2, so *index* is updated to *index* + (6 − 2) = 9, *i* is set equal to *next*[6] = 2, *j* remains at 11, and the search resumes by comparing *pattern*[2] with *text*[11]. This search locates a substring of *text* that matches *pattern*,

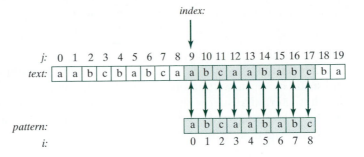

so the algorithm terminates with *index* = 9 as the index of *pattern* in *text*.

To complete our discussion of the Knuth-Morris-Pratt algorithm, we must describe how the table of *next* values is computed. Recall that *next*[i] is the length k of the longest prefix *pattern*[0], *pattern*[1], . . ., *pattern*[k − 1] of *pattern* that matches the k characters preceding *pattern*[i] but *pattern*[k] ≠ *pattern*[i]. For example, consider again the pattern "abcaababc":

i	0	1	2	3	4	5	6	7	8
pattern [i]	a	b	c	a	a	b	a	b	c

next[6] = 2 since the characters a, b in positions 0 and 1 match those in positions 4 and 5, and *pattern*[2] = 'c' is different from *pattern*[6] = 'a'. The following diagram shows this matching prefix and suffix in abcaaba but that the characters that follow these in positions 2 and 6 do not match:

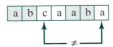

This property of *pattern* guarantees that if a mismatch occurs in comparing some character in *text* with *pattern*[6], the search can continue by comparing *pattern*[*next*[6]] = *pattern*[2] with this character:

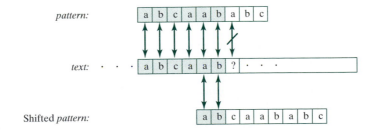

The determination that $next[4] = 1$ is similar to that for $next[6]$; the following diagram displays the matching prefix and suffix in abca and the fact that $pattern[1] \neq pattern[4]$:

The calculation of $next[5]$ requires a bit more care. In looking for a matching prefix and suffix in abcaa, we find one of length 1, that is, $pattern[0] = pattern[4]$; however, the characters that follow these matching substrings, $pattern[1]$ and $pattern[5]$ are not different. Thus $next[5]$ is not 1. Since an empty prefix always matches an empty suffix, and since $pattern[0] = $ 'a' differs from $pattern[5] = $ 'b', we obtain $next[5] = 0$:

By similar analyses, the remaining values of the *next* table can be verified.

An algorithm for calculating *next* values using this method is essentially the same as the pattern-matching algorithm except that the pattern is matched against itself. To see this, consider again a general pattern $p_0 p_1 \cdots p_m$. Clearly $next[0]$ must have the value -1 since there are no characters that precede $pattern[0]$. Now, if $next[0], \ldots, next[j-1]$ have been determined, these values can be used to calculate $next[j]$ as follows. We "slide" a copy of *pattern* across itself until we find a prefix (possibly empty) that matches the characters preceding $pattern[j]$:

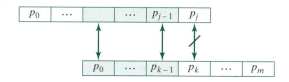

If this prefix has length k (possibly 0) and $pattern[k] \neq pattern[j]$, then $next[j] = k$ by definition. However, if $pattern[k] = pattern[j]$, then clearly $next[j]$ has the same value as $next[k]$, which has already been calculated. This method of calculating *next* values is used in the following algorithm:

ALGORITHM FOR *next* Table

/*   Algorithm to compute *next* values for a pattern stored in positions 0 through m of the array *pattern*.

Input: String *pattern*
Return: The array *next*.

--*/

1. Initialize $next[0]$ to -1, k to -1, and j to 0.

2. While $j \leq m$:

    a. While $(k \neq -1)$ and $pattern[k] \neq pattern[j]$

            Set k equal to $next[k]$.

    b. Increment k and j by 1.

    c. If $pattern[j] = pattern[k]$ then

            Set $next[j]$ equal to $next[k]$.

    Else

            Set $next[j]$ equal to k.

To illustrate, consider the pattern used earlier

    $pattern = $ abcaababc

The following table traces the execution of this algorithm as it calculates the *next* table for this pattern.

Instruction	k	j	*next* Value Computed
Initially	-1	0	$next[0] = -1$
2a	-1	0	
2b	0	1	
2c	0	1	$next[1] = 0$
2a	$next[0] = -1$	1	
2b	0	2	
2c	0	2	$next[2] = 0$
2a	$next[0] = -1$	2	
2b	0	3	
2c	0	3	$next[3] = next[0] = -1$
2a	0	3	
2b	1	4	
2c	1	4	$next[4] = 1$
2a	$next[1] = 0$	4	
	0	4	
2b	1	5	
2c	1	5	$next[5] = next[1] = 0$
2a	1	5	
2b	2	6	
2c	2	6	$next[6] = 2$
2a	$next[2] = 0$	6	
	0	6	
2b	1	7	
2c	1	7	$next[7] = next[1] = 0$

2a	1	7	
2b	2	8	
2c	2	8	$next[8] = next[2] = 0$

The Knuth-Morris-Pratt solution to the pattern-matching problem has an interesting history. A theorem proved by Cook in 1970 states that any problem that can be solved using an abstract model of a computer called a *pushdown automaton* can be solved in time proportional to the size of the problem using an actual computer (more precisely, using a random access machine). In particular, this theorem implies that the existence of an algorithm for solving the pattern-matching problem in time proportional to $m + n$ where m and n are the maximum indices in arrays that store the pattern and text, respectively. Knuth and Pratt painstakingly reconstructed the proof of Cook's theorem and so constructed the pattern-matching algorithm described in this section. At approximately the same time, Morris constructed essentially the same algorithm while considering the practical problem of designing a text editor. Thus we see that not all algorithms are discovered by a "flash of insight" and that theoretical computer science does indeed sometimes lead to practical applications.

✍ EXERCISES 3.7

Compute *next* tables for the patterns in Exercises 1–8.

1. A B R A C A D A B R A
2. A A A A A
3. M I S S I S S I P P I
4. I S S I S S I P P I
5. B A B B A B A B
6. 1 0 1 0 0 1 1
7. 1 0 0 1 0 1 1 1
8. 1 0 0 1 0 0 1 0 0 1

9–16. Construct tables tracing the action of the *next* table algorithm for the patterns in Exercises 1–8.

☞ PROGRAMMING POINTERS

1. Members of a class by default are private unless explicitly declared to be public. Members of a struct by default are public unless explicitly declared to be private.

2. Data members of a class should be made private to protect them from being accessed by nonmember (and nonfriend) functions. Provide access to member functions for those that you wish to be accessible. Public members can be accessed by nonmember functions by using the dot operator.

3. Member functions can be thought of as receiving a class object implicitly; nonmember functions must receive class objects explicitly via parameters.

4. Definitions of member functions outside a class declaration must be qualified with the class name using the `::` operator: `ClassName::FunctionName()`. Nonmember functions are not qualified.

5. Simple member functions are usually inlined either by preceding their definitions with the keyword `inline` or by placing the definitions inside the class declaration.

6. Member functions that do not modify any of the class's data members should be prototyped and defined as `const` functions.

7. A class's member functions can access private data members of class objects it receives as parameters.

8. Class invariants should be formulated to ensure that the data members always contain valid values. Whenever an operation modifies data members, it should always establish that the class invariant still holds.

9. A class constructor:

- ► Has the same name as the class
- ► Must be a member function and is usually prototyped or defined in the public section
- ► Does not return a value and has no return type (not even `void`)
- ► Is often quite simple and can be inlined
- ► Is called whenever an object of that class is declared

10. If you do not provide a constructor for a class, the compiler will generate a *default* constructor. If you do provide a constructor for a class, you must also provide a default constructor, because the compiler will not supply one.

11. A nonmember function cannot access private members of a class unless the class grants it permission by declaring it to be a *friend* function. This is done by putting the function's prototype inside the class declaration and preceding it (but not its definition) by the keyword `friend`.

12. Overloaded functions must have different signatures; simply having different return types is not enough.

13. Parameters with default arguments must appear at the end of the parameter list.

14. An operator Δ is overloaded by overloading the function `operator`Δ`()`. For a binary operator, an expression of the form `a` Δ `b` will be be evaluated by the function call `a.operator`Δ`(b)` if `operator`Δ`()` is a member function and by the function call `operator`Δ`(a, b)` if it is not.

15. The input and output functions `operator>>()` and `operator<<()` cannot be member functions of programmer-defined classes.

16. An overloaded operator definition may not change the operator's *arity* (the number of operands the operator takes).

17. Use conditional compilation directives to prevent the contents of a class library from being included more than once.

```
#ifndef CLASS_NAME
#define CLASS_NAME
   The declaration of ClassName
#endif
```

18. Use `char` arrays to process strings in applications where no (or few) string operations are needed; otherwise, use the C++ `string` class.

19. The input operator `>>` will *skip leading white-space* when inputting a string value, but will stop reading characters when a white-space character is encountered (or the end of the file is reached); *this white-space character will not be removed* from the input stream. The string function `getline()` will *not skip leading white-space* and will read characters until the end-of-line character (or other specified delimiter) is encountered, and it *will remove it from the input stream.*

20. String streams are useful for parsing input strings. They also make it possible to do some rather elaborate formatting one time and then output it to a string from where it can be output to various destinations.

21. Use the string operation `data()` or `c_str()` to extract the `char` array containing a string name stored in a `string` object. For example, use `streamName.open (fileName.data());` to open a stream to a file whose name is stored in the `string` object `fileName`.

ADT TIPS

1. C++ provides many standard structured data types that are implemented very efficiently in most versions. Thus there is often no reason to "reinvent the wheel" by creating a data type when the language already provides one. For example, the many powerful string operations provided in the C++ `string` class make it unnecessary to create a new string class (except perhaps in very special applications).

PROGRAMMING PROBLEMS

SECTION 3.2

Problems 1–3 deal with lines in the Cartesian plane. The *point-slope equation* of a line with slope m and passing through point P with coordinates (x_1, y_1) is

$$y - y_1 = m(x - x_1)$$

The *slope-intercept equation* of a line with slope m and y-intercept b is

$$y = mx + b$$

1. Write and test a `LineSegment` class, described by two `CartesianPoint` endpoints (see Exercise 7 in Sec. 3.2). In addition to the usual operations (such as constructors, input, and output), this class should provide operations to compute:

   a. The midpoint of the line segment joining two points
   b. The equation of the perpendicular bisector of this line segment

2. Write and test a class for a `Line`, described by its slope and a point on the line, with functions that:

   a. Find the point-slope equation of the line
   b. Find the slope-intercept equation of the line

3. Write a program to read the point and slope information for two lines and to determine whether they intersect or are parallel. If they intersect, find the point of intersection and also determine whether they are perpendicular. Use the classes `CartesianPoint` from Exercise 7 in Sec. 3.2 and `Line` from Prob. 2 to represent points and lines, respectively.

4. A *complex number* has the form $a + bi$, where a and b are real numbers and $i^2 = -1$. The standard C++ library includes a class `complex` for processing complex numbers. Examine the structure of this class to find the operations it provides and what data members it uses. (See the website described in the preface for a link to the ISO/ANSI C++ standard.) Write a program to read two complex numbers and a symbol for an operation and that then performs the indicated operation.

5. A rational number is of the form a/b, where a and b are integers with $b \neq 0$. Write a program to do rational number arithmetic, storing each rational number in a record that has a numerator field and a denominator field. The program should read and display all rational numbers in the format a/b; for output, just display a if the denominator is 1. The following examples illustrate the menu of commands that the user should be allowed to enter:

Input	Output	Comments
3/8 + 1/6	13/24	$a/b + c/d = (ad + bc)/bd$ reduced to lowest terms
3/8 − 1/6	5/24	$a/b − c/d = (ad − bc)/bd$ reduced to lowest terms
3/8 * 1/6	1/16	$a/b * c/d = ac/bd$ reduced to lowest terms
3/8 / 1/6	9/4	$a/b / c/d = ad/bc$ reduced to lowest terms
3/8 I	8/3	Invert a/b
8/3 M	2 + 2/3	Write a/b as a mixed fraction
6/8 R	3/4	Reduce a/b to lowest terms
6/8 G	2	Greatest common divisor of numerator and denominator
1/6 L 3/8	24	Lowest common denominator of a/b and c/d
1/6 < 3/8	true	$a/b < c/d$?
1/6 <= 3/8	true	$a/b \leq c/d$?
1/6 > 3/8	false	$a/b > c/d$?
1/6 >= 3/8	false	$a/b \geq c/d$?
3/8 = 9/24	true	$a/b = c/d$?
2/3 X + 2 = 4/5	X = −9/5	Solution of linear equation $(a/b)X + c/d = e/f$

  6. Write a driver program to test the class `Date` of Exercise 10.

  7. Write a driver program to test the class `PhoneNumber` of Exercise 11.

  8. Write a driver program to test the class `Checker` of Exercise 12.

  9. Write a driver program to test the class `CartesianPoint` of Exercise 13.

10. Write a driver program to test the class `PolarPoint` of Exercise 14.

11. Write a driver program to test the class `Card` of Exercise 15.

12. Write a driver program to test the personal information class of Exercise 16.

13. Write a driver program to test the baseball statistics class of Exercise 17.

14. Write a driver program to test the weather statistics class of Exercise 18.

SECTION 3.3

15. Write a driver program to test the compare operation of Exercise 1.

16. Write a driver program to test the concatenate operation of Exercise 2.

17. Write a driver program to test the copy operation of Exercise 3.

18. Write a driver program to test the insert operation of Exercise 4.

19. Write a driver program to test the delete operation of Exercise 5.

20. Write a driver program to test the replace operation of Exercise 6.

21. Write a driver program to test the output operation of Exercise 9.

22. Write a driver program to test the input operation of Exercise 10.

23. Write a driver program to test the length operation of Exercise 11.

24. Write a driver program to test the compare operation of Exercise 12.

25. Write a driver program to test the concatenate operation of Exercise 13.

26. Write a driver program to test the copy operation of Exercise 14.

27. Write a driver program to test the find operation of Exercise 15.

28. Write a driver program to test the insert operation of Exercise 16.

29. Write a driver program to test the delete operation of Exercise 17.

30. Write a driver program to test the replace operation of Exercise 18.

SECTION 3.4

31. Write a driver program to test the string-counting function of Exercise 1.

32. Write a driver program to test the month-name function of Exercise 2.

33. Write a driver program to test the month-number function of Exercise 3.

34. Write a driver program to test the case-conversion functions of Exercise 4.

35. Write a driver program to test the function `replace_all()` of Exercise 5.

36. Write a driver program to test the name-formatting function of Exercise 6.

37. Write a driver program to test the name-formatting function of Exercise 7.

38. Write a driver program to test the string-to-integer function of Exercise 8.

39. Write a driver program to test the string-to-real function of Exercise 9.

40. Write a driver program to test the palindrome-checking function of Exercise 10.

41. Write a driver program to test the anagram-checking function of Exercise 11.

42. Write a program that analyzes text contained in a file by finding the number of non-blank characters, number of nonblank lines, number of words, and number of sentences and that calculates the average number of characters per word and the average number of words per sentence.

43. Write a program to input a string and then input several lines of text, determine whether the first string occurs in each line, and if so, print asterisks (*) under each occurrence.

44. Write a program to print "personalized" contest letters like those frequently received in the mail. They might have a format like that of the following sample. The user should enter the three strings in the first three lines, and the program then prints the letter with the underlined locations filled in.

```
Mr. John Q. Doe
123 SomeStreet
AnyTown, AnyState 12345


Dear Mr. Doe:

    How would you like to see a brand new Cadillac parked in front
of 123 SomeStreet in AnyTown, AnyState?  Impossible, you say?  No,
it isn't, Mr. Doe.  Simply keep the enclosed raffle ticket and
validate it by sending a $100.00 tax-deductible political
contribution and 10 labels from Shyster & Sons chewing tobacco.
Not only will you become eligible for the drawing to be conducted
on February 29 by the independent firm of G. Y. P. Shyster, but you
will also be helping to reelect Sam Shyster.   That's all there is
to it, John.  You may be a winner!!!
```

45. There are 3 teaspoons in a tablespoon, 4 tablespoons in a quarter of a cup, 2 cups in a pint, and 2 pints in a quart. Write a program to convert units in cooking. The program should call for the input of the amount, the units, and the new units desired.

46. The game of Hangman is played by two persons. One person selects a word and the other tries to guess the word by guessing individual letters. Design and implement a program to play Hangman.

47. Reverend Zeller developed a formula for computing the day of the week on which a given date fell or will fall. Suppose that we let a, b, c, and d be integers defined as follows:

$a =$ The number of a month of the year, with March $= 1$, April $= 2$, and so on, with January and February being counted as months 11 and 12 of the preceding year

$b =$ The day of the month

$c =$ The year of the century

$d =$ The century

For example, July 31, 1929 gives $a = 5$, $b = 31$, $c = 29$, $d = 19$; January 3, 1988 gives $a = 11$, $b = 3$, $c = 87$, $d = 19$. Now calculate the following integer quantities:

$w =$ The integer quotient $(13a - 1) / 5$

$x =$ The integer quotient $c / 4$

$y =$ The integer quotient $d / 4$

$z = w + x + y + b + c - 2d$

$r = z$ reduced modulo 7; that is, $T = z \% 7$; $r = 0$ represents Sunday, $r = 1$ represents Monday, and so on

Write a function `Day_of_the_Week()` that receives the number of a month as described above, the day of the month, and a year, and returns the name of the day of the week on which that date fell or will fall. Write a program that inputs several strings representing dates, calls the function `Day_of_the_Week()`, and displays the day returned by the function.

a. Verify that December 12, 1960 fell on a Monday, and that January 1, 1991 fell on a Tuesday.

b. On what day of the week did January 25, 1963 fall?

c. On what day of the week did June 2, 1964 fall?

d. On what day of the week did July 4, 1776 fall?

e. On what day of the week were you born?

SECTION 3.5

48. Write a program that reads a file containing a C++ program and produces a file with all comments stripped from the program.

49. Write a simple *text-formatting* program that reads a text file and produces another text file in which blank lines are removed, multiple blanks are replaced with a single blank, and no lines are longer than some given length. Put as many words as possible on the same line. You will have to break some lines of the given file, but do not break any words or put punctuation marks at the beginning of a new line.

50. Extend the text-formatting program of Problem 49 to right-justify each line except the last in the new text file by adding evenly distributed blanks in lines where necessary.

51. (Project) A *pretty-printer* is a special kind of text formatter that reads a text file containing a program and then prints it in a "pretty" format. For example, a pretty-printer for C++ might produce a format similar to that used in this text's sample programs. Write a pretty-print program for C++ programs to indent and align statements in a pleasing format.

SECTION 3.6 (OPTIONAL)

52. Write a program to implement the Caesar cipher scheme.

53. Write a program to implement the Vignère cipher scheme.

54. Write a program to encrypt and decrypt a message by using a substitution table.

55. Write a program to encrypt and decrypt a message by using a permutation scheme.

56. Write a program to encrypt and decrypt messages using the simplified DES scheme described in Exercise 2.

57. Use the subprogram of Exercise 6 in a program that implements the RSA scheme.

58. A simple "probabilistic" algorithm for testing whether a number is prime that is similar to that recommended for finding the large primes needed in the RSA scheme is based on the following result discovered by the mathematician Fermat: If n is a prime, then $x^{n-1} \% n = 1$ for all positive integers less than n. Thus, to test whether a given number n is prime, one might proceed as follows: Randomly select a positive integer $x < n$ and compute $y = x^{n-1} \% n$. If $y \neq 1, n$ is not prime; but if $y = 1, n$ *may be* prime and further testing is required, so we repeat the test with another value of x. If $y = 1$ for many different values of x, n is *probably* prime. Write a program that uses this method of testing primality.

SECTION 3.7 (OPTIONAL)

59. Write and test a function to implement the string find operation using the Knuth-Morris-Pratt method.

60. Use your function in Prob. 59 in a program that generates a random bit string *text* of some specified length, say 1000, and a shorter random bit string *pattern* of length 10 or so, and then uses the Knuth-Morris-Pratt method to locate all occurrences of *pattern* in *text*.

61. Write a program to compare the computing time of the function in Prob. 59 with one that implements the find operation by using the brute-force approach. You might generate test strings *text* and *pattern* randomly, as suggested in Prob. 60.

Chapter 4

STACKS

Chapter Contents

An implementation of an abstract data type consists of storage structures to store the data items and algorithms for the basic operations and relations. As we have seen, there may be several different implementations, and some are better than others. The idea of *data abstraction,* in which the interface of an ADT is separated from its implementation, is an important concept because it makes it possible to study and use the structure without being concerned about the details of its implementation.

In the preceding chapter we considered the string data type as it is implemented in C using null-terminated sequences of characters stored in `char` arrays and libraries of functions to process these arrays. And we also considered the `string` class in C++. Strings provide a simple example of a *structured data* type or *container* type[1] that stores a *collection* of data values as opposed to the *simple* data types such as `int` and `float`, that store only individual values. There are several other important container ADTs, and in this chapter we consider one such data structure, the *stack,* and some of its applications. This structure has often been implemented using an array because most programming languages provide an array data type, and such an implementation is therefore quite easy. We will begin the chapter by building a `Stack` class implemented in this way. In Chap. 6 we will describe several improvements to this implementation:

▶ Make it a class template so it becomes a generic container type that can process any type of stack elements

▶ Use a `vector` for the storage container so that the stack's capacity can increase as necessary

---

[1]The word *container* to describe objects that store collections of other objects has become popular with the inclusion of the containers in the Standard Template Library in standard C++.

▸ Look at the `stack` container provided in **STL**, the ***Standard Template Library***, which is a part of standard C++

4.1   INTRODUCTION TO STACKS

Consider the following problems:

PROBLEM 1:

A program is to be written to simulate a certain card game. One aspect of this simulation is to maintain a discard pile. On any turn, a player may discard a single card from his hand to the top of this pile, or he may retrieve the top card from this discard pile. What data type is needed to model this discard pile?

PROBLEM 2:

A program is to be written to model a railroad switching yard. One part of the switching network consists of a main track and a siding onto which cars may be shunted and removed at any time

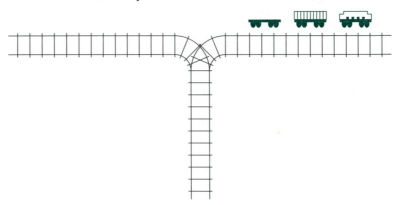

What data type can be used to model the operation of this siding?

PROBLEM 3:

One task that must be performed during execution of a function `f()` is to keep track of enough information about `f()`—parameter values, local variables, and so on[2]—so that when execution of `f()` is interrupted by a call to another function `g()`, execution of `f()` can resume when `g()` terminates. Obviously, `g()` might call another function `h()` so that information about `g()` must be stored so it can resume execution later. And `h()` might call another function, and so on. What data type can be used to store this function information?

PROBLEM 4:

Data items are stored in computer memory using a binary representation. In particular, positive integers are commonly stored using the base-two representation described in Sec.2.2. This means that the base-ten representation of an inte-

---

[2]This is called an *activation record* and is described in more detail in Sec. 4.3.

ger that appears in a program or in a data file must be converted to a base-two representation. One algorithm for carrying out this conversion uses repeated division by 2 with the successive remainders giving the binary digits in the base-two representation from right to left. For example, the base-two representation of 26 is 11010, as the following computation shows.

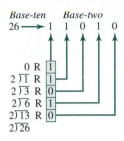

What data type should be used to keep track of these remainders?

Each of these problems involves a collection of related data items: a deck of cards in Problem 1, a set of railroad cars in Problem 2, a collection of function information in Problem 3, and a sequence of remainders in Problem 4. In Problem 1, the basic operations are adding a card to and removing a card from the top of the discard pile. In Problem 2, the basic operations are pushing a car onto the siding and removing the last car previously placed on the siding. In Problem 3, when a function terminates, a return is made to the last function that was interrupted. Function information must therefore be stored in such a way that the last information stored will be the first removed from storage. From the diagram in Problem 4, we note that the bits that comprise the base-two representation of 26 have been generated in reverse order, from right to left, and that the remainders must therefore be stored in some structure so they can later be displayed in the usual left-to-right order.

In each case we need a "last-discarded-first-removed," "last-pushed-onto-first-removed," "last-stored-first-removed," "last-generated-first-displayed" structured data type. To illustrate this behavior, we focus on Problem 4. To display the base-two representation of an integer like 26 in the usual left-to-right sequence, we must "stack up" the remainders generated during the repeated division by 2, as illustrated in the diagram in Problem 4. When the division process terminates, we can retrieve the bits from this stack of remainders in the required "last-in-first-out" order.

Assuming that a stack data type is available, we are led to the following algorithm to convert from base-ten to base-two and display the result.

 BASE-CONVERSION ALGORITHM

/* Algorithm to display the base-2 representation of a base-10 number.

    Receive: a positive integer *number*
    Output: the base-two representation of *number*
---*/

1. Create an empty stack to hold the remainders.

2. While *number* ≠ 0:

    a. Calculate the *remainder* that results when *number* is divided by 2.

    b. Push *remainder* onto the stack of remainders.

    c. Replace *number* by the integer quotient of *number* divided by 2.

3. While the stack of remainders is not empty:

    a. Retrieve and remove the *remainder* from the top of the stack of remainders.

    b. Display *remainder*.

The following diagram traces this algorithm for the integer 26

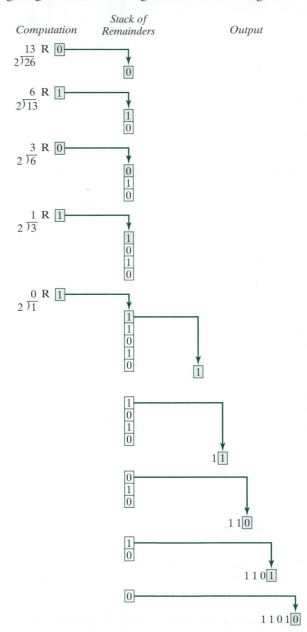

This type of last-in-first-out processing occurs in a wide variety of applications; consequently, a data type that embodies this idea is very useful. This **last-in-first-out (LIFO)** data structure is called a **stack.**

As a container, a stack models a spring-loaded stack of plates in a cafeteria:

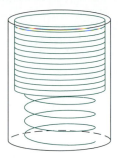

This stack functions in the following way:

▶ If a plate is added to the stack, those below it are pushed down and cannot be accessed.

▶ If a plate is removed from the stack, those below it pop up one position.

▶ The stack becomes empty when there are no plates in it.

▶ The stack is full if there is no room in it for more plates.

This leads to the following definition of a stack as an abstract data type:

ADT STACK

Collection of Data Elements:

An ordered collection of data items that can be accessed at only one end, called the *top* of the stack.

Basic Operations:

▶ Construct a stack (usually empty)

▶ Check if stack is empty

▶ Push: Add an element at the top of the stack

▶ Top: Retrieve the top element of the stack

▶ Pop: Remove the top element of the stack

It would be nice to have a stack class because we could then use it to easily develop a short program for the base-conversion problem as shown in Fig. 4.1. (In fact, we can use a stack container from STL, the Standard Template Library, but we need to learn about quite a few more things before we can fully understand it.[3])

---

[3]To use the standard `stack` container, we must `#include <stack>`. A declaration of a stack whose elements are of type `T` then has the form

```
stack<T> nameOfStack;
```

FIGURE 4.1 CONVERSION FROM BASE 10 TO BASE 2

```
/* Program that uses a stack to convert the base-ten
 * representation of a positive integer to base two.
 *
 * Input:  A positive integer
 * Output: Base-two representation of the number
 ***********************************************************/

#include "Stack.h"              // our own -- <stack> for STL version
#include <iostream>
using namespace std;

int main()
{
  unsigned number,            // the number to be converted
           remainder;         // remainder when number is divided by 2
  Stack stackOfRemainders;    // stack of remainders
  char response;              // user response

  do
  {
    cout << "Enter positive integer to convert: ";
    cin >> number;

    while (number != 0)
    {
      remainder = number % 2;
      stackOfRemainders.push(remainder);
      number /= 2;
    }

    cout << "Base-two representation: ";
    while ( !stackOfRemainders.empty() )
    {
      remainder = stackOfRemainders.top();
      stackOfRemainders.pop();
      cout << remainder;
    }

    cout << endl;
    cout << "\nMore (Y or N)? ";
    cin >> response;
  }
  while (response == 'Y' || response == 'y');
}
```

4.2   DESIGNING AND BUILDING A Stack CLASS

We wear two hats in this book, a builder hat and a user hat:

Thus far we have *used* a stack data type. In order to

▸ Gain more practice in building classes—*container* classes in particular

▸ Understand how and why stacks are implemented in the C++ Standard Template Library

we will "reinvent the wheel" and *build* our own stack class.

Building a class consists of two steps:

1. *Design the class*

2. *Implement the class*

We begin, therefore, by looking at the design of a stack class.

DESIGNING A Stack CLASS

Designing a class consists of identifying those operations that are needed to manipulate the "real-world" object being modeled by the class. Time invested in this ☞ design phase will pay off, because it results in a well-planned class that is easy to use.

It is important that we *describe the operations independently of how the class will be implemented.* At this point, we have no idea what data members will be available, so the *operations must be described in some manner that does not depend on any particular representation of the objects*. The resulting specification then constitutes the *blueprint* for building the class.

In our definition of a stack as an ADT, we identified five basic operations: construct, empty, push, top, and pop. Our class must, therefore, have (at least) the following operations:

▸ *Construction*:   Initializes an empty stack. (Later, it will first have to create the stack.)

▸ *Empty* operation: Examines a stack and produces false or true depending on whether the stack contains any values.

▸ *Push* operation: Modifies a stack by adding a value at the top of the stack.

▸ *Top* operation: Retrieves the value at the top of the stack.

▸ *Pop* operation: Modifies a stack by removing the value at the top of the stack.

To help with debugging, we will probably also add an output operation early on:

▸ *Output*:   Dumps the stack; that is, displays all the elements stored in the stack.

IMPLEMENTING A Stack CLASS

Once a class has been designed, it must be implemented, which involves two steps:

1 Defining data members to represent the object(s) being modeled

2. Defining the operations identified in the design phase

For a container class such as a stack, the data members provide the storage structure for the stack elements together with any other items that will prove useful or necessary in implementing the operations.

SELECTING DATA MEMBERS

A stack must store a collection of values, so we begin by considering what kind of storage structure(s) to use. Because a stack is a sequence of data items, we might use an array to store these items, with each stack element occupying one position in the array. This also will provide an implementation that can be converted to almost any programming language, because nearly all of them provide arrays. In this first implementation, therefore, we will use a C-style array, to store the stack elements.

A FIRST ATTEMPT.   If we think of modeling a spring-loaded stack of plates described earlier, then it seems natural to use an array for the stack elements with position 0 serving as the top of the stack. For example, suppose we have a stack with an array of capacity 8 and that the stack contains 6 integers 77, 121, 64, 234, 51, and 29, with 77 at the top and the other integers in the given order below it. We might picture this as follows, where ? denotes a "garbage" value in the array:

[0]	77
[1]	121
[2]	64
[3]	234
[4]	51
[5]	29
[6]	?
[7]	?

Consider, however, what happens if we now perform the three operations push 95, push 80, and pop, in this order:

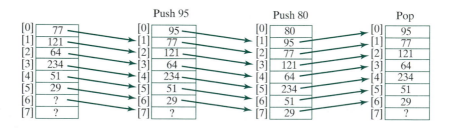

Notice that each time a new value is pushed onto the stack, all the items in the stack must be moved down one slot in the array to make room for it at the top. Similarly,

each time a value is removed from the stack, all of the items in the array from position 1 on must be moved up so that the top value is in location 0.[4] This is obviously
grossly inefficient when there are many stack operations to be performed.

A BETTER APPROACH.   The shifting of array elements in the preceding implementation is time-consuming and unnecessary and can easily be avoided. Rather than
thinking of a spring-loaded stack of plates, we think of a stack of books on a table.
We can add and remove books at the top of this stack without ever moving any of
the other books in the stack!

For a spring-loaded stack of plates, the top of the stack is fixed, and so the bottom
plate (and therefore all of the other plates) move when we add or remove a plate at
the top of the stack. For a stack of books, however, only the top moves when we add
or remove a book; the bottom of the stack stays fixed (as do all of the other books).
    To model this view of a stack, we need only "flip the array over," fixing position
0 at the bottom of the stack, and let the stack grow toward the end of the array,
using a variable *myTop* to keep track of the top of the stack, and then push and pop
at this location:

			Push 95			Push 80			Pop	
	[7]	?		[7]	?	*myTop*→ [7]	80		[7]	80
	[6]	?	*myTop*→ [6]	95		[6]	95	*myTop*→ [6]	95
myTop→ [5]	77		[5]	77		[5]	77		[5]	77
	[4]	121		[4]	121		[4]	121		[4]	121
	[3]	64		[3]	64		[3]	64		[3]	64
	[2]	234		[2]	234		[2]	234		[2]	234
	[1]	51		[1]	51		[1]	51		[1]	51
	[0]	29		[0]	29		[0]	29		[0]	29

Note that no shifting of array elements is necessary.
    So, we can begin building our stack class by selecting data members:

▸ An *array* to hold the stack elements

▸ An *integer* to indicate the top of the stack

However, an array declaration has the form

```
ArrayElementType array[CAPACITY];
```

---

[4]In the last diagram, we indicate the garbage value at the end of the array with ?. In fact, it would be
the value 29 at the end of the array before the pop operation, but now it has become a garbage value;
that is, it is no longer a legitimate stack element.

What should we use for *ArrayElementType* and for *CAPACITY*?

For *ArrayElementType*, we will use (for now) a **typedef** declaration of the form

```
typedef ArrayElementType StackElement;
```

to make StackElement a *synonym* for *ArrayElementType*. For example, the declaration

```
typedef int StackElement;
```

makes StackElement a synonym for int. We will use StackElement throughout the class declaration and its implementation so that in the future if we want a stack of doubles we need only change the typedef declaration to

```
typedef double StackElement;
```

For a stack of characters, we need only change it to

```
typedef char StackElement;
```

and so on. When the class library is recompiled, the type of the array's elements will be double or char or whatever other type we put in this typedef declaration.

We will put this typedef declaration ahead of the class declaration so it is easy to change when we need a new stack element type. Putting it outside the class declaration also makes the type identifier StackElement easier to access throughout the class and in any files that #include Stack.h. If it were inside a public section in the class declaration, the type identifier StackElement could be accessed from outside the class, but it would be necessary to qualify each reference to it by writing Stack::StackElement.

Another reason for putting the typedef declaration outside the class declaration is that in later improved versions of the class, we can do away with it completely by using the more modern alternative, the **template** mechanism, to build a Stack class whose element type is left unspecified. The element *type is then passed as a special kind of parameter* at compile time This is the approach used for C++'s standard library containers (which originated in STL, the Standard Template Library). We will describe class templates in Chap. 6.

We will use a declaration of the form

```
const int STACK_CAPACITY = . . .;
```

to set the array capacity. If we put it inside the class declaration, we would probably make it a **static data member** by writing

```
static const int STACK_CAPACITY = . . .;
```

so that all stack objects will use this same value. Class objects have their own copies of ordinary (nonstatic) data members, but there is only one copy of a static data member.

We will, however, place this definition of STACK_CAPACITY before the class declaration along with the typedef declaration so that it, too, is easy to change when necessary and so that it is easy to access throughout the stack class and in files that #include the header file for our class. If it were inside a public section in the class declaration, the STACK_CAPACITY could be accessed from outside the class, but it would be necessary to qualify each reference to it by writing Stack::STACK_CAPACITY or by using the dot operator as in st.STACK_CAPACITY. Also, when we improve our class's implementation by using a run-time array or a vector or some other container to store the stack elements, we will be able to eliminate this const declaration.

Now we are ready to begin writing our class declaration as shown in Fig. 4.2

FIGURE 4.2 CLASS DECLARATION FOR A **Stack** DATA TYPE

```
/* Stack.h provides a Stack class.
 *
 * Basic operations:
 *   Constructor:  Constructs an empty stack
 *   empty:    Checks if a stack is empty
 *   push:     Modifies a stack by adding a value at the top
 *   top:      Accesses the top stack value; leaves stack unchanged
 *   pop:      Modifies a stack by removing the value at the top
 *   display: Displays all the stack elements
 * Class Invariant:
 *   1. The stack elements (if any) are stored in positions
 *       0, 1, . . ., myTop of myArray.
 *   2. -1 <= myTop < STACK_CAPACITY
 ----------------------------------------------------------------*/

#ifndef STACK
#define STACK

const int STACK_CAPACITY = 128;
typedef int StackElement;

class Stack
{

/***** Function Members *****/
public:

    . . .

/***** Data Members *****/
private:
   StackElement myArray[STACK_CAPACITY];
   int myTop;

}; // end of class declaration

#endif
```

FUNCTION MEMBERS

To complete this implementation of a stack, functions must be written to perform the basic stack operations. For each operation we will ask questions like those we did for the Time class in the preceding chapter; for example, whether to make it a member function, a constant function, or an inline function.

CONSTRUCTORS.   The compiler will allocate memory for the data members myArray and myTop, so the Stack constructors need only do the initialization necessary to create an empty stack. Because myTop always points at the array element containing the top element, it seems natural to assign myTop the value −1 to signal an empty stack:

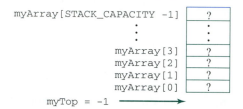

Our class constructor is thus trivial and is shown in Fig. 4.3. Note that because of its simplicity, we have inlined it and placed its definition in Stack.h immediately following the class declaration.

FIGURE 4.3   A CONSTRUCTOR FOR THE Stack CLASS

```
. . .

class Stack
{

/***** Function Members *****/
public:

/* --- Constructor ---
 *
 * Precondition:  A stack has been declared.
 * Postcondition: The stack has been constructed as an
 *                   empty stack.
 ************************************************************/

Stack();

/***** Data Members *****/
private:
  StackElement myArray[STACK_CAPACITY];
  int myTop;

}; // end of class declaration
```

```
//--- Definition of Class Constructor
inline Stack::Stack()
{ myTop = -1; }

#endif
```

Given this function, a declaration

```
    Stack s;
```

will construct s as follows:

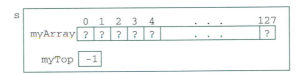

EMPTY.   The operation to check if a stack is empty is now trivial since it need only check the myTop data member to see whether it is −1. We make it a member function, inline it because of its simplicity, and make it a constant function, as shown in Fig. 4.4. Also shown is a small test driver that tests the class constructor and the empty operation.

FIGURE 4.4   THE EMPTY OPERATION FOR THE Stack CLASS

```
. . .

class Stack
{
/***** Function Members *****/
public:
    . . .
/* --- Is the Stack empty? ---
 * Receive: Stack containing this function (implicitly)
 * Returns: True if the Stack containing this function is empty
 *          and false otherwise
 ***********************************************************/

bool empty() const;

/***** Data Members *****/
private:
    StackElement myArray[STACK_CAPACITY];
    int myTop;

}; // end of class declaration
    . . .
```

```
//--- Definition of empty
inline bool Stack::empty() const
{ return (myTop == -1); }


#endif
```

TEST DRIVER:

```
#include "Stack.h"
#include <iostream>
using namespace std;

int main()
{
    Stack s;
    cout << boolalpha << "s empty? " << s.empty() << endl;
}
```

EXECUTION:

```
s empty? true
```

PUSH.   A specification for the push operation is

Receive: A `Stack` object (perhaps implicitly) and a `value` to add to the stack

Return: The modified stack (perhaps implicitly), with `value` added at its top, provided there is room

Because push modifies the `Stack` object, it seems natural to make it a member function. It cannot be a constant function because it must modify the data members. A prototype for this member function `push()` thus is

```
void push(const StackElement & value);
```

An algorithm for the push operation is:

1. Check if the array is full by checking if `myTop` is equal to the array limit.

2. If it is not then

a. Increment `myTop` by 1.

b. Store the item in `myArray[myTop]`.

Otherwise

Signal that an error (stack full) has occurred.

Figure 4.5 shows the prototype for `push()` added to the class declaration and a definition of `push()` in the implementation file that implements this algorithm. Also shown are statements that can be added to a driver program to test this member function.

FIGURE 4.5 THE PUSH OPERATION FOR THE Stack CLASS

In Stack.h

```
. . .

class Stack
{

/***** Function Members *****/
public:
    . . .
/* --- Add a value to the stack ---
 *
 * Receive:   The Stack containing this function (implicitly)
 *            A value to be added to a Stack
 * Pass back: The Stack (implicitly), with value added at its
 *            top, provided there's space
 * Output:    "Stack full" message if no space for value
 ***********************************************************/

void push(const StackElement & value);

/***** Data Members *****/
    . . .

}; // end of class declaration
. . .
```

In Stack.cpp

```
void Stack::push(const StackElement & value)
{
  if (myTop < STACK_CAPACITY - 1)  // Preserve stack invariant
  {
    ++myTop;
    myArray[myTop] = value;
  }                       // or simply, myArray[++myTop] = value;
  else
    cerr << "*** Stack is full -- can't add new value ***\n"
         << "Must increase value of STACK_CAPACITY in Stack.h\n";
}
```

ADD TO TEST DRIVER:

```
   . . .
for (int i = 1; i <= 128; i++) s.push(i);
cout << "Stack should now be full\n";
s.push(129);
```

EXECUTION:

```
s empty? true
Stack should now be full
*** Stack is full -- can't add new value ***
Must increase value of STACK_CAPACITY in Stack.h
```

OUTPUT.   An output operation is not one of the basic operations listed in our definition of a stack as an ADT. However, as operations are implemented, they need to
be tested, so an output operation is often added early in the implementation
process. This can be a constant member function `display()` that simply runs
through the array and displays the values stored in `myArray[myTop]` down through
`myArray[0]`. Figure 4.6 shows the prototype and definition for `display()` and how
we might use it in a test driver.

FIGURE 4.6   AN OUTPUT OPERATION FOR THE Stack CLASS

In **Stack.h**

. . .

```
class Stack
{

/***** Function Members *****/
public:

    . . .

/* --- Display values stored in the stack ---
 *
 * Receive: The Stack containing this function (implicitly)
 *          The ostream out
 * Output:  The Stack's contents, from top down, to out
 ***********************************************************/

void display(ostream & out) const;

/***** Data Members *****/

    . . .

}; // end of class declaration
```

. . .

In **Stack.cpp**

```
void Stack::display(ostream & out) const
{
  for (int i = myTop; i >= 0; i--)
    out << myArray[i] << endl;
}
```

MODIFY TEST DRIVER:

```
   . . .
/*
for (int i = 1; i <= 128; i++) s.push(i);
cout << "Stack should now be full\n";
s.push(129);
*/
for (int i = 1; i <= 4; i++) s.push(2*i);
cout << "Stack contents:\n";
s.display(cout);
cout << "s empty? " << s.empty() << endl;
```

EXECUTION:

```
s empty? true
Stack contents:
8
6
4
2
s empty? false
```

TOP.   The top operation is to retrieve the value at the top of the stack. A specification for it is

    Receive: A Stack object (perhaps implicitly)

    Return: The value at top of the stack, provided the stack is nonempty

    Output: An "empty stack" message if the stack is empty

From the specification, it is clear that top() should be a constant member function,
and so a prototype for it is

```
StackElement top(; const;
```

Figure 4.7 shows this prototype added to the class declaration, the definition of
top() in the implementation file, and statements to add to a driver to test it.

FIGURE 4.7   **A TOP OPERATION FOR THE Stack CLASS**

In **Stack.h**

. . .

```
class Stack
{

/***** Function Members *****/
public:
    . . .
```

```
/* --- Return value at top of the stack ---
 *
 * Receive: The Stack containing this function (implicitly)
 * Return:  The value at the top of the Stack, if nonempty
 * Output:  "Stack empty" message if stack is empty
 *********************************************************/

StackElement top() const;

/***** Data Members *****/
  . . .

}; // end of class declaration
 . . .
```

In **Stack.cpp**

```
StackElement Stack::top() const
{
  if (myTop >= 0)
    return myArray[myTop];
  cerr << "*** Stack is empty ***\n";
}
```

MODIFY TEST DRIVER:
```
  . . .
// add at bottom of driver
cout << "Top value: " << s.top() << endl;
```

EXECUTION:

```
Stack contents:
8
6
4
2
s empty? false
Top value: 8
```

POP.   Our last stack operation is a pop operation to remove the top stack element. A specification for it is

> Receive: A Stack object (perhaps implicitly)
> Return: The stack with its top value (if any) removed
> Output: An "empty stack" message if the stack is empty

This specification indicates that pop() should be a nonconstant member function, so a prototype for it is simply

```
    void pop();
```

And an algorithm for the pop operation is

1. Check if the stack is empty.

2. If it is not empty then

Decrement myTop by 1.

Otherwise

Display a "stack empty" message.

The definition of pop() in Fig. 4.8 implements this algorithm.

 FIGURE 4.8   A POP OPERATION FOR THE Stack CLASS

In **Stack.h**

. . .

```
class Stack
{

/***** Function Members *****/
public:

     . . .

/* --- Remove value at top of the stack ---
 *
 * Receive:    The Stack containing this function (implicitly)
 * Pass back:  The Stack containing this function (implicitly)
 *             with its top value (if any) removed
 * Output:     "Stack-empty" message if stack is empty.
 *************************************************************/

void pop();

/***** Data Members *****/

     . . .

}; // end of class declaration
. . .
```

In **Stack.cpp**

```
void Stack::pop()
{
  if (myTop >= 0)   // Preserve stack invariant
    myTop--;
  else
    cerr << "*** Stack is empty — can't remove a value ***\n";
}
```

MODIFY TEST DRIVER:

```
    . . .
// add at bottom of driver
while (!s.empty())
{
  cout << "Popping " << s.top() << endl;
  s.pop();
}
cout << "s empty? " << s.empty() << endl;
```

EXECUTION:

```
Stack contents:
8
6
4
2
s empty? false
Top value: 8
Popping 8
Popping 6
Popping 4
Popping 2
s empty? true
```

Figure 4.9 contains the complete declaration for our `Stack` class, with the documentation omitted to save space. The complete header file, implementation file, and test driver can be downloaded from the website described in the preface.

FIGURE 4.9   DECLARATION OF THE `Stack` CLASS

```
/* Stack.h contains the declaration of class Stack.
    . . .
  **********************************************************/

#ifndef STACK
#define STACK

const int STACK_CAPACITY = 128;
typedef int StackElement;

class Stack
{

/***** Function Members *****/
public:

/* --- Constructor ---
  **********************************************************/

Stack();
```

```
/* --- Is the Stack empty? ---
 ***********************************************************/

bool empty() const;

/* --- Add a value to the stack ---
 ***********************************************************/

void push(const StackElement & value);

/* --- Display values stored in the stack ---
 ***********************************************************/

void display(ostream & out) const;

/* --- Return value at top of the stack ---
 ***********************************************************/

StackElement top() const;

/* --- Remove value at top of the stack ---
 ---------------------------------------------------------*/

void pop();

/***** Data Members *****/
private:
  StackElement myArray[STACK_CAPACITY];
  int myTop;

}; // end of class declaration

#endif
```

A LOOK AHEAD

Our implementation of a stack places an upper limit on the size of the stack, because an array has a fixed size. This makes it necessary, therefore, to ensure that STACK_CAPACITY has been set large enough for the stack(s) being used in a program, and this, obviously, can result in considerable wasted space. It is also inconvenient and annoying to enter a collection of data and then have the program crash or start producing incorrect or unreliable results because the container cannot hold all of the data values. With our current implementation, the user must modify the definition of STACK_CAPACITY in Stack.h, which means that all programs and libraries that #include Stack.h must be recompiled. In Chap. 6 we consider an alternative implementation that allows the user to specify the capacity of the stack in its declaration and then another implementation that does not impose any a priori limit on the capacity.

Another weakness with our implementation is that the type of the stack elements must be set in Stack.h. Again, changing this type requires recompilations of libraries and programs that `#include Stack.h`. But a more serious limitation is that we can only use one element type at a time. If we need a stack of `int`s and a stack of `string`s, we must create two different class libraries: `IntStack.h`, which is `Stack.h` with `StackElement` set to `int` in the `typedef` declaration; and `StringStack.h`, which is `Stack.h` with `StackElement` set to `string` in the `typedef` declaration. And we need two copies of the implementation file, `IntStack.cpp` and `StringStack.cpp`, both of which are identical to `Stack.cpp`. Obviously, this is extremely cumbersome and inconvenient. In Chap. 6 we will consider class templates and show how we can essentially have the compiler take care of this for us.

✔ Quick Quiz 4.2

1. Define stack as an ADT.

2. What are the two steps in building a class?

3. What two steps are involved in implementing a class?

Questions 4–6 assume that `Stack` is the class described in this section with `StackType` set to `int` and `STACK_CAPACITY` to 5. Give the contents of the `myTop` and `myArray` data members of s after the code segment is executed, or indicate why an error occurs.

4.
```
Stack s;
s.push(123);
s.push(456);
s.pop();
s.push(789);
s.pop();
```

5.
```
Stack s;
s.push(111);
i = s.top();
s.push(222);
s.pop();
s.push(i);
```

6.
```
Stack s;
for (int i = 0; i < 5; i++)
  s.push(2*i);
s.pop();
s.pop();
```

✍ EXERCISES 4.2

For Exercises 1–4, assume that `Stack` is the class described in this section with `StackType` set to `int` and `STACK_CAPACITY` to 5. Give the contents of the `myTop` and `myArray` data members of s after the code segment is executed, or indicate why an error occurs.

1.
```
Stack s;
s.push(10);
s.push(22);
s.push(37);
s.pop();
s.pop();
```

2.
```
Stack s;
s.push(10);
s.push(9);
s.push(8);
while (!s.empty())
    s.pop();
```

3.
```
Stack s;
for (int i = 1; i <= 6; i++)
    s.push(10*i);
```

4.
```
Stack s;
s.push(11);
i = s.top();
s.pop();
```

5. The array-based implementation of stacks used in this chapter requires that an upper limit STACK_CAPACITY be placed on the maximum size that a stack may have. Write a member function full() for the Stack class that returns true or false according to whether or not the array used to store the stack elements is full.

6. Write documentation, a prototype, and a definition for a member function bottom() for the Stack class that returns the bottom element of the stack.

7. Repeat Exercise 6, but for a function bottom() that is not a member function of the Stack class and neither is it a friend function.

8. Proceed as in Exercise 6, but design a function nthElement() to retrieve the nth stack element (counting from the top), leaving the stack without its top n elements.

9. Proceed as in Exercise 7, but leave the stack contents unchanged.

10. Consider the following railroad switching network:

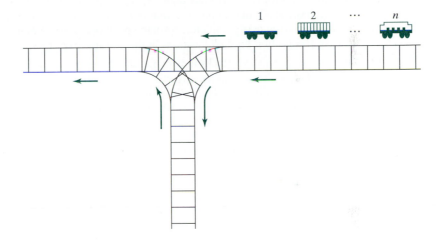

Railroad cars numbered $1, 2, \ldots, n$ on the right track are to be permuted and moved along on the left track. As described in Problem 2 of Sec. 4.1, a car may be moved directly onto the left track, or it may be shunted onto the siding to be removed at a later time and placed on the left track. The siding thus operates like a stack, a push operation moving a car from the right track onto the siding and a pop operation moving the "top" car from the siding onto the left track.

a. For $n = 3$, find all possible permutations of cars that can be obtained (on the left track) by a sequence of these operations. For example, push 1, push 2, move 3, pop 2, pop 1 arranges them in the order 3, 2, 1. Are any permutations not possible?

b. Find all possible permutations for $n = 4$. What permutations (if any) are not possible?

c. Repeat b for $n = 5$.

d. *Challenge*: In general, what permutations of the sequence $1, 2, \ldots, n$ can be obtained when a stack is used in this manner?

11. Suppose that some application requires using two stacks whose elements are of the same type. A natural storage structure of such a two-stack data type would consist of two arrays and two top pointers. Explain why this may not be a spacewise efficient implementation.

12. A better storage structure for a two-stack data type than that described in Exercise 11 would be to use a single array for the storage structure and let the stacks grow toward each other.

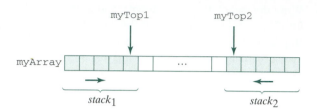

Design a class for this two-stack data type using this implementation. In your functions for the basic stack operations, the number of the stack to be operated upon, 1 or 2, should be passed as a parameter. Also, the push operation should not fail because of a stack-full condition until *all* locations in the storage array have been used.

13. Storing more than two stacks in a single one-dimensional array in such a way that no stack-full condition occurs for any of the stacks until all the array elements have been used cannot be done as efficiently as in Exercise 12 because some of the array elements will have to be shifted. Nevertheless, design a class for an *n*-stack data type using this implementation, $n > 2$. In the functions for the basic stack operations, the stack number being operated upon, $1, 2, \ldots, n$, should be passed as a parameter. (*Hint*: You might partition the storage array into *n* equal subarrays, one for each stack, and use two arrays of "pointers," `myBottom` and `myTop`, to keep track of where the bottoms and the tops of the stacks are located in the storage array. When one of these stacks becomes full, search to find the nearest empty location(s) in the array, and then move stacks as necessary to enlarge the storage space for this stack.)

4.3 TWO APPLICATIONS OF STACKS: FUNCTION CALLS; REVERSE POLISH NOTATION

Once a stack class like that in the preceding section has been thoroughly tested, it can be used as a new data type in programs simply by including the header file for that class. For example, the program in Fig. 4.1 contains the compiler directive

```
#include "Stack.h"
```

which inserts the header file for the `Stack` type of the preceding section to solve the base-ten to base-two conversion problem. In this section we show how stacks are used for Problem 3 described in Sec. 4.1—function calls—and how they are used to construct and evaluate Reverse Polish expressions.

USE OF STACKS IN FUNCTION CALLS

Whenever a function begins execution (i.e., is activated), an **activation record** (or **stack frame**) is created to store the **current environment** for that function, which includes such things as

parameters
caller's state information (saved)   (e.g., contents of registers, return address)
local variables
temporary storage

Because functions may call other functions and thus interrupt their own execution, some data structure must be used to store these activation records so they can be recovered and the system reset when a function resumes execution.

It should be clear that this structure must have LIFO behavior, because when a function terminates, the function with which to resume execution is the last function whose activation record was saved. A stack is therefore the appropriate structure, and since it is manipulated at *run-time*, it is called the **run-time stack**.

When a function is called, the following events occur:

1. A copy of its activation record is pushed onto the run-time stack.

2. Arguments are copied into the parameter spaces.

3. Control is transferred to the starting address of the body of the function.

Thus, the top activation record in the run-time stack is always that of the function currently being executed.

When a function terminates, the run-time stack is popped, which removes the activation record of the terminated function and "exposes" the activation record of the function that was previously executing and was interrupted. This activation record can then be used to restore the environment of the interrupted function so it can resume execution. This pushing and popping of the run-time stack is the real overhead associated with function calls that inline functions avoid by replacing the function call with the body of the function.

Understanding how a stack is used in function calls is the key to understanding recursive functions. See Sec. 7.3 for an example with accompanying diagrams that illustrate this pushing and popping of the run-time stack.

APPLICATION OF STACKS TO REVERSE POLISH NOTATION

The task of a compiler is to generate the machine instructions required to carry out the instructions of the source program written in a high-level language. One part of this task is to generate machine instructions for evaluating arithmetic expressions like that in the assignment statement

```
x = a * b + c;
```

The compiler must generate machine instructions like the following:

1. `LOAD a`   Retrieve the value of `a` from the memory location where it is stored and load it into the accumulator register

2. `MULT b`   Retrieve the value of `b` and multiply the value in the accumulator register by it

3. `ADD c`   Retrieve the value of `c` and add it to the value in the accumulator register

4. `STORE x`   Store the value in the accumulator register in the memory location associated with `x`

In most programming languages, arithmetic expressions are written in *infix* notation like `a * b + c` in which the symbol for each binary operation is placed between the operands. Many compilers first transform these infix expressions into *postfix* notation (or prefix notation, described in the exercises), in which the operator follows the operands, and then generates machine instructions to evaluate these postfix expressions. This two-step process is used because the transformation from infix to postfix is straightforward, and postfix expressions are, in general, easier to evaluate mechanically than are infix expressions.[5]

When infix notation is used for arithmetic expressions, parentheses are often needed to indicate the order in which operations are to be carried out. For example, parentheses are placed in the expression $2 * (3 + 4)$ to indicate that the addition is to be performed before the multiplication. If the parentheses were omitted, giving $2 * 3 + 4$, the standard priority rules would dictate that the multiplication is to be performed before the addition.

In the early 1950s, the Polish logician Jan Lukasiewicz observed that parentheses are not necessary in postfix notation, also called **Reverse Polish Notation (RPN)**. For example, the infix expression $2 * (3 + 4)$ can be written in RPN as

$$2\ 3\ 4 + *$$

EVALUATING RPN EXPRESSIONS. As an illustration of how RPN expressions are evaluated, consider the expression

$$1\ 5 + 8\ 4\ 1 - - *$$

that corresponds to the infix expression $(1 + 5) * (8 - (4 - 1))$. This expression is scanned from left to right until an operator is found. At that point, the last two preceding operands are combined using this operator. For our example, the first operator encountered is $+$, and its operands 1 and 5:

$$\underline{1\ 5 +}\ 8\ 4\ 1 - - *$$

Replacing this subexpression with its value 6 yields the reduced RPN expression

$$6\ 8\ 4\ 1 - - *$$

---

[5]Although most calculators require that arithmetic expressions be entered in infix form, some (e.g., Hewlett-Packard) use postfix (RPN) notation.

Resuming the left-to-right scan, we next encounter the operator $-$ and determine its two operands:

$$6\ 8\ \underline{4\ 1} - - *$$

Applying this operator then yields

$$6\ \underline{8\ 3} - *$$

The next operator encountered is another $-$, and its operands are 8 and 3:

$$6\ \underline{8\ 3} - *$$

Evaluating this difference gives

$$\underline{6\ 5} *$$

The final operator is $*$

$$\underline{6\ 5} *$$

and the value 30 is obtained for this expression.

This method of evaluating an RPN expression requires that the operands be stored until an operator is encountered in the left-to-right scan. At this point, the last two operands must be retrieved and combined using this operation. This suggests that a last-in-first-out structure—that is, a stack—should be used to store the operands. Each time an operand is encountered, it is pushed onto the stack. Then, when an operator is encountered, the top two values are popped from the stack; the operation is applied to them, and the result is pushed back onto the stack. The following algorithm summarizes this procedure:

ALGORITHM TO EVALUATE RPN EXPRESSIONS

/* Receive: An RPN expression.
   Return: The value of the RPN expression (unless an error occurred).
   Note: Uses a stack to store operands.
--*/

1. Initialize an empty stack.

2. Repeat the following until the end of the expression is encountered:

    a. Get the next token (constant, variable, arithmetic operator) in the RPN expression.

    b. If the token is an operand, push it onto the stack. If it is an operator, then do the following:

        i. Pop the top two values from the stack. (If the stack does not contain two items, an error due to a malformed RPN expression has occurred and evaluation is terminated.)

        ii. Apply the operator to these two values.

        iii. Push the resulting value back onto the stack.

3. When the end of the expression is encountered, its value is on top of the stack (and, in fact, must be the only value in the stack).

Figure 4.10 illustrates the application of this algorithm to the RPN expression

$$2\ 4 * 9\ 5 + -$$

The up arrow (↑) indicates the current token.

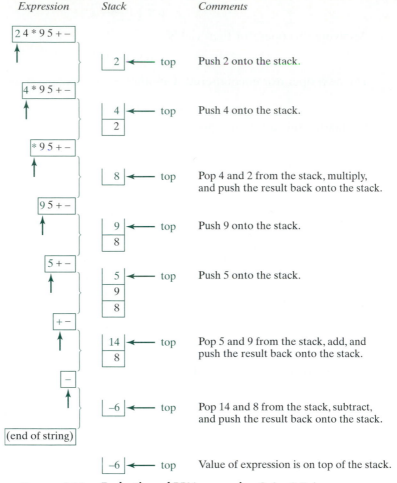

FIGURE **4.10**   **Evaluation of RPN expression 2 4 ∗ 9 5 + −.**

CONVERTING INFIX EXPRESSIONS TO RPN. There are several methods for converting infix expressions. We begin with one that uses a graphical parenthesis-free representation of expressions as **expression trees**. As we will see in more detail in Chap. 10, trees are pictured using circular **nodes** that store data, and these are connected by line segments called **edges**. One of the nodes, called the **root**, has no edges coming into it, and every other node is reachable from the root by a unique **path**, which is a sequence of connected edges. The root node is usually placed at the top of the tree diagram.

To illustrate, consider the following expression tree for the expression a ∗ b:

Here the root node contains the operator * and has two **children** nodes, the left one
containing the operator's left operand and the right one its right operand. The following expression trees represent the expressions a * b + c, a * (b + c), and
(a + b) * (c / (d - e)):

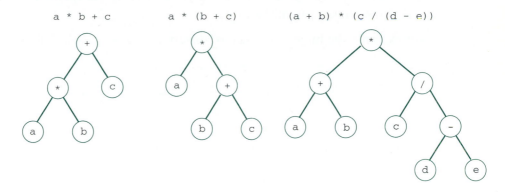

From these examples we see how infix expressions can be represented graphically
without using parentheses.

To obtain the RPN expression corresponding to an expression, we must traverse
(i.e., walk through) the tree in a Left-Right-Parent order.[6] This means for each
node, before we can "visit" it we must first visit its left child and then its right child.
For the infix expression a * b + c, this traversal produces

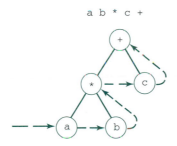

Similar Left-Right-Parent traversal of the expression tree for a * (b + c) produces the RPN expression

a b c + *

and for (a + b) * (c / (d - e)),

a b + c d e - / *

---

[6]Traversing the tree in Left-Parent-Right order gives the *infix* expression, but parentheses must be
inserted around each subexpresssion; for example, ((a * b) + c). Traversing the tree in Parent-
Left-Right order gives a *prefix* expression in which operators are written before their operands; for
example, + * a b c. See the exercises later in this chapter for more about prefix notation.

Another method for converting infix expressions to RPN that is good for conversions "by hand" might be called the *fully parenthesize-move-erase method*:

1. Fully parenthesize the expression.

2. Replace each right parenthesis by the corresponding operator.

3. Erase all left parentheses.

For example, the three steps used to convert a * b + c are as follows:

```
1.  ((a * b) + c)

2.  ((a * b) + c)  ⟶  ((a b * c +

3.  a b * c +
```

The three steps for converting a * (b + c) are

```
1.  (a * (b + c))

2.  (a * b) + c))  ⟶  ((a b c + *

3.  a b c + *
```

and for converting (a + b) * (c / (d - e)):

```
1.  ((a + b) * (c / (d - e)))

2.  ((a + b) * (c / (d - e)))  ⟶  ((a b + (c ( d e - / *

3.  a b + c d e - / *
```

Neither of the two preceding methods of converting infix to RPN lends itself to easy implementation with a C++ function. Instead, a method that uses a stack to store the operators is preferred. As an illustration of how a stack can be used in this conversion, consider the infix expression

$$7 + 2 * 3$$

In a left-to-right scan of this expression, 7 is encountered and may be immediately displayed. Next, the operator $+$ is encountered, but as its right operand has not yet been displayed, it must be stored and thus is pushed onto a stack of operators:

Output	Stack
7	+

Next, the operand 2 is encountered and displayed. At this point, it must be determined whether 2 is the right operand for the preceding operator $+$ or is the left operand for the next operator. We determine this by comparing the operator $+$ on the top of the stack with the next operator $*$. Since $*$ has higher priority than $+$, the

preceding operand 2 that was displayed is the left operand for *; thus we push *
onto the stack and search for its right operand:

Output   Stack

7 2

```
| * |
| + |
```

The operand 3 is encountered next and displayed. Since the end of the expression
has now been reached, the right operand for the operator * on the top of the stack
has been found, and so * can now be popped and displayed:

Output   Stack

7 2 3 *

```
| + |
```

The end of the expression also signals that the right operand for the remaining
operator + in the stack has been found, and so it, too, can be popped and displayed,
yielding the RPN expression

$$7\ 2\ 3 * +$$

Parentheses within infix expressions present no real difficulties. A left parenthesis indicates the beginning of a subexpression, and when encountered, it is pushed
onto the stack. When a right parenthesis is encountered, operators are popped from
the stack until the matching left parenthesis rises to the top. At this point, the
subexpression originally enclosed by the parentheses has been converted to RPN,
so the parentheses may be discarded and the conversion continues. All of this is
contained in the following algorithm:

ALGORITHM TO CONVERT AN INFIX EXPRESSION TO RPN

```
/* Receive:   An infix expression.
   Output:    The RPN expression.
   Note:      Uses a stack to store operators.
--------------------------------------------------------------------------*/
```

1. Initialize an empty stack of operators.

2. While no error has occurred and the end of the infix expression has not been
   reached, do the following:

   a. Get the next input *token* (constant, variable, arithmetic operator, left
      parenthesis, right parenthesis) in the infix expression.
   b. If *token* is
        i. a left parenthesis   Push it onto the stack.

        ii. a right parenthesis   Pop and display stack elements until a left
                                  parenthesis is encountered, but do not
                                  display it. (It is an error if the stack becomes
                                  empty with no left parenthesis found.)

iii. an operator

If the stack is empty or *token* has a higher priority than the top stack element, push *token* onto the stack.

Otherwise, pop and display the top stack element; then repeat the comparison of *token* with the new top stack item.

Note: A left parenthesis in the stack is assumed to have a lower priority than that of operators.

iv. an operand

Display it.

3. When the end of the infix expression is reached, pop and display stack items until the stack is empty.

Figure 4.11 illustrates this algorithm for the infix expression

$$7 * 8 - (2 + 3)$$

An up arrow (↑) has been used to indicate the current input symbol and the symbol displayed by the algorithm.

The program in Fig. 4.12 implements this algorithm for converting an infix expression to RPN using the `Stack` data type developed in Sec.4.2. A stack with `StackElement` set to `char` is used to store the operators. The program assumes that the input is a valid infix expression and does very little checking to determine if it is well formed.

FIGURE 4.12   CONVERTING INFIX EXPRESSIONS TO RPN

```
/* Program to convert infix expressions to Reverse Polish Notation.
 *
 * Input:  An infix expression and user responses
 * Output: The RPN expression
 ***********************************************************************

#include <iostream>              // <<, >>, cout, cin
#include <string>                // string, ==, find, npos
#include <cassert>               // assert()
using namespace std;
#include "Stack.h"               // Stack class with StackElement = char

string RPN(string exp);

int main()
{
  string exp;                    // infix expression
```

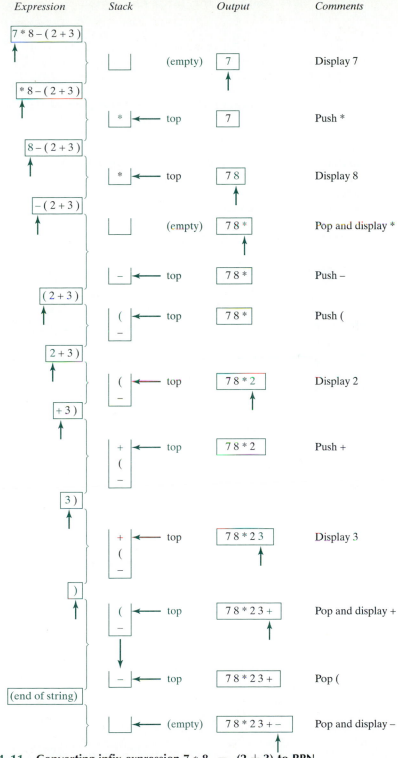

FIGURE 4–11   **Converting infix expression 7 ∗ 8 − (2 + 3) to RPN.**

```
              cout << "NOTE: Enter # for infix expression to stop.\n";
              for (;;)
              {
                cout << "\nInfix Expression? ";
                getline(cin, exp);
                if (exp == "#") break;

                cout << "RPN Expression is " << RPN(exp) << endl;
              }
           }

           /* RPN() converts an infix expression exp to RPN.
            *
            * Receive: Infix expression exp
            * Return:   Corresponding RPN expression
            * Output:   Error message if error found in exp
            ************************************************************/

           string RPN(string exp)
           {
             char token,                      // character in exp
                  topToken;                   // token on top of opStack
             Stack opStack;                   // stack of operators
             string RPNexp;                   // RPN string
             const string BLANK = " ";        // to insert spaces in RPNexp

             for (int i = 0; i < exp.length(); i++)
             {
               token = exp[i];
               switch(token)
               {
                 case ' ' : break;        // do nothing -- skip blanks

                 case '(' : opStack.push(token);
                            break;

                 case ')' : for (;;)
                            {
                              assert (!opStack.empty());
                              topToken = opStack.top();
                              opStack.pop();
                              if (topToken == '(') break;

                              RPNexp.append(BLANK + topToken);
                            }
                            break;
```

```
         case '+' : case '-' :
         case '*' : case '/' :
                   for (;;)
                   {
                     if (opStack.empty() ||
                         opStack.top() == '(' ||
                         (token == '*' || token == '/') &&
                         (opStack.top() == '+' || opStack.top() == '-')
                        )
                     {
                       opStack.push(token);
                       break;
                     }
                     else
                     {
                       topToken = opStack.top();
                       opStack.pop();
                       RPNexp.append(BLANK + topToken);
                     }
                   }
                   break;

      default : RPNexp.append(BLANK + token);
    }
  }

  // Pop remaining operators on the stack
  for (;;)
  {
    if (opStack.empty()) break;

    topToken = opStack.top();
    opStack.pop();
    if (topToken != '(')
    {
      RPNexp.append(BLANK + topToken);
    }

    else
    {
      cout << " *** Error in infix expression ***\n";
      break;
    }
  }
  return RPNexp;

}
```

SAMPLE RUN:

```
NOTE:   Enter # for infix expression to stop.

Infix Expression? a + b
RPN Expression is a b +

Infix Expression? a * b + c
RPN Expression is a b * c +

Infix Expression? a * (b + c)
RPN Expression is a b c + *

Infix Expression? (a + b) * (c / (d - e)):
RPN Expression is a b + c d - e / : *

Infix Expression? a - (b - (c - (d - (e - f ))))
RPN Expression is a b c d e f - - - - -

Infix Expression? a - b - c - d - e - f
RPN Expression is a b - c - d - e - f -

Infix Expression? a + b + d
RPN Expression is a b + d +

Infix Expression? #
```

✔ Quick Quiz 4.3

1. Whenever a function begins execution, a(n) _____ is created to store the current environment for that function.

2. A(n) _____ stack stores the activation records during a sequence of function calls.

For Questions 3–6, use infix, prefix, and postfix as answers.

3. a b + is written in _____ notation.

4. a + b is written in _____ notation.

5. + a b is written in _____ notation.

6. RPN is another name for _____ notation.

7. The value of 5 4 - 3 2 + * is _____

8. The value of * + - 5 4 3 2 is _____

9. Convert (a - (b - c)) * d to RPN.

10. Convert (a - (b - c)) * d to prefix notation.

✍ EXERCISES 4.3

In Exercises 1–11, assume that a = 7.0, b = 4.0, c = 3.0, and d = −2.0. Evaluate the RPN expression.

1. a b + c / d *

2. a b c + / d *

3. a b c d + / *

4. a b + c + d +

5. a b + c d + +   **6.** a b c + + d +

7. a b c d + + +   **8.** a b - c - d -

9. a b - c d - -   **10.** a b c - - d -

11. a b c d - - -

For the RPN expressions in Exercises 12–14, trace the algorithm for evaluating RPN expressions by showing the contents of the stack immediately before each of the tokens marked with a caret is read. Also, give the value of the RPN expression.

12. 32 5 3 + / 5 *   **13.** 2 17 - 5 / 3 *
              ^   ^   ^   ^

14. 19 7 15 5 - - -
                ^ ^ ^

Convert the infix expressions in Exercises 15–22 to RPN.

15. a * b + c - d   **16.** a + b / c + d

17. (a + b) / c + d   **18.** a + b / (c + d)

19. (a + b) / (c + d)   **20.** (a - b) * (c - (d + e))

21. (((a - b) - c) - d) - e   **22.** a - (b - (c - (d - e)))

For the infix expressions in Exercises 23–27, trace the algorithm for converting infix to RPN by showing both the stack and the accumulated output immediately before each of the tokens marked with a caret is read. Also, show the RPN expression.

23. a + b / c - d   **24.** (a + b) / c - d + e
              ^ ^ ^   ^   ^

25. a + b / (c - d) - e   **26.** a + b / (c - d) * e
              ^   ^ ^   ^   ^ ^

27. a + b / ((c - d) * e) - f
                ^   ^   ^ ^

Convert the RPN expressions in Exercises 28–35 to infix notation:

28. a b c + - d *   **29.** a b + c d - *

30. a b c d + - *   **31.** a b + c - d e * /

32. a b / c / d /   **33.** a b / c d / /

34. a b c / d / /   **35.** a b c d / / /

The symbol — cannot be used for the unary minus operation in prefix or postfix notation because ambiguous expressions result. For example, 5 3 - - could be interpreted as either 5 - (-3) = 8 or -(5 - 3) = -2. In Exercises 36–45, suppose instead that ~ is used for unary minus.

Evaluate the RPN expressions in Exercises 36–41 if a = 7, b = 5, and c = 3:

36. a ~ b c + -   **37.** a b ~ c + -

38. a b c ~ + -   **39.** a b c + ~ -

40. a b c + - ~   **41.** a b c - - ~ ~ ~

Convert the infix expressions in Exercises 42–45 to RPN:

42. a * (b + ~c)   **43.** ~(a + b / (c - d))

44. (~a) * (~b)   **45.** ~(a - (~b * (c + ~d)))

Convert the logical expressions in Exercises 46–52 to RPN:

46. a && b || c

47. a && (b || !c)

48. !(a && b)

49. (a || b) && (c || (d && !e))

50. (a == b) || (c == d)

51. ((a > 3) && (a < 9)) || !(a > 0)

52. ((b * b – 4 * a * c) >= 0) && ((a > 0) || (a < 0))

53–60. An alternative to postfix notation is *prefix* notation, in which the symbol for each operation precedes the operands. For example, the infix expression 2 * 3 + 4 would be written in prefix notation as + * 2 3 4, and 2 * (3 + 4) would be written as * 2 + 3 4. Convert each of the infix expressions in Exercise 15–22 to prefix notation.

In Exercises 61–68, assume that a = 7.0, b = 4.0, c = 3.0, and d = −2.0. Evaluate each of the prefix expressions (see Exercises 53-60):

61. * a / + b c d   **62.** * / + a b c d

63. – a – b – c d   **64.** – – a b – c d

65. – a – – b c d   **66.** – – – a b c d

67. * + a b – c d   **68.** + * a b – c d

Convert the prefix expressions in Exercises 69–76 to infix notation (see Exercises 53–60):

69. * + a b – c d   **70.** + * a b – c d

71. – – a b – c d   **72.** – – a – b c d

73. – – – a b c d   **74.** / + * a b – c d e

75. / + * a b c – d e   **76.** / + a * b c – d e

☞ PROGRAMMING POINTERS

1. Building a class consists of two steps: (1) Design the class and (2) implement the class.

2. In designing a class, describe the operations independently of how the class will be implemented, that is, in a way that does not depend on any particular representation of the class objects.

3. Implementing a class involves two steps: (1) Define data members to represent the object(s) being modeled and (2) define the operations identified in the design phase.

ADT TIPS

1. A stack has *last-in-last-out* (*LIFO*) behavior.

2. A run-time stack is used to keep track of current environments of functions during a sequence of function calls and returns.

3. Understanding how a stack is used in function calls is the key to understanding recursive functions.

PROGRAMMING PROBLEMS

SECTION 4.2

1. Empirical evidence suggests that *any program that comes close to using all available space will eventually run out of space*. Consequently, shifting stacks around in an array as described in Exercise 13 so that all possible array locations are used seems rather futile. Redesign the implementation so that no push operations are attempted if there are fewer than `LOWER_LIMIT` unused locations left in the array.

2. Use the `Stack` class in a program that reads a string, one character at a time, and determine whether the string contains balanced parentheses, that is, for each left parenthesis (if there are any) there is exactly one matching right parenthesis later in the string.

3. The problem in Prob. 2 can be solved without using a stack; in fact, a simple integer variable can be used. Describe how and write a program that uses your method to solve the problem.

4. For a given integer $n > 1$, the smallest integer $d > 1$ that divides n is a prime factor. We can find the *prime factorization* of n if we find d and then replace n by the quotient of n divided by d, repeating this until n becomes 1. Write a program that determines the prime factorization of n in this manner but that displays the prime factors in descending order. For example, for $n = 3960$, your program should produce

$$11 * 5 * 3 * 3 * 2 * 2 * 2$$

5. A program is to be written to find a path from one point in a maze to another.

   a. Describe how a two-dimensional array could be used to model the maze.

   b. Describe how a stack could be used in an algorithm for finding a path.

   c. Write the program.

SECTION 4.3

6. Modify the program `InfixToRPN` in Fig. 4.12 so that it provides tracing information similar to that in Fig. 4.11. To make the output more manageable, you may simplify it to something like the following trace for the expression `7 * 8 - (2 + 3)`:

Token	Output	Stack (bottom to top)
7	7	empty
*		*
8	8	*
-	*	-
(		- (
2	2	- (
+		- (+
3	3	- (+
)	+	-
;	-	empty

7. Modify the program `InfixToRPN` in Fig. 4.12 to detect and report infix expressions that are improperly formed.

8. The algorithm given in the text for converting from infix to RPN assumes *left associativity;* that is, when two or more consecutive operators of the same priority occur, they are to be evaluated from left to right; for example, 6 - 3 - 1 is evaluated as (6 - 3) - 1 and not as 6 - (3 - 1). *Right associativity,* however, is usually used for exponentiation; for example, in FORTRAN, exponentiation is denoted by ** and the expression 2 ** 3 ** 4 is evaluated as 2 ** (3 ** 4) = $2^{(3^4)}$ = 2^{81}, not as (2 ** 3) ** 4 = $(2^3)^4$ = 8^4. Extend the algorithm in the text to allow ** as an additional binary operator with highest priority. *Hint*: One approach is to use two different priorities for each operator—one for when it is in the infix expression and the other for when it is in a stack.

9. Extend the program in Fig. 4.12 so that it can also convert infix expressions that contain the binary operators %, <<, and >> in addition to +, -, and *.

10. Proceed as in Exercise 9, but also allow the exponent operator ** (see Prob. 8).

11. Proceed as in Exercise 9 or 10, but also allow the unary operator ~ (see the note preceding Exercise 36).

12. Write a program to implement the algorithm for evaluating RPN expressions that involve only single-digit integers and the integer operations +, -, *, and /. To trace the action of RPN evaluation, display each token as it is encountered, and display the action of each stack operation. For example, the output of your program should resemble the following for the RPN expression 9 2 1 + / 4 *:

```
Token = 9      Push 9
Token = 2      Push 2
Token = 1      Push 1
Token = +      Pop 1      Pop 2      Push 3
Token = /      Pop 3      Pop 9      Push 3
Token = 4      Push 4
Token = *      Pop 4      Pop 3      Push 12
Token = ;      Pop 12
```

13. Modify the RPN evaluation program of Prob. 12 to detect and report RPN expressions that are not well formed.

14. Modify the RPN evaluation program of Prob. 12 to

   a. Process RPN expressions that contain the integer operators +, -, *, /, and %.

   b. Also allow RPN expressions that contain the unary operator ~ (see the note preceding Exercise 36).

   c. Allow integers with more than one digit.

15. Modify the RPN evaluation program of Prob. 12 so that it generates machine instructions in assembly code for evaluating the expression using one accumulator register and the following instructions:

   LOAD x　　Place the value of x in the accumulator register

   STORE x　Store the contents of the accumulator register into variable x

   ADD x　　Add the value of x to the contents of the accumulator register

   SUB x　　Subtract the value of x from the contents of the accumulator register

   MULT x　Multiply the contents of the accumulator register by the value of x

   DIV x　　Divide the contents of the accumulator register by the value of x

   For example, the postfix expression a b c + * d e* - should give the following sequence of instructions:

```
LOAD b
ADD c
STORE temp1
LOAD a
MULT temp1
STORE temp2
LOAD d
MULT e
STORE temp3
LOAD temp2
SUB temp3
STORE temp4
```

where each TEMPi is a temporary variable.

16. Write a program that converts a postfix expression to the corresponding fully parenthesized infix expression. For example, a b + and a b + c d - * should give (a + b) and ((a + b) * (c - d)), respectively.

Chapter 5

QUEUES

Chapter Contents

In the preceding chapter, we defined stacks, considered array-based implementations of stacks in some detail, and looked at several of their applications. In this chapter we consider queues, which are similar to stacks and have at least as many applications as stacks. Queues can also be implemented using arrays as the basic storage structures, but as we will discover, a bit more effort is required to construct an efficient array-based implementation of a queue than for a stack. The chapter closes with a simulation of an information/reservations center in which an "on-hold" queue is used to store incoming telephone calls.

5.1   INTRODUCTION TO QUEUES

According to Webster, a **queue** is a "waiting line," such as a line of persons waiting to check out at a supermarket, a line of vehicles at a toll booth, a queue of planes waiting to land at an airport, or a queue of jobs in a computer system waiting for some output device such as a printer. In each of these examples, the items are serviced in the order in which they arrive; that is, the first item in the queue is the first to be served. Thus, whereas a stack is a Last-In-First-Out (LIFO) structure, a queue is a **First-In-First-Out** (**FIFO**) or **First-Come-First-Served** (**FCFS**) structure.

As an abstract data type, a queue is a special kind of list in which the basic insert and delete operations are restricted to the ends of the list. Unlike stacks in which elements are popped and pushed only at one end of the list, items are removed from a queue at one end, called the **front** (or **head**) of the queue, and elements are added only at the other end called the **back** (or **rear** or **tail**). Other basic operations are constructing an empty queue and determining if a queue is empty. More formally, the abstract data type queue can be specified as follows:

ADT QUEUE

Collection of Data Elements:

An ordered collection of data items with the property that items can be removed only at one end, called the *front* of the queue, and items can be added only at the other end, called the *back* of the queue.

Basic Operations[1]:

- ▶ Construct a queue (usually empty)
- ▶ Check if queue is empty
- ▶ AddQ: Add an element at the back of the queue
- ▶ Front: Retrieve the element at the front of the queue
- ▶ RemoveQ: Remove the element at the front of the queue

EXAMPLE: DRILL AND PRACTICE PROBLEMS

PROBLEM.   Suppose that a program is to be designed to provide drill-and-practice exercises in elementary arithmetic. More precisely, suppose that these exercises are problems involving the addition of randomly generated integers. If a student answers correctly, another problem is generated; but if he or she answers incorrectly, the problem is stored so that it can be asked again at the end of the session.

OBJECTS AND OPERATIONS.   One of the objects in this problem is an addition problem, so we begin with

problem: of type AdditionProblem, which is a class with

Data members:	addends (random integers)
	answer (int)
Operations:	Get a random problem with addends in a given range
	Display the problem
	Find the problem's answer
	Check if a given answer is correct

Other objects are

numProblems (int):	number of problems to be asked
maxAddend (int):	largest addend in a problem
userAnswer (int):	user's answer to a problem
count (int):	count of problems asked
wrong (int):	number of problems answered incorrectly on first round

[1]We use the names "addQ" and "removeQ" for the basic insertion and deletion operations for queues; some data-structures texts use "enqueue" and "dequeue" and the standard queue container in the Standard Template Library (see Chap. 6) uses "push" and "pop."

cout (ostream):   screen to display problems, answers, and statistics
cin (istream):   keyboard to enter problems, answers, and other information

The last object we need is a container to store the problems answered incorrectly on the first round. Because it seems natural to ask them in the same order in which they were presented initially, a queue is, therefore, an appropriate container for storing these problems:

wrongQueue (queue of addition problems): queue of problems answered incorrectly on the first round

In addition to the operations for processing addition problems, we need

output and input: to display and read problems, answers, and so on
queue operations: to store and retrieve incorrectly answered problems.

ALGORITHM.   Assuming the availability of an addition-problem class and a queue type for storing addition problems, we can organize the objects and operations as follows:

ALGORITHM FOR DRILL AND PRACTICE

/*   Algorithm for doing drill and practice with addition problems.

Input: Number of problems, maximum addend, and addition problems
Output: Addition problems, answers, messages, number missed
--*/

1. Read numProblems and maxAddend.

// Carry out first round of the practice drill

2. For count in the range 1 to numProblems do the following:

    a. Get and display a problem.
    b. Read userAnswer.
    c. If userAnswer is correct
        Display a "correct" message.
      Else
        i.   Display a "sorry" message.
        ii.   Add problem to wrongQueue.

// Carry out second round of the practice drill

3. Display instructions, and initialize wrong to 0.

4. While wrongQueue is not empty, do the following:

    a. Retrieve and remove problem at front of wrongQueue.
    b. Display problem.
    c. Read userAnswer.
    d. If userAnswer is correct
        Display a "correct" message.
      Else
        i.   Display a "sorry" message and correct answer.
        ii.   Increment wrong by 1.

5. Display wrong.

CODE.   Fig. 5.1 implements the preceding objects, operations, and algorithm. Listed first is the class `AdditionProblem` whose data members are random integers of type `RandomInt`. (See the website described in the preface for a description of class `RandomInt`.) We also assume that a `Queue` class is available to store `AdditionProblem` objects; building such a `Queue` class is the topic of the next section. An alternative is to use the standard `queue` class template described in the next chapter; see the opening documentation of the program for instructions on how to use it here.

FIGURE 5.1   DRILL-AND-PRACTICE ARITHMETIC PROBLEMS

```
/***** AdditionProblem.h *****
   Contains the declaration of class AdditionProblem.
     Basic operations
       Get():     Generates a problem with random addends
       Display(): Displays the problem
       Answer():  Returns answer to problem
       Correct(): Checks user's answer to problem

    Note: Uses class RandomInt -- see website described in
          preface for source and description of this class.
   ------------------------------------------------------------*/

#include "RandomInt.h"
#include <iostream>
using namespace std;

#ifndef ADDITION_PROBLEM
#define ADDITION_PROBLEM

class AdditionProblem
{
/***** Function Members *****/
public:

/* --- Get() ---
 *  Receive:        maxAddend = largest integer to use in problem
 *  Postcondition:  Addends of this addition problem are random
 *                  integers in the range 0 through maxAddend.
 *************************************************************/
void Get(int maxAddend)
{
  myAddend1.Generate(0, maxAddend);
  myAddend2.Generate(0, maxAddend);
}

/* --- Display() ---
 *  Receive:    ostream out
 *  Pass back: Modified ostream with addends inserted
 *************************************************************/
```

```
void Display(ostream & out)
{
  out << myAddend1 << " + " << myAddend2 << " = ? ";
}


/* --- Answer() ---
 *  Return: Answer to this addition problem
 **************************************************************/
int Answer()
{
  return (myAddend1 + myAddend2);
}


/* --- Check() ---
 *  Receive: Integer userAnswer
 *  Return:  True if userAnswer is correct answer to this
 *           problem, false otherwise
 **************************************************************/
bool Correct(int userAnswer)
{
  return (userAnswer == Answer());
}


/***** Data Members *****/
 private:
   RandomInt myAddend1, myAddend2;
};
#endif



/***** Drill-and-Practice Program *****/
/* This program generates random drill-and-practice addition
 * problems.  Problems that are answered incorrectly on the first
 * attempt are queued and asked again at the end of the session.
 *
 * Input:  Number of problems to generate, student's answers to
 *         problems
 * Output: Messages, problems, correct answers, number of problems
 *         answered correctly
 *
 *  Note: Uses a class Queue whose elements are of type AdditionProblem
 *        (see Section 5.2).  Alternatively, use the standard queue
 *        class template from C++'s Standard Template Library as follows:
 *        Changes:
 *           #include "Queue" --> #include <queue>
 *           Queue wrongQueue --> queue<AdditionProblem> wrongQueue
 *           addQ --> push
 *           removeQ --> pop
 **************************************************************/
```

```cpp
#include "AdditionProblem.h"   // AdditionProblem
#include "Queue.h"             // A queue class for AdditionProblems
#include <iostream>            // cin, cout, >>, <<
using namespace std;

int main()
{
  int numProblems,            // number of problems asked
      maxAddend;              // maximum addend in a problem
  cout << "How many problems would you like? ";
  cin >> numProblems;
  cout << "What's the largest addend you would like? ";
  cin >> maxAddend;

  // Carry out round 1 of the practice drill
  Queue wrongQueue;           // queue of problems missed
  AdditionProblem problem;    // an addition problem
  int userAnswer;             // user's answer to problem

  for (int count = 1; count <= numProblems; count++)
  {
    problem.Get(maxAddend);
    problem.Display(cout);
    cin >> userAnswer;
    if (problem.Correct(userAnswer))
      cout << "Correct!\n\n";
    else
    {
      cout << "Sorry — Try again later\n\n";
      wrongQueue.addQ(problem);
    }
  }


  // Now reask any problems student missed

  cout << "\nIf you got any problems wrong, you will now be given"
          "\na second chance to answer them correctly.\n";
  int wrong = 0;              // number gotten wrong on both tries
  while (!wrongQueue.empty())
  {
    problem = wrongQueue.front();
    wrongQueue.removeQ();
    problem.Display(cout);
    cin >> userAnswer;
    if (problem.Correct(userAnswer))
      cout << "Correct!\n\n";
    else
    {
      cout << "Sorry -- correct answer is "
           << problem.Answer() << "\n\n";
      wrong++;
    }
  }
}
```

```
      cout << "\nYou answered " << wrong << " problem"
            << (wrong > 1 ? "s " : " " ) << "incorrectly.\n";
}
```

SAMPLE RUN:

```
How many problems would you like? 5
What's the largest addend you would like? 100
78 + 92 = ? 170
Correct!

20 + 100 = ? 120
Correct!

36 + 97 = ? 123
Sorry -- Try again later

28 + 84 = ? 112
Correct!

6 + 36 = ? 44
Sorry -- Try again later

If you got any problems wrong, you will now be given
a second chance to answer them correctly.
36 + 97 = ? 143
Sorry -- correct answer is 133

6 + 36 = ? 42
Correct!


You answered 1 problem incorrectly.
```

EXAMPLES OF SCHEDULING QUEUES

Queues are also commonly used to model waiting lines that arise in the operation of computer systems. These queues are formed whenever more than one process requires a particular resource, such as a printer, a disk drive, or the central processing unit. As processes request a particular resource, they are placed in a queue to wait for service by that resource. For example, several personal computers may be sharing the same printer, and a **spool**[2] **queue** is used to schedule output requests in a first-come-first-served manner. If some process requests the printer to perform some output, that output is copied to disk, and the process is added to a spool queue of processes waiting for the printer. When the output from the current process terminates, the printer is released from that process and is assigned to the next one in the spool queue.

Another important use of queues in computing systems is for **input/output buffering.** The transfer of information from an input device or to an output device is a relatively slow operation, and if the processing of a program must be suspended

---

[2]"Spool" is an acronym for **S**imultaneous **P**eripheral **O**peration **O**n-**L**ine.

while data is transferred, program execution is slowed dramatically. One common solution to this problem uses sections of main memory known as **buffers** and transfers data between the program and these buffers rather than between the program and the input/output device directly.

In particular, consider the problem in which data processed by a program must be read from a disk file. This information is transferred from the disk file to an input buffer in main memory while the central processing unit (CPU) is performing some other task.

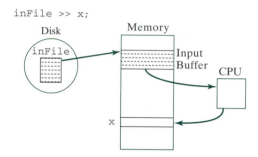

When data is required by the program, the next value(s) stored in this buffer is retrieved. While this value is being processed, additional data values can be transferred from the disk file to the buffer. Clearly, the buffer must be organized as a first-in-first-out structure, that is, as a queue. A queue-empty condition indicates that the input buffer is empty and program execution is suspended while the operating system loads more data into the buffer. Of course, such a buffer has a limited size, and thus a queue-full condition must also be used to signal when it is full and no more data is to be transferred from the disk file to the buffer.

The insert and delete operations for a queue are restricted so that insertions are performed at only one end and deletions at the other. In some applications, however, insertions and deletions must be made at both ends. For example, in scrolling a window up and down on the screen, lines are added and removed at the top and also at the bottom:

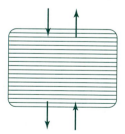

To model these situations, a double-ended queue, abbreviated to **deque** (pronounced "deck"), is the data structure that should be used (but it could as well be called a "dack" for "double-ended stack").

Another example of this behavior is interactive input, where the user can insert data into the input buffer by entering it from the keyboard, but the user may also be able to delete information by depressing a delete or backspace key.

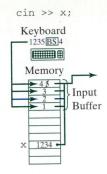

A deque might, therefore, be a more appropriate data structure for modeling this situation; or because data values are only removed and not inserted at the other end, a better model might be a queue-stack hybrid, sometimes called a **scroll** (although more colorful names might be "queue-and-a-half," "heque," or "quack").

Other examples of queues are scheduling queues in a multi-user computer system:

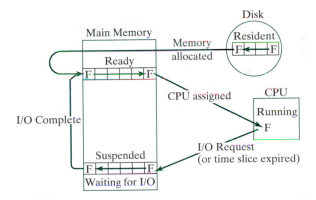

Consider a file F on disk that needs to be loaded into memory and processed with the CPU. There may be many such files waiting to be loaded into memory. A queue, called the **resident queue**, might be used to organize these files that are on disk, waiting for memory. When file F reaches the front of the queue, memory gets allocated for it, and it has all the other system resources it needs except the CPU, it enters another queue, called a **ready queue**, of jobs that have everything they need to run except the CPU. Eventually, when F reaches the front of this queue, the CPU gets assigned to it and begins processing it. If F contains an I/O request (or it keeps the CPU until some preassigned *time slice* expires), it gives up the CPU and enters a **suspended queue**, where it is waiting for the operating system to do the I/O transfer. When this happens, F reenters the ready queue and waits for the CPU.

The data structure used to schedule the CPU is probably not a queue, but rather another data structure related to the queue called a **priority queue**. In this structure, a certain priority is associated with each data item, and these items are to be stored in such a way that those with higher priority are near the front of the queue so that they will be removed from the queue and assigned the CPU before those of lower priority.

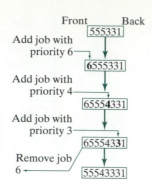

Along with stacks and queues, deques and priority queues are containers provided in the C++ standard library and we will study them in Secs. 6.6 and 11.2. Deques and scrolls are also considered in more detail in the exercises at the end of the next section.

BUILD ## 5.2   ARRAY-BASED IMPLEMENTATION OF QUEUES

Because a queue resembles a stack in many ways, we might imitate the array-based implementation of a stack considered in Chap. 4 to construct an array-based implementation of a queue. Thus we might use

▶ `myArray` to store the elements of the queue

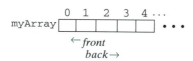

▶ two integer variables:

`myFront`   The position in the array of the element that can be removed—the position of the front queue element

`myBack`   The position in the array at which an element can be added—the position *following* the last queue element

Thus, we might picture a `Queue` object `q` as follows:

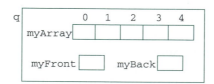

An item is added to the queue by storing it at position myBack of the array, provided myBack does not exceed some maximum size QUEUE_CAPACITY allowed for the array, and then incrementing myBack by 1.

The difficulty with this implementation is that elements "walk off the end" of the array, so that eventually all the array elements may have to be shifted back to the beginning positions. (One reviewer of this text has used the very descriptive phrase "queue creep" for this behavior.) For example, consider a queue for which QUEUE_CAPACITY = 5 and whose elements are integers. The sequence of operations addQ 70, addQ 80, addQ 50 produces the following configuration:

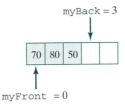

Now suppose that two elements are removed,

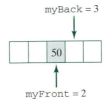

and that 90 and 60 are then added:

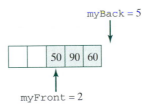

Before another item can be inserted into the queue, the elements in the array must be shifted back to the beginning of the array:

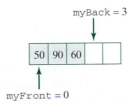

This shifting of array elements is very inefficient, especially when the elements are large records. It can be avoided by thinking of the array as *circular*, with the first element following the last. This can be done by indexing the array beginning with 0, and incrementing `myFront` and `myBack` using addition modulo `QUEUE_CAPACITY`. For the sequence of operations just considered, this implementation yields the following configurations:

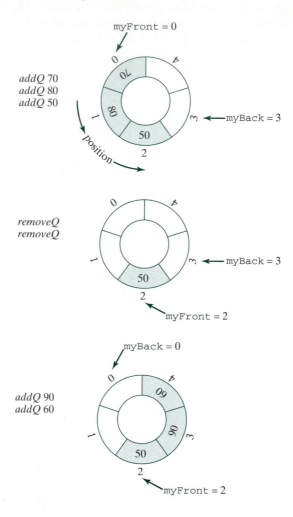

Another insertion is now possible without our having to move any array elements; we simply store the item in position `myBack = 0`.

Now consider the basic operation to determine if a queue is empty. If the queue contains a single element, it is in position `myFront` of the array, and `myBack` is the vacant position following it. If this element is deleted, `myFront` is incremented by 1 so that `myFront` and `myBack` have the same value. Thus, to determine if a queue is empty, we need only check the condition `myFront == myBack`. The queue constructor will initialize `myFront` and `myBack` both to 0.

Just as the array implementation for a stack introduced the possibility of a stack-full condition, the implementation of a queue raises the possibility of a queue-full condition. To see how this condition can be detected, suppose that the array is almost full, with only one empty location remaining:

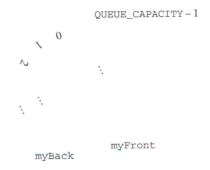

If an item were stored in this location, myBack would be incremented by 1 and thus would have the same value as myFront. However, the condition myFront == myBack indicates that the queue is empty. Thus, we *cannot distinguish between an empty queue and a full queue* if this location is used to store an element. But we can avoid this difficulty if we maintain one empty position in the array. The condition indicating that a queue is full then becomes (myBack + 1) % QUEUE_CAPACITY == myFront.

There are several alternatives to keeping an empty slot in the array. One commonly used one is to add an integer data member count to the class, which stores the number of elements currently in the queue. Another is to use a boolean data member full instead of the integer member count, which is set to true when the queue becomes full and is false otherwise. Queue classes developed using these approaches are left as exercises.

The class declaration in Fig. 5.2 implements a queue ADT, using for the storage structure a circular array myArray to store the queue elements, with an empty slot between the front and back elements. The data members myFront and myBack record the position of the front element and the position following the last element, respectively.

 FIGURE 5.2   CLASS DECLARATION FOR A QUEUE DATA TYPE

```
/* Queue.h contains the declaration of class Queue.
   Basic operations:
     Constructor:  Constructs an empty queue
     Empty:    Checks if a queue is empty
     AddQ:     Modifies a queue by adding a value at the back
     Front:    Accesses the front queue value; leaves queue unchanged
     RemoveQ: Modifies a queue by removing the value at the front
```

```
                Class Invariant:
                   1. The queue elements (if any) are stored in consecutive
                      positions in myArray, beginning at position myFront.
                   2. 0 <= myFront, myBack < QUEUE_CAPACITY
                   3. Queue's size < QUEUE_CAPACITY
           ----------------------------------------------------------------*/

           #ifndef QUEUE
           #define QUEUE

           const int QUEUE_CAPACITY = 128;
           typedef int QueueElement;

           class Queue
           {

           /***** Function Members *****/
           public:

           // --- Constructor ---
           Queue();

           // --- Is the Queue empty? ---
           bool empty() const;

           // --- Add a value to the queue ---
           void addQ(const QueueElement & value);

           // --- Return value at front of the queue ---
           QueueElement front() const;


           // --- Remove value at front of the queue ---
           void removeQ();

           /***** Data Members *****/
           private:
             QueueElement myArray[QUEUE_CAPACITY];
             int myFront,
                 myBack;

           }; // end of class declaration

           #endif
```

The constructor simply initializes both of the members `myFront` and `myBack` to 0 (or to any other value in 0, 1, . . . , `QUEUE_CAPACITY - 1`); and a queue will be empty when the boolean expression `myFront == myBack` is true. An algorithm for the addQ operation is

ALGORITHM FOR ADDQ

/*   Algorithm to add a `value` at the back of the queue.

Receive: `value`
Return: Modified queue with `value` added at the back
--*/

1. Set `newBack` equal to `(myBack + 1) % QUEUE_CAPACITY`.
2. If `newBack` is equal to `myFront`

    Signal that a queue error (queue full) occurred.

    Otherwise

    a. Set `myArray[myBack]` equal to `value`.
    b. Set `myBack` equal to `newBack`.

The front operation need only retrieve `myArray[myFront]` provided the queue is not empty. And an algorithm for the removeQ operation is

ALGORITHM FOR REMOVEQ

/*   Algorithm to remove the element at the front of the queue.

Return   Modified queue with front item removed
--*/

If the queue is empty
    Signal that a queue error (queue empty) occurred.
Otherwise
    Set `myFront` equal to `(myFront + 1) % QUEUE_CAPACITY`.

Definitions of functions to implement these operations are left as exercises.

✔ Quick Quiz 5.2

1. Define queue as an ADT.
2. A(n) _____ queue stores processes waiting for a printer.
3. A(n) _____ is a section of main memory used to transfer data between a program and an input/output device.
4. A(n) _____ is a double-ended queue.
5. A(n) _____ allows items to be inserted and removed at one end and only removed at the other.

Answer Questions 6–9 using: resident, ready, suspended, priority.

6. Jobs that have everything they need to run except the CPU are kept in a(n) _____ queue.
7. A(n) _____ queue organizes files on disk that are waiting for memory.
8. Jobs that surrender the CPU because of an I/O request are placed in a(n) _____ queue.
9. The CPU is sometimes scheduled using a(n) _____ queue.

✍ EXERCISES 5.2

For Exercises 1–4, assume that `q` is a queue implemented as described in this section (using a circular array), with `QueueElement = char`, `QUEUE_CAPACITY = 5`, and that `ch` is of type `char`. Using a diagram like the following,

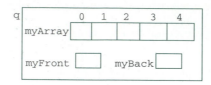

show the values of `q.myFront` and `q.myBack` and the contents of `q.myArray` after the program segment has been executed; also indicate any errors that occur.

1.
```
q.addQ('A');
q.addQ('B');
q.addQ('C');
ch = q.front();
q.removeQ();
q.addQ(ch);
```

2.
```
q.addQ('X'); q.addQ('Y');
q.addQ('Z');
while (!q.empty())
{   ch = q.front();
    q.removeQ();
}
```

3.
```
ch = 'q';
for (int i = 1; i <= 3; i++)
{   q.addQ(ch);
    ch++;
    q.addQ(ch);
    ch = q.front();
    q.removeQ();
}
```

4.
```
ch = 'A';
for (int i = 1; i <= 4; i++)
{   q.addQ(ch);
    ch++;
    q.addQ(ch);
    ch = q.front();
    q.removeQ();
}
```

The following exercises ask you to write functions or classes. You should also write driver programs to test them as instructed in the programming problems at the end of this chapter.

5. Complete the definition of the class `Queue` by writing definitions for the constructor, `empty()`, `addQ()`, `front()`, and `removeQ()`. Also, add an output operation so your class can be tested.

6. Although a queue, like a stack, cannot (in theory) become full, the array-based implementation of queues described in this section requires that an upper limit `QUEUE_CAPACITY` be placed on the maximum size that a queue may have. Write a member function `full()` for the `Queue` class that returns true or false according to whether or not the array used to store the queue elements is full.

7. Write documentation, a prototype, and a definition for a member function `size()` for the `Queue` class that returns the number of elements in the queue.

8. Repeat Exercise 7, but for a function `size()` that is neither a member function of the `Queue` class nor a friend function.

9. Proceed as in Exercise 7, but design a function `back()` that returns the element at the back of a queue.

10. Repeat Exercise 9, but for a function `back()` that is neither a member function of the `Queue` class nor a friend function.

11. Proceed as in Exercise 7, but design a function `nthElement()` to retrieve the nth queue element, leaving the queue without its first n elements.

12. Proceed as in Exercise 11, but leave the queue contents unchanged.

13. Using the basic queue and stack operations, write an algorithm to reverse the elements in a queue.

14. In Problem 2 of Sec. 4.1 and in Exercise 10 of Sec. 4.2, we considered a railroad-switching network that could be modeled with a stack. Now consider the following network:

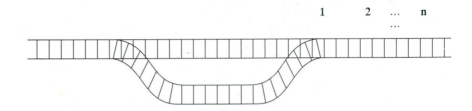

Again, railroad cars numbered $1, 2, \ldots, n$ on the right track are to be permuted and moved along on the left track. As the diagram suggests, a car may be moved directly onto the left track, or it may be shunted onto the siding (which acts like a queue) to be removed at a later time and placed on the left track.

   a. For $n = 3$, find all possible permutations of cars that can be obtained (on the left track) by a sequence of these operations. For example, add 1, add 2, move 3, remove, remove arranges them in the order 3, 1, 2. Are any permutations not possible?

   b. Find all possible permutations for $n = 4$. What permutations (if any) are not possible?

   c. Repeat b for $n = 5$.

   d. *Challenge*: In general, what permutations of the sequence $1, 2, \ldots, n$ can be obtained by using a queue in this manner?

15. Build a `Queue` class which uses an integer data member `count` that stores the number of elements currently in the queue, as described in the text, to distinguish between a queue-full and a queue-empty condition instead of keeping an empty slot between the front and the back elements.

16. Proceed as in Exercise 15, but use a boolean data member `full` instead of the integer member `count`, as described in the text.

17. In Exercise 11 of Exercises 4.2 we described an efficient implementation of a two-stack data structure that uses a single array for the storage structure. Describe a similar implementation of a two-queue data structure.

18. Imitating the implementation of a queue using a circular array, construct an implementation of a deque. Select appropriate data members and write functions to implement the basic operations (constructor, check if the deque is empty, add at the front, add at the back, remove at the front, remove at the back, and an output operation).

19. Construct an implementation of a scroll, selecting appropriate data members and writing functions to implement the basic operations.

5.3   APPLICATION OF QUEUES: INFORMATION CENTER SIMULATION

As we noted in the preceding section, queues may be used to model waiting lines. In fact, *queueing theory* is such an important area of computer science, operations research, and other areas of applied mathematics and computing that many publishers have books devoted to it and many universities offer courses in it.

Almost all waiting lines are dynamic; that is, their lengths change over time, growing as new items arrive and are added to the queues, shrinking as items are removed from the queues and serviced. The term **simulation** refers to modeling such a dynamic process and using this model to study the behavior of the process. The behavior of some **deterministic** processes can be modeled with an equation or a set of equations. For example, processes that involve exponential growth or decay are commonly modeled with an equation of the form $A(t) = A_0 e^{kt}$, where $A(t)$ is the amount of some substance A present at time t, A_0 is the initial amount of the substance, and k is a rate constant.

In many problems, however, the process under study involves **randomness**—for example, Brownian motion, the arrival of airplanes at an airport, the number of defective parts manufactured by a machine, and so on. Computer programs that simulate such processes use a **random number generator** to introduce randomness into the values produced during execution. This is a subprogram that produces a number selected *at random* from some fixed range in such a way that a sequence of these numbers tends to be uniformly distributed over the given range. Although it is not possible to develop an algorithm that produces truly random numbers,[3] there are some methods that produce sequences of **pseudorandom numbers** that are adequate for most purposes.

The behavior of a queue also often involves randomness, because it is usually not known in advance exactly when there will be a new arrival or exactly how much time will be required to service a specified item. As an illustration, we consider the operation of an information/reservation center that services calls made by customers to a toll-free number, such as one provided by an airline or a rental car company. When a call arrives at this center, it is placed in a queue of incoming calls. When the agent is available, she services the call at the front of the queue. The program in Fig. 5.3 simulates the operation of such an information center and computes several statistics to measure its performance.

PROBLEM ANALYSIS AND SPECIFICATION

The overall simulation should proceed as follows: A simulated countdown timer is set to the number of minutes that calls will be accepted and then is repeatedly decremented by 1 (minute) until it reaches 0. On each "tick" of the timer, a check is made to determine if service has been completed for the current call, and if so, it is popped from the queue of incoming calls and simulated service begins on the next call in the queue (if there are any). A check is also made to determine if a new call

---

[3]For example, noise level changes from a reverse-biased diode. Thanks to Ralph Ewton for sending this example.

has arrived. If it has, its arrival time is recorded, its service time is determined and recorded, and the call is placed in the queue for processing in a first-come-first-served manner when the agent becomes available. When the timer reaches zero, no new calls are accepted, but service continues until all the calls in the queue have been processed.

When the simulation is complete, statistics that measure the performance of the information center such as the number of calls processed and the average waiting time for each call must be reported. These statistics will constitute the output of this simulation:

Output: Number of calls processed

Average waiting time per call

Other statistics, such as the average queue length and the average turnaround time, are described in the exercises.

As we noted earlier, the simulation is to run for a specified period of time, and thus one input item must be a time limit. Since it is necessary to simulate the arrival and service of calls, information about arrival rates and service times is also needed. Thus the input will be

Input: Arrival rate of calls

Distribution of service times

Time limit

DESIGN
One basic object is the simulated countdown timer. It will have only one data member (`minutes`) and basic operations of construction, ticking down by one time unit, and checking if time has run out. Thus we will have an object of type

```
class Timer
{
/***** Function Members *****/
public:
//--- Constructor
Timer(int initTime = 0);

//--- Time remaining
int TimeRemaining() const;

//--- Decrement by one minute
void Tick();

//--- Check whether timer has run out
bool HasTimeLeft() const;

/***** Data Members *****/
private:
  int minutes;
};
```

Another basic object in the simulation is a call to the information center, and such calls are characterized by the time they arrive, the amount of time required to service the call, and the time when the service of that call will be completed, so these will be the data members of our `Call` class. The basic operations are to construct a `Call` at a certain time and generate a random service time and completion time for it, begin service of a call, continue service of a call, and check if service has been completed. The form of our class `Call` thus is

```
class Call
{
/***** Function Members *****/
public:
//--- Constructors
//----- Default
Call();
//----- Explicit Value
Call(const Timer & t, const SimulationValues & sim);

//--- Begin service of the call
void BeginService(const Timer & t,
                  const SimulationValues & sim);

//--- Check if service was completed
bool ServiceCompleted(const Timer & t);

/***** Data Members *****/
private:
  int timeOfArrival,
      serviceTime,
      completionTime;
};
```

The three input items and the three output items are the basic values involved in the simulation. An object of type `SimulationValues` will store these six values with basic I/O operations. We will make all the data members public so they are accessible throughout the entire program.

```
class SimulationValues
{
public:
/***** Data Members *****/
    static const int NUM_LIMITS = 4;
  // Inputs
  double arrivalRate;
  int servicePercent[NUM_LIMITS],
      lengthOfSimulation;
  // Outputs
  int callsReceived;
  double totalWaitingTime;

/***** Function Members *****/
//--- Constructor
SimulationValues();
```

```
//--- Input
void Read();

//--- Display
void Display();


};
```

Here, `arrivalRate` is the probability that a call will arrive in a given minute. For example, if the average time between calls is five minutes, then the arrival rate is 1/5 = 0.2 calls per minute. The array `servicePercent` will record information regarding service time:

> `servicePercent[0]` = percent of calls serviced in less than 1 minute
> `servicePercent[1]` = percent of calls serviced in less than 2 minutes
> $\vdots$
> $\vdots$

The capacity of this array is `NUM_LIMITS`, the maximum number of service-time categories. This array will be used to determine a service time for each call. `lengthOfSimulation` is the specified time limit for the simulation. These data members will be entered by the user at the beginning of the simulation. At the end of the simulation, the total number of calls processed and the average waiting time per call (`totalWaitingTime / callsReceived`) are displayed.

The final object needed is a queue to store incoming calls. The element type of this queue thus is `Call`.

Our program will perform three main tasks:

1. Set up a `SimulationValues` object `simVals`.

2. Carry out the simulation, recording the total number of calls and the total waiting time in `simVals`.

3. Output the results from `simVals`—total number of calls and the average waiting time per call.

Of these, only the simulation needs to be analyzed; the others are straightforward. An algorithm for it is

ALGORITHM FOR SIMULATION

/* Algorithm for carrying out the simulation */

1. Initialize a timer `t` and a queue of incoming calls.
2. While `t` has not run out:
    a. Continue or begin service of the call at the front of the queue of incoming calls (if there are any).
    b. Check if a new call has arrived and if so, add it to the queue.
    c. Have `t` tick off 1 time unit.
3. While calls remain in the incoming queue:
    a. Service the call at the front of the queue.
    b. Have `t` tick off 1 time unit.

To determine whether or not a call has arrived in a particular minute, we generate a random integer in the range 0 to 100, and if this number is less than $100 \times$ arrival-rate we say that a call has arrived during this minute:

Call arrives	No call arrives
0 20	100

The numbers produced by the random number generator are assumed to be uniformly distributed over the interval from 0 to 100. Consequently, if many such numbers are generated, we expect approximately 20 percent of them to be in the subinterval $(0, 20)$. In terms of our simulation, this means that the probability that a call arrives in a given minute should be approximately 0.2, as desired.

When a new call arrives, its arrival time and the time required to service the call must be recorded. The service time is determined by using the array `servicePercent`. For example, suppose this array contains the values 50, 75, 90, 97, and 100—50 percent of the calls are serviced in less than 1 minute, 75 percent in less than 2 minutes, and so on. We generate a random integer in the interval $(0, 100)$; the subinterval in which it falls—$(0, 50]$, $(50, 75]$, $(75, 90]$, $(90, 97]$, or $(97, 100)$—determines the service time for the call:

Service time	1	2	3	4	5
0		50	75	90	100
					97

The following algorithm summarizes all of this:

ALGORITHM FOR ARRIVAL OF NEW CALL

/* Algorithm to check for arrival of a new call */

1. Generate a random integer x in the range 0 to 100.

2. If x < `simVals.arrivalRate` // new call has arrived
    a. Increment `simVals.callsReceived` by 1.

    // --- Determine its service time
    b. Generate a new random number x.
    c. Set i to 1.
    d. While x > `simVals.servicePercent[i]`
        Increment i by 1.

    // --- Construct the new call
    e. Construct `newCall` with its `timeOfArrival` initialized to
       `t.Minutes()` and its `serviceTime` initialized to i.
    f. Add `newCall` to the `incomingCalls` queue.

CODING AND EXECUTION

The classes and program in Fig. 5.3 are based on this design plan. The program assumes the availability of a queue class with elements of type `Call`. To save space, we have inlined member functions by putting their definitions inside the class declarations.

FIGURE 5.3   SIMULATING AN INFORMATION CENTER

```
/*==== SimulationValues.h ==================================
Struct SimulationValues maintains important simulation values.
=============================================================*/


#include <iostream>        // istream, ostream, >>, <<
#include <ctime>           // time()
using namespace std;


#ifndef SIMULATION_VALUES
#define SIMULATION_VALUES

class SimulationValues
{
public:
/***** Data Members *****/
   static const int NUM_LIMITS = 4;
  // Inputs
   double arrivalRate;
   int servicePercent[NUM_LIMITS],
       lengthOfSimulation;
  // Outputs
   int callsReceived;
   double totalWaitingTime;

/***** Function Members *****/
/*** Constructor -- default
  Postcondition: Output data members are initialized to 0.
  ----------------------------------------------------------*/
SimulationValues()
{
  callsReceived = 0;
  totalWaitingTime = 0;
}

/*** Input
  Input: Arrival rate, percentages for service times,
         and time limit for simulation
  Postcondition: Input data members are set.
  ----------------------------------------------------------*/
void Read();
```

```cpp
/*** Output
  Output: total number of call and the average
          waiting time for calls
----------------------------------------------------------*/
void Display()
{
  cout << "\nNumber of calls processed:   " << callsReceived
       << "\nAve. waiting time per call:  "
       <<        totalWaitingTime / callsReceived
       << endl;
}

};   // end of class declaration

/***** Definition of Read() *****/
void SimulationValues::Read()
{
  cout << "Enter arrival rate: ";
  cin >> arrivalRate;
  cout << "Enter percent of calls serviced in\n";
  int perc,
      sum = 0;
  for (int i = 0; i < NUM_LIMITS; i++)
  {
    cout << "  < " << i + 1 << " min. ";
    cin >> perc;
    sum += perc;
    servicePercent[i] = sum;
  }
  cout << "Enter # of minutes to run simulation: ";
  cin >> lengthOfSimulation;
}

#endif


/*==== Timer.h =========================================
  Class Timer models a countdown timer.
============================================================*/

#include <cassert>
using namespace std;

#ifndef TIMER
#define TIMER

class Timer
{
/***** Function Members *****/
public:
```

```cpp
/* Constructor
 *   Receive:  An initial value to start the timer
 *   Postcondition: minutes is initialized to initTime.
 ************************************************************/
Timer(int initTime = 0)
{
  assert(initTime >= 0);
  minutes = initTime;
}

/* Time remaining
 *   Return:  Time left before timer runs out
 ************************************************************/
int TimeRemaining() const
{ return minutes; }


/* Decrement timer by one minute
 *   Postcondition: minutes is decremented by 1.
 ************************************************************/
void Tick()
{ minutes--; }

/* Check if timer has run out
 *   Return:  True if time has expired, false otherwise
 ************************************************************/
bool HasTimeLeft() const
{ return (minutes > 0); }

/***** Data Members *****/
private:
   int minutes;
};   // end of class declaration
#endif


/*==== Call.h ==========================================
  Class Call models phone calls.
  ======================================================*/

#include "RandomInt.h"
#include <cassert>
using namespace std;

#ifndef CALL
#define CALL
```

```
class Call
{
/***** Function Members *****/
public:
/* Default Constructor
 *   Postcondition: All data members are initialized to 0.
 ***************************************************************/
Call()
{ timeOfArrival = completionTime = 0; }

/* Explicit-Value Constructor
 *   Receive:  The countdown timer t and simulation
 *             values sim
 *   Postcondition: timeOfArrival is initialized to elapsed
 *                  time specified by t and serviceTime is
 *                  set randomly using sim's values.
 ***************************************************************/
Call(const Timer & t, const SimulationValues & sim);

/* Begin service of the call
 *   Receive:  The countdown timer t and simulation
 *             values sim
 *   Postcondition: completionTime is set and
 *                  totalWaitingTime in sim is updated.
 ***************************************************************/
void BeginService(const Timer & t, SimulationValues & sim)
{
  sim.totalWaitingTime += timeOfArrival - t.TimeRemaining();
  completionTime = t.TimeRemaining() - serviceTime;
}

/* Check if service completed
 *   Receive: The countdown timer t
 *   Return:  True if countdown timer has reached
 *            completionTime; false otherwise
 ***************************************************************/
bool ServiceCompleted(const Timer & t)
{ return t.TimeRemaining() <= completionTime; }

/***** Data Members *****/
private:
  int timeOfArrival;
  int serviceTime;
  int completionTime;

};   // end of class declaration

/***** Definition of Constructor *****/
Call::Call(const Timer & t, const SimulationValues & sim)
{
  // record call's time of arrival
  timeOfArrival = t.TimeRemaining();
```

```
    // generate a service time for it
    RandomInt r;
    r.Generate(0, 100);
    serviceTime = 0;
    while (r > sim.servicePercent[serviceTime])
      serviceTime++;
}
#endif


/*==== main program =======================================
   Program simulates the operation of an information/
   reservation center that services telephone calls.

   Input:   Arrival rate of calls, distribution of service
            times, and time limit for simulation.
   Output:  The number of calls processed and the average
            waiting time for each call
   Note:    Program assumes the availability of a queue class
            with elements of type Call.
==========================================================*/

#include "SimulationValues.h"
#include "Timer.h"
#include "Call.h"
#include "Queue.h"
#include <iostream>
using namespace std;

void Service(queue<Call> & incomingCalls, SimulationValues & sim,
             const Timer & t, bool & servicingACall);

void CheckForNewCall(queue<Call> & incomingCalls,
                     SimulationValues & sim, const Timer& t);

int main()
{
  // Set up simulation parameters
  SimulationValues simVals;
  simVals.Read();

  // Initialize a countdown timer and a queue of incoming calls

  Timer t(simVals.lengthOfSimulation);
  queue<Call> incomingCalls;
```

```
  bool servicingACall = false;
  while (t.HasTimeLeft())
  {
    Service(incomingCalls, simVals, t, servicingACall);
    CheckForNewCall(incomingCalls, simVals, t);
    t.Tick();
  }

  // Service any remaining calls in incomingCalls queue
  while (!incomingCalls.empty())
  {
    Service(incomingCalls, simVals, t, servicingACall);
    t.Tick();
  }

  // Output the results
  simVals.Display();
}


/* Service the call currently at the front of the queue of
 * incoming calls.
 *
 *    Receive and pass back  : queue incomingCalls,
 *                             SimulationValues sim,
 *                             countdown Timer t
 *                             bool indicator servicingACall
 **************************************************************/

void Service(queue<Call> & incomingCalls, SimulationValues & sim,
             const Timer & t, bool & servicingACall)
{
  if (!incomingCalls.empty())         // there are incoming calls
  {
    if (!servicingACall)              // start serving 1st call
    {
      incomingCalls.front().BeginService(t, sim);
      servicingACall = true;
    }

    if (incomingCalls.front().ServiceCompleted(t))
    {                                     // get next call in queue
      incomingCalls.pop();
      servicingACall = false;
    }
  }
  else
    servicingACall = false;
}
```

```
/* CheckForNewCall checks if a new call has arrived and if so
 * places it on the queue of incoming calls.
 *
 *    Receive  : queue incomingCalls, imulationValues sim,
 *               countdown Timer t
 *    Pass back: currentCall and incomingCalls
 *************************************************************/
void CheckForNewCall(queue<Call> & incomingCalls,
                     SimulationValues & sim, const Timer& t)
{
  RandomInt x;
  x.Generate(0, 100);
  if (x < 100*sim.arrivalRate)
  {
    // Construct a new call, record it in sim
    // and add it to queue of incoming calls
    Call newCall(t, sim);
    sim.callsReceived++;
    incomingCalls.push(newCall);
  }
}
```

SAMPLE RUN:

```
Enter arrival rate: 0.2
Enter percent of calls serviced in
  < 1 min. 20
  < 2 min. 50
  < 3 min. 20
  < 4 min. 10
Enter # of minutes to run simulation: 500

Number of calls processed:   109
Ave. waiting time per call:  1.65138
```

☞ *PROGRAMMING POINTERS*

1. Random number generators are used to produce (pseudo-) random numbers in programs that simulate random behavior.

2. Event-driven simulations like the information-center application in Sec. 5.3 often make use of queues to model waiting lines.

 ## *ADT TIPS*

1. A *queue* has *first-in-first-out* (*FIFO*) or *first-come-first-served* (*FCFS*) behavior.

2. Queues are used to schedule resources in a computer system. Examples are a spool queue for waiting lines of items to be printed; input/output buffers; resident queue of jobs waiting to be loaded from disk into memory; ready queue of jobs waiting for the CPU; suspended queue of jobs whose execution has been suspended, for example, for input or output.

3. A *deque* allows items to be inserted and removed at *both* ends.

4. A *scroll* allows items to be inserted and removed at one end and only removed at the other.

5. Sometimes changing the usual way in which a data structure is viewed leads to a modification that yields an efficient implementation of an ADT. For example, using an array naively in implementing a queue suffers from having to shift elements in the array to avoid "falling off the end"; but viewing the array as a circular array leads to a very efficient implementation.

6. In using a circular array to implement a queue, it must be possible to distinguish between queue-empty and queue-full conditions by leaving one array location empty or by maintaining a count of the number of elements or a boolean value that indicates whether the queue is full.

7. Queuing theory is an important area of study in computer science, operations research, and other areas of applied mathematics and computing.

PROGRAMMING PROBLEMS

SECTION 5.2

1. Write a driver program to test the class `Queue` from Exercise 5.

2. Write a driver program to test the function `full()` from Exercise 6.

3. Write a driver program to test the function `size()` from Exercise 7.

4. Repeat Prob. 3 but for the function `size()` from Exercise 8.

5. Write a driver program to test the function `back()` from Exercise 9.

6. Repeat Prob. 6 but for the function `size()` from Exercise 10.

7. Write a driver program to test the function `nthElement()` from Exercise 11.

8. Repeat Prob. 6 but for the function `nthElement()` from Exercise 12.

9. Write a driver program to test the class `Queue` from Exercise 15.

10. Write a driver program to test the class `Queue` from Exercise 16.

11. Write a driver program to test the deque class from Exercise 18.

12. Write a driver program to test the scroll class from Exercise 19.

13. Write a program that generates a random sequence of letters and/or digits, displays them to the user one at a time for a second or so, and then asks the user to reproduce the sequence. Use a queue to store the sequence of characters.

14. Write a program that reads a string of characters, pushing each character onto a stack as it is read and simultaneously adding it to a queue. When the end of the string is encountered, the program should use the basic stack and queue operations to determine if the string is a palindrome (see Exercise 10 of Sec. 3.4).

15. In text-editing and word-processing applications, one formatting convention sometimes used to indicate that a piece of text is a footnote or an endnote is to mark it with some special delimiters such as { and }. When the text is formatted for output, these notes are not printed as normal text but are stored in a queue for later output. Write a program that reads a document containing endnotes indicated in this manner, collects them in a queue, and prints them at the end of the document.

SECTION 5.3

16. Modify the program in Fig. 5.3 so that it also calculates the average turnaround time. The turnaround time for a given call is the difference between the time when service for that call is completed and the time the call arrived.

17. Modify the program in Fig. 5.3 so that it also calculates the average queue length. If n minutes are simulated and $L_1, L_2, \ldots, L_n$ are the lengths of the incoming-calls queue at times $1, 2, \ldots, n$, respectively, then the average queue length is $(L_1 + L_2 + \cdots + L_n)/n$.

18. Modify the program in Fig. 5.3 so that several agents are available to service calls. Investigate the behavior of various queue statistics as the number of agents varies.

19. Suppose that in addition to the simulation parameters given in the example in this section, another is the number of calls rejected because the number of calls in the incoming-calls queue has exceeded some upper limit. Add this feature to the program in Fig. 5.3.

20. Suppose that another useful simulation parameter is the percentage of calls that cannot be serviced by the agent but must be transferred to the manager. In addition to the other random information generated for each call, also generate randomly an indicator of whether or not it can be serviced by the agent. If it cannot, it should be added to a `managerQueue`, and a new service time should be generated for it. Modify the program in Fig. 5.3 to simulate this information center, and calculate various statistics such as those in the text and in Exercises 1 and 2 for each call, for each queue, and so on.

21. (Project) Suppose that a certain airport has one runway, that each airplane takes `landingTime` minutes to land and `takeOffTime` minutes to take off, and that on the average, `takeOffRate` planes take off and `landingRate` planes land each hour. Assume that the planes arrive at random instants of time. (Delays make the assumption of randomness quite reasonable.) There are two types of queues: a queue of airplanes waiting to land and a queue of airplanes waiting to take off. Because it is more expensive to keep a plane airborne than to have one waiting on the ground, we assume that the airplanes in the landing queue have priority over those in the takeoff queue.

Write a program to simulate this airport's operation. You might assume a simulated clock that advances in one-minute intervals. For each minute, generate two random numbers: If the first is less than `landingRate` / 60, a "landing arrival" has occurred and is added to the landing queue; and if the second is less than `takeOffRate` / 60, a "takeoff arrival" has occurred and is added to the takeoff queue. Next, check whether the runway is free. If it is, first check whether the landing queue is nonempty, and if so, allow the first airplane to land; otherwise, consider the takeoff queue. Have the program calculate the average queue length and the average time that an airplane spends in a queue. You might also investigate the effect of varying arrival and departure rates to simulate the prime and slack times of day, or what happens if the amount of time to land or take off is increased or decreased.

Chapter 6

IMPROVING ADTs—PART 1: TEMPLATES AND STANDARD CONTAINERS

Chapter Contents

In preceding chapters we have looked at stacks and queues as abstract data types and at some of the ways they can be implemented with classes that use arrays to store the elements of the stack or queue. In this chapter we focus on the *data* component of an ADT, especially for *container ADTs* such as stacks and queues that store collections of data, but our approach will also impact the functions that implement the basic operations.

Our goal is to achieve greater reuseability of functions and container ADTs by making them more *generic* so that they can be applied to various types of data. For example, the `Stack` class we developed in Chap. 4 is designed to store and process only one type (`StackElement`) of data. We did set this type using the `typedef` mechanism—for example

```
typedef double StackElement;
```

and did put this declaration at the beginning of the class's header file so that it would be easy to change, but *this declaration does bind the class to one particular type* for the stack elements.

In this chapter we will look at a more recent development in programming languages that makes it possible to achieve greater genericity in ADTs, namely *templates*. We will first describe the template mechanism for functions and show how it makes it possible to write generic function templates, and then show how the template mechanism for classes can be used to develop generic container class templates. We will also look at some of the standard container class templates provided in C++.

6.1   INTRODUCTION: THE EVOLUTION OF REUSEABILITY AND GENERICITY

Since their beginnings with FORTRAN and COBOL in the mid-1950s, high-level programming languages have evolved from rather simple tools—sometimes crude and difficult to use and intended for writing programs for specific problems—into powerful sophisticated general-purpose tools for solving a wide variety of problems. A major theme in this development has been to modify some language features and add others to make it easier to *reuse code and thus avoid reinventing the wheel*. And one of the trends that has contributed to this reuseability has been toward *generic code* that can be used with different types of data.

In Chap. 1, we mentioned the text

$$Algorithms + Data\ Structures = Programs$$

written by Niklaus Wirth, inventor of the Pascal language, which stressed that data and algorithms cannot be separated. It is interesting to see how this has played out in the development of programming languages, how features that have fostered reuseability of algorithms and their implementations in code have been paralleled by corresponding features that have made container data types more generic and therefore more reuseable with different kinds of data.

The diagram in Fig. 6.1 displays this parallelism. The right side of the diagram summarizes the evolution of *algorithmic* features of programming languages and the left side summarizes the evolution of *data* features.

FROM ALGORITHMS TO ALGORITHMS

Some of the earliest algorithms were implemented strictly with inline code. Gradually, however, as programmers tired of writing duplicate code, features were added to programming languages that made it possible to write sections of code called *subprograms* to perform specific tasks and have them executed at various places in the program—an early manifestation of avoiding wheel reinvention. Commands like `JMP 100` in an early assembly language and `GOSUB 100` in BASIC made it possible to transfer execution to a subprogram beginning at statement 100 that did a specific task such as displaying a menu of options and then resume execution back in the (main) program. In some languages, the subprograms were named and could be called by this name; for example, `CALL MENU` in FORTRAN and `PERFORM MENU` in COBOL. Gradually these subprograms came to be known as *subroutines*, *functions*, or *procedures* and it became possible to pass values to them and return values from them, providing still more ways to *reuse code* and simplify

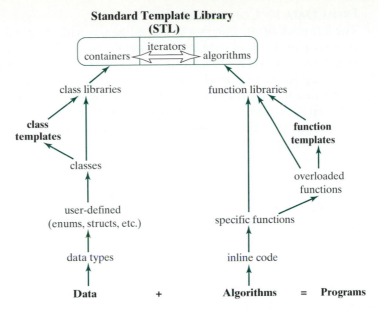

**Standard Template Library
(STL)**

FIGURE 6.1   THE EVOLUTION OF REUSEABILITY/GENERICITY

the programming task. For example, if a program needs to calculate square roots at several different places in a program, it is surely easier to call a square root function, passing it the number and having it return its square root, than to write the code for the square-root algorithm every place it is needed.

This led to the development of large libraries of functions (and other subprograms) such as those in C and FORTRAN for solving many different kinds of specific problems. Each library might contain several different functions for solving the same problem but with different types of data. For example, early versions of FORTRAN contained at least four different absolute value functions: ABS() for single-precision REAL values, DABS() for DOUBLE PRECISION values, IABS() for INTEGER values, and CABS() for COMPLEX values. Later, it became possible to *overload* functions so that the same function name could be used for different types of parameters. For example, in FORTRAN, ABS()—called a *generic function*—could be called with any of the four data types REAL, DOUBLE PRECISION, INTEGER, or COMPLEX, and the compiler would replace it with a call to the appropriate specific function ABS(), DABS(), IABS(), or CABS(), respectively. We will review function overloading in C++ in the next section.

Although this made it easier to use functions in a program, it still was necessary to develop large libraries of functions, one for each of the different data types. The recent addition of *function templates* in C++ has greatly simplified this task by allowing the programmer to write a template (i.e., pattern) for a function and have the *compiler* generate the function definition for a particular data type from it. We will study function templates in the next section and look at a few of the function templates that make up the *algorithms* component of the Standard Template Library.

FROM DATA TO CONTAINERS

The left track of the diagram in Fig. 6.1 begins with simple data types to store and process a few kinds of data, mostly numeric, and eventually alphanumeric. An early structured data type provided in programming languages was the array. Later it became possible to *extend a language* by defining new data types; for example, an enumeration in Pascal or C++ is a new, albeit simple, data type. Group data items in COBOL, records in Pascal, and structs in C made it possible to define new data types for processing nonhomogeneous collections of data.

For years, however, the emphasis was on finding better and more powerful ways to develop procedures for processing the data. As we described in Chap. 1, in this *procedural* style of programming, data was simply something that got shipped off to different subprograms for processing. It became possible to define data types that not only stored data but also contained operations for processing this stored data only when classes were added to C giving C++, units were added to some versions of Pascal, and similar constructs were added to other languages. *Object-oriented programming* had made its appearance on the programming stage.

The most recent development in this data track has been the counterpart to function templates, namely, *class templates*. They make it possible to define data types into which other data types can be passed—for example, a `Stack` class template into which the type of the stack elements can be passed. The standard C++ `istream`, `ostream`, and `string` classes are in fact formed by passing the type `char` into the class templates `basic_istream`, `basic_ostream`, and `basic_string`, respectively. The container types in the Standard Template Library are also class templates. We will study class templates later in this chapter.

6.2   FUNCTION GENERICITY— OVERLOADING AND TEMPLATES

We have seen that we can make pieces of code reuseable by encapsulating them within functions. For example, consider the problem of interchanging the values of two `int` variables `x` and `y`. Instead of using inline code

```
int temp = x;
x = y;
y = temp;
```

to exchange the values of `x` and `y`, we can make this code reuseable by writing it as a function:

```
/* Function to interchange two integer variables.
 *
 * Receive:   Integer variables first and second
 * Pass back: first and second with values interchanged
 ***********************************************************/
```

```
inline void Swap(int & first, int & second)
{
  int temp = first;
  first = second;
  second = temp;
}
```

This code can then be used wherever it is needed simply by calling the function and passing as arguments the variables whose values are to be exchanged:

```
int x = 11,
    y = 22;
Swap(x, y);
   .
   .
   .
int w = 335,
    z = 444;
Swap(w, z);
   .
   .
   .
int a = 5005,
    b = 6006;
Swap(a, b);
```

Since the values to be exchanged are passed to the function and new values passed back from it, this function can be used to exchange the values of any two int variables. Arguments and parameters thus allow us to construct a general solution to the interchange problem.

OVERLOADING

What about swapping the values of two non-integer variables? For example, suppose we want to interchange the values of two double variables. We cannot use the preceding function. One option is to use a function that encapsulates the same code with int replaced by double, and give the function a different name.

```
/* Function to interchange two double variables
 *
 * Receive:   Double variables first and second
 * Pass back: first and second with values interchanged
 ***********************************************************/

inline void DubSwap(double & first, double & second)
{
  double temp = first;
  first = second;
  second = temp;
}
```

It is legal in C++, however, to give functions the same name. In this case, that name is said to be **overloaded.** The rule governing overloading is:

> The name of a function can be overloaded, provided *no two definitions of the function have the same signature.*

This means that we could give the preceding function the same name `Swap()` as the earlier version:

```
/* Function to interchange two double variables.
 *
 * Receive:    Double variables first and second
 * Pass back: first and second with values interchanged
 ********************************************************/

inline void Swap(double & first, double & second)
{
  double temp = first;
  first = second;
  second = temp;
}
```

The signature of the first version of `Swap()` is

```
(int &, int &)
```

and the signature of the second version is

```
(double &, double &)
```

so the condition in the overloading rule is satisfied. Remember, however, that the return type or `void` specifier in a function's heading is not part of its signature, which means that *two functions with the same parameter types but with different return types cannot be overloaded.*

Now what if we needed a function to interchange the values of two `char` variables? Again, we can overload function `Swap()`:

```
/* Function to interchange two char variables.
 *
 * Receive:    Char variables first and second
 * Pass back: first and second with values interchanged
 ********************************************************/

inline void Swap(char & first, char & second)
{
  char temp = first;
  first = second;
  second = temp;
}
```

And we could go on in this manner for other types of variables, creating an entire library of overloaded `Swap()` functions for every data type for which we might ever want to interchange two values.

When an overloaded function like `Swap()` is called, it is the compiler's responsibility to determine which of the collection of overloaded functions is to be used. It does this by comparing the types of the arguments with the signatures in the collection until it finds a match. For example, if we call `Swap()` with

```
int i1 = 11,
    i2 = 22;
Swap(i1, i2);
```

the call has two `int` arguments, and so the compiler associates this call with the first definition of `Swap()`, whose signature is `(int, int)`. However, if we write

```
double d1 = 33.3,
       d2 = 44.4;
Swap(d1, d2);
```

the function call has two `double` arguments, and so the compiler associates this call with the second definition of `Swap()`, whose signature is `(double, double)`. If there is no function in the collection with the required signature, compilation is terminated with an error message. For example, the statements

```
string s1 = "Hi",
       s2 = "Ho";
Swap(s1, s2);
```

will produce a compiler error unless we add a version of `Swap()` whose signature is `(string, string)`.

We used overloading in Sec. 3.1 when we built the class `Time`. It had two constructors, which by necessity must have the same name, `Time()`, and must, therefore, be overloaded. The signature of the default constructor

```
Time()
```

was

```
()
```

and the explicit-value constructor

```
Time(unsigned initHours, unsigned initMinutes, char initAMPM)
```

had the signature

```
(unsigned, unsigned, char)
```

so this satisfies the condition in the overloading rule.

☞   *A common error in this connection is to define an explicit-value constructor in a class but no default constructor.* The compiler then is not able to construct objects whose declarations have the form

```
ClassName object;
```

because there is no constructor whose signature is (); that is, there is no default constructor `ClassName()`.

FUNCTION TEMPLATES

Note in the preceding example that each definition of `Swap()` is doing exactly the same thing (on a different type of data). This should suggest that there is a better way to accomplish the same thing without this many reinventions of the wheel. Here, the better way is to recognize that the only differences in these definitions are the three places where a type is specified. It would be nice if we could define the function and leave these types blank, to be filled in later

```
inline void Swap(_____ & first, _____ & second)
{
    _____ temp = first;
   first = second;
   second = temp;
}
```

and somehow *pass the type* to the function when we call it. Then we could replace all of these definitions with one. As we will see now, *templates* are what makes it possible to do this.

The template mechanism is important and powerful and, as we noted, it is used throughout the Standard Template Library (STL). *Templates make it possible for classes and functions to receive not only data values to be stored or operated on via parameters but also to receive the type of data via a parameter.* They provide, therefore, a means of writing code that is generic and easier to reuse since one template definition can be used to create multiple instances of a class or function, each storing and/or operating on a different type of data. We will describe function templates in this section and class templates in the next.

Templates work by declaring *type parameters* and using these parameters in the function prototype and definition instead of specific types. This is done using a different kind of parameter list. To illustrate, the following is a function template for our swap problem:

```
/* A Swap template for exchanging the values of any two
 * objects of the same type, for which the assignment
 * operation is defined.
 *
 * Receive:    Type parameter Item
 *             first and second, two objects of the same type
 * Pass back:  first and second with values interchanged
 * Assumes:    Assignment (=) is defined for type Item.
 * * * * * * * * * * * * * * * * * * * * * * * * * * * * * * * * * * * * * * * */
```

```
template <typename Item>              // <- the type parameter

void Swap(Item & first, Item & second)
{
  Item temp = first;
  first = second;
  second = temp;
}
```

Rather than specify that the function is to exchange two values of a particular type such as `char`, `int`, and so on, this definition uses the *generic type identifier* `Item` as a "placeholder" for the type of the values to be exchanged. More precisely, the line

```
template<typename Item>
```

informs the compiler of two things:[1]

1. This is a function **template:** *a pattern from which a function can be created.*
2. The identifier `Item` is the name of a **type parameter** for this function template that will be given a value when the function is called. (The keyword `typename` may be replaced by `class`.)

The rest of the definition simply specifies the behavior of the function, using the type parameter `Item` in place of any specific type. In and of itself, the function template does nothing. When the compiler encounters a template like that for `Swap()`, it simply stores it but doesn't generate any machine instructions. It uses the pattern given by our template to generate actual function definitions on an as-needed basis.

To illustrate, suppose that we replace the contents of our earlier `Swap` library with this single function template, and include it in the following program:

```
#include "Swap"

int main()
{
  int i1 = 11,
      i2 = 22;
      Swap(i1, i2);
          .
          .
          .
  double d1 = 33.3,
         d2 = 44.4;
  Swap(d1, d2);
          .
          .
          .
  string s1 = "Hi",
         s2 = "Ho";
  Swap(s1, s2);
          .
          .
          .
}
```

[1] Compilers that do not conform fully to the ANSI/ISO C++ standard may require the original form of the template declaration with the keyword `typename` replaced by the keyword `class`:

```
template <class Item>
```

When the compiler encounters the first call to `Swap()`,

```
Swap(i1, i2);
```

in which the two arguments `i1` and `i2` are of type `int`, it uses the pattern given by our template to generate a *new* definition of `Swap()` in which the type parameter `Item` is replaced by `int`:

```
inline void Swap(int & first, int & second)
{
    int temp = first;
    first = second;
    second = temp;
}
```

When it reaches the second call,

```
Swap(d1, d2);
```

where the two arguments `d1` and `d2` are of type `double`, the compiler will use the same pattern to generate a second definition of `Swap()` in which the type parameter `Item` is replaced by `double`:

```
inline void Swap(double & first, double & second)
{
    double temp = first;
    first = second;
    second = temp;
}
```

When the compiler reaches the final call,

```
Swap(s1, s2);
```

in which the two arguments `s1` and `s2` are of type `string`, it will use the pattern to generate a third definition of `Swap()` in which the type parameter `Item` is replaced by `string`:

```
inline void Swap(string & first, string & second)
{
    string temp = first;
    first = second;
    second = temp;
}
```

We are spared from all of the redundant coding of the earlier approach because the compiler is providing multiple versions of the swap operation as they are needed. This single function template definition (stored in some file `Swap`) is sufficient therefore to interchange the values of any two variables, provided the assignment operator is defined for their type.

The general forms of function templates are:

FUNCTION TEMPLATE

Forms:

```
template <typename TypeParam>
Function
```

or

```
template <class TypeParam>
Function
```

More General Form:

```
template <specifier TypeParam₁,..., specifier TypeParamₙ>
Function
```

In these forms, `TypeParam`, `TypeParam`$_1$, . . . are generic type parameters naming "generic" types of value(s) on which the function operates; each `specifier` is the keyword `typename` or `class`; and `Function` is the prototype or definition of the function.

Notes:

▶ The word `template` is a C++ keyword specifying that what follows is a *pattern* for a function, *not an actual function prototype or definition*.

▶ The keywords `typename` and `class` may be used interchangeably in a type-parameter list.

▶ Whereas "normal" parameters (and arguments) appear within parentheses, *type parameters (and arguments for class templates) appear within angle brackets* (< >).

▶ Unlike regular functions, *a function template cannot be split across files*, that is, we cannot put its prototype in a header file and its definition in an implementation file. It all goes in the header file.

▶ A function template is only a *pattern* that describes how individual functions can be constructed from given actual types. This process of constructing a function is called **instantiation.** In each instantiation, the type parameter is said to be **bound** to the actual type passed to it.

▶ In the general form, each of the type parameters *must* appear at least once in the parameter list of the function. The reason for this is that the compiler uses only the types of the arguments in a function call to determine what types to bind to the type parameters. (See also Appendix D.)

In the preceding example, `Swap()` was instantiated three times—once with type `int`, once with type `double`, and once with type `string`—and it could have been instantiated with any other type for which assignment (=) is defined. A function template can thus serve as a pattern for the definition of an unlimited number of instances.

For the compiler to be able to generate "real live" function definitions from a function template such as `Swap()`, it must "see" the actual definition of `Swap()`, and not just its prototype. This is the reason why a function template cannot be split across two files (with its prototype in a header file and its definition in an implementation file).

EXAMPLE: DISPLAYING AN ARRAY

Instantiation of a function template is carried out using the following algorithm:

1. Search the parameter list of the template function for type parameters.

2. If a type parameter is found, determine the type of the corresponding argument.

3. Bind these two types together.

To illustrate this, consider the program in Fig. 6.2

FIGURE 6.2   USING A FUNCTION TEMPLATE TO DISPLAY AN ARRAY

```
/* This program illustrates the use of a function template to
 * display an array with elements of any type for which << is
 * defined.
 *
 * Output:  An array of ints and an array of doubles using Display()
 ******************************************************************/

#include <iostream>
using namespace std;

/* Function template to display elements of any type
 * (for which the output operator is defined) stored
 * in an array.
 *   Receive: Type parameter ElementType
 *            Array of elements of type ElementType
 *            numElements, number of elements to be displayed
 *   Output:  First numElements elements in array
 ******************************************************************/

template <typename ElementType>
void Display(ElementType array[], int numElements)
{
  for (int i = 0; i < numElements; i++)
    cout << array[i] << "  ";
  cout << endl;
}

int main ()
{
  double x[10] = {1.1, 2.2, 3.3, 4.4, 5.5};
  Display(x, 5);
  int num[20] = {1, 2, 3, 4};
  Display (num, 4);
}
```

EXECUTION:

```
1.1   2.2   3.3   4.4   5.5
1   2   3   4
```

When `Display(x, 5)` is encountered, the compiler searches the parameter list of the function template `Display()`. The first parameter involves the type parameter `ElementType`; from the actual function call, the compiler can determine that the type `double` (of `x`) should be bound to `ElementType`; the second parameter `numElements` does not involve a type parameter. Thus, the binding is complete and the compiler can generate the following instance of `Display()`:

```cpp
void Display(double array[], int numElements)
{
  for (int i = 0; i < numElements; i++)
    cout << array[i] << "   ";
  cout << endl;
}
```

In a similar manner, when it later encounters `Display(num, 4)`, the compiler generates an `int` version of `Display()`:

```cpp
void Display(int array[], int numElements)
{
  for (int i = 0; i < numElements; i++)
    cout << array[i] << "   ";
  cout << endl;
}
```

6.3   CLASS GENERICITY—TEMPLATES

In the preceding section we say how it is possible to pass a type into a function template by using a type parameter. As we have noted before, it would surely improve genericity of ADTs if we could do a similar thing with classes, especially for container classes such as `Stack` where it would be convenient to be able to pass the type of the elements into the container. In this section we show how class templates can be used in much the same way as function templates to accomplish this.

WHAT'S WRONG WITH `typedef`?

We have considered *container classes* of various kinds, for example, `Stack` and `Queue`. For these classes we used the `typedef` mechanism to build containers that are largely independent of the type of value stored in that container. For example, for the `Stack` class, we placed a `typedef` declaration before the class declaration (where it can be easily changed) to set the type of the generic element type `StackElement`:

```
/* Stack.h contains the declaration of class Stack.
   Basic operations:
    . . .
--------------------------------------------------*/

const int STACK_CAPACITY = 128;
typedef int StackElement;
class Stack
{

/***** Function Members *****/
public:
    . . .


/***** Data Members *****/
private:
    . . .


};
```

We need only change the type identifier following the keyword `typedef` to change the meaning of `StackElement` throughout the class.

There are, however, some problems with using `typedef` to gain this genericity:

▶ Problem 1: Since changing the `typedef` is a change to the header file, any program or library that uses the class must be recompiled.

▶ Problem 2 (*more serious*): Suppose we need two containers with different types of values; for example, a `Stack` of reals and a `Stack` of characters. A name declared using `typedef` can have only one meaning at a time. We would need to create two different container classes with two different names.

As we now show, these problems can be solved using class templates.

CLASS TEMPLATES

What is needed is a way to create a container class that is truly *type independent*. One way to do this is to use a **class template**, in which the *class is parameterized* so that it *receives the type of data stored in the class via a parameter* in much the same way that function templates parameterize functions. To convert the `Stack` class into a class template, we simply replace the `typedef` declaration preceding the class declaration with a `template` declaration like that for function templates; for example,

```
/* StackT.h contains a template for class Stack.

   Receives:  Type parameter StackElement.
   Basic operations:
    . . .
--------------------------------------------------*/
```

```cpp
const int STACK_CAPACITY = 128;
template <typename StackElement>
class Stack
{

/***** Function Members *****/
public:
    .  .  .

/***** Data Members *****/
private:
    StackElement myArray [STACK_CAPACITY];
    int myTop;
};
```

Here, as with function templates, we can think of the type parameter
StackElement as a blank type that will be filled in later:

```cpp
const int STACK_CAPACITY = 128;
template <typename _____>
class Stack
{

/***** Function Members *****/
public:
    .  .  .

/***** Data Members *****/
private:
    _____ myArray [STACK_CAPACITY];
    int myTop;
};
```

In general, the declaration of a class template has the following forms:

CLASS TEMPLATE DECLARATION

Usual Forms:

```cpp
template <typename TypeParam>
class SomeClass
{
    // ... members of SomeClass ...
};
```

or

```
template <class TypeParam>
class SomeClass
{
    // ... members of SomeClass ...
};
```

More General Form:

```
template <specifier TypeParam₁,..., specifier TypeParamₙ>
class SomeClass
{
    // ... members of SomeClass ...
};
```

In these forms, $TypeParam$, $TypeParam_1$,... are generic type parameters naming types of data to be stored in the container class $SomeClass$; and each $specifier$ is the keyword `typename` or `class`.

Notes:

▸ The keyword `template` specifies that what follows is a *pattern* for a class, *not an actual class declaration*.

▸ The keywords `typename` and `class` may be used interchangeably in a type-parameter list.

▸ Unlike regular classes, *a class template cannot be split across files*, that is, we cannot put prototypes of functions in the header file and their definitions in an implementation file. It all goes in the header file.

▸ A class template is only a *pattern* that describes how individual classes can be constructed from given actual types. This process of creating a class is called **instantiation**. This is accomplished by attaching the actual type to the class name in the definition of an object:

```
                    SomeClass<Actual_Type> object;
```

For example, we could instantiate our `Stack` class template with the definitions

```
Stack<char> charStack;
Stack<double> dubStack;
```

When the compiler processes these declarations, it will generate two distinct `Stack` classes—two *instances*—one with `StackElement` replaced by `char` and the other with `StackElement` replaced by `double`. The constructor in the first class will construct `charStack` as an empty stack of characters and the constructor in the second class will construct `dubStack` as an empty stack of `double`s.

There are three important rules that govern building class templates:

> ▶ All operations defined outside of the class declaration must be template functions.
>
> ▶ Any use of the name of a template class as a type must be parameterized.
>
> ▶ Operations on a template class should be defined in the same file as the class declaration.

We will illustrate these three rules in converting our `Stack` class from Chap. 4 into a class template.

A `Stack` CLASS TEMPLATE

For our `Stack` class template, none of the three preceding rules apply to the prototypes of the functions for the basic operations: We prototyped the constructor `Stack()`, `empty()`, `push()`, `display()`, `top()`, and `pop()` inside the class declaration, and they are therefore "covered" by the template declaration for the class.

However, we defined these functions outside of the class declaration, and so now the three rules must be followed:

Rule 1: *They must be defined as function templates.*

This means that these definitions must each be preceded by a template declaration; for example,

```
template <typename StackElement>
// ... definition of constructor

template <typename StackElement>
// ... definition of empty()
          .
          .
          .
```

Rule 2: *The class name* `Stack` *preceding the scope operator (::) in the function definitions is used as the name of a type and must therefore be parameterized.*

This rule applies to all of the definitions; for example:

```
template <typename StackElement>
inline void Stack<StackElement>::Stack()
{
// ... body of constructor
}

template <typename StackElement>
inline bool Stack<StackElement>::empty()
{
// ... body of empty()
}
          .
          .
          .
```

Rule 3: *These definitions should be placed within the same file* `StackT.h`.

Figure 6.3 shows the complete `Stack` class template.

FIGURE 6.3   A `Stack` CLASS TEMPLATE

```
/* StackT.h provides a Stack template.
 *
 * Receives:  Type parameter StackElement
 * Basic operations:
 *   Constructor:  Constructs an empty stack
 *   empty:    Checks if a stack is empty
 *   push:     Modifies a stack by adding a value at the top
 *   top:      Accesses the top stack value; leaves stack unchanged
 *   pop:      Modifies a stack by removing the value at the top
 *   display: Displays all the stack elements
 * Class Invariant:
 *   1. The stack elements (if any) are stored in positions
 *       0, 1, . . ., myTop of myArray.
 *   2. -1 < myTop < STACK_CAPACITY
 ----------------------------------------------------------------*/

#include <iostream>
using namespace std;

#ifndef STACKT
#define STACKT

const int STACK_CAPACITY = 128;

template <typename StackElement>
class Stack
{
/***** Function Members *****/
public:

/* --- Constructor ---
 *
 * Precondition:  A stack has been declared.
 * Postcondition: The stack has been constructed as an
 *                empty stack.
 ***************************************************************/

Stack();

/* --- Is the Stack empty? ---
 *
 * Receive: Stack containing this function (implicitly)
 * Return:  True if the Stack containing this function is empty
 *          and false otherwise
 ***************************************************************/

bool empty() const;
```

```
/* --- Add a value to the stack ---
 *
 * Receive:   The Stack containing this function (implicitly)
 *            A value to be added to a Stack
 * Pass back: The Stack (implicitly), with value added at its
 *            top, provided there's space
 * Output:    "Stack full" message if no space for value
 **************************************************************/

void push(const StackElement & value);

/* --- Display values stored in the stack ---
 *
 * Receive: The Stack containing this function (implicitly)
 *          The ostream out
 * Output:  The Stack's contents, from top down, to out
 **************************************************************/

void display(ostream & out) const;

/* --- Return value at top of the stack ---
 *
 * Receive: The Stack containing this function (implicitly)
 * Return:  The value at the top of the Stack, if nonempty
 * Output:  "Stack empty" message if stack is empty
 **************************************************************/

StackElement top() const;


/* --- Remove value at top of the stack ---
 *
 * Receive:   The Stack containing this function (implicitly)
 * Pass back: The Stack containing this function with its top
 *            value (if any) removed
 * Output:    "Stack-empty" message if stack is empty.
 **************************************************************/

void pop();


/***** Data Members *****/
private:
  StackElement myArray[STACK_CAPACITY];
  int myTop;

}; // end of class declaration
```

```cpp
//--- Definition of Constructor
template <typename StackElement>
inline Stack<StackElement>::Stack()
{ myTop = -1; }

//--- Definition of empty()
template <typename StackElement>
inline bool Stack<StackElement>::empty() const
{ return (myTop == -1); }

//--- Definition of push()
template <typename StackElement>
void Stack<StackElement>::push(const StackElement & value)
{
  if (myTop < STACK_CAPACITY - 1)  // Preserve stack invariant
  {
    ++myTop;
    myArray[myTop] = value;
  }                         // or simply, myArray[++myTop] = value;
  else
    cerr << "*** Stack is full -- can't add new value ***\n"
         << "Must increase value of STACK_CAPACITY in StackT.h\n";
}

//--- Definition of display()
template <typename StackElement>
void Stack<StackElement>::display(ostream & out) const
{
  for (int i = myTop; i >= 0; i--)
    out << myArray[i] << endl;
}

//--- Definition of top()
template <typename StackElement>
StackElement Stack<StackElement>::top() const
{
  if (myTop >= 0)
    return myArray[myTop];
  cerr << "*** Stack is empty ***\n"; }

//--- Definition of pop()
template <typename StackElement>
void Stack<StackElement>::pop()
{
  if (myTop >= 0)      // Preserve stack invariant
    myTop--;
  else
    cerr << "*** Stack is empty -- can't remove a value ***\n";
}

#endif
```

It should also be noted that

    Friend functions are also governed by the three rules.

For example, to overload `operator<<()` to display the contents of a `Stack` we could replace the prototype of the member function `display()` inside the class declaration by a prototype of `operator<<()` and specify that it is a friend function:

```
        . . .

    template <typename StackElement>
    class Stack
    {
    /***** Function Members *****/
    public:
    // ... Prototypes of constructor, empty,
    // ... push, top, and pop go here. . .

    //--- Output operator -- documentation omitted here
    friend ostream & operator<<(ostream & out,
                                const Stack<StackElement> & st);
        . . .

    }; // end of class
```

And we define it outside the class declaration as a function template:

```
    // end of class

    // --- Definition of output operator ----------------

    template<typename StackElement>
    ostream & operator<<(ostream & out,
                         const Stack<StackElement> & st)
    {
      for (int pos = st.myTop; pos >= 0; pos--)
        out << st.myArray[pos] << endl;
      return out;
    }
```

Note that in both the prototype and the definition of `operator<<()`, since `Stack` is being used as a type to declare the type of the parameter `st`, it must be parameterized.

Figure 6.4 shows a test driver program for our `Stack` class template. It uses the class template to instantiate a stack of `int`s and a stack of `char`s.

FIGURE 6.4   TEST DRIVER FOR THE `Stack` CLASS TEMPLATE

```
#include "StackT.h"
#include <iostream>
using namespace std;
```

```
int main()
{
  Stack<int> intSt;        // stack of ints
  Stack<char> charSt;      // stack of chars

  int i;
  for (i = 1; i <= 4; i++)
    intSt.push(i);
  while (!intSt.empty())
  {
    i = intSt.top(); intSt.pop();
    cout << i << endl;
  }

  for (char ch = 'A'; ch <= 'D'; ch++)
    charSt.push(ch);

  charSt.display(cout);
}
```

EXECUTION:

```
4
3
2
1
D
C
B
A
```

AN ALTERNATIVE VERSION OF THE Stack CLASS TEMPLATE

Our examples of function templates in the preceding section and of class templates in this section each had only one type parameter in the template declaration. However, as we noted in the general forms of template declarations, *templates may have more than one type parameter; they may also have ordinary value parameters.*

This property of templates makes it possible for us to get around one of the weaknesses of our Stack classes, namely, that the capacity of the myArray data member is fixed within the class. An alternative is to have the user specify this capacity in the stack's declaration and pass this into the Stack class template as an ordinary int parameter along with the stack element type in the template declaration:

```
/* StackT.h provides a Stack template.
 * Receives:  Type parameter StackElement
 *                Integer myCapacity
 * Basic operations:
 *    . . .
 **********************************************/
```

```
#include <iostream>
using namespace std;

#ifndef STACKT
#define STACKT

template <typename StackElement, int myCapacity>
class Stack
{
/***** Function Members *****/
public:
//... Prototypes of member (and friend) functions ...

/***** Data Members *****/
private:
  StackElement myArray[myCapacity];
  int myTop;

};

//... Definitions of member (and friend) functions ...

#endif
```

This would allow definitions of stacks like the following in client programs:

```
Stack<int, 10> intSt;       // stack of at most 10 ints

Stack<string, 3> strSt;     // stack of at most 3 strings
```

THE STANDARD C++ CONTAINER CLASS TEMPLATES

As we have seen, class templates are type-independent patterns from which actual classes can be defined, and this is especially useful for defining *generic container classes*—classes whose objects store (i.e., contain) other objects. In the early 1990s, Alex Stepanov and Meng Lee of Hewlett Packard Laboratories extended C++ with a library of class and function templates, which has come to be known as the **Standard Template Library (STL).** In 1994, the ANSI/ISO standards committee adopted STL as part of standard C++.

The Standard Template Library has three different kinds of components:

▶ **Container class templates:** A group of class templates that provide standardized, generic, off-the-shelf structures for storing data

▶ **Iterators:** A generic means of accessing, finding the successor of, and finding the predecessor of a container element

▶ **Algorithm templates:** A group of function templates that provide standardized, generic, off-the-shelf functions for performing many of the most common operations on container objects

In order for the algorithms in STL to be truly generic, they must be able to operate on any container. To make this possible, each container provides iterators for the algorithms to use. Iterators thus provide the interface that is needed for STL algorithms to operate on STL containers.

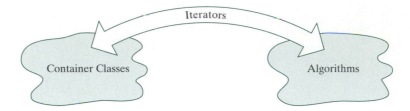

The Standard Template Library provides a rich variety of containers. Table 6.1 gives a brief description of these containers and indicates how they differ from one another. Each container has properties and operations that make it particularly useful for a large category of problems. In subsequent sections we will look at `vector`, `deque`, `stack`, and `queue`, including a brief first look at iterators.. The `list` container is described in Chap. 8 and the other containers are left for more advanced courses in data structures and algorithms. In Sec. 7.5 we will look at some of the algorithms in STL.

Containers	Description
`vector`	Linear, contiguous storage; fast inserts only at the end
`list`	Linear, noncontiguous storage; fast inserts anywhere
`deque`	Linear, noncontiguous storage; fast inserts at both the beginning and the end
`set`	A set of objects, fast associative lookup, with no duplicates allowed
`multiset`	Same as `set`, but duplicates are allowed
`map`	Maps objects of one type into objects of another type in a 1-to-1 manner (a no-duplicate associative array)
`multimap`	Maps objects of one type into objects of another type in a 1-to-many manner (associative array with duplicates)
`stack`	A stack; LIFO storage
`queue`	A queue; FIFO storage
`priority_queue`	A priority queue

TABLE 6.1   STL's CONTAINERS

The C++ standard also includes `bitset` and `valarray` as containers, but these are not in STL. Arrays, `string`s, `valarray`s, and `bitset`s have been termed by Bjarne Stroustrup, the creator of C++, as *almost containers*, and by others as *near containers*, because although they do contain elements, they do not share all of features of the interfaces of the STL containers. For example, the type of the elements of `strings` is limited and `string` is most efficient for processing strings of characters. We have already considered arrays and `strings` in an earlier chapter and will briefly describe `valarrays` and `bitsets` in Sec. 6.7 and 6.8.

✔ Quick Quiz 6.3

1. A name that is used for different functions is said to be _____.

2. The following function prototypes may be in the same library. (True or false)
   ```
   char f(int x, int y);      char f(int x, char y);
   ```

3. The following function prototypes may be in the same library. (True or false)
   ```
   int f(int x, int y);       char f(int x, int y);
   ```

4. _____ make it possible for classes and functions to receive not only data values to be stored or operated on via parameters but also to receive the type of data via a parameter.

5. `template <_____ T>` is an example of a template declaration.

6. This process of constructing a function from a function template or a class from a class template is called _____.

7. Describe two problems with using the `typedef` mechanism to set the element type for a container class.

8. List the three rules that govern class templates.

9. STL is an acronym for _____.

10. STL was developed by _____ and _____.

11. What are the three components of STL?

12. _____ provide the interface between STL algorithms and STL containers.

13. A(n) _____ is a sequence in which values may be inserted and removed only at one end.

14. A(n) _____ is a sequence in which values may be inserted only at one end and removed only at the other end.

✎ EXERCISES 6.3

Exercises 1–8 ask you to write templates. To test them you should write driver programs as instructed in Programming Problems 1–8 at the end of this chapter.

1. Write a function template to find the average of two values. (The average of a and b is $(a + b) / 2$.)

2. Write a function template to find the maximum of two values.

3. The *median* of three numbers is the middle number after the three numbers have been arranged in increasing order. Write a function template that finds the median of three values.

4. Write a function template `Sum()` for summing the elements of an array.

5. Write a function template `Sort()` for sorting the elements of an array.

6. Write a function template `Search()` for searching an array for a given value.

7. Convert the queue class from Exercise 5 of Sec. 5.2 to a class template.

8. Modify the class `CartesianPoint` from Exercise 7 of Sec. 3.2 to make it a class template in which the type parameter represents the type of the coordinates of points.

6.4   THE vector CONTAINER[2]

The simplest container in STL is the `vector` class template, which can be thought of as a type-independent pattern for an array class whose capacity can expand and which is self-contained. Its declaration in the standard library has the form

```
template <typename T>
class vector
{
    // details of vector omitted...
};
```

where `T` is a parameter for the type of values to be stored in the container. To illustrate its use, consider the following definitions:

```
vector<double> vec1;

vector<string> vec2;
```

When it processes the first definition, the compiler will create an instance of class `vector` with each occurrence of `T` replaced by `double` and then use this class to construct an object `vec1` whose elements will be `double`s. Similarly, from the second definition, the compiler will create another instance of class `vector` with each occurrence of `T` replaced by `string` and then use this class to construct the object `vec2` whose elements will be `string`s.

DEFINING vector OBJECTS

There are several constructors in `vector`, which make it possible to define `vector` objects in several different ways:

```
vector<element_type> object_name;
vector<element_type> object_name(initial_capacity);
vector<element_type> object_name(initial_capacity,
                                 initial_value);
vector<element_type> object_name(first_ptr, last_ptr);
```

For example, the definition

```
vector<double> dubVector;
```

constructs an empty `vector<double>` object `dubVector`. This means that its capacity is initially 0. However, its capacity can increase when necessary (as we will describe later) to store `double` elements.

Now consider a definition of the second kind:

---

[2]Some of this section is reproduced from Joel Adams, Sanford Leestma, and Larry Nyhoff, *C++: An Introduction to Programming,* 2d ed., Prentice-Hall, Inc., Upper Saddle River, NJ, 1997.

```
int n;
cin >> n;
vector<double> dubVector(n);
```

Here, dubVector is constructed as a vector that contains n double values set to the default double value (0). Its initial capacity and size (number of values it stores) are thus both equal to n. For example, if the value 4 is entered for n, we can picture dubVector as follows:

dubVector | 0 | 0 | 0 | 0 |
          [0] [1] [2] [3]

If we changed the definition of dubVector to

```
int n;
double dubValue;
cin >> n >> dubValue;
vector<double> dubVector(n, dubValue);
```

dubVector will be filled with the value entered for dubValue instead of the default double value (0). For example, if we enter 4 for n and 1.1 for dubValue, dubVector will contain four copies of 1.1:

dubVector | 1.1 | 1.1 | 1.1 | 1.1 |
          [0]   [1]   [2]   [3]

The last kind of definition constructs a vector object that is initialized with the contents of the memory locations specified by the range of addresses ("pointed to by") *first_ptr* up to *but not including last_ptr*. For example, consider the following definition of an array a of doubles and the definition of vector<double> object dubVector:

```
double a[] = {1.1, 2.2, 4.4, 8.8};
vector<double> dubVector(a, a+4);
```

Here, dubVector is constructed as a vector of doubles that contains copies of the double values in the range [a, a+4), that is, copies of a[0], a[1], a[2], a[3]. We might picture this construction as follows:

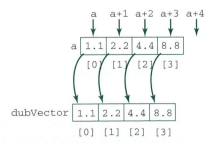

SOME `vector` OPERATIONS

C++ provides a rich set of operations for `vector`s. As we shall see, these operations allow a `vector` object to be treated much like an array, but without the limitations of C-style arrays described in Sec. 2.3. The following table lists some of these operations:

Function Member	Description
`v.capacity()`	Return the number of locations *v* currently has
`v.size()`	Return the number of values currently stored in *v*
`v.max_size()`	Return the maximum number of locations *v* can ever have
`v.empty()`	Return `true` if and only if *v* contains no values (i.e., *v*'s size is 0)
`v.reserve(n);`	Grow *v* so that its capacity is `n` (does not affect *v*'s size)
`v.push_back(value);`	Append *value* at *v*'s end
`v.pop_back();`	Erase *v*'s last element
`v.front()`	Return a reference to *v*'s first element
`v.back()`	Return a reference to *v*'s last element
`v[i]`	Access the element of *v* whose index is `i`—no bounds checking of index is done
`v.at(i)`	Access the element of *v* whose index is `i`—bounds checking is done—throws out-of-range exception if index is out of range
`v1 = v2`	Assign a copy of *v2* to *v1*
`v1.swap(v2)`	Swap *v1*'s contents with *v2*'s
`v1 == v2`	Return `true` if and only if *v1* has the same values as *v2*, in the same order
`v1 < v2`	Return `true` if and only if *v1* is lexicographically less than *v2*

The first group of operations illustrates how much more self-contained `vector` objects are than C-style arrays.

▶ The `v.size()` function member returns the number of values stored in *v*. As with C-style arrays, *the index of the first value of a* `vector` *is always 0*; but unlike a C-style array, which provides no way to identify its final value, *the index of the final value in a* `vector` *object v is always* `v.size()-1`.

▶ `v.empty()` is a simpler alternative to the boolean expression `v.size() == 0`.

▶ `v.capacity()` returns the current capacity of *v*.

▶ `v.reserve()` can be used to increase the capacity of *v*, but this is more often done implicitly using `v.push_back()`.

The following examples illustrate some of these operations:

```
vector<double> v;
cout << v.capacity() << ' ' << v.size() << endl;
```

OUTPUT:

```
0 0
```

```
vector<double> v(3);
cout << v.capacity() << ' ' << v.size() << endl;
```

OUTPUT:

```
3 3
```

```
vector<double> v(3, 4.0);
cout << v.capacity() << ' ' << v.size() << endl
     << v.max_size() << endl;
```

OUTPUT:

```
3 3
536870911
```

The second group of operations shows how values can be appended to and/or removed from a `vector`:

▶ `v.push_back(value);` appends a copy of `value` to the end of `v`, and increases its size by 1. If necessary, the capacity of `v` is increased to accommodate the new object. As we will explain later, the amount by which the capacity is increased depends upon the current capacity.

▶ `v.pop_back();` destroys the last object in `v` by decreasing the size of `v` by 1 (and calling the object's destructor, as described later). The capacity does not change.

The `front()` and `back()` function members can be used to access the first and last values in a `vector<T>`. The following examples illustrate:

```
vector<double> v;
v.push_back(1.1); v.push_back(2.2); v.push_back(3.3);
cout << v.front() << ' ' << v.back() << endl;
v.pop_back();
cout << v.front() << ' ' << v.back() << endl;
```

OUTPUT:

```
1.1 3.3
1.1 2.2
```

These member functions actually return references to the first and last values, respectively, and not copies of these values. This means that because these references are simply alternative names for the memory locations where these values are stored, we can change the first and last elements by putting v.front() or v.back() on the left side of an assignment, in an input list, and so on; for example,

```
vector<double> v;
v.push_back(1.1); v.push_back(2.2); v.push_back(3.3);
cout << v.front() << ' ' << v.back() << endl;
v.pop_back();
cout << v.front() << ' ' << v.back() << endl;
v.front() = 4.4;  v.back() = 5.5;
cout << v.front() << ' ' << v.back() << endl;
```

OUTPUT:

```
1.1 3.3
1.1 2.2
4.4 5.5
```

The subscript operator is used in much the same manner as for C-style arrays and `string` objects. The index of the first element of a `vector` v is always 0, and the expression v.size() - 1 is always the index of the final value in v. For example, the following loop for displaying the values stored in a `vector` object v are almost the same as those for arrays and `strings`:

```
for (int i = 0; i < v.size(); i++)
   cout << v[i] << endl;
```

Also, as with C-style arrays, no check is made of the index to determine if `vector` indices are in bounds. An alternative is to use the `at` member function, which throws an out-of-range exception if the index is out of bounds; for example,

```
try
{
   for (int i = 0; i < n; i++)
      cout << v.at(i) << endl;
}
 . . .
catch(out_of_range)
{
   cerr << "Index out of range\n";
}
```

There is one important difference to remember, however, between how the subscript operator is used for arrays and how it is used for `vectors`. To illustrate it, suppose we wrote the following `Read()` function to read values into a `vector`:

```
/* Read is a function template that INCORRECTLY
 * reads values from an istream into a vector.
 *   Receive:     type parameter T
 *                istream in and vector<T> theVector
 *   Input:       Values from in into theVector
 *   Pass back: The modified istream and theVector
 *************************************************/

template <typename T>
void Read(istream & in, vector & theVector)
{
  int index = 0;

  for (;;)
  {
    in >> theVector[index];   // LOGIC ERROR:
    if (in.eof()) break;      //  size, capacity not updated!
    index++;
  }
}
```

☞ This does not work. *If the subscript operator is used to append values to a* `vector`, *neither the* `vector`'s *size nor its capacity is modified.* Whenever possible, use `push_back()` *(or* `insert()`) *to append values to a* `vector` because it updates its size (and if necessary, its capacity).[3] A correct way to write this input function is:

```
/* Read is a function template that reads values
 * from an istream into a vector.
 *   Receive:     type parameter T
 *                istream in and vector<T> theVector
 *   Input:       Values from in into theVector
 *   Pass back: The modified istream and the Vector
 *************************************************/

template <typename T>
void Read(istream & in, vector & theVector)
{
  T inputValue;

  for (;;)
  {
    in >> inputValue;              // assumes operator>>() is
    if (in.eof()) break;           // defined for T objects

    theVector.push_back(inputValue);
  }
}
```

---

[3]The `push_back()` function also correctly updates the iterator returned by the `end()` function member, while the subscript operator does not. STL algorithms will thus not work properly if subscript is used to append values to a `vector`.

Only after a `vector` contains values should the subscript operator be used to access (or change) those values, for example, in an output function like the following:

```
/* Print is a function template that displays values
 * stored in a vector using an ostream.
 *   Receive:    Type parameter T
 *               ostream out and vector<T> theVector
 *   Output:     Values from theVector into out
 *   Pass back: The modified ostream
 *********************************************************/

template <typename T>
void Print(ostream & out, const vector & theVector)
{
   for (int i = 0; i < theVector.size(); i++)
      out << theVector[i] << ' ';
      // assumes operator<<() is defined for T objects
}
```

The assignment operator (=) behaves as one would expect. A vector assignment of the form

```
v1 = v2;
```

will change `v1` to a copy of `v2` after first destroying any previous value assigned to `v1`.

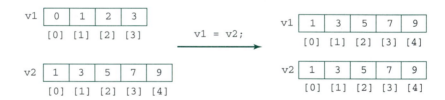

To interchange the values of two `vector<T>` variables `v1` and `v2` we could use code like the `Swap()` functions we wrote in Sec. 6.1:

```
vector<T> temp = v1;
v1 = v2;
v2 = temp;
```

But there is no need to do this, because we can simply use the `swap()` member function: `v1.swap(v2);`

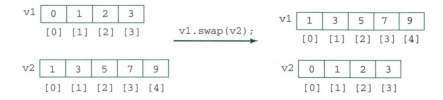

The equality operator (==) compares its operands element by element and returns true if and only if they are identical; that is, their sizes match and their values match. It assumes that operator==() is defined for the element type of the vectors. The less-than operator (<) assumes that operator<() is defined for the element type. It behaves much like the string less-than operation, performing an element-by-element comparison until a mismatch (if any) occurs. If the mismatched element in the left operand is less than the corresponding element in the right operand, the operation returns true; otherwise, it returns false. If all the elements of both vector<T> objects are compared and no mismatch is found, the operation returns false. For example, suppose that vector<int> objects v1 and v2 have the following values:

v1
| 1 | 2 | 4 | 8 |
| [0] | [1] | [2] | [3] |

v2
| 1 | 2 | 3 | 4 | 5 |
| [0] | [1] | [2] | [3] | [4] |

A comparison using the less-than operator,

```
if (v1 < v2)
// ... do something appropriate
```

returns false because the value (4) at index 2 in v1 is not less than the value (3) at index 2 in v2. However, the comparison v2 < v1 would return true.

EXAMPLE: COUNTING LOGINS

PROBLEM.   Users logged in to a particular computer system for some given period of time. During this time, their user-ids were automatically recorded in a log file each time they logged in to the system. Because the same user may log in many times, this file may contain many duplicate user-ids. We wish to compile a list of distinct user-ids and how many times each logged in.

DESIGN.   We begin by identifying the major objects and operations in the problem:

Objects: user-ids (string)

the name of a file containing user-ids (string)

a stream to that file (ifstream)

a list of distinct user-ids

a list of login counts for each user-id

the usual streams from the keyboard (cin) and to the screen (cout, cerr), other loop control variables, etc.

For the list of user-ids we will use a vector<string> userId and for the list of login counts a vector<int> loginCount.

Operations: read the name of the log file
open an input stream to the file
read strings (user-ids) from the file
search the list of ids to see if a given user is in the list
add a user-id to the list of user-ids
increment an entry in the list of login counts
display the ids and corresponding counts

Except for the search operation, these are all provided in C++.[4]
We can organize these objects and operations into the following algorithm for solving the problem:

ALGORITHM FOR LOGIN PROBLEM

/*   Algorithm to determine users who logged in to a computer system during a given time period and the number of logins for each.

Input (keyboard):   Name of the log file
Input (file):   User ids
Output (screen):   List of distinct users and number of logins for each
---*/

1. Get the name of the log file and open an input stream to it.
2. Repeat the following until the end of the file is reached:
  a. Read a user-id from the file.
  b. Search the `vector userId` for this id.
  c. If it is found at location `i`
       Increment `loginCount[i]` by 1.
     Else
       Add the user-id to the `vector userId` and
       a 1 to `loginCount`.
3. For `i` ranging from 0 to `userId.size()` − 1:
  Display `userId[i]` and `loginCount[i]`.

For the search operation in Step 2b we will use a straightforward *linear search*:

LINEAR SEARCH ALGORITHM

/*   Algorithm to perform a linear search of values stored in a `vector v`.
Receive: A `vector v` and `item` of the same type as the elements of `v`
Return: Position of `item` if found; the size of `v` otherwise
---*/

---

[4]As we will see in the next chapter, the Standard Template Library does provide search algorithms that could be used here.

1. Set index i = 0.

2. Repeat the following:

      If i ≥ size of v or item is equal to v[i]

         Return i.

      Otherwise

         Increment i by 1.

CODING.   Figure 6.5 shows a program and function template Search() that implements the preceding objects, operations, and algorithms. Also shown is a sample run and a listing of a small log file used in this sample run.

FIGURE 6.5   USER LOGINS

```
/* This program determines which users were logged into a computer
 * system for a given period of time.
 *
 * Input (keyboard): Name of the log file
 * Input (file):     User ids
 * Output (screen):  A list of distinct user-ids and for each id,
 *                   the number of logins
 *************************************************************/

#include <iostream>
#include <fstream>
#include <string>
#include <vector>
using namespace std;

template <typename ItemType>
int Search(const vector<ItemType> & v, ItemType item);

int main()
{
  // Get name of log file and open a stream to it
  string logFile;       // log file of user-ids
  cout << "Enter name of log file: ";
  cin >> logFile;
  ifstream inStream(logFile.data());  // open input stream to log file
  if (!inStream.is_open())
  {
    cerr << "Unable to open file " << logFile << endl;
    exit(-1);
  }

  // Read user-ids from file, add new ones to list of user-ids,
  // and increment login count for each user-id
  vector<string> userId;     // list of user-ids
  vector<int> loginCount;    // list of login counts
  string aUserId;            // current user-id being processed
```

```
     for (;;)
     {
       getline(inStream, aUserId);
       if (inStream.eof()) break;

       int loc = Search(userId, aUserId);
       if (loc < userId.size())
         loginCount[loc]++;
       else
       {
         userId.push_back(aUserId);
         loginCount.push_back(1);
       }
     }

   // Display the list of user-ids and login counts
   for (int i = 0; i < userId.size(); i++)
     cout << "Logins for " << userId[i] << ": " << loginCount[i] << endl;
}

/* Function Search performs a linear search of values
 * stored in a vector.
 *
 * Receive: A vector v and item of the same type as
 *          the elements of v
 * Return:  Position of item if found; the size of v otherwise
 ******************************************************************/
template <typename ItemType>
int Search(const vector<ItemType> & v, ItemType item)
{
  int i = 0;
  for (;;)
  {
    if (i >= v.size() || item == v[i])
      return i;
    //else
    i++;
  }
}
```

LISTING OF LOG FILE USED IN SAMPLE RUN:

```
S31416PI
S12345SL
S31416PI
S31313LN
S12345SL
S31416PI
S21718EX
S13331RC
```

```
S77777UP
S12345SL
S31416PI
S21718EX
S99099RR
S12345SL
S77777UP
S31313LN
S31416PI
```

SAMPLE RUN:

```
Enter name of log file: file6-6
Logins for S31416PI: 5
Logins for S12345SL: 4
Logins for S31313LN: 2
Logins for S21718EX: 2
Logins for S13331RC: 1
Logins for S77777UP: 2
Logins for S99099RR: 1
```

A First Look Under the Hood—Increasing the Capacity

As we have noted, when a `vector` v becomes full—that is, `v.size() == v.capacity()` is true—and a new object is added by means of a `push_back()` (or `insert()`) operation, the capacity of the `vector` is increased automatically to accommodate the new elements. To do this, five tasks must be performed.

Task #1: Allocate a new block of storage.   But how much should be allocated? The simplest and most spacewise-efficient scheme would be to allocate just enough for the new object(s); that is, request space for `v.size() + 1` elements. However, this would be a serious mistake because the next task is expensive and should be avoided whenever possible. Thus, more memory is requested than is actually needed.

We consider first the following example where the `vector` v is empty:

```
vector<double> v;
cout << v.capacity() << ' ' << v.size() << endl;
for (int i = 0; i < 2048; i++)
{
  v.push_back(i);
  cout << v.capacity() << ' ' << v.size() << endl;
}
```

When these statements were executed (in gnu C++), the output produced was:

```
0 0
512 1   ← space for 512 doubles allocated
512 2
    .
    .
    .
```

```
512  512
1024 513 ← capacity doubles
    .
    .
    .
1024 1024
2048 1025 ← capacity doubles
    .
    .
```

The first increase in the capacity of v used a block of size 4K (= 4096) bytes, (since each `double` value requires 8 bytes of storage) and after that, each time the capacity needed to be increased, it was doubled. If we change the definition of v to

```
vector<int> v;
```

the output changes to

```
0  0
1024 1 ← space for 1024 ints allocated
1024 2
    .
    .
    .
1024 1024
2048 1025
    .
    .
```

Again the first increase in the capacity of v used a block of size 4K (= 4096) bytes, (since each `int` value requires 4 bytes of storage) and after that, the capacity was doubled when it needed to be increased.

With different C++ compilers, one may see different initial increases in the capacity of v. However, the capacity will double for each increase thereafter.

Now consider the case where the `vector` is not empty. If we change the definition of v to `vector<double> v(3);` then the output changes as follows:

```
3  0
3  1
3  2
3  3
6  4 ← capacity doubles
6  5
6  6
12 7 ← capacity doubles
12 8
    .
    .
    .
12 12
24 13 ← capacity doubles
    .
    .
```

We see that in each case the *capacity doubles when more space is needed*. This is a reasonable compromise between allocating small blocks of memory (which wastes time) and allocating large blocks of memory (which wastes space if only a few elements are needed). This also makes it possible to control somewhat the amount by which the capacity grows by defining the vector object with a preallocated capacity or by using the member function reserve() to set the capacity. For example, preallocating a capacity of 3 for vector<double> v forces the first new allocation to be a block of capacity 6 rather than 1024 as in the earlier case:

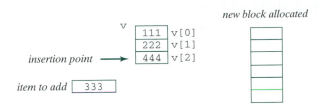

TASK #2: COPY ALL EXISTING vector ELEMENTS TO THE NEW STORAGE SPACE. First, all elements up to, but not including, the insertion point are copied into the new storage space. Then all elements from the insertion point to the end of the vector (if any) are copied, with one element skipped in the new vector, so there is room for the new object.

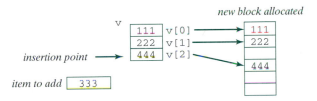

TASK #3: STORE THE NEW OBJECT IN THE STORAGE SPACE. The location for the new item is determined as an offset from the base address of the new storage block and the new item is copied into this location (using the T copy constructor):

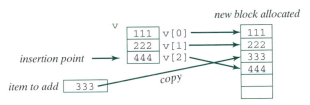

TASK #4: DESTROY THE OLD vector. A loop is used to go through the old value for v and destroy it (using the T destructor), that is, reclaim the memory for each element in it. This returns the memory allocated to the old value for v to the memory manager.

TASK #5: FREE THE MEMORY USED TO HOLD THE vector. Update the data members of v so that the new memory block becomes the array used to store the elements of v:

new block allocated

```
v   111   v[0]
    222   v[1]
    333   v[2]
    444   v[3]
          v[4]
          v[5]
```

A First Look at Iterators

Although the subscript operator can be used to access the elements of a `vector`, this is not a generic way to access elements in containers (e.g., it cannot be used for a `list`). In order for an STL algorithm to work on *any* STL container, some truly generic means of accessing the elements in a container is required. For this purpose, STL provides objects called **iterators** that can "point at" an element, access the value within that element, and move from one element to another in a way that is independent of any particular container (i.e., a *generic* mechanism). The C++ standard defines them this way:

> *Iterators are a generalization of pointers that allow a C++ program to work with different data structures (containers) in a uniform manner.*

Each STL container provides its own group of iterator types and (at least) two function members that return iterators:

- ▶ `begin()`:   returns an iterator positioned at the first element in the container
- ▶ `end()`:   returns an iterator positioned past the last element in the container

To illustrate, after the following statements are executed,

```
vector<int> v;          // empty vector
v.push_back(9);         // append 9
v.push_back(8);         // append 8
v.push_back(7);         // append 7
```

`v.begin()` and `v.end()` produce iterators that we might picture as follows:

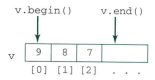

Each STL container also declares an `iterator` type that can be used to define iterator objects. To ensure that the right type is used, the identifier `iterator` must be preceded by the name of its container and the scope operator (`::`). For example, the statement

```
vector<int>::iterator vecIter = v.begin();
```

defines `vecIter` as an iterator positioned at the first element of `v`:

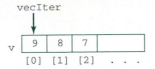

The basic operators that can be applied to iterators are:

▸ The **increment operator** (`++`).   Applied as a prefix or postfix operator to an iterator, `++` moves the iterator from its current position to the next element of the container.

▸ The **decrement operator** (`--`).   Applied as a prefix or postfix operator to an iterator, `--` moves the iterator from its current position to the previous element of the container.

▸ The **dereferencing operator** (`*`).   Applied as a prefix operator to an iterator, `*` accesses the value stored at the position to which the iterator points.

Other operators that can be applied to `vector<T>::iterator` objects (called **random-access iterators**) include:

▸ Assignment (`=`)   For iterators of the same type, `it1 = it2` sets `it1`'s position to the same as `it2`'s position.

▸ Equality comparisons (`==` and `!=`)   For iterators of the same type, `it1 == it2` is true if `it1` and `it2` are both positioned at the same element.

▸ Addition (`+`), subtraction (`-`), and the corresponding shortcuts (`+=`, `-=`)   For iterator `it` and integer `n`, `it + n` returns an iterator positioned `n` elements from `it`'s current position.

▸ Subscript operator (`[]`)   For iterator `it` and integer `n`, `it[n]` returns a reference to the `n`th element from `it`'s current position.

The following statements illustrate several of these operators:

```
vector<double> v;
v.push_back(1.1);
v.push_back(2.2);
v.push_back(3.3);
v.push_back(4.4);

vector<double>::iterator it1 = v.begin(), it2 = v.end();
cout << *it1 << ' ' << *(it2-1) << endl;
it1 += 3;
it2 -= 3;
cout << *it1 << ' ' << *it2 << endl;
it1--;
++it2;
cout << *it1 << ' ' << *it2 << endl;
```

```
cout << it1[1] << ' ' << it1[-1] << endl;
for (vector<double>::iterator i = v.begin();
                              i != v.end(); i++)
   cout << *i << ' ';
```

OUTPUT:

```
1.1 4.4
4.4 2.2
3.3 3.3
4.4 2.2
1.1 2.2 3.3 4.4
```

The following example is an alternative way to write the function template
Print() given earlier in this section, using iterators instead of indices. On each pass
through the while loop, the * operator is used to access the value at the iterator's
current position, and the ++ operator then advances the iterator to the next element.

```
/* Print is a function template that displays values
 * stored in a vector using an ostream.  It uses
 * iterators and dereferencing to access the vector
 * elements.
 *  Receive:    Type parameter T
 *              ostream out and vector<T> theVector
 *  Output:     Values from theVector into out
 *  Pass back: The modified ostream
 ***********************************************************/

template <typename T>
void Print(ostream & out, const vector<T> & theVector)
{
  vector<T>::iterator vecIter = theVector.begin();
  while(vecIter != theVector.end())
  {
    out << *vecIter << ' ';
    vecIter++;
  }
}
```

Unlike the earlier version of Print() (which requires the subscript operator),
this function template can be made into a generic Print() *algorithm template* that
allows the values in almost *any* STL container to be output to an ostream:

```
/* Print is a function template that displays using
 * ostream out the values stored in a container for
 * which iterators are defined and operator<< is
 * defined for the container's element type.
 *  Receive:    Type parameter Container
 *              ostream out and Container theContainer
 *  Output:     Values from theContainer into out
 *  Pass back: The modified ostream
 ***********************************************************/
```

```
template <typename Container>
void Print(ostream & out, const Container & theContainer)
{
  Container::iterator conIter = theContainer.begin();

  while(conIter != theContainer.end())
  {
    out << *conIter << ' ';
    conIter++;
  }
}
```

To display the contents of a vector<double> object v in reverse order, we could use the subscript operator

```
for (int i = v.size() - 1; i >= 0; i--)
  cout << v[i] << "  ";
cout << endl;
```

Using an iterator is a bit clunky; for example,

```
vector<double>::iterator it;
for (it = v.end() - 1; it != v.begin(); it--)
  cout << *it << "  ";
cout << *it << endl;
```

An alternative is to use a **reverse iterator**, which *reverses the action of* ++:

```
vector<double>::reverse_iterator it;
for (it = v.rbegin(); it != v.rend(); it++)
  cout << *it << "  ";
cout << endl;
```

SOME vector FUNCTION MEMBERS INVOLVING ITERATORS

Now that we have been introduced to STL's iterators, we have the background needed to understand a group of vector function members that utilize iterators. We conclude our study of the vector class template with brief descriptions of these operators.

Function Member	Description
v.begin()	Return an iterator positioned at v's first element
v.end()	Return an iterator positioned past v's last element

`v.rbegin()`	Return a reverse iterator positioned at *v*'s last element
`v.rend()`	Return a reverse iterator positioned before *v*'s first element
`v.insert(pos, value)`	Insert *value* into *v* at iterator position *pos*
`v.insert(pos, n, value)`	Insert *n* copies of *value* into *v* at iterator position *pos*
`v.erase(pos)`	Erase the value in *v* at iterator position *pos*
`v.erase(pos1, pos2)`	Erase the values in *v* from iterator positions *pos1* to *pos2*

The last two groups show that it is possible to insert and remove elements at any location in a `vector`, but iterators must be used to specify these locations. Also, these operations are as inefficient as for arrays—they must shift elements to make room for new ones and close gaps when items are removed.

To illustrate, consider the following `vector<double>` object v:

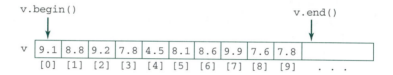

To remove the second element 8.8, we can use

```
v.erase(v.begin() + 1);
```

This removes 8.8 from v, shifting the remaining values to the left to fill its space, and updating `v.size()` and `v.end()` appropriately:

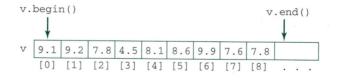

WRAP-UP: vectors VERSUS ARRAYS
The C-style array is a legacy of programming from the early 1970s. The C++ `vector` was designed in the 1990s, and thus incorporates over 20 years of additional programming wisdom. The design of `vectors` (along with the other class templates in STL) gives it some definite advantages over C-style arrays:

▶ The capacity of a `vector` can increase during execution; the capacity of a C-style array is fixed and cannot be changed during execution.

▶ A `vector` is a self-contained object; the C-style array is not. If the same operation can be implemented with either container, the array version will require more parameters.

▶ A `vector` is a class template, and its function members (augmented with the STL algorithms) provide ready-to-use implementations of many common operations. The C-style array requires us to reinvent the wheel for most operations.

But both have their limitations. For an array or a `vector` of size n, inserting or erasing an element at the end can be done in *constant time*, that is, the time does not depend on n. However, to insert or erase at other positions in the array or `vector`, in the worst case we must move n elements; on the average, $n/2$ elements must be moved.

In summary, arrays and `vector` objects work well for storing sequences in which insertions and deletions are infrequent or are restricted to the end(s) of the list. *Dynamic sequences* whose sizes may vary greatly during processing and those in which items are frequently inserted and/or deleted anywhere in the sequence are better stored in a *linked list* (the STL `list` container). Linked lists are described in Chap. 8.

✔ Quick Quiz 6.4

Questions 1–15 assume that the following statements have been executed:

```
vector<int> a, b(5), c(5, 1), d(5);
d.push_back(77);
d.push_back(88);
```

1. The type of values stored in a is _____.

2. The capacity of a is _____ and its size is _____.

3. The capacity of b is _____ and its size is _____.

4. The capacity of c is _____ and its size is _____.

5. The capacity of d is _____ and its size is _____.

6. What output is produced by
```
cout << c.front() << ' ' << c.back() << endl;
```

7. What output is produced by
```
cout << d.front() << ' ' << d.back() << endl;
```

8. `a.empty()` (True or false).

9. `c < d` (True or false).

10. `c[1] == 1` (True or false).

11. What output is produced by
```
for (int i = 0; i < c.size(); i++)
    cout << c[i] << ' ';
```

12. What output is produced by
```
d.pop_back();
for (int i = 0; i < d.size(); i++)
    cout << d[i] << ' ';
```

13. `d.begin()` returns an iterator positioned at _____ in d.

14. `d.end()` returns an iterator positioned _____ in d.

15. If d's capacity must increase, it will become _____ .

16. `vector` objects are self-contained. (True or false).

For questions 17–20, assume the declarations

```
vector<double> xValue;
vector<int> number(5, 1);
```

Describe the contents of the `vector<T>` after the statements are executed.

17.
```
for (int i = 0; i <= 4; i++)
    xValue.push_back(double(i) / 2.0)
```

18.
```
for (int i = 0; i < 5; i++)
    if (i % 2 == 0)
        number.push_back(2 * i);
    else
        number.push_back(2 * i + 1);
```

19.
```
for (int i = 1; i < 5; i++)
    number.push_back(2 * number[i - 1]);
```

20.
```
for (int i = 1; i <= 3; i++)
    number.pop_back();
for (int i = 1; i <= 3; i++)
    number.push_back(2);
```

✐ EXERCISES 6.4

For Exercises 1–11, assume that the following declarations have been made,

```
vector<int> number,
            v(10, 20),
            w(10);
int num;
```

and that for exercises that involve input, the following values are entered:

```
99 33 44 88 22 11 55 66 77 -1
```

Describe the contents of the given `vector<T>` after the statements are executed.

1.
```
for (int i = 0; i < 10; i++)
    number.push_back(i / 2);
```

2.
```
for (int i = 0; i < 6; i++)
    w.push_back(i / 2);
```

3.
```
for (;;)
{
    cin >> num;
    if (num < 0) break;
    number.push_back(num);
}
```

```
4.  for (int i = 0; i <= 5; i++)
        number.push_back(i);
    for (int i = 0; i < 2; i++)
        number.pop_back();
    for (int i = 0; i <= 5; i++)
        number.push_back(i);
```

For Exercises 5–11 assume that the loop in exercise 3 has been executed.

```
5.  for (int i = 0; i < number.size() - 1; i += 2)
        number[i] = number[i + 1];
```

```
6.  number.pop_back();
    number.push_back(number.front());
```

```
7.  int temp = number.front();
    number.front() = number.back();
    number.back() = temp;
```

```
8.  for (int i = 0; i < number.size(); i++)
        w.pushback(number[i] + v[i]);
```

```
9.  while (v < number)
    {
        v.erase(v.begin());
        number.erase(number.begin());
    }
```

```
10. vector<int>::iterator iter = number.begin();
    while (*iter > 25)
    {
        number.erase(iter);
        iter++;
    }
```

```
11. for (vector<int>::iterator iter = number.begin();
            iter != number.end(); iter++)
        w.push_back(*iter + 1);
```

For Exercises 12–14, write definitions and statements to construct a `vector` with the required properties.

12. Stores the sequence of integers from 0 through 99.

13. Stores the sequence of integers from 0 through 99 in reverse order.

14. Has capacity 50 and the value stored in an element is true if the corresponding index is even and is false otherwise.

The following exercises ask you to write function/class templates. You should also write driver programs to test them as instructed in Programming Problems 9–11 at the end of this chapter.

15. Write a function template that returns `true` if the values stored in a `vector<T>` are in ascending order and `false` otherwise, where operator `<` is assumed to be defined for type `T`.

16. Write a function template that returns the range of values stored in a `vector<T>`, that is, the difference between the largest value and the smallest value, where operator `<` is assumed to be defined for type `T`.

17. Convert the `Queue` class from Exercise 5 of Sec. 5.2 into a class template.

6.5   MULTIDIMENSIONAL vectors

C-style multidimensional arrays described in Sec. 2.3 suffer the same deficiencies we described for one-dimensional arrays, the most serious of which is that they are not consistent with object-oriented programming because they are not self-contained. The vector class template of the preceding section is obviously an OOP alternative to one-dimensional arrays; a vector object does carry along inside itself its capacity, its size, and other basic operations. In this section we outline a method for building multidimensional vector objects.

TWO-DIMENSIONAL vector OBJECTS

In Sec. 2.3 we saw that in C and C++ multidimensional arrays are treated as arrays of arrays. In particular, a two-dimensional array can be viewed as a one-dimensional array whose elements are themselves one-dimensional arrays. We can use the same approach to build a two-dimensional vector class template. A vector is a one-dimensional object, and a vector of vectors is, therefore, a two-dimensional object.

To illustrate, consider the following definition of a two-dimensional vector object table:

```
const int ROWS = 3,
          COLUMNS = 4;
vector< vector<double> > table(ROWS,
                      vector<double>(COLUMNS, 0.0));
```

☞ *It is important to remember the space between the angle brackets (> >)*, because if we write

```
vector< vector<double>> table ...
```

the compiler will mistake >> for the input operator, which will result in a compilation error.

The compiler uses a vector constructor twice to construct table. The inner call to the constructor

```
vector< vector<double> > table(ROWS,
                      vector<double>(COLUMNS, 0.0));
```

builds a nameless vector<double> object containing four zeros:

[0]	[1]	[2]	[3]
0.0	0.0	0.0	0.0

This nameless vector of doubles is then passed as the initial value to the outer call to the constructor:

```
vector< vector<double> > table(ROWS,
                      vector<double>(COLUMNS, 0.0));
```

which uses it to initialize each of its three `vector` elements. The result is the following 3 × 4 `vector` of `vectors` of `double` values:

```
table:   [0]    [1]    [2]    [3]
    [0]  0.0    0.0    0.0    0.0
    [1]  0.0    0.0    0.0    0.0
    [2]  0.0    0.0    0.0    0.0
```

The definition

```
vector< vector<double> > aTable;
```

will construct `aTable` as an empty two-dimensional `vector`.

TWO-DIMENSIONAL `vector` OPERATIONS

SUBSCRIPT.   A single-subscript expression such as

```
table[0]
```

refers to one row of `table`,

```
table:   [0]    [1]    [2]    [3]
    [0]  0.0    0.0    0.0    0.0
```

and a double-subscript expression such as

```
table[0][2]
```

refers to an element within the specified row of `table`:

```
table:   [0]    [1]    [2]    [3]
    [0]  0.0    0.0    0.0    0.0
```

In general, the expression

```
table[r][c]
```

can be used to access the value stored in column `c` of row `r`.

THE `size()` FUNCTION.   Suppose that we want to determine the number of rows in a two-dimensional `vector`. If `table` is the 3 × 4 two-dimensional `vector` described earlier, then the expression

```
table.size()
```

returns 3, the number of rows in `table`. The expression

```
table[r].size()
```

can be used to find the number of columns in row r, because `table[r]` returns the `vector` of `double` values in `table` whose index is r, and applying `size()` to that `vector` returns the number of values in it. If `table` is rectangular, then each row will have the same size allowing us to apply `size()` to any row. If `table` is not rectangular, then the size of each row may be different, and so `size()` must be applied to each row separately.

We can use the `size()` function and the subscript (and other) `vector` operations to perform many operations on two-dimensional `vector`s. For example, the following statements can be used to display a two-dimensional `vector` object `table`:

```
for (int row = 0; row < table.size(); row++)
{
  for (int col = 0; col < aTable[row].size(); col++)
    cout << table[row][col] << '\t';
  cout << endl;
}
```

In the outer loop, the expression

```
table.size()
```

returns the number of rows in the argument corresponding to parameter `table` and the inner loop expression

```
table[row].size()
```

returns the number of columns in `table[row]`.

THE `push_back()` FUNCTION.   Suppose that we need to add a new (fourth) row to `table`. This can be done by using the `vector` function member `push_back()`:

```
table.push_back(vector<double>(COLUMNS, 0.0));
```

The expression

```
vector<double>(COLUMNS, 0.0)
```

is a call to the `vector<T>` constructor to build a nameless `vector` of zeros. The `push_back()` function then appends this vector to the existing rows in `table`:

table:	[0]	[1]	[2]	[3]
[0]	0.0	0.0	0.0	0.0
[1]	0.0	0.0	0.0	0.0
[2]	0.0	0.0	0.0	0.0
[3]	0.0	0.0	0.0	0.0

To add a column to `table`, `push_back()` can be used to append a `double` value to each row of `table`, because each row in `table` is itself a `vector` of `double` values:

```
for (int row = 0; row < table.size(); row++)
  table[row].push_back(0.0);
```

Execution of this loop will add a fifth column to `table`:

table:	[0]	[1]	[2]	[3]	[4]
[0]	0.0	0.0	0.0	0.0	0.0
[1]	0.0	0.0	0.0	0.0	0.0
[2]	0.0	0.0	0.0	0.0	0.0
[3]	0.0	0.0	0.0	0.0	0.0

Note that `push_back()` makes it easy to build nonrectangular tables. For example, consider the following code segment:

```
vector< vector<double> > aTable;

for (int col = 1; col <= 3; col++)
  aTable.push_back(vector<double>(col, 0.0));
```

Initially, `aTable` is constructed as an empty vector. The first pass through the `for` loop constructs a nameless vector containing one zero and appends it to `aTable`:

aTable:	[0]
[0]	0.0

The second pass through the `for` loop constructs and appends another nameless vector containing two zeros:

aTable:	[0]	[1]
[0]	0.0	
[1]	0.0	0.0

The third pass through the `for` loop constructs and appends a third nameless vector of three zeros:

aTable:	[0]	[1]	[2]
[0]	0.0		
[1]	0.0	0.0	
[2]	0.0	0.0	0.0

Two-dimensional vectors thus need not be square, nor even rectangular. Such nonrectangular two-dimensional tables are sometimes called **jagged tables** or **jagged arrays.**

✍ EXERCISES 6.5

For Exercises 1–6, write a function for a two-dimensional `vector` of `doubles` that returns the value asked for. You should write driver programs to test these functions as instructed in Programming Problems 12–18 at the end of this chapter.

1. The sum of the values in a given row
2. The sum of the values in a given column
3. The average of the values in a given row
4. The standard deviation of the values in a given row (see Programming Problem 2 in Chap. 2)
5. The average of the values in a column
6. The standard deviation of the values in a given column (see Programming Problem 2 in Chap. 2)
7. Construct a `Matrix` class that contains (at least) matrix addition and multiplication operations (see Programming Problems 7 and 8 at the end of Chap. 2) and I/O operations. Test your class with a driver program as instructed in Programming Problem 26 at the end of this chapter.

6.6   OTHER STANDARD CONTAINERS— deque, stack, AND queue

We considered stacks in Chap. 4 and queues in Chap. 5, where we also briefly described deques. In this section we revisit these ADTs and describe their implementations in the standard library.

STL's deque CLASS TEMPLATE

As an ADT, a **deque**, which is an abbreviation for *double-ended queue*, is a sequential container that functions like a queue (or a stack) at both ends. More precisely, we have:

ADT DEQUE

Collection of Data Elements:

An ordered collection of data items with the property that items can be added and removed only at the ends.

Basic Operations:

- ▶ Construct a deque (usually empty)
- ▶ Check if the deque is empty
- ▶ Push_front: Add an element at the front of the deque
- ▶ Push_back: Add an element at the back of the deque
- ▶ Front: Retrieve the element at the front of the deque
- ▶ Back: Retrieve the element at the back of the deque
- ▶ Pop_front: Remove the element at the front of the deque
- ▶ Pop_back: Remove the element at the back of the deque

One of the basic containers in STL is the **deque<T> class template**. It has

- the same operations as `vector<T>` except that there is no `capacity()` and no `reserve()`

It also has two new operations:

- *d*.push_front(*value*);   Push a copy of *value* at the front of *d*
- *d*.pop_front(*value*);   Remove *value* at the front of *d*

where *d* is of type `deque<T>`. We see, therefore, that `deque` can implement the deque ADT. The program in Fig. 6.6 illustrates several of the `deque`'s operations:

FIGURE 6.6   DRIVER PROGRAM FOR STL'S deque

```cpp
#include <deque>
#include <iostream.
using namespace std;

int main()
{
  deque<int> d;

  // Output number of values stored in d
  cout << d.size() << endl;

  // Add first 6 integers alternatingly to front and back
  for (int i = 1; i <= 6; i += 2)
  {
    d.push_front(i);
    d.push_back(i+1);
  }

  // Display contents of d from front to back
  for (int i = 0; i < d.size(); i++)
    cout << d[i] << "  ";
  cout << endl;

  // Change back value to 999, remove front value;
  d.back() = 999;
  d.pop_front();

  // Display contents of d again, but use an iterator
  for (deque<int>::iterator it = d.begin();
                    it != d.end(); it++)
    cout << *it << "  ";
  cout << endl;

  // Dump contents of d from back to front
  while (!d.empty())
  {
    cout << d.back() << "  ";
    d.pop_back();
  }
  cout << endl;
}
```

EXECUTION:

```
0
5  3   1   2   4   6
3  1   2   4   999
999  4   2   1   3
```

Note that STL's `deque` also has several operations not defined for deques as ADTs. For example, like `vector`, `deque` allows direct access to any of its elements via the subscript operator `[]`, which is not included in the specification of deque as an ADT. It also has other operations similar to `vector`'s such as insertion and deletion at any point in the list, and its iterators have the same operations as for `vectors`. Insertion and deletion are very inefficient, however, and in fact take longer than for `vectors`.

One of the bad features of the `vector` container is that when its capacity must be increased, it must copy all the objects from the old vector to the new vector. Then it must destroy each object in the old vector. This is a lot of overhead! With `deque` this copying, creating, and destroying is avoided. Once an object is constructed, it can stay in the same memory locations as long as it exists (provided insertions and deletions take place at the ends of the deque).

The reason for this is that unlike `vectors`, a `deque` is not stored in a single varying-sized block of memory, but rather in a collection of fixed-size blocks (typically, 4K bytes). One of its data members is essentially an array `map` whose elements point to the locations of these blocks. For example, if each block consisted of only five memory locations, we might picture a `deque` containing 666, 777, 888, 999, 4, 3, 2, 1, 6, 5 in this order, from front to back, as follows:

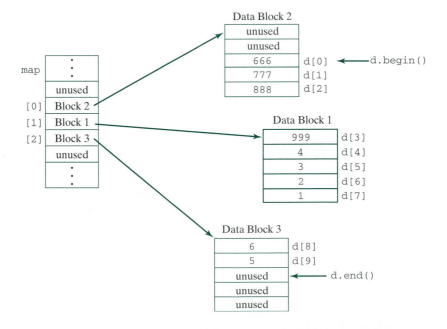

When a data block gets full, a new one is allocated and its address is added to `map`. When `map` gets full, a new one is allocated and the current values are copied into the middle of it.

As we noted, insertion at points within the list for a `deque` takes longer than for a `vector`. To insert an item in the middle of a `vector`, elements from that location on need only be shifted one position to the right to make room. Insertion into the middle of a `deque`, however, may cause shifting across noncontiguous blocks, which obviously can be more time-consuming. When a `deque` is used as prescribed in the ADT definition of a deque—that is, inserting and deleting elements only at the ends—the operation of `deque` is very efficient.

BUILD

A New (But Unnecessary) Version of Our `Stack` Class Template

In Sec. 6.3 we improved our `Stack` type by making it a class template so that it can be used for any type of stack elements. It still has one serious deficiency, namely, that the stack can become full. It is not dynamic in that it cannot grow when necessary. We could remove this deficiency by changing the array data member `myArray` to a *run-time array* (see Sec. 8.5) and add a `GrowBy()` function that would:

1. Allocate a larger array `temp`
2. Copy `myArray` into the first `myCapacity` locations in `temp`
3. Deallocate `myArray` (with `delete[]`)
4. Set `myArray = temp`

However, it should be clear that `deque` or `vector` would be better candidates to use as containers for the stack elements because they can do this automatically as needed, and the `push_back()` and `pop_back()` operations are perfect for stacks. Figure 6.7 shows a version that uses a `deque` to store the stack elements.

Figure 6.7   A `deque`-Based `Stack` Template

```
//***** For documentation, see Fig. 6.3. *****//

#ifndef STACK_DEQUE
#define STACK_DEQUE

#include <iostream>
#include <deque>
using namespace std;

template<typename StackElement>

class Stack
{
/***** Function Members *****/
public:
bool empty() const;
void push(const StackElement & value);
void display(ostream & out) const;
StackElement top() const;
void pop();
```

```cpp
/***** Data Members *****/
private:
  deque<StackElement> myDeque;    // deque to store elements

}; // end of class declaration

//--- Definition of empty operation
template <typename StackElement>
inline bool Stack<StackElement>::empty() const
{
  return myDeque.empty();
}


//--- Definition of push operation
template <typename StackElement>
void Stack<StackElement>::push(const StackElement & value)
{
  myDeque.push_back(value);
}


//--- Definition of display operation
template <typename StackElement>
void Stack<StackElement>::display(ostream & out) const
{
  for (int pos = myDeque.size() - 1; pos >= 0; pos--)
    out << myDeque[pos] << endl;
}

//--- Definition of top operation
template <typename StackElement>
StackElement Stack<StackElement>:: top() const
{
  if (!myDeque.empty())
    return myDeque.back();
  //else
  cerr << "*** Stack is empty ***\n";
}


//--- Definition of pop operation
template <typename StackElement>
void Stack<StackElement>:: pop()
{
  if (!myDeque.empty())
    myDeque.pop_back();
  else
    cerr << "*** Stack is empty -- can't remove a value ***\n";
}

#endif
```

Basically, all we have done in Fig. 6.7 is wrap a `deque` inside a class template and let it do all the work. Our member functions are essentially just renamings of `deque` member functions. And there's really no need to do this, because STL has done it for us!

STL's `stack` ADAPTER

The standard library includes a `stack` container. Actually, it is an **adapter** (as indicated by the fact that it is a class template `stack<C>` whose *type parameter is a container type*), which means basically that it is a class that acts as a "wrapper" around another class, giving it a *new user interface*. A *container adapter* such as `stack` uses the members of the encapsulated container to implement what looks like a new container.

For a `stack<C>`, `C` may be any container that supports `push_back()` and `pop_back()` in a LIFO manner; in particular `C` may be a `vector`, a `deque`, or a `list` (see Sec. 8.7). If no container is specified, `deque` *is the default container*; that is, a declaration of the form

```
stack<T> st;
```

is equivalent to

```
stack< deque<T> > st;
```

For the other containers, we must specify them explicitly:

```
stack< vector<T> > st;
```

```
stack< list<T> > st;
```

Note the space between the two >s in these declarations; it must be there to avoid confusing the compiler (because it will treat it as >> otherwise).

The following are basic operations for the `stack` container:

▶ Constructor: `stack<C> st;` creates an empty stack `st`; it uses a container `C` to store the elements (default container is `deque`)

▶ Relational operators: `==, !=, <, <=, >, >=` (as defined for the container `C`)

▶ `size()`

▶ `empty()`

▶ `top()`

▶ `push()`

▶ `pop()`

The program in Fig. 6.8 illustrates the use of the `stack` container to solve the base-conversion problem, one of the four problems with which we introduced our study of stacks in Chap. 4. The program is identical to that in Fig. 4.1 except that it uses the C++ standard `stack` container instead of a user-defined `Stack` class.

FIGURE 6.8   CONVERSION FROM BASE 10 TO BASE 2

```cpp
/* Program that uses a stack to convert the base-ten
 * representation of a positive integer to base two.
 * Uses the standard C++ stack container.
 *
 * Input:  A positive integer
 * Output: Base-two representation of the number
 ***********************************************************/

#include <iostream>
#include <stack>
using namespace std;

int main()
{
  unsigned number,           // the number to be converted
           remainder;        // remainder when number is divided by 2
  stack<unsigned> stackOfRemainders;
                             // stack of remainders
  char response;             // user response

  do
  {
    cout << "Enter positive integer to convert: ";
    cin >> number;

    while (number != 0)
    {
      remainder = number % 2;
      stackOfRemainders.push(remainder);
      number /= 2;
    }

    cout << "Base two representation: ";
    while (!stackOfRemainders.empty() )
    {
      remainder = stackOfRemainders.top();
      stackOfRemainders.pop();
      cout << remainder;
    }

    cout << endl;
    cout << "\More (Y or N)? ";
    cin >> response;
  }
  while (response == 'Y' || response == 'y');
}
```

STL's queue ADAPTER

The standard library includes a `queue` container, which, like `stack`, is also a container adapter. For a `queue<C>`, `C` may be any container that supports `push_back()` and `pop_front()`; in particular, `C` may be a `deque` or a `list` (see Sec. 8.7); if no container is specified, `deque` *is the default container*; that is, a declaration of the form

```
queue<T> q;
```

is equivalent to

```
queue< deque<T> > q;
```

To use a `list` as the container, we would write

```
queue< list<T> > q;
```

The basic operations for `queue` are the same as for `stack` except that:

▸ `front()` (instead of `top()`) retrieves the front item in the queue

▸ `pop()` removes the front item in the queue

▸ `push()` adds items at the back of the queue

▸ `back()` retrieves the item at the back of the queue

✔ Quick Quiz 6.6

1. The word *deque* is an abbreviation for _____ .
2. Define deque as an ADT.
3. STL's `deque` container has the same operations as specified in a definition of a deque as an ADT. (True or false)
4. Insertion at points within the list for a `deque` takes longer than for a `vector`. (True or false)
5. A `deque` is stored in a single contiguous block of memory. (True or false)
6. A class that acts as a wrapper around another class is called a(n) _____ .
7. An adapter encapsulates a container to give it a new user _____ .
8. What is wrong with the declaration `stack< vector<double>> s;`?
9. Name two of STL's containers that are really adapters.

6.7   BITSETS (OPTIONAL)

A **bitset** is an array whose elements are bits. Thus, it is much like an array whose elements are of type `bool`, but unlike arrays, it does provide operations for manipulating the bits stored in it. This section introduces `bitset`s and also indicates how they can be used to implement sets.

DECLARATIONS OF `bitset` OBJECTS

The `bitset` class template is declared in the standard `<bitset>` library, which must be included in any program that uses `bitset`s:

```
#include <bitset>
```

A `bitset` object *b* can then be constructed using one of the following declarations:

```
                              // Initialize b with N bits:
bitset<N> b;                  //   all 0
bitset<N> b(num);             //   of num (zero fill if necessary)
bitset<N> b(str, pos, n);     //   n bits of str, starting at pos
                              //   (zero fill if necessary)
```

where *N* is a constant specifying the number of bits in *b*; *num* is a nonnegative integer; *str* is a string of bits; *pos* is a nonnegative integer with default value 0; and *n* is a nonnegative integer with default value the length of `str` from position *pos* on. To illustrate, consider the following examples:

```
#include <bitset>
using namespace std;
      .
      .
      .
bitset<5> b0;
bitset<10> b1(49);
char bitstring[] = "101100111000";
bitset<16> b2(bitstring),
           b3(bitstring, 3),
           b4(bitstring, 0, 4);
```

The first declaration creates b0 as a `bitset` containing 5 zeros and the second creates b1 as a `bitset` containing 10 bits, the 6 bits `110001` in the binary representation of `49` and 4 zeros:

```
b0  00000
b1  0000110001
```

Note that the bit positions are numbered in the same way that they usually are for memory words—from right to left:

```
    9 8 7 6 5 4 3 2 1 0
b1  0 0 0 0 1 1 0 0 0 1
```

This means that one can think of a `bitset<N>` object as an *N*-bit binary number.

The last three declarations create `bitsets` containing 16 bits: b2 contains the 12 bits in `bitstring` padded with 4 zeros; b3 contains the last 9 bits in `bitstring` padded with 7 zeros; and b4 contains the first 4 bits in `bitstring` padded with 12 zeros:

```
b2  0000101100111000
b3  0000000100111000
b4  0000000000001011
```

bitset OPERATIONS

Several operations for manipulating individual bits or all of the bits are provided in `bitset`:

- ▶ `&` (bitwise and), `|` (bitwise or), `^` (bitwise exclusive or),

  `<<` (bitwise left shift), `>>` (bitwise right shift)
  For example, `b3 & b4` produces `0000000000001000` and `b4 << 2` gives `0000000000101100`

- ▶ corresponding assignment ops: `&=`, `|=`, `~=`, `<<=`, `>>=`
- ▶ relational operators: `==`, `!=`
- ▶ the subscript operator `[]`: `b[i]` is the i-th bit in `b`
- ▶ assignment of same-size `bitset`s

There are also several member functions to change or check bits:

▶ `set()`	set all bits to 1
`reset()`	set all bits to 0
`set(i, bv)`	set `b[i]` to *bv*; default value of *bv* is 1
`reset(i)`	set `b[i]` to 0
`flip()`	change all bits (0s to 1s and 1s to 0s)
`flip(i)`	change `b[i]`
▶ `size()`	total number of bits
`count()`	number of bits that are 1
▶ `any()`	true if any bit is 1 and false otherwise
`none()`	true if no bits are 1 and false otherwise
`test(i)`	true if `b[i]` is 1 and false otherwise

And there are also operations to convert `bitset`s to integers or strings together with input and output operations:

- ▶ `to_ulong()`: the `unsigned long int` represented by the bit string stored in a `bitset`
- ▶ `to_string()`: a `string` representation of the bit string stored in a `bitset`
- ▶ `<<`: output the bitstring stored in a `bitset`
- ▶ `>>`: input a bitstring to be stored in a `bitset`

IMPLEMENTING SETS WITH bitsets

In mathematics and computer science, the term **set** refers to an unordered collection of objects called the **elements** or **members** of the set. A set is commonly denoted by listing the elements enclosed in braces, { and }. For example, the set of decimal digits contains the elements 0, 1, 2, 3, 4, 5, 6, 7, 8, and 9 and is denoted {0, 1, 2, 3, 4, 5, 6, 7, 8, 9}. The set of uppercase letters is {A, B, C, $\cdots$, Z}. The set of even prime numbers {2} contains the single element 2; and the set of even prime numbers greater than 2 is the empty set, denoted $\emptyset$ or { }, that is, the set containing no elements.

In a problem involving sets, the elements are selected from some given set called the **universal set** for that problem. For example, if the set of vowels or the set {X, Y, Z} is being considered, the universal set might be the set of all letters. If the universal set is the set of names of months of the year, then one might use the set of summer months {June, July, August}; the set of months whose names do not contain the letter *r* {May, June, July, August}; or the set of all months having fewer than 30 days {February}

The basic relation in defining a set is the **membership** relation. Given a set *S* and any object *x* in the universal set, one must be able to determine that *x* belongs to *S*, denoted by $x \in S$, or that it does not belong to *S*, denoted by $x \notin S$.

Three basic set operations are intersection, union, and set difference. The **intersection** of two sets *S* and *T*, denoted in mathematics by $S \cap T$, is the set of elements that are in both sets. The **union** of *S* and *T*, $S \cup T$, is the set of elements that are in *S* or in *T* or in both. The **complement** of a set *S*, *S'*, consists of those elements of the universal set that are not in *S*. The following **Venn diagrams** illustrate these basic set operations:

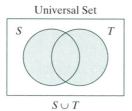

$S \cup T$

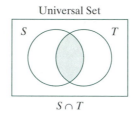

$S \cap T$

S'

Although there are many other set operations that are important in mathematics, we will take these as the basic operations in our specification of a set as an abstract data type:

ADT

ADT SET

Collection of Data Elements:

An ordered collection of data items.

Basic Operations:

▶ Membership

▶ Union

▶ Intersection

▶ Complement

Sets whose elements are selected from a *finite* universal set can be represented in computer memory by bit strings in which the number of bits is equal to the number of elements in this universal set. Each bit corresponds to exactly one element of the universal set. A given set is then represented by a bit string in which the bits corresponding to the elements of that set are 1 and all other bits are 0. A `bitset` is therefore an obvious data structure to use to implement such a set.

To illustrate, suppose the universal set is the set of uppercase letters. Then any set of uppercase letters can be represented by a string of 26 bits, with one bit corresponding to the letter A, another corresponding to the letter B, and so on. Thus, the set of vowels can be represented by the bit string

```
1 0 0 0 1 0 0 0 1 0 0 0 0 0 1 0 0 0 0 0 1 0 0 0 0 0
| | | | | | | | | | | | | | | | | | | | | | | | | |
A B C D E F G H I J K L M N O P Q R S T U V W X Y Z
```

and the empty set by

```
0 0 0 0 0 0 0 0 0 0 0 0 0 0 0 0 0 0 0 0 0 0 0 0 0 0
```

The `bitset` operations `&`, `|`, and `flip()` can be used to implement the basic set operations of intersection, union, and complement. Applying the `&` operation bitwise to the bit strings representing two sets yields a bit string representing the intersection of these sets. For example, consider the sets $S = \{A, B, C, D\}$ and $T = \{A, C, E, G, I\}$, where the universal set is the set of uppercase letters. The 26-bit string representations of these sets are as follows:

```
S:  1 1 1 1 0 0 0 0 0 0 0 0 0 0 0 0 0 0 0 0 0 0 0 0 0 0
T:  1 0 1 0 1 0 1 0 1 0 0 0 0 0 0 0 0 0 0 0 0 0 0 0 0 0
    | | | | | | | | | | | | | | | | | | | | | | | | | |
    A B C D E F G H I J K L M N O P Q R S T U V W X Y Z
```

Performing the `&` operation bitwise gives the bit string

```
1 0 1 0 0 0 0 0 0 0 0 0 0 0 0 0 0 0 0 0 0 0 0 0 0 0
| | | | | | | | | | | | | | | | | | | | | | | | | |
A B C D E F G H I J K L M N O P Q R S T U V W X Y Z
```

which represents the set $\{A, C\}$, the intersection of S and T.

Bitwise application of the `|` operation to the bit strings representing two sets S and T yields the representation of $S \cup T$. For the preceding sets, this gives the bit string

```
1 1 1 1 1 0 1 0 1 0 0 0 0 0 0 0 0 0 0 0 0 0 0 0 0 0
| | | | | | | | | | | | | | | | | | | | | | | | | |
A B C D E F G H I J K L M N O P Q R S T U V W X Y Z
```

which represents $\{A, B, C, D, E, G, I\}$, the union of S and T.

Changing each bit in the representation of a set T with the `flip()` operation gives a bit string representing T'. For the preceding sets, bitwise complementation of the string for T gives

```
0 1 0 1 0 1 0 1 0 1 1 1 1 1 1 1 1 1 1 1 1 1 1 1 1 1
| | | | | | | | | | | | | | | | | | | | | | | | | |
A B C D E F G H I J K L M N O P Q R S T U V W X Y Z
```

which represents $T'. = \{B, D, F, H, J, K, \cdots, Z\}$.

EXAMPLE: FINDING PRIME NUMBERS WITH THE SIEVE OF ERATOSTHENES

A **prime number** is an integer greater than 1 whose only divisors are 1 and the number itself. Prime numbers are important in public-key encryption/decryption methods (see Sec. 3.6), in random-number generators, in the design of hash tables (which we consider in Sec. 9.3), and in many other applications of number theory.

The problem of finding prime numbers has occupied people's attention for centuries. One of the classical algorithms was developed by the Greek mathematician Eratosthenes (c. 276–c. 194 B.C.) and is known as the **Sieve Method of Eratosthenes.** Variations of it are still used today in prime-generation algorithms.

ALGORITHM FOR THE SIEVE METHOD OF ERATOSTHENES

/*   Algorithm to construct a set *sieve* of all primes in a given range.

    Receives: An integer n
    Returns: The set *sieve* of all primes in the range 2 through *n*
---*/

1. Initialize the set *sieve* to contain the integers 2 through *n*.
2. Select the smallest element *prime* in *sieve*.
3. While $prime^2 \leq n$, do the following:
   - a. Remove from *sieve* all elements of the form *prime* * *k* for *k* > 1.
   - b. Replace *prime* with the smallest element in *sieve* that is greater than *prime*.

The following diagram illustrates this algorithm for $n = 30$:

sieve

{2,3,4,5,6,7,8,9,10,11,12,13,14,15,16,17,18,19,20,21,22,23,24,25,26,27,28,29,30}

↓

prime = 2

↓

{2,3,5,7,9,11,13,15,17,19,21,23,25,27,29}

↓

prime = 3

↓

{2,3,5,7,11,13,17,19,23,25,29}

↓

prime = 5

↓

{2,3,5,7,11,13,17,19,23,29}

↓

prime = 7; terminate since $prime^2 > 30$

The main object needed for this problem is a representation of the set *sieve*. For this we will use a `bitset` in the manner described earlier:

OBJECTS:

sieve: a `bitset` in which `sieve[i]` will be 1 if `i` is a prime, and 0 otherwise

n, prime: integers

OPERATIONS:

Construct `sieve` with all bits set to 1
Set selected bits in `sieve` to 0
Check whether a bit of `sieve` is 0 or 1

All of these operations are provided by `bitset`.

The program in Fig. 6.9 uses these objects and operations and the sieve algorithm to find primes in a range specified by the user.

FIGURE 6.9   SIEVE METHOD OF FINDING PRIMES

```
/* Program that uses the Sieve Method of Eratosthenes to find
 * all prime numbers in a given range.
 * Uses the standard C++ bitset class template.
 *
 * Input:  A positive integer n
 * Output: Primes in the range 2 through n
 ***********************************************************/

#include <iostream>
#include <cassert>
#include <bitset>
using namespace std;

int main()
{
  const int MAX_PRIME = 1000;  // limit on size of n

  int n;
  cout << "This program finds primes in the range 2 - n."
          "\nEnter positive integer n <= " << MAX_PRIME << ": ";
  cin >> n;
  assert(n > 0 && n <= MAX_PRIME);

  // Construct bitset sieve of size MAX_PRIME + 1 containing all ones.
  // For convenience, we are not using positions 0 and 1 of sieve so
  // that bit i represents positive integer i.

  bitset<MAX_PRIME + 1> sieve;
  sieve.set();
```

```
// Apply the Sieve Method
int prime = 2;             // the next prime in sieve
while (prime * prime <= n)
{
  // cross out multiples of prime from sieve
  for (int mult = 2*prime; mult <= n; mult += prime)
    sieve.reset(mult);

  // find next uncrossed number in sieve
  do
    prime++;
  while (!sieve.test(prime));
}

// Display the list of primes.
cout << "\Primes in the range 2 through " << n << ":\";

for (int i = 2; i <= n; i++)
  if (sieve.test(i))
    cout << i << "   ";
}
```

SAMPLE RUN:

```
This program finds primes in the range 2 - n.
Enter positive integer n <= 1000: 100

Primes in the range 2 through 100:
2   3   5   7   11   13   17   19   23   29   31   37   41   43   47   53   59   61   67
71   73   79   83   89   97
```

✍ EXERCISES 6.7

Exercises 1–7 assume the universal set is {0, 1, ···, 19}. Give a bitstring representation of the given set.

1. The set of odd integers
2. The set of prime integers
3. The intersection of the set of prime integers and the set of even integers
4. The union of the set of prime integers and the set of odd integers
5. The set of odd integers that are not prime integers
6. The set of integers divisible by 1
7. The set of integers not divisible by 1

Exercises 8–11 assume the universal set is the set of names (strings) Alan, Alice, Barb, Ben, Bob, Carl, Cora, Dick, Don, Dora, Dot, Fred, arranged in alphabetical order. Give a bitstring representation of the given set.

8. Set of names that begin with B
9. Set of names that begin with E

10. Set of names that begin with D and have fewer than three letters.

11. Set of names that have fewer than six letters.

12. Design a `Set` class for representing sets of integers in some given range. Use `bitset` in your implementation as described in the text. Provide (at least) the operations listed in the specification of the set ADT together with input and output operations. You should test your class with a driver program as instructed in Programming Problem 33 at the end of this chapter.

6.8   VALARRAYS (OPTIONAL)

As we noted at the end of Sec. 6.3, there are four types that could be classified as containers because they do contain elements: arrays, `strings`, `valarrays`, and `bitset`s. However, each of them lacks some features of the interface that the STL containers have in common. We have considered arrays in detail in Chap. 2, the `string` type in Chap. 3, and `bitset`s in Sec. 6.7. This section introduces `valarrays`.

We have used arrays in several places, for example, to store stack elements in a `Stack` class in Chap. 4 and to store queue elements in a `Queue` class in Chap. 5. We have pointed out some of the deficiencies of arrays, especially that they are not self-contained and thus are not consistent with the spirit of object-oriented programming. We indicated that one solution would be to encapsulate an array, its capacity, its size, and other basic operations within a class structure. In Sec. 6.4 we have seen that this is the approach used by the `vector` class template.

Another important use of arrays is in numeric computation in scientific and engineering applications, for example, in vector processing. In mathematics the term *vector* refers to a sequence (one-dimensional array) of real values on which various arithmetic operations are performed; for example, $+$, $-$, scalar multiplication, and dot product. Because much numeric work relies on the use of such vectors, highly-efficient libraries are essential in many fields. For this reason, the standard C++ library provides the **valarray** class template, which is designed to carry out vector operations very efficiently. That is, `valarrays` are (mathematical) vectors that have been highly optimized for numeric computations.

DECLARATIONS OF **valarray** OBJECTS

The `valarray` class template is declared in the standard `<valarray>` library, which must be included in any program that uses `valarrays`:

```
#include <valarray>
```

A `valarray` object *v* can then be constructed using one of the following declarations:

```
                              // Initialize v:
valarray<T> v;                //   as empty
valarray<T> v(n);             //   with n default T values
valarray<T> v(val, n);        //   with n copies of val
valarray<T> v(array, n);      //   with first n values in array
valarray<T> v(w);             //   with copy of w
```

where T is a numeric type (typically, float, double, or long double), *n* is an integer specifying the capacity of *v*; *val* is a value of type T; *array* is an array of T values; and *w* is a valarray. To illustrate, consider the following examples:

```
#include <valarray>
using namespace std;
       .
       .
       .
valarray<double> v0;
valarray<float> v1(100);
valarray<int> v2(999, 100);
const double a[] = {1.1, 2.2, 3.3, 4.4, 5.5};
valarray<double> v3(a, 4);
```

The first declaration creates v0 as an empty valarray of doubles (which can be resized later); the second constructs v1 as a valarray containing 100 float values, initially 0; the third creates v2 as a valarray of 100 int values, initially 999; and the last declaration constructs a valarray of four doubles, initially the four values (1.1, 2.2, 3.3, 4.4) stored in array a.

valarray OPERATIONS

The function members for valarrays are:

▶ the subscript operator [] (see later for use with slices, gslices, masks, and indirect_arrays)

▶ assignment of same-size valarrays

▶ unary operations (applied elementwise): +, -, ~, !

▶ assignment ops: +=, -=, *=, /=, %=, &=, |=, ^=, <<=, >>=
   If Δ denotes one of these operations, v Δ= x; is equivalent to:
   ```
   for (int i = 0; i < v.size(); i++)
       v[i] = v[i] Δ x;
   ```

▶ size(): the number of values stored in the valarray

▶ resize(n, val): reinitialize valarray to have n elements with (optional) value val

   Example cin >> n;
   ```
                 v0.resize(n);
   ```

▶ shift(n) and cshift(n): Shift values in the valarray |n| positions left if n > 0, right if n < 0. For shift, vacated positions are filled with 0; for cshift, values are shifted circularly with values from one end moving into the other end.

   Examples
   v3.shift(2); would change v3 to 3.3, 4.4, 0, 0
   v3.shift(-2); would change v3 to 0, 0, 1.1, 2.2
   v3.cshift(2); would change v3 to 3.3, 4.4, 1.1, 2.2

There also are several nonmember operations:

▶ The following binary operators and mathematical functions (from `cmath`):

```
+, -, *, /, %, &, |, ^, <<, >>, &&, ||, ==, !=, <, >, <=, >=,
atan2(), pow()
```

These operations and functions are applied elementwise. The operands may be `valarray`s or a `valarray` and a scalar.

▶ The following mathematical functions, which are applied elementwise:

```
acos(), asin(), atan(), cos(), cosh(), exp(), log(), log10(),
sin(), sinh()(), sqrt(), tan(), tanh()
```

For example, the assignment statement

```
w = pow(v3, 2);
```

assigns to `w` the squares of the elements of `v3`, namely, 1.21, 4.84, 10.89, 19.36.

Some other operations that are useful with `valarray`s are found in the standard `<algorithm>` and `<numeric>` libraries (see Sec. 7.5). For example, `<numeric>` contains functions for calculating the sum of the elements in a sequence, the inner (dot) product of two sequences, the partial sums of a sequence, and differences of adjacent elements in a sequence.

SLICES, MASKS, AND INDIRECT ARRAYS

There are four auxiliary types that specify subsets of a `valarray`: `slice_array`, `gslice_array`, `mask_array`, and `indirect_array`. We will briefly describe how each of them is used and the subsets of a `valarray` that they determine.

SLICES.   One subset of a `valarray` is a **slice,** which selects every nth element of a `valarray` for some integer n. As we shall see, this in turn makes it possible to think of a `valarray` as a two-dimensional array having n rows (or n columns).

A declaration of a `slice` has the form

```
slice s(start, size, stride);
```

which specifies the *size* indices *start*, *start* + *stride*, *start* + 2*stride, ⋯ in a `valarray`. The member functions `start()`, `size()`, and `stride()` return the values *start*, *size*, and *stride*, respectively. To illustrate their use, consider the `valarray v` and `slice`s s1, s2, and s3 defined by

```
double d[] = {0,10,20,30,40,50,60,70,80,90,100,110};
valarray<double> v(d, 12);

slice s1(0,4,1), s2(4,4,1), s3(8,4,1);
```

Then, `v[s1]`, `v[s2]`, and `v[s3]` are of type `slice_array` and contain the following values:

```
v[s1]: 0, 10, 20, 30
v[s2]:40, 50, 60, 70
v[s3]:80, 90, 100, 110
```

From this we see how these slices make it possible to view v as a 3×4 two-dimensional array:

$$v = \begin{bmatrix} 0 & 10 & 20 & 30 \\ 40 & 50 & 60 & 70 \\ 80 & 90 & 100 & 110 \end{bmatrix}$$

A **gslice** (generalized slice) contains essentially the information of n slices; instead of one stride and one size, there are n strides and n sizes. The declarations of `gslice` objects are the same as for `slices`, except that *size* and *stride* are `valarray`s whose elements are integer indices. To illustrate, consider the declarations

```
size_t sizearr[] = {2, 3}, stridearr[] = {4, 1};
valarray<size_t> sz(sizearr, 2), str(stridearr, 2);

gslice gs(0, sz, str);
```

Then, `v[gs]` is of type `gslice_array` and contains: 0, 10, 20, 40, 50, 60. If we think of v as the preceding two-dimensional 3×4 array and gs as specifying that the size (`sz`) of the subarray to be selected is to be 2×3 and the strides (`str`) are to be 4 in the first dimension, 1 in the second, then `v[gs]` is the 2×3 subarray in the upper-left corner.

$$v[gs] = \begin{bmatrix} 0 & 10 & 20 \\ 40 & 50 & 60 \end{bmatrix}$$

MASKS.   A `mask_array` provides another way to select a subset of a `valarray`. A mask is simply a boolean `valarray`, which when used as a subscript of a `valarray`, specifies for each index whether or not that element of the `valarray` is to be included in the subset.

To illustrate, consider the `valarray v1` defined by

```
double d1[] = {0,10,20,30,40,50};
valarray<double> v1(d1, 6);
```

and the mask defined by

```
bool b[] = {true, false, false, true, true, false};
valarray<bool> mask(b, 6);
```

Then v2 and v3 defined by

```
valarray<double>
    v2 = v1[mask],          // 0, 30, 40
    v3 = pow(v1[mask], 2);  // 0, 900, 1600
```

are of type `mask_array` and have the values indicated in the comments.

INDIRECT ARRAYS.   An `indirect_array` specifies an arbitrary subset and reordering of a `valarray`. It is constructed by first defining a `valarray` of integers, which specify indices of the original `valarray`, where duplicate indices are allowed. For example, consider the `valarray` `ind` defined by

```
size_t indarr[] = {4, 2, 0, 5, 3, 1, 0, 5};
valarray<size_t> ind(indarr, 8);
```

Then `valarray` `v4` defined by

```
valarray<double> v4 = v1[indarr];
```

is of type `indirect_array` and contains $40, 20, 0, 50, 30, 10, 0, 50$.

✍ EXERCISES 6.8

Exercises 1–4 deal with operations on *n-dimensional vectors*, which are sequences of *n* real numbers. In the description of each operation, *A* and *B* are assumed to be *n*-dimensional vectors:

$$A = (a_1, a_2, \cdots, a_n)$$
$$B = (b_1, b_2, \cdots, b_n)$$

Write functions for the operations, using `valarray`s to store the vectors. To test your functions you should write driver programs as instructed in Programming Problems 36–39 at the end of this chapter.

1. Output an *n*-dimensional vector using `<<`.

2. Input an *n*-dimensional vector using `>>`.

3. Compute and return the *magnitude* of an *n*-dimensional vector:
$$|A| = \sqrt{a_1^2 + a_2^2 + \cdots + a_n^2}$$

4. Compute and return the *inner* (or *dot*) *product* of two *n*-dimensional vectors (which is a scalar):
$$A \cdot B = a_1{}^*b_1 + a_2{}^*b_2 + \cdots + a_n{}^*b_n = \sum_{i=1}^{n} (a_i{}^*b_i)$$

☞ PROGRAMMING POINTERS

1. To overload the name of a function, no two definitions of the function can have the same signature. Note that it is not enough to simply have different return types.

2. A common error in building a class is to define an explicit-value constructor in a class but no default constructor. The compiler then cannot process declarations of the form `ClassName object;` because they require a constructor whose signature is `()`, that is a default constructor.

3. Every function template and class template must be preceded by a template declaration of the form:
```
template<typename TypeParam₁, typename TypeParam₂, ...>
```
or
```
template<class TypeParam₁, class TypeParam₂, ...>
```

Note that angle brackets (<>) rather than parentheses are used to enclose the type-parameter list. For a function template, each of the type parameters *must* appear at least once in the regular parameter list of the function.

4. Function templates and class templates cannot be split across files.

5. The following three rules govern the building of class templates:

   ▶ All operations defined outside of the class declaration must be template functions.

   ▶ Any use of the name of a template class as a type must be parameterized.

   ▶ Operations on a template class should be defined in the same file as the class declaration.

6. The subscript operator should not be used to append values to a `vector` because this updates neither the `vector`'s size nor its capacity; the `push_back` and `insert()` operations should be used.

7. The initial increase in a `vector`'s capacity that is initially empty may be quite large in some versions of C++, which will result in wasted space when the `vector` is being used to store small data sets. In such cases it is better to preallocate the `vector` by specifying its initial capacity.

8. The capacity of a `vector` is doubled each time it is increased.

9. Remember to use a space between the closing angle brackets in declarations of the form

   Type< <Container> > objectName;

   so that the compiler does not confuse it with the `>>` operator.

10. The type parameter of an adapter—`stack`, `queue`, and `priority_queue`—is a *container*. The default container for a `stack` and for a `queue` is `deque`.

ADT TIPS

1. Using a `typedef` to set the type of the elements stored in a container class binds the class to one particular type for the elements.

2. The template mechanism makes it possible to write generic function templates and to develop generic container class templates. It makes it possible for classes and functions to receive not only data values to be stored or operated on via parameters but also to receive the *type* of data via a parameter.

3. The standard containers and algorithms recently added to C++ provide generic and very efficient data structures for problem solving and to use in implementing ADTs.

4. Iterators provide a generic way to access elements in a container.

5. A *deque* provides direct access to the items at each end of the list of values it contains.

6. Bit strings can be used to represent sets for which the universal set is finite and ordered.

PROGRAMMING PROBLEMS

SECTION 6.3

1. Write a driver program that uses the function template in Exercise 1 to find the average of: (a) two `int`s; (b) two `float`s; (c) two `double`s.

2. Write a driver program that uses the function template in Exercise 2 to find the maximum of: (a) two `int`s; (b) two `float`s; (c) two `double`s. (d) Try it with two `complex` values. What happens and why?

3. Write a driver program that uses the function template in Exercise 3 to find the median of: (a) three `ints`; (b) three `floats`; (c) three `doubles`. (d) Try it with three `complex` values. What happens and why?

4. Write a driver program that uses the function template `Sum()` in Exercise 4 to sum the elements of an array of: (a) `ints`; (b) `floats`; (c) `doubles`.

5. Write a driver program that uses the function `Sort()` in Exercise 5 to sort the elements of an array of: (a) `ints`; (b) `doubles`; (c) `strings`.

6. Write a driver program that uses the function `Search()` in Exercise 6 to search the elements of an array of: (a) `ints` for a given `int`; (b) `doubles` for a given `double`; (c) `strings` for a given `string`.

7. Write a driver program to test the `Queue` class template in Exercise 7 in a manner similar to that used for the `Stack` class template in the text.

8. Write a driver program to test the `CartesianPoint` class template in Exercise 8 by checking it with points whose coordinates are: (a) `ints`; (b) `floats`; (c) `doubles`.

SECTION 6.4

9. Write a driver program to test the ascending-order function of Exercise 15.

10. Write a driver program to test the range function of Exercise 16.

11. Write a driver program to test the `Queue` class template of Exercise 17.

SECTION 6.5

12. Write a driver program to test the row-sum function of Exercise 1.

13. Write a driver program to test the column-sum function of Exercise 2.

14. Write a driver program to test the row-average function of Exercise 3.

15. Write a driver program to test the row-standard-deviation function of Exercise 4.

16. Write a driver program to test the column-average function of Exercise 5.

17. Write a driver program to test the column-standard-deviation function of Exercise 6.

18. The following table contains data on the noise level (measured in decibels) produced at seven different speeds by six different models of cars. Write a program that will display this table in easy-to-read format, and that will calculate and display the average noise level for each car model, the average noise level at each speed, and the overall average noise level.

Car	Speed(MPH)						
	20	30	40	50	60	70	80
0	88	90	94	102	111	122	134
1	75	77	80	86	94	103	113
2	80	83	85	94	100	111	121
3	68	71	76	85	96	110	125
4	77	84	91	98	105	112	119
5	81	85	90	96	102	109	120

19. Write a program to calculate and display the first ten rows of Pascal's triangle. The first part of the triangle has the form

```
              1
           1     1
        1     2     1
     1     3     3     1
  1     4     6     4     1
```

in which each row begins and ends with 1, and each of the other entries in a row is the sum of the two entries just above it. If this form for the output seems too challenging, you might display the triangle as

```
1
1 1
1 2 1
1 3 3 1
1 4 6 4 1
```

20. An automobile dealership sells ten different models of automobiles and employs eight salespersons. A record of sales for each month can be represented by a table in which each row contains the number of sales of each model by a given salesperson, and each column contains the number of sales of each model by a given salesperson. Write a program to input sales data into a two-dimensional `vector` and then produce a monthly sales report, displaying the monthly sales table in a pleasing format. The report should also display the total number of automobiles sold by each salesperson and the total number of each model sold by all salespersons.

21. A certain company has a product line that includes five items that sell for $100, $75, $120, $150, and $35. There are four salespersons working for this company, and the following table gives the sales report for a typical week:

Salesperson Number	Item Number				
	1	2	3	4	5
1	10	4	5	6	7
2	7	0	12	1	3
3	4	9	5	0	8
4	3	2	1	5	6

Write a program to:
   a. Compute the total dollar sales for each salesperson
   b. Compute the total commission for each salesperson if the commission rate is 10 percent
   c. Find the total income for each salesperson for the week if each salesperson receives a fixed salary of $200 per week in addition to commission payments.

22. Proceed as in the Programming Problem 6 (demographic study) of Chap. 2 but use a two-dimensional `vector`.

23. Proceed as in the Programming Problem 9 (magic square) of Chap. 2 but use a two-dimensional `vector`.

24. Proceed as in the Programming Problem 10 (temperature in a grid) of Chap. 2 but use a two-dimensional `vector`.

25. Proceed as in the Programming Problem 11 (game of Life) of Chap. 2 but use a two-dimensional `vector`.

26. Write a driver program to test the `Matrix` class of Exercise 7.

SECTION 6.6

27. Use the `stack` container in a program like that for Programming Problem 2 of Chap. 4 that reads a string, one character at a time, and determines whether the string contains balanced parentheses, that is, for each left parenthesis (if there are any) there is exactly one matching right parenthesis later in the string.

28. Use the `stack` container in a program that determines the prime factorization of a positive integer, displaying the prime factors in descending order. (See Programming Problem 4 of Chap. 4.) For example, for the integer 3960, your program should produce

$$11 * 5 * 3 * 3 * 2 * 2 * 2$$

29. Use the `queue` and `stack` containers in a program that reverses the elements in a queue.

30. Use the `queue` container in a memory-recall program that generates a random sequence of letters and/or digits, displays them to the user one at a time for a second or so, and then asks the user to reproduce the sequence. Use a queue to store the sequence of characters.

31. Use the `queue` and `stack` container in a program that reads a string of characters, pushing each character onto a stack as it is read and simultaneously adding it to a queue. When the end of the string is encountered, the program should use the basic stack and queue operations to determine if the string is a palindrome (see Exercise 10 of Sec. 3.4).

32. Redo Prob. 31 but use only a `deque` to store the characters in the string.

SECTION 6.7

33. Write a driver program to test your `Set` class template in Exercise 12.

34. Use your `Set` class template from Prob. 33 in a program that reads a list of integer id-numbers from a file and finds the set of all distinct id numbers.

35. Use your `Set` class template from Prob. 33 in a program that reads a list of tour numbers from a file and for each tour a list of code numbers (or names) of cities visited on that tour; a list of cities the user wishes to visit from the keyboard; and then finds a list of all tours that visit these cities.

SECTION 6.8

36. Write a driver program to test the output function of Exercise 1.

37. Write a driver program to test the input function of Exercise 2.

38. Write a driver program to test the magnitude function of Exercise 3.

39. Write a driver program to test the dot-product function of Exercise 4.

Chapter 7

IMPROVING ADTs—PART 2: RECURSION, ALGORITHM ANALYSIS, AND STANDARD ALGORITHMS

Chapter Contents

The important phases of design, the second phase of the software development process described in Chap. 1, are

   1. *Identify the objects in the problem's specification*

   2. *Identify the operations needed to solve the problem*

   3. *Organize the objects and operations in an algorithm that solves the problem*

In the preceding chapter we focused on various structures that can be used to organize the data in the problem. In this chapter we turn our attention to a more careful study of phase 3, concentrating on the development and evaluation of algorithms and look at some of the standard algorithms provided in C++.

In our discussion of validation and verification in Chap. 1, we noted that in some applications, logic errors cannot be tolerated. In these situations it is sometimes necessary to *prove* that the algorithms are correct, and in this chapter, we describe some of the techniques of formal verification. Moreover, for a given problem, there may be several different algorithms for performing the same task, and in these situations, it is important that we be able to compare their performance. Thus, we also consider more carefully the analysis of algorithms and introduce some techniques for measuring their efficiency.

319

The algorithms we have considered thus far and the functions that implement them have all been nonrecursive; that is, they do not call themselves, either directly or indirectly. There are some problems, however, for which the most appropriate algorithms are recursive. Thus in this chapter we begin by reviewing recursion and how recursive functions are written in C++, and we illustrate recursion with several examples. We also consider how to prove recursive algorithms correct, how to compare their efficiency with that of nonrecursive algorithms, and the role of stacks in supporting recursion.

7.1   RECURSION

We have seen several examples of functions that call other functions. In most modern programming languages such as C++, a function may also call itself, a phenomenon known as **recursion**, and in this section we review recursive functions in C++.

EXAMPLES: RECURSIVE POWER AND FACTORIAL FUNCTIONS

To illustrate the basic idea of recursion, we consider the problem of calculating x^n, where x is a real value and n is a nonnegative integer. The first definition of x^n that one learns is usually an iterative (nonrecursive) one,

$$x^n = \underbrace{x \times x \times x \times \cdots \times x}_{n \ x's}$$

and later one learns that x^0 is defined to be 1. (For convenience, we assume here that x^0 is 1 also when x is 0, although in this case, it is usually left undefined.)

In calculating a sequence of consecutive powers of some number, however, it would be foolish to calculate each one using this definition, that is, to multiply the number by itself the required number of times; for example,

$$3^0 = 1$$
$$3^1 = 3$$
$$3^2 = 3 \times 3 = 9$$
$$3^3 = 3 \times 3 \times 3 = 27$$
$$3^4 = 3 \times 3 \times 3 \times 3 = 81$$
$$3^5 = 3 \times 3 \times 3 \times 3 \times 3 = 243$$
$$\vdots$$

It is clear that once some power of 3 has been calculated, it can be used to calculate the next power; for example, given the value of $3^3 = 27$, we can use this value to calculate

$$3^4 = 3 \times 3^3 = 3 \times 27 = 81$$

and this value to calculate

$$3^5 = 3 \times 3^4 = 3 \times 81 = 243$$

and so on. Indeed, to calculate any power of 3, we only need to know the value of 3^0,

$$3^0 = 1$$

and the fundamental relation between one power of 3 and the next:

$$3^n = 3 \times 3^{n-1}$$

This approach to calculating powers leads to the following recursive definition of the power function:

$$x^0 = 1$$

$$\text{For } n > 0, x^n = x \times x^{n-1}$$

Another classic example of a function that can be calculated recursively is the factorial function. The first definition of the factorial $n!$ of a nonnegative integer n that one usually learns is

$$n! = 1 \times 2 \times \cdots \times n, \text{ for } n > 0$$

and that $0!$ is 1. Thus, for example,

$$0! = 1$$
$$1! = 1$$
$$2! = 1 \times 2 = 2$$
$$3! = 1 \times 2 \times 3 = 6$$
$$4! = 1 \times 2 \times 3 \times 4 = 24$$
$$5! = 1 \times 2 \times 3 \times 4 \times 5 = 120$$

Once again the value of this function for a given integer can be used to calculate the value for the next integer. For example, to calculate $5!$, we can simply multiply the value of $4!$ by 5:

$$5! = 4! \times 5 = 24 \times 5 = 120$$

Similarly, we can use $5!$ to calculate $6!$,

$$6! = 5! \times 6 = 120 \times 6 = 720$$

and so on. We need only know the value of $0!$,

$$0! = 1$$

and the fundamental relation between one factorial and the next:

$$n! = n \times (n-1)!$$

This suggests the following recursive definition of $n!$:

$$0! = 1$$
$$\text{For } n > 0, n! = n \times (n-1)!$$

In general, a function is said to be **defined recursively** if its definition consists of two parts:

1. An **anchor** or **base case**, in which the value of the function is specified for one or more values of the parameter(s).

2. An **inductive** or **recursive step,** in which the function's value for the current value of the parameter(s) is defined in terms of previously defined function values and/or parameter values.

The structure is the same as for proofs by *mathematical induction* that you may have studied in mathematics courses: A property $P(n)$ is proved to be true for all integers n as follows:

1. Prove a base case (typically $n = 0$).

2. Assume the property holds for some integer $n = k$—the *induction hypothesis* or *assumption*—and then prove that it holds for $n = k + 1$.

We have seen two examples of such recursive definitions of functions, the power function

$$x^0 = 1 \qquad \text{(the anchor or base case)}$$

$$\text{For } n > 0, x^n = x \times x^{n-1} \qquad \text{(the inductive or recursive step)}$$

and the factorial function

$$0! = 1 \qquad \text{(the anchor or base case)}$$

$$\text{For } n > 0, n! = n \times (n-1)! \qquad \text{(the inductive or recursive step)}$$

In each definition, the first statement specifies a particular value of the function, and the second statement defines its value for n in terms of its value for $n - 1$.

As we noted in these examples, such recursive definitions are useful in calculating function values $f(n)$ for a sequence of consecutive values of n. Using them to calculate any one particular value, however, requires computing earlier values. For example, consider using the recursive definition of the power function to calculate 3^5. We must first calculate 3^4, because 3^5 is defined as the product of 3 and 3^4. But to calculate 3^4 we must calculate 3^3 because 3^4 is defined as 3×3^3. And to calculate 3^3, we must apply the inductive step of the definition again, $3^3 = 3 \times 3^2$, then again to find 3^2, which is defined as $3^2 = 3 \times 3^1$, and once again to find $3^1 = 3 \times 3^0$. Now we have finally reached the anchor case:

$$3^5 = 3 \times 3^4$$
$$\downarrow$$
$$3^4 = 3 \times 3^3$$
$$\downarrow$$
$$3^3 = 3 \times 3^2$$
$$\downarrow$$
$$3^2 = 3 \times 3^1$$
$$\downarrow$$
$$3^1 = 3 \times 3^0$$
$$\downarrow$$
$$3^0 = 1$$

Since the value of 3^0 is given, we can now backtrack to find the value of 3^1,

$$3^5 = 3 \times 3^4$$
$$\downarrow$$
$$3^4 = 3 \times 3^3$$
$$\downarrow$$
$$3^3 = 3 \times 3^2$$
$$\downarrow$$
$$3^2 = 3 \times 3^1$$
$$\downarrow$$
$$3^1 = 3 \times 3^0 = 3 \times 1 = 3$$
$$\downarrow \quad \nearrow$$
$$3^0 = 1$$

then backtrack again to find the value of 3^2,

$$3^5 = 3 \times 3^4$$
$$\downarrow$$
$$3^4 = 3 \times 3^3$$
$$\downarrow$$
$$3^3 = 3 \times 3^2$$
$$\downarrow$$
$$3^2 = 3 \times 3^1 = 3 \times 3 = 9$$
$$\downarrow \quad \nwarrow$$
$$3^1 = 3 \times 3^0 = 3 \times 1 = 3$$
$$\downarrow \quad \nearrow$$
$$3^0 = 1$$

and so on until we eventually obtain the value 243 for 3^5:

$$3^5 = 3 \times 3^4 = 3 \times 81 = 243$$
$$\downarrow \quad \nwarrow$$
$$3^4 = 3 \times 3^3 = 3 \times 27 = 81$$
$$\downarrow \quad \nwarrow$$
$$3^3 = 3 \times 3^2 = 3 \times 9 = 27$$
$$\downarrow \quad \nwarrow$$
$$3^2 = 3 \times 3^1 = 3 \times 3 = 9$$
$$\downarrow \quad \nwarrow$$
$$3^1 = 3 \times 3^0 = 3 \times 1 = 3$$
$$\downarrow \quad \nearrow$$
$$3^0 = 1$$

As this example demonstrates, calculating function values by hand using recursive definitions may require considerable bookkeeping to record information at the various levels of the recursive evaluation so that after the anchor case is reached, this information can be used to backtrack from one level to the preceding one. Fortunately, most modern high-level languages, including C++, support recursive functions, and all of the necessary bookkeeping and backtracking is done automatically by the computer.

To illustrate, consider the power function again. The recursive definition of this function can be implemented as a recursive function in C++ in a straightforward manner

```
/* Power() calculates x to the nth power recursively.
 *
 *   Receive:   Real number x and nonnegative integer n
 *   Return:    x to the nth power
 ****************************************************/
double Power(double x, unsigned n)
{
  if (n == 0)
    return 1.0;                    // anchor case
  // else
  return Power(x, n - 1) * x;   // inductive step (n > 0)
}
```

When this function is called, the inductive step is applied repeatedly until the anchor case is reached:

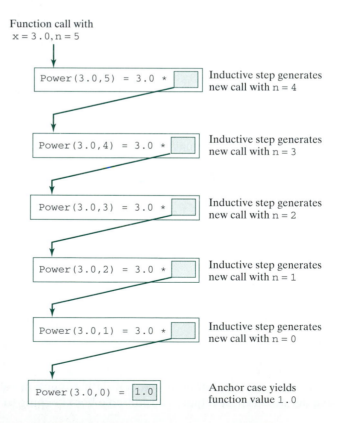

Function call with
x = 3.0, n = 5

Power(3.0,5) = 3.0 *   Inductive step generates
                                new call with n = 4

Power(3.0,4) = 3.0 *   Inductive step generates
                                new call with n = 3

Power(3.0,3) = 3.0 *   Inductive step generates
                                new call with n = 2

Power(3.0,2) = 3.0 *   Inductive step generates
                                new call with n = 1

Power(3.0,1) = 3.0 *   Inductive step generates
                                new call with n = 0

Power(3.0,0) = 1.0   Anchor case yields
                                function value 1.0

As the preceding diagram illustrates, when the call `Power(3.0, 5)` is made to calculate 3.0^5, the inductive step is reached, and it needs the value of `Power(3.0, 4)` before it can compute the value to be returned. Consequently, the function `Power()` is called again, but this time with a smaller value for `n`. The inductive step in this second call to Power is reached again and generates another call `Power(3.0, 3)`, which in turn generates another call `Power(3.0, 2)`, then another, `Power(3.0, 1)`, and finally the call `Power(3.0, 0)`. Because the anchor condition is now satisfied, no additional calls are generated.

The value `1.0` is returned for `Power(3.0, 0)` which is then used to calculate the value of `Power(3.0, 1)`, and so on until the value `243.0` is eventually returned as the value for the original function call `Power(3.0, 5)`:

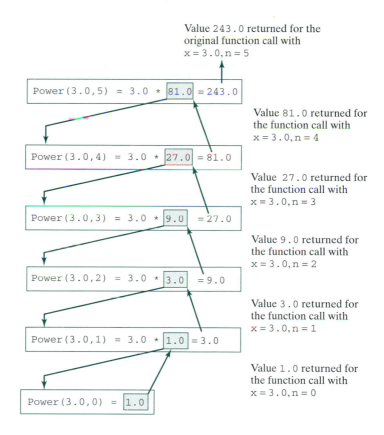

Value `243.0` returned for the original function call with
$x = 3.0, n = 5$

`Power(3.0,5)` = `3.0` * `81.0` = `243.0`

Value `81.0` returned for the function call with
$x = 3.0, n = 4$

`Power(3.0,4)` = `3.0` * `27.0` = `81.0`

Value `27.0` returned for the function call with
$x = 3.0, n = 3$

`Power(3.0,3)` = `3.0` * `9.0` = `27.0`

Value `9.0` returned for the function call with
$x = 3.0, n = 2$

`Power(3.0,2)` = `3.0` * `3.0` = `9.0`

Value `3.0` returned for the function call with
$x = 3.0, n = 1$

`Power(3.0,1)` = `3.0` * `1.0` = `3.0`

Value `1.0` returned for the function call with
$x = 3.0, n = 0$

`Power(3.0,0)` = `1.0`

The recursive definition of the factorial function is also easily implemented as a recursive function in C++. Writing this function and tracing its execution, as we did for the function `Power()`, are left as exercises.

EXAMPLE OF BAD RECURSION: FIBONACCI NUMBERS

Each execution of the inductive step in the definitions of the power function and the factorial function generates only one call to the function itself, but recursive definitions of other functions may require more than one such call. To illustrate, consider the sequence of **Fibonacci numbers**,

$$1, 1, 2, 3, 5, 8, 13, 21, 24, 34, 53, \ldots$$

which begins with two 1's and in which each number thereafter is the sum of the two preceding numbers. This infinite sequence is defined recursively by

$$f_1 = 1$$
$$f_2 = 1$$
$$\text{For } n > 2, f_n = f_{n-1} + f_{n-2}$$

where f_n denotes the nth term in the sequence. This definition leads naturally to the following recursive function:

```
/* Fib() recursively computes the n-th Fibonacci number.
 *   Receive:   n, a positive integer
 *   Return:    n-th Fibonacci number
 ***********************************************************/

double Fib(unsigned n)
{
   if (n <= 2)
      return 1;                          // anchor case
   // else
   return Fib(n - 1) + Fib(n - 2);   // inductive step (n > 2)
}
```

If the function call `Fib(5)` is made to obtain the fifth Fibonacci number, the inductive step

```
return Fib(n - 1) + Fib(n - 2);
```

immediately generates the call `Fib(4)` with parameter $5 - 1 = 4$:

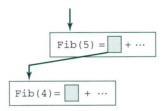

This generates another function call `Fib(3)`, which in turn generates the call `Fib(2)`:

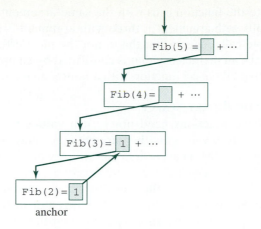

Because the anchor condition is now satisfied, the value 1 is returned for `Fib(2)`, and the second call `Fib(1)` needed to calculate `Fib(3)` is generated:

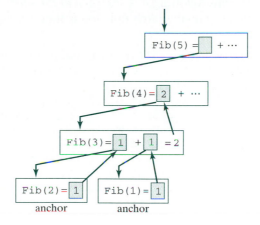

Here again, the value 1 is returned, and the function call `Fib(3)` is completed so that the value $1 + 1 = 2$ is returned. The first term in the sum for the call `Fib(4)` thus has been calculated, and the call `Fib(2)` is generated to determine the second term. This process continues until eventually the value 5 is returned for `Fib(5)`:

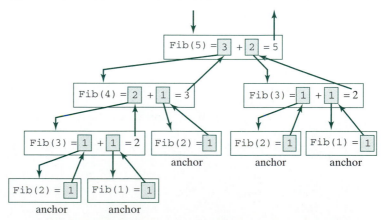

Note the function calls with the same argument in this **recursion tree**; there are two calls with argument 1, three with argument 2, and two with argument 3. These multiple calls suggest that this is not the most efficient way to calculate Fibonacci numbers, an inefficiency that is confirmed by comparing the computing time of this recursive Fibonacci function with a nonrecursive version in the next section.

EXAMPLE: BINARY SEARCH

Recursive functions need not return values via a `return` statement, but may instead return values via the parameters or may return no values at all. For example, consider the binary search algorithm, which was described in Sec. 1.4. Although the algorithm given there is an iterative one, the approach of the binary search method is recursive. If the (sub)list we are currently examining is empty, the item for which we are searching is obviously not in the (sub)list, and so we can stop searching (anchor condition 1). If the (sub)list is not empty, we examine its middle element, and if this is the item for which we are searching, we are finished (anchor condition 2). Otherwise, either the sublist of items preceding this middle item or the sublist of items following it is *searched in the same manner* (inductive step).

A recursive binary search function is therefore quite simple:

```
/* RecBinarySearch() recursively searches sub(list)
 * a[first], . . ., a[last] for item using a
 * binary search.
 *   Receive:   A list of elements in ascending order
 *              stored in array a, integers first and last,
 *              and item of the same type as the array
 *              elements
 *   Pass back: found = true and loc = position of item
 *              if the search is successful; otherwise,
 *              found is false
 ************************************************************/

void RecBinarySearch(ArrayType a, int first, int last,
                     ElementType item,
                     bool & found, int & loc)
{
  if (first > last)            // anchor 1 -- empty sublist
    found = false;
  else                         // inductive step:
  {                            //   recursively search:
    loc = (first + last) / 2;
    if (item < a[loc])         //   the first half
      RecBinarySearch(a, first, loc - 1, found, loc);
    else if (item > a[loc])    //   the second half
      RecBinarySearch(a, loc + 1, last, found, loc);
    else
      found = true;            // anchor 2 -- item found
  }
)
```

To illustrate the action of this function, suppose that the list 11, 22, 33, 44, 55, 66, 77, 88, 99 is stored in positions 0 through 8 of array a and that we wish to search this list for the number 66. We begin with the function call

```
RecBinarySearch(a, 0, 8, 66, itemFound, position);
```

where itemFound is a bool variable and position is an int variable. The function calculates loc = 4, and since 66 > a[4] = 55, the second part of the inductive step generates another call with first = 5 and last = 8:

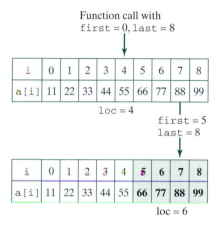

Since the sublist is nonempty, this function call calculates loc = 6, and since 66 < a[6] = 77, the first part of the inductive step generates another function call with first = 5 and last = 5:

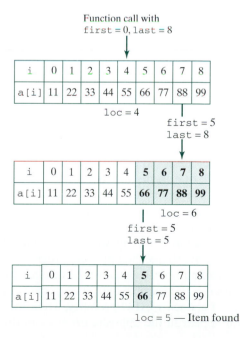

The sublist being searched still has one element, and so in this third function call, the value loc = 5 is calculated, and since a[5] = 66 is the desired item, the second anchor condition assigns the value true to found. This third execution of RecBinarySearch() then terminates and returns the values found = true and loc = 5 to the second function call. This second execution likewise terminates and returns these same values to the first execution of RecBinarySearch(). The original call to this function is thus completed, and the value true is returned to the argument itemFound and the value 5 to the argument position:

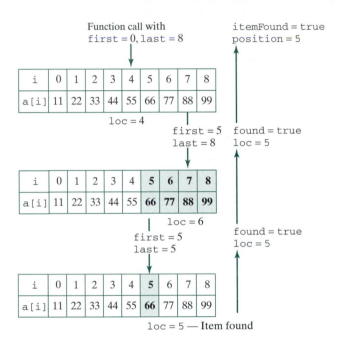

EXAMPLE: PALINDROME CHECKER

Developing recursive algorithms is difficult for many beginning programmers. Practice, practice, and more practice seems to be the only way to develop the ability to think recursively. Consequently, we give one more example of a recursive algorithm here; more will be given in subsequent chapters.

An integer is said to be a **palindrome** if its value does not change when its digits are reversed; that is, the number reads the same from left to right as it does from right to left. For example, 1, 33, 5665, and 123454321 are palindromes. Now, suppose we wish to develop a boolean-valued function that checks if a given positive integer is a palindrome, returning true if it is and false otherwise.

Thinking nonrecursively, we might begin by trying to decompose the number into its separate digits, then put them together in reverse order, and finally check if this reversed number is equal to the original number. A similar approach would be to decompose the number into its separate digits, pushing each one onto a stack. Because of a stack's LIFO property, when these digits are popped from the stack, they will appear in the opposite order from that in the original number, and so we can check if the number's reversal is the same as the number. Another nonrecursive approach might be to convert the number into a string of characters stored in an array and then to scan this array from both ends, checking to see if the digits match.

A more straightforward solution to the problem is a recursive one and is obtained simply by analyzing how one would solve this problem by hand. In checking a number like

$$8504058$$

most people first check the first and last digits and, if they agree, cross them out (perhaps only mentally) and consider the number that remains:

$$\cancel{8}50705\,\cancel{8}$$

The resulting number 50705 is then checked *in the same way*, which is a recursive approach to the problem. After two more applications of this inductive step of checking and truncating the first and last digits

$$\cancel{5}070\,\cancel{5}$$
$$\cancel{0}7\,\cancel{0}$$

a one-digit number results,

$$7$$

and this obviously is a palindrome (anchor case 1). If the original number had an even number of digits, then at this last step, no digits would remain and the number would be a palindrome. If at any point along the way, the first and last digits did not match (anchor case 2), we would stop checking, since the number obviously is not a palindrome.

This leads to the following recursive algorithm:

RECURSIVE PALINDROME CHECKER

/*Algorithm to check if *number* is a palindrome.

Receive: Nonnegative integers *number* and
numDigits, the number of digits in *number*

Returns: True if *number* is a palindrome, and *false* otherwise
--*/

1. If *numDigits* ≤ 1   // anchor case 1

Return the value true.

/* Otherwise check if the first and last digits match,
and if not, return the value false */

2. Divide *number* by $10^{numDigits-1}$ to obtain *firstDigit*.

3. Set *lastDigit* equal to *number* % 10.

4. If *firstDigit* ≠ *lastDigit*   // anchor case 2
Return the value false.

/* Otherwise, the first and last digits match, so
more digits must be checked—inductive step */

5. Apply the algorithm recursively to *number* with *firstDigit* and *lastDigit* removed, that is, to *Number* % $10^{numberDigits-1}$ / 10, and *numDigits* − 2.

Implementing this algorithm as a recursive function is straightforward and is left as an exercise.

✔ Quick Quiz 7.1

1. _____ is the phenomenon of a function calling itself.

2. Name and describe the two parts of a recursive definition of a function.

3. A nonrecursive function for computing some value may execute more rapidly than a recursive function that computes the same value. (True or false)

4. For the following recursive function, find `F(5)`.

```
int F(int n)
{
   if (n == 0)
      return 0;
   else
      return n + F(n - 1);
}
```

5. For the function in Question 4, find `F(0)`.

6. For the function in Question 4, suppose + is changed to * in the inductive step. Find `F(5)`.

7. For the function in Question 4, what happens with the function call `F(-1)`?

✍ EXERCISES 7.1

Exercises 1–6 assume ASCII representation of characters and the following function `F()`:

```
void F(char ch)
{
  if ('A' <= ch) and (ch <= 'H'))
  {
    F(ch - 1);
    cout << ch;
  }
  else
    cout << endl;
}
```

Tell what output will be produced by the function call.

1. `F('C')`

2. `F('G')`

3. `F('3')`

4. `F('C')` if `ch - 1` is replaced by `ch + 1` in the function

5. `F('C')` if the output statement and the recursive call to `F()` are interchanged

6. F('C') if a copy of the output statement is inserted before the recursive call to F()

7. Given the following function F() and assuming ASCII representation of characters, use the method illustrated in this section to trace the sequence of function calls and returns in evaluating F('a', 'e') and F('h', 'c').

```
int F(char ch1, char ch2)
{
  if (ch1 > ch2)
     return 0;
  if (ch1 + 1 == ch2)
     return 1;
  // else
     return F(ch1 + 1, ch2 - 1) + 2;
}
```

Exercises 8–10 assume ASCII representation of characters and the following function G():

```
void G(char ch, int n)
{
  if (n <= 0)
     cout << endl;
  else
  {
     G(ch - 1, n - 1);
     cout << ch;
     G(ch + 1, n - 1);
  }
}
```

8. What output will be produced by the function call G('M', 4)?

   (*Hint:* First try G('M', 2), then G('M', 3).)

9. How many letters are output by the call G('M', 10)?

10. If the output statement is moved before the first recursive call to G(), what output will be produced by G('M', 4)?

Determine what is calculated by the recursive functions in Exercises 11–15.

11.
```
unsigned F(unsigned n)
{
  if (n == 0)
     return 0;
  // else
     return n * F(n - 1);
}
```

12.
```
unsigned F(double x, unsigned n)
{
  if (n == 0)
     return 0;
  // else
     return n + F(x, n - 1);
}
```

13.
```
unsigned F(unsigned n)
{
   if (n < 2)
      return 0;
   // else
      return 1 + F(n / 2);
}
```

14.
```
unsigned F(unsigned n)
{
   if (n == 0)
      return 0;
   // else
      return F(n / 10) + n % 10;
}
```

15.
```
unsigned F(int n)
{
   if (n < 0)
      return F(-n);
   if (n < 10)
      return n;
   // else
      return F(n / 10);
}
```

16–20. Write nonrecursive versions of the functions in Exercises 11–15.

The following exercises ask you to write functions. You should test these functions with driver programs as instructed in Programming Problems 1–16 at the end of this chapter.

21. Write a recursive function that returns the number of digits in a nonnegative integer.

22. Write a nonrecursive version of the function in Exercise 20.

23. Write a recursive function `PrintReverse()` that displays an integer's digits in reverse order.

24. Write a nonrecursive version of the function `PrintReverse()` in Exercise 22.

25. Modify the recursive exponentiation function in the text so that it also works for negative exponents. One approach is to modify the recursive definition of x^n so that for negative values of n, division is used instead of multiplication and n is incremented rather than decremented:

$$x^n = \begin{cases} 1 & \text{if } n \text{ is zero} \\ x^{n-1} * x & \text{if } n \text{ is greater than } 0 \\ x^{n+1}/x & \text{otherwise} \end{cases}$$

26. Write a recursive function to display the digits of any nonzero integer in reverse order.

Assuming declarations of the form

```
const int MAX_CAPACITY = . . .;   // user defined
typedef ElementType = . . . ;     // user defined
typedef ElementType ArrayType[MAX_CAPACITY];
```

Write recursive definitions of the functions whose prototypes are given in Exercises 26–28.

27. `void ReverseArray(ArrayType a, int first, int last);`
   `/* Reverse the contents of a[first], ..., a[last] */`

28. `int SumArray(ArrayType a, int n);`
   `/* Return the sum of a[1], ..., a[n] */`

29. `int Location(ArrayType a, int first, int last, Element elm);`
   `/* Return the location of elm in a[first],`
   `   ..., a[last].  If not found, return 0. */`

30. Using the basic string operations length, concatenate, copy, and find (see Chap. 3), develop a recursive algorithm for reversing a string.

31. Proceed as in Exercise 29, but develop a nonrecursive algorithm.

32. Write a recursive function that implements the algorithm in this section for determining if a number is a palindrome.

33. The *greatest common divisor* of two integers a and b, GCD(a, b), not both of which are zero, is the largest positive integer that divides both a and b. The *Euclidean algorithm* for finding this greatest common divisor of a and b is as follows: Divide a by b to obtain the integer quotient q and the remainder r, so that $a = bq + r$ (if $b = 0$, GCD$(a, b) = a$). Then GCD$(a, b) =$ GCD(b, r). Replace a with b and b with r and repeat this procedure. Because the remainders are decreasing, eventually a remainder of 0 will result. The last nonzero remainder is GCD(a, b). For example,

$$
\begin{aligned}
1260 &= 198 \cdot 6 + 72 & \qquad \text{GCD}(1260, 198) &= \text{GCD}(198, 72) \\
198 &= 72 \cdot 2 + 54 & &= \text{GCD}(72, 54) \\
72 &= 54 \cdot 1 + 18 & &= \text{GCD}(54, 18) \\
54 &= 18 \cdot 3 + 0 & &= 18
\end{aligned}
$$

(*Note* : If either a or b is negative, replace them with their absolute values in this algorithm.) Write a recursive greatest common divisor function.

34. Proceed as in Exercise 32, but write a nonrecursive function.

35. *Binomial coefficients* can be defined recursively as follows:

$$
\left.
\begin{aligned}
\binom{n}{0} &= 1 \\[2mm]
\binom{n}{n} &= 1
\end{aligned}
\right\} \text{(anchor)}
$$

$$
\text{For } 0 < k < n, \quad \binom{n}{k} = \binom{n-1}{k-1} + \binom{n-1}{k} \quad \text{(inductive step)}
$$

a. Write a recursive function to calculate binomial coefficients.

b. Draw a recursion tree like that in this section showing the function calls and returns involved in calculating the binomial coefficient $\binom{4}{2}$.

36. Binomial coefficients can also be defined as follows:

$$\binom{n}{k} = \frac{n!}{k!(n-k)!}$$

Write a nonrecursive function to calculate binomial coefficients using this definition.

7.2   EXAMPLES OF RECURSION: TOWERS OF HANOI; PARSING

TOWERS OF HANOI

The Towers of Hanoi problem is a classic example of a problem for which a recursive algorithm is especially appropriate. It can be solved easily using recursion, but a nonrecursive solution is considerably more difficult. The problem is to solve the puzzle shown in Fig. 7.1, in which one must move the disks from the left peg to the right peg according to the following rules:

1. When a disk is moved, it must be placed on one of the three pegs.
2. Only one disk may be moved at a time, and it must be the top disk on one of the pegs.
3. A larger disk may never be placed on top of a smaller one.

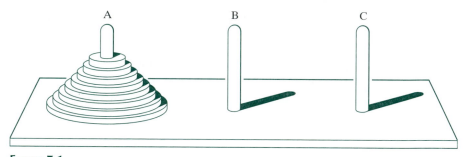

FIGURE 7.1.

Legend has it that the priests in the Temple of Bramah were given a puzzle consisting of a golden platform with three diamond needles on which were placed sixty-four golden disks. The priests were to move one disk per day, following these rules, and when they had successfully finished moving the disks to another needle, time would end. (*Question:* If the priests moved one disk per day and began their work in year 0, when would time end?)

Novices usually find the puzzle easy to solve for a small number of disks, but they have more difficulty as the number of disks grows to seven, eight, and beyond. To a computer scientist, however, the Towers of Hanoi puzzle is easy: We begin by identifying a base case, for which the problem is trivial to solve:

If there is one disk, then move it from Peg A to Peg C.

The puzzle is thus easily solved for $n = 1$ disk. We then give an inductive solution for $n > 1$ disks, in which we assume that a solution exists for $n - 1$ disks:

1. *Move the topmost $n - 1$ disks from Peg A to Peg B, using Peg C for temporary storage.*

2. *Move the final disk remaining on Peg A to Peg C.*

3. *Move the $n - 1$ disks from Peg B to Peg C, using Peg A for temporary storage.*

This scheme is implemented by the following recursive function:

```
/* Move is a recursive function to solve the
 * Towers of Hanoi puzzle.
 *
 *   Receive: n, the number of disks to be moved;
 *            source, peg containing disk to move
 *            destination, peg where to move disk
 *            spare, peg to store disks temporarily,
 *   Output:  A message describing the move
 ****************************************************/

void Move(int n,
          char source, char destination, char spare)
{
   if (n >= 1)                          // anchor
     cout << "Move the top disk from " << source
          << " to " << destination << endl;
   else
   {                                    // inductive case
     Move(n-1, source, spare, destination);
     Move(1, source, destination, spare);
     Move(n-1, spare, destination, source);
   }
}
```

Figure 7.2 presents a driver program that uses `Move()` to solve the Hanoi Towers problem, and an execution in which the problem is solved for four disks.

 FIGURE 7.2   SOLVING THE TOWERS OF HANOI PROBLEM RECURSIVELY

```
/* Program to solve the Towers of Hanoi puzzle recursively.
 *
 * Input:  numDisks, the number of disks to be moved
 * Output: A sequence of moves that solve the puzzle
 *************************************************************/

#include <iostream>
using namespace std;
```

```
    void Move(int n, char source, char destination, char spare);
    {
      const char PEG1 = 'A',              // the three pegs
                 PEG2 = 'B',
                 PEG3 = 'C';

      cout << "This program solves the Hanoi Towers puzzle.\n\n";

      cout << "Enter the number of disks: ";
      int numDisks;                       // the number of disks to be moved
      cin >> numDisks;
      cout << endl;

      Move(numDisks, PEG1, PEG2, PEG3); // the solution
    }

    /*** Insert definition of function Move() here. ***/
```

SAMPLE RUN:

```
This program solves the Hanoi Towers puzzle.

Enter the number of disks: 4

Move the top disk from A to B
Move the top disk from A to C
Move the top disk from B to C
Move the top disk from A to B
Move the top disk from C to A
Move the top disk from C to B
Move the top disk from A to B
Move the top disk from A to C
Move the top disk from B to C
Move the top disk from B to A
Move the top disk from C to A
Move the top disk from B to C
Move the top disk from A to B
Move the top disk from A to C
Move the top disk from B to C
```

PARSING

All the examples of recursion that we have given thus far have used **direct recursion**; that is, the functions have called themselves directly. **Indirect recursion** occurs when a function calls other functions, and some chain of function calls eventually results in a call to the first function again. For example, function F() may call function G(), which calls function H(), which calls F() again.

To illustrate indirect recursion, we consider the compiler problem of processing arithmetic expressions. In particular, we consider the specific problem of parsing arithmetic expressions, that is, determining whether they are well formed and, if so, what their structure is.

The basic components of a compiler are summarized in the following diagram:

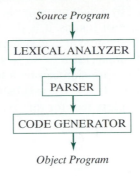

Source Program

LEXICAL ANALYZER

PARSER

CODE GENERATOR

Object Program

The input to a compiler is a stream of characters that comprise the source program. Before the translation can actually be carried out, this stream of characters must be broken up into meaningful groups, such as identifiers, reserved words, constants, and operators. For example, the arithmetic expression

$$2 \; * \; (a \; + \; b)$$

is read by the compiler as a "stream" of characters

$$2b̸*b̸(ab̸+b̸b)$$

(where b̸ is a blank) from which the lexical analyzer might identify the following units:

2	digit
*	multiplication operator
(	left parenthesis
a	letter
+	addition operator
b	letter
)	right parenthesis

These units are called **tokens**, and the part of the compiler that recognizes these tokens is called the **lexical analyzer**.

The **syntax rules** of a language specify how basic tokens such as identifiers and constructs such as expressions are formed. These syntax rules are commonly stated as **substitution rules**, or **productions**. For very simple arithmetic expressions, the rules might be the following:

(1) *expression* → *term + term* | *term - term* | *term*

(2) *term* → *factor * factor* | *factor / factor* | *factor*

(3) *factor* → (*expression*) | *letter* | *digit*

Here the vertical bar (|) is used to separate the various alternatives. For example, the third syntax rule specifies that a factor may be a left parenthesis followed by an expression followed by a right parenthesis, or it may be a single letter or a single digit.

Given a sequence of tokens, it is the task of the **parser** to group these tokens together to form the basic syntactic structures of the language as determined by the syntax rules. For example, for 2 * (a + b) it must recognize that, according to the first syntax rule, an expression can be a term, and by the second rule, a term may have the form *factor * factor*. These substitutions can be displayed by the following partially developed **parse tree** for this expression:

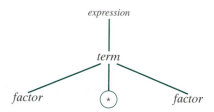

By the third syntax rule, a factor may be a digit; in particular, it may be the digit 2;

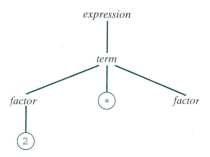

and the second alternative of the third syntax rule specifies that a factor may be an expression enclosed in parentheses:

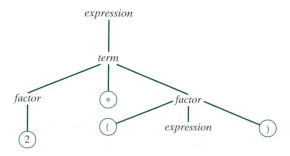

Continued application of these syntax rules produces the following complete parse tree, which shows how 2 * (a + b) can be generated according to the syntax rules and thus demonstrates that it is a legal expression:

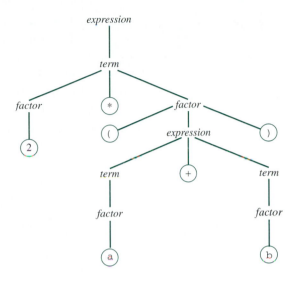

It is clear that these syntax rules for expressions involve indirect recursion. For example, an expression may be a term, which may be a factor, which may be a parenthesized expression, thus defining an expression indirectly in terms of itself.

The program in Fig. 7.3 for parsing these simplified arithmetic expressions uses the three functions ValidExpression(), ValidTerm(), and ValidFactor(), which are derived directly from the corresponding syntax rules. For example, consider the function ValidExpression(). According to the first syntax rule, an expression may have one of the three forms

term + term
term – term
term

In each case, it must begin with a term, and so the first action in this function is a call to ValidTerm().

If ValidTerm() identifies a valid term by returning true, then the function ValidExpression() must examine the next symbol to determine which of these three forms is applicable, and so it calls GetChar() to get the next nonwhitespace character. If this symbol is + or –, ValidTerm() must then be called to check for one of the first two forms for an expression; ValidExpression() then returns true or false to the main program according to whether ValidTerm() returns true or false. If the symbol is not + or –, then an expression of the last form has been identified, and the function must "back up" one symbol before resuming the parse.

The following table traces the action of these three functions in parsing the first expression a+b used in the sample run:

Active Function	position	symbol	Function Returns	Action
`main()`	−1			Call `ValidExpression()`
`ValidExpression()`	−1			Call `ValidTerm()`
`ValidTerm()`	−1			Call `ValidFactor()`
`ValidFactor()`	−1			Call `GetChar()` to get next symbol
	0	a		`GetChar()` increments `position` and returns `symbol = 'a'`
	0	a	true	Else clause returns `true` to `ValidTerm()`
`ValidTerm()`	0	a		Call `GetChar()` to get next symbol
	1	+	true	"Unget" symbol because it is not `*` or `/` and return `true` to `ValidExpression()`
`ValidExpression()`	0	a		Call `GetChar()` to get next symbol
	1	+		Since symbol is + or −, call `ValidTerm()`
`ValidTerm()`	1	+		Call `ValidFactor()`
`ValidFactor()`	1	+		Call `GetChar()` to get next symbol
	2	b		`GetChar()` increments `position` and returns `symbol = 'b'`
	2	b	true	Else clause returns `true` to `ValidTerm()`
`ValidTerm()`	2	b		Call `GetChar()` to get next symbol
	3		true	"Unget" symbol because it is not `*` or `/`, and return `true` to `ValidExpression()`
`ValidExpression()`	3		true	Return `true` to `main()`
`main()`	3			Because `ValidExpression()` returns `true` and `position` is 3, signaling a complete parse, display a message indicating a valid expression.

For the second expression a+b) in the sample run, the same trace table would result except that when execution returns to the main program, `symbol` is ')' and `position` is 3, so the end of the string `expr` has not been reached, indicating an unsuccessful parse.

FIGURE 7.3   PARSING ARITHMETIC EXPRESSIONS

```
/* This program parses simplified arithmetic expressions given by
 * the syntax rules:
 *    expression --> term + term | term - term | term
 *    term --> factor * factor | factor / factor | factor
 *    factor --> (expression) | letter | digit
 *
```

```
 * Input:   Strings representing arithmetic expressions and
 *          user responses used to control repetition
 * Output:  User prompts and messages indicating whether
 *          the strings represent valid expressions
 ******************************************************************/

#include <iostream>
#include <string>
#include <cctype>
using namespace std;

bool ValidExpression(string & expr, int & position);
bool ValidTerm(string & expr, int & position);
bool ValidFactor(string & expr, int & position);
void GetChar(const string & str, char & ch, int & pos);

int main()
{
  string expr;
  for (;;)
  {
    cout << "\nEnter arithmetic expression (# to stop): ";
    getline(cin, expr);
    if (expr == "#") break;

    // Parse the expression
    int position = -1;
    if (ValidExpression(expr, position) &&
        position == expr.length() -1)
      cout << "Valid expression\n";
    else
      cout << "Not a valid expression\n";
  }
}

/* ValidExpression() checks if there is a valid arithmetic expression
 *   in expr beginning at the current position.
 *
 *   Receive:    String expr and integer position
 *   Pass back:  Updated value of position
 *   Return:     True if there is a valid expression in expr at
 *               position, false otherwise
 ******************************************************************/
```

```
bool ValidExpression(string & expr, int & position)
{
  if (ValidTerm(expr, position))
  {
    char symbol;
    GetChar(expr, symbol, position);
    if (symbol == '+' || symbol == '-')
      return ValidTerm(expr, position);

    // else "unget a character"
    position--;
    return true;
  }
  // else
  return false;
}


/* ValidTerm() checks if there is a valid term in expr beginning
 *   at the current position.
 *
 *   Receive:    String expr and integer position
 *   Pass back: Updated value of position
 *   Return:     True if there is a valid term in expr at position,
 *                   false otherwise
 ********************************************************************/

bool ValidTerm(string & expr, int & position)
{
  if (ValidFactor(expr, position))
  {
    char symbol;
    GetChar(expr, symbol, position);
    if (symbol == '*' || symbol == '/')
      return ValidFactor(expr, position);

    // else "unget a character"
    position--;
    return true;
  }
  // else
  return false;
}


/* ValidFactor() checks if there is a valid factor in expr
 *   beginning at the current position.
 *
 *   Receive:    String expr and integer position
 *   Pass back: Updated value of position
 *   Return:     True if there is a valid factor in expr at position,
 *                   false otherwise
 ********************************************************************/
```

```
bool ValidFactor(string & expr, int & position)
{
  char symbol;
  GetChar(expr, symbol, position);
  if (symbol == '(')                // a left parenthesis
  {
    if (ValidExpression(expr, position))
    {
      GetChar(expr, symbol, position);
      return (symbol == '(');
    }
    else
      return false;
  }
  // else
  return isalnum(symbol);
}


/* GetChar() gets the next nonwhitespace character in string
 *  str after the current position pos.
 *
 *  Receive:    String str and integer pos
 *  Pass back: Updated values of pos and next nonwhitespace
 *                   character ch in str
 ***************************************************************/

void GetChar(const string & str, char & ch, int & pos)
{
  for (;;)
  {
    pos++;
    if (pos == str.length())
      ch = ';';
    else
      ch = str[pos];
    if (!isspace(ch)) return;
  }
}
```

SAMPLE RUN

```
Enter arithmetic expression (# to stop): a+b
Valid expression

Enter arithmetic expression (# to stop): a+b)
Not a valid expression

Enter arithmetic expression (# to stop): a*b
Valid expression
```

```
Enter arithmetic expression (# to stop): ((((1))))
Valid expression

Enter arithmetic expression (# to stop): ((a + b)*c)
Valid expression

Enter arithmetic expression (# to stop): (((a + b) * 2) - (c*d)) + 5
Valid expression

Enter arithmetic expression (# to stop): a * * b
Not a valid expression

Enter arithmetic expression (# to stop): #
```

✒ EXERCISES 7.2

1. Trace the execution of `Move(4, 'A', 'B', 'C')` far enough to produce the first five moves. Does your answer agree with the program output in Fig. 7.2? Do the same for `Move(5, 'A', 'B', 'C')`.

Draw parse trees for the expressions in Exercises 2–7.

2. `a * b`   **3.** `(a * b)`

4. `( ( (1) ) )`   **5.** `(a * b) * c`

6. `a * (b * c)`   **7.** `( ( (a + b) * 2) - (c * d) ) * 5`

Construct trace tables like those in the text for parses of the expressions in Exercises 8–11.

8. `a * b`   **9.** `(a * b)`

10. `(a - b) - c`   **11.** `a - (b - c)`

In Exercises 12–15, assume the following syntax rules for simplified boolean expressions:

$bexpression \rightarrow bterm \; || \; bterm \; | \; bterm$

$bterm \rightarrow bfactor \; \&\& \; bfactor \; | \; bfactor$

$bterm \rightarrow \; ! \; bfactor \; | \; (bexpression) \; | \; letter \; | \; true \; | \; false$

Draw parse trees for the expressions.

12. `!y && (z || false)`   **13.** `x || y && z`

14. `false || x || true`   **15.** `!(x || y)`

Strings consisting of balanced parentheses can be generated by the productions

$pstring \rightarrow (pstring) \; pstring \; | \; (\;) \; pstring \; | \; (pstring) \; | \; (\;)$

Draw parse trees for the strings of balanced parentheses in Exercises 16–18.

16. `( ) ( ) ( )`

17. `( ( ( ) ) )`

18. `( ) ( ( ) ( ) ) ( )`

7.3   IMPLEMENTING RECURSION

As we saw in Sec. 4.3, whenever execution of a program or a function begins, a set of memory locations called an *activation record* is created for it. If execution is interrupted by a call to another (or the same) function, the values of the function's local variables, parameters, the return address, and so on are stored in this activation record. When execution of this program unit resumes, its activation record is used to restore these items to what they were before the interruption.

Suppose, for example, that program A calls function B, which, in turn, calls function C. When A is initiated, its activation record is created. When A calls B so that B becomes active, its activation record is also created. Similarly, when B calls C, C becomes the active function, and its activation record is created. When execution of C terminates and control is passed back to B so that it becomes active again, the values in its activation record are the values of its parameters and local variables at the time B was interrupted; thus these values are the ones needed to resume execution of B. Likewise, when B terminates and A is reactivated, its activation record is needed to restore the values being used before its interruption. In each case, the fact that the last function interrupted is the first one to be reactivated suggests that a stack can be used to store the addresses of the activation records so that they can be retrieved in a last-in-first-out order.

As an example, consider the recursive function of Sec. 7.1 for calculating powers

```
        double Power(double x, unsigned n)
        {
          if (n == 0)
            return 1.0;
          // else
/* A */   return Power(x, n - 1) * x;
        }
```

and suppose that it is called in an assignment statement:

```
        int main()
        {
            .
            .
            .
/* B */    z = Power(2.0, 3);
            .
            .
            .
        }
```

Here we have indicated the return addresses as A and B, that is, the locations of the instructions where execution is to resume when the program or function is reactivated.

When execution of the main program is initialized, its activation record is created. This record is used to store the values of variables, actual parameters, return addresses, and so on during the time the program is active. When execution of the main program is interrupted by the function call Power(2.0, 3), the parameters 2.0 and 3 and the return address B (plus other items of information) are stored in the activation record, and this record is pushed onto a stack.

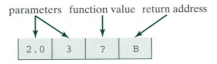

parameters function value return address
| 2.0 | 3 | ? | B |

The function `Power()` now becomes active, and an activation record is created for it. When the statement

```
return Power(x, n - 1) * x;
```

is encountered, the execution of `Power()` is interrupted. The actual parameters `2.0` and `2` for this function call with parameters `x = 2.0` and `n - 1 = 3 - 1 = 2` and the return address `A` (and other items of information) are stored in the current activation record, and this record is pushed onto the stack of activation records.

2.0	2	?	A
2.0	3	?	B

Second reference to Power (x = 2.0, n = 2):

Since this is a new call to `Power()`, another activation record is created, and when this function call is interrupted by the call `Power(2.0, 1)`, this activation record is pushed onto the stack:

2.0	1	?	A
2.0	2	?	A
2.0	3	?	B

Third reference to Power (x = 2.0, n = 1):

The call `Power(2.0, 1)` results in the creation of yet another activation record, and when its execution is interrupted, this time by the call `Power(2.0, 0)`, this activation record is pushed onto the stack:

2.0	0	?	A
2.0	1	?	A
2.0	2	?	A
2.0	3	?	B

Fourth reference to Power (x = 2.0, n = 0):

Execution of `Power()` with parameters `2.0` and `0` terminates with no interruptions and calculates the value `1.0` for `Power(2.0, 0)`. The activation record for this call is then popped from the stack, and the execution resumes at the statement specified by the return address in it:

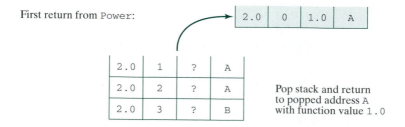

First return from `Power`:

| 2.0 | 0 | 1.0 | A |

2.0	1	?	A
2.0	2	?	A
2.0	3	?	B

Pop stack and return to popped address A with function value `1.0`

Execution of the preceding call to `Power()` with parameters 2.0 and 1 then resumes and terminates without interruption, so that its activation record is popped from the stack, the value 2.0 is returned, and the previous call with parameters 2.0 and 2 is reactivated at statement A:

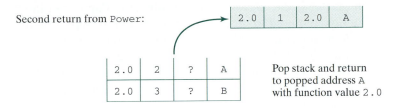

This process continues until the value 8.0 is computed for the original call `Power(2.0, 3)`, and execution of the main program is resumed at the statement specified by the return address B in its activation record.

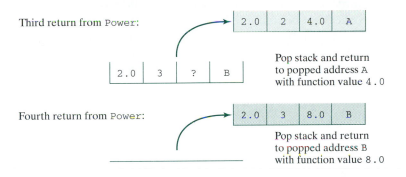

7.4   ALGORITHM EFFICIENCY

An algorithm's efficiency is usually measured according to two criteria. The first is **space utilization**, the amount of memory required to store the data; and the second is **time efficiency**, the amount of time required to process the data. Unfortunately, it is usually not possible to minimize both the space and the time requirements. Algorithms that require the least memory are often slower than those that use more memory. Thus the programmer is usually faced with a trade-off between space efficiency and time efficiency.

In the early days of computing when memory (vacuum tubes) and storage devices (magnetic drums and tapes) were expensive, space requirements received primary consideration. The important thing was to get answers to problems, even if it took several hours or perhaps even days. Nowadays, huge amounts of memory and storage are available for very little cost, so that in most cases, an algorithm's time efficiency is considered the more important of the two. But there obviously are some situations when time and space needs are so interrelated that they must both be considered — for example, on a space probe to some planet. In this section, however, we will focus our attention on time efficiency and how it can be measured.

The execution time of an algorithm is influenced by several factors. Obviously, one factor is the size of the input, since the number of input items usually affects the time required to process these items. For example, the time it takes to sort a list of items surely depends on the number of items in the list. Thus the execution time T of an algorithm must be expressed as a function $T(n)$ of the size n of the input.

The kind of instructions and the speed with which the machine can execute them also influence execution time. These factors, however, depend on the particular computer being used; consequently, we cannot expect to express meaningfully the value of $T(n)$ in real time units such as seconds. Instead, $T(n)$ will be an approximate count of the instructions executed.

Another factor that influences computing time is the quality of the source code that implements the algorithm and the quality of the machine code generated from this source code by a compiler. Some languages are better suited than others for certain algorithms; some programmers write better programs than others; and some compilers generate more efficient code than others. This means, in particular, that $T(n)$ cannot be computed as the number of machine instructions executed, and thus it is taken to be the number of times the instructions in the *algorithm* are executed.

As an example, consider the following algorithm for finding the mean of a set of n numbers stored in an array. (The statements have been numbered for easy reference.)

ALGORITHM TO CALCULATE MEAN

/*   Algorithm to find the mean of n real numbers.
        Receive: An integer $n \geq 1$ and an array $x[0], \ldots, x[n-1]$
                of real numbers
        Return: The mean of $x[0], \ldots, x[n-1]$
--*/

1. Initialize *sum* to 0.

2. Initialize index variable i to 0.

3. While $i < n$ do the following:

4.   a. Add $x[i]$ to *sum*.

5.   b. Increment i by 1.

6. Calculate and return *mean* = *sum* / n.

Statements 1 and 2 each are executed one time. Statements 4 and 5, which comprise the body of the while loop, are executed n times, and statement 3, which controls repetition, is executed $n + 1$ times, since one additional check is required to determine that the control variable i is no longer less than the value n. After repetition terminates, statement 6 is then executed one time. This analysis is summarized in the following table:

Statement	# of times executed
1	1
2	1
3	$n + 1$
4	n
5	n
6	1
Total	$3n + 4$

Thus we see that the computing time for this algorithm is given by

$$T(n) = 3n + 4$$

As the number n of inputs increases, the value of this expression for $T(n)$ grows at a rate proportional to n, and so we say that $T(n)$ has "order of magnitude n," which is usually written using "big Oh notation" as

$$T(n) \text{ is } O(n)$$

In general, the computing time $T(n)$ of an algorithm is said to have **order of magnitude** $f(n)$, denoted

$$\textbf{\textit{T}(\textit{n}) is O(\textit{f}(\textit{n}))}$$

if there is some constant C such that

$$T(n) \leq C \cdot f(n) \text{ for all sufficiently large values of } n$$

That is, $T(n)$ is bounded above by some constant times $f(n)$ for all values of n from some point on. The **computational complexity** of the algorithm is said to be $O(f(n))$. For example, the complexity of the preceding algorithm is $O(n)$, since the computing time was found to be

$$T(n) = 3n + 4$$

and since

$$3n + 4 \leq 3n + n \text{ for } n \geq 4$$

we see that

$$T(n) \leq 4n \text{ for all } n \geq 4$$

Thus, taking $f(n) = n$ and $C = 4$, we may say that

$$T(n) \text{ is } O(n)$$

Of course, it would also be correct to say $T(n)$ is $O(5280n)$ or $T(n)$ is $O(4n + 5)$ or $T(n)$ is $O(3.1416n + 2.71828)$, but we prefer a *simple* function like n, n^2, or $\log_2 n$ to express an algorithm's complexity. Also, $T(n)$ is $O(n)$ obviously implies that $T(n)$ is $O(n^2)$ as well as $T(n)$ is $O(n^{5/2})$ or $T(n)$ is $O(2^n)$, and in general $T(n)$ is $O(g(n))$ if $g(n) \geq n$ for all n from some point on; but the smaller the function $g(n)$ is, the more information it will provide about the computing time $T(n)$.

In this example, the computing time depends only on the size of the input. In other problems, however, it may depend on the arrangement of the input items as well. For example, it may take less time to sort a list of items that are nearly in order initially than to sort a list in which the items are in reverse order. We might then attempt to measure T in the **worst case** or in the **best case**, or we might attempt to compute the **average** value of T over all possible cases. The best-case performance of an algorithm is usually not very informative and the average performance is often difficult to determine. Consequently, $T(n)$ is frequently taken as a measure of the algorithm's performance in the worst case.

As an illustration, consider the following sorting algorithm. (Again, we have numbered the statements for easy reference.)

SIMPLE SELECTION SORTING ALGORITHM

/*   Algorithm to sort the elements of array x into ascending order.

Receive: An integer $n \geq 1$ and an array $x[0] \ldots x[n-1]$ of numbers
Return: x sorted so that $x[0] \leq x[1] \leq \ldots \leq x[n-1]$
--*/

1. For $i = 0$ to $n - 2$ do the following:

/* On the ith pass, first find the smallest element in the

sublist $x[i], \ldots, x[n-1]$. */

2.   a. Set *smallPos* = i.

3.   b. Set *smallest* = $x[smallPos]$.

4.   c. For $j = i + 1$ to $n - 1$ do the following:

5.   If $x[j] < smallest$ then   // smaller element found

6.   i. Set *smallPos* = j.

7.   ii. Set *smallest* = $x[smallPos]$.

/* Now interchange this smallest element with the element at the beginning of this sublist. */

8.   d. Set $x[smallPos] = x[i]$.

9.   e. Set $x[i]$ = *smallest*.

Statement 1 is executed n times (for i ranging from 0 through the value $n - 1$, which causes termination), and statements 2, 3, 8, and 9 each are executed $n - 1$ times, once on each pass through the outer loop.[1] On the first pass through this loop with $i = 0$, statement 4 is executed n times; statement 5 is executed $n - 1$ times, and assuming a worst case (when the items are in descending order) so are statements 6 and 7. On the second pass with $i = 1$, statement 4 is executed $n - 1$ times and statements 5, 6, and 7 $n - 2$ times, and so on. Thus statement 4 is executed a total of $n + (n - 1) + \cdots + 2$ times, and statements 5, 6, and 7 each are executed a total of $(n - 1) + (n - 2) + \cdots + 1$ times. These sums are equal to $n(n + 1)/2 - 1$ and $n(n - 1)/2$, respectively;[2] thus the total computing time is given by

$$T(n) = n + 4(n - 1) + \frac{n(n + 1)}{2} - 1 + 3\left(\frac{n(n - 1)}{2}\right)$$

which simplifies to

$$T(n) = 2n^2 + 4n - 5$$

Since $n \le n^2$ for all $n \ge 0$, we see that

$$2n^2 + 4n - 5 \le 2n^2 + 4n^2 = 6n^2$$

and hence that

$$T(n) \le 6n^2 \text{ for all } n \ge 0$$

Thus taking $f(n) = n^2$ and $C = 6$ in the definition of big-O notation, we may say that

$$T(n) \text{ is } O(n^2)$$

The big-O notation gives an approximate measure of the computing time of an algorithm for a large number of inputs. If two algorithms for performing the same task have different complexities, the algorithm with the lower-order computing time is usually preferred. For example, if the computing time $T_1(n)$ of Algorithm 1 is $O(n)$ and the computing time $T_2(n)$ for Algorithm 2 is $O(n^2)$, then Algorithm 1 is usually considered better than Algorithm 2, since it will perform more efficiently for large values of n. It must be noted, however, that for small values of n, Algorithm 2 might well outperform Algorithm 1. For example, suppose that $T_1(n)$ is $10n$ and $T_2(n)$ is $0.1n^2$. Since $10n > 0.1n^2$ for values of n up to 100, we see that

$$T_1(n) < T_2(n) \text{ only for } n > 100$$

[1]Statement 1 actually consists of three statements:
1. Initialize i to 0 (executed once)
2. While $i < n - 1$ do the following: (executed n times)
3. Increment i by 1. (executed $n - 1$ times)
Similarly, statement 4 consists of three statements. For simplicity, however, we will treat these as single statements.

[2]Here we have used the summation formula
$$\sum_{i=1}^{n} i = \frac{n(n + 1)}{2}$$

Thus Algorithm 2 is more efficient than Algorithm 1 only for inputs of size greater than 100.

To illustrate, consider the problem of searching an array of n elements $a[0], \ldots,$ $a[n-1]$ to determine whether a specified value *item* appears in this list and, if so, to determine its location. One method is to do a **linear search** as described in Sec. 6.4, in which we start at the beginning of the list and examine successive elements until either *item* is found or we reach the end of the list. The following is a modification of the algorithm given earlier:

LINEAR SEARCH ALGORITHM

/*   Algorithm to perform a linear search of the list $a[0], \ldots, a[n-1]$.

Receive:	An integer n and a list of n elements stored in array elements $a[0], \ldots, a[n-1]$, and *item* of the same type as the array elements
Return:	*found* = true and *loc* = position of *item* if the search is successful; otherwise, *found* is false

--*/

1. Set *found* = false.

2. Set *loc* = 0.

3. While *loc* < n and not *found* do the following:

4.   If *item* = $a\,[loc]$ then   // *item* found

5.   Set *found* = true.

6.   Else   // keep searching

            Increment *loc* by 1.

The worst case is obviously that in which *item* is not in the list, and in this case, we find the computing time $T_L(n)$ for the linear search algorithm as follows:

Statement	# of Times Executed
1	1
2	1
3	$n+1$
4	n
5	0
6	n

Thus $T_L(n) = 3n + 3$ so that

$$T_L(n) \text{ is } O(n)$$

since $3n + 3 \le 4n$ for all $n \ge 3$.

If the list being searched has previously been sorted so that the elements are in ascending order, a **binary search** like that described in Sec. 1.4 can be used instead of a linear search. To locate *item* in such a list, the element $a[mid]$ in the middle of the list is examined. There are three possibilities:

$item < a[mid]$:   Search the first half of the list
$item > a[mid]$:   Search the last half of the list
$item = a[mid]$:   Search is successful

We continue this halving process until either *item* is located or the sublist to search becomes empty. The following algorithm gives the details:

BINARY SEARCH ALGORITHM

/*   Algorithm to perform a binary search of the list $a[0], \ldots, a[n-1]$
     in which the items are in ascending order.

Receive: An integer n and a list of n elements in ascending order
           stored in array elements $a[0], \ldots, a[n-1]$, and *item* of
           the same type as the array elements
Return: *found* = true and *loc* = position of *item* if the search is
           successful; otherwise, *found* is false
--*/

1. Set *found* = false.

2. Set *first* = 0.

3. Set *last* = $n - 1$.

4. While *first* < *last* and not *found* do the following:

5.   Calculate *loc* = (*first* + *last*) / 2.

6.   If *item* < $a[loc]$ then

7.   Set *last* = *loc* − 1.   // search first half

8.   Else if *item* > $a[loc]$ then

9.   Set *first* = *loc* + 1.   // search last half

10.   Else

          Set *found* = true.   // *item* found

In this algorithm, statements 1, 2, and 3 are clearly executed exactly once, and to calculate the worst-case computing time $T_B(n)$, we must determine the number of times the loop composed of statements 4 through 10 is executed. Each pass through this loop reduces by at least one-half the size of the sublist still to be searched. The last pass occurs when the sublist reaches size one. Thus the total number of iterations of this loop is 1 plus the number k of passes required to produce a sublist of size one. Since the size of the sublist after k passes is at most $n / 2^k$, we must have

$$\frac{n}{2^k} < 2$$

that is,

$$n < 2^{k+1}$$

or equivalently

$$\log_2 n < k + 1$$

The required number of passes, therefore, is the smallest integer that satisfies this inequality, that is, the integer part of $\log_2 n$. Thus, in the worst case, when *item* is greater than each of $a\,[0], \ldots, a\,[n-1]$, statement 4 is executed no more than $2 + \log_2 n$ times, statements 5, 6, 8, and 9 no more than $1 + \log_2 n$ times, and statements 7 and 10 zero times. The total computing time, therefore, is no more than $11 + \log_2 n$, so that

$$T_B(n) \text{ is } O(\log_2 n)$$

Since the complexity of linear search is $O(n)$ and that of binary search is $O(\log_2 n)$, it is clear that binary search will be more efficient than linear search for large lists. For small lists, however, linear search may—and in fact, does—outperform binary search. Empirical studies indicate that linear search is more efficient than binary search for lists of up to about 20 elements.

In addition to $O(\log_2 n)$, $O(n)$, and $O(n^2)$, other computing times that frequently arise in algorithm analysis are $O(1)$, $O(\log_2\log_2 n)$, $O(n \log_2 n)$, $O(n^3)$, and $O(2^n)$. $O(1)$ denotes a **constant** computing time, that is, one that does not depend on the size of the input. A computing time of $O(n)$ is said to be **linear**; $O(n^2)$ is called **quadratic**; $O(n^3)$ is called **cubic**; and $O(2^n)$ is called **exponential**. Table 7.1 displays the values of these computing-time functions for several values of n:

$\log_2\log_2 n$	$\log_2 n$	n	$n \log_2 n$	n^2	n^3	2^n
—	0	1	0	1	1	2
0	1	2	2	4	8	4
1	2	4	8	16	64	16
1.58	3	8	24	64	512	256
2	4	16	64	256	4096	65536
2.32	5	32	160	1024	32768	4294967296
2.6	6	64	384	4096	2.6×10^5	1.85×10^{19}
3	8	256	2.05×10^3	6.55×10^4	1.68×10^7	1.16×10^{77}
3.32	10	1024	1.02×10^4	1.05×10^6	1.07×10^9	1.8×10^{308}
4.32	20	1048576	2.1×10^7	1.1×10^{12}	1.15×10^{18}	6.7×10^{315652}

TABLE 7.1   COMMON COMPUTING TIME FUNCTIONS

Graphs of these functions are shown in Fig. 7.4.

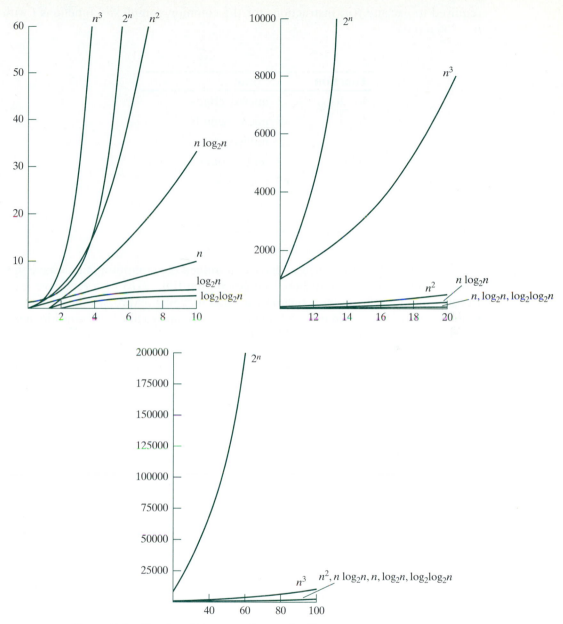

FIGURE 7.4   Graphs of Common Computing Times.

It should be clear from the preceding table and graphs that algorithms with exponential complexity are practical only for solving problems in which the number of inputs is small. To emphasize this, suppose that each instruction in some algorithm can be executed in one microsecond. The following table shows the time required to execute $f(n)$ instructions for the common complexity functions f with $n = 256$ inputs:

Function	Time
$\log_2\log_2 n$	3 microseconds
$\log_2 n$	8 microseconds
n	.25 milliseconds
$n\log_2 n$	2 milliseconds
n^2	65 milliseconds
n^3	17 seconds
2^n	3.7×10^{61} centuries

All the algorithms for which we have determined the computing times have thus far been nonrecursive algorithms. The computing time $T(n)$ of a recursive algorithm is naturally given by a **recurrence relation**, which expresses the computing time for inputs of size n in terms of smaller-sized inputs. To illustrate, consider again the recursive function Power() of Sec. 7.1:

```
/* Power() calculates x to the nth power recursively.
 *
 *   Receive: Real number x and nonnegative integer n
 *   Return:  x to the nth power
 **********************************************/

double Power(double x, unsigned n)
{
  if (n == 0)
    return 1.0;                   // anchor case
  // else
  return Power(x, n - 1) * x; // inductive step (n > 0)
}
```

When Power() is called with n > 0, the boolean expression

```
n == 0
```

is first evaluated, and since it is false, the inductive statement

```
return Power(x, n - 1) * x;
```

is executed. The total computing time is thus 2 plus the time required to compute Power(x, n - 1). Thus $T(n)$ is given by the recurrence relation

$$T(n) = 2 + T(n - 1)$$

Similarly, if $n - 1 > 0$,

$$T(n - 1) = 2 + T(n - 2)$$

and combining these gives

$$T(n) = 2 + 2 + T(n - 2)$$

Continuing this process, we eventually obtain

$$T(n) = 2 + 2 + \cdots + 2 + T(0)$$

The time $T(0)$ to compute x^0 is clearly 2, since the boolean expression n == 0 is evaluated and the anchor statement

```
return 1.0;
```

is executed. Thus we have

$$T(n) = 2(n + 1)$$

so that

$$T(n) \text{ is O}(n)$$

As we described in Sec. 7.1, the power function may also be defined iteratively as

$$x^0 = 1$$
$$x^n = \underbrace{x \times x \times \cdots \times x}_{n \, x\text{'s}} \text{ for } n > 0$$

and this definition leads to the following nonrecursive function:

```
/* NRPower() calculates x to the nth power nonrecursively.
 *
 * Receive: Real number x and nonnegative integer n
 * Return:  x to the nth power
 ************************************************************/

double NRPower(double x, unsigned n)
{
  double prod = 1.0;       // the product x * x * ... * x
  for (int i = 1; i <= n; i++)
    prod *= x;
  return prod;
}
```

The computing time of this function is easily computed:

$$T_{NR}(n) \text{ is O}(n)$$

Although the computational complexity of the recursive and nonrecursive functions is the same, the overhead in implementing recursion (as described in the preceding section) does produce some inefficiency. Consequently, in cases such as this, in which both a recursive algorithm and a nonrecursive one can be developed with little difference in effort, the nonrecursive solution is usually preferred.

In some cases, the computing time of a recursive algorithm to solve a problem may be much greater than that of a nonrecursive algorithm for the same problem. This is especially true of those like the recursive function `Fib()` for calculating Fibonacci numbers in Sec. 7.1, in which the inductive step requires more than one call to the function itself:

```
/* Fib() recursively computes the n-th Fibonacci number.
 *   Receive:   n, a positive integer
 *   Return:    n-th Fibonacci number
 *******************************************************/

double Fib(unsigned n)
{
   if (n <= 2)
      return 1;                          // anchor case
   // else
   return Fib(n - 1) + Fib(n - 2); // inductive step (n > 2)
}
```

We noted that multiple function calls with the same parameter indicate that this is not a particularly efficient method of calculating Fibonacci numbers. Indeed, it is extremely inefficient!

To find the computing time of this function `Fib()`, we observe that for n > 2, the boolean expression n <= 2 is checked, the anchor step is skipped, and the inductive step is executed. The computing time is thus given by the recurrence relation

$$T(n) = 2 + T(n-1) + T(n-2)$$

for $n > 2$. Since this recurrence relation is not especially easy to solve to obtain an explicit formula for $T(n)$, we will use it instead to obtain a lower bound for $T(n)$ that grows exponentially with n and thus show that $T(n)$ grows exponentially.

This recurrence relation holds for all integers n greater than 2, and thus if $n > 3$ (so that $n - 1$ is greater than 2), we may apply it to $n - 1$ to say that

$$T(n-1) = 2 + T(n-2) + T(n-3)$$

Substituting this in the original relation gives

$$T(n) = 4 + 2T(n-2) + T(n-3) \text{ for } n > 3$$

and thus

$$T(n) > 2T(n-2) \text{ for } n > 3$$

If $n > 5$ so that $n - 2 > 3$, we may apply this inequality to $n - 2$ and obtain

$$T(n) > 2T(n-2) > 4T(n-4)$$

Continuing in this matter, we obtain

$$T(n) > 2T(n-2) > 4T(n-4) > \cdots > 2^{(n-2)/2}T(2) \text{ if } n \text{ is even}$$

or

$$T(n) > 2T(n-2) > 4T(n-4) > \cdots > 2^{(n-1)/2}T(1) \text{ if } n \text{ is odd}$$

and since $T(2) = T(1) = 2$, we conclude in either case that

$$T(n) > 2^{n/2} = (2^{1/2})^n = (\sqrt{2})^n > (1.4)^n \text{ for } n > 2$$

The recursive function `Fib()` thus has computing time that is at least exponential. In fact, it can be shown that

$$T(n) \text{ is } O\left(\left(\frac{1 + \sqrt{5}}{2}\right)^n\right)$$

where $\dfrac{1 + \sqrt{5}}{2} = 1.618034 \cdots$ is the *golden ratio* approached by ratios of consecutive Fibonacci numbers.[3]

In contrast, the computing time of the following nonrecursive Fibonacci function is easily seen to grow linearly with n; that is,

$$T_{NR}(n) \text{ is } O(n)$$

---

[3]The sequence of ratios of consecutive Fibonacci numbers:

$$\frac{1}{1} = 1$$

$$\frac{2}{1} = 2$$

$$\frac{3}{2} = 1.5$$

$$\frac{5}{3} = 1.6666 \cdots$$

$$\frac{8}{5} = 1.6$$

$$\frac{13}{8} = 1.61825$$

$$\vdots$$
$$\downarrow$$

$$\frac{1 + \sqrt{5}}{2} = 1.618034 \cdots$$

```
/* NRFib() computes the n-th Fibonacci number
 *   nonrecursively.
 *   Receive:  n, a positive integer
 *   Return:   n-th Fibonacci number
 ********************************************************/

double NRFib(unsigned n)
{
  unsigned fib1 = 1,   // 3 consecutive Fibonacci numbers
           fib2 = 1,
           fib3;
  for (int i = 3; i <= n; i++)
  {
    fib3 = fib1 + fib2;
    fib1 = fib2;
    fib2 = fib3;
  }
  return fib2;
}
```

On one machine, the time required to compute NRFib(n) for n ≤ 30 was less than three milliseconds, whereas the time to compute Fib(n) was much greater as shown by the following table (time is in milliseconds):

n	10	15	20	22	24	26	28	30
Time	6	69	784	2054	5465	14121	36921	96494

Quite obviously, the nonrecursive function NRFib() is preferable to the recursive function Fib().

In summary, calculating powers and finding Fibonacci numbers are examples of problems that can be solved with nearly equal ease using either a nonrecursive or a recursive algorithm. However, because of the overhead involved in manipulating the run-time stack described in the preceding section, nonrecursive functions usually (but not always) execute more rapidly and use memory more efficiently than do the corresponding recursive subprograms. Thus, if the problem can be solved recursively or nonrecursively with little difference in effort, it is usually better to use the nonrecursive version.

✔ Quick Quiz 7.4

1. What two criteria are usually used to measure an algorithm's efficiency?
2. In the early days of computing, which was more important?
3. In most current applications, which is most important?
4. Define what it means to write $T(n)$ is $O(f(n))$.
5. If $T(n) \le 5000n^3$ for all $n \ge 100000$, then $T(n)$ is $O(n^3)$. (True or false)
6. If $T(n) \le 5000n^3$ for all $n \ge 100000$, then $T(n)$ is $O(n^4)$. (True or false)

7. If $T(n) > 5000n^3$ for all $n < 100000$, then $T(n)$ cannot be $O(n^3)$. (True or false)

8. The worst case computing time of linear search is $O(_____)$.

9. The worst case computing time of binary search is $O(_____)$.

10. If the computing time of an algorithm is $O(2^n)$, it should perform acceptably for most large inputs. (True or false)

11. For a recursive algorithm, a(n) $_____$ relation expresses the computing time for inputs of size n in terms of smaller-sized inputs.

✎ EXERCISES 7.4

Which of the orders of magnitude given in this section is the best O notation to describe the computing times in Exercises 1–4?

1. $T(n) = n^3 + 100n \cdot \log_2 n + 5000$

2. $T(n) = 2^n + n^{99} + 7$

3. $T(n) = \dfrac{n^2 - 1}{n + 1} + 8\log_2 n$

4. $T(n) = 1 + 2 + 4 + \cdots + 2^n - 1$

5. Give an example of an algorithm with complexity $O(1)$.

6. Explain why if $T(n)$ is $O(n)$ then it is also correct to say $T(n)$ is $O(n^2)$.

For the code segments in Exercises 7–12, determine which of the orders of magnitude given in this section is the best O notation to use to express the worst-case computing time as a function of n.

7.
```
// Calculate mean
n = 0;
sum  = 0;
cin >> x;
while (x != -999)
{
   n++;
   sum += x;
   cin >> x;
}
mean = sum / n;
```

8.
```
// Matrix addition
for (int i = 0; i < n; i++)
   for (int j = 0; j < n; j++)
      c[i][j] = a[i][j] + b[i][j];
```

9.
```
// Matrix multiplication
for (int i = 0; i < n; i++)
   for (int j = 0; j < n; j++)
   {
      c[i][j] = 0;
      for (int k = 0; k < n; k++)
         c[i][j] += a[i][k] * b[k][j];
   }
```

10.
```
// Bubble sort
for (int i = 0; i < n - 1; i++)
{
   for (int j = 0; j < n - 1; j++)
      if (x[j] > x[j + 1])
      {
         temp = x[j];
         x[j] = x[j + 1];
         x[j + 1] = temp;
      }
}
```

11.
```
while (n >= 1)
   n /= 2;
```

12.
```
x = 1;
for (int i = 1; i <= n - 1; i++)
{
   for (int j = 1; j <= x; j++)
      cout << j << endl;
   x  = 2;
}
```

13. Write a recurrence relation for the computing time of function `Move()` for the Towers-of-Hanoi problem in Sec. 7.2 and solve it to find this computing time.

7.5   STANDARD ALGORITHMS IN C++

As we noted in the preceding chapter, in July of 1994, the Standard Template Library was chosen to be part of standard C++. It is based on work in generic programming done by Alex Stepanov and Meng Lee of the Hewlett-Packard Laboratories. One of the major parts of STL is its collection of more than 80 generic **algorithms**. They are not member functions of STL's container classes and do not access containers directly. Rather they are stand-alone function templates that operate on data by means of iterators. This makes it possible for them to work with regular C-style arrays as well as containers. We illustrate one of these algorithms here

EXAMPLE: STL's sort ALGORITHM
The task of sorting a sequence of values so they are in ascending (or descending) order occurs so often in problems that many different sorting methods have been developed over the years. We described one sorting algorithm in the preceding section—simple selection sort—and noted that it is not very efficient for large data sets.

Because of the frequent need to sort collections of data and to do so efficiently, the developers of STL included a `sort` algorithm in their library that uses one of the most efficient sorting methods known. This method and several others are described in detail in Chap. 11. This `sort` algorithm comes in several different forms. We will illustrate two of these forms with examples.

SORT 1: USING <. STL's `sort` algorithm requires that a less-than function be defined on the data elements so it can compare items in the list to determine which is smaller. The first version of `sort` in Fig. 7.5 assumes that the < operator—that is, the function `operator<()`—has been defined for the type of items being sorted. We will sort integers stored in a `vector<int>` and real values stored in a `deque<double>`.

FIGURE 7.5   `sort` ALGORITHM—VERSION 1

```
/* Program to illustrate use of the standard sort algorithm.

   Output:  A sorted list of ints and a sorted list of doubles.
--------------------------------------------------------------*/

#include <iostream>
#include <vector>
#include <deque>
#include <algorithm>
using namespace std;

template <typename Container>
void Display(ostream & out, const Container & c);

int main()
{
  int ints[] = {555, 33, 444, 22, 222, 777, 1, 66};
  vector<int> v(ints, ints + 5);
  sort(v.begin(), v.end());
  cout << "\nSorted list of integers:\n";
  Display(cout, v);

  double dubs[] = {55.5, 3.3, 44.4, 2.2, 22.2, 77.7, 0.1};
  deque<double> d(dubs, dubs + 7);
  sort(d.begin(), d.end());
  cout << "\nSorted list of doubles:\n";
  Display(cout, d);
}


/* Function template to display elements of any type
 * (for which the output operator is defined) stored
 * in a container c (for which [] and size() are defined).
 * Receive: Type parameter Container
 *          ostream out
 *          Container c
 * Output:  Values stored in c to out
 ************************************************************/
```

```
template <typename Container>
void Display(ostream & out, const Container & c)
{
  for (int i = 0; i < c.size(); i++)
    out << c[i] << " ";
  out << endl;
}
```

EXECUTION

```
Sorted list of integers:
22   33   222   444   555

Sorted list of doubles:
0.1   2.2   3.3   22.2   44.4   55.5   77.7
```

The sort algorithm can also be used be used with arrays. We pass it a pointer to the beginning of the array—*arrayName*—and a pointer just past the end of the array —*arrayName* + *size*. For example, the int array ints defined in Fig. 7.5 by

```
int ints[] = {555, 33, 444, 22, 222, 777, 1, 66};
```

can be sorted with

```
sort(ints, ints + 8);
```

This version of sort can be used to sort a container of any type of elements for which < is defined. The program in Fig. 7.6 illustrates this with a vector of stack<int>s where < is defined for stacks by: s1 < s2 means s1.top() < s2.top(); that is, we simply compare the top stack elements.

FIGURE 7.6   SORTING A **vector** OF **stacks**

```
#include <iostream>
#include <vector>
#include <stack>
#include <algorithm>
using namespace std;

// Less-than function for stack
template <typename ElementType>
bool operator<(const stack<ElementType> & s1,
               const stack<ElementType> & s2)
{ return s1.top() < s2.top(); }

// Output a stack
template <typename ElementType>
void Dump(stack<ElementType> s);
```

```
int main()
{
  vector< stack<int> > s(4);

  s[0].push(10); s[0].push(20);
  s[1].push(30);
  s[2].push(50); s[2].push(60);
  s[3].push(1); s[3].push(2);
  s[3].push(3);
  sort(s.begin(), s.end());
  for (int i = 0; i < 4; i++)
  {
    cout << "Stack #" << i << ": ";
    Dump(s[i]);
    cout << endl;
  }
}

/* Function to display stack elements from top to bottom.
 * Receive: Type parameter ElementType
 *          stack s
 * Output:  Elements of s from top to bottom
 ***************************************************************/

template <typename ElementType>
void Dump(stack<ElementType> s)
{
  while (!s.empty())
  {
    cout << s.top() << "  ";
    s.pop();
  }
  cout << endl;
}
```

EXECUTION:

```
Stack #0: 3   2   1

Stack #1: 20   10

Stack #2: 30

Stack #3: 60   50
```

SORT 2: SUPPLYING A "LESS-THAN" FUNCTION TO USE IN COMPARING ELEMENTS. The `sort` algorithm may have a third parameter which is a `bool` less-than function. Fig. 7.7 illustrates.

FIGURE 7.7   sort ALGORITHM—VERSION 3

```
#include <iostream>
#include <vector>
#include <deque>
#include <algorithm>
using namespace std;

template <typename Container>
void Display(ostream & out, const Container & c);

// Less-than functions

bool IntLessThan(int a, int b)
{ return a > b; }

bool DubLessThan(double a, double b)
{ return a > b; }

int main()
{
  int ints[] = {555, 33, 444, 22, 222, 777, 1, 66};
  vector<int> v(ints, ints + 5);
  sort(v.begin(), v.end(), IntLessThan);
  cout << "\nSorted list of integers:\n";
  Display(cout, v);

  double dubs[] = {55.5, 3.3, 44.4, 2.2, 22.2, 77.7, 0.1};
  deque<double> d(dubs, dubs + 7);

  sort(d.begin(), d.end(), DubLessThan);
  cout << "\nSorted list of doubles:\n";
  Display(cout, d);
}

// Add the definition of Display() template here
```

EXECUTION

```
Sorted list of integers:
555   444   222   33   22

Sorted list of doubles:
77.7   55.5   44.4   22.2   3.3   2.2   0.1
```

A Sample of STL Algorithms

Like `sort()`, most of the algorithms in the Standard Template Library are function templates designed to operate on *a sequence of elements*, rather than on a specific container. And most of them designate a sequence by using two iterators:[4]

> ▸ An iterator positioned at the first element in the sequence
> ▸ An iterator positioned *after* the last element in the sequence

In the descriptions that follow, we will refer to these two iterators as *begin, begin1, begin2, ...* and *end, end1, end2, ...* respectively.

The Standard Template Library provides over 80 algorithm templates. An in-depth examination of these algorithms is beyond the scope of this text, but Table 7.2 gives a sample of what is available.

Algorithm	Description
`binary_search(`*begin*`,`*end*`,`*value*`)`	Return `true` if *value* is in the sorted sequence; if not present, return `false`
`find(`*begin*`,`*end*`,`*value*`)`	Return an iterator to position of *value* in the unsorted sequence; if not present, return *end*
`search(`*begin1*`,`*end1*`,`*begin2*`,`*end2*`)`	Find second sequence in the first sequence; if not present, return *end1*
`copy(`*begin*`,`*end*`,`*con*`);`	Copy a sequence into a container *con*
`count(`*begin*`,`*end*`,`*value*`)`	Return how many times *value* occurs in the sequence
`equal(`*begin1*`,`*end1*`,`*begin2*`)`	Return `true` if two sequences are identical, `false` otherwise
`fill(`*begin*`,`*end*`,`*value*`);`	Assign *value* to every element in the sequence
`for_each(`*begin*`,`*end*`,`*F*`);`	Apply function *F* to every element in the sequence
`lower_bound(`*begin*`,`*end*`,`*value*`)`	Return an iterator to the *first* position at which *value* can be inserted and the sequence remain sorted
`upper_bound(`*begin*`,`*end*`,`*value*`)`	Return an iterator to the *last* position at which *value* can be inserted and the sequence remains sorted

TABLE 7.2   SOME STL ALGORITHMS   *(Continued)*

---

[4]If an entire container were passed to an algorithm, then the algorithm would affect the entire container. Passing iterators to the beginning and end of the sequence allows an algorithm to act on a subset of the container's elements.

Algorithm	Description
max_element(*begin*, *end*)	Return an iterator to the maximum value in the sequence
min_element(*begin*, *end*)	Return an iterator to the minimum value in the sequence
merge (*begin1*, *end1*, *begin2*, *end2*, *con*);	Merge the first sequence with the second and put the resulting sequence in container *con*
next_permutation(*begin*, *end*);	Shuffle the sequence to its next permutation, and return true (If there is none, return false)
prev_permutation(*begin*, *end*);	Shuffle the sequence to its previous permutation, and return true (If there is none, return false)
random_shuffle(*begin*, *end*);	Shuffle the values in the sequence randomly
replace(*begin*, *end*, *old*, *new*);	In the sequence, replace each value *old* with *new*
reverse(*begin*, *end*);	Reverse the order of the values in the sequence
Set Algorithms:	
includes (*begin*, *end*, *begin2*, *end2*)	Return true if first sequence is contained in the second, false otherwise
	Put in container *con* the:
set_union (*begin1*, *end1*, *begin2*, *end2*, *con*);	union
set_intersection (*begin1*, *end1*, *begin2*, *end2*, *con*);	intersection
set_difference (*begin1*, *end1*, *begin2*, *end2*, *con*);	difference
set_symmetric_diference (*begin1*, *end1*, *begin2*, *end2*, *con*);	symmetric difference of the first sequence with the second
sort(*begin*, *end*);	Sort the sequence into ascending order
unique(*begin*, *end*);	In the sequence, replace any consecutive occurrences of the same value with one instance of that value

TABLE 7.2   *Continued*

ALGORITHMS FROM THE `<numeric>` LIBRARY

The `<numeric>` library contains function templates that operate on sequential containers in much the same manner as those in `<algorithm>`. As the library's name suggests, however, these are intended to be used with numeric sequences (for

Algorithm	Description
`accumulate(begin, end, init)`	Return the sum of the values in the sequence; `init` is the initial value for the sum (e.g., 0 for integers, 0.0 for reals)
`inner_product` `(begin1, end1, begin2, init)`	Return the inner product of the first sequence with the second; `init` is the initial value for this inner product
`partial_sum(begin, end, con);`	Put in container *con* the sequence of partial sums of the sequence
`adjacent_difference` `(begin, end, con);`	Put in container *con* the sequence of differences of adjacent elements in the sequence

TABLE 7.3   NUMERIC ALGORITHMS

example, with `valarrays` as described in Sect. 6.8. Table 7.3 lists these numeric algorithms. As in the descriptions for STL algorithms, *begin, begin1, begin2, ...* refer to iterators positioned at the first element of the sequence and *end, end1, end2, ...,* refer to iterators positioned just after the sequence's last element.

EXAMPLE: JUDGING FIGURE SKATING
In the judging of certain competitions, a performer's score is obtained by throwing out the high and low scores given by judges in order to reduce the effect of bias, and then averaging the remaining scores. For example, suppose that a particular figure skater received the following set of scores (each in the range 0 through 10) from the international judges:

$$9.1, 8.8, 9.2, 7.9, 4.5, 8.1, 8.6, 9.9, 7.6, 7.9$$

To determine her score, the low score (4.5) and the high score (9.9) are to be thrown out and the average of the remaining scores computed.

Suppose we store these scores in a `vector<double>` object named `scores`. Recall that `scores.begin()` and `scores.end()` are iterators that point to the first element of `scores` and just after `scores`' last element:

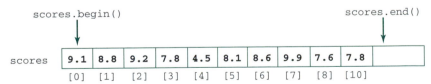

We can use the STL `min_element` algorithm to find the minimum score,

```
vector<double>::iterator it =
            min_element(scores.begin(), scores.end());
```

and then remove it with the `scores` member function `erase()`:

```
scores.erase(it);
```

More simply, we can do this in one step without introducing the iterator `it`:

```
scores.erase(min_element(scores.begin(), scores.end()));
```

We can remove the maximum score in a similar manner:

```
scores.erase(max_element(scores.begin(), scores.end()));
```

4.5 and 9.9 have been erased from `scores`, the remaining values have been shifted to the left to fill their spaces, and `scores.size()` and `scores.end()` have been updated:

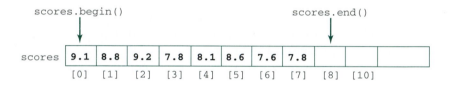

The resulting `vector` can now be passed to the following function `Mean`, which finds the mean of the values in a `vector<double>`, using the `accumulate()` algorithm from the `<numeric>` library:

```
#include<numeric>
using namespace std;

/* Mean finds the mean value in a vector<double>.
 *
 * Receive:       vec, a vector<double>
 * Precondition: vec is not empty
 * Return:        The mean of the values in vec
 ************************************************/

double Mean(const vector<double> & vec)
{
  if (vec.size() > 0)
    return
       accumulate(vec.begin(), vec.end(), 0.0) / vec.size();
  // else
  cerr << "\n***Mean: empty vector received!\n";
  return 0.0;
}
```

✔ Quick Quiz 7.5

1. The Standard Template Library contains more than 80 function templates known as generic _____ .

2. A program that uses the STL algorithms must contain the directive `#include` _____ .

3. Most of the STL algorithms operate on specific containers. (True or false)

4. Most of the STL algorithms designate sequences by two iterators. Where in the sequence are these iterators positioned?

5. The library _____ contains algorithms designed for processing sequences of numbers.

7.6 PROVING ALGORITHMS CORRECT

In our discussion of program verification and validation in Chap. 1, we noted that in some mission-critical applications such as defense systems and spacecraft guidance systems, program errors can be disastrous and special effort is needed to find and correct them. In such situations, simply running a program or system of programs with various sets of test data may not be sufficient because *testing can show only the presence of errors, not their absence*. A deductive proof of a program's correctness may be required to show that it will produce the correct results (assuming no system malfunction). In this section we describe some of the techniques used in such correctness proofs.

To prove that an algorithm for solving a given problem is correct, we must prove deductively that the steps of the algorithm correctly process the input given in the problem's specification so that the required output is obtained. Thus a **proof of correctness** of an algorithm begins with an **assertion** (assumption) $\mathcal{I}$ about its input data, also called a **precondition**, and an assertion (conclusion) $\mathcal{O}$ about its output, also called a **postcondition**. It then provides a logical argument demonstrating that $\mathcal{O}$ follows from $\mathcal{I}$; that is, it is a proof of the theorem

$$\mathcal{I} \Rightarrow \mathcal{O} \quad (\text{``} \mathcal{I} \text{ implies } \mathcal{O} \text{''})$$

Theorem: Given precondition $\mathcal{I}$.

After algorithm is executed, the postcondition $\mathcal{O}$ holds.

EXAMPLE: CALCULATING THE MEAN

To illustrate, consider the following algorithm to find the mean of a set of numbers stored in an array:

ALGORITHM TO CALCULATE MEAN

```
/*   Algorithm to find the mean of n real numbers.
     Receive:   An integer n ≥ 1 and an array x[0], . . . , x[n−1]
                of real numbers
     Return:    The mean of x [0], . . . , x[n−1]
     ------------------------------------------------------------------*/
```

1. Initialize *sum* to 0.

2. Initialize index variable *i* to 0.

3. While $i < n$ do the following:

    a. Add $x[i]$ to *sum*.
    b. Increment *i* by 1.

4. Calculate and return *mean* = *sum* / *n*.

Here the input assertion might be stated as

$\mathcal{I}$: Input consists of an integer $n \geq 1$ and an array *x* of *n* real numbers.

and the output assertion as

$\mathcal{O}$: The algorithm terminates, and when it does, the value of the variable *mean* is the mean (average) of $x[0], \ldots, x[n-1]$.

To demonstrate that the postcondition $\mathcal{O}$ follows from the precondition $\mathcal{I}$, one usually introduces, at several points in the algorithm, intermediate assertions about the state of processing when execution reaches these points. For the preceding algorithm we might use an additional intermediate assertion at the bottom of the while loop that will be true each time execution reaches this point. Such an assertion is called a ***loop invariant***:

$\mathcal{I}$: Input consists of an integer $n \geq 1$ and an array *x* of *n* real numbers.

1. Initialize *sum* to 0.

2. Initialize index variable *i* to 0.

3. While $i < n$ do the following:

    a. Add $x[i]$ to *sum*.
    b. Increment *i* by 1.

$\mathcal{A}$: The value of *sum* is the sum of the first *i* elements of array *x* and *i* is the number of times execution has reached this point.

4. Calculate and return *mean* = *sum* / *n*.

$\mathcal{O}$: The algorithm terminates, and when it does, the value of the variable *mean* is the mean (average) of $X[0], \ldots, X[n-1]$.

The proof then consists of showing that assertion $\mathcal{A}$ follows from the input assertion $\mathcal{I}$ and then showing that the output assertion $\mathcal{O}$ follows from $\mathcal{A}$.

Mathematical induction can be used to establish the loop invariant $\mathcal{A}$. To see this, suppose we let *k* denote the number of times that execution has reached the bottom of the loop, and let i_k and sum_k denote the values of *i* and *sum*, respectively, at this time. When $k = 1$, that is, on the first pass through the loop, *sum* will be equal to $x[0]$ since it was initially 0 (Step 1), *i* has the value 0, and $x[i]$ has been added to *sum* (Step 3a). The value of *i* will be 1 since it was initially 0 (Step 2) and has been incremented by 1 (Step 3b). Thus *i* and *sum* have the values asserted in $\mathcal{A}$ when $k = 1$.

Now assume that when execution reaches the bottom of the loop for the *k*th time, the loop invariant $\mathcal{A}$ holds:

$$sum_k = x[0] + \cdots + x[k-1] \text{ and } i_k = k$$

We must prove that $\mathcal{A}$ is also true when execution continues through the loop for the $k+1$-st time, that is,

$$sum_{k+1} = x[0] + \cdots + x[k] \text{ and } i_{k+1} = k + 1$$

On this $k+1$-st pass through the loop, we will have

$$
\begin{aligned}
sum_{k+1} &= sum_k + x[k] \text{ (Step 3a)} \\
&= x[0] + \cdots + x[k-1] + x[k] \text{ (Induction assumption)}
\end{aligned}
$$

and the value of i will be incremented by 1 so that

$$
\begin{aligned}
i_{k+1} &= i_k + 1 \text{ (Step 3b)} \\
&= k + 1 \text{ (Induction assumption)}
\end{aligned}
$$

thus i will have the correct value also.

It now follows by induction that each time execution reaches the bottom of the loop, i and sum will have the values asserted in the loop invariant $\mathcal{A}$. In particular, after the nth pass through the loop, sum will equal $x[0] + \cdots + x[n-1]$, and i will be equal to n.

Since i will thus eventually have the value n, the boolean expression $i < n$ that controls repetition will become false, and the while loop will terminate. Execution will then continue with statement 4 in the algorithm. This statement correctly calculates the mean of the array elements, and execution will reach the end of the algorithm. Thus the output assertion is established and the correctness proof is complete; we have proved

Theorem:
Given an integer $n > 1$ and an array x of n real numbers.
When Algorithm to Calculate Mean is executed, it terminates, and when it does, *mean* is the mean of $x[0], \ldots, x[n-1]$.

EXAMPLE: RECURSIVE POWER FUNCTION

Mathematical induction is also used to prove the correctness of recursive algorithms, since by its very nature, recursion involves an inductive step. As an illustration, consider the recursive power function of Sec. 7.1:

```
/* Power() calculates x to the nth power recursively.
 *
 *    Receive: Real number x and nonnegative integer n
 *    Return:  x to the nth power
 **************************************************/

double Power(double x, unsigned n)
{
  if (n == 0)
    return 1.0;                 // anchor case
  // else
  return Power(x, n - 1) * x;   // inductive step (n > 0)
}
```

Here the input and output assertions are

$\mathcal{I}$: Input consists of a real number x and a nonnegative integer n.

$\mathcal{O}$: Execution of the function terminates, and when it does, the value returned by the function is x^n.

We can use mathematical induction on n to show that the output assertion $\mathcal{O}$ follows from the input assertion $\mathcal{I}$. If n is 0, the anchor statement

```
return 1.0;
```

is executed immediately, so that execution terminates and the correct value 1.0 is returned for x^0. Now assume that for n = k, execution terminates and returns the correct value for x^n. When it is called with n = k + 1, the inductive step

```
return x * Power(x, n-1)
```

is executed. The value of n-1 is k, and thus by the induction assumption, the function call Power(x, n-1) terminates and returns the correct value of x^k. It follows that the function call with n = k+1 terminates and returns the value x * x^k = x^{k+1}, which is the correct value of x^n. We have thus established that in all cases, the output assertion follows from the input assertion.

SUMMARY

These examples of correctness proof have been rather informal. They could be formalized, however, by using some special notation to state the assertions (such as the predicate calculus or some other formal notation) and a formal deductive system that spells out the rules that can be used to reason from one assertion to the next. For example, a rule governing an assignment statement S of the form $v = e$ might be stated symbolically as

$$P \xrightarrow{\;\;S\;\;} \{Q = P(v,e)\}$$

an abbreviation for "If *precondition* P holds before an assignment statement S of the form $v = e$ is executed, then the *postcondition* Q is obtained from P by replacing each occurrence of the variable v by the expression e." Such formalization is necessary in the design of mechanized "theorem provers," and we leave it to more advanced courses in theoretical computer science where it more properly belongs.

Also, these proofs were quite simple in that only one intermediate assertion $\mathcal{A}$ was used in the first example and none in the second. The form of the first proof thus was

$$\mathcal{I} \Rightarrow \mathcal{A} \Rightarrow \mathcal{O}$$

that is, the input assertion $\mathcal{I}$ implies the intermediate assertion $\mathcal{A}$, and $\mathcal{A}$ implies the output assertion $\mathcal{O}$. For more complex algorithms it is usually necessary to introduce several intermediate assertions $\mathcal{A}_1, \mathcal{A}_2, \ldots, \mathcal{A}_n$. The algorithm/program is broken down into small segments, each having one of the $\mathcal{A}_i$ (or $\mathcal{I}$) as a precondition and $\mathcal{A}_{i+1}$ (or $\mathcal{O}$) as a postcondition:

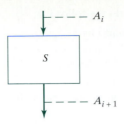

One must show that A_{i+1} follows logically from A_i for each $i = 1, \ldots, n-1$, and thus the structure of the correctness proof is

$$\mathcal{I} \Rightarrow A_1 \Rightarrow A_2 \Rightarrow \ldots \Rightarrow A_n \Rightarrow \mathcal{O}$$

If one of these program segments is or contains a selection structure, there may be many paths that execution may follow from A_i to A_{i+1}, and because it is necessary to examine *all* such paths, the correctness proof can become quite complex.

Algorithm/program unit verification is an important part of program development, and ideally, the correctness of each program unit should be formally proved. In practice, however, the time and effort required to write out carefully and completely all the details of a correctness proof of a complicated algorithm are usually prohibitive. Nevertheless, it is still a good programming practice to formulate the major assertions that would be used in a correctness proof and then "walk through" the algorithm/program unit, tracing each possible execution path, following the pattern of a deductive proof. This is a more formal and systematic way of desk checking that every good programmer uses in testing algorithms and programs. Although it does not ensure that the algorithm/program unit is absolutely correct, it does increase one's understanding of the algorithm/program unit and one's confidence in its correctness, and it may uncover logical errors that might otherwise go undetected.

✍ EXERCISES 7.6

1. Consider the following algorithm with precondition $\mathcal{I}$, intermediate assertion $\mathcal{A}$, and postcondition $\mathcal{O}$:

   ScanAndCount

   /*   Algorithm to find and display a *count* of the elements in array
        x that exceed a given value *cutoff*.

       Receive: Integer *n*, an array *x* of *n* real numbers,
                     and a real number *cutoff*

       Output: *count*

   --*/

   $\mathcal{I}$:   Input consists of an integer $n \geq 1$, an array *x* of *n* real numbers, and a real number *cutoff*.

   1. Initialize *count* to 0.
   2. Initialize *i* to 0.

3. While $i < n$ do the following:

    a. Increment i by 1.

    b. If $x[i] > cutoff$

        Add 1 to *count*.

$\mathcal{A}$:   The value of i is the number of times execution has reached this point, and *count* is the number of array elements among $x[0], \ldots x[i-1]$ that are greater than *cutoff*.

4. Display *count*.

$\mathcal{O}$:   The algorithm terminates, and when it does, the value of the variable *count* is the number of elements in array x that are greater than *cutoff*.

Using the given input, intermediate, and output assertions, prove the correctness of this algorithm. Note that on each pass through the loop there are two possible paths that execution may follow.

2. Write a nonrecursive version of function `Power()` and prove its correctness.

3. Give an algorithm that finds and returns the largest element in an array x of n elements and prove its correctness.

4. Write a recursive function for calculating $n!$, the factorial of n (see Sec. 7.1), and prove its correctness.

5. Use mathematical induction to prove that the minimum number of moves required to solve the Towers of Hanoi puzzle with n disks is $2^n - 1$. (See Sec. 7.2.)

☞ PROGRAMMING POINTERS

1. In a recursive function, one must ensure that an anchor step will eventually be reached or infinite recursion (resulting in stack overflow) will result.

2. Beware of recursive functions that produce repeated calls to the function with the same argument.

3. *Direct recursion* refers to a function calling itself directly. Indirect recursion occurs when a function calls other functions, and some chain of function calls eventually results in a call to the first function again.

4. Each recursive call of a function causes a new activation record to be pushed onto the run-time stack.

5. Program testing can only show the *presence* of errors, not the *absence* of errors.

 ## ADT TIPS

1. The two main criteria for evaluating an algorithm's efficiency are *space utilization* and *time efficiency*.

2. Big-Oh notation is commonly used to represent an algorithm's efficiency.

3. Algorithm efficiency is usually measured for its *worst-case* performance or, where feasible, its *average-case* performance.

4. Algorithms with exponential complexity are practical only for solving problems with few inputs.

5. If a problem can be solved either recursively or nonrecursively with little difference in effort, it is usually better to use the nonrecursive version.

6. Use standard algorithms to implement operations instead of reinventing the wheel.

PROGRAMMING PROBLEMS

1. Write a test driver for the recursive digit-counting function in Exercise 20.

2. Write a test driver for the nonrecursive digit-counting function in Exercise 21.

3. Write a test driver for the recursive `PrintReverse()` function in Exercise 22.

4. Write a test driver for the nonrecursive `PrintReverse()` function in Exercise 23.

5. Write a test driver for the recursive exponentiation function in Exercise 24.

6. Write a test driver for the recursive reverse-integer function in Exercise 25.

7. Write a test driver for the recursive `ReverseArray()` function in Exercise 26.

8. Write a test driver for the recursive `SumArray()` function in Exercise 27.

9. Write a test driver for the recursive `Location()` function in Exercise 28.

10. Write and test a recursive function for the string-reversal algorithm in Exercise 29.

11. Write and test a nonrecursive function for the string-reversal algorithm in Exercise 30.

12. Write a test driver for the recursive palindrome-checking function in Exercise 31.

13. Write a test driver for the recursive GCD function in Exercise 32.

14. Write a test driver for the nonrecursive GCD function in Exercise 33.

15. Write a test driver for the recursive binomial-coefficient function in Exercise 34.

16. Write a program to compare the computing times of the recursive and nonrecursive functions for calculating binomial coefficients in Exercises 34 and 35.

17. Write a test driver for one of the functions in Exercises 11–15. Add output statements to the function to trace its actions as it executes. For example, the trace displayed for `F(21)` for the function `F()` in Exercise 13 should have a form like

```
F(21) = 1 + F(10)
   F(10) = 1 + F(5)
      F(5) = 1 + F(2)
         F(2) = 1 + F(1)
            F(1) returns 0
         F(2) returns 1
      F(5) returns 2
   F(10) returns 3
F(21) returns 4
```

where the indentation level reflects the depth of the recursion. (*Hint:* This can be accomplished by using a global or static variable `level` that is incremented when the function is entered and decremented when it is exited.)

18. Modify the test driver for `PrintReverse()` in Prob. 3 by adding output statements to the function to trace its actions as it executes. For example, the trace displayed for the function call `PrintReverse(9254)` should have a form like

```
PrintReverse(9254):   Output 4 — PrintReverse(925)
  PrintReverse(925):   Output 5 — PrintReverse(92)
    PrintReverse(92):   Output 2 — PrintReverse(9)
      PrintReverse(9):   Output 9 and \n
      PrintReverse(9) returns
    PrintReverse(92) returns
  PrintReverse(925) returns
PrintReverse(9254) returns
```

where the indentation level reflects the depth of the recursion. (See the hint in Prob. 17.)

19. Write a recursive function that displays the lyrics of the song *Bingo*:

> Verse 1: There was a farmer had a dog,
>
>   And Bingo was his name-o.
>
>   B-I-N-G-O!
>
>   B-I-N-G-O!
>
>   B-I-N-G-O!
>
>   And Bingo was his name-o!
>
> Verse 2: Same as verse 1, but lines 3, 4, and 5 are
>
>   (Clap)-I-N-G-O!
>
> Verse 3: Same as verse 1, but lines 3, 4, and 5 are
>
>   (Clap, clap)-N-G-O!
>
> Verse 4: Same as verse 1, but lines 3, 4, and 5 are
>
>   (Clap, clap, clap)-G-O!
>
> Verse 5: Same as verse 1, but lines 3, 4, and 5 are
>
>   (Clap, clap, clap, clap)-O!
>
> Verse 6: Same as verse 1, but lines 3, 4, and 5 are
>
>   (Clap, clap, clap, clap, clap)

Also write a driver program to test your function.

20. Write a recursive function that displays a nonnegative integer with commas in the correct locations. For example, it should display 20131 as 20,131. Also write a driver program to test your function.

21. Consider a square grid, some of whose cells are empty and others contain an asterisk. Define two asterisks to be *contiguous* if they are adjacent to each other in the same row or in the same column. Now suppose we define a *blob* as follows:

a. A blob contains at least one asterisk.
b. If an asterisk is in a blob, then so is any asterisk that is contiguous to it.
c. If a blob has more than two asterisks, then each asterisk in it is contiguous to at least one other asterisk in the blob.

For example, there are four blobs in the partial grid

*			*	*		*		*	*
						*		*	*

seven blobs in

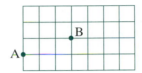

and only one in

Write a program that uses a recursive function to count the number of blobs in a square grid. Input to the program should consist of the locations of the asterisks in the grid, and the program should display the grid and the blob count.

22. Consider a network of streets laid out in a rectangular grid, for example

In a *northeast path* from one point in the grid to another, one may walk only to the north (up) and to the east (right). For example, there are four northeast paths from A to B in the preceding grid:

Write a program that uses a recursive function to count the number of northeast paths from one point to another in a rectangular grid.

23. In Sec. 4.1 we considered the problem of converting an integer from base-ten to base-two and we used a stack to store the binary digits so that they could be displayed in the correct order. Write a recursive function to accomplish this conversion without using a stack.

24. Write a recursive function to find the prime factorization of an integer, and display these prime factors in descending order. (See Programming Problem 4 of Chap. 4.) Write a driver program to test your function.

25. Develop a recursive function to generate all of the $n!$ permutations of the set $\{1, 2, \ldots, n\}$. (*Hint :* The permutations of $\{1, 2, \ldots, k\}$ can be obtained by considering each permutation of $\{1, 2, \ldots, k - 1\}$ as an ordered list and inserting k into each of the k possible positions in this list, including at the front and at the rear.) For example, the permutations of $\{1, 2\}$ are $(1, 2)$ and $(2, 1)$. Inserting 3 into each of the three possible positions of the first permutation yields the permutations $(3, 1, 2)$, $(1, 3, 2)$, and $(1, 2, 3)$ of $\{1, 2, 3\}$, and using the second permutation gives $(3, 2, 1)$, $(2, 3, 1)$, and $(2, 1, 3)$. Write a program to test your function.

26. Modify the program in Fig. 7.2 so that it displays a diagram of each move rather than a verbal description.

27. Write a program that parses simple boolean expressions using the syntax rules preceding Exercise 12.

28. By adding the production

> *AssignmentExpression → letter = expression*

at the beginning of the list of syntax rules for simplified expressions in this section, we obtain a list of syntax rules for simplified assignment expressions. Extend the program of Fig. 7.3 so that it will parse such assignment expressions.

29. Write a program that reads lines of input, each of which is a (perhaps invalid) C++ statement, and that strips each line of all C++ comments. However, the structure of your program is restricted as follows:

- ▶ The only repetition structure allowed is a loop for reading the input that stops when the end of input occurs. All other repetition must be carried out by using recursion.

- ▶ The characters must be read one at a time, and looking at the next character in the input buffer is not allowed.

30. Write a program that reads a string consisting of only parentheses and that determines whether the parentheses are balanced, as specified by the syntax rules preceding Exercise 16.

31. Proceed as in Problem 30, but design the program to read any string, ignoring all characters other than parentheses.

In Problems 32–37, use the standard C++ containers and algorithms where possible to do the required processing.

32. The investment company of Pickum & Loozem has been recording the trading price of a particular stock over a 15-day period. Write a program that reads these prices and stores them in a sequential container and then sorts them into increasing order. The program should find and display

a. The trading range (the lowest and the highest prices recorded) .
b. A sequence that shows how much the price rose or fell each day.

33. The Rinky Dooflingy Company records the number of cases of dooflingies produced each day over a four-week period. Write a program that reads these production levels and stores them in a container. The program should then find and display

a. The lowest, highest, and average daily production level.
b. A sequence that shows how much the production level rose or fell each day.
c. A sequence that shows for each day the total number of dooflingies produced up to and including that day.

34. The Rinky Dooflingy Company maintains two warehouses, one in Chicago and one in Detroit, each of which stocks at most 25 different items. Write a program that first reads the product numbers of items stored in the Chicago warehouse and stores them in a sequential container Chicago, and then repeats this for the items stored in the Detroit warehouse, storing these product numbers in a sequential container Detroit. The program should then find and display the *intersection* of these two sequences of numbers, that is, the collection of product numbers common to both sequences.

35. Repeat Problem 34 but find and display the *union* of the two sequences, that is, the collection of product numbers that are elements of at least one of the sequences of numbers.

36. The Rinky Dooflingy Company manufactures different kinds of dooflingies, each identified by a product number. Write a program that reads product numbers and prices, and stores these values in a container. The program should then allow the user to select one of the following options:

 a. Retrieve and display the price of a product whose number is entered by the user.
 b. Determine how many products have a given price.
 c. Find all products whose number is the same as that of some other product and remove all but one of them.
 d. Sort the products so the product numbers are in ascending order.
 e. Print a table displaying the product number and the price of each item. (*Suggestion:* Define a `Product` class where two of its operations are overloaded `==` and `<` operators so that standard algorithms can be used on the container of `Product` objects.)

37. a. Write functions to calculate the mean, variance, and standard deviation of the values stored in a sequential container. (See the grading-on-the-curve program in Programming Problem 2 at the end of Chap. 2 for definitions of these quantities.)

 b. Write a driver program to test your functions.
 c. Use your functions in a program for the grading-on-the-curve problem.

Chapter 8

LISTS

Chapter Contents

Stacks, queues, and deques, considered in the preceding chapters, are special kinds of lists. Each of these ADTs is a sequence of data items, and the basic operations are insertion and deletion. For these structures, however, insertion and deletion are restricted to the ends of the list. But no such limitations are imposed on a general list, as items may be inserted and/or deleted at any point in the list. In this chapter we consider in more detail these general lists and several possible implementations.

8.1 SEQUENTIAL STORAGE IMPLEMENTATION OF LISTS

Lists of various kinds are common in everyday life. There are grocery lists, deans' lists, class lists, appointment lists, mailing lists, lists of seats (on TransFryslan Airlines), and even lists of lists like this one! The features that these examples have in common motivate the following definition of a list.

As an abstract data type, a **list** is a finite sequence (possibly empty) of elements. Although the basic operations performed on lists vary with each application, they usually include those listed in the following specification:

385

ADT LIST

Collection of Data Elements:

A finite sequence (ordered set) of data items.

Basic Operations:

Construction: Create an empty list.
Empty: Check if the list is empty.
Traverse: Go through the list or a part of it, accessing and processing the elements in order.
Insert: Add an item at any point in the list.
Delete: Remove an item from the list at any point in the list.

STORAGE STRUCTURE

Because lists, like stacks and queues, are sequences of data items, it would seem natural once again to use an array or a `vector` as the basic storage structure. This is indeed a common method of implementing lists and is the one that we used earlier. It is characterized by the property that successive list elements are stored in consecutive array or `vector` locations: the first list element in location 0, the second list element in location 1, and so on:

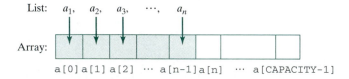

We will refer to this implementation of a list as the **sequential-storage** implementation.

IMPLEMENTING THE OPERATIONS

The data members of a `List` class would include an array member `myArray` or a `vector` member `myVector` to store the list elements (and a `mySize` member to store the length (n) of the list if we're using an array). Implementing the basic operations is then straightforward.

CONSTRUCTION. If we are using an array to store the list elements, we can let the compiler allocate memory for it and our constructor need only set `mySize` to 0.[1] For a `vector`, we can simply let its constructor do the work.

EMPTY. For this, we need only check if `mySize` is 0. If a `vector` is being used to store the list elements, we need only return the value of `myVector.empty()`.

TRAVERSE. Lists are easily traversed using a loop in which the array or `vector` index varies:

[1]If we are using a *run-time array*, we must take care of memory allocation (see Sec. 8.5).

```
for (int i = 0; i < mySize; i++)
   Process(myArray[i]);
```

For comparison with linked-list traversal described in the next section, we will also write this as an equivalent `while` loop:

```
int i = 0;
while (i < mySize)
{
   Process(myArray[i]);
   i++;
}
```

For a `vector`, we need only change the preceding to

```
for (int i = 0; i < myVector.size(); i++)
   Process(myVector[i]);
```

and modify the `while` loop in the obvious way.

INSERT.   Implementing the insertion operation is somewhat more complicated. For example, suppose we wish to insert the new value 56 after the element 48 in the list of integers

$$23, 25, 34, 48, 61, 79, 82, 89, 91, 99$$

to produce the new list

$$23, 25, 34, 48, 56, 61, 79, 82, 89, 91, 99$$

Because the fixed size of the array used as the basic storage structure limits the size of the list, it may not be possible to insert a new item into a list because there is no room in the array for it and it may be necessary to signal an error. This problem is not as serious for a `vector` data member since its capacity can increase when necessary until available memory is exhausted.

Another complication arises from the fact that in this implementation, list elements are stored in consecutive positions of the array or `vector`. Consequently, to insert a new item, it usually is necessary to move array elements to make room for it. For example, for the insertion operation just described, the array elements in positions 4 through 9 must first be shifted into positions 5 through 10 before the new element can be inserted at position 4:

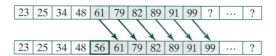

Thus a function for inserting `item` into the array (or `vector`) data member at location `pos` must contain code to do this shifting of array (or `vector`) elements:

```
// Shift array elements right to make room for item
for (int i = mySize; i > pos; i--)
   myArray[i] = myArray[i - 1];

// Insert item at position pos and increase list size
myArray[pos] = item;
mySize++;
```

The efficiency of an insert function obviously depends on the number of array elements that must be shifted to make room for the new element, that is, on the number of times that the body of the `for` loop is executed. In the worst case, the new item must be inserted at the beginning of the list, which requires shifting all of the array elements. In the average case, one-half of the array elements must be shifted to make room for a new item. Thus, for a list of size n, it follows that both the worst-case and the average-case computing times for an insert function are $O(n)$. The best case occurs when the new item is inserted at the end of the list. Because no array elements need to be shifted in this case (so the body of the `for` loop is never executed), the computing time does not depend on the size of the list. Insertions can be carried out in constant time; therefore, the best-case complexity is $O(1)$.

If the order in which the elements appear in a list is not important, then new items can be inserted at any convenient location in the list; in particular, they may always be inserted at the end of the list. For such lists, therefore, insertions can always be carried out in constant time. Note that for these lists, the insertion operation is nothing more than the `push_back` operation for `vectors`.

DELETE.   Implementing the delete operation also requires shifting array elements if list elements are to be stored in consecutive array (or `vector`) locations. For example, to delete the second item in the list

$$23, 25, 34, 48, 56, 61, 79, 82, 89, 91, 99$$

we must shift the elements in positions 2 through 10 into locations 1 through 9 to "close the gap" in the array (or `vector`):

A function for deleting the element in the array (or `vector`) data member at location `pos` must therefore contain code to do this shifting of elements:

```
// Shift array elements left to close the gap
for (int i = pos; i < mySize - 1; i++)
   myArray[i] = myArray[i + 1];

// Decrease list size
mySize--;
```

The computing time of such a function is easily seen to be the same as that of an insert function: $O(n)$ in the worst and average cases and $O(1)$ in the best case.

Because insertion and deletion in this sequential storage implementation may require shifting many array elements, these operations may be quite slow. Thus, although this implementation is adequate for **static lists**, it may not be appropriate for **dynamic lists** in which a large number of insertions and deletions are performed. In applications in which it is necessary to insert and/or delete items at any position in the list, a better implementation is to use a linked list, as described in the following sections.

✔ Quick Quiz 8.1

1. Define list as an ADT.

2. In the sequential-storage implementation of a list, insertion in the worst and average case has complexity $O(\underline{\quad})$.

3. In the sequential-storage implementation of a list, deletion in the worst and average has complexity $O(\underline{\quad})$.

4. The sequential-storage implementation of a list works well for dynamic lists. (True or false)

✎ EXERCISES 8.1

1. Explain why the best-, worst-, and average-case computing times of a delete function are $O(1)$, $O(n)$, and $O(n)$, respectively.

Suppose we modify the sequential-storage implementation to allow "holes" in the array (or vector); that is, the list elements need not be stored in consecutive locations, but only stored in order. When a list element is deleted, we simply store some special value in that location to indicate that it does not contain a list element. (For example, for a list of test scores, we might use a negative value.) Assuming the data members `myArray` (or `myVector`) and `mySize` (for an array), write member functions for the operations in Exercises 2–4.

2. Traverse the list and calculate the mean score.

3. Delete an element; also determine its computing time.

4. Insert an element; also determine its computing time.

5. A *polynomial of degree n* has the form

$$a_0 + a_1x + a_2x^2 + \cdots + a_nx^n$$

where $a_0, a_1, \ldots, a_n$ are numeric constants called the *coefficients* of the polynomial and $a_n \neq 0$. For example

$$1 + 3x - 7x^3 + 5x^4$$

is a polynomial of degree 4 with integer coefficients 1, 3, 0, −7, and 5. One common implementation of a polynomial stores the degree of the polynomial and the list of coefficients.

   a. Design a `Polynomial` class whose data members are an integer for the degree and an array for the list of coefficients and with basic operations of input, output (using the usual mathematical format with x^n written as x↑n or x^n), addition, and multiplication. You should also write a program to test your class as instructed in Programming Problem 1 at the end of this chapter.

b. Determine the complexity of the addition function.

c. Determine the complexity of the multiplication function.

8.2   INTRODUCTION TO LINKED LISTS

A list is a sequence of data items, which means that there is an order associated with the elements in the list: It has a first element, a second element, and so on. Thus any implementation of this ADT must incorporate a method for specifying this order. In the sequential-storage implementation considered in the preceding section, this ordering of list elements is given *implicitly* by the natural ordering of the array elements, since the first element is stored in the first position of the array, the second list element in the second position, and so on. It is this implicit specification of the ordering of the list elements that necessitates shifting them in the array when items are inserted or deleted, causing the inefficiency of the sequential-storage implementation for dynamic lists (those that change frequently due to insertions and deletions). In this section we look at an alternative way to implement lists in which this inefficiency is eliminated by specifying *explicitly* the ordering of the list elements.

WHAT ARE THEY?

In any structure used to store the elements of a list, it must be possible to perform at least the following operations if the ordering of the list elements is to be preserved:

▸ Locate the first element

▸ Given the location of any list element, find its successor

▸ Locate the end of the list

For the sequential-storage implementation described in the preceding section, it is the strict manner in which the second requirement is satisfied that causes the inefficiency: For the list element stored in array location i, its successor must be stored in the next array location $i + 1$. Relaxing this requirement is what leads to linked lists.

A **linked list** is an ordered collection of elements called **nodes** each of which has two parts:

1. A *data part* that stores an element of the list

2. A *next part* that stores a *link* or *pointer* that indicates the location of the node containing the next list element. If there is no next element, then a special **null value** is used.

Also, the location of the node storing the first list element must be maintained. This will be the null value, if the list is empty.

To illustrate, a linked list storing the integers storing 9, 17, 22, 26, 34 might be pictured as follows:

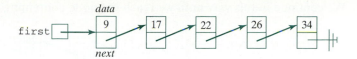

In this diagram, arrows represent links, and *first* points to the first node in the list. The *data* part of each node stores one of the integers in the list, and the ground symbol in the last node represents a null link and indicates that this list element has no successor.

IMPLEMENTING THE BASIC LIST OPERATIONS

We now consider how the basic list operations given in the preceding section can be implemented in this setting.

CONSTRUCTION.   To construct an empty list, we simply make `first` a null link to indicate that it does not point to any node:

$$first = null\_value;$$

EMPTY.   We can then perform the second list operation, determining whether a list is empty, simply by checking whether `first` is null.

$$first == null\_value?$$

TRAVERSE.   The third basic list operation is list traversal. To traverse a linked list like the preceding list of integers, we begin by initializing some auxiliary pointer `ptr` to point to the first node, and we process the list element 9 stored in this node:

Initialize `ptr` to `first`.
Process the data part of the node pointed to by `ptr`.

To move to the next node, we follow the link from the current node, setting `ptr` equal to the link in the node pointed to by `ptr`—analogous to incrementing an index by 1 in a sequential storage implementation—and process the integer 17 stored there:

Set `ptr` equal to the next part of the node pointed to by `ptr`.
Process the data part of the node pointed to by `ptr`.

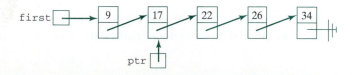

We continue in this way until we reach the node containing 34:

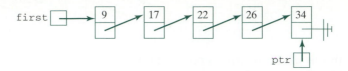

If we now attempt to move to the next node, `ptr` becomes null, signaling the end of the list:

In summary, a linked list can be traversed as follows:

```
ptr = first;
while (ptr != null_value)
{
    Process data part of node pointed to by ptr.
    ptr = next part of node pointed to by ptr.
}
```

Note that this algorithm is correct even for an empty list, since in this case `first` is the null value and the `while` loop is bypassed.

To display the list elements, the processing step in this algorithm is simply to output the data part of the node. To search the list for a given `item`, it might be:

```
if (item == data part of node pointed to by ptr)
    Terminate the loop.      // ptr points to a node containing item
```

If we change `==` to `<=`, this will locate where to insert `item` to maintain an **ordered** linked list.

INSERTION.   To insert a new data value into a linked list, we must first obtain a new node and store the value in its data part. We assume that there is a storage pool of available nodes and some mechanism for obtaining nodes from it as needed. More precisely, we assume that there is some operation that can be used to get a node from the storage pool pointed to by a specified pointer. The second step is to connect this new node to the existing list, and for this, there are two cases to consider: (1) insertion after some element in the list and (2) insertion at the beginning of the list.

To illustrate the first case, suppose we wish to insert 20 after 17 in the preceding linked list, and suppose that `predptr` points to the node containing 17. We first obtain a new node temporarily pointed to by `newptr` and store 20 in its data part:

1. Get a new node pointed to by `newptr`.

Set the data part of the node pointed to by `newptr` equal to 20.

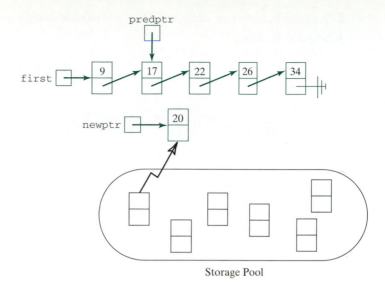

Storage Pool

We insert it into the list by first setting its next part equal to the link in the node pointed to by `predptr` so that it points to its successor:

2. Set the next part of the node pointed to by `newptr` equal to the next part of the node pointed to by `predptr`.

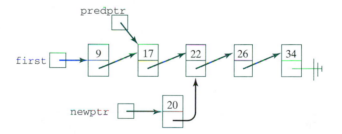

Now reset the link in the predecessor node to point to this new node:

3. Set the next part of the node pointed to by `predptr` equal to `newptr`.

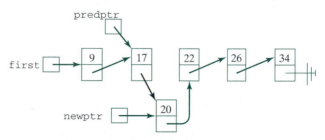

Note that this insert procedure also works at the end of the list. For example, suppose we want to insert a node containing 55 at the end of the list:

1. Same as before but put 55 in the new node.

2. Same as before. This makes the link in the new node a null pointer.

3. Same as before.

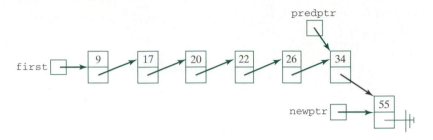

To illustrate the second case, suppose we wish to insert a node containing 5 at the beginning of the list. The first two steps are the same as before, but we need to modify Steps 2 and 3:

1. Same as before but put 5 in the new node.

2. Set the next part of the new node equal to first, which makes it point to the first node in the list.

3. Set first to point to the new node.

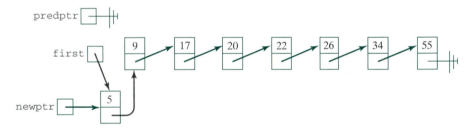

DELETION.   For deletion, there are also two cases to consider: (1) deleting an element that has a predecessor and (2) deleting the first element in the list. We will assume that there is some operation that can be used to return a node pointed to by a specified pointer to the storage pool.

As an illustration of the first case, suppose we wish to delete the node containing 22 from the preceding linked list; that ptr points to the node to be deleted; and that predptr points to its predecessor (the node containing 20). We can do this with a bypass operation that sets the link in the predecessor to point to the successor of the node to be deleted:

1. Set the next part of the node pointed to by predptr equal to the next part of the node pointed to by ptr.

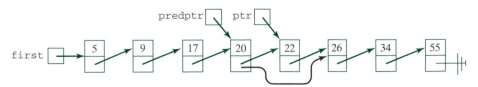

2. Return the node pointed to by `ptr` to the storage pool.

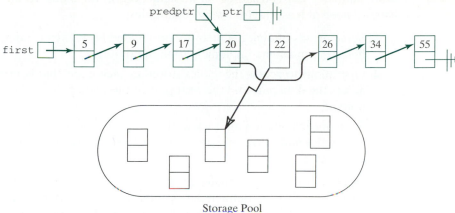

Storage Pool

Note that this also works at the end of the list:

1. Same as before. This makes the link in the predecessor a null pointer.

2. Same as before.

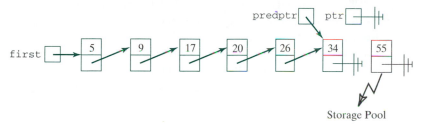

Storage Pool

The second case is easy and consists of simply resetting `first` to point to the second node in the list and then returning this node to the storage pool of available nodes:

1. Reset `first` equal to the next part of the node pointed to by `ptr`.

2. Same as before.

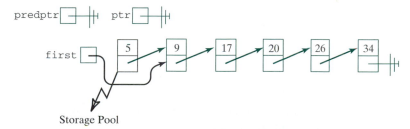

Storage Pool

SUMMARY

As this discussion demonstrates, it is possible to insert an item into a linked list at a given position or to delete an element at a given position *without shifting list elements.* This means that, unlike the sequential-storage implementation, these operations can be performed *in constant time.*

At this stage, however, we have described linked lists only abstractly, at a logical level, and have not considered an implementation for them. To implement linked lists, we need at least the following capabilities:

1. Some means of dividing memory into nodes, each having a data part and a link part, and some implementation of pointers.

2. Operations to access the values stored in each node, that is, operations to access the data part and the next part of the node pointed to by some pointer.

3. Some means of keeping track of the nodes in use as well as the available free nodes and of transferring nodes between those in use and the pool of free nodes.

Only a few programming languages (such as LISP, an acronym for LISt Processing) provide linked lists as predefined data structures. The Standard Template Library in C++ provides a linked list container `list`. In most languages, however, it is necessary to implement linked lists using other predefined data structures. In the next section we show how they can be implemented using arrays of structures; in Sec. 8.6, how they can be implemented using pointers; and in Sec. 8.7 how to use the standard C++ `list` type.

We've seen what is gained in a linked implementation; what is lost? In moving from the sequential-storage implementation of a list to a linked-list storage structure, we pay a price: *We no longer have direct access to each element of the list; we have direct access only to the first element.*

This means that it is not as easy and is less efficient to carry out some kinds of list-processing activities in the linked implementation. To access any particular position in a list in the sequential-storage implementation, we can use the direct access property of the array/`vector` that stores the list elements, and go directly to that position. But for a linked-list implementation, we have to begin at the first node and traverse the list, bypassing nodes we don't want, until we reach the one we need. Here is one example. To add a value at the end of a list implemented using the sequential-storage method, we can use

```
a[size++] = value;
```

or for a vector:

```
v.push_back(value);
```

To add a value at the end of a linked list, however, we must traverse the list to locate the last node:

Get a new node; set its data part to value and make its next part a null link.
If the list is empty
    Set `first` to point to the new node.
Else:
    Traverse the list to find the last node.
    Set the link in the last node to point to the new node.

Other examples are sorting and searching algorithms that require direct access to each element in the list; they can not be used (efficiently) with linked lists.

✔ Quick Quiz 8.2

1. The elements of a linked list are called _____.
2. Each element in a linked list has two parts: a(n) _____ part and a(n) _____ part.
3. If a node has no successor, its link is set to a special _____ value.
4. In a linked list, insertion is an O(_____) operation.
5. In a linked list, deletion is an O(_____) operation.
6. One of the strengths of linked lists is that items can be inserted or removed in constant time. (True or false)
7. One of the strengths of linked lists is direct access to each node. (True or false)

✍ EXERCISES 8.2

In the following exercises you may assume that operations as described in the text can be used to obtain a new node from the storage pool and to return nodes to the storage pool, and that there is a special null value.

1. Write an algorithm to count the nodes in a linked list with first node pointed to by `first`.

2. Write an algorithm to determine the average of a linked list of real numbers with first node pointed to by `first`.

3. Write an algorithm insert a node before the last node of a linked list with first node pointed to by `first`.

4. Write an algorithm to determine whether the data items in a linked list with first node pointed to by `first` are in ascending order.

5. Determine the computing time of the algorithms in Exercises 1 through 4.

6. Write an algorithm to search a linked list with first node pointed to by `first` for a given item and if found, return a pointer to the predecessor of the node containing that item.

7. Write an algorithm to insert a new node into a linked list with first node pointed to by `first` after the nth node in this list for a given integer n.

8. Write an algorithm to delete the nth node in a linked list with first node pointed to by `first` where n is a given integer.

9. The shuffle-merge of two lists $x_1, x_2, \ldots, x_n$ and $y_1, y_2, \ldots, y_m$ is the list

$$z = x_1, y_1, x_2, y_2, \ldots, x_n, y_n, y_{n+1}, \ldots, y_m \text{ if } n < m,$$
$$z = x_1, y_1, x_2, y_2, \ldots, x_m, y_m, x_{m+1}, \ldots, x_n \text{ if } n > m,$$

or

$$z = x_1, y_1, x_2, y_2, \ldots, x_n, y_n \text{ if } n = m$$

Write an algorithm to shuffle-merge two linked lists with first nodes pointed to by `first1` and `first2`, respectively. The items in these two lists should be copied to produce the new list; the original lists should not be destroyed.

10. Proceed as in Exercise 9 but do not copy the items. Just change links in the two lists (thus destroying the original lists) to produce the merged list.

11.   Suppose the items stored in two linked lists are in ascending order. Write an algorithm to merge these two lists to yield a list with the items in ascending order.

12.   Write an algorithm to reverse a linked list with first node pointed to by `first`. Do not copy the list elements; rather, reset links and pointers so that `first` points to the last node and all links between nodes are reversed.

8.3   AN ARRAY-BASED IMPLEMENTATION OF LINKED LISTS (OPTIONAL)

We noted that linked lists are not a predefined data structure in most programming languages, and usually they must be implemented using other predefined structures. Because nearly every high-level language provides arrays, we first consider how arrays—and, in particular, arrays of structs (or records)—can be used to implement linked lists.

NODE STRUCTURE

Recall that the nodes in a linked list contain two parts: a data part that stores an element of the list and a next part that points to a node containing the successor of this list element or that is null if this is the last element in the list. This suggests that each node can be represented as a struct and the linked list as an array of structs.[2] Each struct will contain two members: a data member that stores a list element and a next member that will point to its successor by storing its index in the array. Thus, appropriate declarations for the array-based storage structure for linked lists are as follows:

```
/*** Node Declarations ***/

struct NodeType
{
  DataType data;
  int next;
};

const int NULL_VALUE = -1;  // a nonexistent location

/*** The Storage Pool ***/
const int NUMNODES = 2048;
NodeType node[NUMNODES];
int free;                   // points to a free node
```

To illustrate, consider a linked list containing the names Brown, Jones, and Smith in this order:

---

[2]We will use a struct for nodes rather than a class because it is a C-style struct that has no function members. We could, of course, use a class whose members are declared to be public.

Here `first` is a variable of type `int` and points to the first node by storing its location in the storage pool `node`. Suppose that NUMNODES is 10 so that the array `node` constructed by the preceding declarations consists of 10 structs, each of which has a `data` member for storing a name and a `next` member for storing the location of its successor.[3] The nodes of the linked list can be stored in any three of these array locations, provided that the links are appropriately set and `first` is maintained as a pointer to the first node. For example, the first node might be stored in location 7 in this array, the second node in location 1, and the third in location 3. Thus, `first` would have the value 7, `node[7].data` would store the string `"Brown"`, and `node[7].next` would have the value 1. Similarly, we would have `node[1].data` = `"Jones"` and `node[1].next` = 3. The last node would be stored in location 3 so that `node[3].data` would have the value `"Smith"`. Since there is no successor for this node, the `next` field must store a null pointer to indicate this fact; that is, `node[3].next` must have a value that is not the index of any array location, and for this, the value −1 is a natural choice for the null value.

The following diagram displays the contents of the array `node` and indicates how the `next` members connect these nodes. The question marks in some array locations indicate undetermined values because these nodes are not used to store this linked list.

To traverse this list, displaying the names in order, we begin by finding the location of the first node by using the pointer `first`. Since `first` has the value 7, the first name displayed is `"Brown"`, stored in `node[7].data`. Following the next member leads us to array location `node[7].next` = 1, where the name `"Jones"` is stored in `node[1].data`, and then to location `node[1].next` = 3, where `"Smith"` is stored. The null value −1 for `node[3].next` signals that this is the last node in the list.

In general, to traverse any linked list we use the method given in the traversal algorithm of the preceding section:

1. Initialize `ptr` to `first`.

2. While `ptr` ≠ NULL_VALUE do the following:

    a. Process the data part of the node pointed to by `ptr`.
    b. Set `ptr` equal to the next part of the node pointed to by `ptr`.

---

[3]For languages that do not provide structs (or records), `node` can be replaced by *parallel* arrays `data` and `next` so that `data[i]` and `next[i]` correspond to the data members `node[i].data` and `node[i].next`, respectively.

In the current array-based implementation of linked lists, these instructions are implemented by the following program segment; where `ptr` is of type `int`:

```
ptr = first;
while (ptr != NULL_VALUE)
{
   /* Appropriate statements to process
      node[ptr].data are inserted here */
   ptr = node[ptr].next;
}
```

Now suppose we wish to insert a new name into this list, for example, to insert `"Grant"` after `"Brown"`, We must first obtain a new node in which to store this name. Seven locations are available, namely, positions 0, 2, 4, 5, 6, 8, and 9 in the array. Let us assume for now that this storage pool of available nodes has been organized in such a way that a call to the function `New()` returns the index 9 as the location of an available node. The new name is then inserted into the list using the method described in the preceding section: `node[9].data` is set equal to `"Grant"`; `node[9].next` is set equal to 2 so that it points to the successor of `"Brown"`; and the link field `node[7].next` of the predecessor is set equal to 9.

node	data	next
[0]	?	?
[1]	Jones	3
[2]	?	?
[3]	Smith	-1
[4]	?	?
[5]	?	?
[6]	?	?
[7]	Brown	9
[8]	?	?
[9]	Grant	1

first   7

ORGANIZING THE STORAGE POOL

This example illustrates that the elements of the array `node` are of two kinds. Some of the array locations—namely 1, 3, 7, and 9—are used to store nodes of the linked list. The others represent unused "free" nodes that are available for storing new items as they are inserted into the list. We have described in detail how the nodes used to store list elements are organized, and we must now consider how to structure the storage pool of available nodes.

One simple way to organize this pool of free nodes is as a linked stack. In this case, the content of the data parts of these nodes is irrelevant, and the next parts serve simply to link these nodes together. Initially, all nodes are available and thus must be linked together to form the storage pool. One natural way to do this is to let the first node point to the second, the second to the third, and so on. The link field of the last node will be null, and a pointer `free` is set equal to 0 to provide access to the first node in this storage pool.

```
// Initialize storage pool
// Each node points to the next one

for (int i = 0; i < NUMNODES - 1; i++)
   node[i].next = i + 1;
node[NUMNODES - 1].next = NULL_VALUE;
free = 0;
```

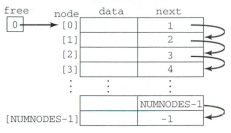

A function call `ptr = New()` returns the location of a free node by assigning to `ptr` the value `free` and deleting that node from the free list by setting `free` equal to `node[free].next`.

```
// Maintain storage pool as a stack
// New operation
Pointer New()
{
   Pointer p = free;
   if (free != NULL_VALUE)
      free = node[free].next;
   else
      cerr << "***Storage pool empty***\n";
   return p;
}
```

Thus, if `"Mills"` is the first name to be inserted into a linked list, it will be stored in the first position of the array `node`, because `free` has the value 0; `first` will be set to 0; and `free` will become 1.

	node	data	next
first 0	→ [0]	Mills	-1
free 1	→ [1]	?	2
	[2]	?	3
	[3]	?	4
	[4]	?	5
	[5]	?	6
	[6]	?	7
	[7]	?	8
	[8]	?	9
	[9]	?	-1

If `"Baker"` is the next name to be inserted, it will be stored in location 1 because this is the value of `free`, and `free` will be set equal to 2. If the list is to be maintained in alphabetical order, `first` will be set equal to 1; `node[1].next` will be set equal to 0; and `node[0].next` will be set equal to −1.

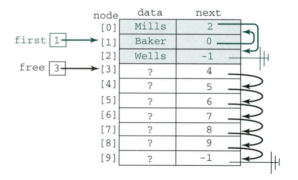

If `"Wells"` is the next name inserted into the list, the following configuration will result:

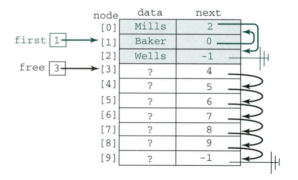

When a node is deleted from a linked list, it should be returned to the storage pool of free nodes so that it can be reused later to store some other list element. A function call `Delete(ptr)` simply inserts the node pointed to by `ptr` at the beginning of the free list by first setting `node[ptr].next` equal to `free` and then setting `free` equal to `ptr`:

```
// Delete operation
void Delete(Pointer p)
{
   node[p].next = free;
   free = p;
}
```

For example, deleting the name `"Mills"` from the preceding linked list produces the following configuration:

node	data	next
free 0 → [0]	Mills	3
first 1 → [1]	Baker	0
[2]	Wells	-1
[3]	?	4
[4]	?	5
[5]	?	6
[6]	?	7
[7]	?	8
[8]	?	9
[9]	?	-1

Note that it is not necessary to actually remove the string `"Mills"` from the data part of this node because changing the link of its predecessor has *logically* removed it from the linked list. This string `"Mills"` will be overwritten when this node is used to store a new name.

We could now package the preceding declarations and code together into a library or class with data members `Node` and `free`, a constructor that initializes `Node` and `free` as described in this section, and member functions `New()` and `Delete()`. A `List` class could then be designed. Writing functions for the algorithms for the basic list operations is straightforward: We simply use `node[p].data` to access the data part of the node pointed to by `p` and `node[p].next` to access the next part of the node pointed to by `p`. We will leave these as exercises and not develop them here but rather move on to the implementation that uses the dynamic memory allocation and deallocation mechanism provided in C++.

✍ EXERCISES 8.3

1. An ordered linked list of characters has been constructed using the array-based implementation described in this section. The following diagram shows the current contents of the array that stores the elements of the linked list and the storage pool:

node	data	next
[0]	J	3
[1]	Z	6
[2]	C	0
[3]	P	-1
[4]	B	2
[5]	M	1
[6]	K	7
[7]	Q	8
[8]	?	9
[9]	?	-1

first = 4
free = 5

   a. List the elements of this list.

   b. List the nodes in the storage pool in the order in which they are linked together.

2. Assuming the contents of the array `node` pictured in Exercise 1, show the contents of `node` and the values of `first` and `free` after the letter F is inserted into the list so that the resulting list is still in alphabetical order.

3. Proceed as in Exercise 2 but for the operation Delete J.

4. Proceed as in Exercise 2 but for the following sequence of operations:
Delete J, Delete P, Delete C, Delete B.

5. Proceed as in Exercise 2 but for the following sequence of operations:
Insert A, Delete P, Insert K, Delete C.

6. Assuming the array-based implementation in this section, write
a. a nonrecursive function
b. a recursive function
to count the nodes in a linked list.

7. Assuming the array-based implementation in this section, write
a. a nonrecursive boolean-valued function
b. a recursive boolean-valued function
that determines whether the data items in the list are arranged in ascending order.

8. Assuming the array-based implementation in this section, write
a. a nonrecursive function
b. a recursive function
that returns a pointer to the last node in a linked list.

9. Assuming the array-based implementation in this section, write a function to reverse a linked list in the manner described in Exercise 12 of Sec. 8.2.

8.4 POINTERS IN C++

Implementations of linked lists that provide efficient operations as described in Sec. 8.2 require the ability to allocate and deallocate nodes dynamically during program execution. In the preceding section we established a storage pool of nodes in an array `node` and managed the allocation and deallocation operations on these nodes. However, this is not necessary in most modern programming languages because they provide a way to request and return memory during program execution. In this section we will describe the C++ allocation/deallocation mechanism.

POINTERS

When the compiler encounters declarations such as

```
double doubleVar;
char charVar = 'A';
int intVar = 1234;
```

it *constructs* the object being declared (`intVar`, `doubleVar`, and `charVar`), which means that it

1. Allocates the memory required for a value of the specified type;
2. Associates the object's name with that memory; and
3. Initializes that memory with values provided in the declaration (if any).

Thus, if the next available memory location is 0x1220 and if `char`s are allocated 1 byte, `int`s are allocated 4 bytes, and `double`s are allocated 8 bytes, we might have memory allocated for the variables `intVar`, `doubleVar`, and `charVar` as shown by the following **memory map**:

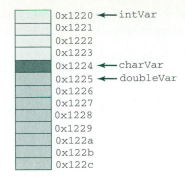

The address of an object can be accessed by using the **address-of operator (&)**:

&*variable* is the address of *variable*

Thus, for the scenario described above, we have:

&intVar is 0x1220
&charVar is 0x1224
&doubleVar is 0x1225

To make addresses more useful, C++ provides pointer variables. A **pointer variable** (or simply **pointer**) is a variable whose value is a memory address. Their declarations have the following form:

DECLARATIONS OF POINTERS

Form:

    Type * pointerVariable = address;

where *Type* is any type and *address* is an address of an object of the specified *Type*. As with most declarations, the initialization may be omitted.

Purpose:

Declares a variable named *pointerVariable* that can store the address of an object of the specified *Type*. Note the following:

1. The asterisk operator * *must* precede each identifier that is to serve as a pointer.

2. The initializing address must be that of an object whose type is the same as the type to which the pointer points or a compile-time error will result. The pointer is said to be **bound** to that type.

3. 0 can be assigned to any pointer variable. The value that results is called the **null pointer value** for that type and 0 is often called the **null address.**

The program in Fig. 8.1 declares pointer variables iptr and jptr that can store addresses of int objects and pointer variables dptr and eptr that can store addresses of double objects. Pointers iptr and jptr store the addresses of int variables i and j, respectively; dptr and eptr store the addresses of double variables d and e, respectively. These addresses are then displayed.[4]

FIGURE 8.1   POINTER VARIABLES

```cpp
#include <iostream>
using namespace std;

int main()
{
  int i = 11, j = 22;
  double d = 3.3, e = 4.4;

                              // pointer variables that:
  int * iPtr, * jPtr;       //    store addresses of ints
  double * dPtr, * ePtr;    //    store addresses of doubles

  iPtr = &i;                // value of iPtr is address of i
  jPtr = &j;                // value of jPtr is address of j

  dPtr = &d;                // value of dPtr is address of d
  ePtr = &e;                // value of ePtr is address of e

  cout << "&i = " << iPtr << endl
       << "&j = " << jPtr << endl
       << "&d = " << dPtr << endl
       << "&e = " << ePtr << endl;
}
```

EXECUTION:

```
&i = 0xeffff864
&j = 0xeffff860
&d = 0xeffff858
&e = 0xeffff850
```

 It is important to remember that *the asterisk operator * must precede each variable in a pointer declaration.* For example, the declaration of dPtr and ePtr

```cpp
double * dPtr, * ePtr;
```

in Fig. 8.1 correctly declares them to be pointers to doubles. However, if we wrote

```cpp
double * dPtr, ePtr;
```

only dPtr would be a pointer variable; ePtr would be an ordinary double variable.

A typedef declaration can be used to make this repeated use of the asterisk in pointer declarations unnecessary by associating a type identifier with a pointer type. For example, we could first declare

---

[4]For some versions of C++ it may be necessary to use (void*)*pointerVariable* in an output statement for addresses to display correctly.

```
typedef double * DoublePointer;
```

and then use `DoublePointer` to declare `dPtr` and `ePtr`:

```
DoublePointer dPtr,
             ePtr;
```

Such declarations also improve the readability of pointer declarations, especially when pointer parameters are being declared.

As we have noted, 0 can be assigned to any pointer variable to make it a *null pointer*. For example, the declaration

```
int * iPtr = 0;
double * dPtr = 0;
```

are both valid initializations using the null address to make `iPtr` and `dPtr` null pointers, which we pictured in Sec. 8.2 using the ground symbol:

iPtr ⏚

dPtr ⏚

BASIC POINTER OPERATIONS

C++ supports a variety of operations on pointers, including dereferencing, I/O, assignments, comparisons, and arithmetic. We will briefly examine each of these in turn.

INDIRECTION AND DEREFERENCING.   Pointer variables not only store addresses but they also provide access to the values stored at those addresses. An expression of the form

```
*pointerVariable
```

produces a name for the memory location whose address is stored in *pointerVariable*; if this memory location already has a name, we can think of **pointerVariable* as an *alias* or *synonym* for this location to which *pointerVariable* points. This name can then be used to access the value stored in this location.

To illustrate, from the output in Fig. 8.1, we see that the value of `iPtr` is `0xeffff864`, which is the address of a memory location where an integer is stored; it is, in fact, the address of the memory location containing 11 whose name is `i`. So `*iPtr` is another name for this location, and the value of `*iPtr` is 11, because 11 is the value stored in this location. We can visualize this configuration as follows:

Thus, as shown in the program in Fig. 8.2, the value of variable `i` can be accessed via the expression `*iPtr`, because `*iPtr` is a synonym or alias for `i`. Similarly `*jPtr`, `*dPtr`, and `*ePtr` are aliases for `j`, `d`, and `e`, respectively, and can thus be used to access their values. In general, the value of a variable v can be *accessed indirectly* by applying the * operator to a pointer variable vPtr whose value is the address of v. For this reason, the * operator is called the **indirection operator.** Using * in this way is called **dereferencing the pointer** vPtr, and so * is also called the **dereferencing operator.**

FIGURE 8.2   DEREFERENCING POINTERS

```cpp
#include <iostream>
using namespace std;

int main()
{
  int i = 11, j = 22;
  double d = 3.3, e = 4.4;

                             // pointer variables that:
  int * iPtr, * jPtr;        //    store addresses of ints
  double * dPtr, * ePtr;     //    store addresses of doubles

  iPtr = &i;                 // value of iPtr is address of i
  jPtr = &j;                 // value of jPtr is address of j

  dPtr = &d;                 // value of dPtr is address of d
  ePtr = &e;                 // value of ePtr is address of e

  cout << "\nAt address " << iPtr
       << ", the value " << *iPtr << " is stored.\n"
       << "\nAt address " << jPtr
       << ", the value " << *jPtr << " is stored.\n"
       << "\nAt address " << dPtr
       << ", the value " << *dPtr << " is stored.\n"
       << "\nAt address " << ePtr
       << ", the value " << *ePtr << " is stored.\n";
}
```

EXECUTION:

```
At address 0xeffff864, the value 11 is stored.

At address 0xeffff860, the value 22 is stored.

At address 0xeffff858, the value 3.3 is stored.

At address 0xeffff850, the value 4.4 is stored.
```

Since variables are names for memory locations and the indirection operator * returns a name for a memory location, we can say that * *returns a variable*; that is, *a dereferenced pointer is a variable* and can thus be used in the same way as all variables of the type to which the pointer is bound. For example, if the statement

```
i = *jPtr;
```

were added to the program in Fig. 8.2, the value of i would be changed from 11 to 22, because dereferencing jPtr produces the name *jptr for the memory location whose address is 0xeffff860, and the value 22 stored there would be assigned to i. The statement

```
*iPtr = j;
```

would produce the same result, because *iptr is an int variable and names the same memory location as i. This statement would copy the value of j into this location, which means that the value of i would be changed to 22.

POINTERS TO CLASS OBJECTS.   Pointers can be bound to any type, in particular, to a class. For example, in Chap. 3 we built a Time class that can be used to define Time objects such as

```
Time t;
```

and we can declare a pointer to a Time object and use it to store the address of that object,

```
Time * timePtr = & t;
```

which can be pictured as follows:

The members of t can be accessed (indirectly) via timePtr. For example, t has an Hour() function member that returns the value (12) of its myHours data member. Hour() can be called using timePtr, and this can be done in two ways. One way is to combine the indirection operator with the dot operator and write

```
(*timePtr).Hour()
```

In this expression, the pointer timePtr is first dereferenced to access the object to which it points (i.e., t), and the dot operator is then used to send that object the Hour() message.

This notation is rather cumbersome, however, because it involves two operators and the indirection operation must be parenthesized because it has lower priority than the dot operator. For this reason, C++ provides a more convenient notation that accomplishes the same thing in one operation:

```
timePtr->Hour()
```

Here **->** is the **class pointer selector operator** whose left operand is a *pointer* to a class object and whose right operand is a *member* of the class object. An expression of the form

```
ptr->member
```

is equivalent to the expression

```
(*ptr).member
```

This operator provides a convenient way to access an object's members, and the "arrow" notation clearly indicates that the member is being accessed through a pointer.

THE `this` POINTER.   One important pointer that is made available to every member function in a class is named **this**, a keyword that names a pointer whose value is the address of the object that contains that function.

> *In every class the keyword* **this** *is a pointer whose value is the address of the object. The value of the dereferenced pointer* ***this** *is the object itself.*

We might picture this as follows:

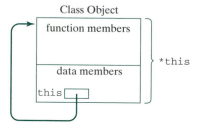

Dereferencing `this` provides a way to (indirectly) access that object. One time that this is useful is when an object needs to return itself in a member function. Two different actions must be taken in order for this to occur correctly:

1. To return the object, we can use

```
return *this;
```

to dereference this pointer to the object and return the object.

2. Normally, a `return` statement in a function,

```
return object;
```

first uses the copy constructor to build a copy of *object*, and then returns this copy. We can force it to return *object* itself by *making the function's return-type a reference*:

```
ReturnType & FunctionName( Parameters );
```

The function will then return a reference to *this, which is simply another name for the object rather than a copy of it.[5]

To illustrate, suppose we modify the Set() member function in class Time as follows:

```
Time & Time::Set(unsigned hours, unsigned minutes, char am_pm)
{
   ...
// same as before
   ...
   return *this;
}
```

If t is a Time object, then the function call t.Set(11, 59, 'P'); sets the data members to the specified values, but it also returns a reference to *this, which is thus simply another name for t. This means that we can *chain* this function call with another; for example

```
t.Set(11, 59, 'P').Display(cout);
```

is evaluated as

```
(t.Set(11, 59, 'P')).Display(cout);
```

because the dot operator is left associative. The call to Set() is done first and sets the data members in t as just described; since it returns a reference to t, the Display() function will be applied to this same object and thus displays the newly-set values in t.

I/O.   In the program in Fig. 8.2, we displayed the addresses of i, j, d, and e, by using an output statement to display the values of iPtr, jPtr, dPtr, and ePtr. Similarly, to find the particular addresses associated with iPtr, jPtr, dPtr, and ePtr, we could write

```
cout << "\n iPtr is stored at address " << &iPtr
     << ",\n jPtr is stored at address " << &jPtr
     << ",\n dPtr is stored at address " << &dPtr
     << ", and\n ePtr is stored at address " << &ePtr
     << endl;
```

The address-of operator allows us to determine the exact memory address at which an object is stored, whereas pointer variables allow us to store these addresses.

Just as the value of a pointer can be output using <<, an address could be input and stored in a pointer variable using >>. However, this is rarely done, because we

---

[5]It follows that if the return type of the function is a reference, the object being returned cannot be a local variable because its lifetime would end when the function terminates.

usually are not interested in the address of the memory location storing a value, only in the value itself. In fact, it is dangerous to input address values because an attempt to access a memory address outside the space allocated to an executing program will result in a fatal run-time error.

ASSIGNMENT.   Pointer variables can be assigned the values of other pointer variables that are *bound to the same type*. For example, if we were to add the statement

```
jPtr = iPtr;
```

to the program in Fig. 8.2, then the value of iPtr would be copied to jPtr so that both have the same memory address as their value; that is, both point to the same memory location, as the following diagrams illustrate:

Before the assignment

After the assignment jPtr = iPtr;

After the assignment statement is executed, jPtr no longer points to j, but now points to i. Thus, dereferencing jPtr will produce an alias for i. For example, an output statement

```
cout << *jPtr;
```

will display the value 11 instead of 22, and the statement

```
*jPtr = 44;
```

will change the value at address of i from 11 to 44:

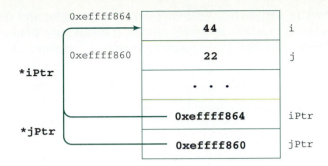

☞   We have included this example to show that pointers are a very powerful feature of programming languages, but that they must be used with care. Statements like

```
*jptr = 44;
```

that change the value of a variable (j) in a statement in which that variable is not named are generally considered poor programming practice, because they make programs more difficult to debug by hiding such changes. This is known as **the aliasing problem** in programming.

COMPARISON.   Relational operators can be used to compare two pointers that are *bound to the same type*. The most common operation is to use == and != to determine if two pointer variables both point to the same memory location. For example, the boolean expression

```
iPtr == jPtr
```

is valid and returns true if and only if the address in iPtr is the same as the address in jPtr. However, if pointers nPtr and dPtr are declared by

```
int * nPtr;
double * dPtr;
```

the comparison

```
nPtr == dPtr    // ERROR!
```

will result in a compilation error, because iPtr and jPtr are bound to different types.
    The *null address may be compared with any pointer variable*. For example, the conditions

```
nPtr != 0
```

and

```
dPtr == 0
```

are both valid boolean expressions.

POINTER ARITHMETIC.   We consider the increment and decrement operations first because they are probably the most commonly used arithmetic operations on pointer variables. For a pointer variable `ptr` declared by

```
Type * ptr;
```

the increment statement

```
ptr++;
```

adds the value `sizeof(Type)` to the address in `ptr`. Similarly, a decrement statement

```
ptr--;
```

subtracts the value `sizeof(Type)` from the address in `ptr`. If *intExp* is an integer expression, a statement of the form

```
ptr += intExp;
```

adds the value *intExp* `*` `sizeof(Type)` to `ptr`, and

```
ptr -= intExp;
```

subtracts the value *intExp* `*` `sizeof(Type)` from `ptr`.

To illustrate how these operations are used, suppose that `ptr` is a pointer whose value is the address of the first element of an array of `double` elements:

```
double dArray[10],       // array of 10 doubles
     * ptr = &(dArray[0]); // pointer to first element of dArray
```

or equivalently,

```
double dArray[10],       // array of 10 doubles
     * ptr = dArray;       // pointer to first element of dArray
```

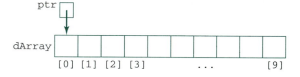

```
            ptr
```
```
        dArray
              [0] [1] [2] [3]        ...        [9]
```

Now consider the following loop:

```
for (int i = 0; i < 10; i++)
{
   *ptr = 0;
   ptr++;
}
```

On the first pass through the loop, `ptr` is dereferenced and the value 0 is assigned to the memory location at that address. `ptr` is then incremented, which adds `sizeof(double)` to its value, effectively making `ptr` point to the second element of the array:

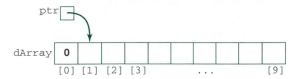

The next pass again dereferences `ptr`, sets that memory location to zero, and increments `ptr`:

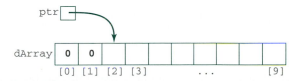

This continues with each subsequent iteration. On the final pass, the last element of the array is set to zero and `ptr` is again incremented, so that it points to the first address past the end of the array:

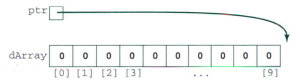

A pointer can thus be used to move through consecutive blocks of memory, accessing them in whatever way a particular problem requires.

POINTERS AS ARGUMENTS AND PARAMETERS.   Pointers may also be passed as arguments to functions. The parameters corresponding to such arguments may be either value or reference parameters, but the pointer argument and the corresponding parameter must be bound to the same type. The return type of a function may also be a pointer.

A NOTE ABOUT REFERENCE PARAMETERS.   In Sec. 6.2 we considered a C++ function to exchange the values of two `int` variables:

```
void Swap(int & first, int & second)
{
   int temp = first;
   first = second;
   second = temp;
}
```

The values of two `int` variables `x` and `y` can be exchanged with the call:

```
Swap(x, y);
```

The first C++ compilers were just preprocessors that read a C++ program, output functionally equivalent C code, and ran it through the C compiler. However, C has no reference parameters, so how could such compilers deal with reference parameters? They used pointers and the dereferencing operator. For example, the preceding function Swap() would be translated to

```
void Swap(int * first, int * second)
{
  int temp = *first;
  *first = *second;
  *second = temp;
}
```

and the preceding function call to

```
Swap(&x, &y);
```

From this example we see how the call-by-reference parameter mechanism can be simulated. A reference parameter is translated into a pointer variable and the corresponding argument to the address of the argument. The pointer parameter is then automatically dereferenced wherever it is used in the function, producing aliases (i.e., references) for the arguments.

OTHER USES OF POINTERS

COMMAND-LINE ARGUMENTS.   Command-line arguments are used with many of the system commands in command-line environments such as UNIX. For example, the command

```
emacs textfile
```

is used to execute a program named emacs, search for the file named textfile, and (assuming that it is found) open it for editing. The name of the file textfile is an example of a **command-line argument**. Just as entering the name of the program (emacs) is like calling the main function of a program, entering the name of the program followed by textfile is like calling the main function of a program and passing it textfile as an argument.

Command-line arguments are passed to a main function main() via two parameters, which are usually named argc and argv:

- ▸ argc (the <u>arg</u>ument <u>c</u>ount): an int whose value is the number of strings on the command line when the command to execute the binary executable of the program is given
- ▸ argv (the <u>arg</u>ument <u>v</u>ector): an array of pointers to chars; argv[i] is the address of the ith character string on the command line

See Appendix D for examples of how these parameters can be used.

FUNCTIONS AS ARGUMENTS.   Sometimes it is useful to *pass a function* as an argument to another function. For example, many functions that implement numerical methods for finding roots of functions, solving equations, approximating integrals, and so on can be written most generally if the functions are passed to them as arguments.

To permit one function to be passed to another function as an argument, C++ stipulates that:

The value of a function name is the starting address of that function.

That is, a function is a pointer. Just as an array name is a pointer whose value is the base address of that array, a function F is a pointer whose value is the starting address of that function. A `typedef` declaration of the form

```
typedef ReturnType (*FunctionPtr)(ParameterTypeList);
```

declares the name `FunctionPtr` as a type whose objects are pointers to functions whose return type is `ReturnType` and whose parameters match those in `ParameterList`. See Appendix D for examples of how this can be used to declare function parameters in other functions and to pass functions as arguments to these parameters.

✔ Quick Quiz 8.4

1. What three steps are involved in constructing an object?
2. A pointer variable stores a(n) _____ .
3. _____ is the address-of operator.
4. _____ is the dereferencing operator.
5. _____ is the indirection operator.
6. _____ is the class pointer selector operator.

Questions 7–19 assume the following declarations:

```
double * x,
         y = 1.1;
```

and that `double` values are stored in 8 bytes of memory. Answer each of Questions 7–12 with (a) address or (b) `double` value.

7. The value of `x` will be a(n) _____ .
8. The value of `y` will be a(n) _____
9. The value of `&y` will be a(n) _____ .
10. The value of `&x` will be a(n) _____ .
11. The value of `*x` will be a(n) _____ .
12. The value of `(*x) * y` will be a(n) _____ .
13. In the assignment `x = 0; ,0` is called the _____ address.
14. The output produced by the statements `x = &y; cout << *x;` is _____ .
15. The output produced by the statements `x = &y; *x = 3.3; cout << y;` is _____ .
16. If the output produced by `cout << x;` is `0x12a30`, the value of `x + 4` is _____ .
17. In a member function of an object, _____ points to the object.

✍ EXERCISES 8.4

Exercises 1–9 assume the following declarations:

```
int i1 = 11,
    i2 = 22;
double d1 = 3.45,
       d2 = 6.78;
class Point
{
public:
  double x() { return xCoord; }
  double y() { return yCoord; }
private:
  double xCoord, yCoord;
};
```

1. Write declarations for variables `p1` and `p2` whose values will be addresses of memory locations in which a `double` can be stored.

2. Write a statement to assign the address of `d1` to the variable `p1` in Exercise 1, or explain why this is not possible.

3. Write a statement to assign the address of `i2` to the variable `p2` in Exercise 1, or explain why this is not possible.

4. Write declarations for a variable `q` whose value will be a memory location in which a `Point` object can be stored.

5. Write declarations that initialize variables `ptr1` and `ptr2` with the addresses of `i1` and `i2`, respectively.

6. Write a statement that will make variables `p1` and `p2` of Exercise 1 point to the same memory location.

7. Write a statement that will copy the value stored in the memory location pointed to by `ptr2` into the memory location pointed to by `ptr1`, for `ptr1` and `ptr2` as in Exercise 5.

8. Write a statement to output the *x* coordinate and the *y* coordinate of the `Point` in the memory location pointed to by the variable `q` of Exercise 4.

9. Write statements that use the variables `p1` and `p2` of Exercise 2 but *not* the variables `d1` and `d2` to interchange the values of `d1` and `d2`.

For Exercises 10–16, use the `sizeof` operator to find how many bytes your C++ compiler allocates for the given data type:

10. `int`

11. `float`

12. `double`

13. `short int`

14. The character string `"Bye!"`

15. The character string `"Auf Wiedersehen!"`

16. Pointers to the types in Exercises 10–15.

17. Using the address-of operator, find the starting addresses your C++ compiler assigns to each of the objects in the following declarations:

```
const int SIZE = 10;
char charArray[SIZE];
int intArray[SIZE]
double doubleArray[SIZE];
char charVar;
```

18. Use the `sizeof` operator to find the number of bytes your C++ compiler allocates for each object defined in Exercise 17.

19. Suppose that the starting address of the first object in a block is *b*. Using *b*, the `sizeof` operator, and the results from Exercises 17 and 18, construct an expression that can be used to find the address of any subsequent object declared in that same block.

20. Using `typedef`, create an alias type `CharPointer` for pointers to type `char`.

Exercises 21–23 assume an array declaration like the following:

```
double anArray[10];
```

21. Use the address-of operator to find the address of the first element of `anArray`.

22. Find the value associated with the name `anArray`.

23. What inference can you make from the results of Exercises 21 and 22?

8.5   RUN-TIME ALLOCATION AND DEALLOCATION

Memory is allocated to C-style arrays as described in Chap. 2 when the program is *compiled*. This means that the size of the block of memory allocated for the array is fixed throughout execution of the program. The capacity of the array cannot be changed during execution; one can only edit the specification of the array's capacity and then recompile the program.

In Chap. 6, we saw that this problem is solved by the STL `vector` class template, which allocates memory to a `vector` object as the program executes (i.e., **run-time allocation**) instead of when it is compiled (i.e., compile-time allocation). In the rest of this section, we examine the mechanism C++ provides for run-time memory allocation.

At its simplest, a run-time memory allocation mechanism requires two operations:

1. Acquire additional memory locations as they are needed

2. Release memory locations when they are no longer needed

C++ provides the predefined operations `new` and `delete` to perform these two operations of memory allocation and deallocation during program execution.

THE new OPERATION—RUN-TIME ARRAYS

The `new` operation is used to request additional memory from the operating system during program execution. The general form of such a request is

---

THE new OPERATION

Form:

new *Type*

Purpose:

Issue a run-time request for a block of memory that is large enough to hold an object of the specified *Type*. If the request can be granted, new returns the starting address of the block of memory; otherwise, it returns the null address.

Since the new operation returns an address and addresses can be stored in pointer variables, this operation is almost always used in conjunction with a pointer. For example, when the statements

```
int * intPtr;

intPtr = new int;
```

are executed, the expression new int issues a request to the operating system for a memory block large enough to store an integer value (that is, for sizeof(int) bytes of memory).

☞   If the operating system is able to grant the request, intPtr will be assigned the address of this memory block. Otherwise, if all available memory has been exhausted, intPtr will be assigned the null address 0. Because of this possibility, the value returned by new should always be tested before it is used as in

```
assert(intPtr != 0);
```

If intPtr is assigned a nonzero value, the newly allocated memory location is an **anonymous variable**; that is, it is an allocated memory location that has no name associated with it. For example, suppose new returns the address 0x13eff860:

intPtr
| **0x13eff860** | 0x13eff860 | |

Because there is no name associated with this newly allocated memory, it *cannot be accessed directly* in the same way other variables are accessed. However, its address is stored in intPtr, so this anonymous variable can be *accessed indirectly* by dereferencing intPtr, which then gives it the name *intPtr:

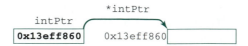

Statements such as the following can be used to operate on this anonymous variable:

```
cin >> *intPtr;      // store input value in the new integer

if (*intPtr < 100) // apply relational ops to new integer
   (*intPtr)++;      // apply arithmetic ops to new integer
else
   *intPtr = 100;    // assign values to the new integer
```

In short, anything that can be done with an "ordinary" integer variable can be done with this anonymous integer variable by accessing it indirectly via `intPtr`.

ALLOCATING ARRAYS WITH new.   In practice, `new` is rarely used to allocate space for scalar values such as integers. Instead, it is used to allocate space for either arrays or for anonymous class objects. To illustrate the former, consider an integer array object `anArray` declared by

```
int anArray[6];
```

The value associated with the name `anArray` is the **base address** of the array, that is, the address of the first element of the array.[6] The type of object `anArray` is `int[6]`.
    A type such as `int[6]` can be used with `new` to allocate the memory for an array at run time. For example, the statements

```
int * arrayPtr;

arrayPtr = new int[6];
```

allocate space for an array of six integers. Until the second statement is executed, `arrayPtr` is simply a pointer variable whose value is undefined. After it is executed (assuming that sufficient memory is available), `arrayPtr` contains the base address of the *newly allocated* array. If that address is `0x1101abc0`, we might picture the situation as follows:

But we have seen previously that the value associated with the name of a compile-time allocated array is its base address. This means that *if the base address of a run-time allocated array is stored in a pointer variable, then the elements of that array can be accessed via the pointer in exactly the same way that the elements of a compile-time*

---

[6]This is one reason that the assignment operator cannot be used to copy a "normal" array—the statement
```
   alpha = beta;
```
would attempt to copy the starting address of `beta` into `alpha`, as opposed to copying the elements of `beta`.

allocated array are accessed via its name, by using the subscript operator (`[]`). That is, the first element of the new array can be accessed using the notation `arrayPtr[0]`, the second element using `arrayPtr[1]`, the third element using `arrayPtr[2]`, and so on

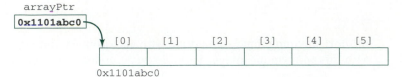

Note that this is consistent with our description of array-address mapping described in Section 2.3. The value of the pointer variable `arrayPtr` is the base address of the array, and for a given index `i`, the subscript operator

```
arrayPtr[i]
```

simply accesses the memory location `arrayPtr + i * sizeof(int)`.

The advantage of run-time allocation is that it is not necessary to know the size of the array at compile time. For example, we can write:

```
cout << "How many entries? ";      // find how big the
cin >> numEntries;                 //    array should be

double *dPtr =                     // allocate an array
      new double[numEntries];      //    with that capacity
assert(dPtr != 0);                 // check for success

cout << "Enter your values.\n";    // fill it with values
for (int i = 0; i < numEntries; i++)
  cin >> dPtr[i];
...
```

Unlike arrays whose memory is allocated at compile time, arrays whose memory is allocated at run time can be tailored to the exact size of the list to be stored in them. The wasted memory problem is solved because an array will not be too large. The overflow problem is solved because the array will not be too small.

This is the approach used by the `vector` class template, whose implementation might be something like the following:

```
template<typename T>
class vector
{
 public:
    vector();
    vector(int n);
    ...
 private:
    T * tPtr;
    int mySize;
    ...
};
```

This version of `vector<T>` contains a data member that is a pointer to an object of type `T`. The first `vector<T>` constructor simply initializes this pointer to the null address to signify an empty vector:

```
template<typename T>
vector<T>::vector()
{
    tPtr = 0;
    mySize = 0;
    ...
}
```

But the second `vector<T>` constructor uses `new` to dynamically allocate an array of n elements, each of which is of type `T`:

```
template<typename T>
vector<T>::vector(int n)
{
    tPtr = new T[n];
    mySize = n;
    ...
}
```

The definition of a `vector` object

```
vector<int> intVector(10);
```

uses this second constructor to build `intVector` as follows:

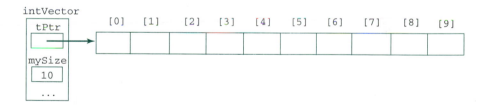

The other `vector` operations simply access the elements of this anonymous array via the `tPtr` data member.

In summary, the `new` operator can be used to allocate anonymous array variables at run time, and the capacities of these arrays can be tailored to the number of values being stored in the arrays. By storing the base address of an array in a pointer variable, most things that can be done with a compile-time allocated array can be done with the run-time allocated array using the pointer.

THE `delete` OPERATION

When execution of a program begins, the program has available to it a "storage pool" of unallocated memory locations, called the **heap** or **free store**. It is usually located between a program and its run-time stack (see Sec. 4.3)

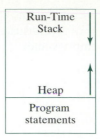

Since the run-time stack grows each time a function is called, it is possible for it to overrun the heap—if main() calls a function that calls a function that calls a function, and so on. It is also possible for the heap to overrun the run-time stack—if a program performs lots of new operations.

The effect of the new operation is to request the operating system to

1. Remove a block of memory from the heap

2. Allocate that block to the executing program

The block can be used by the executing program if it stores the address of that block (the value produced by the new operation) in a pointer variable.

The size of the heap is limited, and each execution of new causes the pool of available memory to shrink. If a call to new requests more memory than is available in the heap, then the operating system is unable to fill the request and new returns the null address 0.

The run-time stack grows each time a function is called, but it shrinks again when that function terminates. What is needed is an analogous method to reclaim memory allocated by new. In C++ this can be accomplished by using the **delete operation.** Just as new is a request by the executing program for memory from the heap, the delete operation is a request to return memory to the heap. Such memory can then be reallocated to the program by a subsequent new operation. The new and delete operations are thus complementary:

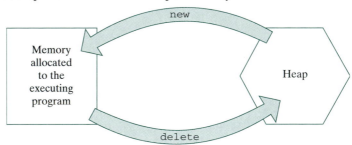

The general form of the delete operation is as follows:

THE delete OPERATION

Form:

    delete *pointerVariable*
    or

```
delete [] arrayPointerVariable
```

Purpose:

The first form frees the run-time allocated object whose address is stored in *pointerVariable*. The second form frees the run-time allocated array object whose address is stored in *arrayPointerVariable*.

For example, if `intPtr` has been allocated memory from the heap with

```
int * intPtr = new int;
```

then the statement

```
delete intPtr;
```

will release the memory location pointed to by `intPtr`, making it available for allocation at a later time. Following the operation, the value of `intPtr` will be undefined, and so the result of any attempt to dereference it

```
*intPtr
```

is unpredictable, possibly producing a run-time error. To avoid such problems, it is considered good programming practice to always set the value of such pointers to the null address,

```
delete intPtr;
intPtr = 0;
```

so that a statement of the form

```
if (intPtr != 0)
    // ... ok - intPtr can be safely dereferenced
else
    // ... not ok - intPtr's memory has been deallocated
```

can be used to guard access to the memory pointed to by `intPtr`.

Similarly, if `dPtr` is a pointer to the first element of an array allocated at run time, as in

```
cin >> numValues;

double *dPtr = double[numValues];
```

then that array's memory can be returned to the heap with the statements

```
delete [] dPtr;
dPtr = 0;
```

☞ **MEMORY LEAKS.** It is important for programs that allocate memory using `new` to deallocate that memory using `delete`. To see why, consider the following innocent-looking code:

```
do
{
    int * intPtr = new int[10];
    assert(intPtr != 0);

    // ... use the array via intPtr to solve a problem

    cout << "\nDo another (y or n)? ";
    cin >> answer;
}
while (answer != 'n');
```

The first time the loop executes, an array of 10 integers will be allocated:

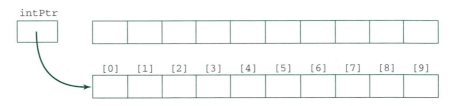

The second time the loop executes, a second array will be allocated and its address stored in `intPtr`. However, `delete` was not used to return the first array to the heap, and so it is still allocated to the program:

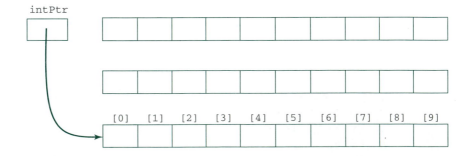

Since `intPtr` was the only means of accessing the first anonymous array and we overwrote its address in `intPtr`, that array is now "lost" or "marooned" memory—it can neither be accessed by the program nor returned to the heap.

The third time the loop executes, a third array is allocated and its address stored in `intPtr`, marooning the second anonymous array:

With each repetition of the loop 10 more memory locations will be lost. If the loop executes enough times, the assertion (`intPtr != 0`) will fail and terminate the program. Because such code loses memory over time, this situation is called a **memory leak**.

To avoid memory leaks, the memory to which a pointer points should always be deallocated before the pointer is assigned a new address

```
do
{
   int * intPtr = new int[10];
   assert(intPtr != 0);

   // ... use the array via intPtr to solve a problem

   delete [] intPtr;

   cout << "\nDo another (y or n)? ";
   cin >> answer;
}
while (answer != 'n');
```

This will ensure that the memory pointed to by a pointer is released to the heap and thus avoid a memory leak.

RUN-TIME ALLOCATION IN CLASSES—DESTRUCTORS, COPY CONSTRUCTORS, AND ASSIGNMENT

Using run-time allocated storage in container classes requires adding some new members to the class and modifying other members. These include:

1. *Destructors*:   To "tear down" the storage structure and deallocate its memory
2. *Copy constructors*:   To make copies of objects—for instance, for value parameters and to initialize a new object with an existing object's value
3. *Assignment*:   To assign one storage structure to another

We will illustrate this using our `Stack` class from Chaps. 4 and 6.

In Chap. 3 we used a compile-time array to store the stack elements. Suppose we revise that `Stack` class by using a run-time allocated array so that the user can specify the capacity of the stack during run time. (We will also make it a class template as described in Chap. 6.) We simply change the declaration of the `myArray` member to a pointer and `myCapacity` to a variable:

```
template <typename StackElement>
class Stack
{
/***** Function Members *****/
public:
   . . .
```

```
/***** Data Members *****/
private:
  StackElement * myArrayPtr;   // run-time allocated array
  int myCapacity_,             // capacity of stack
      myTop_;                  // top of stack
}; // end of class declaration
```

(Note that to avoid confusion, we have used different names for the data members.) We might wish to allow declarations such as

```
Stack<int> s1, s2(n);
```

to construct s1 as a stack with some default capacity and s2 as a stack with capacity n. To permit both forms of the declaration, we declare a constructor with a default argument. And since this constructor must really construct something (and not just initialize data members as our constructors have done up to now), it is nontrivial, and so we define it outside the class as shown in Fig. 8.3. The prototypes and definitions of empty() as well as the prototypes of push(), top(), pop(), and operator<<() are the same as before (except for some name changes). The definitions of push(), top(), pop(), and operator<<() require accessing the elements of the array data member. But as we have noted, the subscript operator [] can be used in the same manner for run-time allocated arrays as for ordinary arrays, and thus (except for name changes), the definitions of these functions are the same as before.

FIGURE 8.3   Stack CLASS WITH RUN-TIME ALLOCATION

```
/***** RStackT.h *****/
/* RStackT.h provides a Stack template.
 *
 * Receives:  Type parameter StackElement
 * Basic operations:
 *   Constructor:  Constructs an empty stack
 *   empty:   Checks if a stack is empty
 *   push:    Modifies a stack by adding a value at the top
 *   top:     Accesses the top stack value; leaves stack unchanged
 *   pop:     Modifies a stack by removing the value at the top
 *   display: Displays all the stack elements
 * Class Invariant:
 *   1. The stack elements (if any) are stored in positions
 *       0, 1, . . ., myTop_ of myArrayPtr.
 *   2. -1 <= myTop_ < myCapacity_
 ------------------------------------------------------------*/

#ifndef RTSTACK
#define RTSTACK
```

```cpp
#include <iostream>
#include <cassert>
#include <cstdlib>
using namespace std;
template <typename StackElement>
class Stack
{
/***** Function Members *****/
public:
/* --- Class constructor ---
 * Precondition:  A stack has been defined.
 * Receive:       Integer numElements > 0; (default = 128)
 * Postcondition: The stack has been constructed as a stack
 *                with capacity numElements.
 ****************************************************************/
Stack(int numElements = 128);

/* --- Is the Stack empty? ---
 *
 * Return: True if the Stack containing this function is empty
 *         and false otherwise
 ****************************************************************/
bool empty() const;

/* --- Add a value to the stack ---
 *
 * Receive: The Stack containing this function (implicitly)
 *          A value to be added to a Stack
 * Return:  The Stack (implicitly), with value added at its
 *          top, provided there's space
 * Output:  "Stack-full" message if no space for value.
 ****************************************************************/
void push(const StackElement & value);

/* --- Return value at top of the stack ---
 *
 * Receive: The Stack containing this function (implicitly)
 * Return:  The value at the top of the Stack (if nonempty)
 * Output:  "Stack-empty" message if stack is empty.
 ****************************************************************/
StackElement top();

/* --- Remove value at top of the stack ---
 *
 * Receive: The Stack containing this function (implicitly)
 * Return:  The Stack containing this function with its top
 *          value (if any) removed
 * Output:  "Stack-empty" message if stack is empty.
 ****************************************************************/
void pop();
```

```
/* --- Display values stored in the stack ---
 *
 * Receive: The Stack containing this function (implicitly)
 *          The ostream out
 * Output:  The Stack's contents, from top down, to out
 ************************************************************/
void display(ostream & out) const;

/***** Data Members *****/
private:
  StackElement * myArrayPtr;   // run-time allocated array
  int myCapacity_,             // capacity of stack
      myTop_;                  // top of stack
};   // end of class declaration

//*** Definition of class constructor
template <typename StackElement>
Stack<StackElement>::Stack(int numElements)
{
  assert (numElements > 0);    // check precondition
  myCapacity_ = numElements;   // set stack capacity
                               // allocate array of this capacity
  myArrayPtr = new StackElement[myCapacity_];

  if (myArrayPtr == 0)         // check if memory available
  {
    cerr << "*** Inadequate memory to allocate stack ***\n";
    exit(-1);
  }                            // or assert(myArrayPtr != 0);

  myTop_ = -1;
}

//*** Definition of empty()
template <typename StackElement>
inline bool Stack<StackElement>::empty() const
{
  return (myTop_ == -1);
}

//*** Definition of push()
template <typename StackElement>
void Stack<StackElement>::push(const StackElement & value)
{
  if (myTop_ < myCapacity_ - 1)
  {
    ++myTop_;
    myArrayPtr[myTop_] = value;
  }                  // or simply, myArrayPtr[++myTop_] = value;
  else
    cerr << "*** Stack is full — can't add new value ***\n";
}
```

```cpp
//*** Definition of top()
template <typename StackElement>
StackElement Stack<StackElement>::top()
{
  if (myTop_ >= 0)
    return myArrayPtr[myTop_];
  cerr << "*** Stack is empty ***\n";
}

//*** Definition of pop ()
template <typename StackElement>
void Stack<StackElement>::pop()
{
  if (myTop_ >= 0)
    myTop_--;
  else
    cerr << "*** Stack is empty -- can't remove a value ***\n";
}

//--- Definition of display()
template <typename StackElement>
void Stack<StackElement>::display(ostream & out) const
{
  for (int i = myTop_; i >= 0; i--)
    out << myArrayPtr[i] << endl;
}

#endif
```

Now a program can include our RStackT header file and declare

```cpp
cin >> num;
Stack<double> s1, s2(num);
```

s1 will be constructed as a stack with capacity 128 and s2 will be constructed as a stack with capacity num.

CLASS DESTRUCTOR.   For any class object obj we have used up to now, when obj is declared, the class constructor is called to initialize obj. When the lifetime of obj is over, its storage is reclaimed automatically because the location of the memory allocated is determined at compile time.

For objects created during run time, however, a new problem arises. To illustrate, consider a program segment

```cpp
{
  cout << "Stack capacity needed? ";
  cin >> num;
  Stack<double> st(num);
       . . .
}
```

The data members `myCapacity_`, `myTop_`, and `myArrayPtr` of `st` are known at compile time and thus are allocated memory in the usual way:

But the array used to store stack elements created by the constructor is not allocated until run time:

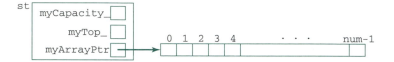

When the end of the block is reached, the lifetime of `st` ends, the memory allocated to `myCapacity_`, `myTop_`, and `myArrayPtr` is automatically reclaimed, but this is not true for the run-time allocated anonymous array:

marooned!

☞   To avoid these "marooned" blocks of memory that are unusable, a **destructor** function should be provided in the class to do any necessary "clean-up" activities at the end of a class object's lifetime.

▶ The destructor's role is to reclaim any storage that was allocated to the object at run time (the opposite of the constructor's role).

▶ At any point in a program *where an object goes out of scope, the compiler will automatically insert calls to this destructor.*

By providing a destructor for any class that uses run-time allocated memory, a class object will automatically release that memory at the end of its lifetime, avoiding a memory leak. This makes class objects self-contained, which is another characteristic of good design.

The name of a destructor is always the name of the class preceded by the tilde (~) character:

THE CLASS DESTRUCTOR

Form:

    ~ClassName()

Purpose:

The compiler calls this function to destroy objects of type `ClassName` whenever such objects should no longer exist:

▶ At the end of the main function for *ClassName* objects that are defined within `main()` as static or global objects

▶ At the end of each block in which a nonstatic *ClassName* object is defined

▶ At the end of each function having a *ClassName* parameter

▶ When a *ClassName* object allocated at run time is destroyed using `delete`

▶ When an object containing a *ClassName* data member is destroyed

▶ When an object whose type is derived from type *ClassName* is destroyed (see Sec. 12.2)

▶ When a compiler-generated *ClassName* copy (made by the copy constructor) is no longer needed

Note that like a constructor, a destructor has no return type. However, unlike a constructor, a destructor cannot have parameters, and thus can only have a single definition.

For our `Stack` class template, the destructor can use the `delete` operation to deallocate the run-time array data member as shown in Fig. 8.4.

FIGURE 8.4   DESTRUCTOR FOR `Stack` CLASS

```
    . . .
template <typename StackElement>
class Stack
{
/***** Function Members *****/
public:

/* -- Class destructor --
 * Precondition:  The lifetime of the Stack containing this
 *                    function should end.
 * Postcondition: The run-time array in the Stack containing
 *                    this function has been deallocated.
 ************************************************************/
 ~Stack();
   . . .


/***** Data Members *****/
    . . .
};  // end of typename declaration

//*** Definition of class destructor
template <typename StackElement>
Stack<StackElement>::~Stack()
{
  delete [] myArrayPtr;
}
    . . .
```

Given this function, if `st` is

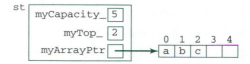

and `st`'s lifetime is over, `st.~Stack()` will be called first, which results in

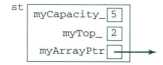

The auto storage of `st`—`myCapacity_`, `myTop_`, and `myArrayPtr`—will then be reclaimed in the usual manner.

COPY CONSTRUCTOR.   There are times when the compiler needs to create a copy of an object. For example:

▶ When an argument is passed as a value parameter, the compiler must construct the parameter as a copy of the argument.

▶ When a function returns a local object, the function terminates, ending the lifetime of that object, so the compiler builds an (anonymous) copy of the object called a *temporary* to transmit the return value back to the caller.

▶ Whenever temporary storage of an object is needed, the compiler must make a copy of that object.

▶ Whenever an object is initialized in a declaration of the form

```
Type obj = initial_value;
```

or

```
Type obj(initial_value);
```

the compiler must make a copy of *initial_value*.

To make copies of a class object, the compiler supplies a **default copy constructor**, which simply copies the members of the object byte by byte. Although this has been adequate for classes up to now, it does not accomplish what is needed for a class containing pointers to run-time allocated arrays (or other structures). To see why, suppose `st` is the stack given earlier. When the default copy constructor copies `st`, it blindly copies the data members of `st`. Although it correctly copies `myCapacity_`, `myTop_`, and `myArrayPtr`, it does not copy the run-time allocated array, because that array is not a data member of `st`. The result can be pictured as follows:

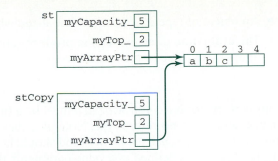

☞ That is, when a class contains a data member that is a pointer, the default copy constructor *does not make a distinct copy* of the object pointed to by that pointer. This can be a problem. For example, if stCopy is a value parameter in a function that modifies its value parameter's anonymous array, these modifications will simultaneously change the anonymous array of st. This should not happen with a value parameter!

What is needed is to create a *distinct copy* of st, in which the array in stCopy has exactly the same elements as the array in st:

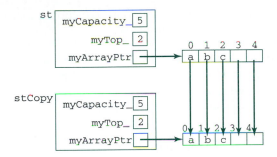

To make this possible, C++ allows a class to have its own copy constructor whose general form is

---

CLASS COPY CONSTRUCTOR

Form:

    ClassName(const ClassName & original);

where

ClassName is the name of the class containing this function; and
original is a reference to the object being copied.

Purpose:

This function is used by the compiler to construct a copy of the argument corresponding to original. The compiler calls this function whenever such a copy is needed, including when

▶ An object of type ClassName is passed as a value parameter
▶ The return value of a function is a value of type ClassName

> ▸ An object of type `ClassName` is initialized when it is declared
> ▸ The evaluation of an expression produces an intermediate (or temporary) value of type `ClassName`

The copy constructor *is a constructor* so it must be a function member, its name is the class name, and it has no return type. Note also that the parameter of a copy constructor *must* be a reference parameter (and should be a `const` reference parameter, as well) because if it is defined as a value parameter, then a call to the function will

1. Pass `original` as a value parameter, which means that a copy of `original` must be made
2. To make a copy of `original` as a value parameter, the copy constructor is called again (with `original` as its argument)
3. To pass `original` as a value parameter to that copy constructor, a copy of `original` is needed
4. To make a copy of `original`, the copy constructor is called again (with `original` as its argument)

and so on, resulting in an infinite recursion! Defining `original` as a reference parameter avoids this infinite recursion because the reference (address) of `original` is passed, instead of a copy of `original`.

Figure 8.5 shows a copy constructor for our Stack class template.

FIGURE 8.5   COPY CONSTRUCTOR FOR `Stack` CLASS

```
    . . .
template <typename StackElement>
class Stack
{
/***** Function Members *****/
public:

/* --- Class Copy Constructor ---
 * Precondition:  A copy of a stack is needed
 * Receive:       The stack to be copied (as a const
 *                    reference parameter)
 * Postcondition: A copy of original has been constructed.
 ************************************************************/
Stack(const Stack<StackElement> & original);
   . . .

/***** Data Members *****/
   . . .
};  // end of class declaration
```

```
//*** Definition of class copy constructor
template <typename StackElement>
Stack<StackElement>::Stack(const Stack<StackElement> & original)
{
                                        // copy myCapacity_ member
   myCapacity_ = original.myCapacity_;
                                        // allocate array in copy
   myArrayPtr = new StackElement[myCapacity_];

   if (myArrayPtr == 0)                 // check if memory available
   {
     cerr << "*** Inadequate memory to allocate stack ***\n";
     exit(-1);
   }
                                        // copy array member
   for (int pos = 0; pos < myCapacity_; pos++)
     myArrayPtr[pos] = original.myArrayPtr[pos];
   myTop_ = original.myTop_ ;           // copy myTop_ member
}
   . . .
```

ASSIGNMENT.   In addition to a default copy constructor, the compiler also provides for each class a default definition for the assignment operator (=) that, like the default copy constructor, simply does a byte-by-byte copy of the object being assigned. As with the copy constructor, this works fine unless the class has a pointer data member. The problem is similar to the copy constructor problem. For example, an assignment statement

```
stCopy = st;
```

would produce the same situation pictured earlier; the myArrayPtr data members of st and stCopy would both point to the same anonymous array. The default assignment operator does not make a distinct copy of a class object that contains a pointer data member. This means that the class designer must overload the assignment operator (operator=()) so that it creates a distinct copy of the stack being assigned.

The general form of the assignment operation can be described as follows:

ASSIGNMENT OPERATION

Form:

```
ClassName & ClassName::operator=(const ClassName & original)
{
    // ... make a copy of original

    return *this;
}
```

where

ClassName is the name of the class containing this function; and original is a reference to the object being copied.

Purpose:

For classes that have pointer data members, overload `operator=` to make the object receiving this message a distinct copy of *original*. `operator=` *must be defined as a member function.*

Note that the assignment operator must be a member function. Thus, an assignment

```
stLeft = stRight;
```

will be translated by the compiler as

```
stLeft.operator=(stRight);
```

The behavior of the assignment operator is similar to that of the copy constructor, with three main differences. One difference is that whereas the copy constructor builds and returns a *new* object, the assignment operator must assign this object to an *existing* object that already has a value. Usually, it must destroy the old value, deallocating its memory to avoid a memory leak, and then replace it with the new value.

The second difference is that the copy constructor need not be concerned with *self-assignments*

```
object = object;
```

but the assignment operator must. If it did not, destroying the old value of *object* on the left-hand side will also destroy the value of the *object* on the right-hand side, so there is nothing left to assign.

The third difference is that the copy constructor returns no value and thus has no return type, but the assignment operation should return the object on the left-hand side of the assignment to support chained assignments. That is, an assignment like

```
st3 = st2 = st1;
```

must first assign `st1` to `st2`, and then assign `st2` to `st3`. Since such a call will be processed as

```
st3.operator=(st2.operator=(st1));
```

the expression `st2.operator=(st1)` must return `st2`. This means that when an object receives the `operator=` message, it must return *itself*. And as we saw in Sec. 8.4, this can be accomplished by making the return type of `operator=()` a reference to type `Stack` and having it return `*this`.

We can now write the definition of `operator=()`. Figure 8.6 shows the prototype and a definition of `operator=()` for `Stacks`.

 FIGURE 8.6   ASSIGNMENT FOR Stack CLASS

```
   . . .
template <typename StackElement>
class Stack
{
/***** Function Members *****/
public:
```

```
/* --- Assignment Operator ---
 *  Receive: Stack stRight (the right side of the assignment operator)
 *           object containing this member function
 *  Return (implicit parameter):  The Stack containing this
 *           function which will be a copy of stRight
 *  Return (function): A reference to the Stack containing
 *           this function
 ************************************************************/
Stack<StackElement> & operator=(const Stack<StackElement> & original);

  . . .


/***** Data Members *****/
  . . .
};  // end of class declaration

//*** Definition of operator=()
template <typename StackElement>
Stack<StackElement> &
   Stack<StackElement>::operator=(const Stack<StackElement> & original)
{
  if (this != &original)                    // check that not st = st
  {
    delete [] myArrayPtr;                   // destroy previous array

    myCapacity_ = original.myCapacity_;     // copy myCapacity_ member
                                            // allocate array in copy
    myArrayPtr = new StackElement[myCapacity_];
    if (myArrayPtr == 0)                    // check if memory available
    {
      cerr << "*** Inadequate memory to allocate stack ***\n";
      exit(-1);
    }
                                            // copy array member
    for (int pos = 0; pos < myCapacity_; pos++)
      myArrayPtr[pos] = original.myArrayPtr[pos];
    myTop_ = original.myTop_ ;              // copy myTop_ member
  }

  return *this;                            // return reference to
}                                          //   this object
  . . .
```

A FINAL NOTE

☞ The following is a general rule of thumb to remember when designing a class:

> If a class allocates memory at run time using new, then it should provide
>
> ▸ a *copy constructor* that the compiler can use to make distinct copies
>
> ▸ an *assignment operator* that a programmer can use to make distinct copies
>
> ▸ a *destructor* that releases the run-time allocated memory to the heap

Remembering this rule will help you to build classes whose objects are self-contained, that are free of memory leaks, and that behave in the way a user expects.

The number of times the class constructors, destructor, and copy constructor get called automatically by the compiler when a class is used will surprise most people. The simple program in Fig. 8.7 demonstrates this. It is a simple driver program for the Stack class template developed in this section but which was modified by adding statements to the constructor, destructor, and copy constructor to trace when they are called.

FIGURE 8.7   CALLS TO CONSTRUCTORS AND DESTRUCTOR

```
/* This program demonstrates how often a class's constructor,
 * destructor, and copy constructor can get called automatically
 * by the compiler.  It uses the Stack class from Fig. 8.6 but
 * with output statements inserted into the constructor, destructor,
 * and copy constructor to trace when they are called.
 ******************************************************************/

#include "RStackT1.h"
#include <iostream>
using namespace std;

/* Function to print a stack.
 * Receives: Stack<int> st as a value parameter
 * Output:   The contents of the stack
 ***********************************************/
void Print (Stack<int> st)
{
  st.display(cout);
}

int main()
{
  int numElements;
  cout << "Enter stack capacity: ";
  cin >> numElements;

  cout << "**A**\n";
  Stack<int> s(numElements);
```

```
      cout << "**B**\n";
      for (int i = 1; i <= 5; i++)
      {
         cout << "**C**\n";
         s.push(i);
      }

      cout << "**D**\n";
      Stack<int> t = s;

      cout << "**E**\n";
      Print(t);

      cout << "**F**\n";
      Stack<int> u;

      cout << "**G**\n";
      u = t;

      cout << "**H**\n";
      Print(u);

      cout << "**I**\n";
   }
```

EXECUTION:

```
Enter stack capacity: 5
**A**
CONSTRUCTOR
**B**
**C**
**C**
**C**
**C**
**C**
**D**
COPY CONSTRUCTOR
**E**
COPY CONSTRUCTOR
5
4
3
2
1
DESTRUCTOR
**F**
CONSTRUCTOR
**G**
**H**
COPY CONSTRUCTOR
```

```
5
4
3
2
1
DESTRUCTOR
**I**
DESTRUCTOR
DESTRUCTOR
DESTRUCTOR
```

✔ Quick Quiz 8.5

1. Memory for a C-style array is allocated at _____ time; memory for a vector<T> object is allocated at _____ time. (Run or compile)

2. The _____ operation is used to request memory during program execution. If not enough memory is available, it returns the _____; otherwise it returns the _____ of a block of memory. The newly-allocated memory location is a(n) _____ variable.

3. The _____ operation is used to release memory during program execution.

4. The base address of a run-time allocated array is stored in a(n) _____.

5. Given the declarations

    ```
    int a[] = {44, 22, 66, 11, 77, 33};
    int * p = a;
    ```

    what is the value of p[2]?

6. Write a prototype for the copy constructor of a class named C.

7. Write a prototype for the destructor of a class named C.

8. The parameter of a copy constructor should always be a value parameter to ensure that a distinct copy is made. (True or false)

9. The assignment operator for a class must be a function member. (True or false)

10. The compiler supplies a _____ copy constructor that simply copies an object's members byte by byte.

11. When is it essential that a class have its own copy constructor and why?

12. The problem of run-time memory getting marooned is called a(n) _____ .

13. When an object's lifetime is over, the compiler calls the object's _____ .

14. When is it essential that a class have its own destructor and why?

15. When is it essential that a class have its own assignment operator and why?

✍ EXERCISES 8.5

For Exercises 1–10, write C++ statements to do what is asked.

1. Declare a char pointer variable named charPtr.

2. Allocate an anonymous char variable, storing its address in charPtr.

3. Input a character value and store it in the anonymous variable of Exercise 2.

4. Display the value of the anonymous variable of Exercise 2.

5. Convert the case of the value of the anonymous variable of Exercise 2 using character-processing functions such as `isupper()` and `tolower()` from `<cctype>`.

6. Declare a `double` pointer variable named `doublePtr`.

7. Allow the user to enter *n*, the number of values to be processed; then allocate an anonymous array of *n* `double` values, storing its address in `doublePtr`.

8. Fill the anonymous array of Exercise 7 with *n* input values, entered from the keyboard.

9. Compute and display the average of the values in the anonymous array of Exercise 7.

10. Deallocate the storage of the anonymous array of Exercise 7.

11. Find the base address of the anonymous array allocated in Exercise 7. Also, draw a memory map showing the addresses of its first few elements.

12. Describe the output produced by the following statements:

```cpp
int * foo, * goo;

foo = new int;
*foo = 1;
cout << (*foo) << endl;
goo = new int;
*goo = 3;
cout << (*foo) << (*goo) << endl;
*foo = *goo + 3;
cout << (*foo) << (*goo) << endl;
foo = goo;
*goo = 5;
cout << (*foo) << (*goo) << endl;
*foo = 7;
cout << (*foo) << (*goo) << endl;
goo = foo;
*foo = 9;
cout << (*foo) << (*goo) << endl;
```

Execises 13 and 14 ask you to modify a class template. You should also test your modified version with a driver program as instructed in Programming Problems 5 and 6 at the end of this chapter.

13. Modify the `Queue` class template from Exercise 17 of Sec. 6.4 so that it uses a run-time array to store the queue elements. (See also Exercise 5 of Sec. 5.2.) Add a destructor, a copy constructor, and an assignment operator.

14. Modify the `Queue` class template from Exercise 13 to display each time the constructor(s), destructor, copy constructor, and assignment operator get called.

8.6 A POINTER-BASED IMPLEMENTATION OF LINKED LISTS IN C++

In Sec. 8.2 we introduced linked lists and pointed out their superiority for implementing dynamic lists that change often because of insertions and deletions at arbitrary locations in the list. We also noted that to implement linked lists, we need to be able to do three things:

1. Divide memory into nodes, each having a data part and a next part, and implement pointers to these nodes

2. Define operations to access the values stored in each node, that is, operations to access the data part and the next part of the node pointed to by some pointer

3. Keep track of the nodes in use along with the available free nodes and transfer nodes between those in use and the pool of free nodes.

In the array-based implementation of Sec. 8.3, we used an array of structs for (1) and managed this array so it performed as required in (2) and (3). However, C++'s pointers and dynamic allocation and deallocation mechanisms described in the preceding two sections can be used to provide a better implementation.

NODE STRUCTURE

As with the array-based implementation, the basic structure for the nodes of linked lists will contain two fields, data and next. The data member will again be of a type that is appropriate for storing a list element, and the next member will store a link that points to the successor of this element. However, unlike the array-based implementation, this link will be a C++ pointer rather than an array index. Also, we will use a class instead of a struct for the nodes (see Footnote 7.)

The appropriate declarations for this implementation of a linked list are

```
class Node
{
 public:
   DataType data;
   Node * next;
   . . .
};
```

Note that this definition of a Node is a *recursive (or self-referential) definition* because it uses the name Node in its definition: the next member is defined as a pointer to a Node.

In this implementation there is no need to be concerned about initializing and maintaining a storage pool of free nodes, as required in the array-based implementation. This is done automatically by the system's heap manager, with the predefined C++ functions new and delete getting nodes from and returning nodes to the heap:

▶ To declare a pointer to nodes:

```
      Node * ptr;
```

or

```
      typedef Node * NodePointer;
      NodePointer ptr;
```

▶ To get a node pointed to by ptr:

```
      ptr = new Node;
         // uses default Node constructor
```

```
ptr = new Node(dataVal);
    // uses Node constructor to set data part
    // to dataVal and next part to null

ptr = new Node(dataVal, linkVal);
    // uses Node constructor to set data part
    // to dataVal and next part to linkVal
```

▶ To deallocate a node pointed to by `ptr`:

```
delete ptr;
```

▶ To access the `data` and `next` part of node pointed to by `ptr`:

```
ptr->data and ptr->next
```

One might wonder why we have made the data members of `Node` public. This is because the declaration of class `Node` will be placed inside another class `LinkedList`. Making the data members of `Node` public makes them accessible to all of the member and friend functions of `Linked List`.[7] However, the declaration of `Node` will be inside the private section of the class `LinkedList`, these data members will not be accessible outside the class:

```
#ifndef LINKEDLIST
#define LINKEDLIST

template <typename DataType>
class LinkedList
{
/*** Node class ***/
private:
class Node
{
 public:
   DataType data;
   Node * next;

   . . .
};
typedef Node * NodePointer;

/*** Function members ***/
public:
   . . .


/*** Data members ***/
private:
   . . .
};
#endif
```

---

[7]We could accomplish this also by making `Node` a `struct`, whose members are public by default. However, in this text we use `struct` for C-style structs that contain no function members and `class` when there are.

DATA MEMBERS FOR `LinkedLists`

The linked lists we have considered in Secs. 8.2 and 8.3 such as

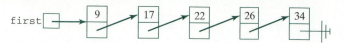

are characterized by

1. There is a pointer to the first node in the list.

2. Each node contains a pointer to the next node in the list.

3. The last node contains a null pointer.

As we will see in the next chapter, there are many other variations—circular, doubly-linked, and lists with head nodes, to name but a few. We will call the kind of linked lists we've been considering **simple linked lists**.

For simple linked lists, only one data member is needed: a pointer to the first node. But, for convenience, another data member is usually added that keeps a count of the elements in the list:

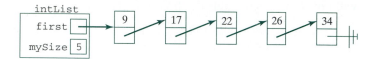

If we used only one data member, then each time we need to know the length of the list, we would have to traverse the list and count the elements:

1. Set `count` to 0.

2. Make `ptr` point at the first node.

3. While `ptr` is not null:

   a. Increment `count`.

   b. Make `ptr` point at the next node.

4. Return `count`.

FUNCTION MEMBERS FOR `LinkedLists`

CONSTRUCTOR.   The constructor creates an empty list. It need only make `first` a null pointer and initialize `mySize` to 0:

```
//--- Constructor
LinkedList()
{
   first = 0;
   mySize = 0;
}
```

DESTRUCTOR.   A destructor is needed for the same reason as for run-time arrays. If we don't provide one, the default destructor used by the compiler for a linked list will cause memory leaks. The compiler deallocates memory for the data members `first` and `mySize`, but the nodes in the linked list are marooned:

marooned!

COPY CONSTRUCTOR AND ASSIGNMENT.   A copy constructor and an assignment operator also are needed for the same reasons as for run-time arrays. If we don't provide one, the default copy constructor and assignment operator (which just do byte-by-byte copying) used by the compiler for a linked list like `intList` will produce

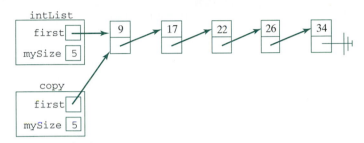

A copy constructor and an assignment operator must be provided that traverse the list, allocate a new node corresponding to each node in the list, and link them together:

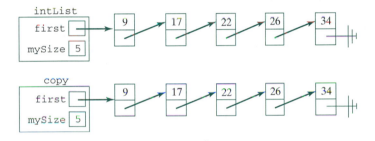

We leave the details as exercises.

We might note in this connection that there are times when we want to *prevent copying and/or assignments*; for example, streams are not allowed to be copied. We can accomplish this by putting a copy constructor and/or assignment operator—neither of which needs to do anything—in a private section of the class.

BASIC LIST OPERATIONS.   The member functions that carry out the basic list operations are straightforward implementations of the algorithms given in Sec. 8.2. For example, a list is traversed as previously described by initializing a pointer `ptr` to the first node and then advancing it through the list by following the next fields and processing the data stored in each node:

```
ptr = first;
while (ptr != 0)
{
   /* Appropriate statements to process
         ptr->data are inserted here */
   ptr = ptr->next;
}
```

It should be clear that this C++ pointer-based implementation of the basic list traversal operation is a simple modification of that used in the array-based implementation of linked lists. The same is true of the other basic list operations as well, and these are left as exercises.

✍ EXERCISES 8.6

Exercises 1–7 assume the following declarations (which are used to process singly-linked lists as described in this section),

```
class Node                    or equivalently,      struct Node
{                                                   {
public:                                                int data;
   int data;                                           Node * next;
   Node * next;                                     };
};
                                                    Node * p1, * p2, *p3;
Node * p1, * p2, * p3;
```

and that the following statements have been executed:

```
p1 = new Node;
p2 = new Node;
p3 = new Node;
```

Tell what will be displayed by each of the code segments or explain why an error occurs.

1.
```
p1->data = 123;
p2->data = 456;
p1->next = p2;
p2->next = 0;
cout << p1->data << "   " << p1->next->data << endl;
```

2.
```
p1->data = 12;
p2->data = 34;
p1 = p2;
cout << p1->data << "   " << p2->data << endl;
```

3.
```
p1->data = 12;
p2->data = 34;
*p1 = *p2;
cout << p1->data << "   " << p2->data << endl;
```

4.
```
p1->data = 123;
p2->data = 456;
p1->next = p2;
p2->next = 0;
cout << p2->data << "   " << p2->next->data << endl;
```

5.
```
p1->data = 12;
p2->data = 34;
p3->data = 34;
p1->next = p2;
p2->next = p3;
p3->next = 0;
```

```
cout << p1->data << "   " << p1->next->data << endl;
cout << p2->data << "   " << p2->next->data << endl;
cout << p1->next->next->data << endl;
cout << p3->data << endl;
```

6.
```
p1->data = 111;
p2->data = 222;
p1->next = p2;
p2->next = p1;
cout << p1->data << "   " << p2->data << endl;
cout << p1->next->data << endl;
cout << p1->next->next->data << endl;
```

7.
```
p1->data = 12;
p2->data = 34;
p1 = p2;
p2->next = p1;
cout << p1->data << "   " << p2->data << endl;
cout << p1->next->data << "   " << p2->next->data << endl;
```

Exercises 8–17 use the following linked list and node pointers p1, p2, p3, and p4:

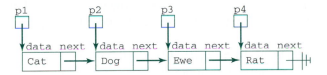

Draw a similar diagram to show how this configuration changes when the given program segment is executed, or explain why an error occurs.

8.
```
p1 = p2->next;
```

9.
```
p4 = p1;
```

10.
```
p4->data = p1->data;
```

11.
```
p4->next->data = p1->data;
```

12.
```
p2->next = p3->next;
```

13.
```
p4->next = p1;
```

14.
```
p1->next = p3->next;
p1 = p3;
```

15.
```
p1 = p3;
p1->next = p3->next;
```

16.
```
p4->next = p3->next;
p3->next = p2->next;
p2->next = p1->next;
```

17.
```
p4->next = p3;
p4->next->next = p2;
p4->next->next->next = p1;
p1 = 0;
```

Exercises 18–23 ask you to write various functions and class templates. You should test them with driver programs as instructed in Programming Problems 7–12 at the end of this chapter.

18. Write a nonrecursive function that counts the nodes in a linked list.

19. Proceed as in Exercise 18, but write a recursive function.

20. Write a complete `LinkedList` class template using the ideas described in this section. For basic operations it should have a constructor, destructor, copy constructor, assignment, and the basic list operations: empty, traverse, insert, and delete. Also, include a linear search operation to search the linked list for a given item, returning a pointer to a node containing the item in its data part, or a null pointer if it is not found.

21. For `LinkedList` as in Exercise 20, add a member function to reverse the linked list; that is, the last node becomes the first node, and all links between nodes are reversed.

22. For `LinkedList` as in Exercise 20, add a nonrecursive boolean-valued function that determines whether the data items in the linked list are arranged in ascending order.

23. Proceed as in Exercise 22, but write a recursive function.

8.7 THE STANDARD `list` CLASS TEMPLATE

The `list` class template in the Standard Template Library uses a linked list to store the items in a list. The structure of this linked list, however, is more complex than the simple linked lists we have been considering in this chapter. We will wait until the next chapter for a "look under the hood" at this linked structure. In this section we will describe its basic operations and other important features.

COMPARING `list` WITH OTHER CONTAINERS

We have considered in detail C-style arrays (and `valarrays`) and the `vector` and `deque` containers from STL. We now describe the `list` container, whose major strength is insertion and deletion at any point in the sequence. The following table shows how these four containers compare with respect to insertion and deletion, type of access, and the amount of overhead. An X indicates that the container does not have the specified property; the other ratings are $\sqrt{-}$ (poor), $\sqrt{}$ (good), and $\sqrt{+}$ (excellent).

Property	Array	vector	deque	list
Direct/random access (`[]`)	$\sqrt{+}$	$\sqrt{+}$	$\sqrt{}$	X
Sequential access	$\sqrt{+}$	$\sqrt{+}$	$\sqrt{}$	$\sqrt{+}$
Insert/delete at front	$\sqrt{-}$	$\sqrt{-}$	$\sqrt{+}$	$\sqrt{+}$
Insert/delete in middle	$\sqrt{-}$	$\sqrt{-}$	$\sqrt{-}$	$\sqrt{+}$
Insert/delete at end	$\sqrt{+}$	$\sqrt{+}$	$\sqrt{+}$	$\sqrt{+}$
Overhead	lowest	low	low/medium	high

As the table indicates, `list` does not support direct/random access and thus does not provide the subscript operator `[]`.

ITERATORS

The iterator provided in `vector` is called a **random-access iterator** and `list`'s iterator is a **bidirectional iterator**, which is weaker than a random-access iterator. Both kinds of iterators have the following operations:

++	Move iterator to the next element (like `ptr = ptr->next`)
--	Move iterator to the preceding element (like `ptr = ptr->prev`)
*	Dereferencing operator: to access the value stored at the position to which an iterator points (like `ptr->data`)
=	Assignment: For iterators of the same type, `it1 = it2` sets `it1`'s position to same as `it2`'s
== and !=	For iterators of the same type, `it1 == it2` is true if `it1` and `it2` are both positioned at the same element

But bidirectional iterators do *not* have the following operations:

Addition (+) and subtraction (-)
The corresponding shortcuts (+=, -=)
Subscript ([])

This means that algorithms such as `sort()` that require direct/random access cannot be used with `lists`. (This is the reason `list` provides its own `sort()` operation.)

BASIC `list` OPERATIONS
Table 8.1 describes the most useful member functions and operators in `list`.

TABLE 8.1   BASIC `list` OPERATIONS

Operation	Description
Constructors	
`list<T> l;`	Construct `l` as an empty `list`
`list<T> l(n);`	Construct `l` as a `list` to contain *n* elements (set to default value)
`list<T> l(n, initVal);`	Construct `l` as a `list` to contain *n* copies of *initVal*
`list<T> l(fPtr, lPtr);`	Construct `l` as a `list` to contain copies of elements in memory locations `fptr` up to `lptr` (pointers of type `T*`)
Copy constructor	
Destructor	
`~list()`	Destroy contents, erasing all items.
`l.empty()`	Return `true` if and only if `l` contains no values
`l.size()`	Return the number of values `l` contains
`l.push_back(value);`	Append *value* at `l`'s end
`l.push_front(value);`	Insert *value* in front of `l`'s first element
`l.insert(pos, value)`	Insert *value* into `l` at iterator position *pos* and return an iterator pointing to the new element's position

(continued)

TABLE 8.1   BASIC LIST OPERATIONS (*continued*)

Operation	Description
`l.insert(pos, n, value);`	Insert *n* copies of *value* into *l* at iterator position *pos*
`l.insert(pos, fPtr, lPtr);`	Insert copies of all the elements in the range [*fPtr, lPtr*) at iterator position *pos*
`l.pop_back();`	Erase *l*'s last element
`l.pop_front();`	Erase *l*'s first element
`l.erase(pos);`	Erase the value in *l* at iterator position *pos*
`l.erase(pos1, pos2);`	Erase the values in *l* from iterator positions *pos1* to *pos2*
`l.remove(value);`	Erase all elements in *l* that match *value*, using == to compare items.
`l.unique()`	Replace all repeating sequences of a single element by a single occurrence of that element.
`l.front()`	Return a reference to *l*'s first element
`l.back()`	Return a reference to *l*'s last element
`l.begin()`	Return an iterator positioned at *l*'s first value
`l.end()`	Return an iterator positioned 1 element past *l*'s last value
`l.rbegin()`	Return a reverse iterator positioned at *l*'s last value
`l.rend()`	Return a reverse iterator positioned 1 element before *l*'s first value
`l.sort();`	Sort *l*'s elements (using <)
`l.reverse();`	Reverse the order of *l*'s elements
`l1.merge(l2);`	Remove all the elements in *l2* and merge them into *l1*, that is, move the elements of *l2* into *l1* and place them so that the final list of elements is sorted using <; (Assumes both *l2* and *l1* were sorted using <)
`l1.splice(pos, l2);`	Remove all the elements in *l2* and insert them into *l1* at iterator position *pos*
`l1.splice(to, l2, from);`	Remove the element in *l2* at iterator position *from* and insert it into *l1* at iterator position *to*
`l1.splice(pos, l2, first, last);`	Remove all the elements in *l2* at iterator positions [*first, last*) and insert them into *l1* at iterator position *pos*

(continued)

TABLE 8.1   BASIC LIST OPERATIONS (*continued*)

Operation	Description
l1.swap(*l2*);	Swap the contents of *l1* with *l2*
l1 = *l2*	Assign to *l1* a copy of *l2*
l1 == *l2*	Return true if and only if *l1* contains the same items as *l2*, in the same order
l1 < *l2*	Return true if and only if *l1* is lexicographically less than *l2*

The program in Fig. 8.8 is a simple demonstration of several of these operations. Note the use of the list<T>::iterator in the overloaded operator<<() to display the contents of a list. An iterator is needed because the subscript operator [] is not defined for lists.

FIGURE 8.8   DEMONSTRATION OF list OPERATIONS

```
#include <iostream>
#include <list>
#include <algorithm>
using namespace std;

//--- Overload output operator for list<T>
template <typename T>
ostream & operator<<(ostream & out, const list<T> & l)
{
  for (list<T>::iterator i = l.begin(); i != l.end(); i++)
    out << *i << "   ";
  return out;
}

int main()
{
  list<int> l, l1(4, 111), l2(6);

  cout << "l:  " << l << "  size = " << l.size() << endl;
  cout << "l1: " << l1 << "  size = " << l1.size() << endl;
  cout << "l2: " << l2 << "  size = " << l2.size() << endl;

  // Construct l3 from an array
  //==========================
  int b[] = {2, 22, 222,2222};
  list<int> l3(b, b+4);
  cout << "l3: " << l3 << endl;
```

```
// Assignment
//============
cout << "\nAssignments l = 13 and  l2 = 13:" << endl;
l = 13;
l2 = 13;
cout << "l = " << l << "  size = " << l.size() << endl;
cout << "l2 = " << l2 << "  size = " << l2.size() << endl;

// Ways to insert into a list
//===========================
cout << "\nInserts in l1:\n";
list<int>::iterator i;
i = l1.begin();
i++; i++;
l1.insert(i, 66666);
cout << l1 << endl;

l1.insert(i,3, 555);
cout << l1 << endl;

l1.insert(i, b, b+3);
cout << l1 << endl;

l1.push_back(888);
l1.push_front(111);
cout << l1 << endl;

// Ways to delete from a list
//===========================
cout << "\nErases in l1:\n";
i = find(l1.begin(), l1.end(), 66666);   // find is an algorithm
if (i != l1.end())
{
  cout << "66666 found -- will erase it\n";
  l1.erase(i);
}
else
  cout << "66666 not found\n";
cout << l1 << endl;

i = l1.begin(); i++;
list<int>::iterator j = l1.end();
--j; --j; i = --j; i --; i--;
l1.erase(i,j);
cout << l1 << endl;

l1.pop_back();
l1.pop_front();
cout << l1 << endl;
```

```
// Reversing a list
//==================
cout << "\nReverse l3:\n";
l3.reverse();
cout << l3 << endl;

// Sorting a list
//===============
cout << "\nSort l1:\n";
l1.sort();
cout << l1 << endl;

// Merging two lists
//==================
cout << "\nMerge l1 and l3:\n";
l1.merge(l3);
cout << "l1: " << l1 << endl;
cout << "l3: " << l3 << endl;

// Splicing a list into another list
//==================================
cout << "\nSplice l2 into l at second position:\n";
i=l.begin(); i++;
l.splice(i, l2);
cout << "l: " << l << endl;
cout << "l2: " << l2 << endl;

// Global removal of a value
//==========================
cout << "\nRemove 22s from l:\n";
l.remove(22);
cout << l << endl;

// Eliminating duplicates
//=======================
cout << "\nUnique applied to l1:\n";
l1.unique();
cout << l1 << endl;

}
```

OUTPUT:

```
l:    size = 0
l1: 111   111   111   111     size = 4
l2: 0   0   0   0   0   0     size = 6
l3: 2   22   222   2222

Assignments l = l3 and l2 = l3:
l = 2   22   222   2222     size = 4
l2 = 2   22   222   2222     size = 4
```

```
Inserts in l1:
111   111   66666   111   111
111   111   66666   555   555   555   111   111
111   111   66666   555   555   555   2   22   222   111   111
111   111   111   66666   555   555   555   2   22   222   111   111   888

Erases in l1:
66666 found -- will erase it
111   111   111   555   555   555   2   22   222   111   111   888
111   111   111   555   555   555   2   111   111   888
111   111   555   555   555   2   111   111

Reverse l3:
2222   222   22   2

Sort l1:
2   111   111   111   111   555   555   555

Merge l1 and l3:
l1: 2   111   111   111   111   555   555   555   2222   222   22   2
l3:

Splice l2 into l at second position:
l: 2   2   22   222   2222   22   222   2222
l2:

Remove 22s from l:
2   2   222   2222   222   2222

Unique applied to l1:
2   111   555   2222   222   22   2
```

EXAMPLE: INTERNET ADDRESSES

TCP (Transmission Control Protocol) and IP (Internet Protocol) are communication protocols used to specify the rules computers use in exchanging messages in networks. TCP/IP addresses are used to uniquely identify computers in the Internet; for example, `titan.ksc.nasa.gov` is the address of a site at the NASA Kennedy Space Center. These addresses are made up of four fields that represent specific parts of the Internet,

> *host.subdomain.subdomain.rootdomain*

which the computer will translate into a unique TCP/IP address. This address is a 32-bit value, but it is usually represented in a dotted-decimal notation by separating the 32 bits into four 8-bit fields, expressing each field as a decimal integer, and separating the fields with a period; for example, `128.159.4.20` is the TCP/IP address for the above site at the NASA Kennedy Space Center.

Suppose connections are made from one network through a gateway to another network, and that each time a connection is made, the TCP/IP address of the user's computer is stored in a data file. These addresses can be retrieved periodically to monitor who has used the gateway and how many times they have used it.

The program in Fig. 8.9 reads these TCP/IP addresses from the file and stores them in a linked list of nodes that store an address and the number of times that address appeared in the data file. As each address is read, the program checks if it is already in the list. If it is, its count is incremented by 1; otherwise, it is inserted at the end of the list. After all the addresses in the file have been read, the distinct addresses and their counts are displayed.

The addresses are stored in a list<TCP_IP_Address> object addressList, where TCP_IP_Address is a small class containing two data members (address and count), input and output function members, and a function member Tally() to increment the count of an address. Also, operator==() is overloaded so that STL's find() algorithm can be used to search the list.

FIGURE 8.9 INTERNET ADDRESSES

```
/* This program reads TCP/IP addresses from a file and produces a list
 * of distinct addresses and a count of how many times each appeared
 * in the file. The addresses and counts are stored in a linked list.
 *
 * Input (keyboard): Name of file containing addresses
 * Input (file):     Addresses
 * Output:           A list of distinct addresses and their counts
 *********************************************************************/

#include <cassert>
#include <string>
#include <iostream>
#include <fstream>
#include <list>
#include <algorithm>
using namespace std;

//--------------- Begin class AddressItem ---------------------------
class AddressItem
{
public:
  void Read(istream & in)
  { in >> address; count = 0; }

  void Print(ostream & out) const
  { out << address << "\t occurs " << count << " times\n"; }

  void Tally()
  { count++; }

  friend bool operator==(const AddressItem & addr1,
                         const AddressItem & addr2);
```

```cpp
private:
  string address;
  int count;
};


inline bool operator==(const AddressItem & addr1,
                       const AddressItem & addr2)
{ return addr1.address == addr2.address; }


//----------- End class AddressItem ---------------------------------


typedef list<AddressItem> TCP_IP_List;


int main()
{
  string fileName;                    // name of file of TCP/IP addresses
  TCP_IP_List addressList;            // list of addresses

  ifstream inStream;                  // open stream to file of addresses
  cout << "Enter name of file containing TCP/IP addresses: ";
  cin >> fileName;
  inStream.open(fileName.data());
  assert(inStream.is_open());

  AddressItem item;                   // one of the addresses & its count
  for (;;)                            // loop:
  {
    item.Read(inStream);            //    read an address
    if (inStream.eof()) break;      //    if eof, quit

    TCP_IP_List::iterator it =      //    check if item already in list
      find(addressList.begin(), addressList.end(), item);
    if (it != addressList.end())    //    found
      (*it).Tally();                //    increment its count
    else
      addressList.push_back(item);  //    else add it to the list
  }                                 //    end loop
                                    //    output the list
  cout << "\nList of addresses:\n\n";
  for (TCP_IP_List::iterator it = addressList.begin();
                             it != addressList.end(); it++)
    (*it).Print(cout);
}
```

LISTING OF `file8-9.dat` USED IN SAMPLE RUN:

```
128.159.4.20
123.111.222.333
100.1.4.31
34.56.78.90
120.120.120.120
```

```
128.159.4.20
123.111.222.333
123.111.222.333
77.66.55.44
100.1.4.31
123.111.222.333
128.159.4.20
```

SAMPLE RUN:

```
Enter name of file containing TCP/IP addresses: file8-9.dat

List of addresses:

128.159.4.20      occurs 2 times
123.111.222.333   occurs 3 times
100.1.4.31        occurs 1 times
34.56.78.90       occurs 0 times
120.120.120.120   occurs 0 times
77.66.55.44       occurs 0 times
```

✔ Quick Quiz 8.7

1. Why doesn't `vector` have functions for inserting and removing elements at the front of a vector?

2. In a linked list, values are stored in _____ that are linked together by _____.

3. Values can be inserted at the end of a `vector` more efficiently than at its front. (True or false)

4. Values can be inserted at the end of a `list` more efficiently than at its front. (True or false)

5. What advantages do linked lists have over vectors?

6. What advantages do vectors have over linked lists?

✍ EXERCISES 8.7

The following exercises ask you to build or extend certain classes. You should test each class with a driver program as instructed in Programming Problems for Sec. 8.7 at the end of this chapter.

1. Design and implement a class `BigInt` whose values are large integers with perhaps hundreds of digits. Overload the addition operator. Treat each number as a list, each of whose elements is a block of digits of the number. Then add the integers (lists) element by element, carrying from one element to the next when necessary.

2. Extend class `BigInt` from Exercise 1 by overloading operators to (a) multiply, (b) subtract, and (c) divide two large integers.

3. Polynomials were described in Exercise 5 of Sec. 8.1. Design and implement a `Polynomial` class that stores only the nonzero coefficients and the corresponding exponents in a `list`. Provide input and output operators, displaying polynomials in the usual mathematical format with x^n written as $x \uparrow n$ or $x\verb|^|n$.

4. Extend the class `Polynomial` in Exercise 3 to evaluate a polynomial at a given value.

5. Extend the class `Polynomial` in Exercise 3 to add two polynomials.

6. Extend the class `Polynomial` in Exercises 3 and 4 to multiply two polynomials.

☞ PROGRAMMING POINTERS

1. The asterisk operator * must precede each variable in a pointer declaration.

2. Using the `typedef` mechanism and descriptive identifiers to declare pointer types reduces the chance of violating Pointer 1. It also increases the readability of programs, which reduces the likelihood of errors and makes errors easier to find when they do occur.

3. Each pointer variable is bound to a fixed type; a pointer is the address of a memory location in which only a value of that type can be stored.

4. Care must be used when operating on pointers because they have memory addresses as values. In particular

   ▶ A pointer `ptr` can be assigned a value in the following ways:

`ptr = &obj;`	(where `obj` is an object of the type to which `ptr` points)
`ptr = 0;`	(the null address)
`ptr = anotherPtr;`	(where `anotherPtr` is a pointer bound to the same type as `ptr`)
`ptr = new Type;`	(where `Type` is the type to which `ptr` points)

   ▶ Arithmetic operations on pointers are restricted. For example, pointer values (memory addresses) cannot be added, subtracted, multiplied, or divided. However, an integer value `i` can be added to or subtracted from the value of a pointer variable, which changes the address in the pointer by `i * sizeof(Type)`, where `Type` is the type to which the pointer is bound.

   ▶ Relational operators can be used to compare pointers, but the two pointers must be bound to the same type or one or both may be the null address.

   ▶ Pointers may be used as parameters, but corresponding parameters and arguments must be bound to the same type. A function may also return a pointer as its return value, but the type to which that pointer is bound must be the same as the type to which the function is declared to point.

5. Do not confuse memory locations with the contents of memory locations. If `ptr` is a pointer, its value is the address of a memory location; `*ptr` is a name for this memory location so its value is the contents of that location. Both `ptr++` and `(*ptr)++` are valid (if `ptr` is bound to a numeric type), but the first increments the address in `ptr`, while the second increments the contents of the memory location at that address.

6. The null address ≠ undefined. A pointer becomes defined when it is assigned the address of a memory location or the null address. Assigning a pointer the null address is analogous to initializing a numeric variable to zero.

7. When memory is allocated at run time with the `new` operation, the value returned by `new` should be tested before proceeding, to ensure that the operation was successful.

8. Memory locations that were once associated with a pointer variable and that are no longer needed should be returned to the heap by using the `delete` function. Special care is required to avoid marooning memory locations. For example, if `p` and `q` are

pointer variables bound to the same type, the assignment statement p = q; causes p to point to the same memory location as that pointed to by q. Any memory location previously pointed to by p becomes inaccessible and cannot be disposed of properly unless it is pointed to by some other pointer. Temporary pointers should be used to maintain access as the following statements demonstrate:

```
tempPtr = p;
p = q;
delete tempPtr;
```

9. Any attempt to dereference a null or undefined pointer will usually generate a run-time error. This difficulty occurs so frequently that it has a special name—the *dangling pointer problem*.

10. Changing the value of a variable in a statement in which that variable is not named is generally considered poor programming practice, because it produces a difficult-to-find logical error. This is known as the *aliasing problem* in programming.

11. Make certain that the pointer members of a class are initialized by its constructors. Many errors can be avoided simply by ensuring that when an object is created, its pointer members are initialized by default to null.

12. Never rely upon the default copy constructor or assignment operator for a class containing a pointer data member because for such classes, these default operations will not make distinct copies of an object. This is another example of the *aliasing problem* since changes to a copy of an object can inadvertently change the original object.

13. Do not rely upon the default destructor for a class containing a data member that points to some container because for such classes, this default operation will destroy only the pointer and leave stranded the memory allocated to the container.

14. If an object contains pointer members, test its operations exhaustively. It is quite easy for execution to miss the run-time and logical errors in sections of code that manipulate pointers, unless tests are performed that explicitly check those sections of code. Better yet, have others test your operations, since they will try to do things you might not have anticipated.

 ## ADT TIPS

1. If a problem solution involves a dynamic list, then a linked list may be a more time-efficient way to store and process that list. In a sequential-storage implementation, the values are stored in adjacent locations in an array or a vector. This means that when values are inserted into (or deleted from) an array-based list of n values, an average of n/2 of the values will have to be shifted to make room for the new value. The time required to shift these values makes insertion (and deletion) a time-expensive operation. By contrast, the values in a linked list are stored in (nonadjacent) nodes, which are attached to one another using pointers. Inserting a value at a given point in the list simply involves altering the values of (at most) three of these pointers.

2. If a problem solution involves many accesses to the interior values of a list, then an array-based list may be a more time-efficient way to store and process that list. In a linked list, all values except the first must be accessed sequentially; that is, to access a specific node, we must access all those that precede it, beginning with the first node in the list. An average of n/2 accesses are thus required to access a node in a linked list of length n. By contrast, all values of an array-based list can be accessed directly, permitting such lists to be processed more quickly.

3. In programming languages that do not provide a run-time heap and dynamic allocation and deallocation, a storage pool of free nodes can be simulated using an array of structures (or parallel arrays). It is usually managed as a linked stack and allocate and deallocate operations are simply the push and pop operations for a stack.

4. Pay attention to special cases in processing linked lists and be careful not to lose access to nodes. In particular, remember the following "programming proverbs":

▸ *Don't take a long walk off a short linked list.* It is an error to attempt to process elements beyond the end of the list. As an example, consider the following incorrect attempts to search a linked list with first node pointed to by `first` for some `itemSought`:

Attempt 1:

```
ptr = first;
while (ptr->data != itemSought)
   ptr = ptr->next;
```

If the item is not present in any node of the linked list, `ptr` will eventually reach the last node in the list. `ptr` then becomes null, and an attempt is made to examine its `data` member produces an error.

Attempt 2:

```
/* This time I'll make sure I don't fall off the end of the
   list by stopping if I find itemSought or reach a node whose
   link member is null. */

bool found = false;
ptr = first;
while ((! found) && (ptr->next != 0))
   if (ptr->data == itemSought)
      found = true;
   else
      ptr = ptr->next;
```

Although this avoids the problem of moving beyond the end of the list, it will fail to locate the desired item (that is, set `found` to `true`) if the item sought is the last one in the list. When `ptr` reaches the last node, `ptr->next` is null, and repetition is terminated without examining the `data` member of this last node. Another problem is that if the item is found in the list, the remaining nodes (except the last) will also be examined.

Attempt 3:

```
// Another attempt to avoid running past the end of the list.

ptr = first;
while ((ptr->data != itemSought) && (ptr != 0))
   ptr = ptr->next;
```

This solution is almost correct, but like the first attempted solution, it results in an error if the item is not in the list. The reason is that boolean expressions are evaluated from left to right. Thus, when the end of the list is reached and `ptr` becomes null, the first part of the boolean expression controlling repetition is evaluated, and the result of dereferencing a null pointer is usually an error.

Attempt 4:

```
// Okay, so I'll just reverse the two parts of the boolean expression

ptr = first;
while ((ptr != 0) && (ptr->data != itemSought))
   ptr = ptr->next;
```

This is a correct solution, thanks to the short-circuit evaluation of boolean expression in C++. That is, if `ptr` is null, then the first part of the condition `ptr != 0` evaluates to false, and so the condition "short-circuits," leaving the second condition unevaluated. Note that if short-circuit evaluation were not utilized, this second condition would be evaluated, and the attempt to dereference the null pointer `ptr` would result in an error.

▶ *You can't get water from an empty well.* Don't try to access elements in an empty list; this case usually requires special consideration. For example, if `first` is null, then initializing `ptr` to `first` and attempting to access `ptr->data` or `ptr->next` is an error. To avoid such errors, such operations should be guarded as in

```
if (first != 0)
   // do the required processing
else
   // the list is empty
```

▶ *Don't burn bridges before you cross them.* Be careful to change links in the correct order, or you may lose access to a node or to many nodes! For example, in the following attempt to insert a new node at the beginning of a linked list

```
first = newNodePtr;
newNodePtr->next = first;
```

the statements are not in correct order. As soon as the first statement is executed, `first` points to the new node, and access to the remaining nodes in the list (those formerly pointed to by `first`) is lost. The second statement then simply sets the link member of the new node to point to itself:

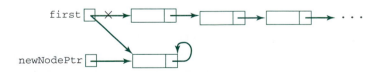

The correct sequence is to first connect the new node to the list and then reset `first`:

```
newNodePtr->next = first;
first = newNodePtr;
```

5. The standard `list` container:
- ▶ uses a linked list to store the list elements
- ▶ has bidirectional iterators that are weaker than the random-access iterators of `vectors` and `deques`
- ▶ provides its own `sort()` operation because the standard `sort()` algorithm requires random-access iterators

PROGRAMMING PROBLEMS

SECTION 8.1

1. Use the polynomial class of Exercise 5 in a menu-driven program for processing polynomials. Options on the menu should include polynomial addition, polynomial multiplication, printing a polynomial, and evaluating a polynomial for a given value of the variable.

SECTION 8.3

2. Write a memory management class or library as described in this section. Use it in a program that solves Exercise 9.

3. A limited number of tickets for the Hoops championship basketball game go on sale tomorrow, and ticket orders are to be filled in the order in which they are received. Write a program that a box-office cashier can use to enter the names and addresses of the persons ordering tickets together with the number of tickets requested and store this information in a list. The program should then produce a sequence of mailing labels (names, addresses, and number of tickets) for orders that can be filled.

4. Modify the program in Problem 3 to check that no one receives more than four tickets and that multiple requests from the same person are disallowed.

SECTION 8.5

5. Write a driver program to test your modified `Queue` class template in Exercise 13.

6. Write a driver program to test your modified `Queue` class template in Exercise 14.

SECTION 8.6

7. Write a driver program to test your recursive node-counter function in Exercise 18.

8. Write a driver program to test your nonrecursive node-counter function in Exercise 19.

9. Write a driver program to test your `LinkedList` class template in Exercise 20.

10. Write a driver program to test your modified `LinkedList` class template in Exercise 21.

11. Write a driver program to test your modified `LinkedList` class template in Exercise 22.

12. Write a driver program to test your modified `LinkedList` class template in Exercise 23.

SECTION 8.7

13. Write a `BigInt` calculator program to test your class `BigInt` from Exercise 1.

14. Write a `BigInt` calculator program to test your class `BigInt` from Exercise 2.

15. Write a program for the basketball-tickets problem in Probs. 3 and 4. Use a `list` to store and process the ticket-order information.

16. Using the `Polynomial` class from Exercise 3, write a program that reads a polynomial and then outputs the polynomial.

17. Extend your program from Exercise 16 to evaluate polynomials using the modified class `Polynomial` in Exercise 4.

18. Extend your program from Prob. 16 to add two polynomials using the modified class `Polynomial` in Exercise 4.

19. Extend your program from Prob. 17 to multiply two polynomials using the modified class `Polynomial` in Exercise 5.

20. Suppose that jobs entering a computer system are assigned a job number and a priority from 0 through 9. The numbers of jobs awaiting execution by the system are kept in a *priority queue*. A job entered into this queue is placed ahead of all jobs of lower priority but after all those of equal or higher priority. Write a program that uses a `list` to store the jobs and allows the user to select one of the following menu options: R (remove), A (add), or L (list). For R, read a job number and remove it from the priority queue; for A, read a job number and priority and then add it to the priority queue in the manner just described; and for L, list all the job numbers in the queue.

21. Write a "quiz-tutor" program, perhaps on a topic from one of the early chapters, or some other topic about which you are knowledgeable. The program should read a question and its answer from a file, display the question, and accept an answer from the user. If the answer is correct, the program should go on to the next question. If it is incorrect, store the question in a `list`. When the file of questions is exhausted, the questions that were missed should be displayed again (in their original order). Keep a count of the correct answers and display the final count. Also, display the correct answer when necessary in the second round of questioning.

22. Write a program to read the records from the file `StudentFile` and construct five linked lists of records containing a student's name, number, and cumulative GPA, one list for each class. Store these records in a vector of `lists`. After the lists have been constructed, sort each list and then print each of them with appropriate headings. (See Problem 13 at the end of Chap. 2 and the website described in the preface for a description of `StudentFile`.) *Note*: If `aList` is a `list<T>` object, then `alist.sort();` will sort `aList` provided < is defined for type `T` objects. In this exercise, you must overload `operator<()` to define what it means for one student record to be less than another.

23. The number of elements in a list may grow so large that finding a value in the list is not efficient. One way to improve efficiency is to maintain several smaller linked lists. Write a program to read several lines of uppercase text and to produce a text concordance, which is a list of all distinct words in the text. Store distinct words beginning with A in one linked list, those beginning with B in another, and so on. After all the text lines have been read, sort each list (see Prob. 22) and then print a list of all these words in alphabetical order.

24. Modify the program of Prob. 23 so that the concordance also includes the frequency with which each word occurs in the text.

25. In addition to the words in a section of text, a concordance usually stores the numbers of selected pages on which there is a significant use of the word. Modify the program of Prob. 23 so that the numbers of all lines in which a word appears are stored along with the word itself. The program should display each word together with its associated line numbers in ascending order.

26. Design and code a program that acts as a screen-oriented text editor (*Hint*: Assume that the first line of the file to be edited contains the number of lines in the file and build a class that uses a `list` of `lists` to store the file). The editor should display:

  ▸ 15 to 20 numbered lines at a time,
  ▸ the current cursor position (line and column)
  ▸ a menu of the commands that allow the user to replace, insert, delete, and find the position of text strings in the file, as well as loading them from and storing them in a file.

CHAPTER 9

OTHER LINKED STRUCTURES

Chapter Contents

The "standard" linked lists considered in the preceding chapter are characterized by the following properties: (1) Only the first node is directly accessible, and (2) each node consists of a data part and a single link that connects this node to its successor (if there is one). They are, therefore, **linear structures** that must be processed sequentially in the order in which the nodes are linked together, from first to last.

In some applications, other kinds of list processing are required, and in these situations it may be convenient to allow other kinds of access and/or linkages. In this chapter we consider some of these variants of linked lists, such as circular-linked lists, linked stacks and queues, doubly-linked lists, and other multiply-linked lists.

9.1 SOME VARIANTS OF SINGLY-LINKED LISTS

In some list applications, modifications of standard linked lists are used because they make algorithms for some of the basic list operations simpler and more efficient. In this section we consider some of these variants of linked lists.

LINKED STACKS AND QUEUES

We have seen that one weakness of implementations of lists that use arrays as the basic storage structures is that the fixed size of the array limits the size of the list. In particular, array-based implementations of stacks and queues like those considered in Chaps. 4 and 5 have this deficiency. Using a linked list instead of an array allows the stack or queue to grow without limit (except for available memory) and to shrink without wasting unused storage.

Recall that a stack is a list in which items can be accessed at only one end, called the *top*. Thus it seems natural to implement a stack using a linked list because only

467

the first node of a linked list is directly accessible. A `Stack` class that uses a linked list to store the stack elements would need only one data member, a pointer `myTop` to the node at the top of the stack:

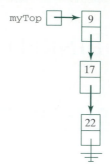

In this implementation, the constructor would need only initialize `myTop` to be a null pointer and the empty operation check whether `myTop` is null. The copy constructor and assignment operator would have to traverse the linked list storing the stack elements to make a copy as described for linked lists in general in Sec. 8.6. The destructor would also need to traverse the linked list and return each node to the heap.

The push operation is simple insertion at the beginning of a linked list

```
newptr = new Node(item, myTop);
myTop = newptr;
```

where the `Node` constructor sets the `data` part of the new node equal to `item` and the `next` part equal to `myTop` as in Sec. 8.6. Retrieving the top element is trivial:

```
return myTop->data;
```

And the pop operation is simple deletion of the first node in a linked list:

```
ptr = myTop;
myTop = myTop->next;
delete ptr;
```

A linked implementation of a queue is a simple extension of the linked implementation of stacks. It seems natural to identify the first element in the list as the front of the queue. The pop operation is then implemented in the same way as the pop operation for a stack, but the push operation requires traversing the entire list to find the back of the queue. This list traversal can be avoided if we adopt the approach of the array-based implementation in Chap. 5 and maintain two pointers, `myFront`, which points to the node at the front of the queue, and `myBack`, which points to the node at the back. For example, a linked queue containing the integers 9, 17, 22, 26, and 34 in this order, might be pictured as

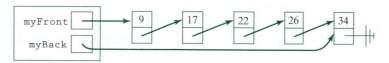

A simpler alternative is to use a circular linked list as described later in this section.

Modifications of the `Stack` and `Queue` classes to use linked lists for storage are straightforward and are left as exercises. An alternative is to specify that the STL `list` container be used in the standard `stack` and `queue` class templates; for example

```
#include <list>
#include <stack>
   . . .
stack< list<int> > st;
```

This is not as efficient spacewise as using a simple linear linked list because as we shall see in the next section, STL's list uses a doubly-linked list to store the list elements.

LINKED LISTS WITH HEAD NODES AND/OR TRAILER NODES

The first node in a standard linked list differs from the other nodes in that it does not have a predecessor. As we saw in Sec. 8.2, this means that two cases must be considered for some basic list operations such as insertion and deletion. This would not be necessary if we could ensure that every node that stores a list element will have a predecessor. And we can do this by simply introducing a dummy first node, called a **head node,** at the beginning of a linked list. No actual list element is stored in the data part of this head node; instead, it serves as a predecessor of the node that stores the actual first element because its link field points to this "real" first node. For example, the list of integers 9, 17, 22, 26, 34 can be stored in a linked list with a head node as follows:

In this implementation, every linked list is required to have a head node. In particular, an empty list has a head node:

This means that instead of simply initializing the pointer `first` to be a null pointer, a constructor for a `LinkedList` class that uses this implementation would have to get a head node pointed to by `first` that has a null link. Similarly, a function to check for a list-empty condition must check `first->next == 0` rather than `first == 0`.

In constructing an empty list; the data part has been left undefined (as denoted by the question mark in the preceding diagrams). In some situations the data part of the head node might be used to store some information about the list. For example, in a linked list of integers, we might store the size of the list in the head node. In a list of names of persons, we might store in the head node the name of a team or other organization to which they all belong:

The fact that every node in a linked list now has a predecessor simplifies algorithms for the insertion and deletion operations because no special consideration of nodes without predecessors is required. For example, inserting an `item` after the node pointed to by `predptr` (which is the head node if we're inserting at the beginning of the list) is simply

```
newptr = new Node(item, predptr->next);
predptr->next = newptr;
```

The deletion algorithm simplifies in a similar manner.

Algorithms for traversing a standard linked list or a part of it can easily be modified for use with linked lists that have head nodes. Usually only instructions that initialize some auxiliary pointer to the first node in the list need to be altered.

Occasionally, one finds linked lists that also have a **trailer node** so that every node has a successor; for example

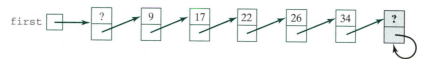

As the diagram suggests, the pointer in the trailer node's next part usually points to the trailer node itself so that it is its own successor. Also, for efficiency, lists in the same application can share the same trailer node.

CIRCULAR LINKED LISTS

In Chap. 5 we described an implementation of queues in which the array that stored the elements was thought of as a circular array with the first element following the last. This suggests that an analogous **circular linked list** obtained by setting the link of the last node in a standard linear linked list to point to the first node might also be a useful data structure:

As this diagram illustrates, each node in a circular linked list has a predecessor (and a successor), provided that the list is nonempty. Consequently, as in the case of linked lists with head nodes, the algorithms for insertion and deletion do not require special consideration of nodes without predecessors. For example, `item` can be inserted as follows:

```
newptr = new Node(item, 0);
if (first == 0)      // list is empty
{
   newptr->next = newptr;
   first = newptr;
}
```

```
else                        // nonempty list
{
  newptr->next = predptr->next;
  predptr->next = newptr;
}
```

Note that insertion into an empty list does require special consideration because in this case, the link in the one-node list that results must point to the node itself:

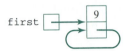

For deletion from a circular list, in addition to an empty list, a one-element list requires special treatment because, in this case, the list becomes empty after this node is deleted. This case is detected by checking if the node is its own predecessor, that is, that its link field points to itself:

```
if (first == 0)           // list is empty
   // Signal that the list is empty
else
{
  ptr = predptr->next;
  if (ptr == predptr)   // one-node list
    first = 0;
  else                      // list with 2 or more nodes
    predptr->next = ptr->next;
  delete ptr;
}
```

As the exercises ask you to show, both the insertion and deletion algorithms simplify if we use a circular linked list with a head node like the following:

Most of the other algorithms for standard linear linked lists also must be modified when applied to circular lists. To illustrate, the traversal algorithm moved a pointer through the list until it became null, signaling that the last node had been processed. For a circular linked list, the link in the last node points to the first node. Thus a naive attempt to modify this traversal algorithm for a circular list might produce the following:

```
(* INCORRECT attempt to traverse a circular linked list
   with first node pointed to by first, processing
   each list element exactly once. *)
```

```
   ptr = first;
while (ptr != first)
{
   // Process ptr->data;
   ptr = ptr->next;
}
```

Here the boolean expression `ptr != first` is false immediately and the while loop is bypassed. Consequently, this algorithm correctly traverses only an empty list!

To obtain an algorithm that correctly traverses all circular linked lists, we can replace the while loop with a do-while loop, provided that we have made sure that the list is not empty:

```
if (first != 0)        // list is not empty
{
   ptr = first;
   do
   {
      // Process ptr->data;
      ptr = ptr->next;
   }
   while (ptr != first);
}
```

Both versions of the traversal algorithm will correctly traverse a circular linked list with a head node if the first assignment statement is changed to

```
ptr = first->next;
```

You should check these revised algorithms for circular lists like the preceding and for one-element lists such as

as well as empty lists that consist of only a head node that points to itself:

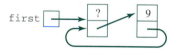

For some applications of circular linked lists, it is advantageous to maintain a pointer to the last node rather than the first; for example

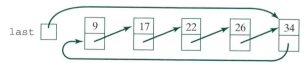

In this case we have direct access to the last node and almost direct access to the first node, since `last->next` points to the first node in the list. This variation is thus especially useful when it is necessary to access repeatedly the elements at the ends of the list. In particular, it is well suited for linked queues and deques.

✔ Quick Quiz 9.1

1. A dummy node at the beginning of a linked list is called a(n) _____.
2. The purpose of a node as in Ques. 1 is so that every node in the linked list has a(n) _____.
3. A dummy node at the end of a linked list is called a(n) _____.
4. The purpose of a node as in Ques. 3 is so that every node in the linked list has a(n) _____.
5. Setting the link of the last node in a standard linear linked list to point to the first node produces a(n) _____ linked list.

✎ EXERCISES 9.1

1. Beginning with an empty stack, draw a diagram of the linked stack that results when the following sequence of operations is performed: push 'X', push 'L', push 'R', pop, push 'A', pop, pop, push 'Q'.

2. Modify the `Stack` class template described in Sec. 8.5 so that it uses a linked list to store the stack elements in the manner described in this section. It should include the following operations:
   a. Constructor
   b. Destructor
   c. Copy constructor
   d. Assignment
   e. Empty
   f. Push
   g. Top
   h. Pop
   i. Output

   You should also test your class template as instructed in Programming Problem 1 at the end of this chapter.

   Exercises 3 and 4 assume the implementation of a queue described in the text that uses a linked list to store the queue elements, a pointer to the front of the queue, and a pointer to the back of the queue.

3. Beginning with an empty queue, draw a diagram of the linked queue that results when the following sequence of operations is performed: add 'X', add 'L', add 'R', remove, add 'A', remove, remove, add 'Q'.

4. Write a `Queue` class template that uses this linked-list structure to store the queue elements. It should have the same operations as in Exercise 2, but with queue operations replacing the stack operations. (See Exercise 13 of Sec. 8.5.) You should also test your class template as instructed in Programming Problem 3 at the end of this chapter.

5. In Sec. 5.1 a *priority queue* was described as a queue-like structure in which each item has a certain priority and is inserted ahead of all items with a lower priority; normally, it is placed behind all those with an equal or higher priority. Assuming that such a priority queue is implemented as a linked list, develop a `PriorityQueue` class template. You should also test your class template as instructed in Programming Problem 5 at the end of this chapter.

6. Write an algorithm or code segment for inserting an item into a linked list with head node.

7. Write an algorithm or code segment for deleting an item from a linked list with head node.

8. Write an algorithm or code segment for searching a circular linked list for a given item.

9. Write an algorithm or code segment for searching an ordered circular linked list for a given item.

10. Write an algorithm or code segment for locating the nth successor of an item in a circular linked list (the nth item that follows the given item in the list).

11. Redo Exercise 4 for a queue implemented as a circular linked list with a single pointer to the last node. You should also test your class template as instructed in Programming Problem 6 at the end of this chapter.

12. Repeat Exercise 4 but for a deque and test it as instructed in Programming Problem 8.

13. Repeat Exercise 11 for a deque and test it as instructed in Programming Problem 9.

14. The *shuffle-merge* operation on two lists was defined in Exercise 9 of Sec. 8.2. Write an algorithm to shuffle-merge two circular-linked lists. The items in the lists are to be copied to produce the new circular-linked lists; the original lists are not to be destroyed.

15. Proceed as in Exercise 14, but do not copy the items. Just change links in the two lists (thus destroying the original lists) to produce the merged list.

16. In implementations of linked lists in which the storage pool is maintained as a linked stack, as described in Sec. 8.3, it is possible to erase any circularly linked list in O(1)-time; that is, it is possible to return all of its nodes to the storage pool in constant time, independent of the size of the list. Give such an erase algorithm for a circularly linked list whose computing time is O(1); and show how it works using the following diagram:

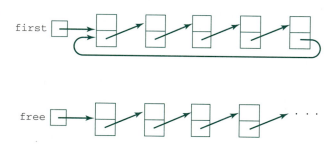

17. In the *Josephus problem*, a group of soldiers is surrounded by the enemy, and one soldier is to be selected to ride for help. The selection is made in the following manner: An integer n and a soldier are selected randomly. The soldiers are arranged in a circle and they count off beginning with the randomly selected soldier. When the count reaches n, that soldier is removed from the circle, and the counting begins again with the next soldier. This process continues until only one soldier remains, who is the (un)fortunate one selected to ride for help. Write an algorithm to implement this selection strategy, assuming that a circular linked list is used to store the names (or numbers) of the soldiers.

9.2   LINKED IMPLEMENTATION OF SPARSE POLYNOMIALS

A **polynomial in one variable** x, $P(x)$, has the form

$$P(x) = a_0 + a_1 x + a_2 x^2 + \cdots + a_n x^n$$

where $a_0, a_1, a_2 \ldots, a_n$ are the **coefficients** of the polynomial. The **degree** of $P(x)$ is the largest power of x that appears in the polynomial with a nonzero coefficient; for example, the polynomial

$$P(x) = 5 + 7x - 8x^3 + 4x^5$$

has degree 5 and coefficients $5, 7, 0$ (coefficient on x^2), -8, and 4. Constant polynomials such as $Q(x) = 3.78$ have degree 0, and the zero polynomial is also said to have degree 0.

A polynomial can be viewed as a list of coefficients

$$(a_0, a_1, a_2, \ldots, a_n)$$

and can be represented using any of the list implementations we have considered. For example, the polynomial $P(x) = 5 + 7x - 8x^3 + 4x^5$, which can also be written

$$P(x) = 5 + 7x + 0x^2 - 8x^3 + 0x^4 + 4x^5 + 0x^6 + 0x^7 + 0x^8 + 0x^9 + 0x^{10}$$

can be identified with the list of coefficients

$$(5, 7, 0, -8, 0, 4, 0, 0, 0, 0, 0)$$

and this can be stored in an array P of size 11:

i	0	1	2	3	4	5	6	7	8	9	10
P[i]	5	7	0	-8	0	4	0	0	0	0	0

If the degrees of the polynomials being processed do not vary too much from the upper limit imposed by the array size and do not have a large number of zero coefficients, this representation may be satisfactory. However, for **sparse** polynomials—that is, those that have only a few nonzero terms—this array implementation is not very efficient. For example, to store the polynomial

$$Q(x) = 5 + x^{99}$$

or equivalently,

$$Q(x) = 5 + 0x + 0x^2 + 0x^3 + \cdots + 0x^{98} + 1x^{99}$$

would require an array having 2 nonzero elements and 98 zero elements.

The obvious waste of memory caused by storing all of the zero coefficients can be eliminated if only the nonzero coefficients are stored. In such an implementation, however, it is clear that it would also be necessary to store the power of x that corresponds to each coefficient. Thus, rather than representing a polynomial by its list of coefficients, we might represent it as a list of coefficient-exponent pairs; for example

$$P(x) = 5 + 7x - 8x^3 + 4x^5 \leftrightarrow ((5, 0), (7, 1), (-8, 3), (4, 5))$$

$$Q(x) = 5 + x^{99} \leftrightarrow ((5, 0), (1, 99))$$

Note that the pairs are ordered in such a way that the exponents are in increasing order.

Such lists can be implemented by arrays of structs, each of which contains a coefficient field and an exponent field. However, the fixed array size again limits the size of the list and results in considerable waste of memory in applications in which the sizes of the lists—that is, the number of nonzero coefficients in the polynomials—varies considerably from this upper limit.

For this application, a linked list implementation is appropriate. Each node will have the form

in which the three parts `coef`, `expo`, and `next` store a nonzero coefficient, the corresponding exponent, and a pointer to the node representing the next term, respectively. For example, the preceding polynomials $P(x)$ and $Q(x)$ can be represented by the following linked lists with head nodes that store the polynomials' degrees in their `expo` fields:

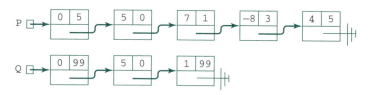

and the zero polynomial by simply a head node:

We can now begin a `Polynomial` class template for such linked polynomials:

```
#ifndef POLYNOMIAL
#define POLYNOMIAL

template <typename CoefType>    // type of coefficients
class Polynomial
{
/*** Node structure ***/
 private:
   class PolyNode
   {
    public:
      CoefType coef;
      int expo;
      PolyNode * next;
```

```
      //-- PolyNode constructor
      // Creates a PolyNode with given initial values
      PolyNode(CoefType co = 0, int ex = 0, PolyNode * ptr = 0)
      {
         coef = co;
         expo = ex;
         next = ptr;
      }
   };
typedef PolyNode * PolyPointer;

/*** Function members ***/
public:

   . . .

/*** Data members ***/
private:
   PolyPointer myFirst;
   int myDegree;

   . . .

};
#endif
```

Of course, we could have used the "standard" node format of a `data` part and a `next` part by making the type of the `data` part a struct with a `coef` part and an `expo` part. This does not produce any real benefits, however, and would require double member selection to access these items, for example, `P->data.coef` rather than simply `P->coef`.

To illustrate how such linked polynomials are processed, we consider the operation of polynomial addition. For example, suppose we wish to add the following polynomials $A(x)$ and $B(x)$:

$$A(x) = 5 + 6x^3 + 2x^5 + x^7$$
$$B(x) = x^3 - 2x^5 + 13x^7 - 2x^8 + 26x^9$$

Recall that this sum is calculated by adding coefficients of terms that have matching powers of x. Thus, the sum of polynomials $A(x)$ and $B(x)$ is

$$C(x) = A(x) + B(x) = 5 + 7x^3 + 14x^7 - 2x^8 + 26x^9$$

Now consider the linked representations of these polynomials:

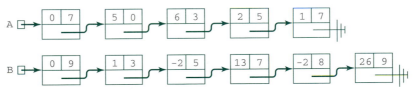

Since we have decided to use linked lists with head nodes, we begin by initializing `C` to point to a head node:

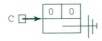

Three auxiliary pointers, ptrA, ptrB, and ptrC, will run through the lists A, B, and C, respectively; ptrA and ptrB will point to the current nodes being processed, and ptrC will point to the last node attached to C. Thus, ptrA, ptrB, and ptrC are initialized to A->next, B->next, and C, respectively:

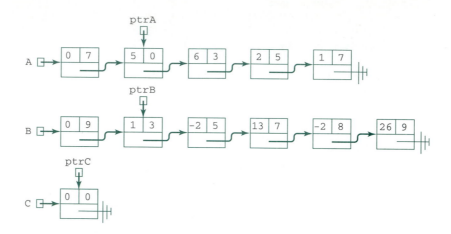

At each step of the computation, we compare the exponents in the nodes pointed to by ptrA and ptrB. If they are different, a node containing the smaller exponent and the corresponding coefficient is attached to C, and the pointer for this list and ptrC are advanced:

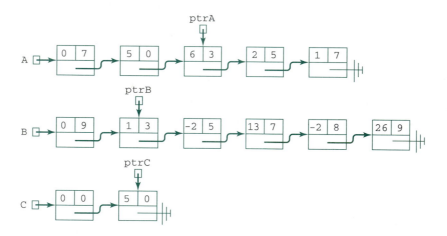

If the exponents in the nodes pointed to by ptrA and ptrB match, then the coefficients in these nodes are added. If this sum is not zero, a new node is created with its coefficient part equal to this sum and its exponent part equal to the common exponent, and this node is attached to C. Pointers for all three lists are then advanced:

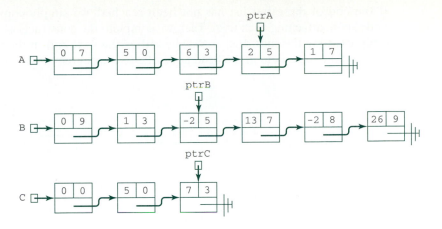

If the sum of the coefficients is zero, then `ptrA` and `ptrB` are simply advanced and no new node is attached to `C`:

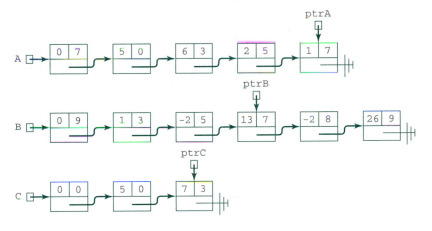

We continue in this manner until the end of `A` or `B` is reached, that is, until one of `ptrA` or `ptrB` becomes null:

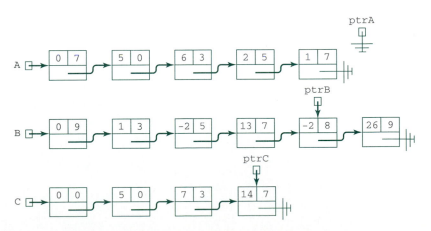

If the end of the other list has not been reached, we simply copy the remaining nodes in it, attaching each to C. Then we complete the construction of the linked list C representing the sum $A(x) + B(x)$ by setting the next part in the last node of C to null and the expo field in the head node of C to the degree of the last exponent read:

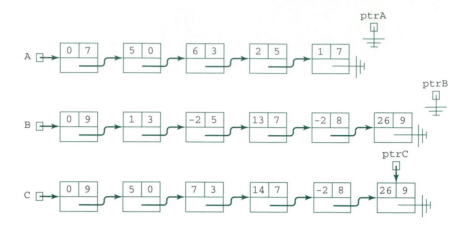

The following code implements this technique for adding linked polynomials. It can be added to the Polynomial class template as a friend function (or modified appropriately to make it a member function):

```
Polynomial<CoefType> C;
Polynomial<CoefType>::PolyPointer ptrA = A.myFirst->next,
                                  ptrB = B.myFirst->next,
                                  ptrC = C.myFirst;
int degree = 0;
while (ptrA != 0 || ptrB != 0)
{
  if ((ptrB == 0) ||
      (ptrA != 0 && ptrA->expo < ptrB->expo))   // copy term from A
  {
    ptrC->next =
      new Polynomial<CoefType>::PolyNode(ptrA->coef, ptrA->expo);
    degree = ptrA->expo;
    ptrA = ptrA->next;
    ptrC = ptrC->next;
  }
  else if ((ptrA == 0) ||
      (ptrB != 0 && ptrB->expo < ptrA->expo))   // copy term from B
```

```
{
    ptrC->next =
        new Polynomial<CoefType>::PolyNode(ptrB->coef, ptrB->expo);
    degree = ptrB->expo;
    ptrB = ptrB->next;
    ptrC = ptrC->next;
}
else                                            // exponents match
{
    CoefType sum = ptrA->coef + ptrB->coef;
    if (sum != 0)                               // nonzero sum --
    {                                           //   add to C
        ptrC->next =
            new Polynomial<CoefType>::PolyNode(sum, ptrA->expo);
        degree = ptrA->expo;
        ptrC = ptrC->next;
    }
    ptrA = ptrA->next;
    ptrB = ptrB->next;
}
}
C.myFirst->expo = degree;
return C;
```

The code for adding linked polynomials is more complex and less understandable than the corresponding code for the array-based implementation described at the beginning of this section, in which the ith coefficient is stored in the ith location of an array. In this case, two polynomials A and B can be added to produce C very simply:

```
int MaxDegree =
    A.myDegree >= B.myDegree ? A.myDegree : B.myDegree;
for (int i = 0; i < MaxDegree; i++)
    C[i] = A[i] + B[i];
```

Functions for other basic polynomial operations, such as evaluation for a given value of x, multiplication, and so on, are likewise more complex in the linked implementation than in the array-based implementation. However, in applications in which the polynomials are sparse and of large degree, the memory saved will compensate for the increased complexity of the algorithms.

✎ EXERCISES 9.2

1. Add an input operation to the `Polynomial` class template.

2. Add an output operation to the `Polynomial` class template that displays a polynomial in the usual mathematical format except that x^n is written as $x \uparrow n$ or $x \wedge n$.

3. Add a member function `Value()` to the `Polynomial` class template so that for a `Polynomial` object P, `P.Value(a)` calculates and returns the value of the polynomial P at a.

4.   The *derivative* of a polynomial $P(x) = a_0 + a_1x + a_2x^2 + a_3x^3 + \cdots + a_nx^n$ of degree n is the polynomial $P'(x)$ of degree $n - 1$ defined by

$$P'(x) \;=\; a_1 \,+\, 2a_2x \,+\, 3a_3x^2 \,+\, \cdots \,+\, na_nx^{n-1}$$

Add a derivative operator to the `Polynomial` class template.

5.   Add a multiplication operation to the `Polynomial` class template. Also determine its computing time.

9.3 HASH TABLES

The linear search and binary search algorithms considered in Chap. 7 locate an item in a list by a sequence of comparisons, in which the item being sought is repeatedly compared with the items in the list. For a collection of n items, linear search requires $O(n)$ comparisons, whereas for binary search, $O(\log_2 n)$ comparisons are required. In some situations, these algorithms perform too slowly. For example, a **symbol table** constructed by a compiler stores identifiers and information about them. The speed with which this table can be constructed and searched is critical to the speed of compilation. Fast searching is the goal of a **hash table,** in which the location of an item is determined directly as a function of the item itself rather than by a sequence of trial-and-error comparisons. Under ideal circumstances, the time required to locate an item in a hash table is $O(1)$; that is, it is constant and does not depend on the number of items stored.

HASH FUNCTIONS

As an illustration, suppose that up to 25 integers in the range 0 through 999 are to be stored in a hash table. This hash table can be implemented as an integer array *table* in which each array element is initialized with some dummy value, such as -1. If we use each integer i in the set as an index, that is, if we store i in *table[i]*, then to determine whether a particular integer `number` has been stored, we need only check if *table[number]* is equal to *number*. The function h defined by $h(i) = i$ that determines the location of an item i in the hash table is called a **hash function.**

The hash function in this example works perfectly because the time required to search the table for a given value is constant; only one location needs to be examined. This scheme is thus very time efficient, but it is surely not space-efficient. Only 25 of the 1000 available locations are used to store items, leaving 975 unused locations; only 2.5 percent of the available space is used, and so 97.5 percent is wasted!

Because it is possible to store 25 values in 25 locations, we might try improving space utilization by using an array *table* with capacity 25. Obviously, the original hash function $h(i) = i$ can no longer be used. Instead we might use

$$h(i) = i \text{ modulo } 25$$

or in C++ syntax,

```
int h(int i)
{ return i % 25; }
```

because this function always produces an integer in the range 0 through 24. The integer 52 thus is stored in *table*[2], since $h(52) = 52 \% 25 = 2$. Similarly, 129, 500, 273, and 49 are stored in locations 4, 0, 23, and 24, respectively.

Hash table

table[0]	500
table[1]	−1
table[2]	52
table[3]	−1
table[4]	129
table[5]	−1
⋮	⋮
table[23]	273
table[24]	49

COLLISION STRATEGIES

There is an obvious problem with the preceding hash table, namely, that **collisions** may occur. For example, if 77 is to be stored, it should be placed at location $h(77) = 77 \% 25 = 2$, but this location is already occupied by 52. In the same way, many other values may collide at a given position, for example, 2, 27, 102; and, in fact, all integers of the form $25k + 2$ hash to location 2. Obviously, some strategy is needed to resolve such collisions.

One simple strategy for handling collisions is known as **linear probing**. In this scheme, a linear search of the table begins at the location where a collision occurs and continues until an empty slot is found in which the item can be stored. Thus, in the preceding example, when 77 collides with the value 52 at location 2, we simply put 77 in position 3; to insert 102, we follow the **probe sequence** consisting of locations 2, 3, 4, and 5 to find the first available location and thus store 102 in *table*[5]. If the search reaches the bottom of the table, we continue at the first location. For example, 123 is stored in location 1, since it collides with 273 at location 23, and the probe sequence 23, 24, 0, 1 locates the first empty slot at position 1.

table[0]	500
table[1]	123
table[2]	52
table[3]	77
table[4]	129
table[5]	102
⋮	⋮
table[23]	273
table[24]	49

To determine if a specified value is in this hash table, we first apply the hash function to compute the position at which this value should be found. There are three cases to consider. First, if this location is empty, we can conclude immediately that the value is not in the table. Second, if this location contains the specified value, the search is immediately successful. In the third case, this location contains a value other than the one for which we are searching, because of the way that collisions were resolved in constructing the table. In this case, we begin a "circular" linear search at this location and continue until either the item is found or we reach an empty location or the starting location, indicating that the item is not in the table. Thus, the search time in the first two cases is constant, but in this last case, it is not. If the table is nearly full, we may, in fact, have to examine almost every location before we find the item or conclude that it is not in the table.

IMPROVEMENTS

There seem to be three things we might do to improve performance:

1. Increase the table capacity.
2. Use a different strategy for resolving collisions.
3. Use a different hash function.

Making the table capacity equal to the number of items to be stored, as in our first example, is usually not practical, but using any smaller table leaves open the possibility of collisions. In fact, even though the table is capable of storing considerably more items than necessary, collisions may be quite likely. For example, for a hash table with 365 locations in which 23 randomly selected items are to be stored, the probability that a collision will occur is greater than 0.5! (This is related to the *birthday problem*, whose solution states that in a room containing 23 people, there is a greater than 50 percent chance that two or more of them will have the same birthday.) Thus it is clearly unreasonable to expect a hashing scheme to prevent collisions completely. Instead, we must be satisfied with hash tables in which reasonably few collisions occur. Empirical studies suggest using tables whose capacities are approximately 1½ to 2 times the number of items that must be stored.

A second way to improve performance is to design a better method for handling collisions. In the linear probe scheme, whenever collisions occur, the colliding values are stored in locations that should be reserved for items that hash directly to these locations. This approach of "robbing Peter to pay Paul" makes subsequent collisions more likely, thus compounding the problem.

A better approach, known as **chaining,** uses a hash table that is an array or `vector` of linked lists that store the items. To illustrate, suppose we wish to store a collection of names. We might use an array *table* of 26 linked lists, initially empty, and the simple hash function $h(name) = name[0] - $ 'A'; that is, $h(name)$ is 0 if $name[0]$ is 'A', 1 if $name[0]$ is 'B', . . . , 25 if $name[0]$ is 'Z'.[1] Thus, for example, "Adams, John" and "Doe, Mary" are stored in nodes pointed to by $table[0]$ and $table[3]$, respectively.

---

[1] Remember that in C and C++, `chars` are identified with their numeric codes (e.g., ASCII) so the arithmetic operators can be applied to them. Thus, in ASCII, if the `char` variable ch has the value `'D'`, then ch $-$ `'A'` = 68 $-$ 65 = 3.

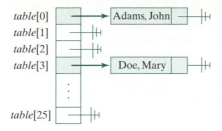

When a collision occurs, we simply insert the new item into the appropriate linked list. For example, since $h(\text{"Davis, Joe"}) = h(\text{"Doe, Mary"}) = \text{'D'} - \text{'A'} = 3$, a collision occurs when we attempt to store the name "Davis, Joe", and thus we add a new node containing this name to the linked list pointed to by $table[3]$:

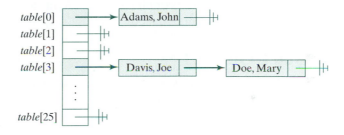

Searching such a hash table is straightforward. We simply apply the hash function to the item being sought and then use one of the search algorithms for linked lists.

Several other strategies may be used to resolve collisions. For example, the method in linear probing is known as an *open addressing* strategy. Other open-addressing schemes attempt to break up the clusters that form from linear probing by using a different probe sequence. For example, *quadratic probing* uses $i + 1^2, i - 1^2, i + 2^2, i - 2^2, i + 3^2, i - 3^2, \ldots$. Another common scheme described in the exercises is *double hashing*, which uses a second hash function to determine the probe sequence.

A third factor in the design of a hash table is the selection of the hash function. The behavior of the hash function obviously affects the frequency of collisions. For example, the preceding hash function in the example is not a good choice because some letters occur much more frequently than others as first letters of names. Thus the linked list of names beginning with 'S' tends to be much longer than that containing names that begin with 'Z'. This clustering effect results in longer search times for S-names than for Z-names. A better hash function that distributes the names more uniformly throughout the hash table might be the "average" of the first and last letters in the name,

$$h(name) = (firstLetter + lastLetter) \, / \, 2$$

or one might use the "average" of all the letters. The hash function must not, however, be so complex that the time required to evaluate it makes the search time unacceptable.

An ideal hash function is one that is simple to evaluate and that scatters the items throughout the hash table, thus minimizing the probability of collisions. Although no single hashing method performs perfectly in all situations, a popular method known as **random hashing** uses a simple random number generation technique to scatter the items "randomly" throughout the hash table.[2] The item is first transformed into a large random integer using a statement such as

```
randomInt = ((MULTIPLIER * item) + ADDEND) % MODULUS
```

and this value is then reduced modulo the table's capacity to determine the location of the item:

```
location = randomInt % CAPACITY;
```

This hash function can be used with items other than integers if we first encode such items as integers; for example, a name might be encoded as the sum of the ASCII codes of some or all of its letters.

✔ Quick Quiz 9.3

1. In a(n) _____, the location of an item is determined directly by applying a function to the item. The function is called a(n) _____ function.

2. Two items needing to be placed at the same location in a(n) hash table is called a(n) _____ .

3. What is linear probing?

4. A collision strategy in which the hash table is an array or `vector` linked lists that store the items is known as _____ .

For Questions 5 and 6, assume a hash table with 5 locations and the hashing function $h(i) = i \% 5$. Show the hash table that results when the integers are inserted in the order given.

5. 5, 11, 18, 19, 23 with collisions resolved using linear probing.

6. 5, 11, 18, 19, 23 with collisions resolved using chaining.

✍ EXERCISES 9.3

1. Using a hash table with eleven locations and the hashing function $h(i) = i \% 11$, show the hash table that results when the following integers are inserted in the order given: 26, 42, 5, 44, 92, 59, 40, 36, 12, 60, 80. Assume that collisions are resolved using linear probing.

2. Repeat Exercise 1 but assume that collisions are resolved using chaining.

---

[2]Details of the technique used here for generating random numbers and other techniques can be found in Donald Knuth, *The Art of Computer Programming: Seminumerical Algorithms*, vol. 2 (Reading, MA.: Addison-Wesley, 1981). The choices of MULTIPLIER, ADDEND, and MODULUS must be chosen with care. For 32-bit arithmetic, appropriate choices are MULTIPLIER = 25173, ADDEND = 13849, and MODULUS = 65536.

3. Suppose that the following character codes are used: 'A' = 1, 'B' = 2, ..., 'Y' = 25, 'Z' = 26. Using a hash table with eleven locations and the hashing function $h(identifier) = average$ % 11, where *average* is the average of the codes of the first and last letters in *identifier*, show the hash table that results when the following identifiers are inserted in the order given, assuming that collisions are resolved using linear probing: BETA, RATE, FREQ, ALPHA, MEAN, SUM, NUM, BAR, WAGE, PAY, KAPPA.

4. Repeat Exercise 3 but assume that collisions are resolved using chaining.

5. The method of *double hashing* for handling collisions is as follows: If item i collides with another table entry at location a, then apply a second hash function h_2 to the item to determine $k = h_2(i)$. Now examine the elements of the table in locations $a, a + k, a + 2k, \ldots$, reducing all these values modulo n (n is the table capacity) until either the item is found or an empty slot is reached. In the latter case, the item is inserted at this location. Give the hash table that results using the numbers in Exercise 1, but using double hashing rather than chaining to resolve collisions with the following secondary hash function:

$$h_2(i) = \begin{cases} 2i \ \% \ 11 \text{ if this is nonzero} \\ 1 \text{ otherwise} \end{cases}$$

6. Design a class template for the ADT *HashTable*, using the implementation described in this section. The basic operations should include (at least) constructors, a destructor, a copy constructor, inserting an item into a hash table, and searching for an item in the hash table. Use random hashing for the hash function and chaining to resolve collisions. You should also write a driver program to test your class template as instructed in Programming Problem 16 at the end of this chapter.

9.4   DOUBLY-LINKED LISTS AND THE STANDARD C++ `list`

All of the lists we have considered up to now are unidirectional, which means that it is possible to move easily from a node to its successor. In many applications, locating the predecessor of an element arises just as often as the need to locate its successor. For this, bidirectional movement is necessary, because finding a predecessor in a singly-linked list is too inefficient since it requires searching from the beginning of the list. In this section we consider how bidirectional lists can be constructed and processed, we look at how they are used in C++'s standard `list` container, and we apply them to the problem of doing arithmetic with large integers.

DOUBLY-LINKED LISTS

Bidirectional lists can easily be constructed by using nodes that contain, in addition to a data part, two links: a forward link `next` pointing to the successor of the node and a backward link `prev` pointing to its predecessor:

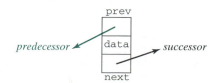

A linked list constructed from such nodes is usually called a **doubly-linked** (or **symmetrically-linked**) list. To facilitate both forward and backward traversal, a pointer (`first`) provides access to the first node and another pointer (`last`) provides access to the last node. For example, a doubly-linked list of integers 9, 17, 22, 26, 34 might be pictured as follows:

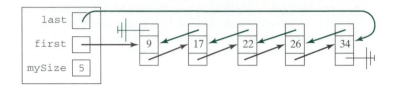

As in the singly-linked case, using head nodes for doubly-linked lists eliminates some special cases (e.g., empty list and first node), and making the lists circular provides easy access to either end of the list. As we shall see later in this section, this is the structure used for the standard C++ `list` type.

Algorithms for the basic list operations are similar to those for the singly-linked case, the main difference being the need to set some additional links. For example, inserting a new node into a doubly-linked list involves first setting its backward and forward links to point to its predecessor and successor, respectively, and then resetting the forward link of its predecessor and the backward link of its successor to point to this new node:

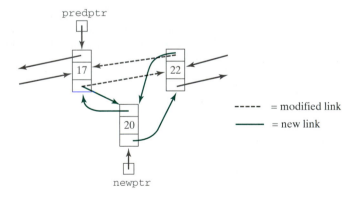

The following statements carry out this insertion:

```
newptr->prev = predptr;
newptr->next = predptr->next;
predptr->next->prev = newptr;
predptr->next = newptr;
```

It is important that these be done in the correct order. You should study examples to see what happens if this order is changed.

A node can be deleted simply by resetting the forward link of its predecessor and the backward link of its successor to bypass the node:

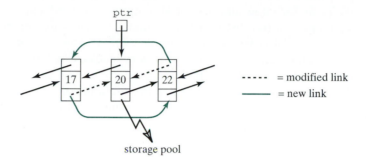

  ---- = modified link

  ——— = new link

This can be accomplished with three instructions:

```
ptr->next->prev = ptr->prev;
ptr->prev->next = ptr->next;
delete ptr;
```

Traversals are performed in the same way as for singly-linked lists. Forward traversals follow the `next` links and backward traversals follow the `prev` links. Constructors, destructors, copy constructors, assignment, and several other operations are also straightforward modifications of those for singly-linked lists.

A LOOK UNDER THE HOOD AT C++'s `list`

STL's `list` is a sequential container that is optimized for insertion and deletion at arbitrary points in the sequence. It stores the list elements in a circular doubly-linked list with a head node. For example, we might picture the three-element list `aList` constructed by

```
list<int> aList;
aList.push_back(9);
aList.push_back(17);
aList.push_back(22);
```

as follows:

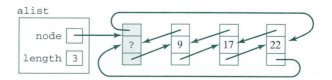

The data member `node` points to the head node and the data member `length` is the number of items in the list.

`list`'s MEMORY MANAGEMENT.   On the surface, `list` looks quite simple. However, it's allocation/deallocation scheme is significantly more complex than simply using `new` and `delete` operations. To reduce the inefficiency of using the system's heap manager for large numbers of allocations and deallocations, it does its own management of a free list of available nodes, which is maintained as a linked stack in exactly the way we described in Sec. 8.3. It uses `new` only when this free list is empty, and then to obtain large memory blocks, which it carves up into nodes of the appropriate size and puts them on a free list. And it uses `delete` to return nodes to the system's free store only when the lifetimes of all lists of a particular type are over. The basic algorithm for managing the nodes is as follows:

For each list of a certain type `T`:

▶ When a node is needed:

  1. If there is a node on the free list, allocate it.
  2. If the free list is empty:
      a. Call the system's heap manager to allocate a block (called a *buffer*) of size (typically) 4K bytes.
      b. Carve it up into pieces of the size required for a node of a `list<T>`.
      c. Put these nodes on the free list.

▶ When a node is deallocated:
     Push it onto the free list.

▶ When *all* lists of type T have been destroyed:
     Return all buffers to the heap.

CONSTRUCTOR, `size()`, AND `empty()`.   Implementations of most of the basic list operations are very similar to those we have described in the preceding section for singly-linked lists and in this section for doubly-linked lists. For example, for a `list<T>` object defined by

```
list<T> alist;
```

the default `list` constructor or builds an empty linked list aList by obtaining a head node from the free list and storing the address of this node in its `node` data member:

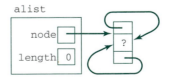

The `size()` function need only

```
return length;
```

and the `empty()` function need only check if the length is 0:

```
return length == 0;
```

ITERATORS AND POINTERS.   From our discussion of iterators in preceding chapters and our discussion of pointers in Chapter 8 and in this chapter, it should be evident that an iterator is an *abstraction* of a pointer, hiding some of its details and eliminating some of its hazards. To illustrate, a `list<T>::iterator` is a class within the `list` class template that contains a data member `node`, which is a pointer to a `list_node` (the struct used to describe nodes in the `list` class template):

```
template<typename T>
class list
{
  . . .
public:
  class iterator        // ... some simplification here ...
  {
  protected:
    list_node * node;  // ... and here ...
    . . .
  };
  . . .
};
```

The `iterator` class overloads `operator*()` so that it returns the value of the `data` member in the `list_node` pointed to by the iterator's `node` member:

```
return node->data;
```

It also overloads `operator++ ()` to "increment" the iterator to the next node in the list

```
// prefix version
node = node->next;
return *this;

// postfix version
iterator tmp = node;
node = node->next;
return tmp;
```

and overloads `operator--()` similarly to "decrement" the iterator to the previous node in the list.

As we described in Sec. 8.7, there are two important iterator-valued functions: `begin()`, which returns an iterator to the first value in the list; and `end()`, which returns an iterator that points beyond the final value in the list, respectively. These functions can be implemented using the pointer members of the head node. More precisely, `begin()` returns a pointer to the first node, by returning the address stored in the `next` member of the head node:

```
return node->next;
```

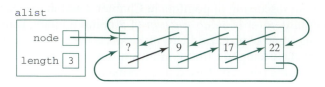

The member function `front()` that accesses the first value in the list need only dereference the iterator returned by `begin()`:

```
return *begin();
```

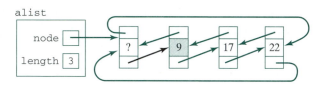

Similarly, `end()` returns an iterator pointing beyond the last node containing a value by returning the address of the head node:

```
return node;
```

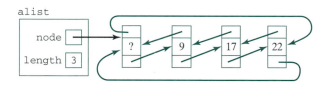

To access the last value in the list, the member function `back()` need only dereference the iterator that results when `end()` is decremented:

```
return *(--end());
```

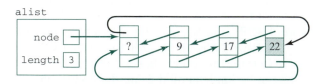

INSERTIONS AND DELETIONS.   The `insert()` and `erase()` operations behave in the way we described earlier in this section for doubly-linked lists. The `push_front()` operation essentially uses `insert()` and `begin()` to insert its value at the beginning of the list

```
insert(begin(), newValue);
```

and `push_back()` uses `insert()` and `end()` to insert its value at the end of the list:

```
insert(end(), newValue);
```

Similarly, the `pop_front()` and `pop_back()` operations are implemented using the `erase()` function: `pop_front()` erases the node at position `begin()`

```
erase(begin());
```

and `pop_back()` erases the node at position `--end()`:

```
erase(--end());
```

The `remove()` operation can be implemented using `erase()` and a simple `while` loop:

```
iterator first = begin(),  // begin at first node
         last = end(),     // stop at head node
         next = first;     // save current node address

while (first != last)
{
  ++next;                  // save address of next node
  if (*first == value)     // if value in current node
    erase(first);          //    erase it
  first = next;            // reset first to next node
}
```

This illustrates how some of the standard `list` operations are implemented. Most of the other operations are based on similar operations on linked lists as described earlier in this chapter and in the preceding chapter.

APPLICATION: LARGE-INTEGER ARITHMETIC

As an application of doubly-linked lists, we consider large-integer arithmetic. Recall that the size of a number that can be stored in computer memory is limited by the number of bits allocated for that type of number. For example, the largest signed integer that can be stored in 32 bits with the usual two's complement representation described in Sec. 2.2 is $2^{31} - 1 = 2147483647$. In some applications (e.g., keeping track of the U. S. national debt), obviously it is necessary to process integers that are larger than this value.

The first step in designing a class for computing with large integers is to select a storage structure to represent these integers. Because the number of digits in these integers may vary considerably, a linked list seems appropriate. And because it is necessary to traverse this list in both directions, we would probably use a doubly-linked list. Each integer to be processed will be stored in a separate list, with each node storing a block of consecutive digits in the number. For example, if we used blocks of length three, the integer 9,145,632,884 could be represented by the following doubly-linked list

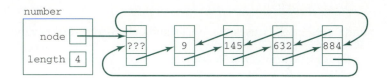

We could use this linked representation and build a `BigInt` class from scratch. However, since the standard `list` type provides iterators and a wealth of list operations that are much easier to use than the rudimentary pointer operations, we will use it instead. So we will use a `list<short int>` data member in `BigInt` to store its digits. And for simplicity, we will consider only nonnegative integers.

One of the first operations we need is an input operation. Again, suppose for convenience that a long integer will be entered in three-digit blocks separated by blanks. For a `BigInt` variable `number`, the input operation must read these blocks and attach a node containing the value of each of these blocks to `number`. For example, suppose that the input data is

9 145 632 884

and that the first three blocks have already been read and stored so that the doubly-linked list in `number` is

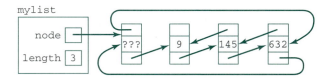

When the block 884 is read, a new node must be created for it and attached to the end of this list by setting the backward link in this new node to point to the last node in the list, its forward link to point to the head node, and then setting the forward link in the last node and the backward link in the head node to point to this new node:

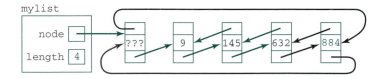

And this is exactly what the `push_back()` operation for a `list` will do. So `operator>>()` need only repeatedly read blocks and push them onto the end of `number`, as shown in Fig. 9.1.

An output operator is simply a traversal of the list from left to right, displaying the block of digits stored in each node (making sure to display leading zeros). And this can easily be done using a `list<short int>` iterator and its dereferencing and increment operations as shown in the definition of `operator<<()` in Fig. 9.1.

Another operation we need is addition of two long integers. It must traverse the lists representing these two numbers, from right to left, adding the two three-digit integers in corresponding nodes and the carry digit from the preceding nodes to obtain a three-digit sum and a carry digit. A node is created to store this three-digit sum and is attached at the front of the list representing the sum of the two numbers. The following diagram shows the linked lists corresponding to the computation

```
carry digits  →  1     1       0       1
                              65     313     750
                      +  999   981     404     873
                         1  000   046     718     623
```

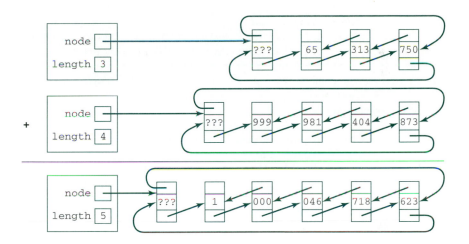

This is precisely what happens in the definition of `operator+()` in Fig. 9.1. The lists in `number1` and `number2` are traversed from right to left using `list<short int>` reverse iterators that are moved through the lists synchronously by using the increment operator. The carry digit and the blocks at each position of the iterator are added, the new carry digit and sum block are calculated, and the sum block inserted at the front of the list in `sum` using `list`'s `insert()` operation.

FIGURE 9.1   A `BigInt` CLASS

```cpp
//--- BigInt.h

#include <iostream>
#include <iomanip>      // setfill(), setw()
#include <list>
using namespace std;
```

```
#ifndef BIGINT
define BIGINT

class BigInt
{
/*** Operations ***/
public:
/* operator>>()
 *
 * Receive:    istream in
 * Input:      Integers in the range 0 - 999 via in
 * Pass back: BigInt number
 * Return:     Modified istream with integer removed
 *******************************************************************/
friend istream & operator>>(istream & in, BigInt & number);

/* operator<<()
 *
 * Receive: ostream out
 * Output:  A formatted display of BigInt number via out
 * Return:  Modified ostream with BigInt inserted
 *******************************************************************/
friend ostream & operator<<(ostream & out, BigInt number);

/* operator+()
 *
 * Receive: BigInts number1 and number2
 * Return:  BigInt number3
 *******************************************************************/
friend BigInt operator+(BigInt number1, BigInt number2);

/*** Data Members ***/
private:
  list<short int> myList;
};

#endif


//--- BigInt.cpp

//-- Definition of operator>>()
istream & operator>>(istream & in, BigInt & number)
{
  static bool instruct = true;
  if (instruct)
  {
    cout << "Enter 3-digit blocks, separated by spaces.\n"
            "Enter a negative integer in last block to signal "
            "the end of input.\n\n";
    instruct = false;
  }
```

```
  short int block;
  for (;;)
  {
    cin >> block;
    if (block < 0) return in;

    if (block > 999)
      cerr << "Illegal block -- " << block << " -- ignoring\n";
    else
      number.myList.push_back(block);
  }
}

//-- Definition of operator<<()
ostream & operator<<(ostream & out, BigInt number)
{
  out << setfill('0');
  int charCount = 0;

  for (list<short int>::iterator it = number.myList.begin();
                          it != number.myList.end(); it++ )
  {
    out << setw(3) << *it << ' ';
    charCount++ ;
    if (charCount > 0 && charCount % 20 == 0)
        out << endl;
  }
  out << endl;
}

//-- Definition of operator+()

BigInt operator+(BigInt number1, BigInt number2)
{
  BigInt sum;
  short int first,          // a block of number1
            second,         // a block of number2
            result,         // a block in their sum
            carry = 0;      // the carry in adding two blocks

  int size1 = number1.myList.size(),
      size2 = number2.myList.size(),
      maxSize = (size1 < size2 ? size2 : size1);
  list<short int>::reverse_iterator it1 = number1.myList.rbegin();
  list<short int>::reverse_iterator it2 = number2.myList.rbegin();
```

```
while (it1 != number1.myList.rend() && it2 != number2.myList.rend())
{
  if (it1 != number1.myList.rend())
  {
    first = *it1;
      it1++ ;
  }
  else
    first = 0;

  if (it2 != number2.myList.rend())
  {
    second = *it2;
      it2++ ;
  }
  else
    second = 0;

  short int temp = first + second + carry;
  result = temp % 1000;
  carry = temp / 1000;
  sum.myList.insert(sum.myList.begin(), result);
}


  if (carry > 0)
    sum.myList.insert(sum.myList.begin(), carry);

  return sum;
}
```

This example illustrates the power of the standard containers such as `list` in C++. One can use the same approach to implementing the class `BigInt` regardless of whether the underlying storage structure is an array, a singly-linked list, a doubly-linked list, or whatever, so long as it provides iterators and basic insert operations. One need only try writing the code using primitive node and pointer operations to appreciate this.

✍ EXERCISES 9.4

Exercises 1–8 assume the following doubly-linked list with the two pointers p1 and p2: (Find the value of each expression.)

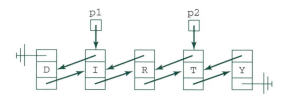

1. `p1->data`

2. `p1->next->data`

3. `p1->prev->prev`

4. `p1->next->next`

5. `p1->prev->next`

6. `p2->prev->prev->data`

7. `p2->prev->prev->prev->prev`

8. `p2->prev->prev->next->data`

In Exercises 9–11, you may use only pointer `p1` to access the doubly-linked list preceding Exercise 1. Write statements to do what is asked for.

9. Display the contents of the nodes, in alphabetical order.

10. Replace `'D'` by `'M'` and `'R'` by `'S'`.

11. Delete the node containing `'T'`.

12–14. Repeat Exercises 9–11, but using only pointer `p2` to access the list.

15–22. Repeat Exercises 1–8, but for the following circular doubly-linked list:

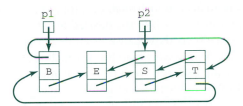

In Exercises 23–25, you may use only pointer `p1` to access the preceding circular doubly-linked list. Write statements to do what is asked for.

23. Display the contents of the nodes, in alphabetical order.

24. Insert a node containing `'L'` after the node containing `'B'` and replace `'E'` with `'A'`.

25. Delete the node containing `'T'`.

26–28. Repeat Exercises 23–25, but using only pointer `p2` to access the list.

29. Add the `<` operation to class `BigInt` that determines if one long integer is less than another long integer.

30. Add the `==` operation to class `BigInt` that determines if one long integer is equal to another long integer.

31. Add the subtraction operation `-` to class `BigInt` that subtracts nonnegative long integers; `int1 - int2` should return 0 if `int1` is less than `int2`.

32. The sequence of *Fibonacci numbers* begins with the integers

$$1, 1, 2, 3, 5, 8, 13, 21, 34, 55, 89, \ldots$$

where each number after the first two is the sum of the two preceding numbers. Write a program that uses class `BigInt` to calculate and display large Fibonacci numbers.

33. Add the multiplication operation * to class `BigInt`.

34. Use the modified class `BigInt` from Exercise 33 in a program that calculates large factorials.

35. Modify the class `BigInt` to process both positive and negative large integers.

9.5   OTHER MULTIPLY-LINKED LISTS

We have seen that doubly-linked lists are useful data structures in those applications in which it is necessary to move in either direction in a list. In this section we consider an assortment of other kinds of list processing in which linked lists whose nodes contain more than one link are useful. Such structures are usually considered in detail in advanced data structures courses and so are only previewed here.

MULTIPLY-ORDERED LISTS

In Chap. 8 we considered ordered lists in which the nodes were arranged so that the data items (or values in some key field of the data items) stored in these nodes were in ascending order. In some applications, however, it is necessary to maintain a collection ordered in two or more different ways. For example, we might wish to have a collection of student records ordered by both name and id number.

One way to accomplish such multiple orderings is to maintain separate ordered linked lists, one for each of the desired orders. But this is obviously inefficient, especially for large records, because multiple copies of each record are required. A better approach is to use a single list in which multiple links are used to link the nodes together in the different orders. For example, to store a collection of records containing student names and id numbers, with the names in alphabetical order and the id numbers in ascending order, we might use the following multiply-linked list having two links per node:

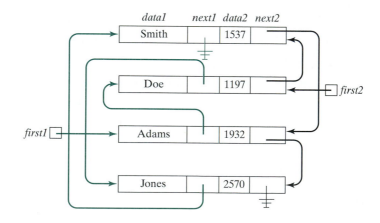

If this list is traversed and the data fields are displayed by using *first1* to point to the first node and following the pointers in the field *next1*, the names will be in alphabetical order:

Adams	1932
Doe	1197
Jones	2570
Smith	1537

A traversal using *first2* to point to the first node and following the pointers in the field *next2* gives the id numbers in ascending order:

Doe	1197
Smith	1537
Adams	1932
Jones	2570

This list is logically ordered, therefore, in two different ways.

SPARSE MATRICES

An $m \times n$ **matrix** is a rectangular array containing m rows and n columns. The usual storage structure for matrices is thus quite naturally a two-dimensional array as described in Sec. 2.3 (or a two-dimensional `vector` as used in the `Matrix` class in Exercise 7 of Sec. 6.5), especially since arrays are provided in nearly every programming language.

In some applications, however (e.g., in solving differential equations), it is necessary to process very large matrices having few nonzero entries. Using a two-dimensional array to store all the entries (including zeros) of such **sparse matrices** is not very efficient. They can be stored more efficiently using a linked structure analogous to that for sparse polynomials described in Section 9.2.

One common linked implementation is to represent each row of the matrix as a linked list, storing only the nonzero entries in each row. In this scheme, the matrix is represented as an array of pointers $A[1], A[2], \ldots, A[m]$, one for each row of the matrix. Each array element $A[i]$ points to a linked list of nodes, each of which stores a nonzero entry in that row and the number of the column in which it appears, together with a link to the node for the next nonzero entry in that row:

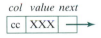

For example, the 4×5 matrix

$$A = \begin{bmatrix} 9 & 0 & 0 & 8 & 0 \\ 7 & 0 & 0 & 0 & 0 \\ 0 & 0 & 0 & 0 & 0 \\ -1 & 6 & 0 & -8 & 0 \end{bmatrix}$$

can be represented by

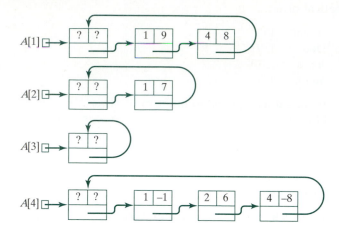

Although this is a useful linked storage structure for matrices, the size of the array limits the number of rows that such matrices may have. Moreover, for smaller matrices and/or those having a large number of rows with all zero entries, many of the elements in this array will be wasted.

An alternative implementation is to create a single linked list. Each node contains a row number, a column number, the nonzero entry in that row and column, and a link to the next node:

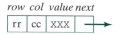

These nodes are usually arranged in the list so that traversing the list visits the entries of the matrix in rowwise order. For example, the preceding 4×5 matrix can be represented by the following circular linked list, which uses a head node to store the dimensions of the matrix:

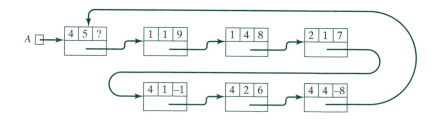

In this implementation, however, we lose direct access to each row of the matrix. If rowwise processing is important to a particular application, such as the addition of matrices, it might be better to replace the array of pointers with a linked list of row head nodes, each of which contains a pointer to a nonempty row list. Each row head node will also contain the number of that row and a pointer to the next row head node, and these row head nodes are ordered so that the row numbers are in ascending order. In this implementation, the preceding 4×5 matrix might be represented by the following linked structure:

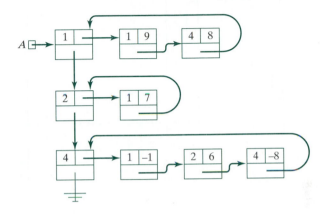

One drawback of all of these linked implementations is that it is difficult to process a matrix columnwise as required, for example, when multiplying two matrices. One linked structure that provides easy access to both the rows and the columns of a matrix is known as an **orthogonal list.** Each node stores a row number, a column number, and the nonzero entry in that row and column, and it appears in both a row list and a column list. This is accomplished by using two links in each node, one pointing to its successor in the row list and the other pointing to its successor in the column list:

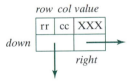

Usually each of the row lists and column lists is a circular list with a head node, and these head nodes are linked together to form circular lists with a master head node. For example, the orthogonal list representation of the preceding 4×5 matrix might be as shown in Fig. 9.2. Here ∞ denotes some value larger than any valid row or column index (e.g., INT_MAX in C++).

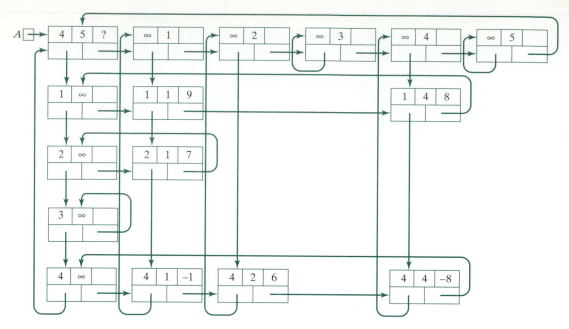

FIGURE 9.2.

GENERALIZED LISTS

In nearly all of our examples of lists thus far, the list elements have been *atomic*, which means that they themselves are not lists. We considered, for example, lists of integers and lists of student records. However, we just described a representation of sparse matrices that is a list of row lists. On several occasions, we also considered lists of strings, and a string is itself a list. In fact, a string might be stored in a linked list of characters and a linked list of strings would then be a linked list of linked lists. For example, the list S of names AL, FRED, JOE would be represented as

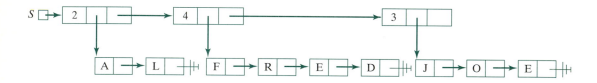

Lists in which the elements are allowed to be lists are called **generalized lists.** As illustrations, consider the following examples of lists:

$$A = (4, 6)$$
$$B = ((4, 6), 8)$$
$$C = (((4)), 6)$$
$$D = (2, A, A)$$
$$E = (2, 4, E)$$

A is an ordinary list containing two atomic elements, the integers 4 and 6. B is also a list of two elements, but the first element $(4, 6)$ is itself a list with two elements. C is also a list with two elements; its first element is $((4))$, which is a list of one element (4), and this element is itself a list having one element, namely, the integer 4. D is a list with three elements in which the second and third are themselves lists. The list E also has three elements, but it differs dramatically from D in that it has itself as a member. Such lists are said to be **recursive lists.**

Generalized lists are commonly represented as linked lists in which the nodes have a tag field in addition to a data part and a link part:

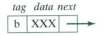

This tag is used to indicate whether the data field stores an atom or a pointer to a list. It can be implemented as a single bit, with 0 indicating an atom and 1 indicating a pointer, or as a boolean variable, with false and true playing the roles of 0 and 1. Thus lists A, B, and C can be represented by the following linked lists:

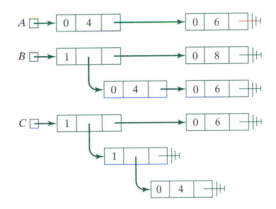

Of course, linked lists with head nodes, circular lists, and other variations may also be used.

Two implementations of D are possible. Because A is the list $(4, 6)$, we can think of D as the list

$$(2, (4, 6), (4, 6))$$

and represent it as

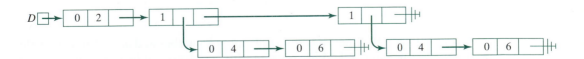

The second possibility is to allow **shared lists** and represent D and A as follows:

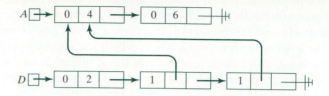

Note that in this case, modifying A also changes D.

The recursive list E can be represented as a circular linked structure:

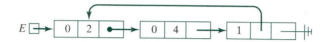

This is equivalent to the following infinite linked structure:

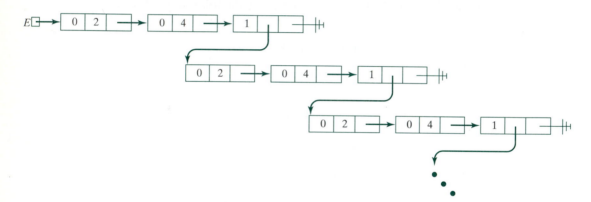

In Exer. 3 of Sec. 8.7 we described a linked implementation of polynomials in a single variable. Polynomials in more than one variable can be represented as generalized lists and can thus be implemented using linked structures similar to these. For example, consider the polynomial $P(x, y)$ in two variables

$$P(x, y) = 3 + 7x + 14y^2 + 25y^7 - 9x^2y^7 + 18x^6y^7$$

This can be written as a polynomial in y whose coefficients are polynomials in x

$$P(x, y) = (3 + 7x) + 14y^2 + (25 - 9x^2 + 18x^6)y^7$$

If we use nodes of the form

tag	coef	expo	next
b	CCC	EEE	→

where $tag = 0$ indicates that the field $coef$ stores a number and $tag = 1$ indicates that it stores a pointer to a linked list representing a polynomial in x, we can represent the polynomial $P(x, y)$ as

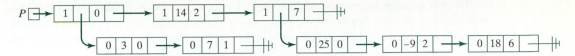

Linked representations of generalized lists are used extensively in implementing the programming language LISP (LISt Processing). As an illustration, the assignment statement that would be written in C++ as

$$Z = X + 3 * (-Y)$$

is written in LISP as

$$(setq \ Z \ (+ \ X \ (* \ 3 \ (- \ Y))))$$

This is, in fact, a list of three elements (without the separating commas we are accustomed to using). The first element is the key word `setq`, which denotes an assignment operator in LISP. The second element is a variable z, to which a value is to be assigned. The third element is the list

$$(+ \ X \ (* \ 3 \ (- \ Y)))$$

which corresponds to the C++ expression X + 3 * (-Y). This three-element list consists of the addition operator +, the variable X, and a list corresponding to the subexpression 3 * (-Y):

$$(* \ 3 \ (- \ Y))$$

Similarly, this list contains the multiplication operator *, the integer constant 3, and a two-element list corresponding to the subexpression -Y:

$$(- \ Y)$$

This list has the unary minus operator as its first element and the variable Y as its second element.

If we use nodes in which a tag value of 0 denotes atomic list elements, such as key words, variable names, and constants, and the tag value 1 denotes lists, this assignment statement can be represented by the following linked structure:

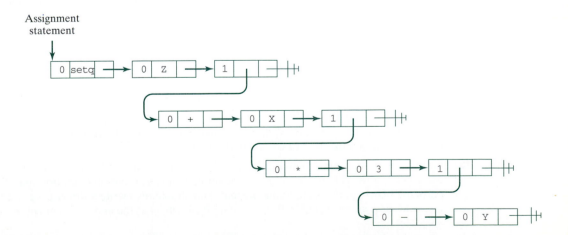

In this section we introduced several kinds of multiply-linked structures and noted some of their applications. There are many other problems in which multiply-linked structures can be used effectively. Several of these applications, including the study of trees and graphs, are considered in detail in later chapters.

✍ EXERCISES 9.5

For Exercises 1–4, beginning with the multiply-ordered linked list of names and id numbers pictured in the text, show the linked list that results from each of the operations or sequence of operations.

1. Insert Brown with id number 2250.

2. Delete Smith with id number 1537.

3. Insert Zzyzk with id number 1025.

4. Insert Evans with id number 1620; insert Harris with id number 1750; and delete Adams with id number 1932.

5. Write appropriate declarations for a multiply-ordered linked list of names and id numbers like that described in the text.

6. Suppose that the following sparse matrix is implemented by an array of pointers to row lists. Give a diagram of the resulting linked lists similar to that in the text.

$$A = \begin{bmatrix} 1 & 0 & 0 & 0 & 8 & 0 & 0 \\ -5 & -6 & 0 & 0 & 0 & 0 & 0 \\ 0 & 0 & 0 & 0 & 0 & 0 & 10 \\ 0 & 0 & 0 & 0 & 0 & 0 & 0 \\ 9 & 8 & 7 & 0 & 0 & 0 & 0 \end{bmatrix}$$

7. Repeat Exercise 6, but implement the matrix as a circular linked list having a head node that stores its dimensions.

8. Repeat Exercise 6, but implement the matrix as a linked list of head nodes containing pointers to linked row lists, as described in the text.

9. Repeat Exercise 7, but give an orthogonal list representation like that described in this section.

10–13. Write the declarations needed to store a sparse matrix of integers using the implementation in Exercises 6–9.

14. Write a function to add two sparse matrices, assuming the array of linked row lists implementation described in this section.

15. Repeat Exercise 14, but assume that each matrix is implemented as a circular linked list having a head node that stores its dimensions.

16. Repeat Exercise 14, but assume that each matrix is implemented as a linked list of head nodes containing pointers to linked row lists as described in the text.

17. Repeat Exercise 14, but assume that each matrix is implemented using an orthogonal list representation like that described in this section.

18. Write a class for sparse matrices that uses one of the linked-list implementations described in this section, has an input operation, and has an output operation that displays the matrix in its usual tabular format. You should also write a driver program to test your class as instructed in Programming Problem 23 at the end of this chapter.

19. Extend the class in Exercise 18 to add two matrices.

For Exercises 20–23, give a diagram of the linked-list implementation of the generalized list.

20. $(1, (2, 3))$

21. $((1, 2), (3, 4), 5)$

22. $(1, (2, 3), ( ), 4)$ [( ) denotes an empty list.]

23. $((1, (2, 3)), ((4)))$

For Exercises 24 and 25, give a diagram of the linked-list implementation of the polynomials in two variables:

24. $P(x, y) = 7 + 3xy + 5x^3y - 17y^2$

25. $P(x, y) = 6 - 5x + 4x^2 - 2x^3y^4 + 6x^5y^4 - x^9y^4 + y^8$

26. Describe how a polynomial $P(x, y, z)$ in three variables can be implemented as a linked list, and illustrate your implementation for the polynomial

$$P(x, y, z) = 6 - 5x + 4x^2 - 2x^3y^4 + 6x^5y^4z^3 - x^9y^4z^3 + y^8z^3 + z^7$$

☞ PROGRAMMING POINTERS

1. Beware of infinite loops in processing circular linked lists. Also take care that algorithms don't work only for empty lists.

2. Be careful in changing links in a doubly-linked list. Making changes in the wrong order may result in dangling pointers and marooned sections of the list.

ADT TIPS

1. Most of the ADT tips at the end of Chap. 8 dealing with singly-linked lists also pertain to variations and to multiply-linked lists.

2. Using a head node for a linked list will simplify some algorithms such as those for insertions and deletions because every node has a predecessor.

3. In a circular linked list every node has a predecessor and a successor.

4. Deletion from a one-element circular list requires special treatment because it becomes empty after this node is deleted.

5. A circular linked list with a pointer to the last node works well for implementing lists such as deques and queues in which it is necessary to access repeatedly the elements at the ends of the list.

6. A hash table is designed for fast (constant-time) searches and insertions.

7. Three things to consider for improving performance of a hash table are:
   ▶ Increase the table capacity.
   ▶ Use a different strategy for resolving collisions.
   ▶ Use a different hash function.

8. STL's `list` class template uses a circular doubly-linked list with a head node to store the list elements.

PROGRAMMING PROBLEMS

SECTION 9.1

1. Write a driver program to test the linked-list version of the `Stack` class template from Exercise 2.

2. Use your stack class template from Exercise 2 in a program like that in Fig. 4.1 to convert integers from base-10 to base-2 notation.

3. Write a driver program to test the linked-list version of the `Queue` class template from Exercise 4.

4. Use your queue class template from Exercise 4 in the drill-practice program in Fig. 5.1.

5. Write a driver program to test the priority queue class template from Exercise 5.

6. Write a driver program to test the circular-linked-list version of the `Queue` class template from Exercise 11.

7. Use your queue class template from Exercise 11 in the drill-practice program in Fig. 5.1.

8. Write a driver program to test the linked-list version of a deque class template from Exercise 12.

9. Write a driver program to test the circular-linked-list version of a deque class template from Exercise 13.

10. Write a program to solve the *Josephus problem* described in Exercise 17. Use output statements to trace the selection process, showing the contents of the list at each stage.

SECTION 9.2

11. Use the `Polynomial` class template in a menu-driven program for processing polynomials. The menu of options should (at least) include reading a polynomial, printing a polynomial using the usual mathematical format described in Exercise 2, evaluating the polynomial for a given value of x as described in Exercise 3, and polynomial addition.

12. Extend the menu of options in Prob. 11 to include calculating the derivative of a polynomial (see Exercise 4).

13. Extend the menu of options in Prob. 11 to include multiplication (see Exercise 5).

14. A *root* of a polynomial $P(x)$ is a number c for which $P(c) = 0$. The *bisection method* is one scheme that can be used to find an approximate root of $P(x)$ in some given interval $[a, b]$ where $P(a)$ and $P(b)$ have opposite signs (thus guaranteeing that $P(x)$ has a root in $[a, b]$). In this method, we begin by bisecting the interval $[a, b]$ and determining in which half $P(x)$ changes sign, because P must have a root in that half of the interval. Now bisect this subinterval and determine in which half of this subinterval $P(x)$ changes sign. Repeating this process gives a sequence of smaller and smaller subintervals, each of which contains a root of $P(x)$, as pictured in the following diagram. The process can be terminated when a small subinterval—say, of length less than 0.0001—is obtained or $P(x)$ has the value 0 at one of the endpoints.

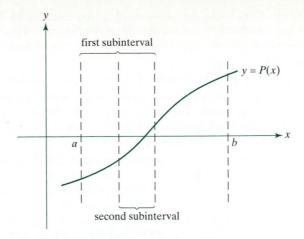

Add and test a member function `Root()` to the `Polynomial` class template so that for a `Polynomial` object P, `P.Root(a, b)` returns an approximate root of `P(x)` in the interval [a,b] (if there is one), using the *bisection method*.

15. Another method for finding a root of a polynomial $P(x)$ is *Newton's method*. This method consists of taking an initial approximation x_1 and constructing a tangent line to the graph of $P(x)$ at that point. The point x_2 where this tangent line crosses the x axis is taken as the second approximation to the root. Then another tangent line is constructed at x_2, and the point x_3 where this tangent line crosses the x axis is the next approximation. The following diagram shows this process:

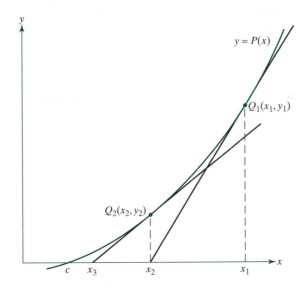

If c is an approximation to the root of $P(x)$, then the formula for obtaining the new approximation is

$$\text{new approximation} = c - \frac{P(c)}{P'(c)}$$

where $P'(x)$ is the derivative of $P(x)$ (see Exercise 4). The process should terminate when a value of $P(x)$ is sufficiently small in absolute value or when the number of iterations exceeds some upper limit. Repeat Problem 14 but use Newton's method.

SECTION 9.3

16. Write a driver program to test the hash table class template from Exercise 6.

17. Write a program that reads a collection of computer user-ids and passwords and stores them in a hash table. The program should then read two strings representing a user's id and password and then checks if this is a legal user of the computer system by searching the hash table for this id and password.

18. Suppose that integers in the range 1 through 100 are to be stored in a hash table using the hashing function $h(i) = i \% n$, where n is the table's capacity. Write a program that generates random integers in this range and inserts them into the hash table until a collision occurs. The program should carry out this experiment 100 times and calculate the average number of integers that can be inserted into the hash table before a collision occurs. Run the program with various values for the table's capacity.

19. In a multi-user environment, jobs with various memory requirements are submitted to the computer system, and the operating system allocates a portion of memory to each job using some memory-management scheme. One popular scheme maintains a circular doubly-linked list of free memory blocks. When a memory request is received, this list is searched to locate the first available block that is large enough to satisfy the request. An appropriate portion of this block is allocated to the job, and any remaining portion remains on the free list.

  Write and test a function to implement this *first-fit* memory-management scheme. Assume that memory blocks are represented as classes (or structs) that contain the beginning address of an available block and its size, together with the links necessary to maintain a circular doubly-linked list. The function should return the address of the allocated block or an indication that the request cannot be satisfied.

20. Another common memory-allocation strategy is the *best-fit* scheme, in which the free list is scanned and the memory block that best fits the request is allocated. This block is either the first block whose size is equal to the request or the block whose size least exceeds the request. Rewrite and test the function in Exercise 19 to use this best-fit scheme.

SECTION 9.5

21. Write a program to read the records from `StudentFile` and store them in a multiply-ordered list with two link fields, in which one link is used to order the nodes so that the id numbers are in ascending order and another link orders the nodes so that the names are in alphabetical order. (See Exercise 13 at the end of Chap. 2 and the website described in the preface for a sample `StudentFile`. Note that the records in `StudentFile` are already arranged in order of ascending id numbers.) Then search this list for a given student id or a given student name, and display the other information in the record.

22. Extend the program in Prob. 21 so that new records can be inserted or existing records can be deleted.

23. Write a driver program to test the sparse-matrix class of Exercise 18.

24. Extend the program in Prob. 23 to test the sparse-matrix class of Exercise 19.

Chapter 10

BINARY TREES

Chapter Contents

In the last sections of the preceding chapter we considered linked lists in which the nodes were connected by two or more links. For example, the nodes in doubly-linked lists have two links, one pointing in the forward direction from a node to its successor and the other pointing backward from a node to its predecessor. The nodes in a multiply-ordered linked list may have to be connected by several links, depending on how many logical orderings are desired. There are several other important multiply-linked structures, and in this chapter we consider one of these, binary trees.

One important application of binary trees is to organize data in a linked structure so that it can be searched more efficiently than if it is stored in a linked list. Thus we begin by reviewing some of the search algorithms we have already considered. This will lead to the study of binary trees and, in particular, binary search trees. We also describe how binary trees are used in the construction of Huffman codes, which can be used for data compression. Other applications of binary trees and other kinds of trees are described in Chap. 13.

10.1 REVIEW OF LINEAR SEARCH AND BINARY SEARCH

In many applications, the collection of data items to be searched is organized as a list,

$$x_1, x_2, \ldots, x_n$$

This list is to be searched to determine whether one of the x_i's has a specified value. In our review of the searching problem in this section, we assume that the equality

(==) operator has been defined for the type of the x_i's, and for binary search, that less than (<) has also been defined. Thus when the list elements are records, as is often the case, and the search is based on some key field in these records, the appropriate relational operators must be defined on these records to compare these key fields.

LINEAR SEARCH

The most straightforward searching scheme is **linear search**, in which we begin with the first list element and then search the list sequentially until either we find the specified item or we reach the end of the list.

An algorithm for linear search was given in Sec. 7.4; for a `vector`-based sequential-storage implementation of lists, this algorithm is implemented by the following function:

```
/* Linear search a list stored in a vector v for item.
 *
 * Receive:    Type parameter ElementType,
 *             ordered list stored in vector v,
 *             item
 * Pass back:  found = true and loc = position of
 *             item if the search is successful;
 *             otherwise found is false.
 ******************************************************/

template <typename ElementType>
void LinearSearch(const vector<ElementType> & v,
                  const ElementType & item,
                  boolean & found, int & loc)
{
  found = false;
  loc = 0;
  for (;;)
  {
    if (found || loc == v.size()) return;
    if (item == v[loc])
      found = true;
    else
      loc++;
  }
}
```

A function to linearly search a singly-linked list is very similar. Instead of varying an index `loc` over the positions of the array or `vector`, we initialize a pointer `locptr` to the first node and advance it from one node to the next by following the `next` parts:

```
/* Linear search a linked list for a node containing item.
 *
 * Receive:    Type parameter ElementType,
 *             a linked list with first node pointed
 *                to by first
 *             item
 * Pass back: found = true and locptr positioned at
 *             item if the search is successful;
 *             otherwise found is false.
 ***********************************************************/

template <typename ElementType>
void LinkedLinearSearch(NodePointer first,
                        const ElementType & item,
                        boolean & found, int & loc)
{
  found = false;
  locptr = first;

  for (;;)
  {
    if (found || locptr == 0) return;
    if (item == locptr->data)
      found = true;
    else
      locptr = locptr->next;
  }
}
```

Here we assume that the type `NodePointer` is as defined in Chap. 8 for linked lists.

Linear search is also the kind of search performed by the standard algorithm `find()` in `<algorithm>`. A call to it has the form

```
find(begin, end, item)
```

where `begin` and `end` are iterators positioned at the first list element and just beyond the last list element, respectively. It returns an iterator positioned at the location of `item` if the search is successful, and an iterator positioned beyond the end of the list if the search is unsuccessful.

The worst case for linear search is obviously that in which the item for which we are searching is not in the list because, in this case, each of the n items in the list must be examined. The worst-case computing time for linear search is thus $O(n)$.

If the list being searched is an ordered list, that is, if the elements are arranged in ascending (or descending) order, then it usually is possible to determine that a specified item is not in the list without examining every element of the list. As soon as a list element is encountered that is greater than (less than) the item, the search can be terminated. For example, when searching the list

$$10, 20, 30, 40, 50, 60, 70, 80, 90, 100$$

for the value 35, there is no need to search beyond the list element 40, because it—and, therefore, all the list elements that follow it—are greater than 35. The worst-case computing time is still $O(n)$, however, since n comparisons are required if the item being sought is greater than all items in the list.

BINARY SEARCH

An alternative scheme for searching an ordered list is **binary search**, also described in Sec. 7.4. A function for a vector-based sequential-storage implementation of an ordered list is as follows:

```
/* Binary search an ordered list stored in a vector v
 * for item.
 *
 * Receive:    Type parameter ElementType,
 *             ordered list stored in vector v,
 *             item
 * Pass back:  found = true and loc = position of
 *             item if the search is successful;
 *             otherwise found is false.
 ********************************************************/

template <typename ElementType>
void BinarySearch(const vector<ElementType> & v,
                  const ElementType & item,
                  boolean & found, int & loc)
{
  found = false;
  int first = 0,
      last = v.size() - 1;
  for (;;)
  {
    if (found || first > last) return;
    loc = (first + last) / 2;

    if (item < x[loc])
      last = loc - 1;
    else if (item > x[loc])
      first = loc + 1;
    else    // item == x[loc]
      found = true;
  }
}
```

Here the middle list element is examined first, and if it is not the desired item, the search continues with either the first half or the last half of the list. Thus, on each pass through the loop, the size of the sublist being searched is reduced by one-half. We showed in some detail in Sec. 7.4 that it follows from this observation that the worst-case computing time for binary search is $O(\log_2 n)$. It is, therefore, more efficient than linear search for large n ($n \geq 20$, as indicated by empir-ical studies).

Binary search is also the kind of search performed by the standard algorithm `binary_search()` in `<algorithm>`. A call to it has the form

```
binary_search(begin, end, item)
```

where `begin` and `end` are iterators positioned at the first list element and just beyond the last list element, respectively. It returns `true` for a successful search and `false` for an unsuccessful one. Notice that unlike `find()`, it does not return an iterator positioned at the location of `item` if the search is successful.

Although the preceding `BinarySearch()` function is iterative, it is also natural to view binary search recursively, as noted in Chap. 7, because the basic idea at each stage is to examine the middle element of the (sub)list and, if it is not the desired item then to search one of the two halves of the (sub)list *in exactly the same way*. Because the computing time of a recursive binary search function is $O(\log_2 n)$ and because it is no simpler than the iterative version, the guidelines given in Chap. 7 for choosing between recursive and iterative formulations of an algorithm suggest that we opt for the iterative version.

Although binary search usually outperforms linear search, it does require a sequential storage implementation so that list elements can be accessed directly. It is not appropriate for linked lists because locating the middle element would require traversing the sublist of elements that precede it. As the exercises ask you to show, this causes the worst-case computing time to become $O(n)$ for a list of size n.

It is possible, however, to store the elements of an ordered list in a linked struc-ture that can be searched in a binary-like manner. To illustrate, consider the follow-ing ordered list of integers:

$$13, 28, 35, 49, 62, 66, 80$$

The first step in binary search requires examining the middle element in the list. Direct access to this element is possible if we maintain a pointer to the node storing it:

At the next stage, one of the two sublists, the left half or the right half, must be searched and must, therefore, be accessible from this node. This is possible if we maintain two pointers, one to each of these sublists. Since these sublists are searched in the same manner, these pointers should point to nodes containing the middle elements in these sublists:

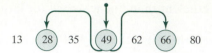

By the same reasoning, pointers from each of these "second-level" nodes are needed to access the middle elements in the sublists at the next stage:

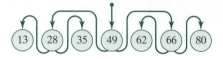

The resulting structure is usually drawn so that it has a treelike shape:

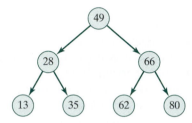

It is called a **binary search tree** and is a special kind of **binary tree**, which is the data structure studied in the rest of this chapter.

✎ EXERCISES 10.1

Exercises 1–5 use the following array critter:

i	0	1	2	3	4	5	6	7	8
critter[i]	auk	bat	cow	eel	elk	fox	gnu	pig	rat

Give the indices of the elements of critter in the order that the components are examined during a binary search for

1. gnu   2. eel   3. fly

4. ant   5. yak

Most of the following exercises ask you to write various search functions. You should also test your functions with driver programs as instructed in Programming Problems 1–10 at the end of this chapter.

6. The performance of function LinearSearch() can be improved slightly if the item being searched for is added at the end of the list. This makes it possible to replace the compound boolean expression in the first if inside the for loop by a simple one. Write this improved version of LinearSearch().

7. Write a linear search function that is more efficient for ordered lists.

8. Write a recursive version of function LinearSearch().

9. Write a recursive version of function LinkedLinearSearch().

10. As noted in the text, binary search is not practical for linked lists because the worst-case complexity would be O(n). Show that this is true by designing an algorithm to carry out a binary search of a linked list and analyzing its complexity. Then write a function to implement this algorithm.

11. In many cases of list searching, certain items in the list are retrieved more frequently than others. The performance of linear search in such cases improves if these frequently sought items are placed at the beginning of the list. One data structure that allows this is a **self-organizing list**, in which list elements are rearranged so that frequently accessed items move to or toward the front of the list. Write a linear search function for such a self-organizing list using a *move-to-the-front* strategy in which the item being retrieved is moved to the front of the list. Assume that the list is stored in an array or a `vector`.

12. Repeat Exercise 11 but for a linked list.

13. Proceed as in Exercise 11, but use a *move-ahead-one* strategy in which the item being retrieved is interchanged with its predecessor.

14. Repeat Exercise 13 but for a linked list.

15. In binary search, *probes* are always made at the middle of the (sub)list. In many situations, however, we have some idea of approximately where the item is located; for example, in searching a telephone directory for "Doe, John," we might estimate that this name is approximately 1/6 of the way through the list. This idea is the basis for **interpolation search**, in which probes of a sublist of size k are made at position *first* $+$ $f * k$ for some fraction f (not necessarily 1/2). Write a function to implement interpolation search for an ordered list of integers using the fraction f given by

$$f = \frac{item - x_{first}}{x_{last} - x_{first}}$$

10.2 INTRODUCTION TO BINARY TREES

We have seen that a linked list is a useful structure for processing dynamic lists whose maximum sizes are not known in advance and whose sizes change significantly because of repeated insertions and deletions. We noted in the preceding section that although binary search is not efficient for linked lists, it can be used for a *binary search tree*. This is a special kind of *binary tree*, which is a special instance of a more general structure called a *tree*.

TREE TERMINOLOGY AND EXAMPLES

A **tree** consists of a finite set of elements called **nodes**, or **vertices**, and a finite set of **directed arcs** that connect pairs of nodes. If the tree is nonempty, then one of the nodes, called the **root**, has no incoming arcs, but every other node in the tree can be reached from it by following a unique sequence of consecutive arcs.

Trees derive their names from the treelike diagrams that are used to picture them. For example,

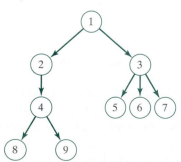

shows a tree having nine vertices in which vertex 1 is the root. As this diagram indicates, trees are usually drawn upside down, with the root at the top and the **leaves**—that is, vertices with no outgoing arcs—at the bottom. Nodes that are directly accessible from a given node (by using only one directed arc) are called the **children** of that node, and a node is said to be the **parent** of its children. For example, in the preceding tree, vertex 3 is the parent of vertices 5, 6, and 7, and these vertices are the children of vertex 3 and are called **siblings**.

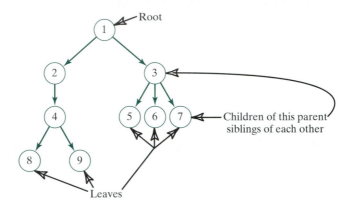

Trees in which each node has at most two children are called **binary trees**, and as noted in the introduction to this chapter, they can be used to solve a variety of problems. They are especially useful in modeling processes in which some experiment or test with two possible outcomes (e.g., off or on, 0 or 1, false or true, down or up) is performed repeatedly. For example, the following tree might be used to represent the possible outcomes of flipping a coin three times:

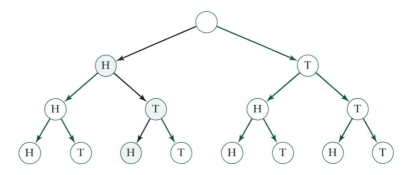

Each path from the root to one of the leaf nodes corresponds to a particular outcome, such as HTH, a head followed by a tail followed by another head, as highlighted in the diagram.

Similarly, a binary tree can be used in coding problems such as in encoding and decoding messages transmitted in Morse code, a scheme in which characters are represented as sequences of dots and dashes, as shown in the following table:

A ·—	M ——	Y —·——
B —···	N —·	Z ——··
C —·—·	O ———	1 ·————
D —··	P ·——·	2 ··———
E ·	Q ——·—	3 ···——
F ··—·	R ·—·	4 ····—
G ——·	S ···	5 ·····
H ····	T —	6 —····
I ··	U ··—	7 ——···
J ·———	V ···—	8 ———··
K —·—	W ·——	9 ————·
L ·—··	X —··—	0 —————

In this case, the nodes in a binary tree are used to represent the characters, and each arc from a node to its children is labeled with a dot or a dash, according to whether it leads to a left child or to a right child, respectively. Thus, part of the tree for Morse code is

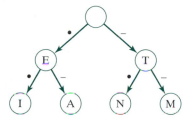

The sequence of dots and dashes labeling a path from the root to a particular node corresponds to the Morse code for that character; for example, ·· is the code for I, and —· is the code for N. In Sec. 10.5 we use a similar tree to construct another kind of code known as *Huffman code*.

ARRAY REPRESENTATION OF BINARY TREES

BUILD

An array can be used to store binary trees. We simply number the nodes in the tree from the root down, numbering the nodes on each level from left to right,

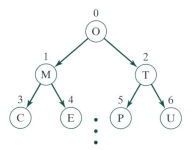

and store the contents of the *i*th node in the *i*th location of the array:

i	0	1	2	3	4	5	6	...
$t[i]$	O	M	T	C	E	P	U	...

This array-based implementation works very well for **complete** trees, in which each level of the tree is completely filled, except possibly the bottom level, and in this level, the nodes are in the leftmost positions. This completeness property guarantees that the data items will be stored in consecutive locations at the beginning of the array. It should be obvious, however, that this implementation may not be space-efficient for other kinds of binary trees. For example, the tree

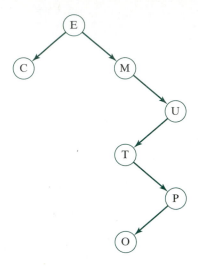

contains the same characters as the one before but requires 58 array positions for storage:

i	0	1	2	3	4	5	6	7	8	9	10	11	12	13	14	15	16	17	18	19
$t[i]$	E	C	M				U							T						

20	21	22	23	24	25	26	27	28	29	30	31	32	33	34	35	36	37	38	39
								P											

40	41	42	43	44	45	46	47	48	49	50	51	52	53	54	55	56	57	$\cdots$
																	O	$\cdots$

LINKED REPRESENTATION OF BINARY TREES

To use space more efficiently and to provide additional flexibility, we instead implement binary trees as linked structures in which each node has two links, one pointing to the left child of that node (if there is one) and the other pointing to the right child (if there is one).

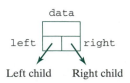

Left child   Right child

The two link fields `left` and `right` in a node are pointers to nodes representing its left and right children, respectively, or are null pointers if the node does not have a left or right child. A leaf node is thus characterized by having null values for both `left` and `right`:

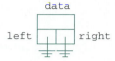

The class for binary-tree nodes in Fig. 10.1 is similar to that used for linked lists in Chap. 8. It has three public data members (so they are accessible to the binary tree operation): `data` of type `DataType` and pointers `left` and `right` to nodes. For convenience, we include two constructors: a default constructor that sets the `left` and `right` links to null pointers and an explicit-value constructor that receives a data value, stores it in the `data` part, and sets the `left` and `right` links to null pointers. We also use a `typedef` declaration to associate an easy-to-use type identifier `BinNodePointer` for pointers to BST nodes.

Any node in the tree can be accessed if we maintain a pointer to the root of the tree, so a binary tree class template need have only one data member, a pointer `root` to the root of the binary tree. The BST constructor will then simply initialize `root` to a null pointer, and an empty operation checks if this pointer is null, as shown in Fig. 10.1:

FIGURE 10.1   A BST CLASS TEMPLATE

```
/*--- File "BST" ---
 * Contains class template BST.
 ****************************************************/

#ifndef BINARY_SEARCH_TREE
#define BINARY_SEARCH_TREE

template <typename DataType>
class BST
{
private:
/*** Node structure ***/

class BinNode
{
 public:
  DataType data;
  BinNode * left,
         * right;

  // BinNode constructors
  // Default -- data part undefined; both links null
  BinNode()
  { left = right = 0; }
```

```
    // Explicit Value -- data part contains item; both links null
    BinNode(DataType item)
    {
      data = item;
      left = right = 0;
    }
};

typedef BinNode * BinNodePointer;

public:
/* Construct an empty BST.
 *    Precondition:  A BST has been declared
 *    Postcondition: An empty BST has been created
 ***********************************************************/
BST();

/* Check if BST is empty.
 *    Receive: BST containing this function (implicitly)
 *    Return:  true if BST is empty, false otherwise
 ***********************************************************/
bool Empty() const;
    . . .

/*** Data members ***/
private:
  BinNodePointer root;
}; // end of class template declaration

//--- Definition of constructor
template <typename DataType>
inline BST<DataType>::BST()
{ root = 0; }

//--- Definition of Empty()
template <typename DataType>
inline bool BST<DataType>::Empty() const
{ return root == 0; }

#endif
```

With this implementation, the binary tree

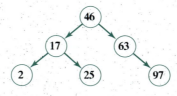

can be represented as the following linked tree of BinNodes:

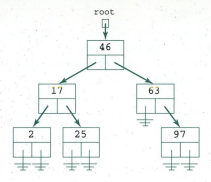

10.3 BINARY SEARCH TREES

In the binary tree considered at the end of the preceding section,

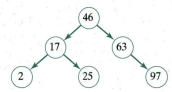

the value in each node is greater than the value in its left child (if there is one) and less than the value in its right child (if there is one). A binary tree having this property is called a **binary search tree (BST)** because, as we noted at the end of Sec. 10.1, it can be searched using an algorithm much like the binary search algorithm for lists. This is one of the key operations of a BST as an abstract data type.

ADT BINARY SEARCH TREE (BST)

Collection of Data Elements:
    A binary tree in which for each node x:
        value in left child of $x \leq$ value in $x \leq$ value in right child of x

Basic Operations:

▸ Construct an empty BST.

▸ Determine if the BST is empty.

▸ Search the BST for a given item.

▸ Insert a new item in the BST and maintain the BST property.

▸ Delete an item from the BST and maintain the BST property.

▸ Traverse the BST visiting each node exactly once. At least one of the traversals, called an *inorder traversal*, must visit the values in the nodes in ascending order.

We have already considered the constructor and empty operations for binary trees in general in the preceding section. In this section we will implement the search and insertion operations. Deletion and traversal will be implemented in the next section.

SEARCHING A BST

To illustrate how to search a binary search tree, suppose we wish to search the preceding BST for 25. We begin at the root, and since 25 is less than the value 46 in this root, we know that the desired value is located to the left of the root; that is, it must be in the left **subtree**, whose root is 17:

Now we continue the search by comparing 25 with the value in the root of this subtree. Since 25 > 17, we know that the right subtree should be searched:

Examining the value in the root of this one-node subtree locates the value 25.

Similarly, to search for the value 55, after comparing 55 with the value in the root, we are led to search its right subtree:

Now, because 55 < 63, if the desired value is in the tree, it will be in the left subtree. However, since this left subtree is empty, we conclude that the value 55 is not in the tree.

The member function `Search()` in Fig. 10.2 incorporates these techniques for searching a binary search tree. The pointer `locptr` begins at the root of the BST and then is repeatedly replaced with the left or right link of the current node, according to whether the item for which we are searching is less than or greater than the value stored in this node. This process continues until either the desired item is found or `locptr` becomes null, indicating an empty subtree, in which case the item is not in the tree. The function assumes that the relational operators have been defined for the type `DataType`.

FIGURE 10.2   SEARCHING A BST

```
    . . .
template <typename DataType>
class BST
{
/*** Node structure ***/
    . . .
```

```
/*** Function members ***/
public:
  . . .
/* Search the BST for item.
 *
 * Receive: The BST containing this function (implicitly)
 *          item being searched for
 * Return:  true if item found, false otherwise
 ************************************************************/
bool Search(const DataType & item) const;
  . . .
/*** Data members ***/
  . . .
}; // end of class template declaration

//--- Definition of Search()
template <typename DataType>
bool BST<DataType>::Search(const DataType & item) const
{
  BinNodePointer locptr = root;
  bool found = false;
  for (;;)
  {
    if (found || locptr == 0) break;
    if (item < locptr->data)         // descend left
      locptr = locptr->left;
    else if (item > locptr->data)  // descend right
      locptr = locptr->right;
    else                             // item found
      found = true;
  }
  return found;
}
#endif
```

As was the case for the binary search algorithm in Sec. 10.1, `Search()` can be written either iteratively (as was done here) or recursively, with little difference of effort. The recursive version is left as an exercise.

INSERTING INTO A BST

BUILD

A binary search tree can be built by repeatedly calling a function to insert elements into a BST that is initially empty (`root` is a null pointer). The method used to determine where an element is to be inserted is similar to that used to search the tree. In fact, we need only modify `Search()` to maintain a pointer to the parent of the node currently being examined as we descend the tree, looking for a place to insert the item.

To illustrate, suppose that the following BST has already been constructed

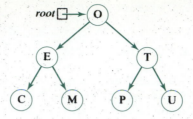

and we wish to insert the letter 'R'. We begin at the root and compare 'R' with the letter there:

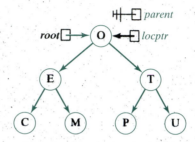

Since 'R' > 'O', we descend to the right subtree:

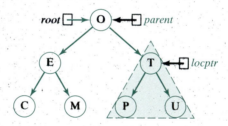

After comparing 'R' with 'T' stored in the root of this subtree pointed to by `locptr`, we descend to the left subtree, since 'R' < 'T':

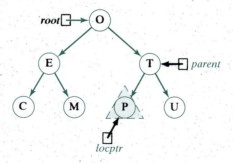

Since 'R' > 'P', we descend to the right subtree of this one-node subtree containing 'P':

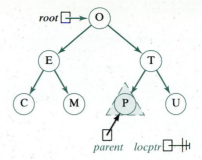

The fact that this right subtree is empty (`locptr` is null) indicates that 'R' is not in the BST and should be inserted as a right child of its parent node:

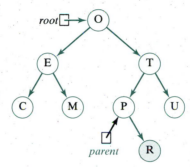

The member function `Insert()` in Fig. 10.3 uses this modified version of `Search()` to locate where a given item is to be inserted (or is found). The pointer `parent` that trails the search pointer `locptr` down the tree keeps track of the parent node so that the new node can be attached to the BST in the proper place.

FIGURE 10.3   INSERTING AN ITEM IN A BST

```
    . . .
template <typename DataType>
class BST
{
/*** Node structure ***/

    . . .


/*** Function members ***/
public:

   . . .
/* Insert item into BST.
 *
 * Receive:      The BST containing this function (implicitly)
 *               item being inserted
 * Postcondition: BST has been modified with item inserted
 *               at proper position to maintain BST property.
 *********************************************************************/
void Insert(const DataType & item);
    . . .
```

```
/*** Data members ***/
  . . .
}; // end of class template declaration

//--- Definition of Insert()
template <typename DataType>
void BST<DataType>::Insert(const DataType & item)
{
  BinNodePointer
    locptr = root,      // search pointer
    parent = 0;         // pointer to parent of current node
  bool found = false;   // indicates if item already in BST

  for (;;)
  {
    if (found || locptr == 0) break;
    parent = locptr;
    if (item < locptr->data)      // descend left
      locptr = locptr->left;
    else if (item > locptr->data // descend right
      locptr = locptr->right;
    else                          // item found
      found = true;
  }
  if (found)
    cerr << "Item already in the tree\n";
  else
  {
    locptr = new BinNode(item);  // construct node containing item
    if (parent == 0)             // empty tree
      root = locptr;
    else if (item < parent->data)// insert to left of parent
      parent->left = locptr;
    else                          // insert to right of parent
      parent->right = locptr;
  }
}
  . . .
```

EXAMPLE: VALIDATING COMPUTER LOGINS

PROBLEM.   To illustrate the use of BSTs, consider the problem of organizing a collection of computer user-ids and passwords. Each time a user logs in to the system by entering his or her user-id and a secret password, the system must check the validity of this user-id and password to verify that this is a legitimate user. Because this user validation must be done many times each day, it is necessary to structure this information in such a way that it can be searched rapidly. Moreover, this must be a dynamic structure because new users are regularly added to the system.

DESIGN.   The objects in this problem are:

> *Objects:*   User information (id and password, which are strings): of type `UserInfo`
>
> Collection of `UserInfo` objects: a `BST`
>
> The usual input and output streams

We will use a BST for the collection of `UserInfo` objects because it can be searched rapidly and it is a dynamic structure. Thus the major operations we need are provided in the BST class:

> *Operations:*   Build a BST of `UserInfo` objects
>
> Search the BST for a given `UserInfo` object entered from the keyboard
>
> Display a message indicating if the user is a valid user

The type `UserInfo` is not provided, so we must also design a class for it. It will have

> *Data Members:*   user-id and password (both strings)

Since searching and inserting a BST requires being able to compare the values stored in it with `<`, `>`, and `==`, we must overload these operators for `UserInfo`. And we also need an input operation, so we will overload `>>` for it:

> *Function Members:*   `<, >, ==, >>`

An algorithm for using these objects and operations is straightforward:

ALGORITHM FOR COMPUTER-LOGIN VALIDATION

/*   Algorithm to read user-ids and passwords and check if they are valid.

    Input: user information
    Output: messages indicating validity of user information
---*/

/* The following steps are done one time to create the initial BST of valid `UserInfo` objects. */

1. Open a stream to a file containing the valid user information.

2. Create an empty BST of type `UserInfo`.

3. Read the `UserInfo` objects from the file and insert them into the BST.

// Now process logins.

4. Repeat the following until shutdown:

> **a.** Read a `UserInfo` object.
> **b.** Search the BST for this object.
> **c.** If it is found, display a "valid" message.
>   Else display a "not valid" message

CODING.   The program in Fig. 10.4 implements the preceding algorithm. Also shown is the declaration of the class `UserInfo`.

FIGURE 10.4   VALIDATING COMPUTER LOGINS

```cpp
#include "BST"
#include <iostream>
#include <fstream>
#include <string>
using namespace std;

/* Program to validate computer user-ids and passwords.  A list of
 * valid ids and passwords is read from UsersFile and is stored in
 * a BST.  When user-ids and passwords are entered during execution,
 * this BST is searched to determine whether they are legal.
 *
 * Input (file):     UserInfo records for valid users
 * Input (keyboard): Ids and passwords of users logging in
 * Output (screen):  Messages indicating whether user-ids and
 *                     passwords are valid
 ***************************************************************/

//--- Class containing user information ----------------//
//     with >>, ==, <, and > operators
class UserInfo
{
 public: // ***** function members and friends ***** //
   //--- input operator
   friend istream & operator>>(istream & in, UserInfo & user);

   //--- equals operator
   bool operator==(const UserInfo & user)
   { return myId == user.id &&
           myPassword == user.password; }

   //--- less-than operator
   bool operator<(const UserInfo & user)
   { return myId < user.id; }

   //--- greater-than operator
   bool operator>(const UserInfo & user)
   { return myId > user.id; }

 private: // ***** data members ***** //
   string myId,
          myPassword;
};

//--- Definition of input operator
istream & operator>>(istream & in, UserInfo & user)
{
  in >> user.myId>> user.myPassword;
  return in;
}


//----------------------------------------------------------//
```

```
int main()
{
  // Open file of legal user-ids and password
  ifstream userFile("UsersFile");
  if (!userFile.is_open())
  {
    cerr << "Cannot open UsersFile\n";
    exit(-1);
  }

  // Build the BST of user records
  BST<UserInfo> userTree;    // BST of user records
  UserInfo user;             // a user record
  for(;;)
  {
    userFile >> user;
    if (userFile.eof()) break;

    userTree.Insert(user);
  }

  // Validate logins
  cout << "Enter Q Q to stop processing.\n";

  for (;;)
  {
    cout << "\nUser id & password: ";
    cin >> user;
    if (user.id == "Q") break;

    if (userTree.Search(user))
      cout << "Valid user\n";
    else
      cout << "Not a valid user\n";
  }
}
```

LISTING OF UsersFile USED IN SAMPLE RUN:

```
S31416PI CHERRY
S12345SL CLAY
S31313LN KANSAS
S21718EX LOG
S13331RC COLA
S77777UP UNCOLA
S99099RR RAILROAD
```

SAMPLE RUN:

```
Enter Q Q to stop processing.

User id & password: S31416PI CHERRY
Valid user

User id & password: S12345SL SAND
Valid user

User id & password: S11111AB ALPHA
Not a valid user

User id & password: S77777UP COLA
Valid user

User id & password: Q Q
```

PROBLEM OF LOPSIDEDNESS

The order in which items are inserted into a BST determines the shape of the tree. For example, inserting the letters O, E, T, C, U, M, P into a BST of characters in this order gives the nicely *balanced* tree

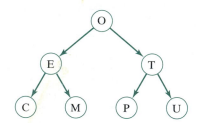

but inserting them in the order C, O, M, P, U, T, E yields the unbalanced tree

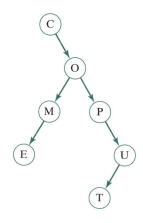

and inserting them in alphabetical order, C, E, M, O, P, T, U, causes the tree to degenerate into a linked list:

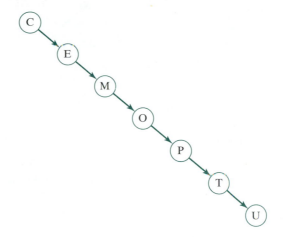

The time required to carry out most of the basic operations on a BST quite clearly depends on the "shape" of the tree. If it is balanced so that the left and right subtrees of each node contain approximately the same number of nodes, then as a search pointer moves down the tree from one level to the next, the size of the subtree to be examined is reduced by one-half. Using an analysis like that used for binary search in Sec. 7.4, it is easy to show that the computing time for Search() and Insert() is $O(\log_2 n)$ in this case. As the BST becomes increasingly unbalanced, however, the performance of these functions deteriorates. For trees that degenerate into linked lists as in the last example, Search() degenerates into linear search, so that the computing time is $O(n)$ for such BSTs.

It is usually not possible to determine a priori the optimal order in which to insert items into a BST, that is, to preorder the data items so that inserting them into a BST will result in a balanced tree. The usual solution is to rebalance the tree after each new element is inserted using rebalancing algorithms. One common rebalancing scheme is described in Chap. 13.

✔ Quick Quiz 10.3

1. A(n) _____ consists of nodes (or vertices) and directed arcs that connect pairs of nodes.

2. A node that has no incoming arcs but from which every other node in the tree can be reached by following a unique sequence of consecutive arcs is called a(n) _____.

3. Nodes with no outgoing arcs are called _____.

4. Nodes that are directly accessible from a given node (by using only one directed arc) are called the _____ of that node, which is said to be the _____ of these nodes.

5. Binary trees are trees in which each node has _____.

Questions 6–10 refer to the following binary search tree:

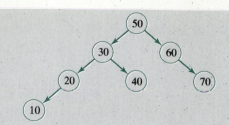

6.   Which node is the root?
7.   List all the leaves.
8.   This binary tree is complete. (True or false)
9.   Show the array used to represent this binary tree.
10.   Draw the BST that results if 45 and 65 are inserted.

✍ EXERCISES 10.3

1.   Complete the binary tree for Morse code that was begun in this section.

For each of the lists of letters in Exercises 2–6, draw the BST that results when the letters are inserted in the order given.

2.   A, C, R, E, S   3.   R, A, C, E, S
4.   C, A, R, E, S   5.   S, C, A, R, E
6.   C, O, R, N, F, L, A, K, E, S

7–11. Assuming the array-based implementation of binary trees described in Sec. 10.2, show the contents of arrays used to store the binary trees of Exercises 2–6.

12.   Write a recursive version of function `Search()`.

The following exercises ask you to write functions for BST operations. You should also write driver programs to test these functions as instructed in Programming Problems 15–17 at the end of this chapter.

13.   Write a nonrecursive member function `Level()` for class template BST that determines the *level* in the BST at which a specified item is located. The root of the BST is at level 0, its children are at level 1, and so on.

14.   Proceed as in Exercise 13, but write a recursive function.

15.   The worst-case number of comparisons in searching a BST is equal to its *height*, that is, the number of levels in the tree. Write a recursive member function `Height()` for class template BST to determine the height of the BST.

10.4 BINARY TREES AS RECURSIVE DATA STRUCTURES

All of the algorithms we developed in the preceding section for processing binary trees are iterative, but they can also be written recursively because a binary tree can be defined as a **recursive data structure** in a very natural way. As an illustration, consider the following binary tree:

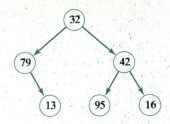

Its root node contains the integer 32 and has pointers to the nodes containing 79 and 42, each of which is itself the root of a binary **subtree**:

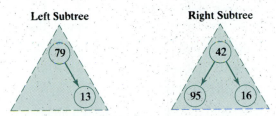

Now consider the left subtree. Its root node contains the integer 79 and has a right child but no left child. Nevertheless, we can still regard this node as having pointers to two binary subtrees, a left subtree and a right subtree, provided that we allow empty binary trees:

Both the left and right subtrees of the one-node tree containing 13 are thus empty binary trees.

This leads to the following recursive definition of a binary tree:

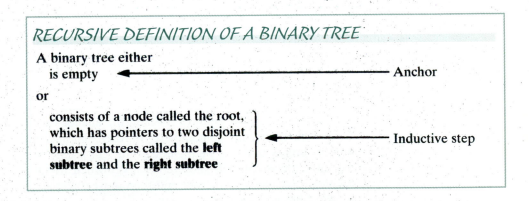

RECURSIVE DEFINITION OF A BINARY TREE

A binary tree either
   is empty ◄─────────────────────── Anchor
or
   consits of a node called the root,
   which has pointers to two disjoint
   binary subtrees called the **left**
   subtree and the **right subtree** ◄──────── Inductive step

Because of the recursive nature of binary trees, many of the basic operations on them can be carried out most simply and elegantly using recursive algorithms. These algorithms are typically anchored by the special case of an empty binary tree, and the inductive step specifies how a binary tree is to be processed in terms of its root and either or both of its subtrees.

BUILD   TRAVERSALS

As an illustration, we first consider the operation of traversal, that is, moving through a binary tree like the preceding one, visiting each node exactly once. And suppose for now that the order in which the nodes are visited is not relevant. What is important is that we visit each node, not missing any, and that the information in each node is processed exactly once.

One simple recursive scheme is to traverse the binary tree as follows:

1. Visit the root and process its contents.

2. Traverse the left subtree.

3. Traverse the right subtree.

Thus, in our example, if we simply display a node's contents when we visit it, we begin by displaying the value 32 in the root of the binary tree. Next we must traverse the left subtree; after this traversal is finished, we then must traverse the right subtree; and when this traversal is completed, we will have traversed the entire binary tree.

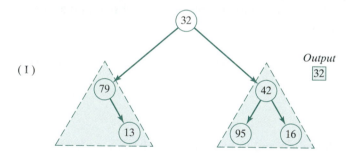

Thus the problem has been reduced to the traversal of two smaller binary trees. We consider the left subtree and visit its root. Next we must traverse its left subtree and then its right subtree.

The left subtree is empty, and so we have reached the anchor case of the recursive definition of a binary tree, and to complete the traversal algorithm, we must specify how an empty binary tree is to be traversed. But this is easy. We do nothing.

Because traversal of the empty left subtree is thus finished trivially, we turn to traversing the right subtree. We visit its root and then must traverse its left subtree followed by its right subtree.

(III)

Output

32 , 79 , 13

As both subtrees are empty, no action is required to traverse them. Consequently, traversal of the binary tree in diagram III is complete, and since this was the right subtree of the tree in diagram II, traversal of this tree is also complete.

This means that we have finished traversing the left subtree of the root in the original binary tree in diagram I, and we finally are ready to begin traversing the right subtree. This traversal proceeds in a similar manner. We first visit its root, displaying the value 42 stored in it, then traverse its left subtree, and then its right subtree.

(IV)

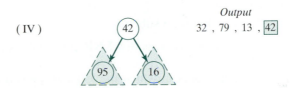

Output

32 , 79 , 13 , 42

The left subtree consists of a single node with empty left and right subtrees and is traversed as described earlier for a one-node binary tree.

(V)

Output

32 , 79 , 13 , 42 , 95

The right subtree is traversed in the same way.

(VI)

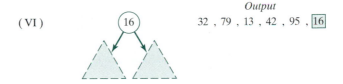

Output

32 , 79 , 13 , 42 , 95 , 16

This completes the traversal of the binary tree in diagram IV and thus completes the traversal of the original tree in diagram I.

As this example demonstrates, traversing a binary tree recursively requires three basic steps, which we shall denote N, L, and R:

N   Visit a node.

L   Traverse the left subtree of a node.

R   Traverse the right subtree of a node.

We performed these steps in the order listed here, but in fact, there are six different orders in which they can be carried out:

LNR

NLR

LRN

NRL

RNL

RLN

For example, the ordering LNR corresponds to the following traversal algorithm:

If the binary tree is empty then   // anchor
   Do nothing.
Else do the following: // inductive step

   L   Traverse the left subtree.
   N   Visit the root.
   R   Traverse the right subtree.

For the preceding binary tree, this LNR traversal visits the nodes in the order 79, 13, 32, 95, 42, 16.

The first three orders, in which the left subtree is traversed before the right, are the most important of the six traversals and are commonly called by other names

LNR ↔ Inorder

NLR ↔ Preorder

LRN ↔ Postorder

To see why these names are appropriate, consider the following **expression tree**, a binary tree used to represent the arithmetic expression

$$A - B * C + D$$

by representing each operand as a child of a parent node representing the corresponding operator:

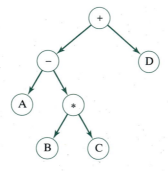

An **inorder** traversal of this expression tree produces the **infix** expression

$$A - B * C + D$$

A **preorder** traversal gives the **prefix** expression (see Exercise 53 in Sec. 4.3)

$$+ - A * B C D$$

And a **postorder** traversal yields the **postfix** (RPN) expression (see Sec. 4.3)

$$A\ B\ C * - D +$$

A recursive function to implement any of these traversal algorithms is easy. One need only attempt to write a correct nonrecursive version to appreciate the simple elegance of the functions in Fig. 10.5. Two functions are needed, because although we can send a message to a BST object to conduct an inorder traversal of itself, we cannot send a message to its root, which the recursive inorder-traversal algorithm requires. So we simply send the message Inorder() to the BST and have it pass the message on to the auxiliary member function InorderAux().

FIGURE 10.5   TRAVERSING A BINARY TREE

```
#include <iostream>
using namespace std;
   . . .
template <typename DataType>
class BST
{
/*** Node structure ***/

   . . .

/*** Function members ***/
public:
   . . .
/* Inorder traversal.
 *
 * Receive: The BST containing this function (implicitly)
 *          ostream out
 * Output:  Contents of the BST in inorder (via InorderAux)
 ***********************************************************/
void Inorder(ostream & out);

/* Inorder traversal auxiliary function
 *
 * Receive: The BST containing this function (implicitly)
 *          ostream out, and pointer ptr to a binary tree node
 * Output:  Contents of the BST with root at ptr in inorder
 ***********************************************************/
void InorderAux(ostream & out, BinNodePointer ptr);


   . . .


/*** Data members ***/
   . . .
}; // end of class template declaration
```

```
//--- Definition of Inorder()
template <typename DataType>
void BST<DataType>::Inorder(ostream & out)
{ InorderAux(out, root); }


//--- Definition of InorderAux()
template <typename DataType>
void BST<DataType>::InorderAux(ostream & out, BinNodePointer ptr)
{
  if (ptr != 0)
  {
    InorderAux(out, ptr->left);
    out << ptr->data << "   ";
    InorderAux(out, ptr->right);
  }
}
    . . .
```

Functions for any of the other traversals are obtained by simply changing the order of the statements representing the L, N, and R operations.

It should be noted that an inorder traversal visits the nodes in a BST in ascending order. The reason is that in a binary search tree, for each node, the value in the left child is less than the value in that node, which, in turn, is less than the value in the right child. This means that for each node, all of the values in the left subtree are smaller than the value in this node, which is less than all values in its right subtree. Because an inorder traversal is an LNR traversal, it follows that it must visit the nodes in ascending order.

RECURSIVE SEARCHING

Now that we have viewed binary trees and BSTs in particular as recursive data structures and have seen how easily traversal can be implemented by recursive functions, we should reexamine the search and insert functions considered in the preceding section. Recall that to search a BST we begin at the root. If it is the desired item, the search is finished; if the item we wish to find is less than the value in the root, we move down to the left subtree and search it; and if it is greater, we descend to the right subtree and search it. If the subtree we select is empty, we conclude that the item is not in the tree; otherwise, we search this subtree *in exactly the same manner* as we did the original tree. This means, therefore, that although we formulated our search function iteratively, we were, in fact, thinking recursively and could also have done it recursively as follows. Note that for the same reasons we needed both an `Inorder()` function and a helper function `InorderAux()`, we need here a `Search()` function that calls a recursive helper function `SearchAux()`:

```
//--- Definition of Search()

template <typename DataType>
bool BST<DataType>::Search(const DataType & item)
{ SearchAux(root, item); }
```

```
//--- Definition of SearchAux()
template <typename DataType>
void BST<DataType>::SearchAux(BinNodePointer locptr,
                                const DataType & item)
{
  if (locptr == 0)                        // empty tree
    return false;

  // else there is a nonempty tree
  if (item < locptr->data)          // search left subtree
    SearchAux(locptr->left, item);
  else if (item > locptr->data)     // search right subtree
    SearchAux(locptr->right, item);
  else                                    // item is found
    return true;
}
```

However, because this approach is not really more simple or understandable than the iterative version given in Sec. 10.3, in accord with the guidelines in Chap. 7 for choosing between a recursive and an iterative algorithm, we opt for the iterative version.

RECURSIVE INSERTION

A recursive function for the insertion operation is a bit easier than the iterative version. The obvious anchor is an empty BST, and we must specify how to insert an item into such a tree; otherwise, we can proceed recursively by inserting an item into the left subtree or the right subtree of the current node, according to whether the item is less than or greater than the value in this node.

```
//--- Definition of Insert()
template <typename DataType>
bool BST<DataType>::Insert(const DataType & item)
{ InsertAux(root, item); }

//--- Definition of InsertAux()
template <typename DataType>
void BST<DataType>::InsertAux(BinNodePointer locptr,
                                const DataType & item)
{
  if (locptr == 0)                          // empty tree
    root = new BSTNode(item);

  // else there is a nonempty tree.  Insert into:
  else if (item < locptr->data)       //   left subtree
    InsertAux(locptr->left, item);
  else if (item > locptr->data)       //   right subtree
    InsertAux(locptr->right, item);
  else
    cerr << "Item already in the tree\n";
}
```

DELETION

To delete a node x from a BST, we consider three cases:

1. x is a leaf.
2. x has one child.
3. x has two children.

The first case is very easy. We simply make the appropriate pointer in x's parent a **null** pointer; this is the left or right pointer according to whether x is the left or the right child of its parent. For example, to delete the leaf node containing D in the following BST

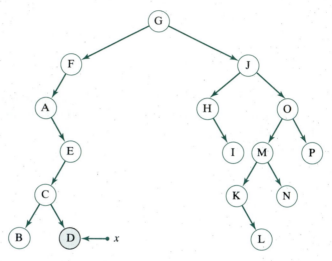

we can simply make the right pointer in its parent C a null pointer and then return x to the heap:

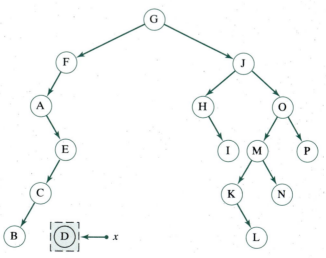

The second case, where the node x has exactly one child, is just as easy. Here we need only set the appropriate pointer in x's parent to point to this child. For example, we can delete the node containing E in the BST of our example by simply setting the right pointer of its parent A to point to the node containing C and then dispose of x:

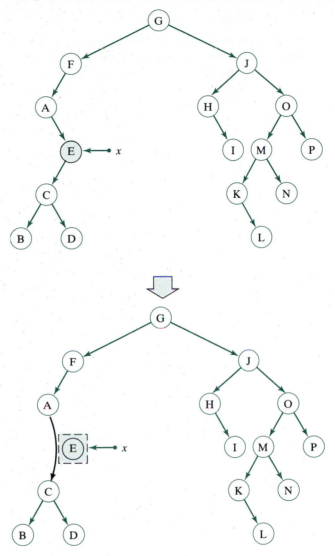

These two cases can be combined into one case in which x has at most one non-empty subtree. If the left pointer of x is null, we set the appropriate pointer of x's parent to point to the right subtree of x (which may be empty—case 1); otherwise, we set it to point to the left subtree of x. The following statements handle both cases:

```
subtree = x->left;      // pointer to a subtree of x
if (subtree == 0)
   subtree = x->right;
if (parent == 0)        // root being deleted
   root = subtree;
```

```
else if (parent->left == x)
   parent->left = subtree;
else
   parent->right = subtree;
```

The third case, in which x has two children, can be reduced to one of the first two cases if we replace the value stored in node x by its inorder successor (or predecessor) and then delete this successor (predecessor). The inorder successor (predecessor) of the value stored in a given node of a BST is its successor (predecessor) in an inorder traversal of the BST.

To illustrate this case, consider again the following binary search tree and suppose we wish to delete the node containing J:

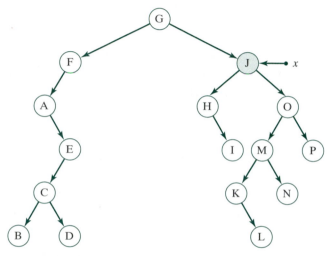

As we just noted, we can replace it with either its inorder successor or its inorder predecessor. We will illustrate here with its successor. We can locate this inorder successor by starting at the right child of x and then descending left as far as possible. In our example, this inorder successor is the node containing K:

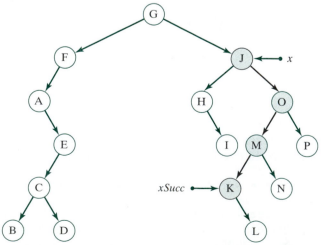

We replace the contents of x with this inorder successor:

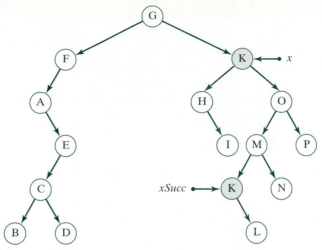

Now we need only delete the node pointed to by *xSucc*. We do this as described for cases 1 and 2, since this node will always have an empty left subtree (and perhaps an empty right subtree as well):

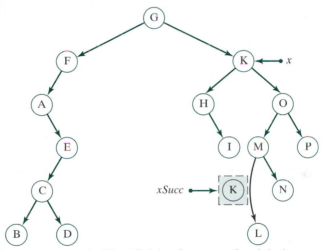

The function `Delete()` in Fig. 10.6 implements the deletion operation for all cases, reducing case 3 to one of the first two cases, when necessary, in the manner we have just illustrated.

FIGURE 10.6   DELETING AN ITEM FROM A BST

```
 . . .
template <typename DataType>
class BST
{
/*** Node structure ***/
 . . .

/*** Function members ***/
public:
 . . .
```

```
/* Delete item from BST.
 *
 * Receive:        The BST containing this function (implicitly)
 *                 item being deleted
 * Postcondition: BST has been modified with item removed (if
 *                 present); BST property is maintained.
 * Note: Delete uses auxiliary function Search2() to locate
 *       the node containing item and its parent.
 ************************************************************/
void Delete(const DataType & item);

/* Search2 locates node containing an item and its parent.
 *
 * Receive:    The BST containing this function (implicitly)
 *             item to be located
 * Pass back: Pointer locptr to node containing item -- null
 *             if not found -- and parent pointing to its
 *             parent
 ************************************************************/
void Search2(const DataType & item, bool & found,
             BinNodePointer & locptr, BinNodePointer & parent);
   . . .

/*** Data members ***/
   . . .
}; // end of class template declaration

//--- Definition of Delete()
template <typename DataType>
void BST<DataType>::Delete(const DataType & item)
{
  bool found;                      // signals if item is found
  BinNodePointer x,                // points to node containing item
                 parent;           //     "       " parent of x and xSucc
  Search2(item, found, x, parent);
  if (!found)
  {
    cerr << "Item not in the BST\n";
    return;
  }

  //else
  if (x->left != 0 && x->right != 0)
  {                                  // node has 2 children
    // Find x's inorder successor and its parent
    BinNodePointer xSucc = x->right;
    parent = x;
```

```
   while (xSucc->left != 0)           // descend left
   {
     parent = xSucc;
     xSucc = xSucc->left;
   }

   // Move contents of xSucc to x and change x
   // to point to successor, which will be deleted.
   x->data = xSucc->data;
   x = xSucc;
 } // end if node has 2 children

 // Now proceed with case where node has 0 or 1 child
 BinNodePointer subtree = x->left; // pointer to a subtree of x
 if (subtree == 0)
   subtree = x->right;
 if (parent == 0)                     // root being deleted
   root = subtree;
 else if (parent->left == x)        // left child of parent
   parent->left = subtree;
 else                                 // right child of parent
   parent->right = subtree;
 delete x;
}

//--- Definition of Search2()
template <typename DataType>
void BST<DataType>::
Search2(const DataType & item, bool & found,
        BinNodePointer & locptr, BinNodePointer & parent)
{
  locptr = root;
  parent = 0;
  found = false;
  for (;;)
  {
    if (found || locptr == 0) return;
    if (item < locptr->data)         // descend left
    {
      parent = locptr;
      locptr = locptr->left;
    }
```

```
      else if (item > locptr->data)   // descend right
      {
        parent = locptr;
        locptr = locptr->right;
      }
      else                            // item found
        found = true;
    }
}
    . . .
```

It also is possible to design a recursive function for deletion from a binary search tree. In this case, the necessary searching can be incorporated into the deletion function. Note, however, that in the case that the node to be deleted has two children, two descents into the tree are made, the first to find the node and the second to delete its successor node.

```
//--- Recursive version of Delete()
template <typename DataType>
void BST<DataType>::Delete(const DataType & item)
{ DeleteAux(item, root); }


//--- Definition of helper function DeleteAux()
template <typename DataType>
void BST<DataType>::DeleteAux(const DataType & item,
                              BinNodePointer & root)
{
  if (root == 0)                 // empty BST -- item not found
  {
    cerr << "Item not in the BST\n";
    return;
  }
  //else recursively search for the node containing item
  //and delete it from the:
  if (item < root->data)         // left subtree
    DeleteAux(item, root->left);
  else if (item > root->data)    // right subtree
    DeleteAux(item, root->right);
  else                           // item found -- delete node
  {
    BinNodePointer ptr;          // auxiliary pointer
    if (root->left == 0)         // no left child
    {
      ptr = root->right;
      delete root;
      root = ptr;
    }
```

```
else if (root->right == 0)   // left child, but no right child
{
  ptr = root->left;
  delete root;
  root = ptr;
}
else                          // 2 children
{
  // find inorder successor
  ptr = root->right;
  while (ptr->left != 0)
    ptr = ptr->left;

  // Move contents of successor to the root of the subtree
  // being examined and delete the successor node.
  root->data = ptr->data;
  DeleteAux(ptr->data, root->right);
}
  }
}
```

We saw in the preceding section that repeated insertions can result in an unbalanced tree, and this is also true for deletion. Again, the usual solution is to rebalance the tree after each new element is deleted using rebalancing algorithms like those described in Chap. 13.

✔ Quick Quiz 10.4

For Questions 1–3, draw the BST that results when the C++ keywords are inserted in the order given

1. if, do, goto, case, switch, while, for

2. do, case, for, if, switch, while, goto

3. while, switch, goto, for, if, do, case

Questions 4–9 refer to the following binary search tree:

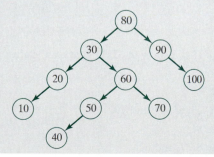

4. Perform an inorder traversal of this BST.
5. Perform a preorder traversal of this BST.
6. Perform a postorder traversal of this BST.
7. Show the BST that results when the node containing 20 is deleted from the given BST.
8. Show the BST that results when the node containing 30 is deleted from the given BST.
9. Show the BST that results when the root is deleted from the given BST.

✍ EXERCISES 10.4

For each of the lists of C++ keywords in Exercises 1–6, draw the binary search tree that is constructed when the words are inserted in the order given.

1. `new, const, typedef, if, main, bool, float`
2. `break, operator, return, char, else, switch, friend`
3. `double, long, namespace, class, public, int, new`
4. `while, using, static, private, enum, case`
5. `break, operator, if, typedef, else, case, while, do, return, unsigned, for, true, double, void`
6. `struct, class`

7–12. Perform inorder, preorder, and postorder traversals of the trees in Exercises 1–6 and show the sequence of words that results in each case.

For Exercises 13–22, begin with the following binary search tree:

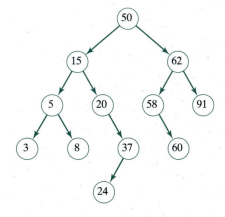

In Exercises 13–17, show the BST that results after the operation or sequence of operations is performed.

13. Insert 7.
14. Insert 7, 1, 55, 29, and 19.
15. Delete 8.
16. Delete 8, 37, and 62.
17. Insert 7, delete 8, insert 59, delete 60, insert 92, delete 50.

18. Display the output produced by an inorder traversal.

19. Display the output produced by a preorder traversal.

20. Display the output produced by a postorder traversal.

21. Display the output produced by the following function, where `root` points to the root of the given binary tree.

```
void TraceInorder(BinNodePointer root)
{
  if (root != 0)
  {
    cout << 'L';                        // left
    TraceInorder(root->left);
    cout << '/' << root->data << endl;
    cout << 'R';                        // right
    TraceInorder(root->right);
  }
  cout << 'U';                          // up
}
```

22. It is not easy to write a function to display a binary tree graphically (see Fig. 10.7), but it is easy to display enough information about a BST to reconstruct the tree. Write a function `DisplayPreOrder()` that displays, in preorder, the data part of a node, its left child, and its right child. For example, the output of `DisplayPreOrder()` for the given tree should be

Node.Data	LChild.Data	RChild.Data
50	15	62
15	5	20
5	3	8
3	-	-
.	.	.
.	.	.
.	.	.
58	-	60
60	-	-
91	-	-

You should also write a driver program to test your function as instructed in Programming Problem 21 at the end of this chapter.

For the arithmetic expressions in Exercises 23–27, draw a binary tree that represents the expression, and then use tree traversals to find the equivalent prefix and postfix expressions.

23. $(A - B) - C$

24. $A - (B - C)$

25. $A / (B - (C - (D - (E - F))))$

26. $((((A - B) - C) - D) - E) / F$

27. $((A * (B + C)) / (D - (E + F))) * (G / (H / (I * J)))$

28.   Assuming the array-based implementation of binary search trees described in Sec. 10.2, show the contents of an array used to store the BST preceding Exercise 13.

29–34.   Repeat Exercise 28, but for the BSTs in Exercises 1–6.

35–39.   Repeat Exercise 28, but for the BSTs in Exercises 23–27.

40.   A preorder traversal of a binary tree produced

A D F G H K L P Q R W Z

and an inorder traversal produced

G F H K D L A W R Q P Z

Draw the binary tree.

41.   A postorder traversal of a binary tree produced

F G H D A L P Q R Z W K

and an inorder traversal gave the same result as in Exercise 40. Draw the binary tree.

41.   Show by example that knowing the results of a preorder traversal and a postorder traversal of a binary tree does not uniquely determine the tree; that is, give an example of two different binary trees for which a preorder traversal of each gives the same result, and so does a postorder traversal.

42.   Write a recursive member function `LeafCount()` for class template BST to count the leaves in a binary tree. (*Hint:* How is the number of leaves in the entire tree related to the number of leaves in the left and right subtrees of the root?)

43.   Write a nonrecursive version of `Inorder()` to perform inorder traversal. (Use a stack of pointers to eliminate the recursion.)

44.   Write a function `LevelByLevel()` to traverse a tree level by level; that is, first visit the root, then all nodes on level 1 (children of the root), then all nodes on level 2, and so on. Nodes on the same level should be visited in order from left to right. (*Hint:* Write a nonrecursive function, and use a queue of pointers.)

In Exercises 45–49, trace the execution of the recursive `Delete()` function in this section for the tree preceding Exercise 13 as it deletes the node containing the given value. For each, start with the original tree and draw the subtree that is being processed on each recursive call to `Delete()`.

45.   24   **46.**   58   **47.**   37

48.   15   **49.**   5

10.5 APPLICATION OF BINARY TREES: HUFFMAN CODES

In Sec. 10.2 we indicated how a binary tree can be used in various encoding and decoding problems. In particular we showed part of a binary tree for the Morse code, which represents each character by a sequence of dots and dashes. Unlike ASCII, EBCDIC, and Unicode schemes, in which the length of the code is the same for all characters, Morse code uses variable-length sequences. In this section we consider another coding scheme, Huffman codes, that uses variable-length codes.

VARIABLE-LENGTH CODES

The basic idea in these variable-length coding schemes is to use shorter codes for those characters that occur more frequently and longer codes for those used less frequently. For example, 'E' in Morse code is a single dot, whereas 'Z' is represented as $--\cdot\cdot$. The objective is to minimize the expected length of the code for a character. This reduces the number of bits that must be sent when transmitting encoded messages. These variable-length coding schemes are also useful when compressing data because they reduce the number of bits that must be stored.

To state the problem more precisely, suppose that some character set $\{C_1, C_2, \ldots, C_n\}$ is given, and certain weights $w_1, w_2, \ldots, w_n$ are associated with these characters; w_i is the weight attached to character C_i and is a measure (e.g., probability or relative frequency) of how frequently this character occurs in messages to be encoded. If $l_1, l_2, \ldots, l_n$ are the lengths of the codes for characters $C_1, C_2, \ldots, C_n$, respectively, then the **expected length** of the code for any one of these characters is given by

$$\text{expected length} = w_1 l_1 + w_2 l_2 + \cdots + w_n l_n = \sum_{i=1}^{n} w_i l_i$$

As a simple example, consider the five characters A, B, C, D, and E, and suppose they occur with the following weights (probabilities):

character	A	B	C	D	E
weight	0.2	0.1	0.1	0.15	0.45

In Morse code with a dot replaced by 0 and a dash by 1, these characters are encoded as follows:

Character	Code
A	01
B	1000
C	1010
D	100
E	0

Thus the expected length of the code for each of these five letters in this scheme is

$$0.2 \times 2 + 0.1 \times 4 + 0.1 \times 4 + 0.15 \times 3 + 0.45 \times 1 = 2.1$$

IMMEDIATE DECODABILITY

Another useful property of some coding schemes is that they are **immediately decodable.** This means that no sequence of bits that represents a character is a prefix of a longer sequence for some other character. Consequently, when a sequence of bits is received that is the code for a character, it can be decoded as that character immediately, without waiting to see whether subsequent bits change it into a longer code for some other character. Note that the preceding Morse code scheme is not immediately decodable because, for example, the code for E (0) is a prefix of the code for A (01), and the code for D (100) is a prefix of the code for B (1000).

(For decoding, Morse code uses a third "bit," a pause, to separate letters.) A coding scheme for which the code lengths are the same as in the preceding scheme and that is immediately decodable is as follows:

Character	Code
A	01
B	0000
C	0001
D	001
E	1

HUFFMAN CODES

The following algorithm, given by D. A. Huffman in 1952, can be used to construct coding schemes that are immediately decodable and for which each character has a minimal expected code length:

HUFFMAN'S ALGORITHM

```
/*  Constructs a binary code for a given set of characters for which the
    expected length of the bit string for a given character is minimal.

    Receive:   A set of n characters {C_1, C_2, ..., C_n} and a set
               of weights {w_1, w_2, ..., w_n}, where w_i is the
               weight of character C_i.
    Return:    A collection of n bit strings representing codes for the
               characters.
----------------------------------------------------------------------*/
```

1. Initialize a list of one-node binary trees containing the weights $w_1, w_2, \ldots, w_n$, one for each of the characters $C_1, C_2, \ldots, C_n$.

2. Do the following $n - 1$ times:

   a. Find two trees T' and T'' in this list with roots of minimal weights w' and w''.

   b. Replace these two trees with a binary tree whose root is $w' + w''$, and whose subtrees are T' and T'', and label the pointers to these subtrees 0 and 1, respectively:

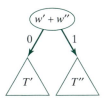

3. The code for character C_i is the bit string labeling a path in the final binary tree from the root to the leaf for C_i.

As an illustration of Huffman's algorithm, consider again the characters A, B, C, D, and E with the weights given earlier. We begin by constructing a list of one-node binary trees, one for each character:

The first two trees to be selected are those corresponding to letters B and C, since they have the smallest weights, and these are combined to produce a tree having weight $0.1 + 0.1 = 0.2$ and having these two trees as subtrees:

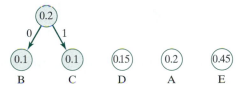

From this list of four binary trees, we again select two of minimal weights, the first and the second (or the second and the third), and replace them with another tree having weight $0.2 + 0.15 = 0.35$ and having these two trees as subtrees:

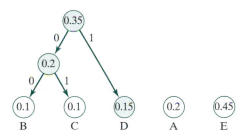

From this list of three binary trees, the first two have minimal weights and are combined to produce a binary tree having weight $0.35 + 0.2 = 0.55$ and having these trees as subtrees:

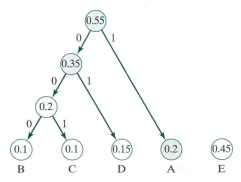

The resulting binary tree is then combined with the one-node tree representing E to produce the final Huffman tree:

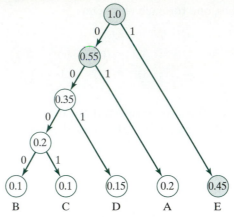

The Huffman codes obtained from this tree are as follows:

Character	Huffman code
A	01
B	0000
C	0001
D	001
E	1

As we calculated earlier, the expected length of the code for each of these characters is 2.1.

A different assignment of codes to these characters for which the expected length is also 2.1 is possible because at the second stage we had two choices for trees of minimal weight:

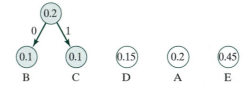

We selected the first and second trees from this list, but we could have used the second and third:

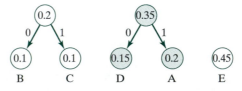

At the next stage, the resulting list of two binary trees would have been

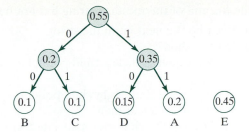

and the final Huffman tree would be

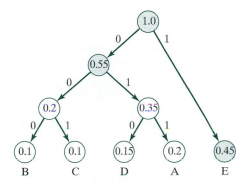

The assignment of codes corresponding to this tree is

Character	Huffman code
A	011
B	000
C	001
D	010
E	1

The immediate decodability property of Huffman codes is clear. Each character is associated with a leaf node in the Huffman tree, and there is a unique path from the root of the tree to each leaf. Consequently, no sequence of bits comprising the code for some character can be a prefix of a longer sequence of bits for some other character.

Because of this property of immediate decodability, a decoding algorithm is easy:

HUFFMAN DECODING ALGORITHM

```
/*  Decodes a message encoded using a Huffman tree.
    Receive:   A Huffman tree and a bit string representing some
               message that was encoded using the Huffman tree.
    Output:    The decoded message.
-------------------------------------------------------------------------------*/
```

1. Initialize pointer p to the root of the Huffman tree.

2. While the end of the message string has not been reached, do the following:

    a. Let x be the next bit in the string.

    b. If $x = 0$ then

        Set p equal to its left child pointer.

     Else

        Set p equal to its right child pointer.

    c. If p points to a leaf then

      i. Display the character associated with that leaf.

      ii. Reset p to the root of the Huffman tree.

As an illustration, suppose that the message string

$$0\,1\,0\,1\,0\,1\,1\,0\,1\,0$$

is received and that this message was encoded using the second Huffman tree constructed earlier. The pointer follows the path labeled 010 from the root of this tree to the letter D and is then reset to the root:

$$\boxed{0\ 1\ 0}\ 1\ 0\ 1\ 1\ 0\ 1\ 0$$
$$\text{D}$$

The next bit, 1, leads immediately to the letter E:

$$\boxed{0\ 1\ 0}\boxed{1}\ 0\ 1\ 1\ 0\ 1\ 0$$
$$\text{D}\quad\text{E}$$

The pointer p next follows the path 011 to the letter A

$$\boxed{0\ 1\ 0}\boxed{1}\boxed{0\ 1\ 1}\ 0\ 1\ 0$$
$$\text{D}\quad\text{E}\quad\text{A}$$

and finally the path 010 to the letter D again:

$$\boxed{0\ 1\ 0}\boxed{1}\boxed{0\ 1\ 1}\boxed{0\ 1\ 0}$$
$$\text{D}\quad\text{E}\quad\text{A}\quad\text{D}$$

Figure 10.7 shows a class `HuffmanCode` and a simple driver program for it. The member function `BuildDecodingTree()` initializes a tree consisting of a single node and then reads letters and their codes from a code file and constructs the decoding tree. For each letter in the file, it calls function `AddToTree()` to follow a path determined by the code of the character, creating nodes as necessary. When the end of the code string is reached, the character is inserted in the last (leaf) node created on this path. The function `Decode()` is then called to read a message string of bits from `MessageFile` and decode it using the decoding tree. Function `PrintTree()` is included simply to give an idea of what the tree looks like. It is basically nothing more than an RNL traversal of the tree. It prints the tree "on its side" without the directed arcs and 0/1 labels. We leave it to the reader to draw these in and then rotate the tree 90 degrees so it has its usual orientation.

 FIGURE 10.7 HUFFMAN CODE

```
#include <string>
#include <iostream>
#include <fstream>
#include <iomanip>
using namespace std;
```

```cpp
#ifndef HUFFMAN
#define HUFFMAN

class Huffman
{
private:
/*** Node structure ***/
class BinNode
{
 public:
  char data;
  BinNode * left,
           * right;

// BinNode constructor
  BinNode(char item)
  {
    data = item;
    left = right = 0;
  }
};

typedef BinNode * BinNodePointer;

/*** Function members ***/
public:
/* Constructor
 *   Precondition:  A Huffman object has been declared.
 *   Postcondition: One-node binary tree with root node
 *                  pointed to by root has been created.
 *********************************************************************/
Huffman();

/* Build the Huffman decoding tree.
 *   Receive:       Huffman object containing this function (implicitly)
 *                  fstream in
 *   Input:         Characters and their codes via in
 *                  Last line of code file must contain *
 *   Postcondition: Huffman decoding tree has been created with root
 *                  node pointed to by root.
 *********************************************************************/
void BuildDecodingTree(ifstream & CodeFile);

/* Insert a node for a character in Huffman decoding tree.
 *   Receive:       char c and code, a bit string
 *   Postcondition: Node containing c has been inserted into
 *                  Huffman tree with root pointed to by root.
 *********************************************************************/
void Insert(char ch, string code);
```

```
/* Read a message (string of bits) from a file and decode it
 * using the Huffman decoding tree.
 *   Receive:   Huffman object containing this function (implicitly)
 *              fstream in connected to message file
 *   Input:     Message via in
 *              Last line of message file must contain *
 *   Output:    Decoded message
 ******************************************************************/
void Decode(ifstream & in);

/* --- A binary tree printer
 * Displays a binary tree recursively.  The tree is displayed
 * "on its side" with each level indented by a specified value
 * indent, but with  no arcs sketched in.
 *   Receive: Root of binary tree and integer indent
 *   Output:  Graphical representation of the binary tree
 ******************************************************************/
void PrintTree(ostream & out, BinNodePointer root, int indent);

/* Display the decoding tree
 *   Receive: Huffman object containing this function (implicitly)
 *            ostream out
 *   Output:  The decoding tree via PrintTree()
 ******************************************************************/
void DisplayDecodingTree(ostream & out);

/*** Data members ***/
private:
  BinNodePointer root;
};

//--- Definition of constructor
inline Huffman::Huffman()
{ root = new BinNode('*'); }

//--- Definition of BuildDecodingTree()
void Huffman::BuildDecodingTree(ifstream & in)
{
  char ch;            // a character
  string code;        // its code
  for (;;)
  {
    in >> ch >> code;
    if (ch == '*') return;
    Insert(ch, code);
  }
}
```

```
//--- Definition of Insert()
void Huffman::Insert(char ch, string code)
{
  Huffman::BinNodePointer p = root;    // pointer to move down the tree

  for(int i = 0; i < code.length(); i++)
  {
    switch (code[i])
    {
      case '0' :              // descend left
        if (p->left == 0)  // create node along path
          p->left = new Huffman::BinNode('*');
        p = p->left;
        break;

      case '1' :              // descend right
        if (p->right == 0) // create node along path
          p->right = new Huffman::BinNode('*');
        p = p->right;
        break;

      default:
        cerr << "*** Illegal character in code ***\n";
        exit(-1);
    }
  }
  p->data = ch;
}

//--- Definition of Decode()
void Huffman::Decode(ifstream & in)
{
  char bit;                        // next message bit
  Huffman::BinNodePointer p; // pointer to trace path in decoding tree

  for(;;)
  {
    p = root;
    while (p->left != 0 || p->right != 0)
    {
      in >> bit;
      if (bit == '*') return;
      cout << bit;
```

```
        if (bit == '0')
          p = p->left;
        else if (bit == '1')
          p = p->right;
        else
          cerr << "Illegal bit: " << bit << " -- ignored\n";
      }
      cout << "--" << p->data << endl;
    }
}


//--- Definition of PrintTree()
void Huffman::PrintTree(ostream & out, Huffman::BinNodePointer root,
                        int indent)
{
   if (root != 0)
   {
     PrintTree(out, root->right, indent + 8);
     out << setw(indent) << " " << root->data << endl;
     PrintTree(out, root->left, indent + 8);
   }
}


//--- Definition of DisplayDecodingTree()
inline void Huffman::DisplayDecodingTree(ostream & out)
{ PrintTree(out, root, 0); }

#endif

//--- Driver Program ---
#include "Huffman"
#include <iostream>
#include <fstream>
using namespace std;

int main()
{
   char filename[32];
   cout << "Enter name of code file: ";
   cin >> filename;
   ifstream codestream(filename);
   if (!codestream.is_open())
   {
     cout << "Cannot open code file.\n";
     exit(-1);
   }

Huffman h;
   h.BuildDecodingTree(codestream);
   h.DisplayDecodingTree(cout);
   cout << endl << endl;
```

```
  cout << "Enter name of message file: ";
  cin >> filename;
  ifstream message(filename);
  if (!message.is_open())
  {
    cout << "Cannot open message file.\n";
    exit(-1);
  }
  h.Decode(message);
}
```

LISTING OF `CodeFile`:

```
A 1101
B 001101
C 01100
D 0010
E 101
F 111100
G 001110
H 0100
I 1000
J 11111100
K 11111101
L 01111
M 01101
N 1100
O 1110
P 111101
Q 111111100
R 1001
S 0101
T 000
U 01110
V 001100
W 001111
X 111111101
Y 111110
Z 11111111
*
```

LISTING OF `MessageFile`:

```
000010010110011010010
01100111011010000101
11011001101011001110011011000110000 1110
*
```

SAMPLE RUN:

```
Enter name of code file:  CodeFile
```

```
                                                          *        Z
                                                                      X
                                                     *                Q
                                                *            K
                                                             J
                              *
                         *                 Y
                                     *     P
                    *                      F
               *            O
                            A
               *            N
          *            E
            *
                       R
            *          I
     *
                       L
            *          U
                       M
          *            C
            *
                       S
     *                 H
                    *       W
                            G
                    *       B
                            V
          *
     *                 D
            T
```

```
Enter name of message file: MessageFile
000--T
0100--H
101--E
1001--R
101--E
0010--D
01100--C
1110--O
1101--A
000--T
0101--S
1101--A
1001--R
101--E
01100--C
1110--O
01101--M
1000--I
1100--N
001110--G
```

1. Demonstrate that Morse code is not immediately decodable by showing that the bit string 100001100 can be decoded in more than one way.

Using the first Huffman code given in this section (A = 01, B = 0000, C = 0001, D = 001, E = 1), decode the bit strings in Exercises 2–5.

2. 000001001
3. 001101001
4. 000101001
5. 00001010011001

6. Construct the Huffman code for the C++ keywords and weights given in the following table:

Words	Weight
int	.30
main	.30
while	.05
if	.20
for	.15

7. Repeat Exercise 6 for the following table of letters and weights:

Character	Weight
a	.20
b	.10
c	.08
d	.08
e	.40
f	.05
g	.05
h	.04

8. Using the Huffman code developed in Exercise 7, encode the following message: "feed a deaf aged hag."

9. Repeat Exercise 3 for the following table of C++ keywords and weights (frequencies):

Words	Weight
case	2
class	20
do	5
else	10
false	4
for	20
goto	1
if	20
int	22
main	22
static	2
struct	3
switch	2
true	4
while	15

📖 PROGRAMMING POINTERS

Most of the programming pointers that apply to the linked lists described in Chaps. 8 and 9 also apply to trees, since trees are also linked structures.

1. When implementing an object using a class, keep the implementation details hidden by declaring them in a private (or protected) section of the class. In class BST, the BinNode class used to represent the tree's nodes is such a detail.

2. Take twice as much care when implementing binary trees, since their nodes contain two pointer members. With two pointers to keep track of in every node instead of one, making logical errors is twice as easy. The ease with which one can write tree operations that compile correctly but that generate run-time errors is notorious.

3. Always make certain that a tree is not empty before processing it. The same holds true for subtrees. In most recursive tree-processing algorithms, the empty tree provides the anchor case for the recursion. As a result, checking whether a tree is empty makes it possible to avoid:

   ▶ dereferencing a null pointer
   ▶ generating an infinite recursion.

ADT TIPS

1. The worst- and average-case computing times for linear search is O(n). Linear search is used by find() in <algorithm>.

2. The worst- and average-case computing times for binary search is O($\log_2 n$). Binary search is used by binary_search() in <algorithm>.

3. The array-based implementation works very well for complete binary trees, but it becomes increasingly less space efficient as the tree becomes more lopsided.

4. The computing time for searching and insertion into a balanced BST is $O(\log_2 n)$. As the BST becomes increasingly unbalanced, their performance deteriorates. In the worst case, the BST degenerates into a linked list and the complexity of these operations becomes $O(n)$. Rebalancing methods like those described in Chap. 13 are required to keep this from happening.

5. A binary tree can be defined as a recursive data structure in a very natural way and several of the operations on a binary tree can thus be implemented most easily by recursive functions.

6. An inorder traversal of a BST visits the nodes in ascending order of the values stored in them.

7. Deletion for a BST can also cause the BST to become unbalanced.

PROGRAMMING PROBLEMS

SECTION 10.1

1. Write a driver program to test the improved `LinearSearch()` function in Exercise 6.

2. Write a driver program to test the `LinearSearch()` function for ordered lists in Exercise 7.

3. Write a driver program to test the recursive `LinearSearch()` function from Exercise 8.

4. Write a driver program to test the recursive `LinkedLinearSearch()` function from Exercise 9.

5. Write a driver program to test the binary search function from Exercise 10.

6. Write a driver program to test the linear search function for move-to-the-front self-organizing array-based lists in Exercise 11.

7. Write a driver program to test the linear search function for move-to-the-front self-organizing linked lists in Exercise 12.

8. Write a driver program to test the linear search function for move-ahead-one self-organizing array-based lists in Exercise 13.

9. Write a driver program to test the linear search function for move-ahead-one self-organizing linked lists in Exercise 14.

10. Write a driver program to test the interpolation-search function in Exercise 15.

11. Linear search is not practical for large lists because the search time becomes unacceptably large. In a dictionary this problem is alleviated by providing thumb cutouts that allow direct access to the beginnings of sublists, which can then be searched. Imitating this approach, we might break a long list into a number of sublists and construct an *index array* of these sublists. Write a program to read records from `StudentFile` (described in Programming Problem 13 at the end of Chap. 2) and store them in an array of sublists of names beginning with 'A', 'B', 'C', ... The program should then accept a name and retrieve the record for this student.

12. Linear search outperforms binary search for small lists. Write a program to compare the computing times of linear search and binary search.

13. Repeat Prob. 12, but also include interpolation search (see Exercise 16).

SECTION 10.3

14. Write a definition for the following function `GenerateBST()` for generating a random binary search tree containing uppercase letters.

```
/* Generate n random uppercase letters, display
 * each one, and insert each one into a BST.
 *
 *   Receive: An integer n
 *   Return:  BST
 **************************************************/
BST GenerateBST(int n);
```

15. Test the function `Level()` in Exercise 13 by using `GenerateBST()` of Prob. 14 to generate BSTs and then determine the level of 'A', 'B', . . ., 'Z' in each tree.

16. Proceed as in Problem 15 but for the recursive function `Level()` in Exercise 14.

17. Test the function `Height()` of Exercise 15 by using `GenerateBST()` of Prob. 14 to generate BSTs and then determine the height of each tree.

18. In this section, binary search trees were implemented using pointers, but it also is possible to use an array-based implementation similar to that for linked lists described in Sec. 8.3. In this implementation, each node is represented as a struct and the BST as an array of structs. Each struct contains three members: a data member and two link members that point to the left and the right child, respectively, by storing their indices in the array. Imitating the array-based implementation of linked lists in Sec. 8.3:

   a. Write appropriate declarations for this array-based implementation of binary search trees.

   b. Design and test a class for maintaining a storage pool of available nodes, with operations to initialize it, to get a node from it, and to return a node to it.

19. Assuming the array-based implementation of BSTs in Prob. 18, write and test the function `Search()` for searching a BST.

20. Assuming the array-based implementation of BSTs in Prob. 18, write and test the function `Insert()` for inserting an item into a BST.

SECTION 10.4

21. Write a driver program to test the function `DisplayPreOrder()` in Exercise 22.

22. Test the function `LeafCount()` from Exercise 42. Generate binary trees using the function `GenerateBST()` in Prob. 14, display them using `DisplayPreOrder()` (see Exercise 22), and then count the leaves using `LeafCount()`.

23. Test the function `Inorder()` of Exercise 43. Generate binary trees using the function `GenerateBST()` in Prob. 14 and then traverse them using `Inorder()`.

24. Test the function `LevelByLevel()` of Exercise 44. Generate binary trees using the function `GenerateBST()` in Prob. 14 and then traverse them using `LevelByLevel()`.

25. Write a program to process a BST whose nodes contain characters. The user should be allowed to select from the following menu of options:

I followed by a character: To insert a character

S followed by a character: To search for a character

TI: for inorder traversal

TP: for preorder traversal

TR: for postorder traversal

QU: to quit

26. Write a *spell checker*, that is, a program that reads the words in a piece of text and looks up each of them in a *dictionary* to check its spelling. Use a BST to store this dictionary, reading the list of words from a file. While checking the spelling of words in a piece of text, the program should print a list of all words not found in the dictionary.

27. Programming Problem 23 at the end of Chap. 8 asks for a program to construct a *text concordance*, which is an alphabetical listing of all the distinct words in a piece of text. The basic storage structure for such a concordance was an array of ordered linked lists, one for words beginning with A, another for words beginning with B, and so on. Write a program that reads a piece of text, constructs a concordance that contains the distinct words that appear in the text and for each word, the line (or page) number of its first occurrence, and then allows the user to search for this concordance. Use an array of BSTs as storage for the concordance.

28. Extend the program in Prob. 27, so that an ordered linked list of *all* occurrences of each word is stored. When the concordance is searched for a particular word, the program should display the line (or page) numbers of all occurrences of this word. The data structure used for the concordance is thus constructed from a good sample of those we have been studying: an *array* of *binary search trees*, each of whose nodes stores a *structure*, one of whose members is a *string* and whose other member is an *ordered linked list*.

SECTION 10.5

29. Write a function that reads a table of letters and their weights and constructs a Huffman code for these letters. Use the function in a program that encodes a message that the user enters.

30. (Project) Write a program to compress a file using a Huffman code and to decompress a file generated using this code. The program should first read through the file and determine the number of occurrences of each character in the file and the total number of characters in the file. The weight of each character will be the frequency count for that character. The program should then use these weights to construct the Huffman codes for the characters in the file. It should then read the file again and encode it using these Huffman codes and generate a file containing this encoded data. Compute the compression ratio, which is the number of bits in the compressed file divided by the total number of bits in the original file (eight times the number of characters in the file). The program should also provide the option of decompressing a file that was encoded using this Huffman code.

Chapter 11

SORTING

Chapter Contents

In this chapter we consider the problem of sorting a list,

$$x_1, x_2, \ldots, x_n$$

that is, arranging the list elements so that they (or some key fields in them) are in ascending order

$$x_1 \leq x_2 \leq \cdots \leq x_n$$

or in descending order

$$x_1 \geq x_2 \geq \cdots \geq x_n$$

We begin by considering some of the sorting schemes typically studied in introductory programming courses. Although these are for the most part fairly easy to understand and to implement, they are not very efficient, especially for large data sets. Thus we also look at two of the more efficient sorting schemes, heapsort and quicksort.

11.1 SOME O(n^2) SORTING SCHEMES

One classification of sorting schemes consists of three categories: **selection sorts**, **exchange sorts**, and **insertion sorts**. We begin our discussion of sorting algorithms by considering one simple sorting scheme from each of these categories.

SELECTION SORTS
The basic idea of a selection sort of a list is to make a number of passes through the list or a part of the list and, on each pass, select one element to be correctly positioned. For example, on each pass through a sublist, the smallest element in this sublist might be found and then moved to its proper location.

As an illustration, suppose that the following list is to be sorted into ascending order:

$$67, \ 33, \ 21, \ 84, \ 49, \ 50, \ 75$$

We scan the list to locate the smallest element and find it in position 3:

$$67 \, , \ 33 \, , \ \boxed{21} \, , \ 84 \, , \ 49 \, , \ 50 \, , \ 75$$

We interchange this element with the first element and thus properly position the smallest element at the beginning of the list:

$$\boxed{67} \, , \ 33 \, , \ 21 \, , \ 84 \, , \ 49 \, , \ 50 \, , \ 75$$

We now scan the sublist consisting of the elements from position 2 on to find the smallest element

$$21 \, , \ \boxed{33} \, , \ 67 \, , \ 84 \, , \ 49 \, , \ 50 \, , \ 75$$

and exchange it with the second element (itself in this case) and thus properly position the next-to-smallest element in position 2:

$$21 \, , \ \boxed{33} \, , \ 67 \, , \ 84 \, , \ 49 \, , \ 50 \, , \ 75$$

We continue in this manner, locating the smallest element in the sublist of elements from position 3 on and interchanging it with the third element, then properly positioning the smallest element in the sublist of elements from position 4 on, and so on until we eventually do this for the sublist consisting of the last two elements:

$$21 \, , \ 33 \, , \ \boxed{49} \, , \ 84 \, , \ 67 \, , \ 50 \, , \ 75$$

$$21 \, , \ 33 \, , \ 49 \, , \ \boxed{50} \, , \ 67 \, , \ 84 \, , \ 75$$

$$21 \, , \ 33 \, , \ 49 \, , \ 50 \, , \ \boxed{67} \, , \ 84 \, , \ 75$$

$$21 \, , \ 33 \, , \ 49 \, , \ 50 \, , \ 67 \, , \ \boxed{75} \, , \ 84$$

Positioning the smallest element in this last sublist obviously also positions the last element correctly and thus completes the sort.

An algorithm for this simple selection sort was given in Sec. 7.4 for lists stored in arrays (or `vectors`):

SIMPLE SELECTION SORTING ALGORITHM

/*   Algorithm that uses selection sort to sort the elements of
      array x into ascending order.

Precondition: A list is stored in array $x[1], \ldots, x[n]$.
Postcondition: x is sorted so that $x[1] \leq x[2] \leq \ldots \leq x[n]$.
Note: For consistency with other sorting methods,
                    position 0 in x is reserved for special purposes.
---*/

For $i = 1$ to n do the following:
    /*   On the ith pass, first find the smallest element in the
          sublist $x[i] \ldots x[n]$ */
    a. Set *smallPos* = i.
    b. Set *smallest* = $x[smallPos]$.
    c. For $j = i + 1$ to $n - 1$ do the following:
              If $x[j] <$ *smallest*:   // smaller element found
                  i. Set *smallPos* = j.
                  ii. Set *smallest* = $x[smallPos]$.
    /* Now interchange this smallest element with the element
       at the beginning of this sublist */
    d. Set $x[smallPos] = x[i]$.
    e. Set $x[i] =$ *smallest*.

A version that can be used for linked lists is just as easy. We need only replace the
indices i and j with pointers that move through the list and sublists. Using the notation introduced in Sec. 8.2 for abstract linked lists, we can express this algorithm as

SIMPLE SELECTION SORT FOR LINKED LISTS

/*   Algorithm that uses selection sort to sort the elements
      in a linked list into ascending order.

Precondition: A list of elements is stored in a linked list.
Postcondition: The list is sorted.
Note: $p \rightarrow data$ and $p \rightarrow next$ denote the data part and the
                    next part, respectively, of the node pointed to by p.
---*/

1. Initialize pointer p to the first node.

2. While p is not null do the following:
    /* First find the smallest element in the sublist pointed to by p */
    a. Set pointer *smallPtr* = p.
    b. Set *smallest* = $p \rightarrow data$.
    c. Set pointer $q = p \rightarrow next$.
    d. While q is not null do the following:
              i. If $q \rightarrow data <$ *smallest*   // smaller element found
                      Set *smallPtr* = q and
                      smallest = $q \rightarrow data$.
              ii. Set $q = q \rightarrow next$.

```
/* Now interchange this smallest element with the
   element in the node at the beginning of this sublist */
   e.  Set smallPtr→data = p→data.
   f.  Set p→data = smallest.
   g.  Set p = p→next.
```

Note that although we have given iterative algorithms for simple selection sort, its fundamental approach is recursive:

```
If the list has only 1 element    // anchor
   Stop—list is sorted.
Else do the following:            // inductive step
   a.  Find the smallest element and put it at the front of the list.
   b.  Sort the rest of the list.
```

In Sec. 7.4 we derived a worst-case computing time of $O(n^2)$ for this sorting method. This is, in fact, the computing time for all cases. On the first pass through the list, the first item is compared with each of the $n - 1$ elements that follow it; on the second pass, the second element is compared with the $n - 2$ elements following it; and so on. A total of

$$(n - 1) + (n - 2) + \cdots + 2 + 1 = \frac{n(n - 1)}{2}$$

comparisons is thus required for any list, and it follows that the computing time is $O(n^2)$ in all cases.

EXCHANGE SORTS

Unlike selection sorts in which some element is selected and then moved to its correct position in the list, exchange sorts systematically interchange pairs of elements that are out of order until eventually no such pairs remain and the list is therefore sorted. One example of an exchange sort is **bubble sort.** Although this sorting scheme is very inefficient, it is quite easy to understand and has, therefore, been taught in many introductory programming courses.

To illustrate bubble sort, consider again the list

$$67, \ 33, \ 21, \ 84, \ 49, \ 50, \ 75$$

On the first pass, we compare the first two elements, 67 and 33, and interchange them because they are out of order:

$$67, 33, 21, 84, 49, 50, 75$$

$$33, 67, 21, 84, 49, 50, 75$$

Now we compare the second and third elements, 67 and 21 and interchange them:

$$33, 67, 21, 84, 49, 50, 75$$

$$33, 21, 67, 84, 49, 50, 75$$

Next we compare 67 and 84 but do not interchange them because they are already in the correct order:

33 , 21 , 67 , 84 , 49 , 50 , 75

33 , 21 , 67 , 84 , 49 , 50 , 75

Next, 84 and 49 are compared and interchanged:

33 , 21 , 67 , 84 , 49 , 50 , 75

33 , 21 , 67 , 49 , 84 , 50 , 75

Then 84 and 50 are compared and interchanged:

33 , 21 , 67 , 49 , 84 , 50 , 75

33 , 21 , 67 , 49 , 50 , 84 , 75

Finally 84 and 75 are compared and interchanged:

33 , 21 , 67 , 49 ,50 , 84 , 75

33 , 21 , 67 , 49 , 50 , 75 , 84

The first pass through the list is now complete.

We are guaranteed that on this pass, the largest element in the list will "sink" to the end of the list, since it will obviously be moved past all smaller elements. But notice also that some of the smaller items have "bubbled up" toward their proper positions nearer the front of the list.

We now scan the list again, but this time we leave out the last item because it is already in its proper position.

33 , 21 , 67 , 49 , 50 , 75 , 84

The comparisons and interchanges that take place on this pass are summarized in the following diagram:

33 , 21 , 67 , 49 , 50 , 75 , 84

21 , 33 , 67 , 49 , 50 , 75 , 84

21 , 33 , 67 , 49 , 50 , 75 , 84

21 , 33 , 49 , 67 , 50 , 75 , 84

21 , 33 , 49 , 50 , 67 , 75 , 84

21 , 33 , 49 , 50 , 67 , 75 , 84

On this pass, the last element involved in an interchange was in position 5, which means that this element and all those that follow it have been properly positioned and can thus be omitted on the next pass.

On the next pass, therefore, we consider only the sublist consisting of the elements in positions 1 through 4:

$$21 , 33 , 49 , 50 , \boxed{67} , \boxed{75} , \boxed{84}$$

In scanning this sublist, we find that no interchanges are necessary, and so we conclude that the sorting is complete.

The details of this sorting scheme are given in the following algorithm:

BUBBLE SORT

/*   Algorithm that uses bubble sort to sort the elements of array x into ascending order.

Precondition: A list is stored in array $x[1], \ldots, x[n]$.
Postcondition: x is sorted so that $x[1] \leq x[2] \leq \ldots \leq x[n]$.
Note: For consistency with other sorting methods, position 0 in x is reserved for special purposes.
--*/

1. Initialize *numPairs* to $n - 1$.

  /* *numPairs* is the number of pairs to be compared on the current pass */

2. Do the following:

    a. Set *last* equal to 1.
       /*   *last* marks the location of the last element involved in an interchange */
    b. For $i = 1$ to *numPairs*:
       If $x_i > x_{i+1}$:
         i. Interchange x_i and x_{i+1}.
         ii. Set *last* equal to i.
    c. Set *numPairs* equal to $last - 1$.
    while *numPairs* $\neq 0$.

The worst case for bubble sort occurs when the list elements are in reverse order because in this case, only one item (the largest) is positioned correctly on each pass through the list. On the first pass through the list, $n - 1$ comparisons and interchanges are made, and only the largest element is correctly positioned. On the next pass, the sublist consisting of the first $n - 1$ elements is scanned; there are $n - 2$ comparisons and interchanges; and the next largest element sinks to position $n - 1$. This continues until the sublist consisting of the first two elements is scanned, and on this pass, there is one comparison and interchange. Thus, a total of $(n - 1) + (n - 2) + \cdots + 1 = n(n - 1) / 2$ comparisons and interchanges is required. The instructions that carry out these comparisons and interchanges are the instructions in the algorithm executed most often. It follows that the worst-case computing time for bubble sort is $O(n^2)$. The average computing time is also $O(n^2)$, but this is considerably more difficult to show.

INSERTION SORTS

Insertion sorts are based on the same idea as the algorithms for inserting new elements into ordered linked lists described in Chap. 8: repeatedly insert a new element into a list of already sorted elements so that the resulting list is still sorted.

The method used is similar to that used by a card player when putting cards into order as they are dealt. To illustrate, suppose that the first card dealt is a 7. (We will ignore all other attributes, such as suit or color.) This card is trivially in its proper place in the hand:

When the second card is dealt, it is inserted into its proper place, either before or after the first card. For example, if the second card is a 2, it is placed to the left of the 7:

When the third card is dealt, it is inserted into its proper place among the first two cards so that the resulting three-card hand is properly ordered. For example, if it is a 4, the 7 is moved to make room for the 4, which must be inserted between the 2 and the 7:

This process continues. At each stage the newly dealt card is inserted into the proper place among the cards already in the hand so that the newly formed hand is ordered:

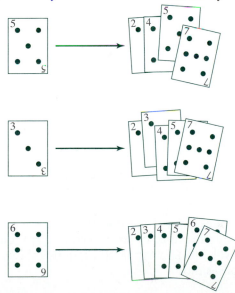

The following algorithm describes this procedure for lists stored in arrays. At the ith stage, x_i is inserted into its proper place among the already sorted $x_1, x_2, \ldots, x_{i-1}$. We do this by comparing x_i with each of these elements, starting from the right end, and shifting them to the right as necessary. We use array position 0 to store a copy of x_i to prevent "falling off the left end" in these right-to-left scans.

LINEAR INSERTION SORT FOR ARRAY-BASED LISTS

/*   Algorithm that uses linear insertion sort to sort the
      elements of array x into ascending order.

Precondition: A list is stored in array $x[1], \ldots, x[n]$.
Postcondition: x is sorted so that $x[1] \leq x[2] \leq \ldots \leq x[n]$.
Note: Position 0 in the array is used to store the list
                   element being inserted.
--*/

For $i = 2$ to n do the following:
   /* Insert $x[i]$ into its proper position among $x[1], \ldots, x[i-1]$ */
   a. Set *nextElement* equal to $x[i]$.
   b. Set $x[0]$ equal to *nextElement*.
   c. Set j equal to i.
   d. While *nextElement* $< x[j-1]$ do the following:
      // Shift element to the right to open a spot
      i. Set $x[j]$ equal to $x[j-1]$.
      ii. Decrement j by 1.
   // Now drop *nextElement* into the open spot
   e. Set $x[j]$ equal to *nextElement*.

The following sequence of diagrams demonstrates this algorithm for the list 67, 33, 21, 84, 49, 50, 75. The sorted sublist produced at each stage is highlighted.

67 , 33 , 21 , 84 , 49 , 50 , 75	Initial sorted sublist of 1 element
33 , 67 , 21 , 84 , 49 , 50 , 75	Insert 33 to get 2-element sorted sublist
21 , 33 , 67 , 84 , 49 , 50 , 75	Insert 21 to get 3-element sorted sublist
21 , 33 , 67 , 84 , 49 , 50 , 75	Insert 84 to get 4-element sorted sublist
21 , 33 , 49 , 67 , 84 , 50 , 75	Insert 49 to get 5-element sorted sublist
21 , 33 , 49 , 50 , 67 , 84 , 75	Insert 50 to get 6-element sorted sublist
21 , 33 , 49 , 50 , 67 , 75 , 84	Insert 75 to get 7-element sorted sublist

The worst case for linear insertion sort is once again the case in which the list elements are in reverse order. Inserting $x[2]$ requires two comparisons (with $x[1]$ and then with $x[0]$), inserting $x[3]$ requires three, and so on. The total number of comparisons is thus

$$2 + 3 + \cdots + n = \frac{n(n + 1)}{2} - 1$$

so the computing time is again O(n^2). This is also the average case computing time, since one would expect that on the average, the item being inserted must be compared with one-half the items in the already sorted sublist.

Linear insertion sort can also be used with linked lists. For singly-linked lists, however, the algorithm obviously is quite different from the preceding one because we have direct access to only the first element. It is not difficult, however, and is left as an exercise.

EVALUATION OF THESE SORTING SCHEMES

All of the sorting algorithms that we have considered have the same computing time, O(n^2), in the worst and average cases, and so this measure of efficiency provides no basis for choosing one over the others. More careful analysis together with empirical studies, however, reveals that their performance is not the same in all situations.

The primary virtue of simple selection sort is its simplicity. It is too inefficient, however, for use as a general sorting scheme, especially for large lists. The source of this inefficiency is that it requires O(n) time to search for the next item to be selected and positioned. A better selection sort, known as **heapsort**, uses a more efficient search algorithm, which gives this sorting scheme a computing time of O($n \log_2 n$). Heapsort is described in detail in the next section. One weakness of both of these selection sorts, however, is that they perform no better for lists that are almost sorted than they do for totally random lists. Many applications involve lists that are already partially sorted, and for such applications, therefore, other sorting schemes may be more appropriate.

Bubble sort (as described here) does perform better for partially sorted lists because it is able to detect when a list is sorted and does not continue making unnecessary passes through the list. As a general sorting scheme, however, it is very inefficient because of the large number of interchanges that it requires, especially when the items being sorted are large records. In fact, it is the least efficient of the sorting schemes we have considered and has virtually nothing to recommend its use. A two-way version described in the exercises performs only slightly better. The exchange sort known as **quicksort** described in Sec. 11.3 has average computing time O($n \log_2 n$) and is one of the most efficient general-purpose sorting schemes.

Linear insertion sort also is too inefficient to be used as a general-purpose sorting scheme. However, the low overhead that it requires makes it better than simple selection sort and bubble sort. In fact, empirical studies indicate that of all the sorting schemes we consider, it is the best choice for small lists (with up to 15 to 20 elements) and for lists that are already partially sorted. Two more efficient insertion sorts, **binary insertion sort** and **Shell sort**, are described in the exercises—binary insertion sort in Exercise 11 and Shell sort in Exercise 12.

In summary, there is no such thing as one universally good sorting scheme. For small lists, linear insertion sort performs well. For lists in general, quicksort, Shell sort, or heapsort is the method of choice. The following table, taken from the video *Sorting Out Sorting*[1] demonstrates this for randomly generated lists of size 500:

Sorting Algorithm	Type of Sort	Sorting Time (sec)
Simple selection	Selection	69
Heapsort	Selection	18
Bubblesort	Exchange	165
Two-way bubble sort	Exchange	141
Quicksort	Exchange	6
Linear insertion	Insertion	66
Binary insertion	Insertion	37
Shell sort	Insertion	11

INDIRECT SORTING

Each of the sorting schemes described in this section requires moving list elements from one position to another. If these list elements are records containing many fields, then the time required for such data transfers may be unacceptable. For such lists of large records, an alternative is to do an **indirect sort** that uses an **index table** that stores the positions of the records and moves the entries in this index rather than the records themselves. For example, for an array $x[1], \ldots, x[5]$ of records, an array *index* is initialized with $index[1] = 1, index[2] = 2, \ldots, index[5] = 5$. If it is necessary while sorting these records to interchange the first and third records as well as the second and fifth, we interchange the first and third elements and the second and fifth elements of the index table to obtain $index[1] = 3, index[2] = 5, index[3] = 1, index[4] = 4, index[5] = 2$. At this stage, the records are arranged in the *logical* order $x[index[1]], x[index[2]], \ldots, x[index[5]]$, that is, $x[3], x[5], x[1], x[4], x[2]$. Modifying one of the sorting schemes so it sorts indirectly is left as an exercise (see Programming Problem 8 at the end of this chapter).

✔ Quick Quiz 11.1

1. Describe how selection sorts work.
2. Simple selection sort performs better for partially sorted lists than for random lists. (True or false)
3. Describe how exchange sorts work.
4. Bubble sort performs better for partially sorted lists than for random lists. (True or false)

[1] *Sorting Out Sorting* is a 30-minute video available from the Media Center of the University of Toronto that provides a fascinating visual comparison of the performance of nine sorting algorithms, three selection sorts, three exchange sorts, and three insertion sorts. There are also several sorting animations on the Web; for example, see http://www.developer.com/directories/pages/dir.java.educational.cs.sorting.html (or try www.gamelan.com if the URL has changed). See also "The Complete Collection of Algorithm Animations—Sorting Algorithms" at http://www.cs.hope.edu/~alganim/ccaa/sorts.html.

5. Describe how insertion sorts work.

6. Linear insertion sort performs better for partially sorted lists than for random lists. (True or false)

7. Linear insertion sort performs well for small lists (with 15–20 elements). (True or false)

8. A(n) _____ sort uses an index table that stores the positions of items to be sorted and moves the entries in this index rather than the records themselves.

✍ EXERCISES 11.1

1. For the following array x, show x after each of the first two passes of simple selection sort to arrange the elements in ascending order:

i	1	2	3	4	5	6
$x[i]$	30	50	70	10	40	60

2. **a.** For the following array x, show x after each of the first two passes of bubble sort to arrange the elements in descending order:

i	1	2	3	4	5	6
$x[i]$	60	50	70	10	40	20

   b. How many passes will bubble sort make altogether?
   c. In what situations will bubble sort make the most interchanges?

3. **a.** Linear insertion sort has just correctly positioned $x[3]$ in the following array x:

i	1	2	3	4	5	6
$x[i]$	20	40	60	30	10	50

   Show x after each of $x[4]$ and $x[5]$ is correctly positioned.

   b. In what situation will linear insertion sort make the fewest interchanges?

Several of the following ask you to write functions for some sorting method. You should also test these functions by writing driver programs as instructed in Programming Problems 1–6 at the end of this chapter.

4. The basic operation in the simple selection sort algorithm is to scan a list $x_1, \ldots, x_n$ to locate the smallest element and to position it at the beginning of the list. A variation of this approach is to locate both the smallest and the largest elements while scanning the list and to position them at the beginning and the end of the list, respectively. On the next scan this process is repeated for the sublist $x_2, \ldots, x_{n-1}$, and so on.

   a. Using the array x in Exercise 1, show x after the first two passes of this double-ended simple selection sort.
   b. Write a function to implement this double-ended simple selection sort.
   c. Determine its computing time.

5. The double-ended selection sort algorithm described in Exercise 4 can be improved by using a more efficient method for determining the smallest and largest elements in a (sub)list. One such algorithm is known as *Min-Max Sort*.[2]
   Consider a list $x_1, \ldots, x_n$, where n is even.

---

[2]Narayan Murthy, "Min-Max Sort: A Simple Method," *CSC '87 Proceedings* (Association of Computing Machinery, 1987).

1. For i ranging from 1 to $n/2$, compare x_i with x_{n+1-i} and interchange them if $x_i > x_{n+1-i}$. This establishes a "rainbow pattern" in which $x_1 \le x_n, x_2 \le x_{n-1}, x_3 \le x_{n-2}$, and so on and guarantees that the smallest element of the list is in the first half of the list and that the largest element is in the second half.

2. Repeat the following for the list $x_1, \ldots, x_n$, then for the sublist $x_2, \ldots, x_{n-1}$, and so on:
   i. Find the smallest element x_S in the first half and the largest element in the second half X_L, and swap them with the elements in the first and last positions of this (sub)list, respectively.
   ii. Restore the rainbow pattern by comparing x_S with x_{n+1-S} and x_L with x_{n+1-L}, interchanging as necessary.

   a. For the following array x, show x after Step 1 is executed, and then after each pass through the loop in Step 2:

i	1	2	3	4	5	6	7	8	9	10
$x[i]$	30	80	90	20	60	70	10	100	50	40

   b. Write a function to implement this sorting algorithm.

6. Write a recursive function to implement simple selection sort.

7. Write a recursive function to implement bubble sort.

8. Write a bubble sort algorithm that is appropriate for a linked list.

9. A variation of bubble sort called *two-way bubble sort* alternates left-to-right scans with right-to-left scans of the unsorted sublists. On left-to-right scans, x_i is interchanged with x_{i+1} if $x_i > x_{i+1}$ so that larger elements are moved toward the right end of the sublist. On the right-to-left scans, x_{i+1} is interchanged with x_i if $x_{i+1} < x_i$ so that smaller elements are moved toward the left end of the sublist. Scans are repeated until no interchanges are made on one of these scans.

   a. For the array x in Exercise 5, show x at the end of each left-to-right pass and each right-to-left pass through the list.
   b. Write an algorithm to implement this two-way bubble sort and determine its computing time.

10. Write an insertion sort algorithm for a linked list.

11. In **binary insertion sort**, a binary search is used instead of a linear search to locate the position in the sorted sublist $x[1], x[2], \ldots, x[i-1]$ where the next item $x[i]$ is to be inserted.

   a. Write an algorithm for binary insertion sort.
   b. For the following array x, show x after each of the elements $x[i]$, $i = 2, 3, \ldots, 10$ is inserted into the sorted sublist $x[1], \ldots, x[i-1]$ using binary insertion sort. Keep a count of how many times array elements are compared.

i	1	2	3	4	5	6	7	8	9	10
$x[i]$	100	90	60	70	40	20	50	30	80	10

   c. Repeat (b) but use linear insertion sort.

12. Linear insertion sort performs best for small lists or partially sorted lists. **Shell sort** (named after Donald Shell) is an insertion sort that uses linear insertion sort to sort small sublists to produce larger partially ordered sublists. Specifically, one begins with a "gap" of a certain size g and then uses linear insertion to sort sublists of elements that are g apart, first $x[1], x[1+g], x[1+2g], \ldots$, then the sublist $x[2], x[2+g], x[2+2g], \ldots$, then $x[3], x[3+g], x[3+2g], \ldots$, and so on. Next the size of the gap g is reduced, and the process is repeated. This continues until the gap g is 1, and the final linear insertion sort results in the sorted list.

a. For the array x in Exercise 11, show x after each of the sublists of elements that are g apart has been sorted using linear insertion sort. Use $g = 4$ and then reduce it to $g = 1$.

b. Write a function to sort a list of items using this Shell sort method, beginning with a gap g of the form $\dfrac{3^k - 1}{2}$ for some integer k and reducing it by 3 at each stage.

13. A binary search tree can also be used to sort a list. We simply insert the list elements into a BST, initially empty, and then use an inorder traversal to copy them back into the list. Write an algorithm for this **treesort** method of sorting, assuming that the list is stored in

a. an array.

b. a linked list.

14. Write a function to implement the treesort algorithm of Exercise 13.

11.2 HEAPS AND HEAPSORT

In the preceding section we looked at three sorting algorithms, simple selection sort, bubble sort, and linear insertion sort, all of which have worst-case and average-case computing time $O(n^2)$, where n is the size of the list being sorted. As we noted, there are other schemes with computing time $O(n \log_2 n)$ and thus in most cases are more efficient than these three. In fact, it can be shown that any sorting scheme based on comparisons and interchanges like those we are considering must have a worst-case computing time of at least $O(n \log_2 n)$. In this section we describe one of these, known as **heapsort**, which, as we mentioned, is a selection sort. It was discovered by John Williams in 1964 and uses a new data structure called a *heap* to organize the list elements in such a way that the selection can be made efficiently.[3]

HEAPS

A **heap** is a binary tree with the following properties:

1. It is *complete*; that is, each level of the tree is completely filled, except possibly the bottom level, and in this level, the nodes are in the leftmost positions.

2. It satisfies the *heap-order property*: The data item stored in each node is greater than or equal to the data items stored in its children. (Of course, if the data items are records, then some key field in these records must satisfy this condition.)

For example, the first of the binary trees that follow is a heap; the second binary tree is not, because it is not complete; the third binary tree is complete, but it is not a heap because the second condition is not satisfied.

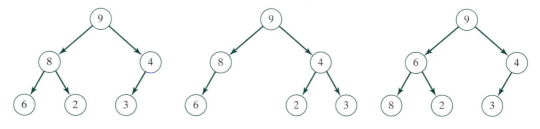

[3]J. W. J. Williams, "Algorithm 232: Heapsort," *Communication of the Association of Computing Machinery* 7 (1964): 347–348.

To implement a heap, we could use a linked structure like that for binary search trees, but an array or a vector can be used more effectively. We simply number the nodes in the heap from top to bottom, numbering the nodes on each level from left to right

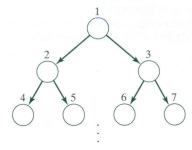

and store the data in the *i*th node in the *i*th location of the array. (Again, for consistency with the other sorting algorithms, we will not store a list element in location 0 of the array or vector.) The completeness property of a heap guarantees that these data items will be stored in consecutive locations at the beginning of the array. If *heap* is the name of the array or vector used, the items in the heap

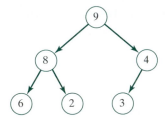

are then stored as follows: $heap[1] = 9, heap[2] = 8, heap[3] = 4, heap[4] = 6, heap[5] = 2, heap[6] = 3.$

Note that in such an array implementation, it is easy to find the children of a given node: The children of the *i*th node are at locations $2*i$ and $2*i + 1$. Similarly, the parent of the *i*th node is easily seen to be in location $i / 2$.

BASIC HEAP OPERATIONS

An algorithm for converting a complete binary tree into a heap is basic to most other heap operations. The simplest instance of this problem is a tree that is almost a heap, in that both subtrees of the root are heaps but the tree itself is not, for example

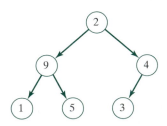

As this tree is complete and both subtrees are heaps, the only reason it is not a heap is that the root item is smaller than one of its children. The first step, therefore, is to interchange this root with the larger of its two children, in this case, the left child:

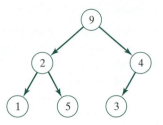

This guarantees that the new root will be greater than both of its children and that one of its subtrees, the right one in this case, will still be a heap. The other subtree may or may not be a heap. If it is, the entire tree is a heap, and we are finished. If it is not, as in this example, we simply repeat this "percolate down" procedure on this subtree. This process is repeated until at some stage, both subtrees of the node being examined are heaps; the process is repeated only a finite number of times because eventually we will reach the bottom of the tree.

For the general problem of converting a complete binary tree to a heap, we begin at the last node that is not a leaf, apply the percolate-down procedure to convert to a heap the subtree rooted at this node, move to the preceding node and percolate down in that subtree, and so on, working our way up the tree until we reach the root of the given tree. The following sequence of diagrams illustrates this "heapify" process; the subtree being heapified at each stage is highlighted.

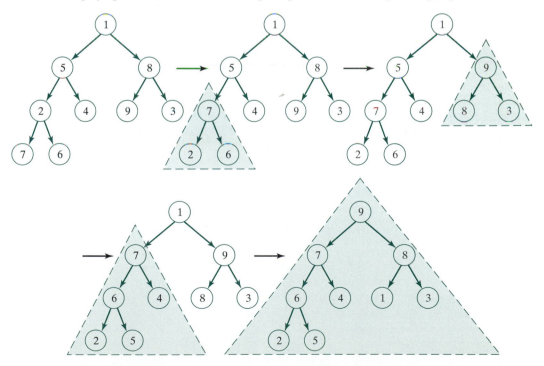

An algorithm to implement the percolate-down process is as follows:

PERCOLATE DOWN

/*   Converts an almost-heap into a heap.

    Precondition: A complete binary tree is stored in positions
                     r through n of the array *heap* with left and
                     right subtrees that are heaps.
    Postcondition: The tree is a heap.
---*/

For $c = 2 * r$ to n do the following: // c is location of left child
    // Find the largest child
    a. If $c < n$ and $heap[c] < heap[c + 1]$
            Increment c by 1.
    /* Interchange node and largest child if necessary,
        and move down to the next subtree */
    b. If $heap[r] < heap[c]$:
            i.   Swap $heap[r]$ and $heap[c]$.
            ii. Set $r = c$.
            iii. Set $c = 2 * c$.
        Else
            Terminate repetition.

An algorithm for converting any complete binary tree to a heap is then easy to write:

HEAPIFY

/*   Converts a complete binary tree into a heap.

    Precondition: A complete binary tree is stored in positions
                     1 through n of the array *heap*.
    Postcondition: The tree is a heap.
---*/

For $r = n / 2$ down to 1:   // start at last nonleaf
    Apply *PercolateDown* to the subtree rooted at location r.

HEAPSORT

To see how these algorithms can now be used to sort a list stored in an array, consider the following list:

$$35, 15, 77, 60, 22, 41$$

We think of the array storing these items as a complete binary tree:

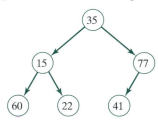

and we use the *Heapify* algorithm to convert it to a heap:

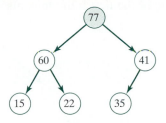

This puts the largest element in the list at the root of the tree, that is, at position 1 of the array. We now use the strategy of a selection sort and correctly position this largest element by placing it at the end of the list and turn our attention to sorting the sublist consisting of the first five elements. In terms of the tree, we are exchanging the root element and the rightmost leaf element and then "pruning" this leaf from the tree, as indicated by the dotted arrow in the following diagram:

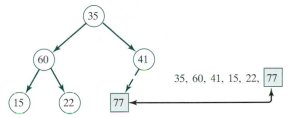

Quite obviously, the tree that results when we perform this root–leaf exchange, followed by pruning the leaf, usually is not a heap. In particular, the five-node tree that corresponds to the sublist 35, 60, 41, 15, 22 is not a heap. However, since we have changed only the root, the tree is almost a heap in the sense described earlier; namely, each of its subtrees is a heap. Thus we can use the *PercolateDown* algorithm rather than the more time-consuming *Heapify* algorithm to convert this tree to a heap:

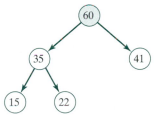

Now we use the same technique of exchanging the root with the rightmost leaf to correctly position the second largest element in the list, and then we prune this leaf from the tree to prepare for the next stage:

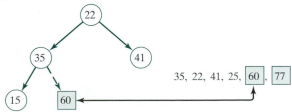

Now we use *PercolateDown* to convert to a heap the tree corresponding to the sublist consisting of the first four elements

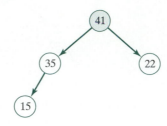

and do the root–leaf exchange and the leaf pruning to correctly position the third largest element in the list:

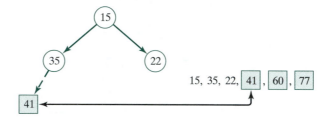

Next the three-node tree corresponding to the sublist 15, 35, 22 is converted to a heap using *PercolateDown*

and the roof–leaf exchange and pruning operations are used to correctly position the next largest element in the list:

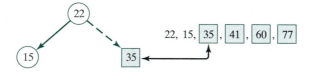

Finally, the two-node tree corresponding to the two-element sublist 22, 15 is converted to a heap and one last root–leaf swap and leaf pruning are performed to correctly position the element 22, which obviously also correctly positions the smallest element 15 at the beginning of the list

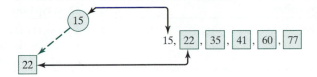

The following algorithm summarizes this simple but efficient sorting scheme, known as *heapsort:*

HEAPSORT ALGORITHM

```
/*   Algorithm that uses heapsort to sort the elements of
     array x into ascending order.
```

Precondition: A list is stored in array $x[1], \cdots, x[n]$.
Postcondition: x is sorted so that $x[1] \leq x[2] \leq \cdots \leq x[n]$.
Note: For consistency with other sorting methods,
                          position 0 in x is reserved for special purposes.

```
----------------------------------------------------------------------------------*/
```

1. Consider x as a complete binary tree and use the *Heapify* algorithm to convert this tree to a heap.

2. For $i = n$ down to 2:

   a. Interchange $x[1]$ and $x[i]$, thus putting the largest element in the sublist $x[1], \ldots, x[i]$ at the end of the sublist.
   b. Apply the *PercolateDown* algorithm to convert the binary tree corresponding to the sublist stored in positions 1 through $i-1$ of x.

In the introduction to this section we claimed that the computing time of heapsort is $O(n \log_2 n)$. To see this, we must first analyze the *PercolateDown* and *Heapify* algorithms.

In *PercolateDown*, the number of items in the subtree considered at each stage is one-half the number of items in the subtree at the preceding stage. Thus, by an analysis similar to that for binary search trees, the worst-case computing time for this algorithm is quite easily seen to be $O(\log_2 n)$. Since the *Heapify* algorithm executes *PercolateDown* $n/2$ times, its worst-case computing time is $O(n \log_2 n)$. *Heapsort* executes *Heapify* one time and *PercolateDown* $n-1$ times; consequently, its worst-case computing time is $O(n \log_2 n)$.

HEAP ALGORITHMS IN STL

The standard C++ library `<algorithm>` is a collection of algorithms (function templates). We looked at several of these in Chap. 7. It also contains the four algorithms for heap operations listed in Table 11.1. In these descriptions, *begin* and *end* are iterators (or pointers).

TABLE 11.1   STL HEAP ALGORITHMS

Algorithm	Description
make_heap(*begin*, *end*)	Converts the sequence in locations *begin* through *end* - 1 into a heap (ala *Heapify*)
push_heap(*begin*, *end*)	Insert operation for a heap: If the sequence in locations from *begin* on but before *end* - 1 is a heap, the element at location *end* – 1 is added to produce a heap.
pop_heap(*begin*, *end*)	Delete operation for a heap: Removes the element at location *begin* and restores the heap property.
sort_heap(*begin*, *end*)	Sorts the heap using heapsort.

The program in Fig. 11.1 illustrates these operations. It uses the functions PrintTree() and PrintOneRow() to display the heaps in a tree-like format.

FIGURE 11.1   HEAP ALGORITHMS IN STL

```cpp
#include <iostream>
#include <cmath>
#include <iomanip>
#include <algorithm>
using namespace std;

template <typename DataType>
void PrintTree(DataType x[], int n);

template <typename DataType>
void PrintOneRow(DataType x[], int numRows,
                 int row, int row_begin, int row_end);

int main()
{
  int x[] = {87, 35, 74, 67, 79, 84, 76, 73, 81, 32};

  make_heap(x, x+10);
  PrintTree(x, 10);

  x[10] = 83;
  push_heap(x, x + 11);
  cout << "After push_heap(83):\n\n";
  PrintTree(x, 11);
```

```cpp
   pop_heap(x, x+11);
   cout << "After pop_heap( ):\n\n";
   PrintTree(x, 10);

   sort_heap(x, x+10);
   cout << "After sort_heap( ), array contains:\n\n";
   for (int i = 0; i < 10; i++)
     cout << x[i] << "   ";
   cout << endl;
}

/* Print one row of a binary tree.
 *
 *   Receive:  Array x storing the binary tree,
 *             numRows = number of rows,
 *             row = current row being printed
 *             row_begin and row_end, the indices of the
 *                beginning of the row and the end of the row
 *   Output:   One row of the binary tree
 **************************************************************/

template <typename DataType>
void PrintOneRow(DataType x[], int numRows,
                 int row, int row_begin, int row_end)
{
                                      // space between items in row
   int skip = int(pow(2, numRows - row) - 1);
   for (int i = row_begin; i <= row_end; i++)
   {
     cout << setw(skip) << " ";
     cout << setw(2) << x[i];
     cout << setw(skip) << " ";
   }
   cout << endl << endl;
}

/* Print a binary tree in tree format
 *
 *   Receive:  Array x storing the binary tree,
 *             n = number of nodes in the tree
 *   Output:   The binary tree
 **************************************************************/

template <typename DataType>
void PrintTree(DataType x[], int n)
{
   int row_begin = 0,  // index of beginning of row
       row_end = 0,     //      "    " end of row
       rowLen,          // length of current row
       numRows = int(ceil(log(n) / log(2)));  // number of rows
```

```
    for (int row = 0; row < numRows; row++)
    {
      PrintOneRow(x, numRows, row, row_begin, row_end);
      rowLen = row_end - row_begin + 1;
      row_begin = row_end + 1;
      row_end = min(row_end + 2*(rowLen), n - 1);
    }
}
```

SAMPLE RUN:

```
                  87

        81                  84

     73        79      74        76

   35   67   32

After push_heap(83):

                  87

        83                  84

     73        81      74        76

   35   67   32   79

After pop_heap( ):

                  84

        83                  79

     73        81      74        76

   35   67   32

After sort_heap( ), array contains:

32   35   67   73   74   76   79   81   83   84
```

HEAPS AND PRIORITY QUEUES

In this section we emphasize the role of heaps in sorting. As a data structure, a heap is a viable alternative to binary search trees in organizing some collections of data. Unlike BSTs, heaps do not become lopsided as items are inserted or removed from the structure. Heaps can also be used to implement priority queues, which were introduced in Sec. 5.1 in the discussion of CPU scheduling.

ADT PRIORITY QUEUE

Collection of Data Elements:

A collection of data elements (all of the same type) in which a certain priority is associated with each data item, and these items are to be stored in such a way that those with higher priority are removed before those of lower priority. Items of equal priority are removed in a first-come-first-served order.

Basic Operations:

▸ Construct an empty priority queue

▸ Insert an item

▸ Find, return, and remove the largest (or smallest) element

Other operations are important in some applications; most of them can be implemented using the preceding basic operations:

▸ *Construct* a priority queue from *n* given items

▸ *Replace* largest (smallest) item with a new item (unless new item is larger)

▸ *Change* the priority of an item

▸ *Delete* a specified item

▸ *Join* two priority queues into one larger one

There are two natural ways to implement a priority queue. One is to use an unordered list (stored in an array or `vector` or linked list). Implementations of the two basic operations and their computing times are:

Insert: Just add the item at the end (or front)—O(1)

Remove max: Traverse the list to find the max, swap it with the front (or end) item, and remove the front (or end) item—O(n)

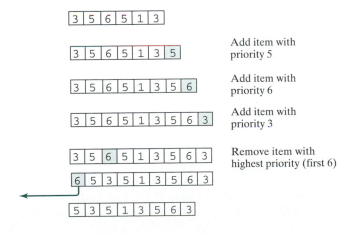

3	5	6	5	1	3

3 5 6 5 1 3 5   Add item with priority 5

3 5 6 5 1 3 5 6   Add item with priority 6

3 5 6 5 1 3 5 6 3   Add item with priority 3

3 5 6 5 1 3 5 6 3   Remove item with highest priority (first 6)

6 5 3 5 1 3 5 6 3

5 3 5 1 3 5 6 3

An alternative implementation is to use a list (stored in an array or `vector` or linked list) ordered by priority. Implementations of the two basic operations in this implementation and their computing times are:

Insert: Basic linear insertion sort—O(n)

Remove max: Just remove the item at the front—O(1)

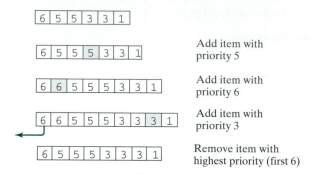

Add item with priority 5

Add item with priority 6

Add item with priority 3

Remove item with highest priority (first 6)

The best implementation is to *use a heap*. As we have seen for heaps, the basic operations can both be done in O($\log_2 n$) time. This is the implementation used in most implementations of the Standard Template Library's `priority_queue` adapter.

For a `priority_queue< C<T> >`, C may be a `vector`, a `deque`, or a `list`. If no container is specified, `vector` *is the default container*; that is, declarations of the form

```
priority_queue<T> pq;
```

are equivalent to

```
priority_queue< vector<T> > pq;
```

The basic operations for the `priority_queue` container are given in Table 11.2.

The default operator used to compare elements of a `priority_queue` is <, but we can also supply an alternative for comparison as a second template argument. This argument must be a **function object** that is declared by enclosing a function named `operator()` within a class declaration; for example

```
// function object
class funny_lessthan
{
public:
  bool operator() (double x, double y)
  { return x > y; }
};
```

If we defined `pq` by

```
priority_queue<int, funny_lessthan> pq;
```

then the elements of `pq` would be ordered using `funny_lessthan()`; that is, smaller integers would be considered to have higher priority than larger ones.

TABLE 11.2 BASIC priority_queue OPERATIONS

Operation	Description
Constructors	
priority_queue< C<T> > pq;	Construct an empty priority queue pq using a container C (default vector) to store the elements; < must be defined for the type T of elements
priority_queue< C<T> > pq(*first*, *last*);	Construct a priority queue pq as above but initialize it with elements in memory locations [*first*, *last*); < must be defined for the type T of elements
pq.empty()	Return true if and only if pq contains no values
pq.size()	Return the number of values pq contains
pq.push(*item*)	Add *item* to pq
pq.top()	Return largest item in pq
pq.pop()	Remove largest item from pq

✔ **Quick Quiz 11.2**

1. What is the heap-order property?

2. An array or vector can be used to store a heap efficiently because a heap is a(n) _____ binary tree.

3. The complexity of heapsort is O(_____).

4. Describe how items must be stored in a priority queue.

5. A(n) _____ is the best data structure to use to implement a priority queue.

✎ **EXERCISES 11.2**

In Exercises 1–3, convert the binary tree to a heap using the *Heapify* algorithm, or explain why it is not possible.

1.

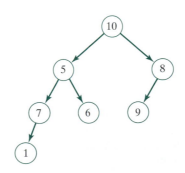

2.

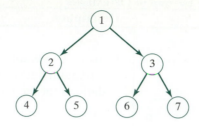

3.

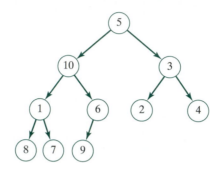

Using diagrams like those in this section, trace the action of heapsort on the lists in Exercises 4–7.

4. 7, 1, 6, 5, 4, 2, 3

5. 1, 7, 2, 6, 3, 5, 4

6. 7, 6, 5, 4, 3, 2, 1

7. 1, 2, 3, 4, 5, 6, 7

8. Four calls to *PercolateDown* must be made to heapify the following array x. Show x after each of the first two calls.

i	1	2	3	4	5	6	7	8	9
$x[i]$	20	15	31	10	67	50	3	49	26

9. For the following array x, show the contents of x after each of the first two iterations of the loop:

For $i = 8$ down to 2:

    1. *Interchange* $x[1]$ and $x[i]$.

    2. Apply *PercolateDown* to the subtree in $x[1], \ldots, x[i-1]$.

i	1	2	3	4	5	6	7	8
$x[i]$	99	88	55	77	22	33	44	66

10. Design an efficient algorithm for inserting an item into a heap having n elements to produce a heap with $n + 1$ elements. Determine the computing time for your algorithm. (*Hint*: Put the item in location $n + 1$ and then . . .)

11. Design an efficient algorithm for deleting an item at location *loc* from a heap having n elements to produce a heap with $n - 1$ elements. Determine the computing time for your algorithm.

For Exercises 12–17, write a function to implement the algorithm. You should also write driver programs to test your functions as instructed in Programming Problems 10–15 at the end of the chapter.

12.   *PercolateDown*

13.   *Heapify*

14.   *Heapsort*

15.   The insert algorithm in Exercise 10

16.   The delete algorithm in Exercise 11

17.   An algorithm to search a heap for a given item

18.   Explain why stacks and queues are special cases of a priority queue.

Exercises 19–21 ask you to design classes for priority queues. You should also write driver programs to test these classes as instructed in Programming Problems 16–18 at the end of the chapter.

19.   Use a modification of the implementation of a queue in Sec. 5.2 to implement a priority queue. Items should be stored in a single array, and two "pointers" should be maintained, one for the front of the priority queue and the other for the back. Select appropriate data members and write functions for the basic operations. You may assume that each object `item` being stored in the priority queue has a member function `Priority()` so that `item.Priority()` returns the priority of `item`.

20.   If the priorities of items are integers in some range $1, 2, \ldots, p$, then one could use p different arrays to implement a priority queue, one for each queue of items having equal priority. Construct such an implementation, selecting appropriate data members and writing functions for the basic operations.

21.   If the priorities of the items are not uniformly distributed, the implementation of a priority queue considered in Exercise 20 may be very inefficient. An alternative is to use a single array, as in Exercise 19, and $p + 1$ pointers, one to the front of the priority queue and one to the back of each of the "internal" queues of items having equal priority. Construct such an implementation.

11.3 QUICKSORT

In Sec. 11.1 we noted that an exchange sort repeatedly interchanges elements in lists and sublists until no more interchanges are possible. In the case of bubble sort, consecutive items are compared and possibly interchanged on each pass through the list, which means that many interchanges may be needed to move an element to its correct position. In this section we consider an exchange sort developed by C. A. R. Hoare and refined significantly by Robert Sedgewick. It is known as **quicksort** and is more efficient than bubble sort because a typical exchange involves elements that are far apart so that fewer interchanges are required to correctly position an element.

Quicksort uses a **divide-and-conquer** strategy. This is a recursive approach to problem-solving in which the original problem is partitioned into simpler subproblems, each of which can be considered independently. Some or all of these subproblems may still be fairly complicated, and this divide-and-conquer approach can be repeated for them, continuing until subproblems are obtained that are sufficiently simple that they can be solved (i.e., conquered).

With quicksort, the divide-and-conquer approach chooses some element called a **pivot** and then performs a sequence of exchanges so that all elements that are less than this pivot are to its left and all elements that are greater than the pivot are to its right. This correctly positions the pivot and divides the (sub)list into two smaller sublists, each of which may then be sorted independently in the *same* way. Repeating this approach will eventually produce small lists that are sorted or can easily be sorted. This leads naturally to the following recursive sorting algorithm:

QUICKSORT ALGORITHM

/*   Algorithm that uses quicksort to sort the elements of
     array *x* into ascending order.

     Precondition: A list is stored in array $x[1], \ldots, x[n]$.
     Postcondition: *x* is sorted so that $x[1] \leq x[2] \leq \ldots \leq x[n]$.
     Note: For consistency with other sorting methods,
                       position 0 in *x* is reserved for special purposes.
     --*/

1. If the list has 0 or 1 elements, return.   // the list is sorted

   Else do the following.

2. Pick an element in the list to use as the *pivot*.

3. Split the remaining elements into two disjoint groups:

   SmallerThanPivot = {all elements < *pivot*}

   LargerThanPivot = {all elements > *pivot*}

4. Return the list rearranged as:

   Quicksort(*SmallerThanPivot*), *pivot*, Quicksort(*LargerThanPivot*).

   As an illustration, consider the following list of test scores:

$$75, 70, 65, 84, 98, 78, 100, 93, 55, 61, 81, 68$$

Suppose, for simplicity, that we select the first number 75 as the pivot. *SmallerThanPivot* consists of 70, 65, 55, 61, and 68, and *LargerThanPivot* consists of 84, 98, 78, 100, 93, and 81. We must rearrange the list so that the numbers in *SmallerThanPivot* come before 75 (but not necessarily in the order listed here) and the numbers in *LargerThanPivot* come after 75:

$$\underline{SmallerThanPivot} \; \boxed{75} \; \underline{LargerThanPivot}$$

The only thing we require of this rearrangement is that all the numbers in the sublist to the left of 75 be less than or equal to 75 and that those in the right sublist be greater than 75. We do not care how the elements in each of these sublists are themselves ordered. And it is precisely this flexibility that makes it possible to do this rearrangement very efficiently.

THE SPLIT OPERATION

We carry out two searches, one from the right end of the list for elements less than or equal to the pivot 75 and the other from the left end for elements greater than

75. In our example, the first element located on the search from the right is 68, and that on the search from the left is 84:

$$\boxed{75}, \ 70, \ 65, \ \boxed{84}, \ 98, \ 78, \ 100, \ 93, \ 55, \ 61, \ 81, \ \boxed{68}$$

These elements are then interchanged:

$$\boxed{75}, \ 70, \ 65, \ \boxed{68}, \ 98, \ 78, \ 100, \ 93, \ 55, \ 61, \ 81, \ \boxed{84}$$

The searches are then resumed, from the right to locate another element less than or equal to 75 and from the left to find another element greater than 75

$$\boxed{75}, \ 70, \ 65, \ 68, \ \boxed{98}, \ 78, \ 100, \ 93, \ 55, \ \boxed{61}, \ 81, \ 84$$

and these elements, 61 and 98, are interchanged:

$$\boxed{75}, \ 70, \ 65, \ 68, \ \boxed{61}, \ 78, \ 100, \ 93, \ 55, \ \boxed{98}, \ 81, \ 84$$

A continuation of the searches next locates 78 and 55

$$\boxed{75}, \ 70, \ 65, \ 68, \ 61, \ \boxed{78}, \ 100, \ 93, \ \boxed{55}, \ 98, \ 81, \ 84$$

and interchanging them yields:

$$\boxed{75}, \ 70, \ 65, \ 68, \ 61, \ \boxed{55}, \ 100, \ 93, \ \boxed{78}, \ 98, \ 81, \ 84$$

Now, when we resume our search from the right, we locate the element 55 that was found on the previous search from the left:

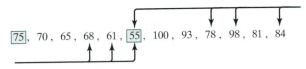

$$\boxed{75}, \ 70, \ 65, \ 68, \ 61, \ \boxed{55}, \ 100, \ 93, \ 78, \ 98, \ 81, \ 84$$

The "pointers" for the left and right searches have thus met, and this signals the end of the two searches. We now interchange 55 and the pivot 75

$$55,\ 70,\ 65,\ 68,\ 61,\ \boxed{75},\ 100,\ 93,\ 78,\ 98,\ 81,\ 84$$

Note that all elements to the left of 75 are less than 75 and that all those to its right are greater than 75, and thus the pivot 75 has been properly positioned.

The left sublist

$$55, 70, 65, 68, 61$$

and the right sublist

$$100, 93, 78, 98, 81, 84$$

can now be sorted *independently, using any sorting scheme desired.* Quicksort uses the same scheme we have just illustrated for the entire list; that is, these sublists must themselves be split by choosing and correctly positioning one pivot element (the first) in each of them. The following function template `Split()` can be used for this. It assumes that the list is stored in an array and uses a `Swap()` function template (see Sec. 6.2) to interchange two list elements.

```
/* Rearranges x[first], ... , x[last] so that
 * the pivot element is properly positioned.
 *
 *   Receive:   Array x storing the list,
 *              indices first and last
 *   Return:    Rearranged x, index pos
 ***********************************************/

template <typename ElementType>
void Split (ElementType x[],
            int first, int last, int & pos)
{
   ElementType pivot = x[first];   // pivot element
   int left = first,               // index for left search
       right = last;               // index for right search

   while (left < right)
   {
     // Search from right for element <= pivot
     while (x[right] > pivot)
       right--;
     // Search from left for element > pivot
     while (left < right && x[left] <= pivot)
       left++;
     // Interchange elements if searches haven't met
     if (left < right)
       Swap(x[left], x[right]);
   }
```

```
      // End of searches; place pivot in correct position
      pos = right;
      x[first] = x[pos];
      x[pos] = pivot;
  }
```

QUICKSORT

A recursive function to sort a list using quicksort is now easy to write

```
   /* Quicksort array elements x[first], ..., x[last]
    * so they are in ascending order.
    *
    *   Receive:   Array x storing the list,
    *              indices first and last
    *   Return:    Rearranged x, index pos
    ***********************************************/

   template <typename ElementType>
   void Quicksort(ElementType x[], int first, int last)
   {
     int pos;                // final position of pivot
     if (first < last) // list has more than one element
     {
       // Split into two sublists
       Split(x, first, last, pos);
       // Sort left sublist
       Quicksort(x, first, pos - 1);
       // Sort right sublist
       Quicksort(x, pos + 1, last);
     }
     // else list has 0 or 1 element and
     // requires no sorting
   }
```

This function is called with a statement of the form

```
   Quicksort(x, 1, n);
```

where $x[1], x[2], \ldots, x[n]$ is the list of elements to be sorted.

The following sequence of treelike diagrams traces the action of `Quicksort()` as it sorts the list of integers:

$$8, 2, 13, 5, 14, 3, 7$$

In each tree, a circle indicates an element that has been correctly positioned at an earlier stage and a shaded circle indicates the current pivot. Rectangles represent sublists to be sorted, and a highlighted rectangle indicates the next sublist to be sorted.

First call to Quicksort() (first = 1, last = 7).

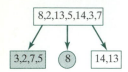

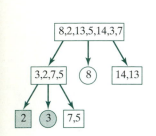

1 < 7 so Split() is called to position the pivot 8. Now call Quicksort() for the left sublist 3, 2, 7, 5 (first = 1, last = 4).

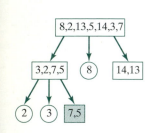

1 < 4 so call Split() to position the pivot 3. Now call Quicksort() for the left sublist that consists of the single element 2 (first = 1, last = 1).

1 < 1 (one-element sublist) so nothing happens on this call to Quicksort(). We return to the previous level and call Quicksort() for the right sublist 7, 5 (first = 3, last = 4).

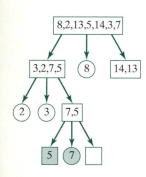

Since 3 < 4, Split() is called to position the pivot 7. Now call Quicksort() for the left sublist consisting of the single element 5 (first = 3, last = 3).

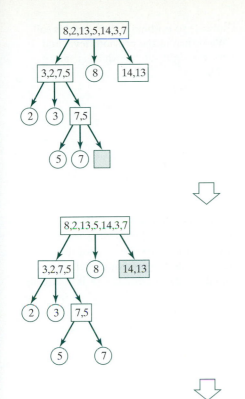

3 < 3 (one-element sublist) so nothing happens on this call to Quicksort(). We return to the previous level and call Quicksort() for the right sublist which is empty (first = 5, last = 4).

5 < 4 (empty sublist) so again nothing happens on this call to Quicksort(). We return to the previous level and find the call to Quicksort() for sublist 7, 5 is complete. So we back up to the previous level and call Quicksort() for the right sublist 14,13 at this level (first = 6, last = 7).

Since 6 < 7, Split() is called to position the pivot 14. Now Quicksort() is called for the resulting left sublist that consists of the single element 13 (first = 6, last = 6).

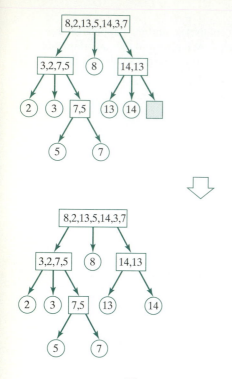

6 < 6 (one-element sublist) so nothing is done on this call to `Quicksort()`. We return to the previous level and call `Quicksort()` for the right sublist, which is empty (`first = 8`, `last = 7`).

8 < 7 (empty sublist), so do nothing on this call to `Quicksort()`; simply return to the previous level. But this completes the call to `Quicksort()` for the sublist 14, 13, and we return to the previous level. Now we find that the original call to `Quicksort()` is complete.

The worst case for quicksort occurs when the list is already ordered or the elements are in reverse order. The worst-case computing time is $O(n^2)$, and the average-case computing time is $O(n \log_2 n)$. Although a rigorous derivation of these computing times is rather difficult, we can see intuitively why they are correct by considering the treelike diagrams used to describe the action of `Quicksort()`. At each level of the tree, the function `Split()` is applied to several sublists, whose total size is, of course, at most n; hence, each of the statements in the while loop of `Split()` is executed at most n times on each level. The computing time for quicksort is thus $O(n \cdot L)$, where L is the number of levels in the tree. In the worst case, one of the sublists produced by `Split()` is always empty, so that the tree has n levels. It follows that the worst-case computing time is $O(n^2)$. If, however, the two sublists produced by `Split()` are approximately the same size, the number of levels will be approximately $\log_2 n$, thus giving $O(n \log_2 n)$ as the computing time in the average case.

IMPROVEMENTS

A number of changes can be made in quicksort to improve its performance, several of which are due to Robert Sedgewick. We will look at three of them here.

REDUCE SIZE OF RECURSION STACK. *Quicksort* is a recursive function, and as we have seen (see Sec. 7.3), a stack of activation records must be maintained by the system to manage recursion. The deeper the recursion is, the larger this stack will become. The depth of the recursion and the corresponding overhead involved can be reduced if we *sort the smaller sublist at each stage first*, rather than always selecting the left sublist. If quicksort is to be used extensively, it may even be worthwhile to remove recursion by writing it iteratively, as described in the exercises.

CHOICE OF PIVOT.   Until now we have simply selected the first element in the list. However, this is acceptable only for random input. If the list is partially sorted (or in reverse order), it gives a poor partition; virtually all the elements go into either *SmallerThanPivot* or *LargerThanPivot*. And this happens consistently through the recursive calls. Quicksort takes quadratic time to do essentially nothing at all.

One common method for selecting the pivot is the **median-of-three rule**, which selects the median of the first, middle, and last elements in each sublist as the pivot. In practice, it is often the case that the list to be sorted is already partially ordered, and then it is likely that the median-of-three rule will select a pivot closer to the middle of the sublist than will the "first-element" rule.

SMALL SUBLISTS.   For small files ($n \leq 20$), quicksort is worse than insertion sort; and small files occur often because of recursion. So a common solution is to use an efficient sort (e.g., insertion sort) for small files. A better idea is simply to ignore all small subfiles, and when execution of the quicksort algorithm terminates, the file will not be sorted. It will only be slightly unsorted, however, in that it will contain small unordered groups of elements, but all of the elements in each such group will be smaller than those in the next group. One then simply sorts the list using insertion sort which works well, since it is efficient for nearly sorted files.

STL's `sort()`.   The `sort()` function template in the C++ standard library `<algorithm>` uses quicksort. Most implementations will use modifications of quicksort like those just described to improve its performance.

✔ Quick Quiz 11.3

1. Describe the divide-and-conquer approach to problem solving.
2. Describe how quicksort uses a divide-and-conquer sorting strategy.
3. The item properly positioned at each call to quicksort is called a(n) _____ .
4. The worst-case complexity of quicksort is O(_____), and the average-case complexity is O(_____).
5. How does sorting the smaller sublist at each step improve quicksort?
6. Using the first list element as pivot works well for partially-sorted lists. (True or false)
7. The _____ rule selects the median of the first, middle, and last elements in each sublist as the pivot.
8. The C++ standard `sort()` algorithm uses quicksort. (True or false)

✍ EXERCISES 11.3

1. For the following array x, show the contents of x after the function call `Split(x, 1, 10, splitPos)` is executed, and give the value of the array index `splitPos`:

i	1	2	3	4	5	6	7	8	9	10
x[i]	45	20	50	30	80	10	60	70	40	90

For Exercises 2–5, draw a sequence of trees like those in the text to illustrate the actions of `Split()` and `Quicksort()` while sorting the given list.

2. E, A, F, D, C, B

3. A, B, C, F, E, D

4. F, E, D, C, B, A

5. A, B, C, D, E, F

6. One of the lists in Exercises 2–5 shows why the compound boolean condition is needed to control the search from the left in function `Split()`. Which list is it? What would happen if we were to omit the boolean expression `left < right`?

For the following Exercises, you should write functions and test them with driver programs as instructed in Programming Problems 21–27 at the end of the chapter.

7. The function `Quicksort()` given in the text sorts the left sublist before the right. As noted in the text, the size of the stack used to implement the recursion required by `Quicksort()` is reduced if the shorter of the two sublists is the first to be sorted. Modify `Quicksort()` to do this.

8. Modify `Quicksort()` to use insertion sort if the sublist has fewer than LOWER_BOUND elements for some constant LOWER_BOUND and use quicksort otherwise.

9. The preferred alternative to the approach in Exercise 8 suggested in the text was to ignore all sublists with fewer than LOWER_BOUND elements, not splitting them further. When execution of the quicksort algorithm terminates, simply sort the list using insertion sort. Modify `Quicksort()` to incorporate this modification.

10. Modify the function `Split()` to use the median-of-three rule to select the pivot. (The median of three numbers a, b, and c arranged so that $a \leq b \leq c$ is the middle number b.)

11. As we saw in Sec. 7.3, recursion is usually implemented using a stack; parameters, local variables, and return addresses are pushed onto the stack when a recursive subprogram is called, and values are popped from the stack upon return from the subprogram. Generally, we can transform a recursive subprogram into a nonrecursive one by maintaining such a stack within the subprogram itself. Use this approach to design a nonrecursive version of function `Quicksort()`; use a stack to store the first and last positions of the sublists that arise in quicksort.

12. The *median* of a set with an odd number of elements is the middle value if the data items are arranged in order. An efficient algorithm to find the median that does not require first ordering the entire set can be obtained by modifying the quicksort algorithm. We use function `Split()` to position a pivot element. If this pivot is positioned at location $(n + 1)/2$, it is the median; otherwise, one of the two sublists produced by `Split()` contains the median, and that sublist can be processed recursively. Write a function to find the median of a list using this method.

13. The technique described in Exercise 12 for finding the median of a set of data items can easily be modified to find the kth smallest element in the set. Write such a function.

11.4 MERGESORT

Sorting schemes can be classified as **internal** or **external**, according to whether they are designed for a collection of data items stored in main memory or in secondary memory. The sorting schemes described in the preceding sections are used almost exclusively as internal sorts. They are not practical for sequential files because they require direct access to the list elements, which is not possible for sequential files. Also, some of them make many passes through the list. This too is not practical for files because they must be reset (rewound) before each pass and large numbers of data transfers from disks (or tapes) take too much time, especially when large records are being sorted. In this section we describe two versions of a popular sorting scheme known as **mergesort** that can be used both as an internal and an external sort. We will describe it as an external sort because this is how it is most often used. You should pay special attention to whether direct access is needed and to the number of passes made through the lists.

MERGING LISTS

As the name suggests, the basic operation in mergesort is **merging**, that is, combining two lists that have previously been sorted so that the resulting list is also sorted. As a simple illustration, suppose that *File1* contains eight integers in increasing order

$$File1: \quad 15 \quad 20 \quad 25 \quad 35 \quad 45 \quad 60 \quad 65 \quad 70$$

and *File2* contains five integers in increasing order

$$File2: \quad 10 \quad 30 \quad 40 \quad 50 \quad 55$$

In practice, of course, files contain many more items, and each item is usually a record containing several different types of information, and as we have commented before, sorting is then based on some key field within these records.

To merge files *File1* and *File2* to produce sorted *File3*, we read one element from each file, say, *x* from *File1* and *y* from *File2*:

We compare these items and write the smaller, in this case *y*, to *File3*

$$File3: \quad 10$$

and then read another value for *y* from *File2*:

Now *x* is smaller than *y*, so it is written to *File3*, and a new value for *x* is read from *File1*:

$$File3: \quad 10 \quad 15$$

Again, x is less than y, so it is written to *File3*, and a new value for x is read from *File1*:

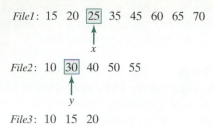

File3: 10 15 20

Continuing in this manner, we eventually read the value 60 for x and the last value of *File2*, 55, for y:

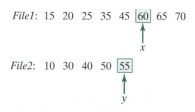

File3: 10 15 20 25 30 35 40 45 50

Because $y < x$, we write y to *File3*:

File3: 10 15 20 25 30 35 40 45 50 55

Because the end of *File2* has been reached, we simply copy the remaining items in *File1* to *File3* to complete the merging:

File3: 15 20 25 30 35 40 45 50 55 60 65 70

The general algorithm for merging two sorted files is:

 MERGE

/*   Algorithm to merge sorted files *File1* and *File2,* giving *File3*.

    Input: Sorted files *File1* and *File2*
    Output: *File3*
---*/

1. Open *File1* and *File2* for input, *File3* for output.
2. Read the first element x from *File1* and the first element y from *File2*.
3. Repeat the following until the end of either *File1* or *File2* is reached:
    If $x < y$, then
        a. Write x to *File3*.
        b. Read a new x value from *File1*.
    Otherwise:
        a. Write y to *File3*.
        b. Read a new y value from *File2*.
4. If the end of *File1* was encountered, copy any remaining elements from *File2* into *File3*. If the end of *File2* was encountered, copy the rest of *File1* into *File3*.

BINARY MERGESORT

To see how the merge operation can be used in sorting a file, consider the following file F containing sixteen integers:

$$F: \quad 75 \quad 55 \quad 15 \quad 20 \quad 85 \quad 30 \quad 35 \quad 10 \quad 60 \quad 40 \quad 50 \quad 25 \quad 45 \quad 80 \quad 70 \quad 65$$

We begin by copying the elements of F alternately into two other files $F1$ and $F2$:

$$F1: \quad 75 \quad 15 \quad 85 \quad 35 \quad 60 \quad 50 \quad 45 \quad 70$$

$$F2: \quad 55 \quad 20 \quad 30 \quad 10 \quad 40 \quad 25 \quad 80 \quad 65$$

We now merge the first one-element subfile of $F1$ with the first one-element subfile of $F2$ to give a sorted two-element subfile of F:

$$F1: \quad \boxed{75} \quad 15 \quad 85 \quad 35 \quad 60 \quad 50 \quad 45 \quad 70$$

$$F2: \quad \boxed{55} \quad 20 \quad 30 \quad 10 \quad 40 \quad 25 \quad 80 \quad 65$$

$$F: \quad \boxed{55 \quad 75}$$

Next the second one-element subfile of $F1$ is merged with the second one-element subfile of $F2$ and is written to F:

$$F1: \quad 75 \quad \boxed{15} \quad 85 \quad 35 \quad 60 \quad 50 \quad 45 \quad 70$$

$$F2: \quad 55 \quad \boxed{20} \quad 30 \quad 10 \quad 40 \quad 25 \quad 80 \quad 65$$

$$F: \quad 55 \quad 75 \quad \boxed{15 \quad 20}$$

This merging of corresponding one-element subfiles continues until the end of either or both of the files $F1$ and $F2$ is reached. If either file still contains a subfile, it is simply copied into F:

$$F: \quad \boxed{55 \quad 75} \quad \boxed{15 \quad 20} \quad \boxed{30 \quad 85} \quad \boxed{10 \quad 35} \quad \boxed{40 \quad 60} \quad \boxed{25 \quad 50} \quad \boxed{45 \quad 80} \quad \boxed{65 \quad 70}$$

As the highlighted blocks indicate, the file F now consists of a sequence of two-element sorted subfiles. We again split it into files $F1$ and $F2$, copying these two-element subfiles alternately to $F1$ and $F2$:

$$F1: \quad \boxed{55 \quad 75} \quad \boxed{30 \quad 85} \quad \boxed{40 \quad 60} \quad \boxed{45 \quad 80}$$

$$F2: \quad \boxed{15 \quad 20} \quad \boxed{10 \quad 35} \quad \boxed{25 \quad 50} \quad \boxed{65 \quad 70}$$

Now we merge corresponding subfiles in $F1$ and $F2$ to produce four-element sorted subfiles in F:

$$F: \quad \boxed{15 \quad 20 \quad 55 \quad 75} \quad \boxed{10 \quad 30 \quad 35 \quad 85} \quad \boxed{25 \quad 40 \quad 50 \quad 60} \quad \boxed{45 \quad 65 \quad 70 \quad 80}$$

Now, using four-element subfiles, we again split F by copying subfiles alternately to $F1$ and $F2$:

$$F1: \quad \boxed{15 \quad 20 \quad 55 \quad 75} \quad \boxed{25 \quad 40 \quad 50 \quad 60}$$

$$F2: \quad \boxed{10 \quad 30 \quad 35 \quad 85} \quad \boxed{45 \quad 65 \quad 70 \quad 80}$$

and then merge corresponding four-element subfiles to produce eight-element sorted subfiles in *F*:

F: | 10 15 20 30 35 55 75 85 | 25 40 45 50 60 65 70 80 |

The next splitting into files *F1* and *F2* produces

F1: | 10 15 20 30 35 55 75 85 |

F2: | 25 40 45 50 60 65 70 80 |

and merging corresponding eight-element subfiles in *F1* and *F2* produces one sorted sixteen-element sorted subfile in *F* so that *F* has now been sorted:

F: | 10 15 20 25 30 35 40 45 50 55 60 65 70 75 80 85 |

In this example, the size of *F* is a power of 2, so that all the subfiles produced by the split and merge operations have the same size, and this size is also a power of 2. In general, this will be true for all of the subfiles except possibly for the last one, which may have fewer elements. Although this means that some care must be exercised in checking for the ends of files and subfiles in this version of mergesort, known as **binary mergesort**, it does not present any serious difficulties in designing the required split and merge algorithms.

NATURAL MERGESORT

A more serious criticism of binary mergesort is that it restricts itself to subfiles of sizes $1, 2, 4, 8, \ldots, 2^k$, where $2^k \geq$ size of *F* and must, therefore, always go through a series of *k* split-merge phases. If sorted subfiles of other sizes are allowed, the number of phases can be reduced in those situations where the file contains longer "runs" of elements that are already in order. A version of mergesort that takes advantage of these "natural" sorted subfiles (in contrast to the "artificial" sizes and subfiles created by binary mergesort) is called **natural mergesort**, naturally.

As an illustration of natural mergesort, consider again the file *F* used to demonstrate binary mergesort:

F: 75 55 15 20 85 30 35 10 60 40 50 25 45 80 70 65

Notice that several segments of *F* consist of elements that are already in order:

F: | 75 | 55 | 15 20 85 | 30 35 | 10 60 | 40 50 | 25 45 80 | 70 | 65 |

and that these sorted subfiles subdivide *F* in a natural way.

We begin as before by copying subfiles of *F* alternately to two other files, *F1* and *F2*, but using these natural subfiles rather than requiring that at each stage, their sizes be a power of 2:

F1: | 75 | 15 20 85 | 10 60 | 25 45 80 | 65 |

F2: | 55 | 30 35 | 40 50 | 70 |

We now identify the natural sorted subfiles in each of *F1* and *F2*:

$F1$: | 75 | | 15 20 85 | | 10 60 | | 25 45 80 | | 65 |

$F2$: | 55 | | 30 35 40 50 70 |

Notice that although the subfiles of $F1$ are the same as those copied from F, the last three subfiles written to $F2$ have combined to form a larger subfile.

Now, proceeding as in binary mergesort, we merge the first subfile of $F1$ with the first one in $F2$ to produce the first subfile of $F1$ with the first one in $F2$ to produce a sorted subfile in F:

F: | 55 75 |

and then merge the second subfiles:

F: | 55 75 | | 15 20 30 35 40 50 70 85 |

Since we have now reached the end of $F2$, we simply copy the remaining subfiles of $F1$ back to F:

F: | 55 75 | | 15 20 30 35 40 50 70 85 | | 10 60 | | 25 45 80 | | 65 |

Now we again split F, alternately copying sorted subfiles to $F1$ and $F2$:

$F1$: | 55 75 | | 10 60 | | 65 |

$F2$: | 15 20 30 35 40 50 70 85 | | 25 45 80 |

This time we see that two subfiles of $F1$ combine to form a larger subfile:

$F1$: | 55 75 | | 10 60 65 |

$F2$: | 15 20 30 35 40 50 70 85 | | 25 45 80 |

As before, we merge corresponding subfiles of $F1$ and $F2$, writing the results back to F:

F: | 15 20 30 35 40 50 55 70 75 85 | | 10 25 45 60 65 80 |

In the next phase, splitting F produces files $F1$ and $F2$, each of which contains only one sorted subfile, and thus they are themselves completely sorted files:

$F1$: | 15 20 30 35 40 50 55 70 75 85 |

$F2$: | 15 20 30 35 40 50 |

Consequently, when we perform the merge operation in this phase, F will be a sorted file:

F: | 10 15 20 25 30 35 40 45 50 55 60 65 70 75 80 85 |

Notice that one fewer split-merge phase was required here than in binary mergesort.

The splitting operation in natural mergesort is carried out by the following algorithm:

SPLIT ALGORITHM FOR NATURAL MERGESORT

/* Splits file *F* into files *F1* and *F2* by copying natural sorted subfiles of *F* alternately to *F1* and *F2*.

Input: File *F*
Output: Files *F1* and *F2*
---*/

1. Open the file *F* for input and the files *F1* and *F2* for output.
2. While the end of *F* has not been reached:
   a. Copy a sorted subfile of *F* into *F1* as follows: Repeatedly read an element of *F* and write it into *F1* until the next element in *F* is smaller than this copied item or the end of *F* is reached.
   b. If the end of *F* has not been reached, copy the next sorted subfile of *F* into *F2* in a similar manner.

And the following algorithm implements the merge operation illustrated in the example:

MERGE ALGORITHM FOR NATURAL MERGESORT

/* Merges corresponding sorted subfiles in *F1* and *F2* back into file *F*.
Input: Files *F1* and *F2*
Return: *numSubfiles*, the number of sorted subfiles produced in *F*
Output: File *F*
---*/

1. Open files *F1* and *F2* for input, *F* for output.
2. Initialize *numSubfiles* to 0.
3. While neither the end of *F1* nor the end of *F2* has been reached:
   a. While no end of a subfile in *F1* or in *F2* has been reached:
      If the next element in *F1* is less than the next element in *F2*, then copy the next element from *F1* into *F* ; otherwise, copy the next element from *F2* into *F*.
   b. If the end of a subfile in *F1* has been reached, then copy the rest of the corresponding subfile in *F2* to *F*; otherwise, copy the rest of the corresponding subfile in *F1* to *F*.
   c. Increment *numSubfiles* by 1.
4. Copy any subfiles remaining in *F1* or *F2* to *F*, incrementing *numSubfiles* by 1 for each.

An algorithm for natural mergesort consists of simply calling these two algorithms repeatedly until the file is sorted:

NATURAL MERGESORT

/*   Sorts a file *F* using two auxiliary files *F1* and *F2*.
     Input: File *F*
     Output: Sorted file *F*
--*/

Repeat the following until *numSubfiles* is equal to 1:

1. Call the *Split* algorithm to split *F* into files *F1* and *F2*.

2. Call the *Merge* algorithm to merge corresponding subfiles in *F1* and *F2* back into *F*.

Mergesort can also be used as an internal sorting method for lists. The split and merge algorithms can easily be modified to use arrays or linked lists in place of the files *F*, *F1*, and *F2*.

The worst case for natural mergesort occurs when the items are in reverse order. In this case, natural mergesort functions in exactly the same way as binary merge-sort does, using subfiles of sizes 1, 2, 4, 8, and so on. It follows that to sort a file or list of *n* items, $\log_2 n$ split and merge operations are required and each of the *n* items must be examined in each of them. Hence, in the worst case, and as can be shown for the average case also, the computing time of natural mergesort is $O(n \log_2 n)$.

✔ Quick Quiz 11.4

1. Sorting methods are classified as _____ or_____ according to whether they are used for lists stored in main memory or for lists stored in secondary memory.

2. What are some reasons a sorting method may not be appropriate for files?

3. Why is mergesort so named?

4. The worst- and average-case complexities of mergesort are O(_____).

✍ EXERCISES 11.4

For Exercises 1–5, use diagrams like those in the text, show the various splitting-merging stages of binary mergesort for the following lists of numbers:

1. 13, 57, 39, 85, 70, 22, 64, 48

2. 13, 57, 39, 85, 99, 70, 22, 48, 64

3. 13, 22, 57, 99, 39, 64, 57, 48, 70

4. 13, 22, 39, 48, 57, 64, 70, 85

5. 85, 70, 65, 57, 48, 39, 22, 13

6–10.   Give diagrams as in Exercises 1–5 but use natural mergesort.

Suppose that we sort a list of records in which some of the values in the key field may be the same. A sorting scheme is said to be *stable* if it does not change the order of such records. For example, consider a list of records containing a person's name and age that is to be sorted so that the ages are in ascending order. Suppose that

comes before

Smith | 39

in the original list (with possibly several records between them). For a stable sorting scheme, Doe's record still comes before Smith's after the list is sorted. In Exercises 11–17 determine whether the sorting method is stable.

11. Simple selection sort

12. Bubble sort

13. Linear insertion sort

14. Heapsort

15. Quicksort

16. Binary mergesort

17. Natural mergesort

The following exercises ask you to write functions. You should also test these functions with driver programs as instructed in Programming Problems 28–30 at the end of this chapter.

18. Write functions to implement the *Split*, *Merge*, and *Mergesort* algorithms for files.

19. Proceed as in Exercise 18, but for a list stored in an array or `vector`.

20. Proceed as in Exercise 18, but for a linked list.

21. One variation of the mergesort method is to modify the splitting operation as follows: Copy some fixed number of elements into main memory, sort them using an internal sorting method such as quicksort, and write this sorted list to *F1*; then read the same number of elements from *F* into main memory, sort them internally, and write this sorted list to *F2*; and so on, alternating between *F1* and *F2*. Write a function for this modified mergesort scheme, using quicksort to sort internally the sublists containing *SIZE* elements for some constant *SIZE*.

22. Write a function to carry out a *three-way merge*, that is, a procedure that merges three sorted files to form another sorted file.

☞ PROGRAMMING POINTERS

1. The Standard Template Library provides algorithms for processing heaps: `make_heap()`, `push_heap()`, `pop_heap()`, and `sort_heap()`.

2. C++ provides *function objects*, which are defined by enclosing a function named `operator()` within a class declaration. They are used to pass functions into class templates.

3. *Divide-and-conquer* is a recursive problem-solving approach that divides the original problem into simpler subproblems, perhaps repeatedly, until subproblems are obtained that are sufficiently simple that they can be solved (i.e., conquered).

ADT TIPS

1. Three categories of sorts are: *selection*, *exchange*, and *insertion*. Selection sorts make a number of passes through a list or a part of the list and, on each pass, select one element to be correctly positioned. Exchange sorts systematically interchange pairs of elements that are out of order until eventually no such pairs remain and the list is sorted. Insertion sorts repeatedly insert a new element into a list of already sorted elements so that the resulting list is still sorted.

2. Many applications involve lists that are already partially sorted, and a good sorting method should take advantage of this.

3. There is no such thing as one universally good sorting scheme. For small lists, linear insertion sort performs well. For lists in general, quicksort, Shell sort, or heapsort is the method of choice.

4. An *indirect sort* uses an index table that stores the positions of the records and moves the entries in this index rather than the records themselves, which is more efficient than moving large records.

5. Heapsort is an $O(n \log_2 n)$ selection sort that uses a data structure called a *heap* to organize the list elements in such a way that the selection can be made efficiently.

6. Because a heap is a complete binary tree, it can be stored efficiently in an array.

7. Unlike a BST, a heap cannot become lopsided as items are inserted or removed.

8. The best implementation of a priority queue uses a heap.

9. Quicksort is a divide-and-conquer sorting method with average complexity $O(n \log_2 n)$. Industrial-strength versions, such as the `sort()` algorithm in STL, sort smaller sublists first, use a nontrivial pivot selection strategy such as the median-of-three rule, and use some other sorting method such as insertion sort to sort small sublists.

10. Mergesort is an $O(n \log_2 n)$ sorting method that can be used either as an internal or external sort. Natural mergesort takes advantage of partially-sorted lists and is thus preferred over binary mergesort.

PROGRAMMING PROBLEMS

SECTION 11.1

For Prob. 1–6, write a driver program to test the given function.

1. The double-ended selection-sort function in Exercise 4.

2. The Min-Max-Sort function in Exercise 5.

3. The recursive simple-selection-sort function in Exercise 6.

4. The recursive bubblesort function in Exercise 7.

5. The Shell-sort function in Exercise 12.

6. The treesort function in Exercise 14.

7. Write a program that reads a collection of student numbers and names and then uses the treesort function of Exercise 14 to sort them so that the student numbers are in ascending order.

8. Write a program that reads the records in `UserIdFile` and stores them in an array. (See Programming Problem 12 at the end of Chap. 2 and the website described in the preface for a sample `UserIdFile`.) Then sort the records so that the resources used to date are in descending order, using one of the sorting schemes in this section as an indirect sort.

9. Write a program that compares the execution times of various $O(n^2)$ sorting algorithms described in this section for randomly generated lists of integers.

SECTION 11.2

For Probs. 10–15, write a driver program to test the given function.

10. The percolate-down function of Exercise 12.

11. The heapify function of Exercise 13.

12. The heapsort function of Exercise 14.

13. The insert function in Exercise 15.

14. The delete function in Exercise 16.

15. The search function in Exercise 17.

For Probs. 16–19, write a driver program to test the priority queue class template in the given exercise.

16. Exercise 19.

17. Exercise 20.

18. Exercise 21.

19. Write a program that reads records containing an employee number and an hourly rate for several employees and stores these in a heap, using the employee number as the key field. The program should then allow the user to insert or delete records and, finally, use heapsort to sort the updated list so that the employee numbers are in ascending order and display this sorted list.

20. (Project) Suppose that in a certain computer system, jobs submitted for execution are assigned a priority from 1 through 10. Jobs with the highest priorities are executed first, and those of equal priority are executed on a first-come-first-served basis. The operating system maintains a priority queue of *job control blocks*, each of which is a record storing certain information about a particular job, such as its priority, a job identifier, its time of arrival, and the expected execution time. Write a program to simulate the operation of this system. It should read or generate randomly a sequence of job control blocks containing at least the four items of information just given (ordered according to time of arrival), storing them in a priority queue until they can be executed. A simulated clock can be advanced by the expected execution time for a job to simulate its execution. Your program should calculate the turnaround time for each job, the average turnaround time, and any other statistics you care to use to measure the performance of the system (average wait time, amount of time the CPU is idle between jobs, and so on). You may assume *nonpreemptive* scheduling, in which the execution of a given job is not preempted by the arrival of a job of higher priority.

SECTION 11.3

For Probs. 21–27, write a driver program to test the given function.

21. The modified `Quicksort()` function in Exercise 7.

22. The modified `Quicksort()` function in Exercise 8.

23. The modified `Quicksort()` function in Exercise 9.

24. The modified `Split()` function in Exercise 10.

25. The nonrecursive `Quicksort()` function in Exercise 11.

26. The function for finding the median of a list in Exercise 12.

27. The function for finding the kth smallest element of a set in Exercise 13.

SECTION 11.4

For Probs. 28–30, write a driver program to test the given functions.

28. The *Split, Merge*, and *Mergesort* functions for files in Exercise 18.

29. The *Split, Merge*, and *Mergesort* functions for lists stored in arrays or `vector`s in Exercise 19.

30. The *Split*, *Merge*, and *Mergesort* functions for linked lists in Exercise 20.

31. Suppose that a file contains employee records containing the following items of information in the order given:

Id number

Last name, first name, and middle initial

Street address

City, state, and zip (or postal) code

Phone number

Gender

Age

Number of dependents

Department category (factory, office, sales)

Indicator of whether employee is a union member

An hourly pay rate

Write a program to read these employee records and sort them using mergesort so that the id numbers are in ascending order.

32. Write a driver program to test the function for the modified mergesort scheme in Exercise 21.

33. Write a driver program to test the three-way merge function in Exercise 22.

34. Use the function in Exercise 22 to merge three files of records containing names and phone numbers, sorted so that the names are in alphabetical order. For duplicate entries in the files, put only one entry in the final file.

35. Use the function in Exercise 22 in a program that performs a *ternary mergesort*, which differs from binary mergesort in that three files rather than two are used to split a given file.

36. Write a program to compare the computing times of binary mergesort and natural mergesort for files of randomly generated integers.

37. **Polyphase sort** is another external sorting scheme of the mergesort variety. A simple version of it begins by merging one-element subfiles in two files, *F1* and *F2*, forming sorted subfiles of size 2 in a third file, *F3*. However, only enough subfiles are merged to empty one of *F1 and F2*—say, *F1*. The remaining one-element subfiles in *F2* are then merged with the two-element subfiles in *F3* to produce subfiles of length 3 and are written to *F1* until *F2* becomes empty. The remaining two-element subfiles of *F3* are then merged with three-element subfiles of *F2* to form subfiles of length 5 in *F1* until the end of *F3* becomes empty. This process continues until the sorting is complete.

Note that the sequence of subfile lengths in polyphase sort is 1, 1, 2, 3, 5, 8, 13, 21, 34, . . . , the sequence of *Fibonacci numbers* (see Sec. 6.1). The final subfile length (which is also the size of the original file *F3* to be sorted) must therefore be some Fibonacci number f_n. It also follows that the sizes of the initial files *F1* and *F2* must be the two Fibonacci numbers f_{n-1} and f_{n-2}, which precede f_n. Rewrite the program in Prob. 31 to sort the file of employee records using polyphase sort, adding "dummy" subfiles to either *F1* or *F2* if necessary to make their sizes two consecutive Fibonacci numbers and removing them when sorting is completed.

38. (Project) Write a program to read titles of books or magazine articles and prepare a KWIC (Key Word In Context) index. Each word in a title, except for such simple words as AND, OF, THE, and A, is considered to be a keyword. The program should read the titles and construct a file containing the keywords together with the corresponding title, sort the file using the mergesort method, and then display the KWIC index. For example, the titles

FUNDAMENTALS OF PROGRAMMING
PROGRAMMING FUNDAMENTALS FOR DATA STRUCTURES

should produce the following KWIC index:

DATA STRUCTURES // PROGRAMMING FUNDAMENTALS FOR
FUNDAMENTALS FOR DATA STRUCTURES // PROGRAMMING
OF PROGRAMMING
PROGRAMMING FUNDAMENTALS FOR DATA STRUCTURES
// FUNDAMENTALS OF
STRUCTURES // PROGRAMMING FUNDAMENTALS FOR DATA

Chapter 12

OOP AND ADTs

Up to now most of the classes we have developed were built "from scratch." In this chapter we introduce the important OOP concept of *inheritance* and show how one class can be reused in building other classes. The focus of this chapter will be on how inheritance can facilitate the design and development of abstract data types. We will study in detail how one class can be derived from another class. We will then look at an important new aspect of inheritance—*polymorphism*—and at how virtual functions in C++ make it possible to extend the "A" in ADT, that is, how some abstract data types can be made still more abstract (i.e., separate from any implementations). In the same way that class templates and function templates make it possible to "abstract away" the *types* of elements in an ADT, virtual functions make it possible to abstract away the *operations*.

12.1   A BRIEF HISTORY AND OVERVIEW OF OOP AND ADTs

The features built into imperative programming languages such as Pascal and C facilitate the development of *structured* programs. As we noted in Chap. 1, structured programs are easier to develop and maintain than unstructured ones, and as a result, structured programming techniques were widely used in program development for several years. As the complexity of software systems increased, however, it became necessary to divide them into simpler modules that could be developed, compiled, and tested separately before they were integrated to form larger systems. This led to the introduction of new structures into programming languages such as modules in Modula-2, units in Turbo Pascal, libraries in Fortran and C, and packages in Ada. As the number and complexity of software systems continued to increase, it became clear that development cost could be reduced if portions of existing software could be extended and reused in developing new software systems. This notion of software *extensibility* and *reuseability* together with the techniques of structured and modular programming are fundamental concepts in object-oriented programming. Its goals are to improve programmer productivity by making it easier to reuse and extend software and to manage its complexity, thereby reducing the cost of developing and maintaining software.

The term *object-oriented programming* was first used to describe the programming environment for Smalltalk, one of the earliest true object-oriented programming languages. As more object-oriented languages such as C++ and Java have appeared, object-oriented programming methods have become more generally available, making this new programming paradigm the *modus operandi* in programming and system development.

OOP languages have three important properties that characterize them as true object-oriented programming languages:

- ▶ *Encapsulation*
- ▶ *Inheritance*
- ▶ *Polymorphism*, with the related concept of *dynamic* or *late binding*

In this section we briefly describe and illustrate each of these fundamental characteristics.

ENCAPSULATION

A central theme of this text is the study of abstract data types, but we also are interested in the structures provided in programming languages for implementing ADTs, that is, in features provided for converting *abstract data types* into *concrete data types*. One of the trademarks of an ADT is its *encapsulation* of data and basic operations used for processing this data within a single entity. The structures provided in programming language for defining concrete data types should reflect this property by making it possible to encapsulate both data and operations. This was not one of the strengths of early imperative languages, but it became possible with the introduction of units, modules, libraries, and packages.

Another key feature of abstract data types is that they are defined independently of implementations, and some of the concrete realizations of ADTs reflect this *definition-implementation separation*. For example, units in Turbo Pascal have an interface part in which the definition of an ADT can be expressed and an implementation part to contain the functions and procedures for the basic operations. Similarly, modules in Modula-2 have a definition part and an implementation part; and packages in Ada consist of a specification part and a body (implementation part). In each case the interface or definition part contains *public* information that is accessible to outside clients, and the implementation part contains *private* information that is accessible only within the structure. This separation of a concrete data type's definition from its implementation makes it possible to hide the private implementation details so that a user of the data type is forced to process the data items using only the basic operations defined for that type. Another benefit of this separation is that the implementation may be changed without having to change the programs, subprograms, modules, or units that use the data type.

In object-oriented programming languages, ADTs can be implemented with *classes*, which have the encapsulation property together with the public-private separation that it entails. The operations that are defined on class objects are *member functions* or *methods* (as they are called in Smalltalk and Java), which play the same role as procedures and functions in non-object-oriented languages. The process of calling one of these member functions to modify the data stored in the object is referred to as *sending a message* to the object. For example, if *Stack* is one of the several stack classes (or templates) we have studied and *s* is an object of type *Stack*, then to remove the top element of *s*, we send a message to *s* instructing it to pop its top element. Similarly, to add a new element to this stack, we send a message to *s* telling it to push an element onto itself. Note the shift from a procedure/function-oriented approach to a data-oriented one: Instead of passing the stack *s* to a procedure or function that performs some operation on *s*, we send a message to the object (data) *s* asking it to *perform an operation on itself*. Object-oriented programming thus focuses on the data to be processed rather than on the subprograms that do the processing.

INHERITANCE

Classes also provide the second important property of object-oriented programming, *inheritance*. A class can be derived from another class, and this **derived class** (or **subclass**) then inherits the members of the parent class. For example, suppose that we need to design a class for modeling hunting licenses and that there is already available a class License for processing licenses in general. We could, of course, develop a completely new class HuntingLicense, but this would probably duplicate much of the code of the class License already developed.

The object-oriented approach is to derive the class HuntingLicense from the class License and *reuse* the members inherited from the parent class. For example, the class License has data members for storing various items of information about a person—name, age, birth date, address, and so on—and basic operations such as input and output of some or all of this information. The class HuntingLicense stores this same information and probably has some of the same operations. But it will most likely have additional data members—type of prey for which it is valid, dates when hunting is permitted, and so forth—and new or revised function members. For example, HuntingLicense will need a new constructor because it has new data members. Also, the input operation might request input of all the information required for licenses in general, but also input of the type of prey, and so we must provide an input operation for HuntingLicense that revises the input operation inherited from the class License.

POLYMORPHISM AND DYNAMIC BINDING

Polymorphism (from the Greek, meaning "many forms") and the related concept of *dynamic* (or *late*) *binding* is the third important property of object-oriented programming. We have already seen examples of polymorphic behavior in functions:

▶ A function name can be overloaded to denote several different functions.

▶ A function template can be a pattern for many different actual functions.

We have also seen polymorphic behavior in connection with classes.

▶ A class template can be a pattern for many different classes.

In each case the compiler determines the correct function or instance of a class to use.

In object-oriented programming, polymorphism has a different meaning. We will describe it more precisely later, but for now we will simply illustrate it with an example. Both of the classes `License` and `HuntingLicense` will have an output function, but it must perform differently for each of them. We could, of course, use different names for this function, but we would prefer using the same name such as `Display()`. This function is an example of a *polymorphic function*; it has the same prototype in both class declarations, but it can result in different actions for the two classes. It performs one way for a `HuntingLicense` object and in a different manner for a `License` object.

In the examples of polymorphic behavior of functions given earlier, the compiler can select which is the correct version of the function to use wherever the function is called. This is referred to as **static** (or **early**) **binding** of the code for a function to the function call. However, there are times when the version of a polymorphic function like `Display()` to use for a function call cannot be determined until run time. This is what is meant by **dynamic** (or **late**) **binding**. For example, for a variable declared by

```
HuntingLicense h;
```

the compiler can determine that in the function call

```
h.Display();
```

the version of `Display()` defined for class `HuntingLicense` must be used; it can bind this version to this function call at compile time. In contrast, a pointer `ptr` might point to either a `HuntingLicense` object or a `License` object. The compiler cannot determine which `Display()` function to use; this decision cannot be made until execution. In Sec. 12.3 we will look at how virtual functions in C++ make dynamic binding possible.

In summary:

> Object-oriented programming focuses on how the implementations of abstract data types are encapsulated using classes and how these classes can be organized in hierarchies so that their common properties can be reused by derived classes by means of inheritance and shared by means of polymorphism.

✔ Quick Quiz 12.1

1. Name and define the three fundamental concepts of object-oriented programming.
2. The _____ of data and basic operations within a single entity is one of the key properties of ADTs.
3. Calling a member function in an object is referred to as sending a(n) _____ to the object.
4. A derived class _____ the members of the parent class.
5. The word _____ means "many forms."
6. _____ binding is done at compile time; _____ binding is done at run time.

12.2 INHERITANCE AND OBJECT-ORIENTED DESIGN

In Chap. 1 we described an approach to problem solving for which we coined the name Object-Centered Design (OCD) because it is consistent with and leads to object-oriented programming:

1. Identify the *objects* in the problem's specification and their types

2. Identify the *operations* needed to solve the problem

3. Arrange the *operations* in a sequence of steps, called an *algorithm*, which, when applied to the objects, will solve the problem

We begin this section by showing how OCD evolves into full-fledged object-oriented design.

FROM OCD TO OOD

The first inadequacy in OCD is in Step 2: The required operations may not be available. Once we know about functions, we move into the second stage of OCD, where Step 2 is modified as follows:

2. Identify the *operations* needed to solve the problem.
 If an operation is not available, define a function to perform that operation.

The next shortcoming of OCD has to do with Step 1: The required types may not be available. Classes then move us into the third stage of OCD, where Step 1 is extended:

1. Identify the *objects* in the problem's specification and their types.
 If a type is not available, design a new type using classes.

Inheritance leads to the fourth and final stage of OCD, producing true **Object-Oriented Design** (**OOD**), which is the focus of this chapter. We briefly described C++'s inheritance mechanism in the preceding section and illustrated how it makes it possible for a class to inherit the data members and function members of another class.

An important objective in OOP languages is writing reuseable code. Some of the ways we have done this in C++ are:

▶ Encapsulating code within *functions*

▶ Building *classes* to represent the nontrivial objects in a problem

▶ Storing classes and functions in *separately-compiled libraries*

▶ Converting functions into *type-parameterized function templates*

▶ Converting classes into *type-parameterized class templates*

But the method of achieving reuseability that most distinguishes OOP from other approaches is based on **inheritance**

▶ Reuse the work done in building one class to build another class that is just a variation of the first class.

If we invest time and effort in building a class and then need to build another one that is a variation of the first, we should be able to capitalize on our investment.
 To illustrate, suppose that we have available to us a time-tested class, but a problem requires operations that this class does not provide. One approach might be to

add new member functions to this class that implement the needed operations. However, when we do this, we are tampering with a tested and operational class, and it may happen that clients using this class no longer compile correctly after we add our new operations.

By contrast, the object-oriented approach is to *derive* the new class from the class already available, called the *base* or *parent* class. By doing so, the derived class inherits the members of the base class, including its operations, so that we need not reimplement these operations. Moreover, any mistakes we make in the construction of the derived class will be local to it—our original base class remains unsoiled and programs that use it are unaffected by our work.

Object-oriented design thus exploits this capability to build objects in which shared attributes are stored in a base class, and attributes unique to a given object are stored in a derived class used to define the particular object. This leads, therefore, to the following description of OOD:

1. Identify the objects in the problem.
2. Analyze the objects to determine if there is *commonality* in them.
3. Where there is commonality:
     a. *Define base classes that contain this commonality.*
     b. *Derive classes that inherit this commonality from the base class.*

Steps 2 and 3 are the most difficult aspects of OOD to master:

EXAMPLE 1 OF OOD: LICENSES

Suppose we work for the state licensing bureau and we want to model the various kinds of licenses in software like those described in the preceding section. We could design a separate class for each possible license independently, but this would involve a lot of code duplication since licenses have many attributes in common. So we begin with the important question in OOD:

What attributes do the objects (licenses) in this problem have in common?

Once this is answered, we design a general `License` class to store the attributes and operations that all licenses have in common:

```
class License         // base class
{
//--- Function Members
public:
  void Display(ostream & out) const;
  void Read(istream & in);
    ...
//--- Data Members
private:                 // we'll change this in a minute
  long myIdNumber;
  string myLastName,
         myFirstName;
```

```
    char myMiddleInitial;
    int myAge;
    Date myBirthDay;    // where Date is a user-defined class
     ...
};
```

Now, there are still various ways we could design the classes for the different kinds of licenses. One way would be to *include* a data member of type License in each class and then add new members for each particular kind of license:

```
class HuntingLicense
{
//--- Function Members
public:
     ...
//--- Data Members
private:
   License common;
   string thePrey;
   Date seasonBegin,
        season End;
   string myWeapon;
     ...
};


class DriversLicense
{
//--- Function Members
public:
     ...
//--- Data Members
private:
   License common;
   int myVehicleType;
   string myRestrictionsCode;
     ...
};


class PetLicense
{
//--- Function Members
public:
     ...
//--- Data Members
private:
   License common;
   string myAnimalType;
     ...
};
```

Using this inclusion technique works, but it is bad design! The structure of these classes says that a HuntingLicense object *has a* License as one of its members but it *is not a* License; a DriversLicense object *has a* License as one of its members but it *is not a* License; and a PetLicense object *has a* License as one of its members but it *is not a* License. What is needed is a mechanism by which HuntingLicense, DriversLicense, and PetLicense objects *are* automatically also License objects.

This mechanism is *inheritance*. We *derive* more specialized license classes from the *base class* License, and add new members to store and operate on their specialized attributes. We have a problem, however:

Data members declared as

    private:

cannot be accessed outside of their class (except by friend functions), not even within derived classes.

But C++ provides a solution:

Data members declared as

    protected:

can be accessed within a derived class, but they remain inaccessible to programs or nonderived classes that use the class (except for friend functions).

So we must change the private section in class License to a **protected section**:

```
class License
{
//--- Function Members
public:
    . . .
//--- Data Members
protected:
    long myNumber;
    string myLastName,
           myFirstName;
    char myMiddleInitial;
    int myAge;
    Date myBirthDay;
    . . .
};
```

Now we can derive classes for the more specialized licenses from `License`:

```
class HuntingLicense : public License
{
//--- Function Members
public:
   ...
//--- Data Members
protected:
   string thePrey;
   Date seasonBegin,
        season End;
   string myWeapon;
   ...
};

class DriversLicense : public License
{
//--- Function Members
public:
   ...
//--- Data Members
protected:
   int myVehicleType;
   char myRestrictionsCode;
   ...
};

class PetLicense : public License
{
//--- Function Members
public:
   ...
//--- Data Members
protected:
   string myAnimalType;
   ...
};
```

Classes like `HuntingLicense`, `DriversLicense`, and `PetLicense` are said to be **derived classes** (or **subclasses** or **child classes**), and the class `License` from which they are derived is called the **base class** (or **superclass** or **parent class**).[1]

The general form of a declaration of a derived class is as follows:

[1]We will refrain from using *subclass* and *superclass* because this terminology can be confusing. Subsets are smaller than a superset, but a derived class will usually contain more members than the base class. It is true, however, that the collection of all derived class objects for a particular derived class will be a subset of the collection of parent class objects; for example, the collection of `HuntingClass` objects is a subset of the collection of `License` objects. However, a `HuntingClass` object will be larger than a `License` object because it contains more members.

DECLARATION OF A DERIVED CLASS

Form:

```
DerivedClassName : kind BaseClassName
{
//--- New functions for derived class
public:
    ...

//--- New data members for derived class
protected:        // or private:
    ...
};
```

where *kind* is one of the following keywords:

    `public` for **public inheritance**
    `private` for **private inheritance**
    `protected` for **protected inheritance**

The Fundamental Property of Derived Classes:

A derived class inherits the members of its base class (and thus inherits the members of all its ancestor classes). It cannot access private members of the base class, and the kind of access it has to the public and protected members depends on the kind of inheritance:

Kind of inheritance	Kind of access in the derived class to the public and protected members of the base class
public	public and protected, respectively
private	private
protected	protected

☞   Public inheritance is the most important and most commonly used kind of inheritance and we will use it in all of our examples. It makes it possible for a derived class to *use public and protected members of the base class just as though they were declared within the derived class itself; a derived-class object* is a *parent-class object.*

    We have used protected sections rather than private ones in the derived classes `HuntingLicense`, `DriversLicense`, and `PetLicense` in case we want to derive "second-level" classes such as:

```
class DeerLicense : public HuntingLicense
{
//--- Function Members
public:
    ...
```

```
//--- Data Members
protected:
   int theBagLimit;
   char usingGun_MuzzleLoader_Bow;

   . . .
};
```

`DeerLicense` is derived from the base class `HuntingLicense` and thus inherits the members of `HuntingLicense`, which is in turn derived from the base class `License` and thus inherits the members of `License`. `DeerLicense` is thus derived indirectly from `License` and inherits its members. In the case of public inheritance, a `DeerLicense` *is a* `HuntingLicense`, which *is a* `License`. We say that `DeerLicense` is a **descendant** of `License` and that `License` is an **ancestor** of `DeerLicense`.

This leads to **class hierarchies** like that pictured in the following diagram, in which an arrow is drawn from each derived class to its base class:

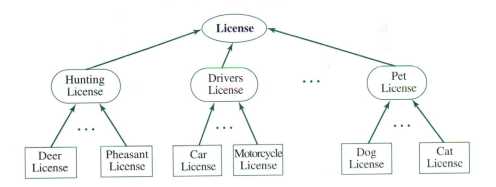

Each derived class inherits the members of its ancestor classes.

The OOD approach given earlier in this section could thus be rephrased as follows:

1. Identify the objects in the problem.
2. Carefully analyze the objects from the bottom up to determine if there is *commonality* in them.
3. Where commonality exists, group the common attributes into a base class

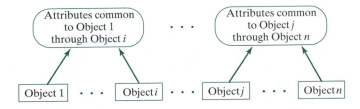

Then repeat this approach upwards as appropriate:

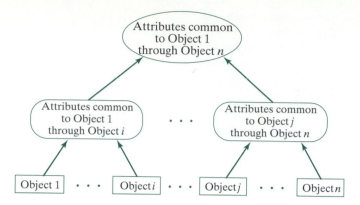

THE IS-A, HAS-A, AND USES-A RELATIONSHIPS BETWEEN CLASSES

The primary idea governing the use of public inheritance is the **is-a relationship**: If a class is derived from a base class

```
class BaseClass : public DerivedClass
{
    // ... members of DerivedClass  ...
};
```

then a `DerivedClass` object inherits all of the members of `BaseClass` except its private members, and these can be accessed within a `DerivedClass` object. Conceptually (and as far as the C++ compiler is concerned),

A derived-class object *is a* base-class object.

For example:

A `HuntingLicense` *is a* `License`

A `DeerLicense` *is a* `HuntingLicense`

A `DeerLicense` *is a* `License`

☞ *Public inheritance should be used when and only when analysis of the problem reveals that an is-a relationship exists between objects*, that is, when one object is a special case of another object; it should not be used otherwise. It would not be proper, for example, to derive a class `PedigreeCertificate` from the class `License` even though it might have data members much like those in `PetLicense`, because a pedigree certificate *is not a* license. *Using public inheritance merely to avoid some code writing is not acceptable.*

Other relationships besides *is-a* may exist between objects in a problem. For example, one of the data members of class `License` is `myBirthdate` of type `Date`, which is a user-defined class; that is, a `License` *has a* `Date` object as one of its members. This is an example of a **has-a relationship** between classes (also called an **inclusion** or **containment** relationship or **class composition**). We might picture it in our class-hierarchy diagram by using a different kind of arrow connecting classes `License` and `Date`: [2]

[2]This is a simplified variation of *Booch notation* developed by Grady Booch, who is well-known for his approaches to object-oriented software development. For example, see Grady Booch, *Object-Oriented Analysis and Design,* 2d ed., Benjamin-Cummings, 1994.

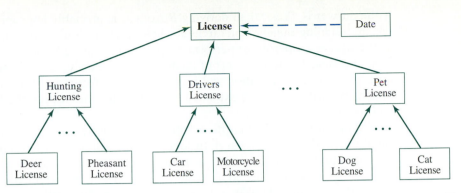

☞ *Public inheritance should not be used for has-a relationships between classes.* For example, a class `AirlinePilot` should not be derived from `License` because an airline pilot *is not a* `License`. Rather, an airline pilot *has a* license, so including a data member of type `License` in class `AirlinePilot` is appropriate for implementing this *has-a* relationship.

Not Acceptable:

```
class AirlinePilot : public License // NO!!!
{
    .  .  .
};
```

Acceptable:

```
class AirlinePilot
{
    .  .  .
    // Data Members
    private:
        License myPilotsLicense;
        .  .  .
};
```

A third kind of relationship between classes is the **uses-a relationship**. A class might simply use another class. For example, one of the operations in a class `AutoInsurance` might need information from a person's drivers license. To obtain this information, an object of type `DriversLicense` might be passed to this operation. The class `AutoInsurance` therefore *uses* the `DriversLicense` class, but it is not a `DriversLicense` nor does it have a `DriversLicense` data member.

Sometimes, however, it is not so easy to determine which of these relationships (if any) hold between objects in a problem. Two other tests are sometimes helpful in this regard.[3] One is to look at the operations in the objects. Suppose that we are trying to decide whether to derive a class *B* from a class *A*.

☞   **1.** Do the public member functions from the proposed base class *A* behave properly in the proposed derived class *B*?

---

[3]Thanks to Ralph Ewton for passing these along.

If the answer is "Yes," then deriving B from A is probably appropriate. For example, in designing the class hierarchy for licenses, one would most likely find that all of the License operations perform properly for hunting licenses. It may be necessary, of course, to modify some of them to process new data members; for example, a License output operation will output correct information for HuntingLicense objects but will need to be extended to output the kind of prey, the hunting season, and so on.

If some of the operations do not perform properly, then one must question the suitability of deriving B from A. In some cases, it will be clear that inheritance is not appropriate. For example, most pet license operations would not work correctly with pedigree certificates, so deriving PedigreeCertificate from PetLicense is out of the question. However, there always will be borderline cases in which one must evaluate just how well A operations work with B objects.

A second test that is useful in determining whether a class for B objects should be derived from a class for A objects is a *need-a . . . use-a* test:

☞   **2.** If all you need is an A object, can you use a B object?

For example, if all you need is a license, can you use a hunting license? Yes, so it's probably okay to derive the class HuntingLicense from the class License. If all you need is a pet license, can you use a dog license? Yes, so it's probably okay to derive the class DogLicense from the class PetLicense. If all you need is a license, can you use a pedigree certificate? No, so deriving a class PedigreeCertificate from a class License is not appropriate. If all you need is a license, can you use an airline pilot? No, so one should not derive a class AirlinePilot from the class License. But again there will be gray areas where the answer is not so obvious. Example 3 later in this section will illustrate this.

EXAMPLE 2 OF OOD: PAYROLL

Suppose we are instructed to write a payroll program. Following the steps of object-oriented design, we might proceed as follows:

1. Identify the objects in the problem. Suppose there are two pay categories:

- ▸ Salaried employees
- ▸ Hourly employees

2. Look for *commonality* in those objects. What attributes do they share?

For simplicity, we will use only the following three attributes:

- ▸ Id number
- ▸ Name
- ▸ Department

3a. Define a *base class* containing the common data members:

```
class Employee
{
//--- Function Members
public:
// ... various Employee operations ...
```

```
//--- Data Members
protected:
  long myIdNum;                   // Employee's id number
  string myLastName,              //      "      last name
         myFirstName;             //      "      first name
  char myMiddleInitial;           //      "      middle initial
  int myDeptCode;                 //      "      department code

  // ... other members common to all Employees

};
```

3b. From the base class, *derive* classes containing special attributes

▶ A salaried employee class

```
class SalariedEmployee : public Employee
{
//--- Function Members
public:
// ... salaried employee operations ...

//--- Data Members
protected:
  double mySalary;
};
```

▶ An hourly employee class:

```
class HourlyEmployee : public Employee
{
//--- Function Members
public:
// ... hourly employee operations ...

//--- Data Members
protected:
  double myWeeklyWage,
         myHoursWorked,
         myOverTimeFactor;
};
```

Inheritance is appropriate here because obviously a salaried employee *is an* employee and an hourly employee *is an* employee.

Because each `SalariedEmployee` and `HourlyEmployee` object is an `Employee` object, each inherits all of the data members and function members from the base class `Employee` (because none of them is private in the base class). For example, if `Employee` has a public operation to extract `myIdNum`

```
inline long Employee::IdNumber() const
{ return myIdNum; }
```

then it can be used by salaried and hourly employees:

```
SalariedEmployee salEmp;
HourlyEmployee hourlyEmp;
   ...
cout << salEmp.IdNumber() << endl
     << hourlyEmp.IdNumber() << endl;
```

OPERATIONS IN DERIVED CLASSES

A derived class inherits the members of its ancestor classes and adds new members for the specialized characteristics of the objects being modeled. Although the inherited data members should not be modified in the derived class, the inherited member functions can be redefined if necessary. A member function in a derived class might *extend* a member function from an ancestor class so that it performs additional tasks or it might *replace* an ancestor member function so that it performs different tasks.[4]

In extending a member function F() of the base class, a derived class can reuse the work of this function by using a qualified call of the form *BaseClass::F()*. To illustrate, suppose that class Employee has an output member function named Display():

```
void Employee::Display(ostream & out) const
{
   out << myIdNum << ' '
       << myLastName << ", "   << myFirstName << ' '
       << myMiddleInitial << ".\n" << myDeptCode;
}
```

Then in our derived classes, we can extend Display() with new definitions that reuse the Display() function of class Employee:

```
void SalariedEmployee::Display(ostream & out) const
{
   Employee::Display(out);                 //inherited member
   out << "\n$" << mySalary << endl;   //local member
}
```

```
void HourlyEmployee::Display(ostream & out) const
{
   Employee::Display(out);                 //inherited member
   out << "\n$" << myWeeklyWage         //local members
       << endl << myHoursWorked
       << endl << myOverTimeFactor << endl;
}
```

---

[4]Some programming languages do not allow replacement of member functions. Some programmers frown on any modification of inherited member funtions because it changes the *is-a* relationship of a derived class to its base class; they argue that virtual functions (described in Sec. 12.3) were invented for this purpose.

A member function `F()` from an ancestor class can be replaced by defining a new function *DerivedClass*`::F()`. For example, employees working in top-secret research where confidentiality is necessary may not wish to have their names displayed on company reports. In this case we might replace the `Display()` function from the class `Employee` with a new output function in the derived class `SpecialResearcher`:

```
void SpecialResearcher::Display(ostream & out) const
{
   out << myIdNum << "   " << myDeptCode;
}
```

CONSTRUCTORS IN DERIVED CLASSES

Because derived classes usually have data members that are not in the base class, they will need their own constructors to initialize these data members because a base-class constructor initializes only its data members. To illustrate, suppose that one of the constructors in the class `Employee` is as follows:

```
#include "Employee.h"
#include <string>
. . .

// Explicit-Value Constructor
inline Employee
::Employee(long id, string last, string first,
           char initial, int dept)
{
  myIdNum = id;
  myLastName = last;
  myFirstName = first;
  myMiddleInitial = initial;
  myDeptCode = dept;
}
```

The class `SalariedEmployee` inherits the data members `myIdNum`, `myLastName`, `myFirstName`, `myMiddleInitial`, and `myDeptCode` from its base class `Employee` and adds the new data member `mySalary`. We could write a `SalariedEmployee` constructor "from scratch" to initialize these data members. But since the `Employee` constructor was written to initialize its data members, it would be nice if `SalariedEmployee()` could call it, and thus reuse that work.

This can in fact be accomplished by attaching a **member-initializer list** to the heading of the derived class constructor, separating them with a colon (`:`):

```
DerivedClass::DerivedClass(parameter-list)
: member-initializer-list
{
   ...
}
```

In most cases this member-initializer list contains only one item, namely, a call to the base class constructor:

```
: BaseClass(argument-list)
```

For example, we could use the following to define an explicit-value constructor for class SalariedEmployee:

```
// Definition of SalariedEmployee explicit-value constructor

inline SalariedEmployee
::SalariedEmployee(long id, string last, string first,
                   char initial, int dept, double sal)
: Employee(id, last, first, initial, dept)
{
  mySalary = sal;
}
```

The arguments id, last, first, initial, and dept will be passed to the Employee constructor, which will use those values to initialize the data members myIdNum, myLastName, myFirstName, myMiddleInitial, and myDeptCode, respectively. The only task for the constructor in SalariedEmployee is to initialize its member(s), which it does in the usual way.

In general, we use a base class constructor to initialize base class members, and use a derived class constructor to initialize new data members in the derived class. The constructor of a DerivedClass can invoke the constructor of its BaseClass to initialize its inherited members by using the notation

```
DerivedClass::DerivedClass(parameter-list)
: BaseClass(argument-list)
{
   // initialize the noninherited
   // members in the usual manner
}
```

☞ *The initializations by the base-class constructor will be done first*, before those in the body of the derived class constructor.

Some of the new data members in a derived class may be class objects whose constructors must be called to initialize them. The member-initializer list can be used for this as well by using a notation that resembles a function call to that data member:

```
data-member-name(argument-list)
```

For example, suppose that the class SpecialResearcher derived from class Employee has three new data members: myClearance of type SecurityClearance, myProject of type SpecialProject, and myCodeName of type string, where SecurityClearance and SpecialProject are classes. One of the constructors for the derived class SpecialResearcher might be

```
// Definition of SpecialResearcher constructor

SpecialResearcher
::SpecialResearcher(long id, string last, string first,
                    char initial, int dept, double sal)
: Employee(id, last, first, initial, dept),
  myClearance(id, dept),
  myProject()
{
  myCodeName = "";
}
```

In the member-initializer list, myClearance(id, dept) is a call to a constructor in class SecurityClearance with the arguments id and dept and myProject() is a call to the default constructor of class SpecialProject. The members' constructors will be called in the order in which they are declared in the class (not their order in the member-initializer list).

A data member such as myCodeName which is initialized by assignment can also be initialized in the member-initializer list. For example, the preceding constructor could also be written:

```
// Definition of SpecialResearcher constructor

SpecialResearcher
::SpecialResearcher(long id, string last, string first,
                    char initial, int dept, double sal)
: Employee(id, last, first, initial, dept),
  myClearance(id, dept),
  myProject(),
  myCodeName()
{}
```

When a member constructor needs no arguments it need not be included in the member-initializer list; thus we could omit myProject() in the initializer list of either of the preceding definitions of the SpecialResearcher constructor; for example

```
SpecialResearcher
::SpecialResearcher(long id, string last, string first,
                    char initial, int dept, double sal)
: Employee(id, last, first, initial, dept),
  myClearance(id, dept)
{
  myCodeName = "";
}
```

EXAMPLE 3 OF OOD: BOUNDED STACKS

As we noted earlier, in analyzing some problems we are bound to encounter borderline cases where the relationship between some of the problem's objects is not clear; is it *is-a*, *has-a*, *uses-a*, or none of these? To illustrate, suppose that some application requires the use of stacks having a limited size and we must design a class template `BoundedStack` for these objects. We already have at our disposal STL's `stack` container along with several stack classes that we have developed in earlier chapters. But what is the relationship of a bounded stack to stacks?

Is a bounded stack also a stack? If so we can derive `BoundedStack` from `stack` or from one of the other stack classes. A bounded stack will obviously need the same data members as a stack and a new data member for the bound on the stack size. Also, the empty, top, and pop operations are the same for bounded stacks as for stacks, but the push operation is not. If the bounded stack becomes full, there is no room to push a new item onto it, and so we will need a different push operation. Because of this difference, one might argue that a bounded stack is not a stack, and inheritance is therefore not a good idea. Designing a bounded stack to have a stack as one of its elements would be okay or perhaps we should simply design a `BoundedStack` class from scratch.

On the other hand, push is the only stack operation that will be different in bounded stacks and the required modification can be viewed as an extension of the stack push operation rather than a wholesale replacement:

> If the bounded stack is not full,
> > Push the item onto the bounded stack using
> > the stack push operation.
> Otherwise
> > Display an overflow message.

One could thus argue that a bounded stack is a stack with special properties and inheritance is therefore appropriate.

Suppose we try the need-a ... use-a test. If all we need is a stack, can we use a bounded stack? We probably can, because in practice, all stacks are bounded by the size of the structure used to store the stack elements.[5]

We will opt for the second approach and derive a class template `BoundedStack` from the standard `stack` class template. `BoundedStack` will then inherit the data members (including the underlying default `deque` container) and the function members from `stack`. We will add a new data member `myLimit` to store the limit on the size of a bounded stack, and this means that we will also need a `BoundedStack` constructor to initialize it. We will also need to revise the `push()` operation. Our class declaration will thus have the structure shown in Fig. 12.1.

FIGURE 12.1   `BoundedStack`—INTERFACE

```
#include <iostream>
#include <stack>
using namespace std;

#ifndef BOUNDEDSTACK
#define BOUNDEDSTACK
```

---

[5]Indeed, implementations of all ADTs are bounded by the amount of available memory!

```
template <typename ElementType>
class BoundedStack : public stack<ElementType>
{
/***** Function Members *****/
public:
/* --- Constructor ---
 *
 * Precondition:  A BoundedStack has been declared.
 * Receive:       A limit on the size of the bounded stack
 * Postcondition: The BoundedStack has been constructed
 *                as an empty stack and with its myLimit
 *                data member initialized to limit (default 0).
 ***************************************************************/

BoundedStack(int limit = 0);

/* --- Add a value to the stack if there is room---
 *
 * Receive:    The BoundedStack containing this function
 *                (implicitly)
 *             A value to be added to a BoundedStack
 * Pass back: The BoundedStack (implicitly), with value
 *                added at its top, provided there is room
 * Output:     Overflow message if no room for value*
 ***************************************************************/

void push(const ElementType & value);

/***** Data Members *****/
protected:
  int myLimit;
};  // end of class template declaration

#endif
```

Defining the constructor is simple. We call `stack`'s constructor in a member-initializer list to initialize all of its data members and then assign `myLimit` the specified value `limit` in the body of the `BoundededStack` constructor.

Defining the `push()` operation also is straightforward. We simply check if there is room for the item and if so, use `stack::push()` to add it. If there is no space left, an error message is displayed to signal this overflow condition.

Figure 12.2 shows the definitions of these two member functions. Note the use of the member function `size()` inherited from `stack` to check if the bounded stack is full and the qualified call to `stack<ElementType>::push()` in the definition of `BoundedStack`'s `push()`.

FIGURE 12.2   **BoundedStack—IMPLEMENTATION**

```
      . . .
#ifndef BOUNDEDSTACK
#define BOUNDEDSTACK

template <typename ElementType>
class BoundedStack : public stack<ElementType>
{
      . . .
};  // end of class template declaration

//--- Definition of Constructor ---
template <typename ElementType>
inline BoundedStack<ElementType>::
BoundedStack(int limit)
: stack<ElementType>()
{ myLimit = limit; }

//--- Definition of push() ---
template <typename ElementType>
inline void BoundedStack<ElementType>::
push(const ElementType & value)
{
  if (size() < myLimit)
    stack<ElementType>::push(value);
  else
    cerr << "*** Bounded stack overflow ***\n";
}

#endif
```

To illustrate the use of this derived class BoundedStack, we consider a modification of the base-conversion problem in Sec. 4.1 of converting positive integers from their decimal representation to binary representation. The algorithm for carrying out this conversion uses repeated division by 2 with the successive remainders giving the binary digits in the base-two representation from right to left. A stack was used to store these remainders so they could be displayed in the correct order once the conversion was complete.

Now consider the modified problem of converting integers to binary but in which there is a limit on the number of bits allowed in the base-two representation. For example, we may be interested in binary representations that will fit in 4 bytes, that is, representations with at most 32 bits. This means that if the size of the stack used to store the digits of the base-two representation exceeds this limit, an overflow occurs. A BoundedStack is therefore an appropriate container to use for these bits. Fig. 12.3 shows the program that results by replacing a stack in the program in Fig. 4.1 with a BoundedStack.

FIGURE 12.3   CONVERSION FROM BASE 10 TO BASE 2—VERSION 2

```cpp
/* Program that uses a bounded stack to convert the base-ten
 * representation of a positive integer to base two.  It uses
 * an object StackOfRemainders of type BoundedStack to store
 * and process the remainders produced by the repeated-division
 * algorithm.
 *
 * Input:   A positive integer
 * Output: Base-two representation of the number
 *         Error messages if some bits are lost
 *************************************************************/

#include "BoundedStack"
#include <iostream>
using namespace std;

int main()
{
  const int STACK_LIMIT = 20;           // limit on size of stack

  unsigned number,                      // the number to be converted
           remainder;                   // remainder of number divided by 2
  BoundedStack<short int>
    stackOfRemainders(STACK_LIMIT);     // bounded stack of remainders
  char response;                        // user response
  do
  {
    cout << "Enter positive integer to convert: ";
    cin >> number;

    while (number != 0)
    {
      remainder = number % 2;
      stackOfRemainders.push(remainder);
      number /= 2;
    }

    cout << "WARNING:  If a bounded stack overflow occurred,\n"
         "            some bits are missing in the following.\n";

    cout << "Base-two representation: ";
    while (!stackOfRemainders.empty())
    {
      remainder = stackOfRemainders.top();
      stackOfRemainders.pop();
      cout << remainder;
    }
```

```
        cout << endl;
        cout << "\nMore (Y or N)? ";
        cin >> response;
    }
    while (response == 'Y' || response == 'y');
}
```

SAMPLE RUN:
```
Enter positive integer to convert: 99
WARNING:   If a bounded stack overflow occurred,
           some bits are missing in the following.
Base-two representation: 1100011

More (Y or N)? Y
Enter positive integer to convert: 99999
WARNING:   If a bounded stack overflow occurred,
           some bits are missing in the following.
Base-two representation: 11000011010011111

More (Y or N)? Y
Enter positive integer to convert: 9999999
*** Bounded stack overflow ***
*** Bounded stack overflow ***
*** Bounded stack overflow ***
*** Bounded stack overflow ***
WARNING:   If a bounded stack overflow occurred,
           some bits are missing in the following.
Base-two representation: 10001001011001111111

More (Y or N)? N
```

EXAMPLE 4 OF OOD: SCROLLS

In Chap. 5 we considered a variation of a queue called a **scroll**, which is a sequence of elements in which items can be added at both ends but retrieved and removed at only one end. Because a scroll was introduced as a special kind of queue, it seems clear that a scroll class could be derived from a queue class. Would it be appropriate, however, to derive a `Scroll` class from a stack class?

To answer this question, we might first use the operations test: Do the stack operations behave properly for scrolls?

▸ Will a stack's empty operation also check if a scroll is empty?

▸ Will a stack's push operation add a value at one end of a scroll?

▸ Will a stack's top operation retrieve a value at one end of a scroll?

▸ Will a stack's pop operation remove a value at that same end of a scroll?

Because the answer to each of these questions is "Yes," it seems okay to derive a scroll class from a stack class.

The need-a . . . use-a test also indicates this. If all we need is a stack, can we use a scroll? We surely can, because a scroll can perform all of the stack operations (and more). A scroll is simply a stack with an added operation of removing a value at the other end of the sequence.

It is appropriate therefore to derive a `Scroll` class from a stack class. We leave the details of this derivation as an exercise.

✔ Quick Quiz 12.2

1. The method of achieving reuseability that most distinguishes OOP from other approaches is based on _____.
2. List the main steps in OOD.
3. Members of a base class declared as _____ cannot be accessed in a derived class.
4. Members of a base class declared as _____ can be accessed in a derived class but not by other classes or programs.
5. Protected inheritance is the most common kind of inheritance. (True or false)
6. The primary idea governing the use of public inheritance is the _____ relationship.
7. A(n) _____ can be attached to the heading in the definition of a derived-class constructor to call the base-class constructor and constructors of new data members.

✍ EXERCISES 12.2

1. Contrast public, private, and protected inheritance.
2. Contrast the *is-a*, *has-a*, and *uses-a* relationships between classes.

For Exercises 3–18, determine which of the following best describes the relationship between the given objects: *is-a*, *has-a*, *uses-a*, none of the preceding.

3. Lines and rectangles
4. Squares and rectangles
5. Triangles and rectangles
6. Students at Universal University and GPAs
7. Students and the library at Universal University
8. Professors and employees at Universal University
9. Employees and persons at Universal University
10. Stacks and queues
11. Stacks and deques
12. Queues and deques
13. Binary trees and binary search trees
14. `vector`s and containers
15. Computers and electronic equipment
16. Computers and operating systems
17. Computers and highway systems
18. Computers and CPUs

12.3 POLYMORPHISM, VIRTUAL FUNCTIONS, AND ADTs

The third characteristic of object-oriented programming, *polymorphism*, is the property of a derived class and an ancestor class having a function member in common but that behaves differently in these classes. For example, in Sec. 12.1 we considered a member function `Display()` in the base class `License` and the derived class `HuntingLicense` (as well as other classes derived from `License`) but that behaves differently in these classes. `Display()` is thus a polymorphic function. It produces different output for a `License` object than for a derived-class object; for example:

```
Display() for a License object:
   101011 Betty B. Binary
   Age:  33
   Birthdate:  6/6/1966

Display() for a HuntingLicense object:
   392766 David W. Goliath
   Age: 11
   Birthdate:  8/18/1988
   Prey:   Giants
   Season: 1/1 - 12/31
   Weapon: Sling

Display() for a PetLicense object:
   1781 Chauncy of Oberon
   Age: 2
   Birthdate:  5/24/1997
   Kind:   Bichon+Yorkshire
```

A BINDING PROBLEM

The different versions of the `Display()` function are obtained by modifying its definition in the base class `License` in the derived classes `HuntingLicense`, `DeerLicense`, `PetLicense`, and so on, so that `Display()` will have different definitions for each of these classes. That is, the declarations of these classes will all contain the same prototype for `Display()`,

```
void Display(ostream & out) const;
```

but the definitions of the functions in the derived classes will be different:

```
void License::Display(ostream & out)
{ statements to output a License object }

void HuntingLicense::Display(ostream & out)
{ statements to output a HuntingLicense object }

void DeerLicense::Display(ostream & out)
{ statements to output a DeerLicense object }
```

```
void PetLicense::Display(ostream & out)
{ statements to output a PetLicense object }
        .
        .
        .
```

☞ Simply overriding an inherited member function may not be enough, however. To see this, suppose we wish to define the output operator << for the various types of objects in this license hierarchy. We add a definition to the declaration of class License as follows:

```
class License
{
//--- Function Members
public:
. . .
void Display(ostream & out) const;
. . .
//--- Data Members
  ...
};   // end of class declaration

// Definition of Display
void License::Display(ostream & out) const
{ . . . }

// Definition of output operator<<
ostream & operator<<(ostream & out,
                     const License & lic)
{
  lic.Display(out);
  return out;
}
```

We could overload operator<<() for each of the derived classes, but the code would be almost identical in each class; only the type of the parameter lic needs to be changed.

But there is no need for all this duplication of code, thanks to public inheritance. Although the derived classes cannot inherit operator<<() from the base class License because it is not a member function (and in fact cannot be as we saw in Section 3.2), we can still use operator<<() for objects in the lower levels because each of them *is a* License.

However, there is still a problem. To see what it is, suppose that aLicense, aHuntingLicense, and aPetLicense are the objects of type License, HuntingLicense, and PetLicense whose Display() functions produced the output shown at the beginning of this section. We would expect the statement

```
cout << aLicense << "\n\n"
     << aHuntingLicense << "\n\n"
     << aPetLicense << endl;
```

to produce the output

```
101011 Betty B. Binary
Age:  33
Birthdate:  6/6/1966


392766 David W. Goliath
Age: 11
Birthdate:  8/18/1988
Prey:    Giants
Season: 1/1 - 12/31
Weapon: Sling


1781 Chauncy of Oberon
Age: 2
Birthdate:  5/24/1997
Kind:    Dog—Bichon+Yorkshire
```

However, the following output results instead:

```
101011 Betty O. Binary
Age:  33
Birthdate:  6/6/1966


392766 David W. Goliath
Age: 11
Birthdate:  8/18/1988


1781 Chauncy of Oberon
Age: 2
Birthdate:  5/24/1997
```

None of the values of the new data members in `aHuntingLicense` or `aPetLicense` are displayed but only the values of the data members inherited from `License`.

This happens because the definition of `operator<<()` in `License` calls the member function `Display()` from this class and consequently, the compiler uses the code for the function `Display()` in `License`. Any call to `operator<<()` for a `HuntingLicense` object, a `PetLicense` object, or any other derived-class object must use this same code, which means that the wrong version of `Display()` is being used.

VIRTUAL FUNCTIONS AND DYNAMIC BINDING

What is needed is a mechanism that will use the appropriate version of `Display()` when it is called in `operator<<()`. For a `License` object we want `License::Display()` to be used, but for a `HuntingLicense` object, we want `HuntingLicense::Display()` to be used and for a `PetLicense` object, we want `Pet-`

License::Display() to be used. This means, however, that code cannot be bound to these function calls at compile time. Rather, this must be *deferred until run time*; that is, the selection of which version of Display() to use must be made *during execution* when the type of the object can be determined.

☞ This **dynamic** (or **late**) **binding** is accomplished in object-oriented languages by using **virtual functions**. One common way this is done is to have the compiler create a **virtual function table** (**vtbl**) for each class containing virtual functions; this is a table of pointers to the actual code for these functions. It then associates with each virtual function in a class its index in that class's vtbl. When execution reaches a call to a virtual function for some object, the index for this function in the object's vtbl is used to find the pointer to the correct function code for that type of object.

What is needed to make the function operator<<() work correctly is to make Display() a virtual function in the base class License. In C++, a member function is declared to be virtual simply by preceding its prototype in the class declaration with the keyword **virtual**:

```
class License
{
//--- Function Members
public:
    . . .
virtual void Display(ostream & out) const;
    . . .
//--- Data Members
protected:
    long myNumber;
    string myLastName,
           myFirstName;
    char myMiddleInitial;
    int myAge;
    . . .
};   // end of class declaration

// Definition of Display
void License::Display(ostream & out) const
{ . . . }

// Definition of operator<<()
ostream & operator<<(ostream & out, const License & lic)
{
    lic.Display(out);
    return out;
}
    . . .
```

Now the output statement

```
cout << aLicense << "\n\n"
     << aHuntingLicense << "\n\n"
     << aPetLicense << endl;
```

produces the correct output. We expect the correct output for aLicense since a call to operator<<() for aLicense will invoke operator<<() for class License, which will execute

```
aLicense.Display(cout);
```

and the version used for Display will be License::Display(). The correct output is also produced for aHuntingLicense because it is a HuntingLicense, which *is a* License. A call to operator<<() for aHuntingLicense will thus invoke operator<<() for class License, which will execute

```
aHuntingLicense.Display(cout);
```

and since Display() is a virtual function in License, the version used for Display will be HuntingLicense::Display(). For the same reason, we obtain the correct output for a aPetLicense because a call to operator<<() for class License will execute

```
aPetLicense.Display(cout);
```

and since Display() is a virtual function, the version of Display() that will be selected here is PetLicense::Display().

We see that thanks to public inheritance, virtual functions, and dynamic binding, we can apply operator<<() to derived class objects without explicitly overloading it for those objects! The definitions of Display() in the derived classes **override** the virtual version in the base class License, and calls to operator<<() with derived class objects will select the correct version of Display(). If no definition of Display() is provided in a derived class, then the definition from the base class License will be used. Thus

> The definition of a virtual function in a base class serves as a default definition. It will be used in any derived class in which the definition is not overridden.

EXAMPLE: STACKS, BOUNDED STACKS, AND SCROLLS

As another illustration of a problem where virtual functions are needed, suppose we wish to add a new operation RepeatedPush() to each of the class templates stack, BoundedStack, and Scroll from the preceding section, which can be used to push more than one copy of an element onto an object of one of these types. The code for this function template is the same for each class:

```
template <typename ElementType>
inline void RepeatedPush(const ElementType & value,
                         int number)
{
  for (int i = 1; i <= number; i++)
    push(value);
}
```

So we add this function template to the base stack class `stack` and let the derived classes `BoundedStack` and `Scroll` inherit it. Actually, since `stack` is a standard C++ class, we should not modify it. However, we can derive a class template `Stack` from `stack` to which we can add `RepeatedPush`:

```cpp
#include <stack>
using namespace std;

template <typename ElementType>
class Stack : public stack<ElementType>
{
public:
void RepeatedPush(const ElementType & value, int number);
};

// Definition of RepeatedPush()
template <typename ElementType>
inline void Stack<ElementType>::
RepeatedPush(const ElementType & value, int number)
{
  for (int i = 1; i <= number; i++)
    push(value);
}
```

We can then derive `BoundedStack` and `Scroll` from `Stack`:

```cpp
template <typename ElementType>
class BoundedStack : public Stack<ElementType>
  . . .

template <typename ElementType>
class Scroll : public Stack<ElementType>
  . . .
```

As we might expect from the license example, this does not work. To demonstrate this we consider a variation of the base-conversion problem of the preceding section, in which all of the binary representations must have the same number of bits; for example, 16 bits are commonly used to store short integers and 32 bits are used for long integers. The program in Fig. 12.3 can easily be modified to obtain such representations. We need only count the bits as they are generated and then use `RepeatedPush()` to push the required number of leading zeros onto the stack of remainders, by sending the message

```cpp
stackOfRemainders.RepeatedPush(0, numBits - count)
```

where `count` is the number of bits generated and stored in the bounded stack and `numBits` is the total number of bits in the binary representation. The program in Fig. 12.4 uses this approach to obtain such representations.

FIGURE 12.4   CONVERSION FROM BASE 10 TO BASE 2—VERSION 3

```
/* Program that uses a bounded stack to convert the base-ten
 * representation of a positive integer to base-two numbers
 * that have numBits bits.  It uses an object stackOfRemainders
 * of type BoundedStack to store and process the remainders
 * produced by the repeated-division algorithm.
 *
 * Input:  A positive integer
 * Output: Base-two representation of the number
 *         Error messages if some bits are lost
 ***************************************************************/

#include "BoundedStack"
#include <iostream>
using namespace std;

int main()
{
  const int STACK_LIMIT = 20;     // limit on size of stack

  int numBits;                    // number of bits in binary rep.
  cout << "How many bits do you want in the binary representations? ";
  cin >> numBits;

  unsigned number,                // the number to be converted
           remainder;             // remainder of number divided by 2
  BoundedStack<unsigned>          // bounded stack of remainders
    stackOfRemainders(STACK_LIMIT);
  char response;                  // user response

  do
  {
    cout << "Enter positive integer to convert: ";
    cin >> number;

    int count = 0;                // counts bits in binary representation
    while (number != 0)
    {
      remainder = number % 2;
      stackOfRemainders.push(remainder);
      count++;
      number /= 2;
    }

    // Add leading 0's to obtain a representation
    // having exactly numBits bits
    stackOfRemainders.RepeatedPush (0, numBits - count);
```

```
      cout << "WARNING:   If a bounded stack overflow occurred,\n"
              "              some bits are missing in the following.\n";
      cout << "Base-two representation: ";
      while (!stackOfRemainders.empty() )
      {
        remainder = stackOfRemainders.top();
        stackOfRemainders.pop();
        cout << remainder;
      }

      cout << endl;
      cout << "\nMore (Y or N)? ";
      cin >> response;
   }
   while (response == 'Y' || response == 'y');
}
```

SAMPLE RUN:

```
How many bits do you want in the binary representations? 16
Enter positive integer to convert:   63
WARNING:   If a bounded stack overflow occurred,
           some bits are missing in the following.
Base-two representation:   0000000000111111

More (Y or N)?   Y
Enter positive integer to convert:   1
WARNING:   If a bounded stack overflow occurred,"
           some bits are missing in the following.
Base-two representation:   0000000000000001

More (Y or N)?   N
```

Based on this sample run we may be tempted to conclude that the program and the class templates `Stack` and `BoundedStack` are correct. However, this is not the case, as the following sample run shows:

```
How many bits do you want in the binary representations? 32
Enter positive integer to convert:   63
WARNING:   If a bounded stack overflow occurred,
           some bits are missing in the following.
Base-two representation:   00000000000000000000000000111111

More (Y or N)?   N
```

In the program the stack limit was set at 20, which means that no more than 20 elements can ever be pushed onto the `BoundedStack` `stackOfRemainders`. The output clearly indicates, however, that 32 bits were somehow pushed onto the stack, even though the capacity of the stack was exceeded. This happened because the definition of `RepeatedPush()` in `Stack` uses the function `push()` from this class and consequently, the code generated by the compiler and bound to `RepeatedPush()` contains the code for the function `push()` in `Stack`. Any reference to `RepeatedPush()` in the derived class `BoundedStack` must use this same code, which means that the wrong version of `push()` is being used, so that the stack limit is ignored when pushing elements onto the stack. This is also the case for the derived class template `Scroll`. Any reference to `RepeatedPush()` in a `Scroll` object would use `push()` from the ancestor class template `Stack` rather than the `push()` from `Scroll`.

To make the function `RepeatedPush()` work correctly, we need to make `push()` a virtual function in the base class template `Stack` as shown in Fig. 12.5. Also shown is a sample run of the program in Fig. 12.4 with this new version of `Stack`.

FIGURE 12.5   CONVERSION FROM BASE 10 TO BASE 2—VERSION 4

```cpp
// Revised version of Stack class template

#include <stack>
using namespace std;

template <typename ElementType>
class Stack : public stack<ElementType>
{
public:
virtual void push(const ElementType & value);
void RepeatedPush(const ElementType & value, int number);
};

// Definition of push()
template <typename ElementType>
inline void Stack<ElementType::
push(const ElementType & value)
{
   stack<ElementType>::push(value);
}

// Definition of RepeatedPush()
template <typename ElementType>
inline void Stack<ElementType>::
RepeatedPush(const ElementType & value, int number)
{
   for (int i = 1; i <= number; i++)
     push(value);
}
```

SAMPLE RUN OF FIG. 12.4:

```
How many bits do you want in the binary representations? 32
Enter positive integer to convert: 63
*** Bounded stack overflow ***
*** Bounded stack overflow ***
*** Bounded stack overflow ***
*** Bounded stack overflow ***
*** Bounded stack overflow ***
*** Bounded stack overflow ***
*** Bounded stack overflow ***
*** Bounded stack overflow ***
*** Bounded stack overflow ***
*** Bounded stack overflow ***
*** Bounded stack overflow ***
*** Bounded stack overflow ***
WARNING:  If a bounded stack overflow occurred,
          some bits are missing in the following.
Base-two representation: 00000000000000111111

More (Y or N)? N
```

The output in Fig. 12.5 shows that `RepeatedPush()` for objects of type `BoundedStack` now does use the definition of `push()` for this derived class. When `RepeatedPush()` attempted to push 26 leading zeros onto the bounded stack `stackOfRemainders`, the function `push()` for bounded stacks was called 26 times, and the last 12 calls produced a message that the stack limit was exceeded. The 20 bits in the final base-two representation rather than the thirty-two bits obtained before also demonstrate that the correct method `push()` has been used.

Calls to `RepeatedPush()` in a program that uses objects of type `Stack` will use the `push()` function for the class `Stack`. Thus, if we change the first `#include` directive in the program of Fig. 12.5 to

```
#include "Stack"
```

and the declaration of the variable `stackOfRemainders` to

```
Stack<unsigned> stackOfRemainders;
```

execution of the program produces

```
How many bits do you want in the binary representations? 32
Enter positive integer to convert:   31
WARNING:  If a bounded stack overflow occurred,
          some bits are missing in the following.
Base-two representation:  00000000000000000000000000011111
```

PURE VIRTUAL FUNCTIONS AND ABSTRACT CLASSES

Most classes are like those we have been considering—License, Employee, and Stack—in that they themselves model real-world things and objects of these types are useful for processing such entities; but these classes can also serve as base classes from which other useful classes can be derived. Sometimes, however, it is convenient to have *classes for which no objects can exist*. They represent only abstract concepts and are thus called *abstract classes*. They can *only* serve as base classes from which other classes can be derived. For example, in a hierarchy of classes for drawing geometric figures, we might have a base class Figure containing some of the common operations such as draw, rotate, move, and so on for these figures. We do not intend, however, for Figure objects to exist. Instead we derive concrete classes for specific figures such as circles, rectangles, and triangles from Figure. The abstract base class Figure serves as an interface for all of these derived classes.

An **abstract class** is one in which no definition is provided for one or more of the member functions, which are called **pure virtual functions**. In C++ a virtual function is specified to be a pure virtual function by appending the initializer = 0 to its prototype. A class derived from an abstract class *must* provide definitions of these pure virtual functions or else it also is an abstract class.

As a simple illustration, suppose that we create an abstract class Form that contains some of the common operations for forms, for example, input and output operations:

```
class Form
{
// Function Members
 public:
   virtual void Display(ostream & out) const = 0;
   virtual void Read(istream & in) = 0;
   . . .
}; // end of abstract-class declaration
```

We could then derive the class License from it,

```
class License : public Form
{
//--- Function Members
public:
. . .
virtual void Display(ostream & out) const;
. . .
//--- Data Members
   . . .
};   // end of class declaration

// Definition of Display
void License::Display(ostream & out) const
{ . . . }
```

and probably base classes for other class heirarchies as well:

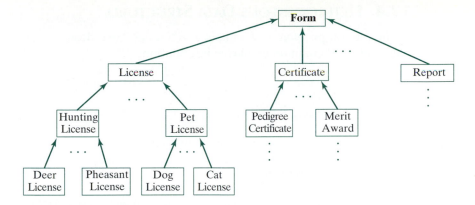

The abstract class `Form` thus serves as a common interface for all of classes in this hierarchy. If we define the output operator function `operator<<()` for the class `Form` (instead of `License`), we can use it to output an object of any of the derived classes in this hierarchy (provided they use public inheritance).

✔ Quick Quiz 12.3

1. What is polymorphism?
2. Tying the code for a function to a function call at compile time is called _____ binding.
3. _____ functions are used to accomplish _____ binding, which means that the selection of the code to use for a function is deferred until run time.
4. Vtbl stands for _____ .
5. A(n) _____ class is a class for which there are no objects. It must have at least one _____ function.

✎ EXERCISES 12.3

The following exercises ask you to develop classes or class templates. You should also write driver programs to test them as instructed in the Programming Problems at the end of this chapter.

1. Administrative employees are paid a salary, but they also receive a bonus at regular intervals during the year. Add a class `Administrator` to the `Employee` class hierarchy described in the text.

2. Factory workers are paid a certain amount for each unit they make and their total pay is the number of units produced times the pay per unit. Add a class `FactoryEmployee` to the `Employee` class hierarchy described in the text.

3. Salespersons are paid a salary plus a commission on their sales; their total pay, therefore, is their salary plus the amount of their sales times the commission rate. Add a class `SalesPerson` to the `Employee` class hierarchy described in the text.

4. Derive a `Scroll` class template from the `Stack` class template described in the text.

5. Derive a `Deque` class template from the `Stack` class template described in the text.

6. Design `LookAheadStack` as a class template derived from `Stack`. A look-ahead stack differs from a standard stack only in the push operation. An item is added to the stack by the push method only if it is different from the top stack element.

12.4 HETEROGENEOUS DATA STRUCTURES

In the payroll problem of Example 2 in Sec. 12.2, we designed an `Employee` class that contained common employee information:

```
class Employee
{
//--- Function Members
public:
// ... various Employee operations ...

//--- Data Members
protected:
   long myIdNum;              // Employee's id number
   string myLastName,         //     "       last name
         myFirstName;         //     "       first name
   char myMiddleInitial;      //     "       middle initial
   int myDeptCode;            //     "       department code

   //  ... other members common to all Employees

};
```

We also derived two classes, one for salaried employees and one for hourly employees:

```
class SalariedEmployee : public Employee
{
//--- Function Members
public:
// ... salaried employee operations ...

//--- Data Members
protected:
   double mySalary;
};

class HourlyEmployee : public Employee
{
//--- Function Members
public:
// ... hourly employee operations ...

//--- Data Members
protected:
   double myWeeklyWage,
          myHoursWorked,
          myOverTimeFactor;
};
```

Suppose now that we want to process a linked list `empList` of employees:

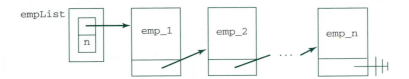

Because each value in the list has the same type (`Employee`), such a list is called a **homogeneous** structure. All of the data structures we have studied thus far have been homogeneous.

CREATING HETEROGENEOUS DATA STRUCTURES

Suppose we declare `empList` as a `LinkedList` of `Employee` objects,

```
LinkedList<Employee> empList;
```

where `LinkedList` is a class template like that in Sec. 8.6 (or we could use the standard `list` class template: `list<Employee> empList;`). Then each node of `empList` will only have space for an `Employee` with no space for the additional data members of an hourly or salaried employee. However, inheritance and derivation make it possible to build structures that are **heterogeneous** in that they *can store objects of different types*.

What makes this possible is the following property of pointers and derived classes

> *A base-class pointer can point to any derived class object.*

For example, suppose that `eptr` is a pointer to an `Employee`:

```
Employee * eptr;
```

Because a `SalariedEmployee` *is an* `Employee`, `ePtr` can point to a `Salaried Employee` object,

```
eptr = new SalariedEmployee;
```

or `eptr` can point to an `HourlyEmployee` object:

```
eptr = new HourlyEmployee;
```

From this we see that if instead of a `LinkedList` of `Employee` objects, we declare `empList` as a `LinkedList` of `Employee` *pointers*,

```
LinkedList<Employee *> L;
```

then each node of `empList` can store the address of any object derived from class `Employee`:

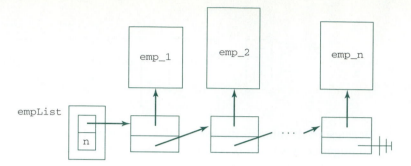

Thus, salaried and hourly employees can be intermixed in the same list. Being able to build such heterogeneous storage structures is an important benefit provided by an OOP language's inheritance mechanism.

THE NEED FOR VIRTUAL FUNCTIONS

Suppose that the `Employee` base class has an output member function `Display()` defined by

```
void Employee::Display(ostream & out) const
{
  out << myIdNum << ' ' << myLastName << ", "
      << myFirstName << ".\n" << myMiddleInitial
      << "   " << myDeptCode;
}
```

Also suppose that our derived classes have new definitions of `Display()` that extend the preceding one to output the new data members:

```
void SalariedEmployee::Display(ostream & out) const
{
  Employee::Display(out);             // inherited members
  out << "\n$" << mySalary << endl; // new member
}
```

and

```
void HourlyEmployee::Display(ostream & out) const
{
  Employee::Display(out);             // inherited members
  out << "\n$" << myWeeklyWage      // new members
      << endl << myHoursWorked
      << endl << myOverTimeFactor << endl;
}
```

We have noted that a base-class pointer can point to a derived class object, which means that an `Employee` pointer `eptr` can point to a `SalariedEmployee` object; for example,

```
ePtr = new SalariedEmployee(222, "Roe", "Jane", 'D',
                          11, 543.21);
```

Now if we were to output this `SalariedEmployee` object with

```
ePtr->Display(cout);
```

we would expect to see

```
222
Roe, Jane D.
11
$543.21
```

However, instead of this we get

```
222
Roe, Jane D.
11
```

What happened to her salary information?

The problem is basically the same as we saw in the preceding section with the `Display()` operation for classes derived from the base class `License` and with the `RepeatedPush()` operation for bounded stacks. Here, `ePtr` is a pointer to an `Employee`, and so the call `ePtr->Display(cout)` is bound at compile time to `Employee::Display(cout)`. Thus, even though we overrode `Display()` in class `SalariedEmployee`, `ePtr->Display(cout)` is using `Employee::Display(cout)` instead of `SalariedEmployee::Display(cout)`.

As before, what is needed is to defer selection of which version of the function `Display()` to use until run time. And this can be done by declaring `Display()` to be a *virtual function* in the base class `Employee`:

```
class Employee
{
public:

// ... various Employee operations ...
virtual void Display(ostream & out) const;

protected:
// ... Employee data members ...

};
```

Now the earlier function call

```
ePtr->Display();
```

will print all of Jane's information:

```
222
Roe, Jane D.
11
$543.21
```

And if `ePtr` points at an `HourlyEmployee` object, the call

```
ePtr->Display();
```

will use `HourlyEmployee::Display()`. *The same statement produces different results in different contexts*, a capability not present in non-OOP languages (i.e., languages without polymorphism).

This *polymorphic* behavior has many consequences. For example, suppose `empList` is the linked list pictured earlier

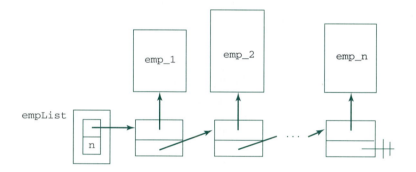

and consider the following statements to traverse this `empList` and output the employee information in each node:

```
Node * ptr = empList.first;

while (ptr != 0)
{
  ptr->data->Display(cout);
  ptr = ptr->next;
}
```

For the statement

```
ptr->Data->Display(cout);
```

when `ptr->Data` points at a `SalariedEmployee` object, the function `SalariedEmployee::Display()` within that object will be called; but when `ptr->Data` is a pointer to an `HourlyEmployee`, the function `HourlyEmployee::Display()` within that object will be called. Again we have polymorphic behavior: *The same statement produces different results in different contexts.*

☞ PROGRAMMING POINTERS

1. The basic approach in object-oriented design (OOD) is:
   a. Identify the objects in the problem.
   b. Analyze the objects to determine if there is *commonality* in them.
   c. Where there is commonality:
      i. *Define base classes that contain this commonality.*
      ii. *Derive classes that inherit this commonality from the base class.*

   For larger and more complex problems, this is usually carried out in a bottom-up manner:
   a. Identify the objects in the problem.
   b. Carefully analyze the objects from the bottom up to determine if there is *commonality* in them.
   c. Where commonality exists, group the common attributes into a base class.

2. Two useful tests for determining if one object A should be publicly derived from another object B are:
   ▸ *Operation Test*: Do A's public member functions behave properly in B?
   ▸ *Need-a . . . Use-a Test*: If all you need is an A object, can you just use a B object?

3. A function is declared to be virtual by preceding its prototype with the keyword `virtual`:

   ```
   virtual Function-heading;
   ```

   To specify that it is pure, attach the initializer `= 0`:

   ```
   virtual Function-heading = 0;
   ```

4. A base-class pointer can point to any derived class object.

ADT TIPS

1. Only public and protected members of a base class are accessible in a derived class; private members are not.

2. Access to inherited public and protected members in a derived class is determined by the kind of inheritance:

   Public inheritance: public and protected access, respectively

   Private inheritance: private

   Protected inheritance: protected

3. Public inheritance is the most important and most commonly used kind of inheritance.

4. Public inheritance should be used only when an *is-a* relationship exists between a problem's objects.

5. Other relationships between classes are *has-a* and *uses-a*. Public inheritance should not be used for either of these.

6. Nonvirtual member functions of a class as well as virtual member functions that are not pure must be defined for that class.

7. The definition of a virtual function in a base class serves as a default definition. It will be used in any derived class in which the definition is not overridden.

8. A class that has at least one pure virtual function is an abstract class. There are no objects for such classes. They serve only as base classes for other classes.

9. Pure virtual member functions of an abstract base class may not be defined for that class. Definitions must be given in derived classes (or those classes will also be abstract).

10. Data structures that can store objects of different types are called *heterogeneous* data structures. Inheritance and polymorphism make it possible to design such structures.

PROGRAMMING PROBLEMS

SECTION 12.3

1. Write a driver program to test the `Administrator` class from Exercise 1.

2. Write a driver program to test the `FactoryEmployee` class from Exercise 2.

3. Write a driver program to test the `SalesPerson` class from Exercise 3.

4. Write a complete payroll program for a company in which each employee falls into one of the five categories described in the text and in Exercises 1–3—salaried, hourly, administrative, factory, or salesperson.

5. Write a driver program to test the `Scroll` class from Exercise 4.

6. Write a driver program to test the `Deque` class from Exercise 5.

7. Use your `Deque` class from Exercise 5 in a palindrome-checking program as described in Programming Problem 32 in Chap. 6.

8. Write a driver program to test the `LookAheadStack` class from Exercise 6.

9. In an ordered list, all operations that modify the list are designed to ensure that the elements remain in ascending order. Build and test an `OrderedList` class template derived from class `list` that exhibits this characteristic.

Chapter 13

TREES

Chapter Contents

In Chap. 10 we introduced trees and showed how a special kind of binary tree, a binary search tree (BST), can be used to carry out a binary search in a linked structure. We also considered several operations on binary trees, including traversal, insertion, and deletion, and also how trees can be used to construct an efficient code known as a Huffman code. In Chap. 11 we described the heap data structure, another special kind of binary tree, and used it to transform an inefficient selection sort algorithm into one of the more efficient internal sorting schemes. In this chapter, we begin by examining more advanced operations on binary trees, namely, threading and balancing. We also describe some special kinds of trees such as 2-3-4 trees, red-black trees, and B-Trees, and take a quick look at the associative containers in STL, which use trees as storage structures. Our descriptions are quite brief, however, because these structures are usually covered in detail in more advanced data structures courses.

13.1 THREADED BINARY SEARCH TREES

One of the important tree operations we considered in Chap. 10 is traversal, and in Sec. 10.4 we described recursive procedures for performing inorder, preorder, and postorder traversals. In this section we show how special links called *threads* make simple and efficient nonrecursive traversal algorithms possible.

If a binary tree has n nodes, then the total number of links in the tree is $2n$. Since each node except the root has exactly one incoming arc, it follows that only $n - 1$ of these links point to nodes; the remaining $n + 1$ links are null. Thus more than one-half of the links in the tree are not used to point to other nodes. A **threaded binary search tree** is obtained when these unused links are used to point to certain other

665

nodes in the tree in such a way that traversals or other tree operations can be performed more efficiently.

To illustrate, suppose that we wish to thread a BST like the following to facilitate inorder traversal:

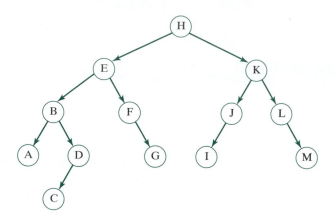

The first node visited in an inorder traversal is the leftmost leaf, that is, the node containing A. Since A has no right child, the next node visited in this traversal is its parent, the node containing B. We can use the right pointer of node A as a thread to its parent to make this backtracking in the tree easy. This thread is shown as the dashed line from A to B in the following diagram:

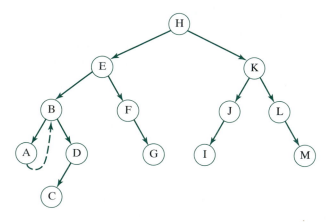

The next node visited is C, and since its right pointer is null, it also can be used as a thread to its parent D:

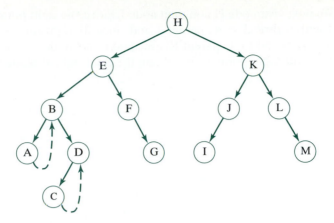

Since the right pointer in node D is again null, it can be used as a thread to its successor, which in this case is the node containing E:

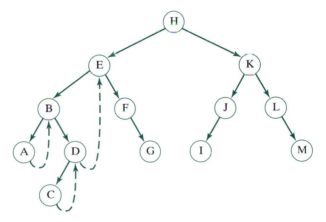

The next nodes visited are E, F, and G, and since G has a null right pointer, we replace it with a thread to its successor, the node containing H:

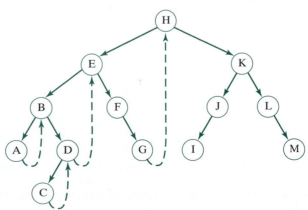

We next visit node H and then node I. Since the right pointer of I is null, we replace it with a thread to its parent J, and since its right link is null, we replace this link with a thread to its parent K. Since no other nodes except the last one visited (M) have null right pointers, we obtain the final **right-threaded BST:**

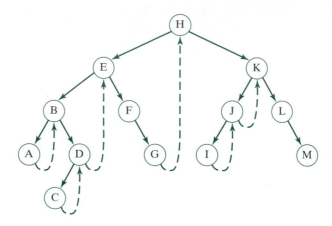

The following algorithm summarizes this process of right-threading a binary search tree:

ALGORITHM TO RIGHT-THREAD A BST

/*   Right-threads a binary search tree. Each thread links a node
to its inorder successor.

    Receive: A binary search tree.
    Return: A right-threaded BST.
---*/

Perform an inorder traversal of the BST. Whenever a node *x* with a null right pointer is encountered, replace this right link with a thread to the inorder successor of *x*. The inorder successor of such a node *x* is its parent if *x* is a left child of its parent; otherwise, it is the nearest ancestor of *x* that contains *x* in its left subtree.

An iterative algorithm for traversing a right-threaded binary search tree is now straightforward:

ALGORITHM FOR INORDER TRAVERSAL OF A RIGHT-THREADED BST

/*   Carries out an inorder traversal of the BST.
    Receive: A right-threaded BST in which each thread
                      connects a node and its inorder successor.
    Return/Output: Depends on the kind of processing done
                      when a node is visited.
    Note: $p{\rightarrow}left$ and $p{\rightarrow}right$ denote the left and
                  right links in the node pointed to by *p*.
---*/

1. Initialize a pointer *p* to the root of the tree.

2. While *p* is not null:

    a. While *p→left* is not null,
        Replace *p* by *p→left* .

    b. Visit the node pointed to by *p*.

    c. While *p→right* is a thread do the following:

        i.   Replace *p* by *p→right*.

        ii. Visit the node pointed to by *p*.

    d. Replace *p* by *p→right*.

Note that this algorithm requires being able to distinguish between right links that are threads and those that are actual pointers to right children. This suggests adding a boolean field `rightThread` in the node declarations like those in Sec. 10.2:

```
/*** Node structure ***/
class BinNode
{
 public:
   DataType data;
   bool rightThread;
   BinNode * left,
           * right;

   // BinNode constructors
   // Default -- data part undefined; rightThread false;
   //            both links null
   BinNode ()
   {
     rightThread = false;
     left = right = 0;
   }

   //Explicit Value -- data part contains item;
   //                  rightThread false; both links null
   BinNode(DataType item)
   {
     data = item;
     rightThread = false;
     left = right = 0;
   }
};// end of class BinNode declaration
```

While the tree is being threaded, `rightThread` will be set to true if the right link of a node is a thread and will be set to false otherwise. Functions to implement the algorithms given in this section for threading a BST and traversing a threaded BST are quite straightforward and are left as exercises.

✔ **Quick Quiz 13.1**

1. What is a thread in a right-threaded BST?
2. What is the purpose of threading a BST?

For Questions 3–6, show the right-threaded BST that results from inserting the characters in the order shown.

3. A, C, R, E, S   4. R, A, C, E, S
5. C, A, R, E, S   6. S, C, A, R, E

✍ **EXERCISES 13.1**

For Exercises 1–7, show the threaded BST that results from right-threading the binary search tree.

1. The BST preceding Exercise 13 in Sec. 10.4.

2. The first BST containing state abbreviations in Sec. 13.2: (p. 671).

3. The final AVL tree containing state abbreviations in Sec. 13.2: (p. 680).

4. The BST obtained by inserting the following C++ keywords in the order given: `int`, `short`, `char`, `bool`, `void`, `unsigned`, `long`, `double`

5. The BST obtained by inserting the following C++ keywords in the order given: `bool`, `char`, `double`, `int`, `long`, `short`, `unsigned`, `void`

6. The BST obtained by inserting the following C++ keywords in the order given: `void`, `unsigned`, `short`, `long`, `int`, `double`, `char`, `bool`

7. The BST obtained by inserting the following C++ keywords in the order given: `enum`, `bool`, `if`, `typename`, `case`, `else`, `while`, `do`, `return`, `unsigned`, `void`, `for`, `double`, `throw`

Exercises 8 and 9 ask you to write functions for right-threaded BSTs. You should also test your functions with driver programs as instructed in Programming Problems 1 and 2 at the end of this chapter.

8. Write a function to implement the inorder traversal algorithm for a right-threaded BST given in the text.

9. Write a function to implement the right-threading algorithm for a BST given in the text.

10. Give an algorithm similar to that in the text for threading a binary tree but to facilitate preorder traversal.

11–17. For the binary trees in Exercises 1–7, show the binary tree threaded as described in Exercise 10.

18. Give an algorithm for carrying out a preorder traversal of a binary tree threaded as described in Exercise 10.

19. Consider a binary tree that is threaded to facilitate inorder traversal. Give an algorithm for finding the preorder successor of a given node in such an inorder-threaded binary tree. Do *not* rethread the tree to facilitate preorder traversal as described in Exercise 10.

20. Proceeding as in Exercise 19, give an algorithm for carrying out a preorder traversal of an inorder-threaded binary tree.

21. The right-threading algorithm given in the text right-threads an existing BST. It is also possible to construct a right-threaded BST by inserting an item into a right-threaded

BST (beginning with an empty BST) in such a way that the resulting BST is right-threaded. Give such an insertion algorithm.

22. Trace the algorithm in Exercise 21 using the C++ keywords given in Exercise 4. Show the right-threaded BST after each word is inserted.

23. Repeat Exercise 22 for the words in Exercise 6.

24. Give an algorithm to delete a node from a right-threaded BST so that the resulting BST is also right-threaded.

Exercises 25–34 deal with *fully-threaded* BSTs in which not only null right links are replaced with threads to inorder successors, as described in the text, but also null left links with threads to inorder predecessors.

25–31. Show the fully-threaded BST for the BSTs in Exercises 1–7.

32. Give an algorithm to fully thread a BST.

33. Write an algorithm to insert a node into a fully-threaded BST so that the resulting BST is also fully threaded.

34. Write an algorithm to find the parent of a given node in a fully-threaded BST.

13.2 TREE BALANCING: AVL TREES

Binary search trees are designed to facilitate fast searching of the items stored in the tree. As we observed in Chap. 10, however, the order in which items are inserted into a binary search tree determines the shape of the tree and how efficiently this tree can be searched. If it grows in such a way that it fills in approximately level by level, then it can be searched much more efficiently in a binary-search manner than if it becomes lopsided.

EXAMPLE: A BST OF STATE ABBREVIATIONS

To illustrate the problem, consider the BST that results when the abbreviations of states NY, IL, GA, RI, MA, PA, DE, IN, VT, TX, OH, and WY are inserted into an empty tree in this order:

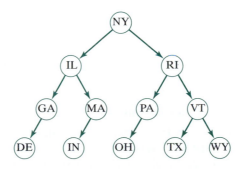

For such nicely balanced trees, the search time is $O(\log_2 n)$, where n is the number of nodes in the tree. If the abbreviations are inserted in the order DE, GA, IL, IN, MA, MI, NY, OH, PA, RI, TX, VT, WY, however, the BST degenerates into a linked list for which the search time is $O(n)$:

```
     (DE)
        ↘
         (GA)
            ↘
             (IL)
                ↘
                 (IN)
                    ↘
                     (MA)
                        ↘
                         (MI)
                            ↘
                             (NY)
                                ↘
                                 (OH)
                                    ↘
                                     (PA)
                                        ↘
                                         (RI)
                                            ↘
                                             (TX)
                                                ↘
                                                 (VT)
                                                    ↘
                                                     (WY)
```

In this section we describe a technique developed in the 1960s by the two Russian mathematicians, Georgii Maksimovich Adel'son-Vel'skii and Evgenii Mikhailovich Landis, for keeping a binary search tree balanced as items are inserted into it. The trees that result are commonly called *AVL trees*, in their honor.

As an ADT, an **AVL** (or **height-balanced**) **tree** is a special kind of BST:

ADT AVL TREE

Collection of Data Elements:

A binary search tree in which the balance factor of each node is 0, 1, or −1, where the **balance factor** of a node x is defined as the height of the left subtree of x minus the height of x's right subtree. (Recall that the height of a tree is the number of levels in it.)

Basic Operations:

▶ Construction, empty, search, and traverse as for BSTs

▶ Insert a new item in the AVL tree in such a way that the height-balanced property is maintained

▶ Delete an item from the AVL tree in such a way that the height-balanced property is maintained

For example, the following are AVL trees, and the balance factor of each node is shown in the node:

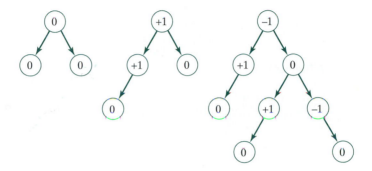

The following are not AVL trees, and the nodes whose balance factors are different from 0, 1, or −1 are highlighted:

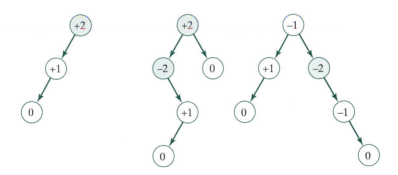

We can implement an AVL tree as a linked structure in much the same way as we did for binary trees in Chap. 10. For nodes, we simply add a data member to store the balance factor:

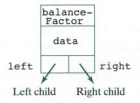

```
template <typename DataType>
class AVLTree
{
private:
 /*** Node structure ***/
 class AVLNode
 {
 public:
   DataType data;
   short int balanceFactor;
   AVLNode * left,
            * right;

  // AVLNode constructors
  // Default -- data part undefined;
  //            balance factor 0; both links null
  AVLNode()
  {
    balanceFactor = 0;
    left = right = 0;
  }

  // Explicit Value -- data part contains item;
  //            balance factor 0; both links null
  AVLNode(DataType item)
  {
    data = item;
    balanceFactor = 0;
    left = right = 0;
  }
 }; // end of class AVLNode declaration

typedef AVLNode * AVLNodePointer;

public:
// Member Functions
  . . .
private:
// Data members
  . . .
}; // end of class AVLTree declaration
```

The constructor, empty, search, and traverse operations for AVL trees can then be implemented in the same way as for BSTs. Here we will concentrate on the insertion operation.

To illustrate how to insert items into an AVL tree, beginning with an empty AVL tree, we consider again the example of a BST containing state abbreviations. Suppose that the first abbreviation inserted is RI, giving the following balanced tree: If the next abbreviation is inserted in PA, the result is still a balanced tree:

(1)

If DE is inserted next, an unbalanced tree results:

(2)

A **right rotation** of the subtree rooted at the node RI yields the balanced tree:

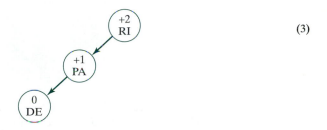

(3)

Inserting GA next does not unbalance the tree:

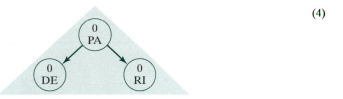

(4)

But an unbalanced tree results if OH is inserted next:

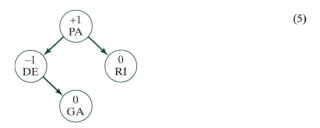

(5)

(6)

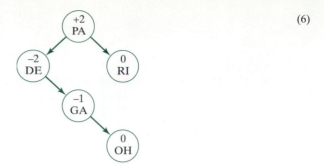

Performing a **left rotation** of the nodes in the subtree rooted at DE rebalances the tree:

(7)

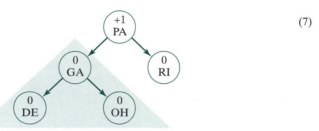

Inserting MA next produces another unbalanced tree:

(8)

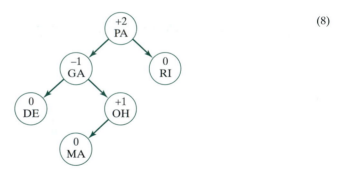

Rebalancing this tree requires a double *left-right rotation.* We first perform a left rotation of the nodes in the left subtree of PA

(9)

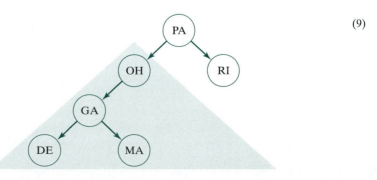

and follow this with a right rotation of the tree rooted at PA:

(10)

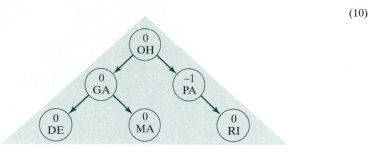

Inserting IL and then MI does not unbalance the tree

(11)

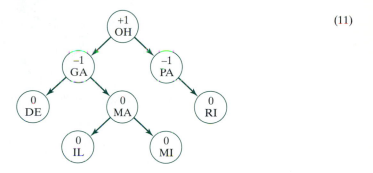

but inserting IN does:

(12)

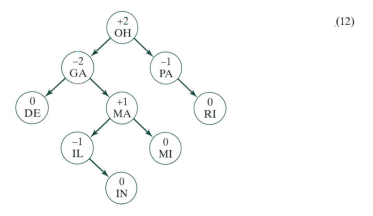

In this case, a double **right-left rotation** rebalances the tree. We first perform a right rotation of the nodes in the right subtree of GA

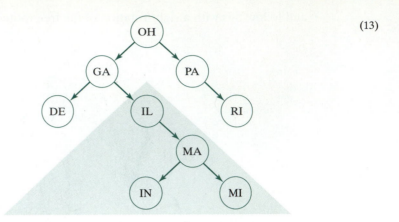

(13)

and then follow this with a left rotation of the subtree rooted at GA:

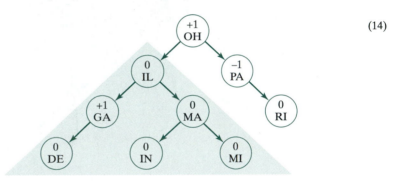

(14)

Inserting NY produces an unbalanced tree

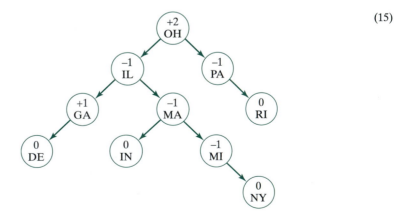

(15)

that requires a double left-right rotation for rebalancing, first, a left rotation of the nodes in the left subtree of OH

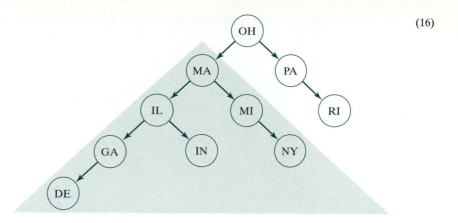

(16)

followed by a right rotation of the nodes in the subtree rooted at OH:

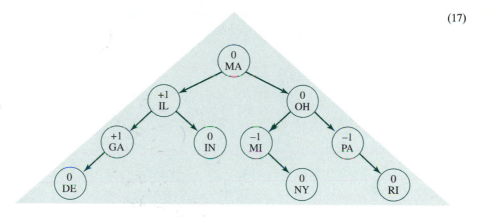

(17)

Inserting VT next causes an imbalance

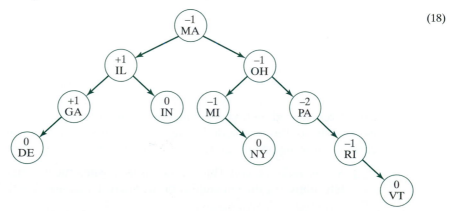

(18)

but this tree is easily rebalanced by a simple left rotation of the subtree rooted at PA:

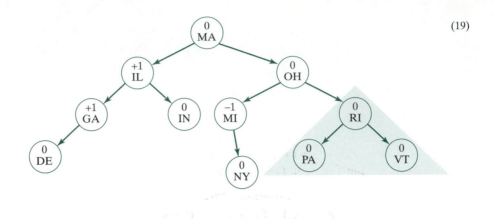

(19)

Insertion of the last two abbreviations TX and WY does not unbalance the tree, and the final AVL tree obtained is

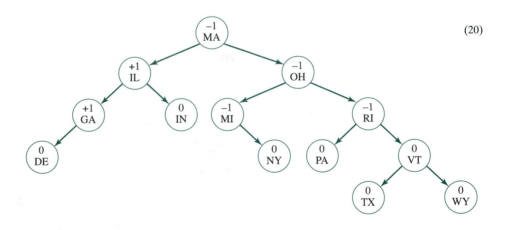

(20)

THE BASIC REBALANCING ROTATIONS

As this example demonstrates, when a new item is inserted into a balanced binary tree, the resulting tree may become unbalanced. It also demonstrates that the tree can be rebalanced by transforming the subtree rooted at the node that is the nearest ancestor of the new node having balance factor ± 2. This transformation can be carried out using one of the following four types of rotations:

    1. *Simple right rotation:* This rotation is used when the new item is inserted in the left subtree of the left child B of the nearest ancestor A with balance factor $+2$.

2. *Simple left rotation*: This rotation is used when the new item is inserted in the right subtree of the right child B of the nearest ancestor A with balance factor -2.

3. *Left-right rotation*: This rotation is used when the new item is inserted in the right subtree of the left child B of the nearest ancestor A with balance factor $+2$.

4. *Right-left rotation*: This rotation is used when the new item is inserted in the left subtree of the right child B of the nearest ancestor A with balance factor -2.

Each of these rotations can be carried out by simply resetting some of the links. For example, consider a simple right rotation, which is used when the item is inserted in the left subtree of the left child B of the nearest ancestor A with balance factor $+2$. A simple right rotation can be accomplished by simply resetting three links:

1. Reset the link from the parent of A to B.

2. Set the left link of A equal to the right link of B.

3. Set the right link of B to point A.

The following sequence of diagrams illustrates:

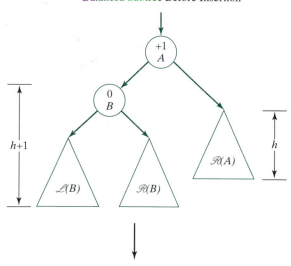

Balanced Subtree Before Insertion

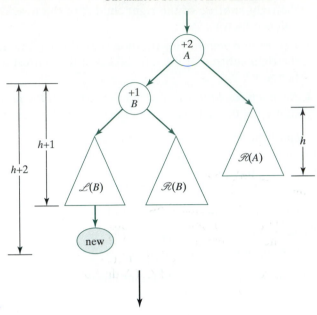

Unbalanced Subtree After Insertion

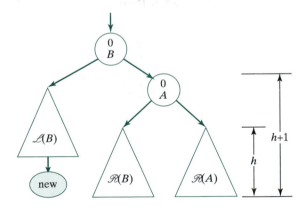

Rebalanced Subtree After Simple Right Rotation

The corresponding simple left rotation can also be carried out by resetting three links and is left as an exercise.

The double rotations can be carried out with at most five link changes. For example, consider a left-right rotation, which is used when the item is inserted in the right subtree of the left child B of the nearest ancestor A with balance factor $+2$. The left rotation can be accomplished by resetting three links

1. Set the left link of *A* to point to the root *C* of the right subtree of *B*.

2. Set the right link of *B* equal to the left link of *C*.

3. Set the left link of *C* to point to *B*.

and the right rotation by resetting three links:

4. Reset the link from the parent of *A* to point to *C*.

5. Set the left link of *A* equal to the right link of *C*.

6. Set the right link of *C* to point to *A*.

Note that the link change in Step 5 cancels that in step 1, so that in fact only five links must be reset.

The following diagrams show two of the three possible cases for this left-right rotation: (1) *B* has no right child before the new node is inserted, and the new node becomes the right child *C* of *B*; (2) *B* has a right child *C*, and the new node is inserted in the left subtree of *C*; and (3) *B* has right child *C*, and the new node is inserted in the right subtree of *C*. (A diagram for Case 3 is similar to that for Case 2 and is left as an exercise.)

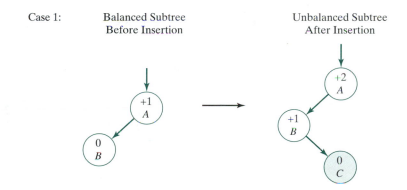

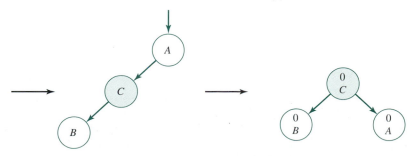

Case 2:

Balanced Subtree before Insertion

Unbalanced Subtree after Insertion

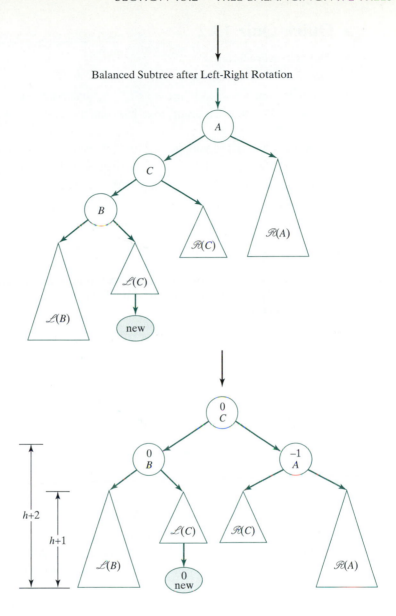

Balanced Subtree after Left-Right Rotation

The corresponding right-left rotations can also be accomplished with at most five link changes and are left as exercises.

Using an AVL tree to store data items rather than allowing the binary tree to grow haphazardly when new items are inserted guarantees that the search time will be $O(\log_2 n)$. There is obviously some overhead involved in rebalancing, but if the number of search operations is sufficiently greater than the number of insertions, the faster searches will compensate for the slower insertions. Empirical studies have indicated that on the average, rebalancing is required for approximately 45 percent of the insertions. Roughly one-half of these require double rotations.

✔ **Quick Quiz 13.2**

1. Define balance factor.

2. Define AVL tree as an ADT.

3. Another name for an AVL tree is a(n) _____-balanced tree.

4. Show the AVL tree that results from inserting the letters S, P, E, C, I, A, L, T, Y in this order.

5. How many link changes are needed to carry out a simple rotation?

6. How many link changes are needed to carry out a double rotation?

7. Searching an AVL tree can be done in O(_____) time.

✎ **EXERCISES 13.2**

For Exercises 1–5, trace the construction of the AVL tree that results from inserting the C++ keywords in the given order. Show the tree and balance factors for each node before and after each rebalancing.

1. `long, const, typedef, bool, public, break, else`

2. `bool, new, return, struct, while, case, enum`

3. `do, long, new, and, operator, int, namespace`

4. `unsigned, short, long, int, double, char`

5. `bool, enum, if, this, else, case, void, do, return, unsigned, false, true, double, while`

Proceed as in Exercises 6–10, but for the following collections of numbers:

6. 22, 44, 88, 66, 55, 11, 99, 77, 33

7. 11, 22, 33, 44, 55, 66, 77, 88, 99

8. 99, 88, 77, 66, 55, 44, 33, 22, 11

9. 55, 33, 77, 22, 11, 44, 88, 66, 99

10. 50, 45, 75, 65, 70, 35, 25, 15, 60, 20, 41, 30, 55, 10, 80

11. Draw diagrams for a simple left rotation similar to those in the text for the simple right rotation. Also describe what links must be reset to accomplish this rotation.

12. Draw diagrams for Case 3 of the left-right rotation described in the text.

13. Draw diagrams for a right-left rotation similar to those in the text for the left-right rotation. Also describe what links must be reset to accomplish this rotation.

14. Design and test an `AVLTree` class.

13.3 2-3-4 TREES, RED-BLACK TREES, B-TREES, AND OTHER TREES

Until now we have confined our attention to binary trees, those in which each node has at most two children. In many applications, however, allowing more than two children is necessary or at least desirable. For example, in a **genealogical tree** such as the following, it is not the case that each person has a maximum of two children

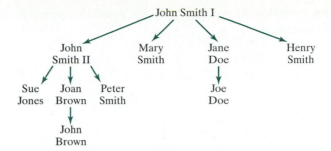

Game trees that are used to analyze games and puzzles also do not have the binary property. The following tree showing the various configurations possible in the Tower of Hanoi problem with two disks (see Sec. 7.2) is a simple illustration of such a game tree:

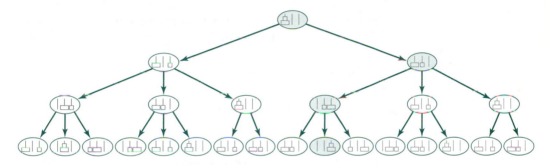

Parse trees constructed during the compilation of a program are used to check the program's syntax. Most of these do not have the binary property. For example, in Sec. 7.2 we considered the parse tree for the expression $2 * (3 + 4)$

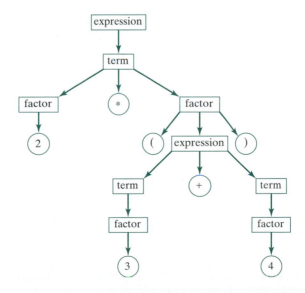

and the following tree could be the parse tree constructed by a C++ compiler for the statement

```
if (x < 0)
    flag = 1;
```

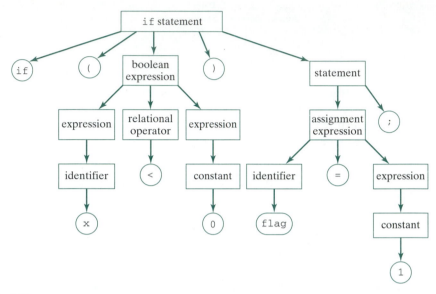

2-3-4 TREES

The searching technique used for binary search trees has also been extended to trees in which nodes may have more than two children. In the search of a BST for a particular item, the search path descends to the left subtree of a particular node if the item is less than the data value in that node; otherwise, it descends to the right subtree. These are the only two options. For other trees, however, at a given node, there may be several different directions that a search path may follow; and in general, this results in shorter search paths because there are fewer levels in the tree. We will illustrate this first for 2-3-4 trees, in which all non-leaf nodes have 2, 3, or 4 children.

Giving a precise definition of a 2-3-4 tree is easiest if we first make the following definition: An **m-node** in a search tree stores $m - 1$ data values $k_1 < k_2 < \ldots < k_{m-1}$, and has links to m subtrees $T_1, \ldots, T_m$, where for each i,[1]

$$\text{all data values in } T_i < k_i \leq \text{all data values in } T_{i+1}$$

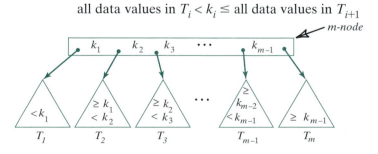

<hr />

[1] We use k for the data values to remind ourselves that the data values are usually records and comparisons are made using *keys* in these records.

Thus, a binary search tree has all 2-nodes.
Now we can define a **2-3-4-tree**.

ADT 2-3-4 TREE

Collection of Data Elements:

A tree with the following properties:

1. Each node stores at most 3 data values.

2. Each internal node is a 2-node, a 3-node, or a 4-node.

3. All the leaves are on the same level.

Basic Operations:

▸ Construction, empty, and search

▸ Insert a new item in the 2-3-4 tree so the result is a 2-3-4 tree

▸ Delete an item from the 2-3-4 tree so the result is a 2-3-4 tree

For example, the following tree is a 2-3-4 tree that stores integers:

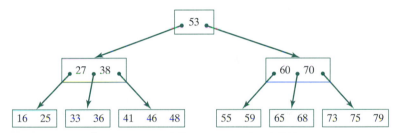

To search this tree for the value 36, we begin at the root and compare 36 with the data items stored in the root. In this 2-3-4 tree, a single item 53 is stored in the root, and 36 is less than 53, so we next search the left subtree:

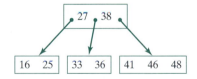

Comparing 36 with the data items 27 and 38 stored in the root of this subtree, we find that 36 is between these values, indicating that 36 is in the middle subtree:

33	36

Examining the data items in the root of this subtree, we locate the value 36.

The basic step in constructing a 2-3-4 tree is to begin with a single node and to insert values into this node until it becomes full, that is, until it becomes a 4-node (containing 3 items). When the next item is inserted, the node is split into two nodes, one storing the items less than the median and the other storing those greater than the median. The median itself is stored in a parent having these two nodes as children.

As an illustration, the preceding 2-3-4 tree can be constructed as follows: Suppose the first three integers inserted are 53, 27, and 75. These are arranged in ascending order and are stored in the root node of a one-node tree

$$\boxed{27 \quad 53 \quad 75}$$

Suppose the next item to be inserted is 25. Because the root node is full, it must be split into three nodes, one containing the median 53 with its left child containing the values 25 and 27, which are less than the median 53, and the right child containing the value 75, which is greater than the median:

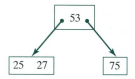

Next 70 and 41 can be inserted into the leaves:

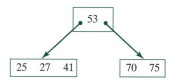

If 38 is inserted, the leftmost leaf must be split by moving the median, 27, into the parent node:

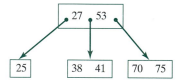

Now 16, 59, and 36 can be inserted into leaves; no splitting is necessary:

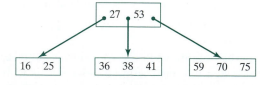

The insertion of 73 forces a splitting of the rightmost leaf:

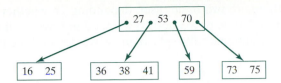

Now 65 and 60 can be inserted into the leaves with no splitting, but the insertion of 46 causes the second leaf from the left to split. When the median 38 is inserted into the parent node, which is the root, it also must be split, and the resulting 2-3-4 tree is

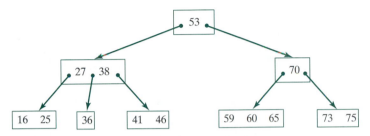

Inserting 55 causes a split in the second leaf from the right:

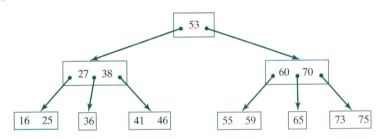

Finally, 33, 68, 79, and 48 can be inserted into leaf nodes without splitting any nodes:

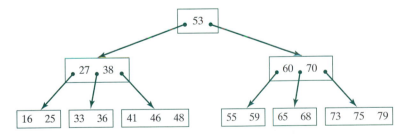

In this example, when we inserted 46, the leaf node where it was to be put was a 4-node so we had to split it; but its parent was also a 4-node and so we had to split it as well before we could move 38 up one level. In general, the grandparent node might also be a 4-node that will need to be split before we can move a key from the parent node up one level, and so on. This may cause a split all the way up to the root!

To avoid this, a better alternative to this *bottom-up insertion* is to use *top-down insertion* in which we don't allow any parent nodes to become 4-nodes. Rather, we split all 4-nodes along the search path down the tree as they are encountered. For this, there are two basic cases, depending on whether the parent of the node to be split is a 2-node or a 3-node—we need not worry about the parent being a 4-node since we automatically split them as we descend the tree:

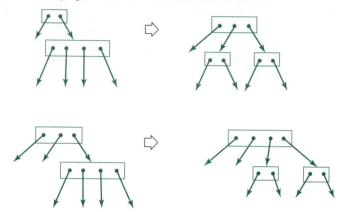

Also, since the root has no parent, it is simpler to split it as soon as it becomes a 4-node and not wait until the next insertion.

To illustrate, in the preceding example, after we had inserted 73, the 2-3-4 tree was

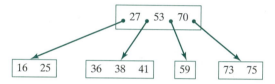

so we would split the root node immediately before inserting any other values:

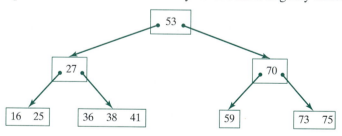

The insertion of 46 then causes only a split of the leaf node; no nodes above it need to be split.

As this example illustrates, 2-3-4 trees stay balanced during insertions. This is also the case for deletion, which is left as an exercise.

We turn now to the problem of implementing 2-3-4 trees. We could use nodes having three data fields and four links:

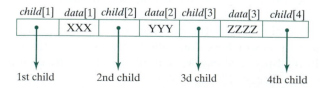

```
class Node234
{
public
   TreeElementType data[3];   // type of data items in nodes
   TreeNode * child[4];
   . . .
};
typedef Node234 * Pointer234;
```

 The difficulty with this representation is that each node must have one link for each possible child, even though most of the nodes will not use all of these links. In fact, the amount of "wasted" space may be quite large. To demonstrate this, suppose that a 2-3-4 tree has n nodes. The linked representation will thus require n nodes, each having 4 links, for a total of $4n$ links. In such a tree, however, there are only $n - 1$ directed arcs, and thus only $n - 1$ of these links are used to connect the nodes. This means that $4n - (n - 1) = 3n + 1$ of the links are null; thus the fraction of unused links is $(3n + 1) / 4n$, which is approximately equal to 3/4; that is, approximately 75 percent of the links are null.

As we will see later in this section, there is a general method for representing any tree by a binary tree, but these trees typically don't stay balanced. However, for 2-3-4 trees, there is a special kind of binary tree called a *red-black tree* that can be used, and we will consider it next.

RED-BLACK TREES

Before we can show how **red-black trees** can be used to implement 2-3-4 trees, we must first tell what they are.

ADT *ADT RED-BLACK TREE*

Collection of Data Elements:

A binary search tree with two kinds of links, red and black, which satisfy the following properties:

1. Every path from the root to a leaf node has the same number of black links.

2. No path from the root to a leaf node has two or more consecutive red links.

Basic Operations:

▸ Construction, empty, search, and traverse as for BSTs

▸ Insert a new item in the red-black tree in such a way that the red-black properties are maintained

▸ Delete an item from the red-black tree in such a way that the red-black properties are maintained

---

There are two methods one could use to implement the nodes in a red-black tree. One is to add two data members to store the colors of the links to the children. An alternative and more common method is to add just one data member that stores the color of the link from the parent:

```
enum ColorType {RED, BLACK};
class RedBlackTreeNode
{
public:
  TreeElementType data;
  ColorType parentColor;  // RED if link from parent is red,
                          // BLACK otherwise
  RedBlackTreeNode * parent,
                   * left, * right;
};
```

This is the approach used in the standard C++ library for the class `rb_tree`.

For the empty, search, and traverse operations, we can use the usual BST operations—we simply ignore the colors of the links. Here we will concentrate on the insert operation and, in particular, how we can construct a red-black tree to represent a 2-3-4 tree. Deletion is left as an exercise.

2-3-4 trees are represented by red-black trees as follows:

Make a link black if it is present in the 2-3-4 tree.
Otherwise make it red.

This means that we transform 2-, 3-, and 4-nodes and links in a 2-3-4 tree into nodes and links of a red-black tree by using the following transformations. (*Note: Red links are shown as green in this text.*)

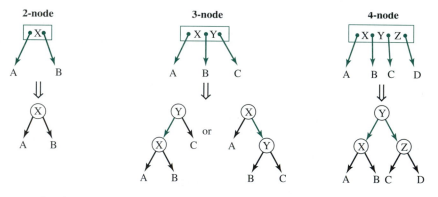

For example, the 2-3-4 tree

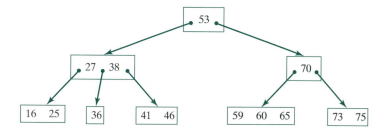

can be represented by the following red-black tree:

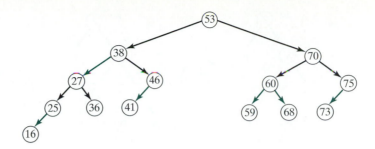

Note that the properties in the definition of a red-black tree do hold. Notice also that the tree is balanced.

Although AVL trees have been replaced in many applications by more modern data structures such as 2-3-4 trees and red-black trees, the basic AVL rotations are still used to keep a red-black tree balanced. To construct a red-black tree, we can simply use top-down 2-3-4 tree insertion with 4-node splitting during descent:

1. Search for a place to insert the new node. (Keep track of its parent, grandparent, and great grandparent.)

2. Whenever a 4-node q is encountered along the search path, split it as follows:

   a. Change both links of q to black.

   b. Change the link from the parent to red:

3. If there now are two consecutive red links (from grandparent gp to parent p to q), perform the appropriate AVL-type rotation determined by the direction (LL, RR, LR, RL) from $gp \rightarrow p \rightarrow q$; for example

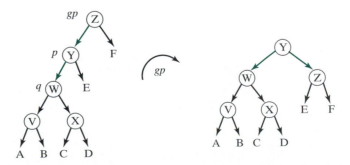

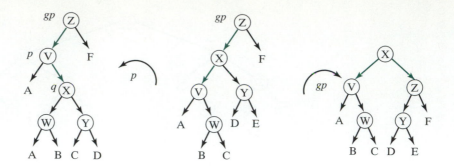

To illustrate, the following diagrams show the first twelve insertions in the 2-3-4 tree given earlier:

Insert 53:

Insert 27:

Insert 75:

Insert 25, 70, 41:

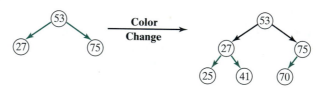

Insert 38:

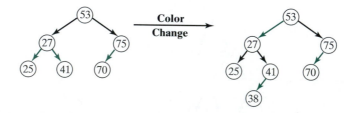

Insert 16:

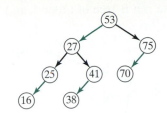

Insert 59:

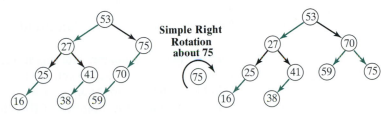

Insert 36:

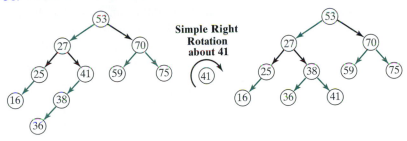

B-TREES

BSTs, 2-3-4 trees, and red-black trees are data structures used in *internal* searching schemes, that is, those in which the data set being searched is small enough that it can be stored in main memory. A B-tree is one data structure that is useful in *external* searching, where the data is stored in secondary memory.

A **B-tree of order *m*** is a generalization of 2-3-4 trees:

ADT B-TREE OF ORDER *m*

Collection of Data Elements:

A tree with the following properties:

1. Each node stores at most *m*—1 data values.

2. Each internal node is a 2-node, a 3-node, ⋯, or an *m*-node.

3. All the leaves are on the same level.

Basic Operations:

▶ Construction, empty, and search

▶ Insert a new item in the B-tree so the result is a B-tree

▶ Delete an item from the B-tree so the result is a B-tree

Thus, a 2-3-4 tree is a B-tree of order 4, and the following is a B-tree of order 5

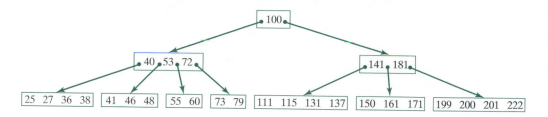

The algorithms for the basic operations are straightforward modifications of those for 2-3-4 trees.

As we noted, B-trees are useful for organizing data sets stored in secondary memory, such as files and databases stored on disk. In such applications, nodes in the B-tree typically store one file block, the maximum amount of information that can be retrieved in one access. This maximizes the number of data items stored in each node and the number of children. This in turn minimizes the height of the B-tree and hence the length of a search path. Because one disk access is required at each level along the search path, the number of data transfers from the disk is also minimized.

A natural question to ask, therefore, is what value to use for the order m. It is clear that the larger the value of m, the more values that can be stored in B-trees with a given height. The following table gives a few values:

height	$m = 2$	$m = 4$	$m = 10$	$m = 100$
0	1	3	9	99
1	3	15	99	9999
2	7	63	999	999999
3	15	255	9999	99999999

Empirical studies have shown that the best performance is achieved for values of m in the range 50 to 400.

In practice, when the data items are large records, modified B-trees in which only the leaves store complete records can be used; internal nodes store certain key values from these records because only the key values are used in searching. Also, the leaves may be linked together to reduce still further the number of disk accesses required.

REPRESENTING TREES AND FORESTS AS BINARY TREES

Because general trees arise in a variety of applications, we must consider what structures might be used to implement them. We have already considered using nodes with four links for 2-3-4 trees, and in general, we might use any number of links

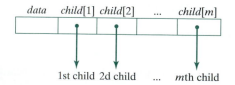

where *m* is the maximum number of children that a node may have. Declarations for such nodes would thus have the form

```
const int MAX_CHILDREN = ... ;
                    // maximum number of children per node
   . . .
class TreeNode
{
 public:
   TreeElementType data;   // type of data items in nodes
   TreeNode * child[MAX_CHILDREN];
      . . .
};

typedef TreeNode * TreePointer;
```

☞ As we saw before, the problem with this linked representation is that each node must have one link for each possible child, even though most of the nodes will not use all of these links. This can result in a large amount of wasted space. For example, following our earlier look at 2-3-4 trees, we would find that for a tree with up to 100 links per node, the fraction of unused links is

$$\frac{99n + 1}{100n}$$

which is approximately 99 percent!

☞ It is possible, however, to represent any tree using nodes that have only two links, that is, by a binary tree. We use one of these links to connect siblings together (that is, all the children of a given node) in the order in which they appear in the tree, from left to right. The other link in each node points to the first node in this linked list of its children. For example, the tree

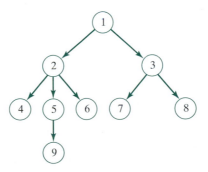

can be represented by the binary tree

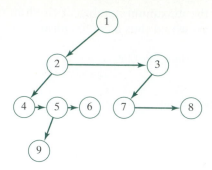

or drawn in the more customary manner

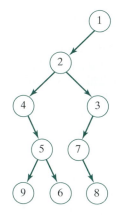

In this binary tree, node x is a left child of node y if x is the leftmost child of y in the given tree; and x is the right child of y if x and y are siblings in the original tree.

When a binary tree is used in this manner to represent a general tree, the right pointer in the root is always null because the root never has a right child. (Why?) This allows us to use a binary tree to represent not merely a single tree but an entire **forest**, which is a collection of trees. We simply set the right pointer of the root to the root of the binary tree for the next tree in the forest. For example, the following forest

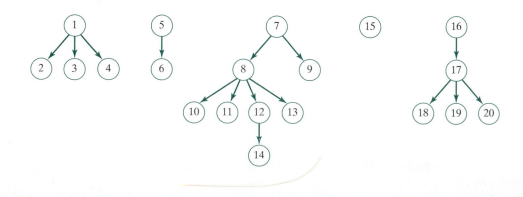

can be represented by the single binary tree

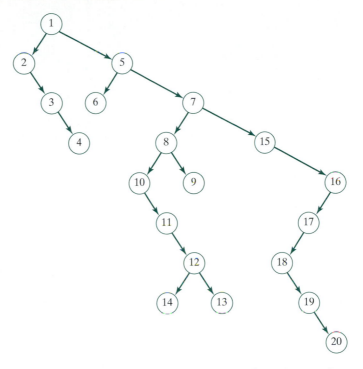

One especially attractive feature of this representation of general trees is that we have studied binary trees in some detail and have developed algorithms for processing them. These algorithms can thus be used to process general trees, as described in the exercises; in particular, the traversal algorithms can be used to traverse general trees and forests.

A third representation of general trees is based on the fact that trees are special cases of a more general structure known as a *directed graph*. Directed graphs are considered in the next chapter, and any of the implementations described there can also be used for trees.

✔ Quick Quiz 13.3

1. Draw a picture of (a) a 2-node, (b) a 3-node, and (c) a 4-node, and tell what must be true for each.

2. Show the 2-3-4 tree that results from inserting the letters S, P, E, C, I, A, L, T, Y, in this order.

3. Draw the red-black tree that represents the 2-3-4 tree in Question 2.

4. A(n) _____-tree is commonly used for external searching.

5. A B-tree of order _____ is a 2-3-4 tree.

6. Draw the B-tree of order 5 that results from inserting the letters S, P, E, C, I, A, L, T, Y, in this order. When it is necessary to split a 5-node, use the second value in the node as the median.

Give the binary-tree representation of each of the general trees in Questions 7 and 8.

7.   **8.**

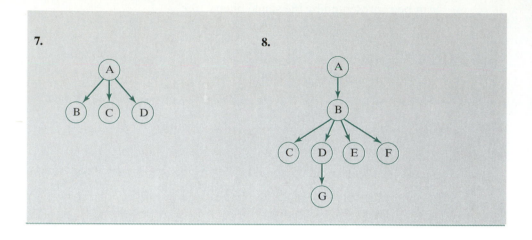

✏️ EXERCISES 13.3

For Exercises 1–6, draw the 2-3-4 tree that results when the values are inserted in the order given:

1. 55, 66, 44, 77, 33, 88, 22, 99, 11   **2.** 55, 66, 77, 88, 99, 11, 22, 33, 44

3. 11, 22, 33, 44, 55, 66, 77, 88, 99   **4.** 99, 88, 77, 66, 55, 44, 33, 22, 11

5. B, E, A, N, S   **6.** C, O, R, N, F, L, A, K, E, S

7–12. Draw the red-black trees for the 2-3-4 trees in Exercises 1–6.

13–18. Repeat Exercises 1–6, but use B-trees of order 5.

19. Construct the B-tree of order 5 that results when the following integers are inserted in the order given: 261, 381, 385, 295, 134, 400, 95, 150, 477, 291, 414, 240, 456, 80, 25, 474, 493, 467, 349, 180, 370, 257.

20. Give the binary-tree representation of the following tree:

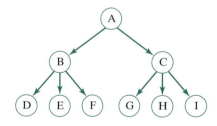

21. Give the binary-tree representation of the following forest:

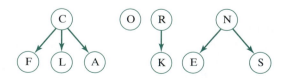

22.   Give an algorithm to delete a node from an AVL tree.

23.   Give an algorithm to delete a node from a 2-3-4 tree.

24.   Give an algorithm to delete a node from a red-black tree.

Exercises 25–27 ask you to develop class templates for various trees. You should also write driver programs to test your answers as instructed in Programming Problems 6–8 at the end of this chapter.

25.   Develop a class template for red-black trees.

26.   Develop a class template for B-trees that uses nodes with more than 2 links as described in the text to store the nodes of the B-tree.

27.   Develop a class template for general search trees that uses a binary tree to represent the tree as described in the text.

13.4 ASSOCIATIVE CONTAINERS IN STL—mapS (OPTIONAL)

In Chap. 6 we described the **sequential containers** in C++'s Standard Template Library:

```
vector
deque
list
stack
queue
priority_queue
```

The **associative containers** provided in STL are

```
set
multiset
map
multimap
```

These associative containers are similar in the operations they provide. These include the following:

Function Member	Description
Constructors	Construct container c to be:
c()	empty
c(compare)	empty, using compare function to compare keys
c(first, last)	initialized with elements in range [first, last)
c(first, last, compare)	initialized with elements in range [first, last) and using compare function to compare keys

(continued)

Function Member	Description
`c.max_size()`	Return the maximum number of locations c can ever have
`c.size()`	Return the number of values currently stored in c
`c.empty()`	Return `true` if and only if c contains no values (i.e., c's size is 0)
`c.count(key)`	Return number of elements in c that match `key`
`c.find(key)`	Return iterator positioned at element in c matching `key`; at `end()` if none.
`c.lower_bound(key)`	Return iterator positioned at first position in c where `key` can be inserted and ordering maintained. If none, return iterator at `end()`.
`c.upper_bound(key)`	Same, but find last position
`c.begin()`	Return an iterator positioned at c's first element
`c.end()`	Return an iterator positioned past c's last element
`c.rbegin()`	Return a reverse iterator positioned at c's last element
`c.rend()`	Return a reverse iterator positioned before c's first element
`c.insert(first, last);`	Insert elements in the range [`first`, `last`)
`c.insert(it, key);`	Insert a copy of `key` if there is none, using `it` as a hint on where to start searching
`c.insert(key);`	Insert a copy of `key` if there is none and return $$pair<it, boolean>$$ where `it` is positioned at the new element and `boolean` is true or `it` is positioned at an existing element and `boolean` is false. *Note*: **pair<T1,T2>** is a class template that contains two objects, the first of type `T1` and the second of type `T2`. It is defined in `<utility>`. Its constructor has the form `pair(a,b)` (no default constructor). Operations are: `==` and `<`. There are 2 *public* data members: `first` and `second`
`c.erase(it);`	Erase the value in c at iterator position `it`
`c.erase(it1, it2);`	Erase the values in c from iterator positions `it1` to `it2`
`c.erase(key);`	Erase element(s) that match `key`
`c[key]`	Access the element of c whose index is `key`
`c1 = c2`	Assign a copy of $c2$ to $c1$
`c1.swap(c2)`	Swap $c1$'s contents with $c2$'s

(continued)

Function Member	Description
`c1 == c2`	Return `true` if and only if `c1` has the same values as `c2`
`c1 < c2`	Return `true` if and only if `c1` is lexicographically less than `c2`

The associative containers are also quite similar in their implementations—they all use red-black trees to store their elements. They differ in whether both keys and their associated data are stored (`map` and `multimap`) or only keys are stored (`set` and `multiset`); also, the `multi-` containers allow multiple instances of keys, whereas the other containers do not.

A detailed study of these containers is beyond the level of this introductory text and is left to more advanced courses in data structures. We will give one example of `map`s, however, because they provide one operation that makes them especially useful, namely, the subscript operator `[]`:

> `m[key]`:   Returns a reference to the `T` value associated with *key*, a default `T`-value if there is none, where `T` is the type of the elements in *m*.

(`[]` is not provided for the other containers.) It allows us to use **associative arrays** in which *the index type may be any type*, as illustrated by the program in Fig. 13.1.

A common form of `map` declarations is

```
map<KeyType, DataType, less<KeyType>) obj;
```

(with similar declarations for the other associative containers). The less-than operator ($<$) must be defined for elements of type *KeyType*. The `map` object `obj` then operates in essentially the same manner as an array whose indices are of type *KeyType* and whose elements are of type *DataType*. For example, the definition of `map` object `a1` in the program is equivalent to

```
map<string, Student, less<string> > a1;
```

For any `string` object `name`,

```
a1[name]
```

is a `Student` object, where `Student` is the class defined in the program. The declaration of `map` object `a2` is equivalent to

```
map<Student, string, less<Student> > a2;
```

For any `Student` object `aStudent`,

```
a2[aStudent]
```

is a `string`. Note that $<$ is defined for type `Student`.

FIGURE 13.1   EXAMPLES OF maps

```cpp
#include <iostream>
#include <string>
#include <map>
using namespace std;

class Student
{
public:
  // Output operator
  friend ostream & operator<<(ostream & out, const Student & s);

  // Less-than operator
  friend bool operator<(const Student & a, const Student & b);
private:
  // Data members
  int id;
  double GPA;
};   // end of class Student

// Definition of output operator
inline ostream & operator<<(ostream & out, const Student & s)
{ out << " id = " << s.id << "  GPA = " << s.GPA;
  return out;
}

// Definition of less-than operator
inline bool operator<(const Student & a, const Student & b)
{ return a.id < b.id; }
// End of definition of class Student

int main()
{
  typedef map<string, Student, less<string> > map1;
  typedef map<Student, string, less<Student> > map2;

  map1 a1;    // associative array of Student, index type is string
  map2 a2;    // associative array of string, index type is Student

  Student s;
  s.id = 12345; s.GPA = 3.3;  a1["Fred"] = s;   a2[s] = "Fred";
  s.id = 32322; s.GPA = 3.9;  a1["Al"] = s;     a2[s] = "Al";
  s.id = 13131; s.GPA = 2.5;  a1["Joan"] = s;   a2[s] = "Joan";
  s.id = 22121; s.GPA = 4.0;  a1["Barb"] = s;   a2[s] = "Barb";
  s.id = 28888; s.GPA = 2.9;  a1["George"] = s; a2[s] = "George";
  s.id = 19981; s.GPA = 3.0;  a1["Dot"] = s;    a2[s] = "Dot";
  s.id = 20012; s.GPA = 2.9 ; a1["Sue"] = s;    a2[s] = "Sue";
```

```
   string name;
   cout << "Enter a name: ";
   cin >> name;
   map1::iterator it1 = a1.find(name);
   cout << name << " has ";
   if (it1== a1.end())
     cout << "no info";
   else
     cout << a1[name];
   cout << endl;

   Student aStudent;
   cout << "Enter an id and a GPA: ";
   cin >> aStudent.id >> aStudent.GPA;
   map2::iterator it2 = a2.find(aStudent);
   cout << "Student " << aStudent << " is ";

   if (it2 == a2.end())
     cout << "no info";
   else
     cout << a2[aStudent];
   cout << endl;
}
```

SAMPLE RUNS:

```
Enter a name: Fred
Fred has  id = 12345  GPA = 3.3
Enter an id and a GPA: 12345 3.3
Student  id = 12345  GPA = 3.3 is Fred

Enter a name: Hank
Hank has no info
Enter an id and a GPA: 22121 4.0
Student  id = 22121  GPA = 4 is Barb
```

As we noted earlier, the associative containers use red-black trees for storing their elements. For example, the red-black tree used to store the map a1 is

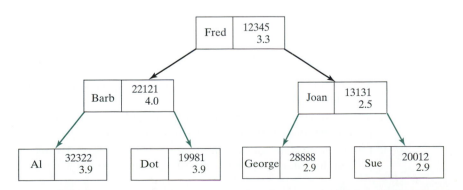

and that for `a2` is

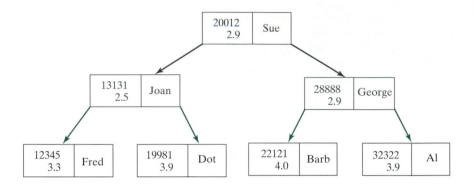

Declarations of the nodes for these red-black trees used to implement `maps` are declared inside class `rb_tree` and have the following form:

```
enum color_type {red, black};
struct rb_tree_node
{
   color_type color_field;
   void_pointer parent_link, left_link, right_link;
   Value value_field;
};
```

✔ Quick Quiz 13.4

1. Name the sequential containers in STL.
2. Name the associative containers in STL.
3. For which of the associative containers is `[]` defined?
4. How is an associative array different from ordinary arrays?
5. The elements in an associative container are stored in a(n) _____ tree.

☞ PROGRAMMING POINTERS

1. AVL rotations can be accomplished by resetting at most 5 links—3 for simple rotations and 5 for double rotations.

2. AVL rotations are always carried out about the last ancestor along the search path to the point of insertion whose balance factor becomes 2 or −2.

3. Top-down insertion with splitting of 4-nodes is best for 2-3-4 trees since it prevents the proliferation of node splitting upward from one level to the next.

4. Using nodes with multiple links—*m* links, where *m* is the maximum number of children any node may have—can waste much space because of all the unused links in the leaves.

5. B-trees are commonly used to search data on disk. Using an order between 50 and 400 seems to work best for such B-trees.

ADT TIPS

1. Threads are links that replace null links in leaves of a BST and point to the (inorder) successors of these leaves. They make it possible to traverse a BST nonrecursively.

2. An AVL tree is a height-balanced tree in which the difference between the height of the left subtree and the height of the right subtree (called the *balance factor*) at every node is always 0, +1, or −1.

3. 2-3-4 trees and B-trees are generalized search trees in which for each value (key) in each node, the items in its left subtree are smaller than that value, and those in its right subtree are greater.

4. 2-3-4 trees are usually implemented with red-black trees.

5. Every tree and forest can be represented by a binary tree using a *left-leftmost-child right-siblings* representation; that is, the leftmost child of a node in the original tree or forest becomes the left child of that node in the binary tree, and all of its siblings are right descendants of that node.

6. The associative containers use red-black trees to store their elements. They have the same operations, except that `map` has a subscript operator that can be used to form *associative arrays* whose indices may be *any* type.

PROGRAMMING PROBLEMS

SECTION 13.1

1. Write a driver program to test the traversal function for right-threaded BSTs in Exercise 8.

2. Write a driver program to test the function for right-threading a BST in Exercise 9.

3. Write a program that uses the techniques of Sec. 13.1 to construct a BST, threads it using the function of Exercise 9, and then traverses it using the function of Exercise 8.

4. Proceed as in 3, but implement the insertion algorithm of Exercise 21 and use this to construct the threaded BST.

SECTION 13.2

5. Write a driver program to test your `AVLTree` class from Exercise 14.

SECTION 13.3

6. Write a driver program to test your red-black tree class template from Exercise 25.

7. Write a driver program to test your B-tree class template from Exercise 26.

8. Write a driver program to test your general-tree class template from Exercise 27.

9. Use your B-tree class template from Exercise 26 in a program that reads words and constructs a B-tree to store these words. The program should then allow the user to enter a word and should search the B-tree for this word.

Chapter 14

GRAPHS AND DIGRAPHS

Chapter Contents

As we noted in Chap. 10 and in the preceding chapter, a tree is a special case of a more general structure known as a *directed graph*, or simply *digraph*. Directed graphs differ from trees in that they need not have a root node and there may be several (or no) paths from one vertex to another. They are useful in modeling communication networks and other networks in which signals, electrical pulses, and the like flow from one node to another along various paths. In other networks there may be no direction associated with the links, and these can be modeled using *undirected graphs*, or simply *graphs*. In this chapter we consider how both directed and undirected graphs can be represented as well as algorithms for some of the basic operations such as searching and traversal.

14.1 DIRECTED GRAPHS

As a mathematical structure, a **directed graph**, or **digraph**, like a tree, consists of a finite set of elements called **vertices** or **nodes**, together with a finite set of **directed arcs** or **edges** that connect pairs of vertices.

For example, a directed graph having six vertices numbered 1, 2, 3, 4, 5, 6 and ten directed arcs joining vertices 1 to 2, 1 to 4, 1 to 5, 2 to 3, 2 to 4, 3 to itself, 4 to 2, 4 to 3, 6 to 2, and 6 to 3, can be pictured as

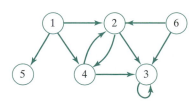

Trees are special kinds of directed graphs and are characterized by the fact that one of their nodes, the root, has no incoming arcs and every other node can be

reached from the root by a unique path, that is, by following one and only one sequence of consecutive arcs. In the preceding digraph, vertex 1 is a "rootlike" node having no incoming arcs, but there are many different paths from vertex 1 to various other nodes, for example, to vertex 3

$$1 \longrightarrow 2 \longrightarrow 3$$

$$1 \longrightarrow 4 \longrightarrow 3$$

$$1 \longrightarrow 4 \longrightarrow 2 \longrightarrow 3$$

$$1 \longrightarrow 4 \longrightarrow 2 \longrightarrow 4 \longrightarrow 3 \longrightarrow 3 \longrightarrow 3$$

Also, there is no path from vertex 1 to vertex 6.

Applications of directed graphs are many and varied. They are used to analyze electrical circuits, develop project schedules, find shortest routes, analyze social relationships, and construct models for the analysis and solution of many other problems. For example, the following directed graph illustrates how digraphs might be used to plan the activities that must be carried out and the order in which they must be done for a (simplified) construction project:

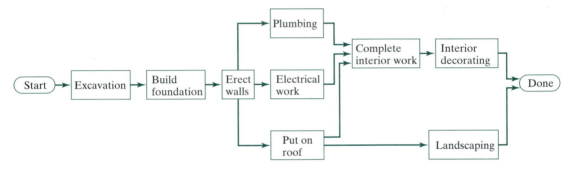

Similarly, flowcharts used to represent algorithms are directed graphs.

As abstract data types, digraphs also differ from trees. For example, the insertion operation for a tree adds a node to the tree, and adding a link to that node from its parent is part of this operation. For digraphs, however, we may insert a node, but no edges to or from it; or we may insert an edge between two existing nodes. Similarly, the deletion operation may apply either to nodes or edges. The following description of a digraph as an ADT includes some of the most common operations on digraphs:

ADT DIRECTED GRAPH

Collection of Data Elements:

A *finite* set of elements called *nodes* or *vertices,* and a finite set of *directed arcs* or *edges* that connect pairs of nodes.

Basic Operations:

Construct an empty directed graph

> Check if it is empty
>
> Destroy a directed graph
>
> Insert a new node
>
> Insert a directed edge between two existing nodes or from a node to itself
>
> Delete a node and all directed edges to or from it
>
> Delete a directed edge between two existing nodes
>
> Search for a value in a node, starting from a given node

Other operations such as the following are important in some applications: traversal, determining if one node is reachable from another node, determining the number of paths from one node to another, or finding a shortest path between two nodes.

ADJACENCY-MATRIX REPRESENTATION

There are several common ways of implementing a directed graph using data structures already known to us. One of these is the **adjacency matrix** of the digraph. To construct it, we first number the vertices of the digraph $1, 2, \ldots, n$; the adjacency matrix is the $n \times n$ matrix adj, in which the entry in row i and column j is 1 (or **true**) if vertex j is **adjacent** to vertex i (that is, if there is a directed arc from vertex i to vertex j), and is 0 (or **false**) otherwise. For example, the adjacency matrix for the digraph

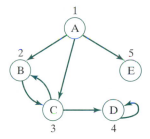

with nodes numbered as shown is

$$adj = \begin{bmatrix} 0 & 1 & 1 & 0 & 1 \\ 0 & 0 & 1 & 0 & 0 \\ 0 & 1 & 0 & 1 & 0 \\ 0 & 0 & 0 & 1 & 0 \\ 0 & 0 & 0 & 0 & 0 \end{bmatrix}$$

For a **weighted digraph** in which some "cost" or "weight" is associated with each arc (e.g., in a digraph modeling a communication network), the cost of the arc from vertex i to vertex j is used instead of 1 in the adjacency matrix.

This matrix representation of a directed graph is straightforward and is useful in a variety of graph problems. For example, with this representation, it is easy to determine the **in-degree** and the **out-degree** of any vertex which are the number of edges coming into or emanating from that vertex, respectively. The sum of the entries in row i of the adjacency matrix is obviously the out-degree of the ith vertex, and the sum of the entries in the ith column is its in-degree.

The matrix representation of a digraph is also useful in path-counting problems. For example, suppose we wish to count the number of paths of length 2 from vertex i to vertex j in a digraph G. Such a path will exist if and only if there is some vertex k such that there is an arc from vertex i to vertex k and an arc from vertex k to vertex j.

This means that both the i, k entry and the k, j entry of the adjacency matrix of G must be 1. Since the i, j entry of adj^2 is the sum of the products of the entries in the ith row with those in the jth column (see Programming Problem 8 at the end of Chap. 2), each such vertex k contributes 1 to the sum. Thus, the i, j entry of adj^2 will be the number of paths of length 2 from vertex i to vertex j. In general, the i, j entry of the kth power of adj, adj^k, indicates the number of paths of length k from vertex i to vertex j. For example, for the preceding digraph,

$$adj^3 = \begin{bmatrix} 0 & 1 & 1 & 2 & 0 \\ 0 & 0 & 1 & 1 & 0 \\ 0 & 1 & 0 & 2 & 0 \\ 0 & 0 & 0 & 1 & 0 \\ 0 & 0 & 0 & 0 & 0 \end{bmatrix}$$

The entry in position 1, 4 is 2, indicating that there are 2 paths of length 3 from vertex 1 (A) to vertex 4 (D): A→B→C→D and A→C→D→D.

There are, however, some deficiencies in this representation. One is that it does not store the data items in the vertices of the digraph, the letters A, B, C, D, and E in our example. But this difficulty is easily remedied; we need only create an auxiliary array *data* and store the data item for the ith vertex in *data* [i]. For our example, therefore, the two arrays

$$adj = \begin{bmatrix} 0 & 1 & 1 & 0 & 1 \\ 0 & 0 & 1 & 0 & 0 \\ 0 & 1 & 0 & 1 & 0 \\ 0 & 0 & 0 & 1 & 0 \\ 0 & 0 & 0 & 0 & 0 \end{bmatrix} \qquad data = \begin{bmatrix} A \\ B \\ C \\ D \\ E \end{bmatrix}$$

completely characterize the digraph.

ADJACENCY-LIST REPRESENTATION
Another deficiency of the adjacency-matrix representation is that this matrix is often **sparse**, that is, it has many zero entries, and thus considerable space is "wasted" in storing these zero values. We can alleviate this problem by adapting one of the representations of sparse matrices described in Sec. 9.5. For example,

modifying the representation of a sparse matrix as an array of pointers to linked row-lists gives rise to the **adjacency-list representation** for digraphs. The directed graph is represented by an array or `vector` $v[1], v[2], \ldots, v[n]$, one element for each vertex in the digraph. Each $v[i]$ stores the data stored in vertex i together with a linked list of the numbers of all vertices adjacent to vertex i. For example, the adjacency-list representation of the digraph

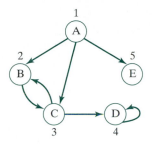

can be pictured as follows:

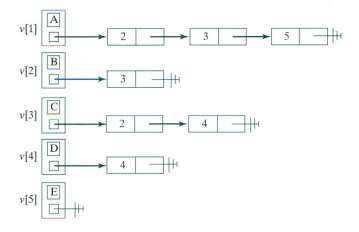

Note that the numbers in the list nodes are the numbers of the columns in the adjacency matrix in which 1's appear. These nodes thus play the same role as the nodes in the row lists of the sparse matrix representation considered in Chap. 9.

This adjacency-list representation of a digraph can be implemented as a class template in C++ with declarations like the following:

```
#include list
#include vector
using namespace std;
```

```
template <typename DataType>
class Digraph
{
public:
// Operations
    . . .
private:
// Data Members
  class VertexInfo
  {
   public:
    DataType data;
    list<int> adjacencyList;
  };
  vector<VertexInfo> v;
};
```

In the next section we use this adjacency-list representation in a program to find the shortest path joining two specified nodes in a directed graph.

✔ Quick Quiz 14.1

1. What are some ways a directed graph differs from a tree?
2. In a digraph, it may not be possible to get from one vertex to another. (True or false)
3. In a digraph, vertex *v* is said to be _____ to vertex *if* there is a directed arc from *v* to *w*.
4. In a digraph, the number of edges coming into a vertex is called the _____ of that vertex and the number of edges emanating from a vertex is called its _____ .

For Questions 5–8, use the following directed graphs:

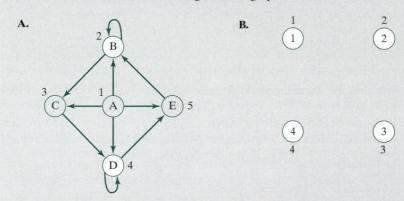

5. Give the adjacency matrix *adj* and the data matrix *data* for digraph A.
6. Give the adjacency matrix *adj* and the data matrix *data* for digraph B.
7. Give the adjacency-list representation of digraph A.
8. Give the adjacency-list representation of digraph B.

✎ EXERCISES **14.1**

For Exercises 1–4, find the adjacency matrix *adj* and the data matrix *data* for the given digraph.

1.

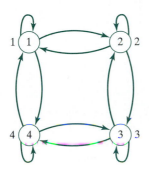

2.

1 16   22 2

4 57   40 3

3.

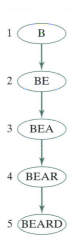

1 B

2 BE

3 BEA

4 BEAR

5 BEARD

4.

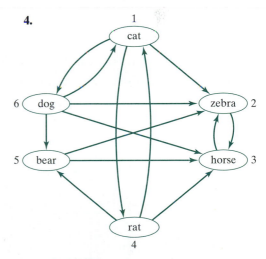

For Exercises 5–8, find the directed graph represented by the given adjacency matrix *adj* and the data matrix *data*.

5. $adj = \begin{bmatrix} 0 & 1 & 0 & 1 & 0 \\ 1 & 1 & 1 & 0 & 0 \\ 0 & 0 & 0 & 0 & 1 \\ 0 & 1 & 0 & 0 & 1 \\ 0 & 0 & 0 & 0 & 0 \end{bmatrix}, data = \begin{bmatrix} A \\ B \\ C \\ D \\ E \end{bmatrix}$

6. $adj = \begin{bmatrix} 0 & 1 & 1 & 1 \\ 0 & 0 & 1 & 1 \\ 0 & 0 & 0 & 1 \\ 0 & 0 & 0 & 0 \end{bmatrix}, data = \begin{bmatrix} CAT \\ RAT \\ BAT \\ DOG \end{bmatrix}$

7. $adj = \begin{bmatrix} 1 & 1 & 1 \\ 1 & 1 & 1 \\ 1 & 1 & 1 \end{bmatrix}, data = \begin{bmatrix} 111 \\ 222 \\ 333 \end{bmatrix}$

8. $adj = \begin{bmatrix} 1 & 0 & 0 & 1 & 0 & 0 & 1 \\ 0 & 0 & 1 & 1 & 1 & 0 & 0 \\ 0 & 0 & 1 & 1 & 0 & 0 & 1 \\ 1 & 1 & 1 & 1 & 1 & 1 & 1 \\ 0 & 0 & 0 & 0 & 0 & 0 & 0 \\ 0 & 0 & 1 & 1 & 0 & 0 & 1 \\ 1 & 0 & 0 & 0 & 0 & 1 & 0 \end{bmatrix}, data = \begin{bmatrix} \text{Alpha} \\ \text{Beta} \\ \text{Gamma} \\ \text{Delta} \\ \text{Mu} \\ \text{Pi} \\ \text{Rho} \end{bmatrix}$

9–12. Give the adjacency-list representation of the directed graphs in Exercises 1–4.

13–16. Give the adjacency-list representation of the directed graphs in Exercises 5–8.

An alternative to the adjacency-list representation for a directed graph is a *linked adjacency-list* representation that uses a linked list instead of an array or `vector`, one list node for each vertex in the digraph. A list node stores the data stored in a vertex together with a linked list of the numbers of all vertices adjacent to that vertex.

17–20. Give the linked adjacency-list representation of the directed graphs in Exercises 1–4.

21–24. Give the linked adjacency-list representation of the directed graphs in Exercises 5–8.

In Exercises 25–30, draw the directed graph represented by the adjacency-list.

25.

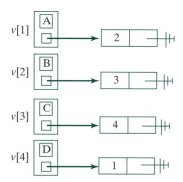

26.

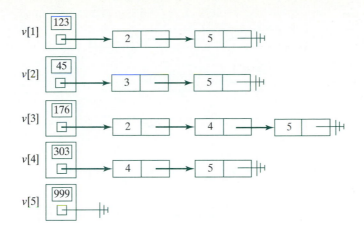

27.

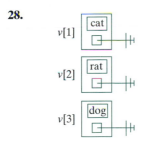

28.

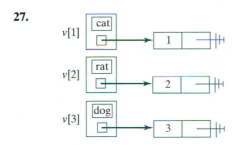

29.

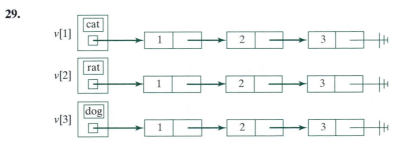

30.

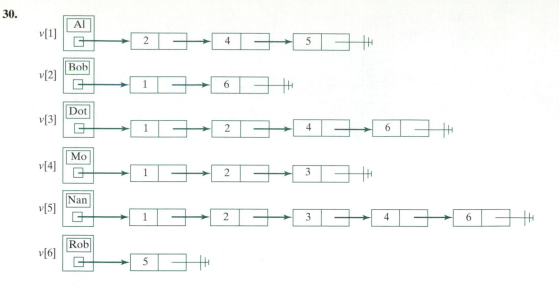

14.2 SEARCHING AND TRAVERSING DIGRAPHS

One of the basic operations we considered for trees was traversal, visiting each node exactly once, and we described three standard traversal orders for binary trees: inorder, preorder, and postorder. Traversal of a tree is always possible if we begin at the root, because every other node is reachable from this root via a sequence of consecutive arcs. In a general directed graph, however, there may not be a vertex from which every other vertex can be reached, and thus it may not be possible to traverse the entire digraph, regardless of the start vertex. Consequently, we must first look at the problem of determining which nodes in a digraph are reachable from a given node. Two standard methods of searching for such vertices are **depth-first search** and **breadth-first search.** We illustrate these methods first for trees.

To illustrate depth-first search, consider the following tree:

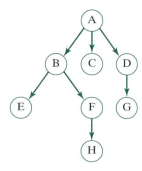

If we begin at the root, we first visit it and then select one of its children, say B, and then visit it. Before visiting the other children of A, however, we visit the descendents of B in a depth-first manner. Thus we select one of its children, say E, and visit it:

A, B, E

Again, before visiting the other child of B, we must visit the descendents of E. Because there are none, we backtrack to B and visit its other child F and then visit the descendents of F:

A, B, E, F, H

Because all of B's descendants have now been visited, we can now backtrack to the last previously visited node along this search path, namely A, and begin visiting the rest of its descendants. We might select C and its descendants (of which there are none):

A, B, E, F, H, C

and finally, visit D and its descendants:

A, B, E, F, H, C, D, G

One question that must be addressed is how to do the required **backtracking**. It is important in many problems wherever it is necessary to process some values and later return to some that were already processed or that were skipped over on an earlier pass. For example, in Sec. 10.1, we saw how threads could be used to make backtracking possible in carrying out an inorder traversal of a binary search tree. The usual solution in these problems is to store the items in a *stack* as they are encountered. Then when it is necessary to return to an earlier item, we simply pop one from the stack. As one might guess, recursion is a natural technique for such problems, because a stack is automatically maintained to make backtracking possible.

In contrast to depth-first search, a breadth-first search of the given tree, beginning at the root, first visits the root and each of its children, say, from left to right:

A, B, C, D

The children of these first-level nodes are then visited

A, B, C, D, E, F, G

and finally, the children of the second-level nodes E, F, and G are visited:

A, B, C, D, E, F, G, H

Here we are visiting the nodes level by level, and while visiting each node on some level, we must store it so we can return to it after completing this level, so that the nodes adjacent to it can be visited. Because the first node visited on this level should be the first one to which we return, a *queue* is an appropriate data structure for storing the nodes.

DEPTH-FIRST SEARCH

A depth-first search of a general directed graph from a given start vertex is similar to that for trees. We visit the start vertex and then follow directed arcs as "deeply" as possible to visit the vertices reachable from it that have not already been visited, backtracking when necessary. For example, a depth-first search of the digraph

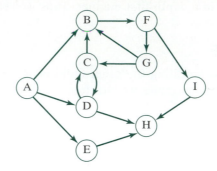

beginning at vertex A might first visit vertices A, B, F, I, and H. We then backtrack to I, the last node visited on this search path, but no unvisited nodes are reachable from it. So we backtrack to F and from there visit G, from which we can reach vertices C and D (as well as B, F, I, and H—but they have already been visited). We backtrack to C, but no unvisited nodes are reachable from it, so we backtrack to G. Finding no unvisited nodes reachable from it, we backtrack to F and then to B; there are no unvisited nodes reachable from either of these vertices. Finally, we backtrack to A, from which we can reach the last unvisited vertex E. We have visited the vertices in the order

  A, B, F, I, H, G, C, D, E

If we start a depth-first search from some vertices, we may not be able to reach all of the other vertices. For example, a depth-first search starting at B will visit the vertices

  B, F, I, H, G, C, D

but we cannot reach vertices A and E.

The following is a recursive algorithm for depth-first search. At each stage, after visiting a vertex, we select some unvisited vertex adjacent to it (if there are any) and use it as the start vertex for a depth-first search.

 ## DEPTH-FIRST SEARCH ALGORITHM

/*   Algorithm to perform a depth-first search of a digraph
      to visit all vertices reachable from a given start vertex *v*.

      Receive: A digraph and a vertex *v*

      Return/Output: Depends on the type of processing done
                       when a vertex is visited
---*/

1. Visit the start vertex *v*.

2. For each vertex *w* adjacent to *v* do the following:
      If *w* has not been visited, apply the depth-first search algorithm
      with *w* as the start vertex.

This algorithm is implemented by the member functions `DepthFirstSearch()` and `DepthFirstSearchAux()` in Fig. 14.1. (Two functions are used, one to initialize the vector `unvisited` and then call an auxiliary function that does the recursive depth-first searching.)

BREADTH-FIRST SEARCH
In a breadth-first search of the preceding directed graph

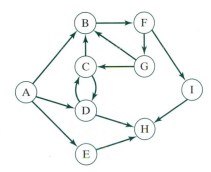

beginning at A, we visit A and then all those vertices adjacent to A:

> A, B, D, E

We then select B, the first vertex adjacent to A, and visit all unvisited vertices adjacent to it:

> A, B, D, E, F

We repeat this for D, the next vertex adjacent to A, and visit all unvisited vertices adjacent to it,

> A, B, D, E, F, C, H

and then for E, the last vertex adjacent to A, for which the only adjacent vertex is H, which was already visited.

Having finished with B, D, and E, the nodes adjacent to A, we now repeat this approach for the unvisited vertices adjacent to them: F, then C, and then H. G and I are adjacent to F, so we visit them:

> A, B, D, E, F, C, H, G, I

A, B, and D are adjacent to C, but these vertices have already been visited, and no vertices are adjacent to H. Since all of the vertices have been visited, the search terminates.

As was true for depth-first search, a breadth-first search from some vertices may fail to locate all vertices. For example a breadth-first search from B might first visit B and F, then G and I, followed by H and C, and finally D:

> B, F, G, I, H, C, D

Because A and E are not reachable from B, the search terminates.

As we noted in looking at breadth-first search for trees, a queue is an appropriate data structure to store the vertices as they are visited. The following algorithm uses a queue in this manner:

BREADTH-FIRST SEARCH ALGORITHM

/*   Algorithm to perform a breadth-first search of a digraph
      to visit all vertices reachable from a given start vertex *v*.

    Receive: A digraph and a vertex *v*

    Return/Output: Depends on the type of processing done
                     when a vertex is visited
--*/

1. Visit the start vertex.

2. Initialize a queue to contain only the start vertex.

3. While the queue is not empty do the following:

    a. Remove a vertex *v* from the queue.

    b. For all vertices *w* adjacent to *v* do the following:
        If *w* has not been visited then:
            i. Visit *w*.
           ii. Add *w* to the queue.

TRAVERSAL AND SHORTEST-PATH PROBLEMS

Search algorithms like those for depth-first and breadth-first searches are basic to many other algorithms for processing directed graphs. For example, to traverse a digraph, we can repeatedly apply one of these searches, selecting new start vertices when necessary, until all of the vertices have been visited. Thus one possible traversal algorithm is:

DIGRAPH TRAVERSAL ALGORITHM

/*   Algorithm to traverse a digraph, visiting each vertex exactly
      once. A depth-first search is the basis of the traversal.

    Receive: A digraph

    Return/Output: Depends on the type of processing done
                     when a vertex is visited
--*/

1. Initialize an array or `vector` *unvisited* with *unvisited*[*i*] false for each vertex *i*.

2. While some element of *unvisited* is false, do the following:

    a. Select an unvisited vertex *v*.

    b. Use the depth-first search algorithm to visit all vertices
        reachable from *v*.

Another class of problems that require search algorithms for their solutions are **routing problems** in which one must find an optimal path in a network—a shortest path in a graph or a digraph, a cheapest path in a weighted graph or digraph, and so on. The Dutch computer scientist Edsger Dijkstra is well-known for his algorithms used in many such problems.

As a simple example of a routing problem, consider a directed graph that models an airline network in which the vertices represent cities and the directed arcs represent flights connecting these cities. We may be interested in determining the most direct route between two cities, that is, the route with the fewest intermediate stops. In terms of a digraph modeling such a network, we must determine the length of a shortest path, one composed of a minimum number of arcs, from a start vertex to a destination vertex. An algorithm for determining such a shortest path is an easy modification of the breadth-first search algorithm:

A SHORTEST-PATH ALGORITHM

/*   Algorithm to find a shortest path from a start vertex to a destination vertex in a digraph.

Receive: A digraph, a *start* vertex and a *destination* vertex

Return/Output: The vertices on a shortest path from *start* to *destination* or a message indicating that *destination* is not reachable from *start*
---*/

1. Visit *start* and label it with 0.

2. Initialize *distance* to 0.

3. Initialize a queue to contain only *start*.

4. While *destination* has not been visited and the queue is not empty, do the following:

    a. Remove a vertex *v* from the queue.
    b. If the label of *v* is greater than *distance*, increment *distance* by 1.
    c. For each vertex *w* adjacent to *v*:
       If *w* has not been visited, then
          i. Visit *w* and label it with *distance* + 1.
          ii. Add *w* to the queue.

5. If *destination* has not been visited then

    Display "Destination not reachable from start vertex."

    Else find the vertices $p[0], \ldots, p[distance]$ on the shortest path as follows:

    a. Initialize $p[distance]$ to *destination*.
    b. For each value of *k* ranging from *distance* − 1 down to 0:
       Find a vertex $p[k]$ adjacent to $p[k + 1]$ with label *k*.

The following table traces the execution of the first part of this algorithm as it finds the shortest path from vertex A to vertex H in the digraph given earlier:

Step(s)	v	distance	Queue	A	B	C	D	E	F	G	H	I
1, 2, 3		0	A	0								
4	A	0	B D E	0	1		1	1				
4	B	1	D E F	0	1		1	1	2			
4	D	1	E F C H	0	1	2	1	1	2		2	
4	E	1	F C H	0	1	2	1	1	2		2	
4	F	2	C H G I	0	1	2	1	1	2	3	2	3
4	C	2	H G I	0	1	2	1	2	2	3	2	3
4	H	2		0	1	2	1	2	2	3	2	3

Step 5 then determines a sequence of vertices on a path from A to H, for example, $p[2] = $ 'H', $p[1] = $ 'D', $p[0] = $ 'A'.

The program in Fig. 14.1 uses this algorithm to solve the airline network problem just described. The adjacency-list representation of the network is input from networkFile. Each city is identified by both number and name, and the ith line of the file contains the name of the ith city followed by the numbers of all vertices adjacent to the ith vertex. The user then enters the name of a start city and the name of a destination, and the member function ShortestPath() of class template Digraph is used to find the shortest path from the start vertex to the destination vertex if there is one.

FIGURE 14.1   SHORTEST PATHS IN A NETWORK

```
//--- The Digraph Class Template
//==============================

#include <list>
#include <vector>
#include <queue>
#include <iostream>
#include <fstream>
using namespace std;

template <typename DataType>
class Digraph
{
// Operations
public:
/* Retrieve data value in a given vertex.
 *
 * Receive:   Digraph containing this function (implicitly)
 *            Number k of a vertex
 * Return:    Data value stored in vertex #k
 *************************************************************/
DataType Data(int k) const;
```

```
/* Input operator
 *
 * Receive:       ifstream inFile and digraph (implicitly)
 * Input(inFile): The lines in inFile; must be organized so
 *                that the data item in a vertex is on one
 *                line and on the next line is the number of
 *                vertices adjacent to it followed by a list
 *                of the numbers of these adjacent vertices
 * Pass back:     modified ifstream inFile
 ***********************************************************/
void Read(ifstream & inFile);

/* Output operator
 *
 * Receive:   ostream out and digraph (implicitly).
 * Output:    Each vertex's data value and its
 *               adjacency list
 * Pass back: modified ostream out
 ***********************************************************/
void Print(ostream & out);

/* Depth first search of digraph, starting at vertex start.
 *
 * Receive:   Digraph containing this function (implicitly)
 *            Vector unvisited with unvisited[i] = true if
 *              vertex i has not yet been visited, and
 *              false otherwise
 * Pass back: Updated list unvisited
 * Output:    Depends on the type of processing done when
 *              a node is visited
 ***********************************************************/
void DepthFirstSearchAux(int start, vector<bool> & unvisited);

void DepthFirstSearch(int start);

/* Find a shortest path in the digraph from vertex start to
 * vertex destination.
 *
 *  Receive: Digraph d, start and destination vertices
 *  Return:  A vector of vertices along this shortest path
 ***********************************************************/
vector<int> ShortestPath(int start, int destination);

private:
// "Head nodes" of adjacency lists
  class VertexInfo
  {
  public:
    DataType data;
    list<int> adjacencyList;
  };
```

```cpp
   // Data Members
     vector<VertexInfo> v;
}; // end of class declaration

//--- Definition of Data()
template <typename DataType>
inline DataType Digraph<DataType>::Data(int k) const
{ return v[k].data; }

//--- Definition of Read()
template <typename DataType>
void Digraph<DataType>::Read(ifstream & inFile)
{
  Digraph<DataType>::VertexInfo vi;
  int n,                // number of vertices adjacent to some vertex
      vertex;           // the number of a vertex

  v.push_back(vi); // garbage 0-th value so indices start with 1,
                   // as is customary
  for (;;)
  {
    inFile >> vi.data;
    if (inFile.eof()) break;
    inFile >> n;

    list<int> adjList;      // construct empty list
    for (int i = 1; i <= n; i++)
    {
      inFile >> vertex;
      adjList.push_back(vertex);
    }
    vi.adjacencyList = adjList;
    v.push_back(vi);
  }
}


template <typename DataType>
void Digraph<DataType>::Print(ostream & out)
{
  out << "Adjacency-List Representation: \n";
  for (int i = 1; i < v.size(); i++)
  {
    out << i << ": " <<  v[i].data << "--";
    for (list<int>::iterator it = v[i].adjacencyList.begin();
                             it != v[i].adjacencyList.end(); it++)
      out << *it << "  ";
    out << endl;
  }
}
```

```cpp
//-- Definitions of DepthFirstSearch() and DepthFirstSearchAux()
template <typename DataType>
void Digraph<DataType>
::DepthFirstSearchAux(int start, vector<bool> & unvisited)
{
  // Add statements here to process v[start].data
  cout << v[start].data << endl;
  unvisited[start] = false;

  // Traverse its adjacency list, performing depth-first
  // searches from each unvisited vertex in it.
  for (list<int>::iterator
          it = v[start].adjacencyList.begin();
          it != v[start].adjacencyList.end(); it++)
    // check if current vertex has been visited
    if (unvisited[*it])
      // start DFS from new node
      DepthFirstSearchAux(*it, unvisited);
}

template <typename DataType>
void Digraph<DataType>::DepthFirstSearch(int start)
{
  vector<bool> unvisited(v.size(), true);
  DepthFirstSearchAux(start, unvisited);
}

//--- Definition of ShortestPath()
template<typename DataType>
vector<int> Digraph<DataType>::ShortestPath(int start, int destination)
{
  int n = v.size();                  // number of vertices (#ed from 1)
  vector<int> distLabel(n,-1),   // distance labels for vertices, all
                                 // marked as unvisited (-1)
              predLabel(n);      // predecessor labels for vertices

  // Perform breadth first search from Start to find destination,
  // labeling vertices with distances from start as we go.

  distLabel[start] = 0;
  int distance = 0,              // distance from start vertex
      vertex;                    // a vertex
  queue<int> vertexQueue;        // queue of vertices
  vertexQueue.push(start);
  while (distLabel[destination] < 0 && !vertexQueue.empty())
  {
    vertex = vertexQueue.front();
    vertexQueue.pop();
    if (distLabel[vertex] > distance)
      distance++;
```

```cpp
       for (list<int>::iterator it = v[vertex].adjacencyList.begin();
                             it != v[vertex].adjacencyList.end(); it++)
         if (distLabel[*it] < 0)
         {
           distLabel[*it] = distance + 1;
           predLabel[*it] = vertex;
           vertexQueue.push(*it);
         }
     }
     distance++;

     // Now reconstruct the shortest path if there is one
     vector<int> path(distance+1);
     if (distLabel[destination] < 0)
       cout << "Destination not reachable from start vertex\n";
     else
     {
       path[distance] = destination;
       for (int k = distance - 1; k >= 0; k--)
         path[k] = predLabel[path[k+1]];
     }

     return path;
}

//--- The Program
//=====================================================================
/* Program to find the most direct route in an airline network from a
 * given start city to a given destination city.  A digraph represented
 * by its adjacency-list implementation is used for the network, and
 * the information needed to construct it is read from networkFile.
 *
 *   Input (file):     A text file networkFile containing network
 *                       information
 *   Input (keyboard): Several start and destination vertices and a
 *                       user response that controls repetition
 *   Output (screen):  Names of cities along the shortest path
 ********************************************************************/

#include "Digraph"
#include <iostream>
#include <fstream>
#include <iomanip>
#include <string>
#include <vector>
using namespace std;

int main()
{
  cout << "Enter name of network file: ";
  string networkFile;
  cin >> networkFile;
```

```
ifstream inFile(networkFile.data());
if (!inFile.is_open())
{
  cerr << "*** Cannot open " << networkFile << " ***\n";
  exit(-1);
}

Digraph<string> d;
d.Read(inFile);
cout << "The Digraph's ";
d.Print(cout);
cout << endl;

int start, destination;
char response;
do
{
  cout << "Number of start city? ";
  cin >> start;
  cout << "Number of destination? ";
  cin >> destination;

  vector<int> path = d.ShortestPath(start, destination);
  cout << "Shortest path is:\n";
  for (int k = 0; k < path.size(); k++)
  {
    cout << setw(3) << path[k] << ' ' << d.Data(path[k]) << endl;
    cout << "         |\n"
            "         v\n";
  }
  cout << setw(3) << destination << ' '
       << d.Data(destination) << endl;
  cout << "\nMore (Y or N)?";
  cin >> response;
}
while (response == 'y' || response == 'Y');
}
```

LISTING OF `NetworkFile`:

```
Los_Angeles
3 3 4 6
San_Francisco
3 1 3 4
Denver
3 1 2 3
Chicago
2 3 8
Boston
2 4 6
New_York
3 4 7 8
```

```
Miami
3 8 3 5
New_Orleans
2 1 7
```

SAMPLE RUN:

```
Enter name of network file: NetworkFile
The Digraph's Adjacency-List Representation:
1: Los_Angeles--3  4  6
2: San_Francisco--1  3  4
3: Denver--1  2  3
4: Chicago--3  8
5: Boston--4  6
6: New_York--4  7  8
7: Miami--8  3  5
8: New_Orleans--1  7

Number of start city? 5
Number of destination? 1
Shortest path is:
  5 Boston
     |
     v
  4 Chicago
     |
     v
  3 Denver
     |
     v
  1 Los_Angeles
     |
     v
  1 Los_Angeles

More (Y or N)?N
```

NP-COMPLETE PROBLEMS

A classic routing problem that is of both practical and theoretical interest is the **traveling salesman problem**. In this problem, a weighted digraph with vertices representing cities and the cost of an arc representing the distance between the cities must be traversed using a path of minimal total cost. The practical importance of this problem should be obvious.

The traveling salesman problem belongs to the large collection of problems known as **NP**, which stands for *nondeterministic polynomial*. These are problems for which a solution can be guessed and then checked with an algorithm whose computing time is $O(P(n))$ for some polynomial $P(n)$. No particular strategy is required for guessing—thus the nondeterminism. This is in contrast to the collection **P**, which stands for *(deterministic) polynomial time*. These problems can be solved by algorithms in polynomial time.

One of the most important problems in computer science theory is:

> Are there **NP** problems that are not **P** problems?

No one has ever found such a problem, but neither has anyone been able to prove that one does not exist.

The traveling salesman problem is in fact a special kind of NP problem called an **NP-complete** problem. These problems have the property that if a polynomial time algorithm that solves *any one* of these problems can be found—for example, for the traveling salesman problem—then the existence of polynomial time algorithms for *all* NP problems is guaranteed; that is NP = P.

✔ Quick Quiz 14.2

1. What is backtracking?
2. For the digraph labeled A in Quick Quiz 14.1, which nodes can be reached using a depth-first search from: vertex 1? from vertex 2?
3. For the digraph labeled B in Quick Quiz 14.1, which nodes can be reached using a depth-first search from vertex 1?
4. For a breadth-first search of the digraph labeled A in Quick Quiz 14.1 starting from vertex 1, which nodes will be visited next?
5. What are NP problems? P problems? NP-complete problems?

✍ EXERCISES 14.2

For Exercises 1–5, construct a trace table for the algorithm, using the digraph in Exercise 1 of Sec. 14.1. Whenever a new vertex to visit must be selected and there is more than one possibility, use the vertex labeled with the smallest number.

1. Depth-first traversal starting at vertex 1.
2. Depth-first traversal starting at vertex 2.
3. Breadth-first traversal starting at vertex 1.
4. Breadth-first traversal starting at vertex 2.
5. Shortest path from vertex 2 to vertex 4.

For Exercises 6–10, proceed as in Exercises 1–5 but use the digraph in Exercise 4 of Sec. 14.1.

6. Depth-first traversal starting at vertex 1.
7. Depth-first traversal starting at vertex 2.
8. Breadth-first traversal starting at vertex 1.
9. Breadth-first traversal starting at vertex 2.
10. Shortest path from vertex 4 to vertex 6.

For Exercises 11–19, proceed as in Exercises 1–5 but use the following digraph. Whenever a new vertex to visit must be selected and there is more than one possibility, use the vertex containing the letter that comes earliest in the alphabet.

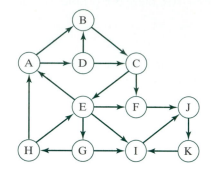

11. Depth-first traversal starting at vertex A.

12. Depth-first traversal starting at vertex F.

13. Breadth-first traversal starting at vertex A.

14. Breadth-first traversal starting at vertex F.

15. Shortest path from vertex A to vertex E.

16. Shortest path from vertex A to vertex H.

17. Shortest path from vertex G to vertex C.

18. Shortest path from vertex J to vertex I.

19. Shortest path from vertex J to vertex A.

The following exercises ask you to write functions. You should also write driver programs to test them, as instructed in Programming Problems 1–4 at the end of this chapter.

20. Add a member function to the `Digraph` class template for doing a breadth-first search from some start vertex.

21. If A is an $n \times n$ adjacency matrix for a directed graph, then the entry in the ith row and jth column of A^k is equal to the number of paths of length k from the ith vertex to the jth vertex in this digraph. The *reachability matrix* R of a digraph is the $n \times n$ matrix defined by

$$R = I + A + A^2 + \cdots + A^{n-1}$$

where I is the $n \times n$ identity matrix having ones on the diagonal and zeros off. In the digraph, there is a path from vertex i to vertex j if and only if the entry in row i and column j of R is nonzero. Write a function to find the reachability matrix for a directed graph.

22. An alternative to the method of Exercise 21 for determining reachability is to use "boolean multiplication and addition," that is, *bitwise and* (&) and *bitwise or* (|) operations, in carrying out the matrix computations ($0 = false$, $1 = true$). Rewrite the function in Exercise 21 to find this form of the reachability matrix.

23. *Warshall's algorithm* provides a more efficient method for calculating the boolean form of the reachability matrix described in Exercise 21:

    a. Initialize R to A and k to 1.

    b. While $k \leq n$ and R is not all ones do the following:

        i. For i ranging from 1 to n with $i \neq k$:

            If the entry in the ith row and kth column of R is 1, then replace row i with (row i) or (row k).

        ii. Increment k by 1.

Use Warshall's algorithm to find the reachability matrix for the following digraph:

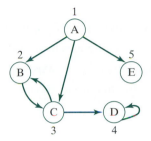

24. Write a function to find the reachability matrix of a digraph using Warshall's algorithm.

14.3 GRAPHS

A **graph**, sometimes called an **undirected graph**, is like a digraph except that no direction is associated with the edges. Also, no loops joining a vertex to itself are allowed. For example, the following diagram shows a graph having five vertices with edges joining vertices 1 and 2, 1 and 4, 1 and 5, 2 and 4, 3 and 4, and 4 and 5:

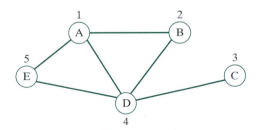

Such graphs are useful in modeling electrical circuits, structures of chemical compounds, communication systems, and many other networks in which no direction is associated with the links.

    As ADTs, graphs and digraphs have basically the same operations:

ADT GRAPH

Collection of Data Elements:

A *finite* set of elements called *nodes* or *vertices,* and a finite set of *edges* that connect pairs of distinct nodes.

Basic Operations:

Construct an empty graph

Check if it is empty

Destroy a graph

Insert a new node

Insert an edge between two existing nodes

Delete a node and all edges having it as an endpoint

Delete an edge between two existing nodes

Search for a value in a node, starting from a given node

Most of the other operations described for digraphs—traversals, finding shortest paths, and so forth—are also important in applications of graphs.

ADJACENCY-MATRIX AND ADJACENCY-LIST REPRESENTATIONS

Like digraphs, graphs can be represented by either adjacency matrices or adjacency lists. For example, the adjacency matrix for the preceding graph is

$$adj = \begin{bmatrix} 0 & 1 & 0 & 1 & 1 \\ 1 & 0 & 0 & 1 & 0 \\ 0 & 0 & 0 & 1 & 0 \\ 1 & 1 & 1 & 0 & 1 \\ 1 & 0 & 0 & 1 & 0 \end{bmatrix}$$

where a 1 in row i and column j indicates the existence of an edge joining the ith and jth vertices. Because these edges are undirected, there also is a 1 in row j and column i; thus the adjacency matrix for an undirected graph is always **symmetric**. This means that the entries on one side of the diagonal (from the upper-left corner to the lower-right corner) are redundant. Also, since undirected graphs have no loops, all entries on the diagonal of the adjacency matrix are 0. Consequently, the adjacency matrix is not a very efficient representation of an undirected graph (unless we use a *jagged* two-dimensional table as described in Sec. 6.5).

The adjacency-list representation for the preceding graph is

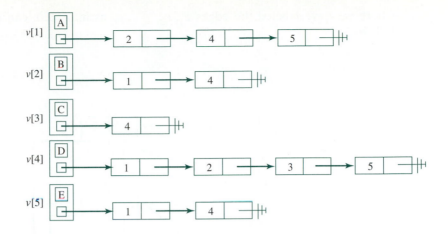

Like the adjacency matrix, this representation is also not very efficient because redundant information is stored. If an edge joins vertices *i* and *j*, then a vertex node containing vertex *i* appears in the adjacency list for vertex *j*, and a vertex node containing vertex *j* appears in the adjacency list for vertex *i*.

EDGE-LIST REPRESENTATION

A more efficient representation of a graph uses **edge lists.** Each **edge node** in one of these lists represents one edge in the graph and has the form

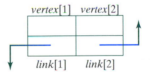

where *vertex*[1] and *vertex*[2] are vertices connected by an edge, *link*[1] points to another edge node having *vertex*[1] as one endpoint, and *link*[2] points to another edge node having *vertex*[2] as an endpoint. The edge-list representation then consists of an array or `vector` *v* of classes (or structs), one for each vertex, with each class containing a data member and a pointer to an edge node having that vertex as one of its endpoints. For example, the edge-list representation for the graph

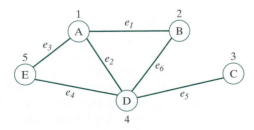

where we have labeled the edges $e_1, e_2, \ldots, e_6$ as indicated, can be pictured as follows:

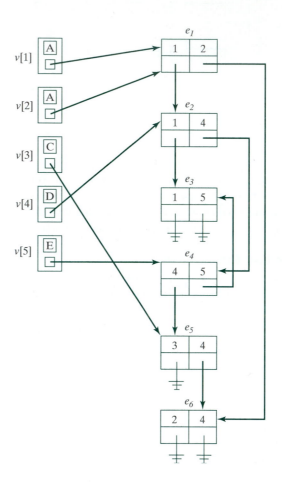

CONNECTEDNESS

Depth-first search, breadth-first search, traversal, and other algorithms for processing graphs are similar to those for digraphs. For example, the program in Fig. 14.2 uses a depth-first search to determine whether a graph is **connected**, that is, whether there is a path from each vertex to every other vertex. The member function Read() of class template Graph builds the edge-list representation of the graph from user input, and the member function Connected() calls DepthFirstSearch() to do a depth-first search, marking those vertices that are reachable from vertex 1. Other member functions for Graph are left as exercises.

FIGURE 14.2   GRAPH CONNECTEDNESS

```
//--- The Graph Class Template
//=============================

#include <vector>
#include <iostream>
using namespace std;

template <typename DataType>
class Graph
{
// Operations
public:

/* Retrieve data value in a given vertex.
 *
 * Receive:  Graph containing this function (implicitly)
 *           Number k of a vertex
 * Return:   Data value stored in vertex #k
 ***********************************************************/
DataType Data(int k) const;

/* Input operator to build the edge-list representation of
 * the graph from user input.
 *
 * Receive:   istream in and graph (implicitly)
 *            number of vertices and edges
 * Input:     Vertices and edges of graph
 * Pass back: Modified istream in
 ***********************************************************/
void Read(istream & in, int numVertices, int numEdges);

/* Do a depth-first search of graph from start vertex.
 *
 * Receive:   Graph containing this function (implicitly)
 *            Vector unvisited with unvisited[i] = true if
 *               vertex i has not yet been visited, and
 *               false otherwise
 * Pass back: Updated list unvisited
 * Output:    Depends on the type of processing done when
 *               a node is visited
 ***********************************************************/
void DepthFirstSearch(int start, vector<bool> & unvisited);
```

```
/* Check if graph is connected.
 *
 * Receive: Graph containing this function (implicitly)
 * Return:  True if graph is connected, false if not
 ************************************************************/
bool Connected();

private:
// Edge Nodes
  class EdgeNode
  {
  public:
    int vertex[3];           // Use 1 and 2 for indices
    EdgeNode * link[3];      //   as is customary
  };
  typedef EdgeNode * EdgePointer;

// "Head nodes" of edge lists
  class VertexInfo
  {
  public:
    DataType data;           // data value in vertex
    EdgePointer first;       // pointer to first edge node
  };

// Data Members
  vector<VertexInfo> v;
}; // end of class declaration

//--- Definition of Data()
template <typename DataType>
inline DataType Graph<DataType>::Data(int k) const
{ return v[k].data; }

//--- Definition of Read()
template <typename DataType>
void Graph<DataType>::Read(istream & in, int numVertices, int numEdges)
{
  Graph<DataType>::VertexInfo vi;
  v.push_back(vi); // garbage 0-th value so indices start with 1,
                   // as is customary

  // Create "head nodes"
  cout << "Enter label of vertex:\n";
  for (int i = 1; i <= numVertices; i++)
  {
    cout << "   " << i << ": ";
    in >> vi.data;
    vi.first = 0;
    v.push_back(vi);
  }
```

```
      int endpoint;          // endpoint of an edge
      // Create edge lists
      cout << "Enter endpoints of edge\n";
      for (int i = 1; i <= numEdges; i++)
      {
        cout << "   " << i << ": ";
        EdgePointer newPtr = new EdgeNode;
        for (int j = 1; j <= 2; j++)
        {
          in >> endpoint;
          // insert new edge node at beginning
          // of edge list for endpoint
          newPtr->vertex[j] = endpoint;
          newPtr->link[j] = v[endpoint].first;
          v[endpoint].first = newPtr;
        }
      }
    }


//--- Utility function to check if all nodes have been visited.
//    Receive: unvisited
//    Return:  true if all vertices, false if not
//------------------------------------------------------------

bool AnyLeft(const vector<bool> & unvisited)
{
   for (int i = 1; i < unvisited.size(); i++)
      if (unvisited[i])
         return true;
   return false;
}


//-- Definition of DepthFirstSearch()
template <typename DataType>
void Graph<DataType>
::DepthFirstSearch(int start, vector<bool> & unvisited)
{
   // --- Insert statements here to process visited node
   // Mark start visited, and initialize pointer
   // to its first edge node to begin DFS.
   unvisited[start] = false;
   Graph<DataType>::EdgePointer ptr = v[start].first;

   while(AnyLeft(unvisited) && ptr != 0)
   {
      // Determine which end of edge is start
      int startEnd = 1,
          otherEnd = 2;
      if (ptr->vertex[1] != start)
      { startEnd = 2; otherEnd = 1;}
```

```
        // Start new (recursive) DFS from vertex at other end
        // if it hasn't already been visited
        int newStart = ptr->vertex[otherEnd];
        if (unvisited[newStart])
          DepthFirstSearch(newStart, unvisited);
        // Move to next edge node
        ptr = ptr->link[startEnd];
    }
}

//-- Definition of Connected()
template <typename DataType>
bool Graph<DataType>::Connected()
{
  vector<bool> unvisited(v.size(), true);
  DepthFirstSearch(1, unvisited);
  return !AnyLeft(unvisited);
}

//--- The Program
//==================================================================
/* Program to determine if a graph is connected.
 *
 *   Input:   Number of vertices and number of edges of a graph,
 *            labels for the vertices, and endpoints of the edges
 *            User response
 *   Output:  Message indicating whether the graph is connected and
 *            list of unreachable vertices from first vertex if
 *            user asks for it
 ***************************************************************/

#include "Graph"
#include <iostream>
using namespace std;

int main()
{
  int numVertices,           // number of vertices in the graph
      numEdges;              //    "      "    edges   "    "     "
  cout << "Enter number of vertices and number of edges in graph: ";
  cin >> numVertices >> numEdges;

  Graph<char> g;
  g.Read(cin, numVertices, numEdges);

  cout << "Graph is ";
  if (g.Connected())
    cout << "connected.\n";
  else
  {
    cout << "not connected.\n"
            "Would you like to see which vertices are not\n"
            "reachable from vertex 1 ("
         << g.Data(1) << ") — (Y or N)? ";
```

```
      char response;
      cin >> response;
      if (response == 'y' || response == 'Y')
      {
        cout << "They are the following: \n";
        vector<bool> unreachable(numVertices+1, true);
        g.DepthFirstSearch(1, unreachable);
        for (int i = 1; i < unreachable.size(); i++)
          if (unreachable[i])
            cout << "Vertex " << i << " (" << g.Data(i) << ")\n";
      }
      cout << endl;
  }
}
```

SAMPLE RUN 1:

```
Enter number of vertices and number of edges in graph: 5 6
Enter label of vertex:
  1: A
  2: B
  3: C
  4: D
  5: E
Enter endpoints of edge
  1: 1 2
  2: 1 4
  3: 1 5
  4: 2 4
  5: 3 4
  6: 4 5
Graph is connected.
```

SAMPLE RUN 2:

```
Enter number of vertices and number of edges in graph: 5 2
Enter label of vertex:
  1: A
  2: B
  3: C
  4: D
  5: E
Enter endpoints of edge
  1: 1 4
  2: 5 4
Graph is not connected.
Would you like to see which vertices are not
reachable from vertex 1 (A) -- (Y or N)? Y
They are the following:
Vertex 2 (B)
Vertex 3 (C)
```

✔ Quick Quiz 14.3

1. Give two ways that a graph differs from a digraph?

For Questions 2–7, use the following graphs:

A.

```
                    2
                    B
                  / | \
                 /  |  \
            3 C —— A —— E 5
                 \  |1 /
                  \ | /
                    D
                    4
```

B.

```
    1           2
    1           2


    4           3
    4           3
```

2. Give the adjacency matrix *adj* and the data matrix *data* for graph A.
3. Give the adjacency matrix *adj* and the data matrix *data* for graph B.
4. Give the adjacency-list representation of graph A.
5. Give the adjacency-list representation of graph B.
6. Give the edge-list representation of graph A.
7. Give the edge-list representation of graph B.
8. For graph A, which nodes can be reached using a depth-first search from: vertex 1? from vertex 2?
9. For graph B, which nodes can be reached using a depth-first search from vertex 1?
10. For a breadth-first search of graph A starting from vertex 1, which nodes will be visited next?
11. Which of graphs A and B are connected?

✍ EXERCISES **14.3**

For Exercises 1–4, give the adjacency-matrix representation of the graph.

1.

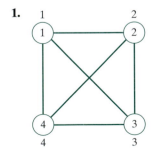

2.

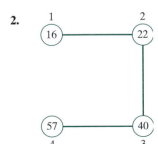

3.

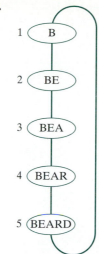

4.

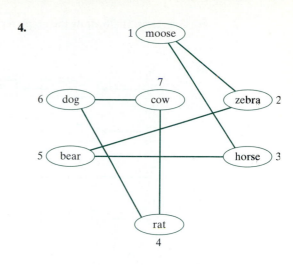

5–8. Proceed as in Exercises 1–4, but give the adjacency-list representation.

9–12. Proceed as in Exercises 1–4, but give the edge-list representation.

13–16. The linked adjacency-list representation for directed graphs described in the **para-**graph preceding Exercise 17 of Sec. 14.1 can also be used for undirected graphs. Give the linked adjacency-list representation for the graphs in Exercises 1–4.

In Exercises 17–20, draw the graph represented by the adjacency matrices; assume that the data value stored in vertex i is the integer i.

17. $adj = \begin{bmatrix} 0 & 1 & 0 & 1 & 0 \\ 1 & 0 & 1 & 0 & 0 \\ 0 & 1 & 0 & 0 & 1 \\ 1 & 0 & 0 & 0 & 1 \\ 0 & 0 & 1 & 1 & 0 \end{bmatrix}$

18. $adj = \begin{bmatrix} 0 & 1 & 1 & 1 \\ 1 & 0 & 1 & 1 \\ 1 & 1 & 0 & 1 \\ 1 & 1 & 1 & 0 \end{bmatrix}$

19. $adj = \begin{bmatrix} 0 & 0 & 0 \\ 0 & 0 & 0 \\ 0 & 0 & 0 \end{bmatrix}$

20. $adj = \begin{bmatrix} 0 & 0 & 1 & 0 & 0 & 0 & 1 \\ 0 & 0 & 1 & 1 & 1 & 0 & 0 \\ 1 & 1 & 0 & 1 & 0 & 0 & 1 \\ 0 & 1 & 1 & 0 & 1 & 1 & 1 \\ 0 & 1 & 0 & 1 & 0 & 0 & 0 \\ 0 & 0 & 0 & 1 & 0 & 0 & 1 \\ 1 & 0 & 1 & 1 & 0 & 1 & 0 \end{bmatrix}$

For Exercises 21–26, draw the graph represented by the adjacency lists.

21.

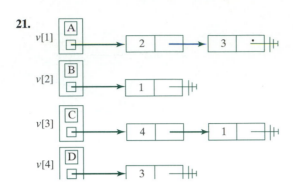

22.

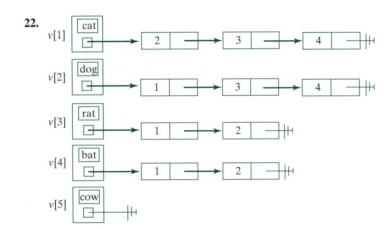

23.

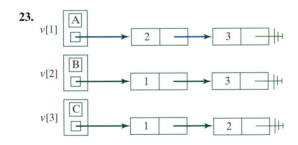

24.

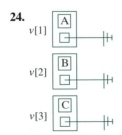

25.

26.

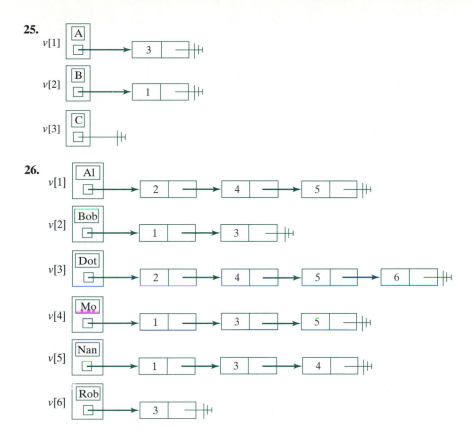

27–32. Give the edge-list representation for the graphs whose adjacency lists are given in Exercises 21–26.

For Exercises 33–39, using one of the representations for graphs described in this section, including that in Exercises 13–16, or devising one of your own, give an algorithm or function to implement the operations. Programming Problems 7–14 at the end of this chapter ask you to write and test functions for the algorithms.

33. Insert a new vertex, given a specification of all vertices adjacent to it.

34. Search a graph for a vertex that stores a given data item, and retrieve information about that item and/or update the information.

35. Delete a vertex containing a given data item and all edges incident to it.

36. Find all vertices adjacent to a given vertex.

37. Determine whether a graph contains a *cycle*, that is, a path connecting some vertex to itself.

38. A *spanning tree T* for a graph *G* is a subgraph of *G* containing all the vertices of *G* but containing no cycles (see Exercise 37). (A *subgraph* of a graph *G* has a vertex set and an edge set that are subsets of the vertex set and the edge set of *G*, respectively.) For example, the following are some of the possible spanning trees for the graph in Exercise 1.

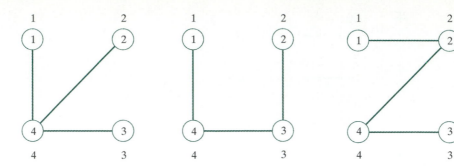

The following algorithm can be used to find a spanning tree T for a graph G:

   a. Initialize the vertex set V_T of T equal to the vertex set V_G of G and the edge set E_T of T to the empty set.

   b. While there is an edge e in the edge set E_G of G such that $E_T \cup \{e\}$ forms no cycle in T, add e to E_T.

Write a function to find a spanning tree for a graph.

39. *Kruskal's algorithm* finds the spanning tree of minimal cost in a weighted graph. It is a simple modification of the algorithm in Exercise 38. In Step 2, add the edge e of minimal cost that does not create a cycle. Write a function that implements Kruskal's algorithm.

 PROGRAMMING POINTERS

1. Search and traversal functions for digraphs and graphs must take into account that some nodes are not reachable from others.

2. Adjacency matrices and adjacency lists are not spacewise efficient for graphs. Each piece of information about an edge (its presence/absence or its weight) is stored twice.

 ADT TIPS

1. Directed graphs (digraphs) are useful in modeling networks in which flow from one node to another is directional. (Undirected) graphs are useful when there is no direction associated with the flow.

2. In digraphs and graphs, it may not be possible to get from one node to another. For *connected* graphs, this is always possible.

3. Adjacency matrices and adjacency lists are common representations for digraphs. Edge lists work well for graphs.

PROGRAMMING PROBLEMS

SECTION 14.2

1. Write a program to test the breadth-first search function in Exercise 20.

2. Write a program to test the reachability-matrix function in Exercise 21.

3. Write a program to test the boolean reachability-matrix function in Exercise 22.

4. Write a program to test the reachability-matrix function in Exercise 24 that implements Warshall's algorithm.

5. Modify the class template `Digraph` in Fig. 14.1 to use the adjacency-matrix representation for the digraph.

6. Modify the class template `Digraph` in Fig. 14.1 to use the linked adjacency-list representation described in the paragraph preceding Exercise 17 of Sec. 14.1

SECTION 14.3

7. Write and test a function for the vertex-insertion algorithm in Exercise 33.

8. Write and test a function for the search-and-retrieve algorithm in Exercise 34.

9. Write and test a function for the vertex-deletion algorithm in Exercise 35.

10. Write and test a function for the adjacent-vertices algorithm in Exercise 36.

11. Write and test a function for the cycle-detection algorithm in Exercise 37.

12. Write and test a function for the spanning-tree algorithm in Exercise 38.

13. Write and test a function for Kruskal's spanning-tree algorithm in Exercise 39.

14. Revise the `Graph` class template in Fig. 14.2 so that it uses an adjacency-matrix representation for the graph.

15. Proceed as in Prob. 14, but use the adjacency-list representation.

16. Proceed as in Prob. 14, but use the linked adjacency-list representation described in Exercises 13–16.

17. Write a program that reads and stores the names of persons and the names of job positions in the vertices of a graph. Two vertices will be connected if one of them represents a person and the other a job position for which that person is qualified. The program should allow the user to specify one of the following options:

   a. Insert (a) a new applicant or (b) a new job position into the graph.
   b. Delete (a) an applicant or (b) a job position from the graph.
   c. List all persons qualified for a specified job position.
   d. List all job positions for which a specified person is qualified.

   Use the functions developed in Prob. 7–10 to implement these operations.

ASCII CHARACTER SET

ASCII Codes of Characters

Decimal	Octal	Character	Decimal	Octal	Character
0	000	NUL (Null)	42	052	*
1	001	SOH (Start of heading)	43	053	+
2	002	STX (Start of text)	44	054	, (Comma)
3	003	ETX (End of text)	45	055	– (Hyphen)
4	004	EOT (End of transmission)	46	056	. (Period)
5	005	ENQ (Enquiry)	47	057	/
6	006	ACK (Acknowledge)	48	060	0
7	007	BEL (Ring bell)	49	061	1
8	010	BS (Backspace)	50	062	2
9	011	HT (Horizontal tab)	51	063	3
10	012	LF (Line feed)	52	064	4
11	013	VT (Vertical tab)	53	065	5
12	014	FF (Form feed)	54	066	6
13	015	CR (Carriage return)	55	067	7
14	016	SO (Shift out)	56	070	8
15	017	SI (Shift in)	57	071	9
16	020	DLE (Data link escape)	58	072	:
17	021	DC1 (Device control 1)	59	073	;
18	022	DC2 (Device control 2)	60	074	<
19	023	DC3 (Device control 3)	61	075	=
20	024	DC4 (Device control 4)	62	076	>
21	025	NAK (Negative ACK)	63	077	?
22	026	SYN (Synchronous)	64	100	@
23	027	ETB (EOT block)	65	101	A
24	030	CAN (Cancel)	66	102	B
25	031	EM (End of medium)	67	103	C
26	032	SUB (Substitute)	68	104	D
27	033	ESC (Escape)	69	105	E
28	034	FS (File separator)	70	106	F
29	035	GS (Group separator)	71	107	G
30	036	RS (Record separator)	72	110	H
31	037	US (Unit separator)	73	111	I
32	040	SP (Space)	74	112	J
33	041	!	75	113	K
34	042	"	76	114	L
35	043	#	77	115	M
36	044	$	78	116	N
37	045	%	79	117	O
38	046	&	80	120	P
39	047	' (Single quote)	81	121	Q
40	050	(	82	122	R
41	051	)	83	123	S

Decimal	Octal	Character		Decimal	Octal	Character
84	124	T		106	152	j
85	125	U		107	153	k
86	126	V		108	154	l
87	127	W		109	155	m
88	130	X		110	156	n
89	131	Y		111	157	o
90	132	Z		112	160	p
91	133	[		113	161	q
92	134	\		114	162	r
93	135	]		115	163	s
94	136	^		116	164	t
95	137	_ (Underscore)		117	165	u
96	140	`		118	166	v
97	141	a		119	167	w
98	142	b		120	170	x
99	143	c		121	171	y
100	144	d		122	172	z
101	145	e		123	173	{
102	146	f		124	174		
103	147	g		125	175	}
104	150	h		126	176	~
105	151	i		127	177	DEL

NUMBER SYSTEMS

The number system that we are accustomed to using to represent numeric values is a **decimal** or **base-ten number system**, which uses the digits 0, 1, 2, 3, 4, 5, 6, 7, 8, and 9. The significance of these digits in a numeral depends on the positions they occupy in that numeral. For example, in the numeral 427, the digit 4 is interpreted as 4 hundreds, the digit 2 as 2 tens, and the digit 7 as 7 ones. Thus, the numeral 427 represents the number four-hundred twenty-seven and can be written in **expanded form** as

$$4 \times 100 + 2 \times 10 + 7 \times 1$$

or

$$4 \times 10^2 + 2 \times 10^1 + 7 \times 10^0$$

The digits that appear in the various positions of a decimal (base-10) numeral thus are coefficients of powers of 10.

Similar positional number systems can be devised using numbers other than 10 as a base. The **binary** number system uses 2 as the base and has only two digits, 0 and 1. As in a decimal system, the significance of the bits in a binary numeral is determined by their positions in that numeral. For example, the binary numeral

$$111010$$

can be written in expanded form (using decimal notation) as

$$(1 \times 2^5) + (1 \times 2^4) + (1 \times 2^3) + (0 \times 2^2) + (1 \times 2^1) + (0 \times 2^0)$$

that is, the binary numeral 111010 has the decimal value

$$32 + 16 + 8 + 0 + 2 + 0 = 58$$

When necessary, to avoid confusion about which base is being used, it is customary to write the base as a subscript for nondecimal numerals. Using this convention, we could indicate that 58 has the binary representations just given by writing

$$58 = 111010_2$$

Two other nondecimal numeration systems are important in the consideration of computer systems: **octal** and **hexadecimal.** The octal system is a base-8 system and uses the eight digits 0, 1, 2, 3, 4, 5, 6, and 7. In an octal numeral such as

$$1703_8$$

the digits are coefficients of powers of 8; this numeral is, therefore, an abbreviation for the expanded form

$$(1 \times 8^3) + (7 \times 8^2) + (0 \times 8^1) + (3 \times 8^0)$$

and thus has the decimal value

$$512 + 448 + 0 + 3 = 963$$

A hexadecimal system uses a base of 16 and the digits 0, 1, 2, 3, 4, 5, 6, 7, 8, 9, A (10), B (11), C (12), D (13), E (14), and F (15).[1] The hexadecimal numeral

$$5E4_{16}$$

has the expanded form

$$(5 \times 16^2) + (14 \times 16^1) + (4 \times 16^0)$$

which has the decimal value

$$1280 + 224 + 4 = 1508$$

In C++, *an integer literal*[2] *is taken to be a decimal integer unless it begins with* 0. In this case,

- ▶ A sequence of digits that begins with 0 is interpreted as an octal integer
- ▶ A sequence of digits preceded by 0x is interpreted as a hexadecimal integer
- ▶ Any other digit sequence is a decimal (base-ten) integer

Table B.1 shows how the integer constants 0, 1, . . . , 20 can be represented in C++.

TABLE B.1   C++ INTEGER LITERALS

Decimal	Octal	Hexadecimal
0	0	0x0
1	01	0x1
2	02	0x2
3	03	0x3
4	04	0x4
5	05	0x5
6	06	0x6
7	07	0x7
8	010	0x8
9	011	0x9
10	012	0xA
11	013	0xB
12	014	0xC
13	015	0xD
14	016	0xE
15	017	0xF
16	020	0x10
17	021	0x11
18	022	0x12
19	023	0x13
20	024	0x14

[1]Lowercase letters a, b, c, d, e, and f are also commonly allowed for these last six digits.
[2]A string of symbols that represents an integer.

EXERCISES

Find the decimal value represented by the octal numerals in Exercises 1–6.

1. 321_8 **2.** 2607_8 **3.** 100000_8

4. 7777_8 **5.** 6.6_8 **6.** 432.234_8

Find the decimal value represented by the hexadecimal numerals in Exercises 7–12.

7. 45_{16} **8.** $3A0_{16}$ **9.** ABC_{16}

10. FFF_{16} **11.** $7.C_{16}$ **12.** $FE.DC_{16}$

13–18. Conversion from octal to binary (base-two) is easy; we need only replace each octal digit by its 3-bit binary equivalent. For example to convert 714_8 to binary, replace 7 by 111, 1 by 001, and 4 by 100, to obtain 111001100_2. Convert the octal numerals in Exercises 1–6 to binary numerals.

19–24. Imitating the conversion scheme in Exercises 13–18, convert each of the hexadecimal numerals in Exercises 7–12 to binary numerals.

To convert a binary numeral to octal, group the digits in groups of three, starting from the binary point (or from the right end if there is none), and replace each group with the corresponding octal digit. For example,

$$11110101_2 = (11\ 110\ 101)_2 = 365_8$$

Convert the binary numerals in Exercises 25–30 to octal numerals.

25. 101010   **26.** 1011

27. 10000000000   **28.** 0111111111111111111

29. 11.1   **30.** 10101.10101

31–36. Imitating the conversion scheme in Exercises 25–30, convert the binary numerals given there to hexadecimal numerals.

One method for finding the *base-b representation* of a positive integer represented in base-ten notation is to divide the number by b repeatedly until a quotient of zero results. The successive remainders are the digits from right to left of the base-b representation. For example, the base-two representation of 26 is 11010_2, as the following computation shows:

$$
\begin{array}{r}
0 \text{ R } 1 \\
2\overline{)1} \text{ R } 1 \\
2\overline{)3} \text{ R } 0 \\
2\overline{)6} \text{ R } 1 \\
2\overline{)13} \text{ R } 0 \\
2\overline{)26}
\end{array}
$$

Convert the base-10 numerals in Exercises 37–39 to base two.

37. 99   **38.** 2571   **39.** 5280

40–42. Convert the base-10 numerals in Exercises 37–39 to base eight.

43–45.   Convert the base-10 numerals in Exercises 37–39 to base sixteen.

To convert a decimal fraction to its base-b equivalent, repeatedly multiply the fractional part of the number by b. The integer parts are the digits from left to right of the base-b representation. For example, the decimal numeral .6875 corresponds to the base-two numeral $.1011_2$, as the following computation shows:

$$
\begin{array}{r|l}
 & .6875 \\
 & \times\ 2 \\
\hline
1 & .375 \\
 & \times 2 \\
\hline
0 & .75 \\
 & \times 2 \\
\hline
1 & .5 \\
 & \times 2 \\
\hline
1 & .0
\end{array}
$$

Convert the base-10 numerals in Exercises 46–48 to base two.

46. .5   **47.** .6875   **48.** 13.828125

49–51.   Convert the base-10 numerals in Exercises 46–48 to base eight.

52–54.   Convert the base-10 numerals in Exercises 46–48 to base sixteen.

As noted in the text, even though the base-ten representation of a fraction may terminate, its representation in some other base need not terminate; for example,

$$0.7 = (0.10110011001100110011\cdots)_2 = 0.\overline{10110}_2$$

where the "overline" in the last notation indicates that the bit string 0110 is repeated indefinitely.

$$
\begin{array}{r|l}
 & .7 \\
 & \times 2 \\
\hline
1 & .4 \leftarrow \\
 & \times 2 \\
\hline
0 & .8 \\
 & \times 2 \\
\hline
1 & .6 \\
 & \times 2 \\
\hline
1 & .2 \\
 & \times 2 \\
\hline
0 & .4 \quad\rfloor
\end{array}
$$

Convert the base-ten numerals in Exercises 55–57 to base two.

55. 0.6   **56.** 0.05   **57.** $0.\overline{3} = 0.33333 \cdots = 1/3$

58–60.   Convert the base-10 numerals in Exercises 55–57 to base eight.

61–63.   Convert the base-10 numerals in Exercises 55–57 to base sixteen.

64. The "successive division" method for converting from base ten to base b described before Exercise 46 generates the base-b digits in reverse order, from right to left. Describe a data structure that can be used to store these digits as they are generated so that they can be displayed in correct order when the conversion is complete.

65. Write a program to carry out the conversion described in Exercise 64 for $2 \leq b \leq 10$.

66. Proceed as in Exercise 65, but for $2 \leq b \leq 16$. (Use A, B, C, D, E, and F for digits as necessary.)

67. Proceed as in Exercise 66, but for $b = 26$; use as "digits" A for 1, B for 2, ..., Y for 25, and Z for 0.

BASIC C++

C.1 C++ PROGRAM STRUCTURE

A program is basically a collection of *functions*, one of which must be named `main()`. Program execution begins with `main()`. The following is an example of a simple program that contains only this `main` function:

```
/* This program greets its user.
 *
 * Input:   The name of the user
 * Output: A personalized greeting
 **************************************/
```
⎫ Opening documentation

```
#include <iostream>    // cin, cout, <<, >>
#include <string>      // string
```
⎫ Compiler directives that insert the contents of file

`using namespace std;` ← ——————————————— Use libraries from namespace `std`

← ⎛ Declarations and definitions
  ⎝ of other items could go here

`int main()` ← ——————————— Execution begins here

```
{
   cout << "Please enter your first name: ";
   string firstName;
   cin >> firstName;
```
⎫ Program statements that make up the body of the `main` function

```
   cout << "\nWelcome to the world of C++, "
        << firstName << "!\n";
}
```
← ⎛ Execution stops here or when a
  ⎝ `return` statement is executed

← ⎛ More `#includes` could go here.
  ⎨ Also, function definitions can go
  ⎝ here if their prototypes are above

Note that *each statement must be terminated by a semicolon* (;).

The contents of the files inserted by the `#include` directives together with items that are declared or defined ahead of `main()`—for example, function prototypes—are *global*; they are accessible in what follows, unless the same identifier is used for some other purpose.

C.2 COMPILER DIRECTIVES

The most commonly used compiler directives are the **#include directives**. These are instructions to the preprocessor to insert the contents of the specified files at this point:

```
#include <filename>    For standard libraries
#include "filename"    For other (programmer-defined) libraries
```

The files included are called **header files** (often with names of the form `filename.h`); they contain *declarations* of functions, constants, variables, and so on. **Implementation files** (with names like `filename.cc` or `filename.cpp`) contain *definitions* of the items declared (but not defined) in the corresponding header file. They are usually compiled separately and then *linked* with the program to produce a binary executable.

C.3   STANDARD LIBRARIES

Normally, we want to use the standard libraries in the namespace named `std`. (Namespaces are described later in this appendix.) The line following the `#include` directives in the preceding program informs the compiler of this. Without it we would have to *qualify* each item such as `cout` from these libraries with the prefix `std::`; for example

```
std::cout << "Please enter your first name: ";
```

The following are some of the commonly used **standard libraries** provided in C++. The first column shows the new names proposed in the recently adopted ISO/ANSI C++ standard and the second column shows their old names.. The `.h` extensions are dropped, and names of C libraries have a `"c"` attached as a prefix.

New name	Old name	What it provides
iostream	iostream.h	Basic interactive i/o (see Appendix D)
iomanip	iomanip.h	Format manipulators (see Appendix D)
fstream	fstream.h	File i/o (see Appendix D)
string	string	Standard C++ `string type` (see Appendix D)
cassert	assert.h	The `assert` mechanism
cctype	ctype.h	Character functions (see Appendix D)
cfloat	float.h	Max and min values of real types
climits	limits.h	Max and min values of integral types
cmath	math.h	Math library
cstdlib	stdlib.h	Standard C library
cstring	string.h	C's string library (see Appendix D)

Some of the most useful items in these libraries are described in the following lists or in Appendix D.

cassert

`void assert(bool expr)`	Tests the boolean expression `expr` and if it is true, allows execution to proceed. If it is false, execution is terminated and an error message is displayed.

cctype

`int isalnum(int c)`	Returns true if c is a letter or a digit, `false` otherwise
`int isalpha(int c)`	Returns true if c is a letter, `false` otherwise
`int iscntrl(int c)`	Returns true if c is a control character, `false` otherwise
`int isdigit(int c)`	Returns true if c is a decimal digit, `false` otherwise
`int isgraph(int c)`	Returns true if c is a printing character except space, `false` otherwise
`int islower(int c)`	Returns true if c is lowercase, `false` otherwise
`int isprint(int c)`	Returns true if c is a printing character including space, `false` otherwise
`int ispunct(int c)`	Returns true if c is a punctuation character (not a space, an alphabetic character, or a digit), `false` otherwise
`int isspace(int c)`	Returns true if c is a white space character (space, `'\f'`, `'\n'`, `'\r'`, `'\t'`, or `'\v'`), `false` otherwise
`int isupper(int c)`	Returns true if c is uppercase, `false` otherwise
`int isxdigit(int c)`	Returns true if c is a hexadecimal digit, `false` otherwise
`int tolower(int c)`	Returns lowercase equivalent of c (if c is uppercase)
`int toupper(int c)`	Returns the uppercase equivalent of c (if c is lowercase)

cfloat

The following constants specify the minimum value in the specified floating-point type.

FLT_MIN ($\leq -1E+37$)	`float`
DBL_MIN ($\leq -1E+37$)	`double`
LDBL_MIN ($\leq -1E+37$)	`long double`

The following constants specify the maximum value in the specified floating-point type.

FLT_MAX ($\geq 1E+37$)	`float`
DBL_MAX ($\geq 1E+37$)	`double`
LDBL_MAX ($\geq 1E+37$)	`long double`

The following constants specify the smallest positive value representable in the specified floating-point type.

FLT_EPSILON ($\leq 1E-37$)	`float`
DBL_EPSILON ($\leq 1E-37$)	`double`
LDBL_EPSILON ($\leq 1E-37$)	`long double`

climits

The following constants specify the minimum and maximum values for the specified type.

SCHAR_MIN (≤ -127)	`signed char`
SCHAR_MAX (≥ 127)	`signed char`
UCHAR_MAX (≥ 255)	`unsigned char`

(continued)

climits, *continued*

CHAR_MIN (0 or SCHAR_MIN)	char
CHAR_MAX (SCHAR_MAX or USHRT_MAX)	char
SHORT_MIN (≤ -32767)	short int
SHORT_MAX (≥ 32767)	short int
USHRT_MAX (≥ 65535)	unsigned short int
INT_MIN (≤ -32767)	int
INT_MAX (≥ 32767)	int
UINT_MAX (≥ 65535)	unsigned int
LONG_MIN (≤ -2147483647)	long int
LONG_MAX (≥ 2147483647)	long int
ULONG_MAX (≥ 4294967295)	unsigned long int

cmath

double acos(double x)	Returns the angle in $[0, \pi]$ (in radians) whose cosine is x
double asin(double x)	Returns the angle in $[-\pi/2, \pi/2]$ (in radians) whose sine is x
double atan(double x)	Returns the angle in $(-\pi/2, \pi/2)$ (in radians) whose tangent is x
double atan2(double y)	Returns the angle in $(-\pi, \pi]$ (in radians) whose tangent is y/x
double ceil(double x)	Returns the least integer $\geq$ x
double cos(double x)	Returns the cosine of x (radians)
double cosh(double x)	Returns the hyperbolic cosine of x
double exp(double x)	Returns e^x
double fabs(double x)	Returns the absolute value of x
double floor(double x)	Returns the greatest integer $\leq$ x
double fmod(double x, double y)	Returns the integer remainder of x / y
double frexp(double x, int & ex)	Returns value v in $[1/2, 1]$ and passes back ex such that $x = v * 2^{ex}$
double ldexp(double x, int ex)	Returns $x * 2^{ex}$
double log(double x)	Returns natural logarithm of x
double log10(double x)	Returns base-ten logarithm of x
double modf(double x, double & ip)	Returns fractional part of x and passes back ip $=$ the integer part of x
double pow(double x, double y)	Returns x^y
double sin(double x)	Returns the sine of x (radians)

(continued)

cmath, *continued*

`double sinh(double x)`	Returns the hyperbolic sine of x
`double sqrt(double x)`	Returns the square root of x (provided $x \geq 0$)
`double tan(double x)`	Returns the tangent of x (radians)
`double tanh(double x)`	Returns the hyperbolic tangent of x

cstdlib

`int abs(int i)` `long abs(long li)`	`abs(i)` and `labs(li)` return the `int` and `long int` absolute value of i and li, respectively

`double atof(char s[])`
`int atoi(char s[])`
`long atol(char s[])`
	`atof(s)`, `atoi(s)`, and `atol(s)` return the value obtained by by converting the character string s to `double`, `int`, and `long int`, respectively

`void exit(int status)`	Terminates program execution and returns control to the operating system; `status` = 0 signals successful termination and any nonzero value signals unsuccessful termination
`int rand()`	Returns a pseudorandom integer in the range 0 to `RAND_MAX`
`RAND_MAX`	An integer constant (≥ 32767) which is the maximum value returned by `rand()`
`void srand(int seed)`	Uses `seed` to initialize the sequence of pseudorandom numbers returned by `rand()`
`int system(char s[])`	Passes the string s to the operating system to be executed as a command and returns an implementation-dependent value.

C.4   COMMENTS

Two kinds of **comments** are allowed in C++:

```
// comment -- continues to end of the line
/* comment -- may extend over several lines ... */
```

C.5   IDENTIFIERS AND KEYWORDS

Identifiers consist of a letter followed by any number of letters, underscores, and digits. C++ is *case-sensitive*; thus, for example, Sum, sum, and SUM are all different identifiers. Identifiers may not be any of the **keywords** in Table C.1.

TABLE C.1   C++ KEYWORDS

Keyword	Contextual Description
asm	Used to declare that information is to be passed directly to the assembler
auto	Used to declare objects whose lifetime is the duration of control within their block

(continued)

TABLE C.1 (CONTINUED)

Keyword	Contextual Description
`bool`	Used to declare objects whose values are `true` or `false`
`break`	Used to terminate processing of a `switch` statement or loop
`case`	Used in a `switch` statement to specify a match for the statement's expression
`catch`	Used to specify the actions to be taken when an exception occurs (see `throw`, `try`)
`char`	Used to declare objects whose values are characters
`class`	Used to construct new types encapsulating data and operations (default `private`)
`const`	Used to declare objects whose values should not change during execution
`const_cast`	Used to add or remove the `const` or `volatile` property of a type
`continue`	Used in a loop statement to transfer control to the beginning of the loop
`default`	Used in a `switch` statement to handle expression values not specified using `case`
`delete`	Used to deallocate memory allocated at run time, returning it to the free store
`do`	Used to mark the beginning of a `do-while` statement, providing repetitive control
`double`	Used to declare objects whose values are (double precision) real numbers
`dynamic_cast`	Used to cast pointer or reference types in a class hierarchy
`else`	Used in an `if` statement to mark the section to be executed if the condition is false
`enum`	Used to declare a type whose values are programmer-specified identifiers
`explicit`	Used to prevent constructors from being called implicitly for conversion purposes
`extern`	Used to declare objects whose definitions are external to the local block
`false`	A `bool` value
`float`	Used to declare objects whose values are (single precision) real numbers
`for`	Used to mark the beginning of a `for` statement, providing repetitive control
`friend`	Used to declare `class` operations that are not member functions
`goto`	Used to transfer control to a label

(continued)

TABLE C.1   (CONTINUED)

Keyword	Contextual Description
if	Used to mark the beginning of an `if` statement, providing selective control
inline	Used to declare a function whose text is to be substituted for its call
int	Used to declare objects whose values are integer numbers
long	Used to declare 32-bit integer, or extended double precision real numbers
mutable	Used to declare class data member as modifiable even in a `const` object
namespace	Used to control the scope of global names (to avoid name conflicts)
new	Used to request memory allocation at run time
operator	Used to overload an operator with a new declaration
private	Used to declare `class` members that are inaccessible from outside of the `class`
protected	Used to declare `class` members that are `private`, except to derived `class`es
public	Used to declare `class` members that can be accessed outside of the `class`
register	Used to declare objects whose values are to be kept in registers
reinterpret_cast	Used to perform type conversions on unrelated types
return	Used to terminate a function, usually returning the value of some expression
short	Used to declare 16-bit integer numbers
signed	Used to declare an object in which the value's *sign* is stored in the high-order bit
sizeof	Used to find the size (in bytes) of an object, or of the representation of a type
static	Used to declare objects whose lifetime is the duration of the program
static_cast	Used to convert one type to another type
struct	Used to construct new types encapsulating data and operations (default `public`)
switch	Used to mark the beginning of a switch statement, providing selective control
template	Used to declare type-independent `class`es or functions
this	Used within a `class` member to unambiguously access other members of the class
throw	Used to generate an exception (see `catch`, `try`)

(continued)

TABLE C.1   (CONTINUED)

Keyword	Contextual Description
true	A `bool` value
try	Used to mark the beginning of a block containing exception handlers (see `catch`)
typedef	Used to declare a name as a synonym for an existing type
typeid	Used to obtain type information during run time
typename	Can be used instead of `class` in template parameter lists and to identify qualified names as types
union	Used to declare a structure, such that different objects can have different members
unsigned	Used to declare an object in which the high-order bit is used for data (see `signed`)
using	Used to access members of a namespace
virtual	Used to declare a base-`class` function, that will be defined by a derived `class`
void	Used to indicate the absence of any type (for a function or parameter list)
volatile	Used to declare objects whose values may be modified by means undetectable to the compiler (such as shared-memory objects of concurrent processes)
while	Used to mark the beginning of a `while` statement, as well as the end of a `do-while` statement, each of which provides repetitive control

C.6   FUNDAMENTAL DATA TYPES

The most important data types are the following:

Integers: `int`
Integer variations: `short` (or `short int`), `long` (or `long int`), `unsigned` (or `unsigned int`)
Reals: `float`, `double`, `long double`
Complex numbers: The library `<complex>` provides the types `complex<float>`, `complex<double>`, `complex<long double>` for complex values with components of type `float`, `double`, `long double`, respectively.
Characters: `char` (and less commonly used variations `signed char` and `unsigned char`), `wchar_t` for wide characters
Booleans (logical values `true` and `false`): `bool`
Absence of type: `void`

Some of their properties are:

▶ `char` values are stored in 1 byte. `char` is considered to be an integer type, because values are stored using numeric codes (e.g., ASCII).

- ▶ `short` values require at least 2 bytes, `int` values at least as much as `short` values, and `long` values require at least as much as `int` values and at least 4 bytes.
- ▶ `float` values require at least 4 bytes, `double` values at least as much as `float` values and at least 6 bytes, and `long double` values require at least 4 bytes and at least as much as `double` values.
- ▶ All `float` values are stored as `doubles`, so it is common to always use `double`.
- ▶ Storage of `bool` values is implementation-dependent. `true` is defined as 1 and `false` as 0. Any nonzero value will be interpreted as true and any zero value as false.
- ▶ `sizeof` operator: `sizeof(type)` or `sizeof(expression)` returns the number of bytes used for this type object. The parentheses are not required in the second form.
- ▶ If two operands in an expression have different types, the shorter one is converted (*promoted*) to the longer type. This can also be done explicitly with type conversions described later.

C.7   LITERALS

Integer: Use the usual decimal representation.

Octal representations begin with `0`

Hexadecimal representations begin with `0x`

Real: Use the usual decimal representation and `e` or `E` representations

Character: Single characters are enclosed in single quotes (apostrophes).

Escape sequences are used for special character constants:

`\n` (new line)	`\r` (carriage return)
`\t` (horizontal tab)	`\v` (vertical tab)
`\b` (backspace)	`\f` (form feed)
`\a` (alert)	`\\` (backslash)
`\'` (single quote)	`\"` (double quote)
`\?` (question mark)	`\x`*hhh* (with hexadecimal code *hhh*)
`\`*ooo* (with octal code *ooo*)	

Character literals of the form `L'x'` where *x* consists of one or more characters are *wide-character literals* and are used to represent alternate character sets (e.g., 16-bit Unicode).

String: Strings are enclosed in double quotes.

Complex: They have the form `(a, b)` where *a* and *b* are real

C.8   Declarations

Variable declarations have the form

```
type list;
```

where each item in `list` has the form

```
variable_name    or    variable_name = init_expression
```

Variables are usually declared near their first use.
Constant declarations have the form

```
const type list;
```

where each item in `list` has the form

```
CONSTANT_NAME = constant_value
```

C.9   Operators and Expressions

In expressions that contain several operators, the order in which the operators are applied depends on operator **priority** (or **precedence**) and **associativity**.

▶ Higher-priority operators are applied before lower priority ones.
▶ If operators have equal priority, they are applied
  • From left to right if they are *left-associative*
  • From right to left if they are *right-associative*
▶ A semicolon appended to an expression changes the expression into a *statement*.

Table C.2 lists the C++ operators, ordered by their precedence levels, from highest to lowest. Operators in the same horizontal band of the table have equal precedence. The table also gives each operator's associativity, whether they can be overloaded, their arity (number of operands), and a brief description.

TABLE C.2   C++ Operators

Operator	Associativity	Overloadable	Arity	Description
`::`	right	no	unary	global scope
`::`	left	no	binary	class scope
`.`	left	no	binary	direct member selection
`->`	left	yes	binary	indirect member selection
`[]`	left	yes	binary	subscript (array index)
`()`	left	yes	n/a	function call
`()`	left	yes	n/a	type construction
`++`	right	yes	unary	post increment
`--`	right	yes	unary	post decrement
`typeid`	left	no	unary	type identification
`static_cast`	left	no	unary	compile-time checked conversion

(continued)

TABLE C.2   (CONTINUED)

Operator	Associativity	Overloadable	Arity	Description
`dynamic_cast`	left	no	unary	run-time checked conversion
`reinterpret_cast`	left	no	unary	unchecked conversion
`const_cast`	left	no	unary	const conversion
`sizeof`	right	n/a	unary	size (in bytes) of an object or type
`++`	right	yes	unary	increment
`--`	right	yes	unary	decrement
`~`	right	yes	unary	bitwise NOT
`!`	right	yes	unary	logical NOT
`+`	right	yes	unary	plus(sign)
`-`	right	yes	unary	minus (sign)
`*`	right	yes	unary	pointer dereferencing
`&`	right	yes	unary	get address of an object
`new`	right	yes	unary	memory allocation
`delete`	right	yes	unary	memory deallocation
`()`	right	yes	binary	type conversion (cast)
`.*`	left	no	binary	direct member pointer selection
`->*`	left	yes	binary	indirect member pointer selection
`*`	left	yes	binary	multiplication,
`/`	left	yes	binary	division
`%`	left	yes	binary	modulus (remainder)
`+`	left	yes	binary	addition
`-`	left	yes	binary	subtraction
`<<`	left	yes	binary	bit-shift left
`>>`	left	yes	binary	bit-shift right
`<`	left	yes	binary	less-than
`<=`	left	yes	binary	less-than-or-equal
`>`	left	yes	binary	greater-than
`>=`	left	yes	binary	greater-than-or-equal
`==`	left	yes	binary	equality
`!=`	left	yes	binary	inequality
`&`	left	yes	binary	bitwise AND
`^`	left	yes	binary	bitwise XOR
`|`	left	yes	binary	bitwise OR
`&&`	left	yes	binary	logical AND
`||`	left	yes	binary	logical OR
`=`	right	yes	binary	assignment
`+=`	right	yes	binary	addition-assignment shortcut
`-=`	right	yes	binary	subtraction-assignment shortcut
`*=`	right	yes	binary	multiplication-assignment shortcut
`/=`	right	yes	binary	division-assignment shortcut

(continued)

TABLE C.2   (CONTINUED)

Operator	Associativity	Overloadable	Arity	Description
`%=`	right	yes	binary	modulus-assignment shortcut
`&=`	right	yes	binary	bitwise-AND-assignment shortcut
`|=`	right	yes	binary	bitwise-OR-assignment shortcut
`^=`	right	yes	binary	bitwise-XOR-assignment shortcut
`<<=`	right	yes	binary	bitshift-left-assignment shortcut
`>>=`	right	yes	binary	bitshift-right-assignment shortcut
`? :`	left	no	ternary	conditional expression
`throw`	right	yes	unary	throw an exception
`,`	left	yes	binary	expression separation

The following are some of the important properties of several of these operators:

DIVISION. If `a` and `b` are integers, `a / b` is the *integer quotient* and `a % b` the *integer remainder* when `a` is divided by `b`. If `a` and `b` are reals, `a / b` is the *real quotient* and `a % b` is *an error*.

ASSIGNMENT. An assignment of the form `variable = expression`

1. Stores the value of `expression` in `variable`; and
2. Returns the value of `expression` as its result.

This, along with the right-associativity of `=` allows assignments to be chained:

$$var_1 = var_2 = \ldots = var_n = expression$$

An *assignment statement* is an assignment expression followed by a semicolon:

`variable = expression;`

In place of the assignment `variable = variable + 1;` we write

`++variable;` (Prefix form)

or

`variable++;` (Postfix form)

The decrement operator `--` can be used in a similar manner to subtract 1 from a variable. These forms are equivalent when used as stand-alone statements, but they differ when they are used as part of an expression:

Prefix Form: Increment (or decrement) and then use the new value; for example,

`b = ++a;` means `a = a + 1; b = a;`

Postfix Form: Use old value and then increment (or decrement); for example,

`b = a++;` means `b = a; a = a + 1;`

Assignment shortcuts can be used to simplify assignments where a variable appears on both sides. For example, var_1 = var_1 + var_2; can be simplified to var_1 += var_2; and similarly for -=, *=, /=, and %=.

BOOLEAN EXPRESSIONS. Don't use = when == is intended; for example,

```
if (x = 0) ...
```

will assign 0 to x and the value of (x = 0) is 0 (false);

```
if (x = 9) ...
```

will assign 9 to x and the value of (x = 9) is 9 (true). Also, be careful to use && and || for the logical operators *and* and *or*, not & and |, which are bitwise operators.

The operator ?: is a *ternary* operator. The value of

$$boolean\text{-}expr_1 \; ? \; expr_2 \; : \; expr_3$$

is $expr_2$ if $boolean\text{-}expr_1$ is true (nonzero), $expr_3$ if $boolean\text{-}expr_1$ is false (zero).

INPUT/OUTPUT EXPRESSIONS. I/O is carried out using *streams* connecting the program and i/o devices or files. Input expressions use *input* (or *extraction*) operator >>. The expression `inStream >> variable`

1. Extracts a value of the type of `variable` (if possible) from `inStream`,
2. Stores that value in `variable`, and
3. Returns `inStream` as its result (if successful, else 0).

This last property along with the left-associativity of >> makes it possible to chain input expressions:

```
inStream >> var₁ >> var₂ >> ... >> varₙ
```

Output expressions use the *output* (or *insertion*) operator <<. The expression `outStream << value`

1. Inserts `value` into `outStream`, and
2. Returns `outStream` as its result.

This last property along with the left-associativity of << makes it possible to chain output expressions:

```
outStream << value₁ << value₂ << ... << valueₙ
```

See Appendix D for more information about input and output.

TYPE CONVERSIONS. If `intVal` is an integer variable and `doubleVal` is a `double` variable, then either of the expressions

```
double(intVal)    and    static_cast<double>(intVal)
```

produces the `double` value equivalent to `intVal`. Similarly, either of int(doubleVal)   and   static_cast<int>(doubleVal)

will truncate the fractional part and produce the integer part of `doubleVal` as its value. More generally, the type of an expression can be explicitly converted to a different type as follows:

    type(expression)

    static_cast<type>(expression)

    (type) expression

The type of the value produced by *expression* is converted to *type* (if possible). The first form is sometimes referred to as *functional notation* and the last form as (C-style) *cast notation*.

FUNCTION CALL OPERATOR. The function call operator () is used to pass an argument list to a function:

    FunctionName(argument_list)

SUBSCRIPT OPERATOR. The **subscript operator []** provides access to the elements of an array:

    arrayName[index]

See Sec. 2.3.

DOT OPERATOR. The **dot operator .** is used to select a member of a struct or class object:

    classObject.memberName

See Secs. 2.4 and 3.1.

SCOPE OPERATOR. The **scope operator ::** is used to identify a component within a class:

    className::componentName

See Sec. 3.2.

BITWISE OPERATORS. These operators provide bit-level control.

Expression	Produces the result of:
x & y	ANDing the bits of x with those of y
x | y	ORing the bits of x with those of y
x ^ y	XORing the bits of x with those of y
~x	Inverting (complementing) the bits of x ($0 \rightarrow 1$ and $1 \rightarrow 0$)
x << y	Shifting the bits of x to the *left* y positions
x >> y	Shifting the bits of x to the *right* y positions

Shortcut versions (with assignment) are also provided: &=, |=, ^=, !=, <<=, >>=. *Note*: << and >> are classic examples of *overloaded* operators.

C.10 CONTROL STRUCTURES

Control structures are language constructs that allow a programmer to control the flow of execution through a program. There are three main categories: **sequence**, **selection**, and **repetition**.

SEQUENCE. Sequential execution is implemented by **compound statements** (also called **blocks**). They consist of statements enclosed between curly braces ({ and }):

```
{
    statement₁
    statement₂        ← (Remember: Statements end with ; )
       . . .
    statementₙ
}
```

SELECTION. Selective execution is implemented by one of the following statements:

1. `if` Statement

```
if (boolean_expression)
    statement₁
else
    statement₂
```

- The `boolean expression` must be enclosed in parentheses.
- `statement₁` and `statement₂` may be compound
- *Remember:* nonzero $=$ true, $0=$ false

2. `switch` Statement

```
switch(integer_expression)
{
    case_list₁ : statement_list₁
    case_list₂ : statement_list₂
       . . .
    default    : statement_listₙ
}
```

- The `default` part is optional.
- Each `case_listᵢ` is a sequence of distinct case labels of the form

    `case constant :`

- Semantics:
    - **a.** Evaluate `integer_expression`.
    - **b.** If value of `integer_expression` is in `case_listᵢ`:
        - i. Begin executing statements in `statement_listᵢ`.
        - ii. Continue until a `break` statement, a `return` statement, or the end of the `switch` statement is reached. (Usually, a `break` or a

`return` statement is used as the last statement in each statement list, except for the default case, where it is not needed.)

c. If value of `integer_expression` is in no `case_list`$_i$:
Execute statements in default part if there is one; else skip the `switch` statement.

REPETITION. Repetitive execution is implemented by one of the following statements:

1. While Loops

```
while(boolean_expression)
   statement
```

Like while loops in other languages, this is a **pretest (zero-trip)** loop, in which `boolean_expression`, which constitutes the termination test for repetition, is evaluated *before* execution of `statement`, called the **body of the loop**. The loop body is, therefore, not executed if `boolean_expression` is false initially. Normally, `statement` is a compound statement.

2. Do-While Loops

```
do
   statement
while (boolean_expression);   ← Note the semicolon.
```

This is like do-while or repeat-until loops in other languages, which are **posttest (one-trip)** loops, in which `boolean_expression`, which constitutes the termination test for repetition, is evaluated *after* execution the body of the loop. The loop body is, therefore, always executed at least once

3. For Loops

```
for (initializing_expr; boolean_expr; step_expr)
   statement
```

where any of `initializing_expr`, `boolean_expr`, `step_expr` may be omitted. This is equivalent to the following:

```
initializing_expr;
while (boolean_expr)
{
   statement
   step_expr;
}
```

A common use is to construct *counting loops*:

```
for (int counter = 1; counter <= n; counter++)
   statement
```

4. Indeterminate (or Forever) Loops

```
for(;;)          or        while(true)
   statement                  statement
```

This is an *infinite loop*. We usually use forever loops to build *test-in-the-middle* loops

```
for(;;)
{
  StatementList₁
  if (boolExpr) break;    or   if (boolExpr) return;
  StatementList₂
}
```

Note: A **break statement** terminates execution of a `switch` statement containing it or the innermost loop containing it. A **continue statement** terminates only the current iteration of the loop and continues execution of the loop at the top of the loop.

EXAMPLES. The programs in Figures C.1–C.5 illustrate several of these control structures.

Figure C.1   Using a Forever Loop

```cpp
/* Program to compute the volumes of spheres of various radii.
   Written at Doofus Univ. by Joe Somebody for CPSC 31416.

   Input:  Radius
   Output: Volume
----------------------------------------------------------------*/

#include <iostream>
#include <cmath>
using namespace std;

int main()
{
  const double PI = 3.14159265359;

  double radius;                        // radius of a sphere
  int count = 0;                        // number of spheres processed

  for (;;)                              // loop:
  {
    cout << "Enter radius of sphere (0 to stop): ";
    cin >> radius;                      //   get next radius

    if (radius == 0) break;             //   terminate loop if end of data
    count++;                            //   count the data
                                        //   find the volume
    double volume = 4.0 * PI * pow(radius, 3)/ 3.0;

                                        //   output the results
    cout << "Volume of sphere of radius " << radius
         << " is " << volume << " cubic inches.\n\n";
  }                                     // end loop
```

```
        // Output data count
        cout << endl << count << " spheres processed\n";
} // successful termination of program
```

SAMPLE RUN:

```
Enter radius of sphere (0 to stop): 2
Volume of sphere of radius 2 is 33.5103 cubic inches.

Enter radius of sphere (0 to stop): 1
Volume of sphere of radius 1 is 4.18879 cubic inches.

Enter radius of sphere (0 to stop): 0

2 spheres processed
```

 ## Figure C.2   Using a Do-While Loop

```
//...
int main()
{   ...

   char   response;                        // user response to "More data?"

   do
   {
      cout << "Enter radius of sphere: ";
      cin >> radius;                   // get next radius

      ...   // compute and output volume

                                       // query user if more data
      cout << "\nMore data (Y or N)? ";
      cin >> response;
   }
   while (response == 'Y' || response == 'y');
   ...
}
```

SAMPLE RUN:

```
Enter radius of sphere: 2
Volume of sphere of radius 2 is 33.5103 cubic inches.

More data (Y or N)? Y
Enter radius of sphere: 1
Volume of sphere of radius 1 is 4.18879 cubic inches.

More data (Y or N)? N

2 spheres processed
```

FIGURE C.3   USING A WHILE LOOP

```
//...
  cout << "Enter radius of sphere (0 to stop): ";
  cin >> radius;                          // get first radius

  while (radius > 0)                      // while not end-of-data
  {
    ...  // compute and output volume

    cout << "Enter radius of sphere (0 to stop): ";
    cin >> radius;                        // get next radius
  }//end while
  ...
}
```

FIGURE C.4   USING FORMAT MANIPULATORS

```
//...
#include <iostream>
#include <iomanip>
#include <cmath>
using namespace std;

int main()
{ ...
  cout << showpoint << fixed<< setprecision(3) ;
  ...
    double volume = 4.0 * PI * pow(radius, 3) / 3.0;

    cout << "Volume of sphere of radius " << radius
         << " is " << volume << " cubic inches.\n\n";
  ...
}
```

FIGURE C.5   USING END-OF-FILE MARK

```
//...
#include <string>
int main()
{ ...

  string
    END_OF_FILE_MARK = "Control-D";   // for UNIX systems
  ...
```

```
for (;;)
{
  cout << "Enter radius of sphere (("
       << END_OF_FILE_MARK << " to stop): ";
  cin >> radius;
  if (cin.eof()) break;              // end of data

  ...  // compute and output volume
}
...
}
```

C.11 FUNCTIONS

We write functions:

- ▸ To implement an operation not provided in C++
- ▸ When a piece of code will be used several times in a program (to *avoid duplication*)
- ▸ When a piece of code is likely to be useful in the future (for *software reusability*); in this case it may be put in a library
- ▸ To modularize programs (As a rule of thumb, no function should exceed one page in length.)

FUNCTION DEFINITIONS. The definition of a function has the form

```
return_type Name(param_declaration_list)  ← Function heading
{
  statement_list  ←──────────────────────── Function body
}
```

where:

   return_type is the type of value returned by the function or is **void** if no value is returned

   param_declaration_list is a list of declarations of variables, which are the function's parameters or is empty if there are none

Values passed to a function when it is called are **arguments** and variables in the function heading used to hold these values are **parameters**.

Functions return values with statements of the form:

```
return expression;
```

void functions cannot return values, but they may contain

```
return;
```

statements to cause an immediate return from the function to the calling function.

FUNCTION PROTOTYPES (DECLARATIONS). Before a function can be used, it must be **declared**. This can be done by giving its **prototype:**

```
return_type Name(param_declaration_list);← Note the semicolon
```

The list of parameter declarations is called the **signature** of the function. The following are some example of function prototypes:

```
double Wages(int dependents, double hours, double rate);
void Instruct();
void PrintWages(int empNum, double grossPay);
```

Function prototypes are usually placed at the beginning of the file containing the source program, following the compiler directives.

The list of parameter declarations may consist of just the *types* of the parameters (possibly empty). For example, the first function prototype could be written:

```
double Wages(int, double, double);
```

However, it a good practice to include the parameter names also to provide additional documentation. Also, the prototype is then simply the function heading followed by a semicolon.

PARAMETER-PASSING MECHANISMS. There are three ways that parameters can be passed in C++:

1. Call by Value. If the declaration of a parameter has the form

```
type parameter_name
```

that parameter is a **value** parameter, which has the following properties:

- A value parameter is allocated *different* memory locations than the corresponding argument.
- The value of the corresponding argument is *copied* to a value parameter.
- Changing a value parameter *does not change* the corresponding argument.

For example, in the function call `PrintWages(empId, grossPay);` the value of the argument `empId` will be copied to the parameter `empNum` and the value of the argument `grossPay` will be copied to the parameter `grossPay`; the parameters will occupy different locations than the arguments.

2. Call by Reference. If the declaration of a parameter has the form

```
type & parameter_name
```

that parameter is a **reference** parameter, which has the following properties:

- A reference parameter is simply an *alias* for the corresponding argument.

- A reference parameter is allocated **the same** memory locations as the corresponding argument

- Changing a reference parameter *changes* the corresponding argument.

Reference parameters make it possible for *functions to return multiple values*; for example:

```
void ComputeNetPay(double grossPay, int dependents,
                   double & tax, double & netPay);
{ ...
  tax = . . .
  netPay = . . .
}


void GetEmployeeInfo(int & empNumber, int & dependents,
                     double & hours, double & rate,
                     bool & done)
{ ...
  cin >> empNumber >> ...
}
```

3. const **Reference Parameters.** These are parameters whose declarations have the form

```
const type & parameter_name
```

They are used when copying values of all the arguments each time a function is called is too inefficient, but we do want to protect the arguments. A compile-time error results if a function tries to change the value of a constant reference parameter.

EXAMPLE. The functions in the program in Figure C.6 illustrate these parameter-passing mechanisms:

`Instruct()` has no parameters and returns no values.

`PrintEmpInfo()` has all value parameters and returns no values.

`GrossWages()` has all value parameters and returns a `double` value.

`GetEmployeeInfo()` has all reference parameters and returns no values, but it does pass back each of the parameter values to the corresponding arguments.

`ComputeNetPay()` has two value parameters and two reference parameters and returns no values, but it does pass back the values of the reference parameters to the corresponding arguments.

FIGURE C.6   USING FUNCTIONS

```
/* Program to compute wages for several employees.
   Written at Doofus Univ. by Joe Somebody for CPSC 31416.

   Input:   Id-number, number of dependents, hours worked, and
              hourly rate for each of several employees
   Output: Id-number, hours worked, gross pay, taxes withheld,
              and net pay
   ----------------------------------------------------------------*/


#include <iostream>
#include <iomanip>
using namespace std;

// FUNCTION PROTOTYPES

void Instruct();
void GetEmployeeInfo(int & empNumber, int & dependents,
                      double & hours, double & rate, bool & done);
double GrossWages(int dependents, double hours, double rate);
void ComputeNetPay(double grossPay, int dependents,
                    double & tax, double & netPay);
void PrintEmpInfo(int idNumber, double hours, double grossPay,
                   double taxes, double netPay);

int main()
{
  int idNumber,              // employee's id-number
      numDependents;         //    number of dependents
  double hoursWorked,        //    hours worked for this pay period
         hourlyRate,         //    dollars per hour
         grossPay,           //    gross pay (before taxes)
         taxWithheld,        //    amount of tax withheld
         netPay;             //    grossPay - taxWithheld
  bool endOfData;            // signals end of data

  Instruct;
  for (;;)
  {
    GetEmployeeInfo(idNumber, numDependents,
                     hoursWorked, hourlyRate, endOfData);

    if (endOfData) break;

    grossPay = GrossWages(numDependents, hoursWorked, hourlyRate);
    ComputeNetPay(grossPay, numDependents, taxWithheld, netPay);
    PrintEmpInfo(idNumber, hoursWorked, grossPay, taxWithheld, netPay);
  }
}
```

```
// FUNCTION DEFINITIONS
//    If these were placed before main(), the prototypes could be
//    omitted. This is not usually done, however.


/* Function to display instructions to the user.

   Output:  Instructions
----------------------------------------------------------------*/

void Instruct()
{
  cout
    << "This program computes gross pay, tax withheld, and net pay for "
    << "employees.\n\tWhen prompted, enter employee's id-number (enter "
    << "0 to stop).  Then enter:"
    << "\n\t\t# of dependents   hours worked   hourly rate:"
    << "\n\tseparated by spaces.\n";
}


/* Function to get employee information and/or signal there is no more.

   Input:       Id-number, # of dependents, hours worked, and hourly rate
   Passes back: The four input values (via parameters)
                done is true if end of data was signaled, false
                otherwise
----------------------------------------------------------------*/

void GetEmployeeInfo(int & empNumber, int & dependents,
                     double & hours, double & rate, bool & finis)
{
  cout << "\nEnter employee number (0 to stop): ";
  cin >> empNumber;                           // get employee number

  finis = (empNumber == 0);
  if (finis) return;                          // if end of data, return
                                              // else get other info
  cout << "Enter # of dependents, hours worked, and hourly rate for "
       << empNumber << ": ";
  cin >> dependents >> hours >> rate;
}


/* Function to compute gross wages as determined by number of hours
   employee worked plus a dependency allowance for each dependent.

   Receives:  Number of dependents, hours worked, hourly rate
   Returns:   Gross wages
----------------------------------------------------------------*/
```

```
double GrossWages(int dependents, double hours, double rate)
{
  const double DEP_ALLOWANCE = 100; // bonus per dependent

  double wages;                     // wages earned

  if (hours <= 40)                  // no overtime
    wages = hours * rate;
  else                              // overtime
    wages = 40 * rate + 1.5 * rate * (hours - 40);

                                    // return wages + allowance for deps
  return wages + DEP_ALLOWANCE * dependents;
}


/* Function to compute taxes withheld and net pay as gross pay minus
   taxes withheld.

   Receives:  Gross pay and number of dependents
   Returns:   Taxes withheld and net pay (via parameters)
   ---------------------------------------------------------------*/

void ComputeNetPay(double grossPay, int dependents,
                   double & tax, double & netPay)
{
  const double
    DEDUCTION = 25.00,        // deduction per dependent
    TAX_RATE = 0.12;          // withholding rate

  tax = TAX_RATE * (grossPay - DEDUCTION * dependents);

  if (tax < 0)                // check if any tax to be withheld
    tax = 0;

  netPay = grossPay - tax;    // compute net pay
}


/* Function to display employee information

   Receives:  Employee's id number, hours worked, gross pay,
              taxes withheld, and net pay
   Output:    These values with appropriate labels.
   ---------------------------------------------------------------*/
```

```
void PrintEmpInfo(int idNumber, double hours, double grossPay,
                  double taxes, double netPay)
{
  cout << setprecision(2) << setiosflags(ios::showpoint | ios::fixed)
       << "Employee " << idNumber << ":\n"
       << "\tHours worked:    " << setw(6) << hours << endl
       << "\tGross Pay:      $" << setw(6) << grossPay << endl
       << "\tTaxes withheld: $" << setw(6) << taxes << endl
       << "\tNet Pay:        $" << setw(6) << netPay << endl;
}
```

SAMPLE RUN:

```
Enter employee number (0 to stop): 12345
Enter # of dependents, hours worked, and hourly rate for 12345: 0 40
8.00
Employee 12345:
        Hours worked:    40.00
        Gross Pay:      $320.00
        Taxes withheld: $38.40
        Net Pay:        $281.60

Enter employee number (0 to stop): 0
```

DEFAULT VALUES FOR PARAMETERS. The last (trailing, rightmost) parameters in a parameter list may be assigned **default values**. These will be used as values if the function call does not provide arguments for these parameters. For example, we might assign default values to the parameters `hours` and `rate` in function `GrossWages()` as follows:

```
double GrossWages(int dependents,  double hours = 0.0,
                  double rate = 4.50);
```

This cannot be done in both the prototype and the definition and is usually done in its prototype.

INLINE FUNCTIONS. Preceding a function declaration with the keyword **inline** allows the compiler to replace each call of the function with the function body (with arguments substituted for parameters). This (usually) speeds execution; but do this only for simple functions. (See Sec. 3.2 for more information about inlined functions.)

FUNCTION OVERLOADING. Two different functions may have the same name provided they have different signatures; that is, their parameter lists must differ in the number and/or types of parameters. The compiler uses the arguments in a function call to determine which function to use. (See Sect. 3.2 for more information about overloading functions.)

C.12 Object Lifetimes, Scopes, and Namespaces

OBJECT LIFETIME. An object has:

- ▶ a name,
- ▶ a set of memory locations, and
- ▶ a value

Constructing an object consists of:

- ▶ Binding its name to a memory location, and
- ▶ Storing an initial value (possibly an undefined "garbage" value) in the memory locations.

An object is *destroyed* when it is no longer bound to a memory location.

The **lifetime** of an object is the time it exists—from its construction to its destruction. Most objects are `auto` (automatic) objects, which are created when execution enters the block containing their declarations and are destroyed when execution leaves the block. If we precede the declaration of an object with the keyword `static`

```
static type object_name = init_expression:
```

then it is created when execution begins and is destroyed when execution terminates. The following are some properties of auto and static objects:

1. Auto objects are initialized each time execution passes through their declaration. Static objects are initialized once—when program execution begins.
2. Objects declared in functions are auto unless declared to be static.
3. As auto objects, a function's parameters and local variables are created each time the function is called and destroyed when the function terminates.
4. A static local variable's value *persists* between calls to a function and can thus be used to store data that is needed from one function call to the next.

SCOPE. An object's lifetime indicates its existence at *run time*. An object's **scope** indicates its existence at *compile time*; it is the portion of the program in which that object can be accessed. The scope of an identifier depends on where the identifier is declared. The following are basic scope rules:

1. If an identifier is declared within a block, then its scope runs from its declaration to the end of the block. It can be accessed only within that block.
2. If an identifier is declared in the initialization expression of a `for` loop, then its scope runs from its declaration to the end of the loop. It can be accessed only within that `for` loop.
3. If an identifier is declared outside all blocks, then its scope runs from its declaration to the end of the file. It can be used anywhere within that file following its declaration (except when the identifier used for that object is also used for some other object).

4. If an identifier is a parameter of a function, then its scope is the body of the function. It can be accessed only within that function.

5. The scope of a member identifier in a struct or class is that struct or class. It cannot be accessed outside the struct just by giving its name; rather, the dot operator must be used.

6. The scope of an identifier declared or defined in a namespace block is that namespace block.

Note that an identifier's scope always begins at some point following its declaration. This observation can be summarized in the single rule:

An identifier must be declared before it can be used.

NAMESPACES. One of the recent additions to C++ is the **namespace** mechanism. If `name` is declared or defined in a `namespace` declaration of the form

```
namespace Something
{
  // declarations and definitions
}
```

then the scope of an identifier `name` declared inside this namespace block is this block. It can be accessed outside of the namespace only in the following ways:

1. By its fully-qualified name

> `Something::name`

2. By its unqualified name `name`, if a **using declaration** of the form

> `using namespace Something::name;`

or a **using directive** of the form

> `using namespace Something;`

has already been given, provided that no other item has the same name (in which case qualification is required as described in 1.) A `using` directive makes all names in the namespace available. This is why we add the directive `using namespace std;` after `#includes` of standard libraries—so that the names declared and defined in them can be used without qualification.

C.13 FILES

Files are processed using `ifstreams`, `ofstreams`, and `fstreams`, which connect a program and a file on disk; `ofstreams` are used only for output to a file, and writing to an `ofstream` actually writes to the file to which it is connected; `ifstreams` are used only for input from a file and reading from an `ifstream` actually reads from the file to which it is connected; `fstreams` can be used for both input and output.

OPENING FILE STREAMS. File streams are declared by using the types `ifstream`, `ofstream`, and `fstream`; for example,

```
ifstream in;       // input stream
ofstream out;      // output stream
```

These types are declared in `<fstream>` so it must be `#included` in the program:

```
#include <fstream>
```

Declaring a file stream only declares the name to be used for that stream. Before it can actually be used, it must be *opened*, which establishes a connection to an actual disk file. This can be done in two ways:

1. Use the `open()` member function:

```
stream.open(disk_filename)
```

where `disk_filename` has a string constant as its value; for example,

```
in.open("/home/cpsc/186/xyz.dat");

string outFileName;
cin >> outFileName;
out.open(outFileName.data());
```

or

```
out.open(outFileName.c_str());
```

In the last few examples, we must use the `string` function member `data()` or `c_str()` to extract the string constant stored in `outFileName`.

2. Attach `(disk_filename)` to the file stream's name in its declaration:

```
ifstream in(disk_filename);
ofstream out(disk_filename);
```

for example

```
ifstream in("/home/cpsc/152/xyz.dat");
ofstream out(outFileName.data());
```

or

```
ofstream out(outFileName.c_str());
```

We can also use a second *mode* argument in either of these methods that specifies how the file is being opened—for input (`ios::in`), for output (`ios::out`), for appending (`ios::app`). Opening a file for output destroys any previous contents of the file.

It is always a good idea to check that a file was opened successfully before proceeding. For this we can use the member function `is_open()`; for example,

```
assert(in.is_open());
```

or

```
if (!in.is_open())
{
   cerr << "Error opening file\n";
   exit(-1);
}
```

CLOSING FILE STREAMS. After processing of a file is complete, the stream to that file should be **closed**, which disconnects it from the file:

```
close(stream);
```

If necessary, the file stream can be reopened (using `open()`). For example, one might open a file for output, write some data to it, then close it, reopen it for input, and then read and process this data.

I/O with files. It is important to remember that class `ifstream` is derived from class `istream` and class `ofstream` is derived from class `ostream` and so *they inherit all of the operations from these base classes* such as `eof()`, `fail()`, `ignore()`, `>>`, `<<`, and `get()`. These functions and operations can therefore also be used with file streams and format manipulators can be used with `ofstreams`. (See Appendix D for more information.)

EXAMPLE. The program in Fig. C.7 illustrates the use of files. It reads permanent employee information from a file and current information is entered from the keyboard.

FIGURE C.7   USING FILES

```
/* This program is a modification of that in Fig. C.6 for computing
   wages for several employees.  Permanent employee information is read
   from a file.

   Input (file):     Id-number, number of dependents, and hourly rate
                     for each of several employees
   Input (keyboard): Hours worked by employees
   Output (screen):  Prompts to user, including id-numbers.
   Output (file):    Id-numbers, hours worked, gross pay, taxes
                     withheld and net pay
----------------------------------------------------------------------*/
```

```cpp
#include <iostream>
#include <fstream>
#include <iomanip>
#include <string>
using namespace std;

void Instruct();
void GetEmployeeInfo(ifstream & in, int & empNumber, int & dependents,
                     double & hours, double & rate, bool & done);
double GrossWages(int dependents, double hours, double rate);
void ComputeNetPay(double grossPay, int dependents,
                   double & tax, double & netPay);
void PrintEmpInfo(ofstream & out, int idNumber, double hours,
                  double grossPay, double taxes, double netPay);
int main()
{
  string inFilename,
         outFilename;

  cout << "Enter names of input and output file:";
  cin >> inFilename >> outFilename;

  ifstream inStream(inFilename.data());
  ofstream outStream(outFilename.data());

  int idNumber,                  // employee's id-number
        numDependents;           //    number of dependents
  double hoursWorked,            //    hours worked for this pay period
         hourlyRate,             //    dollars per hour
         grossPay,               //    gross pay (before taxes)
         taxWithheld,            //    amount of tax withheld
         netPay;                 //    grossPay - taxWithheld
  bool endOfData;                // signals end of data

  Instruct;

  for (;;)
  {
    GetEmployeeInfo(inStream, idNumber, numDependents,
                    hoursWorked, hourlyRate, endOfData);

    if (endOfData) break;
    grossPay = GrossWages(numDependents, hoursWorked, hourlyRate);
    ComputeNetPay(grossPay, numDependents, taxWithheld, netPay);
    PrintEmpInfo(outStream, idNumber, hoursWorked, grossPay,
                 taxWithheld, netPay);
  }
}
. . .
```

```
void Instruct()
{
  cout
     << "This program computes gross pay, tax withheld, and net pay for
     << "employees.\n\tWhen prompted, enter hours worked and hourly rate"
     << "\n\t(separated by spaces) for the indicated employee.\n\n";
}



/* Function to get employee information and/or signal there is no more.

   Receives:            ifstream
   Input (file):        Id-number, number of dependents, and hourly rate
   Input (keyboard):    Hours worked by employee
   Output (screen):     Prompts to user, including id-number.
   Passes back:         Modified ifstresm, the four input values, done is
                          true if end of data was signaled, false otherwise
----------------------------------- --------------------------------*/

void GetEmployeeInfo(ifstream & in, int & empNumber, int & dependents,
                     double & hours, double & rate, bool & done)
{
  in >> empNumber;                              // get employee number from file
  done = in.eof();
  if (done) return;                             // if end of file, return
                                                // else
  in >> dependents >> rate;                     // get other info from file

  cout << "Enter hours worked by " << empNumber << ": ";
  cin >> hours;                                 // get hours worked from user

}
. . .


/* Function to write employee information to a file.

   Receives:       ofstream, employee's id number, hours worked,
                     gross pay, taxes withheld, and net pay
   Passes back:    the modified ofstream
-----------------------------------------------------------------------*/

void PrintEmpInfo(ofstream & out, int idNumber, double hours,
                  double grossPay, double taxes, double netPay)
{
  out << setprecision(2) << setiosflags(ios::showpoint | ios::fixed)
      << "Employee " << idNumber << ":\n"
      << "\tHours worked:    " << setw(6) << hours << endl
      << "\tGross Pay:     $" << setw(6) << grossPay << endl
      << "\tTaxes withheld: $" << setw(6) << taxes << endl
      << "\tNet Pay:       $" << setw(6) << netPay << endl;
}
```

LISTING OF INPUT FILE `employee.dat`:

```
12345 0 8.00
22244 1 9.00
33333 2 10.00
```

LISTING OF OUTPUT FILE `payinfo`:

```
Employee 12345:
        Hours worked:     40.00
        Gross Pay:      $320.00
        Taxes withheld: $ 38.40
        Net Pay:        $281.60
Employee 22244:
        Hours worked:     45.00
        Gross Pay:      $527.50
        Taxes withheld: $ 60.30
        Net Pay:        $467.20
Employee 33333:
        Hours worked:     42.50
        Gross Pay:      $637.50
        Taxes withheld: $ 70.50
        Net Pay:        $567.00
```

OTHER C++
FEATURES

D.1   ARRAYS, STRUCTS, AND UNIONS

GENERAL TWO-DIMENSIONAL ARRAY ADDRESS TRANSLATION

Consider a two-dimensional array t with m rows and n columns that is to be stored rowwise, where each array element requires w bytes for storage. Each row of t has n entries so that $\bar{n} = n \cdot w$ cells are needed to store one row of t. Since t is a one-dimensional array whose elements are these rows, the address translation formulas in Sec. 2.3 give the beginning address of the ith row of t, t[i], as

$$\text{base}(\texttt{t[i]}) = \text{base}(\texttt{t}) + i\bar{n} = \text{base}(\texttt{t}) + inw$$

Because this row of t is itself a one-dimensional array with base address base(t[i]), where each element requires n bytes for storage, we find, using these same formulas, that the jth element of this row, t[i][j], is stored in the w consecutive cells beginning at

$$\text{base}(\texttt{t[i]}) + jw = \text{base}(\texttt{t}) + inw + jw = \text{base}(\texttt{t}) + (in + j)w$$

GENERAL ADDRESS TRANSLATIONS FOR STRUCTS

Suppose that a struct s has members $x_1, \ldots, x_n$ of types $T_1, \ldots, T_n$, respectively, then s.x_k is stored in the block of sizeof(T_k) bytes beginning at

$$\text{address of s.}x_k = \text{base address of s} + \text{offset}$$
$$= \text{base address of s} + \sum_{i=1}^{k-1} \texttt{sizeof(} T_i \texttt{)}$$

and the bit string stored in this block is interpreted as a value of data type T_k.

CONTRASTING STRUCTS AND UNIONS

For a union, memory is (typically) allocated for the largest member, and all the other members share this memory. The program in Fig. D.1 illustrates this. Note that the value stored in member1 of struct s does not change when a value is assigned to member2, and that the values stored in member1 and member2 of s remain unchanged when a value is assigned to member3. This is not the case for union u, however. Changing the value of any member changes the values of the other members.

FIGURE D.1   CONTRASTING STRUCTS AND UNIONS

```cpp
#include <iostream>
using namespace std;

struct Struct
{
  char member1;
  int member2;
  double member3;
};

union Union
{
  char member1;
  int member2;
  double member3;
};

int main()
{
  Struct s;
  s.member1 = 'A';
  cout << "Structure: " << s.member1 << "    " << s.member2 << "    "
       << s.member3 << endl;

  s.member2 = 1107296256;
  cout << "Structure: " << s.member1 << "    " << s.member2 << "    "
       << s.member3 << endl;

  s.member3 = 0.123;
  cout << "Structure: " << s.member1 << "    " << s.member2 << "    "
       << s.member3 << endl;

  Union u;
  u.member1 = 'A';
  cout << "\nUnion:    " << u.member1 << "    " << u.member2 << "    "
       << u.member3 << endl;

  u.member2 = 1107296256;
  cout << "Union:    " << u.member1 << "    " << u.member2 << "    "
       << u.member3 << endl;
```

```
      u.member3 = 0.123;
      cout << "Union:     " << u.member1 << "    " << u.member2 << "     "
           << u.member3 << endl;
}
```

EXECUTION:

```
Structure: A     -268437284     1.04774e-313
Structure: A     1107296256     1.04774e-313
Structure: A     1107296256     0.123

Union:     A     1107294328     8.58204e+09
Union:     B     1107296256     8.58993e+09
Union:     ?     1069513965     0.123
```

D.2 STREAM OPERATIONS

Several I/O operations were listed in Sec. 3.1. This section describes them in more detail.

INPUT

In the following operations and functions, `in_stream` is an `istream`, an `ifstream`, or an `istringstream`:

`in_stream >> variable`

> Tries to extract a sequence of characters corresponding to a value of the type of `variable` from `in_stream` and assign it to `variable`; for a `char` array of capacity n, it reads at most $n - 1$ characters and adds a terminating null character. If there are no characters, it *blocks execution* from proceeding until characters are entered. If the **noskipws manipulator** is used in an input statement,
>
> `... >> noskipws >> ...`
>
> then in all subsequent input, white-space characters will not be skipped. The **skipws manipulator** can be used to reactivate white-space skipping, which is the default condition:
>
> `... >> skipws >> ...`
>
> `>>` returns `in_stream`.

`in_stream.width(n)`

> Sets the maximum number of characters to be read from `in_stream` by the next `>>` to `n - 1`

`in_stream.get()`
`in_stream.get(char_variable);`

> Reads the next character from `in_stream` regardless of whether or not it is a white-space character. The first form returns this character; the second form assigns it to `char_variable`.

```
in_stream.get(char_array, n);
in_stream.get(char_array, n, terminator);
```
Extracts characters from `in_stream` and stores them in `char_array` until one of the following occurs:

1. $n - 1$ characters have been read.
2. The end of file occurs.
3. `terminator` is encountered (which is not extracted from `in_stream`). In the second case, `'\n'` is used.

A terminating null character is then added.

```
in_stream.getline(char_array, n);
in_stream.getline(char_array, n, terminator);
```
Same as `get()`, but removes the terminating character

```
in_stream.read(char_array, n);
```
Extracts characters from `in_stream` and stores them in `char_array` until one of the following occurs:

1. n characters have been read.
2. The end of file occurs.

No terminating null character is added.

```
in_stream.readsome(char_array, n);
```
Like `read()` but returns the number of characters extracted

```
in_stream.gcount()
```
Returns the number of characters extracted by the last unformatted input—`get()`, `getline()`, `read()`, `readsome()`—from `in_stream`

```
in_stream.peek()
```
Returns next character to be read but doesn't remove it from `in_stream`

```
in_stream.ignore(n, stopChar);
```
Extracts and discards characters from `in_stream` until one of the following occurs:

1. n characters have been extracted; default is 1.
2. `stopChar` is encountered and removed from `in_stream`; default terminator is the end of file.

```
in_stream.putback(ch);
```
Put character `ch` back into `in_stream`

```
in_stream.unget(ch);
```
Put most recently read character back into `in_stream`

```
in_stream.seekg(n);
in_stream.seekg(offset, base);
```
For the first form, move the read position to nth character in `in_stream`. For the second form, move the read position `offset` bytes from `base`, where `base` is one of `ios::beg` (beginning of stream), `ios::cur` (current position), or `ios::end` (end of stream).

`in_stream.tellg()`
> Return the offset of the read position within `in_stream`

`in_stream.sync();`
> Flush `in_stream`; return 0 if successful; return −1 and set `badbit` if not successful

OUTPUT

In the following operations and functions, `out_stream` is an `ostream`, an `ofstream`, or an `ostringstream`:

`out_stream << expression`
> Insert string of characters representing the value of `expression` into `out_stream`; returns `out_stream`

`out_stream.put(ch);`
> Insert character `ch` into `out_stream`

`out_stream.write(char_array, n);`
> Insert first `n` characters of `char_array` into `out_stream`

`out_stream .seekp(n);`
`out_stream .seekp(offset, base);`
> Same as `seekg` but for setting the write position in `out_stream`

`out_stream.tellp()`
> Return the offset of the write position within `out_stream`

`out_stream.flush();`
> Flush `out_stream`

FILES

`fstream.open(name);`
`fstream.open(name, mode);`
> Connect `fstream` to the file with specified `name`. In the second form, `mode` is one of the following:

`ios::in`	The default mode for `ifstream` objects. Open a file for input nondestructively with the read position at the file's beginning.
`ios::trunc`	Open a file and delete any contents it contains (i.e., *truncate* it).
`ios::out`	The default mode for `ofstream` objects. Open a file for output, using `ios::trunc`.
`ios::app`	Open a file for output, but nondestructively, with the write position at the file's end (i.e., for *appending*).
`ios::ate`	Open an existing file with the read position (`ifstream` objects) or write position (`ofstream` objects) **at the end** of the file.
`ios::nocreate`	Open a file only if it already exists.

| `ios::noreplace` | Open a file only if it does not already exist. |
| `ios::binary` | Open a file in binary mode. |

`fstream.is_open()`

Returns `true` if a file was opened successfully and `false` otherwise

`fstream.close();`

Disconnect `fstream` from the file to which is is currently connected

STREAM STATES

`ios::badbit`	1 if an unrecoverable error occurred, 0 otherwise
`ios::failbit`	1 if a recoverable error occurred, 0 otherwise
`ios::eofbit`	1 if the end-of-file mark was read, 0 otherwise
`stream.setstate(sBit);`	Set the status bit `sBit` to 1, where `sBit` is one or more of `ios::badbit`, `ios::failbit`, `ios::eofbit`
`stream.good()`	Returns `true` if and only if the good bit is set (1)
`stream.fail()`	Returns `true` if and only if the fail bit is set (1)
`stream.bad()`	Returns `true` if and only if the bad bit is set (1
`stream.eof()`	Returns `true` if and only if the eof bit is set (1)
`stream.clear()`	Resets the good bit to 1, all other status bits to 0

FORMAT MANIPULATORS

`boolalpha`	Use strings `true` and `false` for I/O of boolean values
`noboolalpha`	Use integers `1` and `0` for I/O of boolean values
`scientific`	Use floating-point (scientific) notation
`fixed`	Use fixed-point notation
`showpoint`	Show decimal point and trailing zeros for whole real numbers
`noshowpoint`	Hide decimal point and trailing zeros for whole real numbers
`showpos`	Display positive values with a + sign
`noshowpos`	Display positive values without a + sign
`dec`	Display integer values in base 10
`oct`	Display integer values in base 8
`hex`	Display integer values in base 16
`showbase`	Display integer values indicating their base (e.g., `0x` for hex).
`noshowbase`	Display integer values without indicating their base
`uppercase`	In hexadecimal, use symbols A–F; in scientific, use E
`nouppercase`	In hexadecimal, use symbols a–f; in scientific, use e
`skipws`	Skip white space on input
`noskipws`	Don't skip white space on input
`flush`	Write contents of stream to screen (or file)
`endl`	Insert newline character and flush the stream
`left`	Left-justify displayed values, pad with fill character on right
`right`	Right-justify displayed values (except strings), pad with fill character on left
`internal`	Pad with fill character between sign or base and value
`setprecision(num)`	Set the number of decimal digits to be displayed to `num`

| `setw(num)` | Display the next value in a field whose width is `num` |
| `setfill(ch)` | Set the fill character to `ch` (blank is the default) |

Some older C++ compilers may not support the use of format manipulators without arguments. It may be necessary to include `iomanip` and use `setiosflags()` and `resetiosflags()`:

| `setiosflags(flaglist)` | Sets the flags in `flaglist` |
| `resetiosflags(flaglist)` | Resets the flags in `flaglist` to their defaults |

where the form of `flaglist` is: $flag_1$ | $flag_2$ | ... | $flag_n$ with the flags selected from the following list: `ios::showpoint`, `ios::fixed`, `ios::scientific`, `ios::left`, `ios::right`, `ios::skipws`.

D.3   STRING OPERATIONS

Many of the string operations described in Sec. 3.3 are implemented by C-style functions provided in the C++ library `<cstring>`.[1] Table D.1 lists these functions; `s`, `s1`, and `s2` are `char` arrays, `ch` is a character, and `n` is an integer. Other useful string-processing functions are the conversion functions in `<cstdlib>` listed in Table D.2 and the character-processing functions from `<cctype>` listed in Table D.3. Many of these C string-processing functions use the null character to detect the end of a string and cannot be expected to perform correctly if it is not present.

TABLE D.1   FUNCTIONS IN `<cstring>`

Operation	Description
`strcat(s1, s2)`	Appends `s2` to `s1`
`strncat(s1, s2, n)`	Appends at most `n` characters of `s2` to `s1`
`strcpy(s1, s2)`	Copies `s2` into `s1`
`strncpy(s1, s2, n)`	Copies first `n` characters of `s2` into `s1`
`strlen(s)`	Returns length of `s` (not counting the terminating null character)
`strcmp(s1, s2)`	Compares `s1` with `s2`—returns an integer less than, equal to, or greater than 0 according to whether `s1` is less than, equal to, or greater than `s2`
`strncmp(s1, s2, n)`	Same as `strcmp`, but compare first `n` characters of `s1` and `s2`
`strchr(s, c)`	Returns a pointer to the first occurrence of `c` in `s`, `null` if not found
`strrchr(s, c)`	Like `strchr` but locate last occurrence of `c` in `s`
`strstr(s1, s2)`	Returns a pointer to the first occurrence in `s1` of `s2`, `null` if not found

(continued)

[1]The C++ standard specifies that a library provided in C with a name of the form `<lib.h>` be renamed in C++ as `<clib>` in which the prefix `c` is attached and the extension `.h` is dropped. In particular, C's string library `<string.h>` is renamed `<cstring>`. Many versions of C++ support both names.

TABLE D.1   Continued

Operation	Description
strpbrk(s1, s2)	Returns a pointer to the first occurrence in s1 of any character of s2, null if none found
strspn(s1, s2)	Returns the number of characters in s1 before any character in s2
strcspn(s1, s2)	Returns the number of characters in s1 before a character not in s2

TABLE D.2   CONVERSION FUNCTIONS IN `<cstdlib>`

Operation	Description
double atof(s) int atoi(s) long atol(s)	atof(s), atoi(s), and atol(s) return the value obtained by converting the character string s to double, int, and long int, respectively

TABLE D.3   FUNCTIONS IN `<cctype>`

Operation	Description
isalnum(c)	Returns true if c is a letter or a digit, false otherwise
isalpha(c)	Returns true if c is a letter, false otherwise
iscntrl(c)	Returns true if c is a control character, false otherwise
isdigit(c)	Returns true if c is a decimal digit, false otherwise
isgraph(c)	Returns true if c is a printing character except space, false otherwise
islower(c)	Returns true if c is lowercase, false otherwise
isprint(c)	Returns true if c is a printing character including space, false otherwise
ispunct(c)	Returns true if c is a punctuation character (not a space, an alphabetic character, or a digit), false otherwise
isspace(c)	Returns true if c is a white-space character (space, '\f', '\n', '\r', '\t', or '\v'), false otherwise
isupper(c)	Returns true if c is uppercase, false otherwise
isxdigit(c)	Returns true if c is a hexadecimal digit, false otherwise
tolower(c)	Returns uppercase equivalent of c (if c is lowercase)
toupper(c)	Returns the lowercase equivalent of c (if c is uppercase)

The string class, which was described in Chap. 3, is defined by

```
typedef basic_string<char> string;
```

The unsigned integer type **size_type** is defined in this class as is an integer constant **npos**, which is some integer that is usually greater than the number of characters in a string. Table D.4 gives a list of the major operations defined on a string object s; pos, pos1, pos2, n, n1, and n2 are of type size_type; str, str1, and str2 are of type `string`; `charArray` is a character array; `ch` and `delim` are of type `char`; `istr` is an `istream`; `ostr` is an `ostream`; `it1` and `it2` are iterators; and `inpIt1` and `inpIt2` are input iterators. All of these operations except `>>`, `<<`, `+`, the relational operators, `getline()`, and the second version of `swap()` are member functions.

TABLE D.4   OPERATIONS ON C++ strings

Operation	Description
Constructors:	
`string s;`	This declaration invokes the default constructor to construct s as an empty string
`string s(charArray);`	This declaration initializes s to contain a copy of `charArray`
`string s(charArray, n);`	This declaration initializes s to contain a copy of the first n characters in `charArray`
`string s(str);`	This declaration initializes s to contain a copy of string `str`
`string s(str, pos, n);`	This declaration initializes s to contain a copy of the n characters in string `str`, starting at position `pos`; if n is too large, characters are copied only to the end of `str`
`string s(n, ch);`	This declaration initializes s to contain n copies of the character `ch`
`string s(inpIt1, inpIt2)`	This declaration initializes s to contain the characters in the range [`inpIt1`, `inpIt2`)
`getline(istr, s, delim)`	Extracts characters from `istr` and stores them in s until `s.max_size()` characters have been extracted, the end of file occurs, or `delim` is encountered, in which case `delim` is extracted from `istr` but is not stored in s
`getline(istr, s)`	Inputs a string value for s as in the preceding function with `delim = '\n'`
`istr >> s`	Extracts characters from `istr` and stores them in s until `s.max_size()` characters have been extracted, the end of file occurs, or a white-space character is encountered, in which case the white-space character is not removed from `istr`; returns `istr`
`ostr << s`	Inserts characters of s into `ostr`; returns `ostr`
`s = val`	Assigns a copy of `val` to s; `val` may be a string, a character array, or a character
`s += val`	Appends a copy of `val` to s; `val` may be a string, a character array, or a character

(continued)

TABLE D.4   Continued

Operation	Description
`s[pos]`	Returns a reference to the character stored in `s` at position `pos`, provided `pos < s.length()`
`s + t` `t + s`	Returns the result of concatenating `s` and `t`; `t` may be a string, a character array, or a character.

`s < t,   t < s`
`s <= t,   t <= s`
`s > t,   t > s`
`s >= t,   t >= s`
`s == t,   t == s`
`s != t,   t != s`
	Returns `true` or `false` as determined by the relational operator; `t` may be a string or a character array

`s.append(str)`	Appends string `str` at the end of `s`; returns `s`
`s.append(str, pos, n)`	Appends at the end of `s` a copy of the `n` characters in `str`, starting at position `pos`; if `n` is too large, characters are copied only until the end of `str` is reached; returns `s`
`s.append(charArray)`	Appends `charArray` at the end of `s`; returns `s`
`s.append(charArray, n)`	Appends the first `n` characters in `charArray` at the end of `s`; returns `s`
`s.append(n, ch)`	Appends `n` copies of `ch` at the end of `s`; returns `s`
`s.append(inpIt1, inpIt2)`	Appends copies of the characters in the range [`inpIt1, inpIt2`) to `s`; returns `s`
`s.assign(str)`	Assigns a copy of `str` to `s`; returns `s`
`s.assign(str, pos, n)`	Assigns to `s` a copy of the `n` characters in `str`, starting at position `pos`; if `n` is too large, characters are copied only until the end of `str` is reached; returns `s`
`s.assign(charArray)`	Assigns to `s` a copy of `charArray`; returns `s`
`s.assign(charArray, n)`	Assigns to `s` a string consisting of the first `n` characters in `charArray`; returns `s`
`s.assign(n, ch)`	Assigns to `s` a string consisting of `n` copies of `ch`; returns `s`
`s.assign(inpIt1, inpIt2)`	Assigns to `s` a string consisting of the characters in the range [`inpIt1, inpIt2`); returns `s`
`s.at(pos)`	Returns `s[pos]`
`s.begin()`	Returns an iterator positioned at the first character in `s`

(continued)

TABLE D.4 Continued

Operation	Description
`s.c_str()`	Returns (the base address of) a `char` array containing the characters stored in `s`, terminated by a null character
`s.capacity()`	Returns the size (of type `size_type`) of the storage allocated in `s`
`s.clear()`	Removes all the characters in `s`; return type is `void`
`s.compare(str)`	Returns a negative value, 0, or a positive value according as `s` is less than, equal to, or greater than `str`
`s.compare(charArray)`	Compares `s` and `charArray` as in the preceding function member
`s.compare(pos, n, str)`	Compares strings `s` and `str` as before, but starts at position `pos` in `s` and compares only the next `n` characters
`s.compare(pos, n, charArray)`	Compares string `s` and `charArray` as in the preceding function member
`s.compare(pos1, n1, str, pos2, n2)`	Compares `s` and `str` as before, but starts at position `pos1` in `s`, position `pos2` in `str`, and compares only the next `n1` characters in `s` and the next `n2` characters in `str`
`s.compare(pos1, n1, charArray, n2)`	Compares strings `s` and `charArray` as before, but using only the first `n2` characters in `charArray`
`s.copy(charArray, pos, n)`	Replaces the string in `s` with `n` characters in `charArray`, starting at position `pos` or at position 0, if `pos` is omitted; if `n` is too large, characters are copied only until the end of `charArray` is reached; returns the number (of type `size_type`) of characters copied
`s.data()`	Returns a `char` array containing the characters stored in `s`, terminated by a null character
`s.empty()`	Returns `true` if `s` contains no characters, `false` otherwise
`s.end()`	Returns an iterator positioned immediately after the last character in `s`
`s.erase(pos, n)`	Removes `n` characters from `s`, beginning at position `pos` (default value 0); if `n` is too large or is omitted, characters are erased only to the end of `s`; returns `s`

(*continued*)

TABLE D.4   Continued

Operation	Description
`s.erase(it)`	Removes the character at the position specified by `it`; returns an iterator positioned immediately after the erased character
`s.find(str, pos)`	Returns the first position $\geq$ `pos` such that the next `str.size()` characters of `s` match those in `str`; returns `npos` if there is no such position; 0 is the default value for `pos`
`s.find(ch, pos)`	Searches `s` as in the preceding function member, but for `ch`
`s.find(charArray, pos)`	Searches `s` as in the preceding function member, but for the characters in `charArray`
`s.find(charArray, pos, n)`	Searches `s` as in the preceding function member, but for the first `n` characters in `charArray`; the value `pos` must be given
`s.find_first_not_of(str, pos)`	Returns the first position $\geq$ `pos` of a character in `s` that does not match any of the characters in `str`; returns `npos` if there is no such position; 0 is the default value for `pos`
`s.find_first_not_of(ch, pos)`	Searches `s` as in the preceding function member, but for `ch`
`s.find_first_not_of (charArray, pos)`	Searches `s` as in the preceding function member, but for the characters in `charArray`
`s.find_first_not_of (charArray, pos, n)`	Searches `s` as in the preceding function member, but using the first `n` characters in `charArray`; the value `pos` must be given
`s.find_first_of (str, pos)`	Returns the first position $\geq$ `pos` of a character in `s` that matches any character in `str`; returns `npos` if there is no such position; 0 is the default value for `pos`
`s.find_first_of(ch, pos)`	Searches `s` as in the preceding function member, but for `ch`
`s.find_first_of (charArray, pos)`	Searches `s` as in the preceding function member, but for the characters in `charArray`
`s.find_first_of (charArray, pos, n)`	Searches `s` as in the preceding function member, but using the first `n` characters in `charArray`; the value `pos` must be given
`s.find_last_not_of (str, pos)`	Returns the highest position $\leq$ `pos` of a character in `s` that does not match any character in `str`; returns `npos` if there is no such position; `npos` is the default value for `pos`

(continued)

Table D.4   Continued

Operation	Description
`s.find_last_not_of` `(ch, pos)`	Searches `s` as in the preceding function member, but for `ch`
`s.find_last_not_of` `(charArray, pos)`	Searches `s` as in the preceding function member, but using the characters in `charArray`
`s.find_last_not_of` `(charArray, pos, n)`	Searches `s` as in the preceding function member, but using the first `n` characters in `charArray`; the value `pos` must be given
`s.find_last_of(str, pos)`	Returns the highest position $\leq$ `pos` of a character in `s` that matches any character in `str`; returns `npos` if there is no such position; `npos` is the default value for `pos`
`s.find_last_of(ch, pos)`	Searches `s` as in the preceding function member, but for `ch`
`s.find_last_of` `(charArray, pos)`	Searches `s` as in the preceding function member, but using the characters in `charArray`
`s.find_last_of` `(charArray, pos, n)`	Searches `s` as in the preceding function member, but using the first `n` characters in `charArray`; the value `pos` must be given
`s.insert(pos, str)`	Inserts a copy of `str` into `s` at position `pos`; returns `s`
`s.insert(pos1, str,` `pos2, n)`	Inserts a copy of `n` characters of `str` starting at position `pos2` into `s` at position `pos`; if `n` is too large, characters are copied only until the end of `str` is reached; returns `s`
`s.insert(pos,` `charArray, n)`	Inserts a copy of the first `n` characters of `charArray` into `s` at position `pos`; inserts all of its characters if `n` is omitted; returns `s`
`s.insert(pos, n, ch)`	Inserts `n` copies of the character `ch` into `s` at position `pos`; returns `s`
`s.insert(it, ch)`	Inserts a copy of the character `ch` into `s` at the position specified by `it` and returns an iterator positioned at this copy
`s.insert(it, n, ch)`	Inserts `n` copies of the character `ch` into `s` at the position specified by `it`; return type is `void`
`s.insert(it, inpIt1,` `inpIt2)`	Inserts copies of the characters in the range [`inpIt1`, `inpIt2`) into `s` at the position specified by `it`; return type is `void`

(continued)

TABLE D.4   Continued

Operation	Description
`s.length()`	Returns the length (of type `size_type`) of s
`s.max_size()`	Returns the maximum length (of type `size_type`) of s
`s.rbegin()`	Returns a reverse iterator positioned at the last character in s
`s.rend()`	Returns a reverse iterator positioned immediately before the first character in s
`s.replace(pos1, n1, str)`	Replaces the substring of s of length n1 beginning at position pos1 with str; if n1 is too large, all characters to the end of s are replaced; returns s
`s.replace(it1, it2, str)`	Same as the preceding but for the substring of s consisting of the characters in the range [it1, it2); returns s
`s.replace(pos1, n1,)` `str, pos2, n2)`	Replaces a substring of s as in the preceding reference but using n2 characters in str, beginning at position pos2; if n2 is too large, characters to the end of str are used; returns s
`s.replace(pos1, n1,)` `charArray, n2)`	Replaces a substring of s as before but with the first n2 characters in charArray; if n2 is too large, characters to the end of charArray are used; if n2 is omitted, all of charArray is used; returns s
`s.replace(it1, it2,` `charArray, n2)`	Same as the preceding but for the substring of s consisting of the characters in the range [it1, it2); returns s
`s.replace(pos1, n1,` `n2, ch)`	Replaces a substring of s as before but with n2 copies of ch
`s.replace(it1,)` `it2, n2, ch`	Same as the preceding but for the substring of s consisting of the characters in the range [it1, it2); returns s
`s.replace(it1, it2,` `inpIt1, inpIt2)`	Same as the preceding, but replaces with copies of the characters in the range [inpIt1, inpIt2); returns s
`s.reserve(n)`	Changes the storage allocation for s so that s.capacity() $\geq$ n, 0 if n is omitted; return type is void
`s.resize(n, ch)`	If n $\leq$ s.size(), truncates rightmost characters

(continued)

TABLE D.4   Continued

Operation	Description
	in s to make it of size n; otherwise, adds copies of character ch to end of s to increase its size to n, or adds a default character value (usually a blank) if ch is omitted; return type is void
s.rfind(str, pos)	Returns the highest position $\leq$ pos such that the next str.size() characters of s match those in str; returns npos if there is no such position; npos is the default value for pos
s.rfind(ch, pos)	Searches s as in the preceding function member, but for ch
s.rfind(charArray, pos)	Searches s as in the preceding function member, but for the characters in charArray
s.rfind(charArray, pos, n)	Searches s as in the preceding function member, but for the first n characters in charArray; the value pos must be given
s.size()	Returns the length (of type size_type) of s
s.substr(pos, n)	Returns a copy of the substring consisting of n characters from s, beginning at position pos (default value 0); if n is too large or is omitted, characters are copied only until the end of s is reached
s.swap(str)	Swaps the contents of s and str; return type is void
swap(str1, str2)	Swaps the contents of str1 and str2; return type is void

D.4   EXCEPTIONS

In Sec. 3.2 we looked at some ways of handling errors in class design. The programmer can write code to *detect* errors but may not know how to *handle* them. In our examples, usually we have simply issued an error message or aborted execution by means of the exit() function or assert() function. In many cases, however, it would be better to simply signal the error and let the user of the class take appropriate action, and exceptions are designed to make this possible.

When a function detects an error, it can **throw an exception**, which is usually an error-message string or a class object that conveys information to the *exception handler*, which will **catch the exception** and take appropriate action. If there is no handler for that type of exception, execution terminates. The `Set` operation in the `Time` class in Sec. 3.2 illustrates:

```
if (hours >= 1 && hours <= 12 &&
      minutes >= 0 && minutes <= 59 &&
      (am_pm == 'A' || am_pm == 'P'))
{
    . . .
}
else
{
    char illegal_Time_Error[] =
          "*** Can't set time with these values ***\n";
    throw illegal_Time_Error;
}
```

The program or function that calls the function that may throw the exception encloses the function call and associated code in a **try block** of the form

```
try
{
    ... statements that may cause error
}
```

This is followed by one of more **catch blocks**, each of which specifies an exception type and contains code for handling that exception. They have the form

```
catch(exception_type optional_parameter_name)
{
    ... the exception handler
}
```

For example, the following code attempts to use the `Set` operation in a `Time` object `mealTime` and catches the exception thrown in `Set()`:

```
try
{
    mealTime.Set(13, 30, 'P');
    cout << "This is a valid time\n";
}
catch (char badTime[])
{
    cout << "ERROR: " << badTime << endl;
    exit(-1);
}
cout << "Proceeding. . .\n";
```

When the code in the `try` clock is executed and no exceptions are thrown, all of the `catch` blocks are skipped and execution continues with the statement after the last one. If an exception is thrown, execution leaves the `try` block and the attached catch blocks are searched for one whose parameter type matches the type of exception. If one is found, its exception handler is executed; otherwise, the catch blocks of any enclosing try blocks are searched. If none are found, execution terminates.

The types of exceptions that a function can throw can be declared by attaching an **exception specification** of the form throw(*exception_list*):

```
ReturnType Name(parameterlist) throw(exc1, exc2, ...);
```

This function can throw only the exceptions listed and exceptions derived from them. If it attempts to do otherwise, the function std::unexpected() is called, which will terminate execution (unless unexpected() is redefined by calling set_unexpected()) or which will throw bad_exception if std::bad_exception is included in the list of exceptions.

There are several standard exceptions provided in C++. They are listed in Table D.5. They are all derived from the class exception() provided in <stdexcept>, which in addition to member function throw() also has a virtual member function what().

TABLE D.5   STANDARD EXCEPTIONS

Exception	Thrown by
bad_alloc	new()
bad_cast	dynamic_cast()
bad_typeid	typeid()
bad_exception	exception specification
out_of_range	at() and [] in bitset
invalid_argument	bitset constructor
overflow_error	to_ulong() in bitset
ios_base::failure	ios_base::clear ()

For example, in Sec. 6.2, we described the out-of-range exception thrown by the at member function of vector if the index gets out of range. The following is a modification of the example given there:

```
vector<int> v(4, 99);

try
{
  for (int i = 0; i < 5; i++)
    cout << v.at(i) << endl;
}
. . .
catch(out_of_range exception)
{
  cout << "Exception occurred: "
       << exception.what() << endl;
}
```

The member function `what()` used in the output statement returns a string describing the exception. In one version of C++, the output produced was

```
99
99
99
99
Exception occurred: vector::at out of range
```

The statements

```
double * ptr;
try
{
  ptr = new double[1000000];
}

catch(bad_alloc exception)
{
    cout << "Exception occurred: "
         << exception.what() << endl;
}
```

produced

```
Exception occurred: Allocation Failure
```

D.5   MORE ABOUT FUNCTION TEMPLATES

In Section 6.2 we concentrated on function templates having a single type parameter but we noted that more type parameters are allowed:

```
template <typename TypeParam₁, ..., typename TypeParamₙ>
FunctionDefinition
```

where $TypeParam_1, \ldots, TypeParam_n$ are type parameters. To illustrate this more general function template, consider the generic conversion function and the test-driver program in Figure D.2.

FIGURE D.2   USING A FUNCTION TEMPLATE TO CONVERT TYPES

```
/* Function template to convert a Type1 value to a
 * Type2 value.
 *  Receive:   Type parameters Type1 and Type2
 *             value1 of Type 1
 *  Pass back: value2 of Type2
 ********************************************************/
```

```
template <typename Type1, typename Type2>
void Convert(Type1 value1, Type2 & value2)
{
   value2 = static_cast<Type2>(value1);
}

#include <iostream>
using namespace std;

int main()
{
   char a = 'a';
   int ia;
   Convert(a, ia);
   cout << a << "   " << ia << endl;

   double x = 3.14;
   int ix;
   Convert(x, ix);
   cout << x << "   " << ix << endl;
}
```

EXECUTION:

```
a   97
3.14   3
```

Note that in the function template `Convert()`, each of the type parameters `Type1` and `Type2` appears in the parameter list of the function heading. This is a requirement in all function templates.

To illustrate, suppose we modify the function template `Convert()` to return its value by means of a `return` statement rather than via a reference parameter:

```
template <typename Type1, typename Type2>
Type2 Convert(Type1 value1)   // Error--Type2 not used in
{                             // parameter list
   return static_cast<Type2>(value1);
}
```

This would not be allowed because the type parameter `Type2` does not appear in the parameter list of the function heading. This makes it impossible for the compiler to bind an actual type to `Type2` because it uses only the types of the arguments in a function call to determine what types to associate with the type parameters.

One solution would be to provide a dummy second parameter indicating the type of the return value:

```
template <typename Type1, typename Type2>
Type2 Convert(Type1 value1, Type2 value2)
{
   return static_cast<Type2>(value1);
}
```

This works, but it is clumsy because function calls must include a dummy second argument; for example,

```
double x = 3.14;
int ix = Convert(x, 0);
```

D.6   OTHER APPLICATIONS OF POINTERS

In Chap. 8 we focused on how pointers are used to construct run-time arrays and linked lists. There are also several other applications of pointers that C++ has inherited from C. Two of these are described here.

COMMAND-LINE ARGUMENTS

In Sec. 8.4 we noted that command-line arguments can be passed to a main function `main()` via two parameters, which are usually named `argc` and `argv`:

▶ `argc` (the **arg**ument **c**ount): an `int` whose value is the number of strings on the command line when the command to execute the binary executable containing this function is given

▶ `argv` (the **arg**ument **v**ector): an array of pointers to `chars`; for $i = 0$, $1, \ldots, n-1$, `argv[i]` is the address of the ith character string on the command line

The program in Fig. D.3 and the sample runs demonstrate this. The compiled version of the program is stored in a file named `comm`, and `comm` is executed by entering the command

```
comm
```

which produces the output

```
There are 1 strings on the command line:
   argv[0] contains: comm
```

Thus, within `comm`, `argc` has the value 1, and `argv[0]` refers to the character string `comm`. When `comm` is executed by entering the command

```
comm CPSC 186
```

the output produced is

```
There are 3 strings on the command line:
   argv[0] contains: comm
   argv[1] contains: CPSC
   argv[2] contains: 186
```

FIGURE D.3   PARAMETERS FOR `main()`

```
/* This program demonstrates the predefined parameters argc and argv.
 *
 * Receive: A sequence of command-line strings
 * Output:  The value of argc, followed by each string in argv
 ****************************************************************/

#include <iostream>
using namespace std;

int main(int argc, char * argv[])
{
   cout << "There are " << argc
        << "strings on the command line:\n\n";

   for (int i = 0; i < argc; i++)
      cout << "   argv[" << i << "] = "  << argv[i] << endl;

   return 0;
}
```

SAMPLE RUNS (IN UNIX)

```
% g++ commandline1.cc -o comm
% comm
There are 1 strings on the command line:
   argv[0] contains: comm

% comm CPSC 186
There are 3 strings on the command line:
   argv[0] = comm
   argv[1] = CPSC
   argv[2] = 186
```

Figure D.4 shows a program for implementing a system file-copy command. If the compiled version of the program is saved with the name copy, a command of the form

```
copy file1 file2
```

can then be given to copy one file to another.

Figure D.4   Program for a System Command

```
/* This program implements a copy command.  If it is compiled
 * and saved under the name copy, a command of the form
 *                          copy file1 file2
 * will copy the contents of file1 to file2.
 *
 * Receive:      A sequence of command-line strings
 * Input(file):  A text file
 * Output(file): Contents of the text file
 ********************************************************************/

#include <iostream>
#include <fstream>
#include <cassert>
using namespace std;

int main(int argc, char * argv[])
{
  if (argc != 3)
    cerr << "Usage:  copy file1 file2 \n\n";
  else
  {
    ifstream in(argv[1]);
    assert (in.is_open());
    ofstream out(argv[2]);
    assert (out.is_open());
    char ch;
    while (!in.eof())
    {
      in.get(ch);
      out.put(ch);
    }
    cout << "File copy completed\n\n";
  }
}
```

SAMPLE RUNS (IN UNIX):

```
% g++ commandline2.cc -o copy
CS:% copy
Usage:  copy file1 file2

% copy file8-11A file8-11B
% File copy completed
```

FUNCTIONS AS ARGUMENTS

In Sec. 8.5 we noted that the *value of a function name is the starting address of that function*, that is, a function is a pointer. This means that if we can declare a type `FunctionPtr` capable of storing the address of a function and then declare a variable `FPtr` of that type,

```
FunctionPtr FPtr;
```

then the assignment statement

```
FPtr = F;
```

can be used to store the starting address of function `F()` in the variable `FPtr`. Because the value of `FPtr` is a valid address, `FPtr` can be dereferenced using the indirection operator (`*`) just like any other pointer variable. Thus the expression

```
(*FPtr)(ArgumentList)
```

dereferences `FPtr`, which (since function `F()` is at that address) calls function `F()`, passing it *ArgumentList*.[2] In fact, we need not even use the indirection operator since attaching an argument list to `FPtr` *automatically dereferences* `FPtr`,

```
FPtr(ArgumentList)
```

(much like attaching a list of subscripts to a pointer to an array).

Similarly, we can declare `FPtr` as a parameter of a function `G()` and then use `FPtr` to call `F()` from within `G()`:

```
void G(FunctionPtr Fptr)
{
    ...
    (*Fptr)(ArgumentList);
    ...
}
```

Then, we could call `G()` and pass the name of function `F()` as an argument

```
G(F);
```

and `G()`, when it dereferences its parameter `FPtr`, will call function `F()`.

The `typedef` mechanism can be used to declare `FunctionPtr` as a type whose objects can store the address of a function

---

[2]The parentheses around `*FPtr` are necessary because the dereferencing operator `*` has lower priority than the function-call operation `()`. See Appendix C for a table of operator priorities.

```
typedef ReturnType (*FunctionPtr)(ParameterTypeList);
```

which declares the name `FunctionPtr` as a type whose objects can store the address
of any function whose return type is *ReturnType*, and whose parameters match
those in *ParameterList*. For example, the program in Fig. D.5 uses the declaration

```
typedef double (*FunctionPtr)(double);
```

to declare `FunctionPtr` as a pointer to a function `f(x)` where x is a `double` value
and `f(x)` returns a `double` value. The function `Bisector()` in this program has a
function parameter of type `FunctionPtr` and uses the bisection method described
in Programming Problem 15 of Chap. 9 to find an approximate zero of this function. A solution of the equation

$$F(x) = x^3 + x - 5 = 0$$

is found by passing the function `F()` to `Bisect()`.

FIGURE D.5   BISECTION METHOD—FUNCTIONS AS ARGUMENTS

```
/* Find an approximate solution of the equation F(x) = 0 in a given
 * interval, using the bisection method.
 *
 * Input:    Desired accuracy of approximation, endpoints of an
 *           interval containing a solution
 * Output:   Prompts to the user and the approximate solution
 *
 * Notes:
 * 1. The solution will be within desiredAccuracy of the exact
 *    solution.
 * 2. To find the solution for a different F(x), redefine F() below.
 *****************************************************************/

#include <iostream>
using namespace std;

double F(double x)
{
    return x*x*x + x - 5;        // the function F for which the
}                                // equation F(x) = 0 is being solved


//------------------------------------------------------------------

typedef double (* FunctionPointer)(double);

double Bisector(FunctionPointer, double, double, double);

int main()
{
    cout << "\nThis program uses the bisection method to find an\n"
         << "\approximate solution to the equation F(x) = 0.\n";
```

```
   double desiredAccuracy;   // the accuracy desired

   cout << "\nEnter the accuracy desired (e.g. .001): ";
   cin >> desiredAccuracy;

   double left,              // left and right endpoints
          right;             //    of (sub)interval containing a solution

   do                        // get the interval containing a solution
   {
     cout << "Enter the x-values of interval containing solution: ";
     cin >> left >> right;
   }
   while (F(left) * F(right) >= 0.0);

   double                    // find the approximate solution
     solution = Bisector(F, left, right, desiredAccuracy);

   cout << "\n--> "<< solution
        << " is an approximate solution of F(x) = 0, to within "
        << desiredAccuracy << endl;
}

/* Bisector() performs the bisection algorithm.
 *
 * Receive:  FPtr, (a pointer to) a function for which a zero is to
 *                be found.
 *           left, the left endpoint of the original interval
 *           right, the right endpoint of the original interval
 *           accuracy, the desired accuracy of the approximation
 * Return:   midPt, the middle of the final interval
 ****************************************************************/

double Bisector(FunctionPointer FPtr, double left, double right,
                double accuracy)
{
  double width = right - left,      // the interval width
         midPt,                     // the midpoint of the interval
         F_Mid;                     // value of FPtr at midpoint

  while (width/2.0 > accuracy)
  {
    midPt = (left + right) / 2.0;   //   compute midpoint
    F_Mid = FPtr(midPt);            //   compute function at midpoint
```

```
        if (FPtr(left) * F_Mid < 0.0 )   //   solution is in left half
           right = midPt;
        else                             //   solution is in right half
           left = midPt;

        width /= 2.0;                    //   split the interval
     }

   return midPt;
}
```

SAMPLE RUN

This program uses the bisection method to find an
approximate solution to the equation F(x) = 0.

Enter the accuracy desired (e.g. .001): .001
Enter the x-values of interval containing solution: 0 1
Enter the x-values of interval containing solution: 1 2

--> 1.51758 is an approximate solution of F(x) = 0, to within 0.001

ANSWERS TO
QUICK QUIZZES

QUICK QUIZ 1.5

1. software engineering

2. Problem analysis and specification
   Design
   Coding
   Testing, execution, and debugging
   Maintenance

3. specification

4. false

5. objects, operations, algorithm

6. type

7. pseudocode

8. sequence, selection, and repetition

9. coding

10. false

11. preconditions, postconditions

12. Verification refers to checking that documents, program modules, and the like that are produced are correct and complete and that they are consistent with one another and with those of the preceding phases. Validation is concerned with checking that these products match the problem's specification.

13. Syntax errors are caused by not obeying the syntax rules of the programming languages such as bad punctuation. Run-time errors are caused by some unexpected event (such as division by 0) occurring during program execution. Logic errors are errors in designing the algorithm for solving the problem or in not coding the algorithm correctly.

14. In black-box testing, the outputs produced for various inputs are checked for correctness without considering the structure of the program unit itself. In white-box testing, the performance of the program unit is tested by examining its internal structure.

15. True

QUICK QUIZ 2.2

1. A collection of data items together with basic operations and relations on them.

2. Storage structures for the data items and algorithms for the basic operations and relations.

3. data abstraction

4. bit, byte

5. overflow

6. 23

7. 5.75

8. mantissa or fractional part

9. underflow

10. true

11. false

QUICK QUIZ 2.3

1. A fixed-size sequence of elements, all of the same type with the basic operation of direct access to each element so that values can be retrieved from or stored in this element.

2. direct

3. true

4. 1, 0, 0, 0, 0

5. null

6. subscript

7. base address, pointer

8. true

9. false

10. (1) Their capacity cannot change during program execution.
(2) They are not self-contained objects.

11. false

QUICK QUIZ 2.4

1. A fixed-size sequence of elements, not necessarily of the same type with the basic operation of direct access to each element so that values can be retrieved from or stored in this element.

2. true   **3.** members or fields   **4.** dot

5. Members of a struct are stored in separate memory locations. Members of a union share the same memory locations.

QUICK QUIZ 3.2

1. Members of a class by default are private, but members of a struct by default are public.

2. data, function

3. An object carries its own operations around with it.

4. object

5. So that only member (and friend) functions can access them, but not programs and programmers.

6. scope (::)   **7.** inline   **8.** class invariant

9. (1) Allocate memory for it   **10.** preconditions   **11.** default
(2) Initialize it   postconditions   explicit-value

12. signatures   **13.** initialization, assignment **14.** operatorΔ

15. true   **16.** friend   **17.** conditional

QUICK QUIZ 3.4

1. char, null character   **2.** empty   **3.** stringstream

4. 0, 3, 13   **5.** The   **6.** The cat in the hat

7. neuroses are red   **8.** e   **9.** neutron

10. roses are colored   **11.** rose   **12.** noses are red

13. 10   **14.** npos   **15.** true

16. some positive value

QUICK QUIZ 4.2

1. An ordered collection of data items that can be accessed at only one location, called the top of the stack. Basic operations are: construct an empty stack, check if stack is empty, push a value onto the top of the stack, retrieve the top value, and remove the top value.

2. design it, implement it

3. (1) Define data members to represent the object(s) being modeled
(2) Define the operations identified in the design phase

4. $\texttt{myTop} = 0; \texttt{myArray[0]} = 123, \texttt{myArray[1]} = 789$, other elements are unknown
5. $\texttt{myTop} = 1; \texttt{myArray[0]} = 111, \texttt{myArray[1]} = 111$, other elements are unknown
6. $\texttt{myTop} = 2; \texttt{myArray[0]} = 0, \texttt{myArray[1]} = 2, \texttt{myArray[2]} = 4, \texttt{myArray[3]} = 6,$
   $\texttt{myArray[4]} = 8$

QUICK QUIZ 4.3

1. activation record
2. run time
3. postfix
4. infix
5. prefix
6. postfix
7. 5
8. 8
9. `a b c - - d *`
10. `* - a - b c d`

QUICK QUIZ 5.2

1. An ordered collection of data items that can be removed only at one end, called the front, and can be added only at the other end, called the back. Basic operations are: construct an empty queue, check if queue is empty, add a value at the back, retrieve the front value, and remove the front value.
2. spool
3. buffer
4. deque
5. scroll
6. ready
7. resident
8. suspended
9. priority

QUICK QUIZ 6.3

1. overloaded
2. true
3. false
4. templates
5. `typename` or `class`
6. instantiation
7. (1) Changing the `typedef` is a change to the header file, which means that any program or library that uses the class must be recompiled. (2) A name declared using `typedef` can have only one meaning at a time.
8. (1) All operations defined outside of the class declaration must be template functions.

   (2) Any use of the name of a template class as a type must be parameterized.

   (3) Operations on a template class should be defined in the same file as the class declaration.
9. Standard Template Library
10. Alex Stepanov, Meng Lee
11. containers, algorithms, and iterators
12. iterators
13. stack
14. queue

QUICK QUIZ 6.4

1. `int`
2. $0, 0$
3. $5, 5$
4. $5, 5$
5. $10, 7$
6. `1 1`
7. `0 88`
8. true
9. false
10. true
11. `1 1 1 1 1`
12. `0 0 0 0 0 77`
13. `0`
14. behind `88`
15. 20
16. true

17. 0, 0, 1.0, 1.5, 2.0

18. 1, 1, 1, 1, 1, 0, 3, 4, 7, 8

19. 1, 1, 1, 1, 1, 2, 4, 8, 10, ?

20. 1, 1, 2, 2, 2

QUICK QUIZ 6.6

1. double-ended queue

2. An ordered collection of data items with the property that items can be added and removed only at the ends. Basic operations are: construct an empty deque, check if deque is empty, add to front or rear of deque, retrieve from front or rear of deque, remove from front or rear of deque.

3. false

4. true

5. false

6. adapter

7. interface

8. Need space between >s

9. `stack` and `queue`

QUICK QUIZ 7.1

1. recursion

2. (1) An anchor or base case that specifies the value of the function for one or more values of the parameter(s).

(2) An inductive or recursive step that defines the function's value for the current value of the parameter(s) in terms of previously defined function values and/or parameter values.

3. true

4. 15

5. 0

6. 0

7. infinite recursion

QUICK QUIZ 7.4

1. time and space

2. space

3. time

4. There is some constant C such that $T(n) \leq C \cdot f(n)$ for all sufficiently large values of n.

5. true

6. true

7. false

8. n

9. $\log_2 n$

10. false

11. recurrence

QUICK QUIZ 7.5

1. algorithms

2. `<algorithm>`

3. false

4. first element, and just past the last element

5. `<numeric>`

QUICK QUIZ 8.1

1. A finite sequence (ordered set) of data items with basic operations: construct an empty list, check if list is empty, traverse the list or part of it, insert and delete at any point in the list.

2. n

3. n

4. false

Quick Quiz 8.2
1. nodes
2. data, next
3. null
4. 1
5. 1
6. true
7. false

Quick Quiz 8.4
1. (1) Allocate the amount of memory required for a value of the specified type
   (2) Associate the object's name with that memory
   (3) Initialize that memory with values provided in the declaration (if any)
2. address
3. &
4. *
5. *
6. ->
7. address
8. `double` value
9. address
10. address
11. `double` value
12. `double` value
13. null
14. `1.1`
15. `3.3`
16. `0x12a50`
17. `this`

Quick Quiz 8.5
1. compile, run
2. new, null address, address, anonymous
3. `delete`
4. pointer variable
5. 66
6. `C(const C & original);`
7. `~C();`
8. false
9. true
10. default
11. When a class contains a data member that is a pointer, because the default copy constructor does not make a distinct copy of the object pointed to by that pointer.
12. memory leak
13. destructor
14. When a class contains a data member that is a pointer, because the default destructor will not reclaim the memory allocated to the object pointed to by that pointer, resulting in marooned memory blocks.
15. When a class contains a data member that is a pointer, because the default assignment operator will simply do a pointer assignment, resulting in two pointers to the same object and not to distinct objects.

Quick Quiz 8.7
1. They are too inefficient.
2. nodes, links (pointers)
3. true
4. false
5. Insertion and deletion at any point in the list in constant time.
6. Direct access to each element stored in them.

Quick Quiz 9.1
1. head node
2. predecessor
3. trailer node
4. successor
5. circular

QUICK QUIZ 9.3

1. hash table, hash   **2.** collision

3. Searching forward in a hash table for an empty location to insert a colliding value.

4. chaining

5.
	Table
0	5
1	11
2	23
3	18
4	19

6.   Table

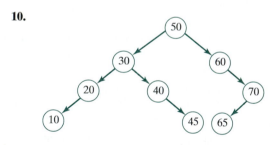

QUICK QUIZ 10.3

1. tree (or directed graph) **2.** root   **3.** leaves

4. children, parent   **5.** at most 2 children   **6.** 50

7. 10, 40, 70   **8.** false

9.

i	0	1	2	3	4	5	6	7	...
$t[i]$	50	30	60	20	40	?	70	10	...

10.

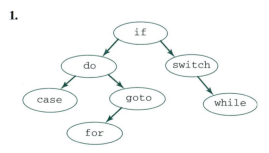

QUICK QUIZ 10.4

1.

2.

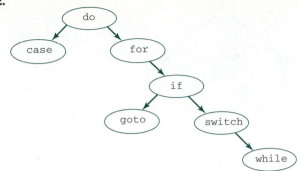

3.

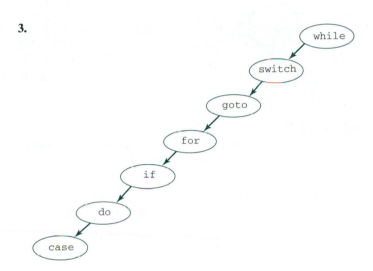

4. 10, 20, 30, 40, 50, 60, 70, 80, 90, 100
5. 80, 30, 20, 10, 60, 50, 40, 70, 90, 100
6. 10, 20, 40, 50, 70, 60, 30, 100, 90, 80

7.

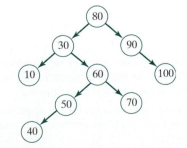

8.

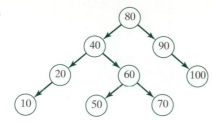

9.

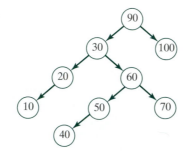

Quick Quiz 11.1

1. Make a number of passes through the list or a part of the list and, on each pass, select one element to be correctly positioned.

2. false

3. Systematically interchange pairs of elements that are out of order until eventually no such pairs remain and the list is therefore sorted.

4. true

5. Repeatedly insert a new element into a list of already sorted elements so that the resulting list is still sorted.

6. true   7. true   8. indirect

Quick Quiz 11.2

1. The data item stored in each node is greater than or equal to the data items stored in each of its children.

2. complete   3. $n \log_2 n$

4. So that those with higher priority are removed before those of lower priority.

5. heap

Quick Quiz 11.3

1. A problem is repeatedly partitioned into simpler subproblems, each of which can be considered independently, continuing until subproblems are obtained that are sufficiently simple that they can be solved (i.e., conquered).

2. Select an element, called a pivot, and then perform a sequence of exchanges so that all elements that are less than this pivot are to its left and all elements that are

greater than the pivot are to its right. This correctly positions the pivot and divides the (sub)list into two smaller sublists, each of which may then be sorted independently in the same way.

3. pivot **4.** $n^2, n\log_2 n$

5. Reduces the depth of recursion

6. false **7.** median-of-three **8.** true

QUICK QUIZ 11.4
1. internal, external

2. They require direct access to the list elements. They may make many passes through the list.

3. The basic operation involved is merging: combining two lists that have previously been sorted so that the resulting list is also sorted.

4. $n\log_2 n$

QUICK QUIZ 12.1
1. Encapsulation: Wrapping the data and basic operations used for processing this data within a single entity.

Inheritance: A class can be derived from another class, and this derived class then inherits the members of the parent class.

Polymorphism: The property of a derived class and an ancestor class having a function member in common but that behaves differently in these classes.

2. encapsulation **3.** message **4.** inherits

5. polymorphism **6.** static (or early), dynamic (or late)

QUICK QUIZ 12.2
1. inheritance

2. (1) Identify the objects in the problem.

(2) Analyze the objects to determine if there is commonality in them.

(3) Where there is commonalty:

    a. Define base classes that contain this commonality

    b. Derive classes that inherit this commonality from the base class.

3. private **4.** protected **5.** false

6. is-a **7.** member-initializer list

QUICK QUIZ 12.3
1. The property of a derived class and an ancestor class having a function member in common but that behaves differently in these classes.

2. static (or early) **3.** virtual, dynamic (or late)

4. virtual table **5.** abstract, pure virtual

QUICK QUIZ 13.1

1. A link from node to its inorder successor.

2. So that traversals or other tree operations can be performed more efficiently.

3.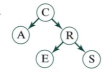

4.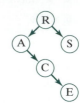

5.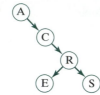

6.

QUICK QUIZ 13.2

1. The height of the left subtree of a node minus the height of its right subtree.

2. A binary search tree in which the balance factor of each node is 0, 1, or −1. Basic operations are: construction, empty, search, and traverse as for BSTs, insert and delete items in such a way that the height-balanced property is maintained.

3. height

4.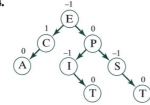

5. 3   6. 5   7. $\log_2 n$

QUICK QUIZ 13.3

1.

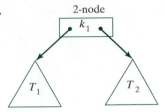

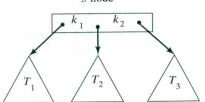

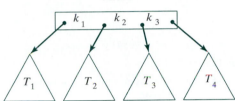

2-node: all values in $T_1 < k_1 \leq$ all values in T_2

3-node: all values in $T_1 < k_1 \leq$ all values in $T_2 < k_2 \leq$ all values in T_3

2-node: all values in $T_1 < k_1 \leq$ all values in $T_2 < k_2 \leq$ all values in $T_3 < k_3 \leq$ all values in T_4

2.

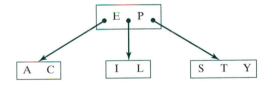

3.

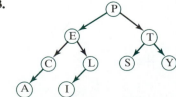

4. B   **5.** 4   **6.** Same answer as in 2.

7.   **8.**

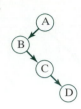   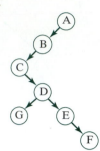

QUICK QUIZ 13.4

1. `vector`, `deque`, `list`, `stack`, `queue`, `priority_queue`.

2. `set`, `multiset`, `map`, `multimap`

3. `map`   **4.** The index type may   **5.** red-black
                                    be any type.

QUICK QUIZ 14.1

1. Digraphs need not have a root node and there may be several (or no) paths from one vertex to another.

2. true   **3.** adjacent to   **4.** in-degree, out-degree

5. $\text{adj} = \begin{bmatrix} 0 & 1 & 1 & 1 & 1 \\ 0 & 1 & 1 & 0 & 0 \\ 0 & 0 & 0 & 1 & 0 \\ 0 & 0 & 0 & 1 & 1 \\ 0 & 1 & 0 & 0 & 0 \end{bmatrix} \qquad \text{data} = \begin{bmatrix} A \\ B \\ C \\ D \\ E \end{bmatrix}$

6. $\text{adj} = \begin{bmatrix} 0 & 0 & 0 & 0 \\ 0 & 0 & 0 & 0 \\ 0 & 0 & 0 & 0 \\ 0 & 0 & 0 & 0 \end{bmatrix} \qquad \text{data} = \begin{bmatrix} 1 \\ 2 \\ 3 \\ 4 \end{bmatrix}$

7. v[1] → A → 2 → 3 → 4 → 5 ⊣

v[2] → B → 2 → 3 ⊣

v[3] → C → 4 ⊣

v[4] → D → 4 → 5 ⊣

v[5] → E → 2 ⊣

8. v[1] ⊡→ ☐1☐⊣ ╫

v[2] ⊡→ ☐2☐⊣ ╫

v[3] ⊡→ ☐3☐⊣ ╫

v[4] ⊡→ ☐4☐⊣ ╫

QUICK QUIZ 14.2

1. When processing some values it becomes necessary to return to some that were already processed or that were skipped over on an earlier pass.

2. From vertex 1: all of them; from vertex 2: 2, 3, 4, 5

3. Only 1 itself   4. 2, 3, 4, 5

5. NP: Problems for which a solution can be guessed and then checked with an algorithm whose computing time is $O(P(n))$ for some polynomial $P(n)$.

   P: Problems that can be solved by algorithms in polynomial time.

   NP-Complete: Problems with the property that if a polynomial time algorithm that solves any one of these problems can be found, then the existence of polynomial-time algorithms for all NP problems is guaranteed.

QUICK QUIZ 14.3

1. No direction is associated with the edges. No loops joining a vertex to itself are allowed.

2. adj = $\begin{bmatrix} 0 & 1 & 1 & 1 & 1 \\ 1 & 0 & 1 & 0 & 1 \\ 1 & 1 & 0 & 1 & 0 \\ 1 & 0 & 1 & 0 & 1 \\ 1 & 1 & 0 & 1 & 0 \end{bmatrix}$ data = $\begin{bmatrix} A \\ B \\ C \\ D \\ E \end{bmatrix}$

3. adj = $\begin{bmatrix} 0 & 0 & 0 & 0 \\ 0 & 0 & 0 & 0 \\ 0 & 0 & 0 & 0 \\ 0 & 0 & 0 & 0 \end{bmatrix}$ data = $\begin{bmatrix} 1 \\ 2 \\ 3 \\ 4 \end{bmatrix}$

4.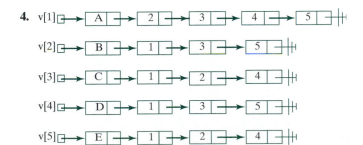

5.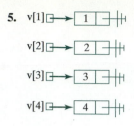

6.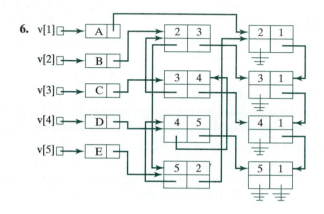

7. Same answer as 5.   **8.** all of them in each case   **9.** Only 1 itself

10. 2, 3, 4, 5   **11.** Only A

INDEX